AF394689

The People's Emperor

The People's Emperor

The Unlikely Rise and Spectacular Fall of Napoléon III

EDWARD SHAWCROSS

faber

First published in 2026
by Faber & Faber Limited
The Bindery, 51 Hatton Garden
London ECIN 8HN

Typeset by Faber & Faber Limited
Printed and bound by CPI Group (UK) Ltd, Croydon, CRO 4YY

A CIP record for this book
is available from the British Library

ISBN 978–0–571–36130–4

2 4 6 8 10 9 7 5 3 1

For Hannah, Ena and Rose

And in loving memory of my father

CONTENTS

Prologue   ix

I: THE MAN WHO WOULD BE EMPEROR

The Wondrous Destiny   3
An Unsentimental Education   22
The Column   37
Some New Napoléon Might Arise   56
Citizen of Nowhere   78
The Eagle Has Landed   99
The Prisoner   112

II: THE WORLD IS A STRANGE THEATRE

Napoléon's Ghost   135
The Chosen One   160
Countdown   178
History of a Crime   198
Vox Populi, Vox Dei   215
The Imperial Cloak   228
War and Peace   243
The Beginning of the Affairs   266
War and Peace Revisited   284

III: TRAGEDY AND FARCE

Blood and Iron   309
The Empire in the Pillory   333

The Liberal Empire   355
War or Peace   374
The Debacle   394
The Terrible Year   416
The End   430

Epilogue   445
Acknowledgements   469
Notes   471
Picture Credits   502
Index   503

PROLOGUE

On 1 September 1870, carnage came to Sedan, a picturesque backwater town in north-eastern France. Wagons, horses and men blocked the roads; shells exploded among them, setting buildings on fire. Wounded men lay screaming on once sedate streets; the dying and the dead had appalling injuries – skulls shattered, limbs blown off, corpses barely held together with rags that were once pristine French army uniforms.

Through the inferno rode Louis-Napoléon, Emperor of the French, known since December 1852 as Napoléon III. As he approached his head-quarters, a shell exploded a few paces away, covering him in a shower of dirt. Another blast knocked several of his entourage and their horses to the ground, leaving two aides dead in the street. An abandoned wagon and its horse blocked the way across a bridge, forcing the emperor to stop. Moments later, a shell detonated in front of the wagon where the emperor would have passed, killing the animal.

That Sedan was in flames was the outcome of Louis-Napoléon's disastrous decision weeks earlier to go to war against the rising German power of Prussia and its allies. Soon three German armies invaded France and defeated the French in every battle they fought. Now the emperor and his forces were trapped in Sedan. As one French general put it with Gallic charm before the fighting started, 'We are in a chamber pot, about to be shat upon.'[1]

Few had predicted the disaster now befalling France, but then few had predicted that Louis-Napoléon would become emperor. He had long been ridiculed for what was seen as his absurd dream that he would recreate the Empire of his uncle, Napoléon Bonaparte: two risible attempts to seize power had ended in pathetic failure. But in 1848 he stunned elites when, aged forty, he won a landslide election to become the first ever directly elected president of France. The political class were horrified at what they saw as an idiot leading one of Europe's greatest nations: a 'dwarf' who 'on the summit of a great wave can reach the top of a cliff that a giant placed on dry ground could not scale', as the famed political theorist Alexis de Tocqueville wrote.[2] France's most celebrated writer, Victor Hugo, lambasted him as 'Napoléon le Pétit'.

These men underestimated Louis-Napoléon. Driven, Machiavellian and with the political instincts of a populist, as president he outmanoeuvred his opponents to rise higher still. Third time lucky, he launched a *coup d'état* on 2 December 1851 against the French Republic he had sworn to defend. Exactly one year later, he realised his oft-mocked dream and proclaimed himself Emperor of the French. The first time as tragedy, the second time as farce, or so Karl Marx put it.

But for millions of French, there was nothing farcical about the Second Empire, the name of the regime Louis-Napoléon created. As one of the most powerful men in the world, the emperor belied his reputation as a ridiculous failed adventurer and transformed France, creating the world's first managed democracy (more than seven million Frenchmen – 75 per cent of all adult males over the age of twenty-one – ratified his decision to become emperor in a plebiscite). The economy roared: between 1848 and 1868, French exports tripled. His radical vision for Paris turned the city into a monumental capital, a centre of modernity and unrivalled luxury envied across the world. Defeating Russia in the Crimean War (1853–6), and then Austria in 1859, France became a European and global superpower after years of decline since his uncle's defeat at the Battle of Waterloo in 1815.

Not only that, but Louis-Napoléon had done what no other French ruler had managed since the revolution of 1789: he had founded a stable regime. By 1870, he had ruled longer than his uncle. In the face of rising opposition many thought would end in revolution, he revitalised his authoritarian reign by creating the Liberal Empire, a political system more democratic than Britain's at the time. It would be hard for any government, democratic or authoritarian, to remain in power for as long as Louis-Napoléon without losing popularity, but when he put his reforms to the French people, once again, more than seven million backed the man who had made France great again.

Months later, however, he was the man who had taken his country into a disastrous war. Now, with his army trapped inside Sedan and outnumbered almost two to one, the situation was desperate. One person who had not given up the fight was the commander of the French army in the thick of the fighting. From here, he penned a message to the emperor. Rather than be taken prisoner, the general wrote, Louis-Napoléon should break out. 'Let your Majesty come and place himself in the middle of his troops. They will be honoured to open a passage for him.'[3] Whenever he was faced with catastrophic defeat, Louis-Napoléon's uncle had run away. Whether in Egypt in 1799, Russia in 1812 or Waterloo in 1815, Napoléon Bonaparte had abandoned his soldiers to their fate and fled to Paris to save his reputation, and himself. Reading the note as shells crashed into the gardens outside his headquarters, Louis-Napoléon had a decision to make.

PART I

THE MAN WHO WOULD BE EMPEROR

1

THE WONDROUS DESTINY

On 12 August 1807, a couple who usually loathed each other had sex. Even though she was resigned to what she euphemistically termed a 'reconciliation', Hortense de Beauharnais could not hide the revulsion she felt for her husband. Hardly a warm character – he described himself as 'cold and taciturn' – Louis, known by his title the comte de Saint-Leu, was rarely as enamoured with his wife as he was on that summer night in the south-western French city of Toulouse.[1]

He had married Hortense five years ago on 4 January 1802, when he was twenty-three years old. 'Never was there a more gloomy ceremony,' he wrote of his wedding day, which he saw as the beginning of 'his misfortunes; of his physical and moral sufferings'. Writing in the third person, he recorded that the marriage 'stamped on his mind and his whole existence a sort of profound melancholy, a dejection, an aridity, so to speak, which nothing ever could, or ever will, remedy'.[2] Needless to say, he was not the life and soul of a party.

This was a shame for his young wife – eighteen when they married – who very much was. She loved playing games, singing, dancing, acting and laughing with friends. This final trait was particularly egregious to her husband, who thought the hilarity was at his expense and chastised her for it in the days after their marriage. 'Thus passed my honeymoon,' sighed Hortense, 'that first month of marriage said to be the happiest in life. Ah, well, sad though it was, it was yet one of the least unhappy of my existence.'[3]

This miserable union had not come about by choice, at least not for those in the marriage. 'I made the greatest sacrifices a man could make,' wrote the comte de Saint-Leu, 'for my family, for my name, for my brother, who is the boss.'[4] The boss tended to get what he wanted. For he was the most powerful man in Europe, Napoléon Bonaparte, Emperor of the French.

Eight months and eight days after the 'reconciliation', Hortense gave birth in Paris to a boy at 1 a.m. on 20 April 1808. The baby was born into splendour, a prince of the imperial Bonaparte dynasty. The father was not present, as his habitual paranoia made him doubt his paternity. The fact that the baby was three weeks premature fuelled the comte de Saint-Leu's suspicions. Plenty of others shared them at the time and since, alleging that the only reason Hortense agreed to sleep with her husband was to provide cover in case she became pregnant from an affair. Whatever the truth, the comte de Saint-Leu came to recognise the boy as his own.

Not that the parents were allowed to call their baby what they wanted. This was for the boss, Napoléon, to decide, and he was busy invading Spain. For six weeks the child had no name. Then, on 2 June, an official arrived at Hortense's home to inform her that her son would be called Charles-Louis-Napoléon Bonaparte, or Louis-Napoléon as he became known, which was confusing because he already had an older brother called Napoléon-Louis.

By 1808, Hortense had had three children and she loved them all. There was, however, something special about the youngest. Her firstborn had died in 1807 before he reached five years old, the devastating grief of both parents driving them, temporarily, back into each other's arms. Her second son was the heir to the kingdom of Holland, which Napoléon Bonaparte had created and where he put the comte de Saint-Leu on the throne in 1806. The third and youngest, Hortense wrote, 'will have nothing at all'.[5] He was all Hortense's.

Louis-Napoléon was a fragile baby – Hortense thought he would die – and he was literally wrapped in cotton wool and bathed in wine for weeks after his birth. He soon gained strength, though, and by the end of 1808 Hortense no longer feared for his health. His earliest years were idyllic. He was inseparable from his older brother, with whom he played whenever he could, watched over by a mother who doted on her two sons and a grandmother, the Empress Joséphine, married to Napoléon.

With beautiful grounds, tropical plants, a revolving cast of famous Frenchmen and women and plenty of troops guarding the imperial family, Malmaison, a chateau to the west of Paris where Joséphine lived and

Napoléon often stayed, was an enchanting playground for Hortense's young boys when they were growing up. Joséphine especially spoiled the children, insisting they do as they pleased at Malmaison. A lover of exotic plants, she let them suck raw the sugar cane that grew there.

It was no surprise, then, that Louis-Napoléon needed a tooth pulled by the dentist as a young boy. The operation was dangerous, and he was still bleeding from the mouth two days later. That night, with tender care, Hortense held him in her arms until he fell asleep and placed him in his bed. Then she left, but, terrified the wound would not close, she returned to his bedside. Seeing there was still a trickle of blood from his mouth as he slept, she placed her finger on the gum and stayed with him the whole night until the bleeding stopped.

Family anecdotes about Louis-Napoléon focused on his kindness, generosity and empathy. His first tutor was a gentle but ineffectual, lacka-daisical and dull teacher. In one lesson he made his student read a fable that had 'metamorphosis' in it. After the word was explained to him, Louis-Napoléon said, 'I should like to be able to change myself into a little bird: I would fly away when it was time for my lesson with you; but I would come back when M. Hase [his German teacher] came.'

'What you say is not very kind towards me,' replied his tutor.

'Oh,' said Louis-Napoléon with the skill of a courtier, 'what I said referred to the lesson, not to the man.'[6]

Louis-Napoléon had to learn charm early, for he had been born into one of the most powerful, cut-throat and mafioso soap operas in modern his-tory, presided over by the terrifying and awe-inspiring figure of his uncle, Napoléon.

———

Napoléon Bonaparte, or Napoleone Buonaparte as he was baptised, was born on 15 August 1769 in Ajaccio, Corsica. He was the second son of eight children, and his father was an obscure but ruthless social climber, Carlo. Furthering his family's position required his sons to leave Corsica and make careers in France. The second son, Napoleone, joined the army. Carlo enrolled him in an officer-training school for the French artillery. He was looked down upon by his fellow students for his humble origins and spoke French badly with a strong Corsican accent; few contemporaries expected him to amount to much.

But the French Revolution created the chaos and flux within which an ambitious, talented man like Napoleone thrived. In 1789, King Louis XVI, whose Bourbon family had ruled France for hundreds of years, headed a bankrupt government. To raise new taxes, he called a meeting of the Estates-General, France's parliament, but it had not met since 1614 and the 1789 meeting resulted in long-pent-up demands for reform. Soon, riots over the price of bread in Paris led to popular insurrection and the storming of the Bastille prison on 14 July. The revolution began.

It became ever more radical. What started as calls for constitutional reform and the ending of aristocratic privilege descended into mob violence, whipped up by political clubs, most famously the Jacobins headed by Maximilien Robespierre. Louis XVI, his Austrian wife Marie Antoinette and their children became virtual prisoners in the palace of the Tuileries in Paris. When in 1791 they tried to flee the capital, they were hauled back and became actual prisoners.

The next year, Austria and Prussia invaded to rescue the monarchs, which mainlined nationalism into the revolution. The monarchy was abolished, a republic was proclaimed, and the Jacobins came to power and painted Louis and Marie Antoinette as counter-revolutionaries, in league with foreigners and enemies of the people. The fact that Louis XVI was royal condemned him: 'One cannot reign innocently . . . every king is a rebel and a usurper,' thundered one leading Jacobin, capturing the mood that, for the revolutionaries at least, pitted a modern, enlightened and meritocratic France based on reason against the archaic European order of kings, feudalism and reaction.[7]

To help usher in a new age of republican virtue, Louis XVI was guillotined on 21 January 1793, his bloody head held aloft as the crowd roared approval. The Terror followed; Robespierre's drive to cleanse the revolution of its enemies resulted in the death of some thirty thousand. Meanwhile, war continued against Austria, Prussia and soon Britain, which placed its wealth and powerful navy behind the forces of order trying to crush the revolution.

This provided opportunities for Napoleone. He positioned himself as a loyal son of the revolution and proved to be a military leader of rare distinction, a meticulous organiser, courageous to the point of foolhardiness and, for someone of small stature and poor French, an unexpectedly charismatic leader. He made a name for himself at the siege of Toulon in 1793, when he helped drive French royalists, and the hated British navy supporting them, from the port.

He soon entered the political fray. In Paris, Robespierre's Terror ended when he was overthrown and then executed in the summer of 1794. After Robespierre came the Directory, the name given to the government that ruled France from 1795. Most thought that this regime would be as ephemeral as those that had gone before. But this one had Napoleone behind it. Since 1789, popular insurrection in Paris, or the threat of it, had determined events, and in October 1795, it looked like the mob would have its way again. There was an uprising that threatened to topple the Directory. Facing down protesters with what he later called the 'whiff of grapeshot', Napoleone broke the power of street politics. As a reward, he was appointed commander of the Army of Italy.

To make his name sound more French, he dropped the final 'e' and added an accent to the first one. Napoléon was invented, and it was in Italy that the Napoleonic legend was made. He turned what was little better than an armed rabble into an invincible army, and his achievements were extraordinary, but he realised they would be even more extraordinary if narrated and embellished by himself. He founded two newspapers, ostensibly to boost army morale, but in reality to boost his reputation. 'Bonaparte flies like lightning and strikes like thunder. He is everywhere and sees everything': reports such as these told the French people of his superhuman exploits.[8] With his victorious soldiers loyal to him and believing his strategic vision greater than that of politicians in Paris, Napoléon acted as a one-man state, concluding treaties, creating republics and almost single-handedly redrawing the political map of the Italian peninsula.

After Italy, Napoléon was looking for a venture that matched his ambition, and the Directory was looking for one that would keep an ambitious general far from Paris. Napoléon invaded Egypt. As usual, he won several battles; one against the backdrop of the pyramids especially fired the imagination of all who read about it. Regardless, the expedition soon turned into a disaster, but it provided brilliant propaganda opportunities for Napoléon, who turned catastrophe into personal triumph – not least by abandoning his men before they were defeated, slipping away to Paris to control the narrative, and shape a new one.

The Directory was not popular. Plots against it were prepared on all sides and the conspiring politicians required a frontman who could manage the military side of things and then return to the background. Instead, they got Napoléon, who brought the necessary martial clout, but pushed the politicians into the background. On 9 November 1799 – 18 Brumaire in the revolutionary calendar – Napoléon launched a *coup d'état*. The conspiracists behind the putsch had expected to rule France. Napoléon had other ideas and became a dictator, though he used another title taken from the Roman Republic, First Consul.

This was an ascension of which Napoléon's Corsican father, who died in 1785, could never have dreamed. Napoléon was the most powerful man in France, and therefore one of the most powerful men in Europe. But this was always a family affair. Napoléon's brothers – the eldest, Joseph; then Lucien; Louis, the comte de Saint-Leu; and the youngest, Jérôme – and his sisters, Elisa, Pauline and Caroline, jostled jealously for his favour and fortune. The squabbles of the Bonaparte siblings were legendary; however, they were united on one thing. They hated Napoléon's wife.

Napoléon married Joséphine de Beauharnais in 1796. Her husband had been guillotined during the Terror; imprisoned, Joséphine would likely have followed if Robespierre had not been ousted. She had a string of affairs with powerful politicians and generals, one of whom introduced her to Napoléon. Thirty-two years old when they met, Marie Josèphe Rose Tascher de La Pagerie, better known as Joséphine, was not a renowned beauty. Born on the Caribbean island of Martinique to a wealthy plantation owner, she developed a taste for sugar which rotted her teeth, and she smiled without opening her mouth. What she lacked in physical beauty, a former lover wrote, she made up for with 'the most refined, the most far-sighted, the most perfected art that the courtesans of Greece or Paris ever employed in the exercise of their profession'.[9] Whatever the truth of that, Napoléon became infatuated, developing a voracious sexual appetite for her alone, initially.

She brought him old-world charm, aristocratic connections and a degree of acceptance in French high society that his Corsican background never could. In return, she got money for her extravagant lifestyle and a guardian for her two young children, Eugène and Hortense. Napoléon ruled his family in the same way he ruled France: despotically. By 1802, family and nation had elided to the point where it seemed a good idea to marry his stepdaughter, Hortense de Beauharnais, to his brother, the comte de Saint-Leu.

———

Napoléon was a father figure to his younger brother the comte de Saint-Leu, taking care of his education and placing him in the army as his aide-de-camp. His sibling was not thankful, however, for the opportunities his brother's success gave him. Rather, he saw Napoléon's ascent as an imposition, pushing him into a life of existential *mauvaise foi* where he was 'always sacrificing his personal interests to those of others'.[10] This was especially the case with his marriage. Napoléon wanted to found a dynasty, but Joséphine was unable to have more children. The solution: marry Hortense and the comte de Saint-Leu.

Hortense was no more enamoured with the idea than the groom, but she was in awe of her stepfather and accepted her fate. As a young girl Hortense had seen mobs roam Paris looking to lynch aristocrats and had watched as crowds mutilated a statue of the Virgin Mary while she hid in a doorway. The role that Napoléon played in Hortense's life mirrored the one that Bonapartist propaganda claimed he performed for France: ending the anarchy of revolution and providing stability. In return, Hortense did what French people were meant to do, and many did: she revered and admired him. For his part, Napoléon trusted, respected and loved his stepchildren, giving them an especial position – much to the chagrin of his own brothers and sisters – within the Empire. Napoléon particularly delighted in Hortense's company. 'You know how well I will always love you, as I have since your childhood,' he wrote to her.[11]

In 1804, Napoléon crowned himself emperor. This act created the French Empire, the name given to the French state Napoléon ruled rather than France's overseas colonies. Far from welcoming his brother's elevation, the comte de Saint-Leu saw it as another step in the campaign to ruin his life. 'The consecration and coronation of the Emperor took place' on

2 December 1804, he wrote, and 'at that time, [I] partly lost the use of the fingers of [my] right hand'. He blamed the 'cold, rheumatism, and the fatigue of all the different ceremonies'. Against his wishes, he complained, he was placed 'near the imperial throne'.[12] Very near, in fact, because Napoléon settled the succession to his Empire: first his brother Joseph and his male children, then the comte de Saint-Leu and his. But as Joseph had no male children, Louis-Napoléon and his brother were next in line for the imperial throne among the younger generation of Bonapartes.

Louis-Napoléon's father had no involvement in his upbringing. In what he considered another afront, Napoléon had bullied the comte de Saint-Leu into becoming King of Holland in 1806. Hortense hated the country almost as much as her husband and spent little time there, preferring to stay in France, especially after the birth of her youngest son. Then, in 1810, believing his brother's rule had insufficiently turned Holland into a French colony, Napoléon lost patience. He got rid of his brother – and Holland, annexing it to France. Fearing his brother's wrath, the comte de Saint-Leu fled to Bohemia, leaving his eldest son behind. Napoléon sent a French official to bring the boy back. 'Come, my son,' said Napoléon when his nephew reached Paris, 'I will be your father. The conduct of your father grieves my heart.'[13] This applied as much to Louis-Napoléon as it did to his older brother: such paternal influence as the children had largely came from the emperor.

By the time Louis-Napoléon was baptised on 4 November 1810, Napoléon was at the apogee of his power. A series of stunning victories over Austria, Russia and Prussia had cowed the great European monarchies into accepting an upstart Corsican dynasty as the ruling house of France. The Treaty of Tilsit, signed in summer 1807 with Tsar Alexander I, brought Russia into Napoléon's continental system, banning trade with Britain. Moreover, with the ascent of Napoléon's brother Joseph to the Spanish throne a year later, French power extended from the Atlantic in the west via a series of client states through to the Duchy of Warsaw, part of modern-day Poland, in the east. Europe had never seen anything like it. Under Napoléon, revolutionary fervour, nationalism and skilled leadership turbocharged French armies as they marched across the continent and tore down old states and feudalism. That this was all done at the behest of a self-made man who had risen from unpromising origins to absolute power merely added to the sense that the world had been turned upside down and a new order created.

At home, Napoléon claimed to have ended the French Revolution, bringing stability after chaos, but he also claimed to safeguard rights won after 1789. Politically, the Empire was an autocracy, but it was dressed up in democratic language and Napoléon considered himself to represent the will of the people. Indeed, the people had spoken, in two plebiscites: once to declare Napoléon consul for life, and then again to create a hereditary empire, where a suspiciously high 99 per cent of those who voted agreed with Napoléon that he should be emperor. But regardless of rhetoric, the Empire was a personal one, centred on the emperor and his family.

Not long after his baptism, Louis-Napoléon's place within this family had become less important. Napoléon was Louis-Napoléon's godfather; through having affairs, however, Napoléon discovered that he could have children of his own. Joséphine, therefore, had been divorced in preference for a dynastic marriage with an Austrian archduchess, Marie Louise. She was Louis-Napoléon's godmother. In March 1811, she gave birth to a boy, Napoléon's heir: Napoléon II, if all went according to plan.

Nonetheless, Hortense's children were still princes in the imperial family and she ensured they venerated the emperor as a god. At breakfasts in the Tuileries, Napoléon would grab them by the head and lift them onto the table, much to the horror of Hortense, who, not unreasonably, hated this unorthodox approach to lifting little boys. She would not, however, complain. Napoléon may have been kind to Hortense, fond of her children, but he was feared as much as he was admired and her children were crucial to his dynastic plans.

Once, she took them to Baden, a spa town in what is today Germany. 'I am very angry', Napoléon wrote to Hortense, 'that you left France without my permission and above all that you took my nephews . . . One hour after receiving this letter, send my two nephews back to [France]. This is the first time I have reason to be unhappy with you; but you should not take steps in regard to my nephews without my permission.'[14]

If the boys revered Napoléon, they adored their mother. Hortense made time for her children in the mornings, refusing to see visitors so that she could be with them. Nonetheless, she still had plenty of entertaining to do as one of the most charming and glamorous members of the spectacular imperial court. In the evenings, as her hairdresser combed her long auburn hair, the little boys would amuse themselves by running through the gaps. Once ready, she kissed them before leaving, the two boys carrying her gloves and shawl, or holding the tail of her long velvet, satin-lined train if she was in full court dress, to her waiting carriage.

Hortense's love was returned with reverential devotion by her youngest son. When playing, he once saw one of the guardsmen had a finger missing. Louis-Napoléon, aged five, asked how he had lost it. The soldier recounted long suffering in various campaigns across Europe and his desire for some leave. 'This would be to see your mother, wouldn't it?' replied Louis-Napoléon. Some days later, the minister of war came to dine and Louis-Napoléon took it upon himself to explain the importance of being allowed to see one's mother. The politician promised to give the soldier leave. When Louis-Napoléon told his governess what he had done he said, 'I am so content. I will have made a man happy in my life.' These were, Hortense wrote to her brother, his own words. 'You judge how sweet it is to see a small, good heart show itself so young.'[15]

When Hortense travelled, the boys' letters to her were full of affection. Three years older, Napoléon-Louis took the lead in writing their news, with Louis-Napoléon adding postscripts; 'Little Louis really loves Maman,' ran a typical one.[16] With the help of his tutor, Louis-Napoléon began writing his own letters. 'It's been a long time since you left,' he wrote to his mother. 'You promised me that you would be back in two months. Two months have passed, are you on your way? Are you well? I have not been very good for the last few days, but I promise to correct myself, and I will keep my word. Farewell my darling Maman, I kiss you with all my heart.'[17]

Although she was at the centre of one of the most powerful regimes in Europe, Hortense wanted her children to grow up self-reliant. Her father had been guillotined, her mother imprisoned and nearly executed and her husband – admittedly much to her relief – had abdicated his throne and fled, abandoning his children. In short, she knew fortunes could change. Governesses and servants were told to call the boys by their names, not their imperial titles. She also impressed on them the need for education and skills. 'If you no longer possessed anything, and were all alone in the world,' she asked her eldest son, 'what would you do?'

'I would become a soldier, and I would fight so well that I would be made an officer.'

Turning to her youngest, she asked the same question. Louis-Napoléon, feeling a musket would be too heavy, opted for a less dangerous, more immediately lucrative and, crucially, less back-breaking career: 'I would sell bouquets of violets like the little boy at the gate of the Tuileries who we buy them from every day.'[18]

Hortense was right to prepare her children for hardship. In 1812, Napoléon launched an invasion of Russia. He led his Grande Armée – more than six hundred thousand men – to Moscow and took it, but Tsar Alexander refused to surrender. After Moscow went up in flames, Napoléon had no choice but to turn his army around for what became a death march through the awful Russian winter. Not that Napoléon stayed for all of it: with his long-suffering men not yet out of enemy territory, Napoléon fled to Paris to shore up his political position. Meanwhile, Hortense's brother Eugène played a key role in bravely leading what remained of the once mighty force as best he could; only some fifty thousand made it back.

Worse was to come. The combined powers of Europe were determined to capitalise on the once unbeatable Napoléon's misfortune. With the British pushing the French out of Spain, and Russia, Prussia and Austria leading the onslaught from the east, Napoléon was caught in a vice that no amount of military genius could counter.

In a show of solidarity, Hortense removed dessert from the boys' dinners, but this failed to stop the advance. By early 1814, armies from across Europe had invaded France. Men deserted from scraped-together, disease-ridden French armies that could not stop the enemy, old men and conscripted boys refused the call-up and the once iron-like grip of imperial authority evaporated. Having raised France to unthinkable glory, the Corsican parvenu now led the country to barely believable ruin. At the end of March 1814, 180,000 soldiers were poised to storm Paris.

———

On the evening of 28 March 1814 in the Tuileries, panicked members of the Bonaparte family debated what to do. Hortense urged Empress Marie Louise, Napoléon's second wife, whom he had left as regent while he fought the armies of Europe, to stay and defend Paris. 'I am leaving and I advise you to do the same,' said the empress, half laughing and half embarrassed. Shocked, Hortense replied, 'At least, sister, remember that you lose your crown. I am glad to see that you sacrifice it with a smile.' The empress leaned close and whispered, 'Perhaps you are right, but thus has it been decided, and if the emperor reproaches anyone, it will not be me.'[19]

Marie Louise was following Napoléon's orders. He wrote to his wife that he would rather see his son and heir at the bottom of the Seine than captured. In the event that Paris might fall, the imperial family must flee. It was an undignified exit, with ladies-in-waiting running from room to room, some crying, desperately packing what they could. Napoléon's son, just turned three, refused to leave. Holding onto the doors of his room, he screamed, 'I don't want to go out!' He had to be forcibly dragged, sobbing uncontrollably. Some interpreted this as a premonition of the end of the Empire he would have one day inherited, although probably not those with experience of toddlers. On the evening of 29 March, Parisians lined the streets, watching in silent disbelief as the imperial family that had brought catastrophic defeat to France after so many victories fled its capital, taking high-ranking officials and treasury with them.

Hortense had a fear far greater than capture by the enemy: her husband. After writing an appalling novel in exile, the comte de Saint-Leu had returned to France without Napoléon's permission. 'This man is mad,' complained the emperor, who had no use for an unhinged writer while trying to save his Empire; 'poor me, for having such an awful family'.[20] Not waiting for his children, the comte de Saint-Leu accompanied Marie Louise in her escape – he was 'in such a state of panic', wrote Marie Louise, 'and so demented that it was embarrassing'.[21]

Hortense kept a cooler head, planning to join the fleeing imperial family later. Leaving Paris at dawn, she heard the sound of guns in the distance. Rushing her children into a carriage, she headed away from the fighting. The road was full of soldiers, wounded men and refugees. As they went, Louis-Napoléon and his older brother played in the carriage, 'as though our flight were a game, and as if at that moment they were not losing their future'.[22] When she reached the rendezvous point, however, her husband and Marie Louise had already gone. Instead of following them, much to her husband's fury, Hortense took her children to join her mother Joséphine.

Meanwhile, with few forces to defend the capital, the remaining imperial authorities surrendered the city on the morning of 31 March. That same day, Tsar Alexander, Frederick William III, King of Prussia, and Karl Philipp, Prince of Schwarzenberg, representing the Austrian Empire, entered Paris. Wearing a green tunic with gold epaulettes, a wide bicorne hat with white feathers and riding a white horse, Tsar Alexander dismounted at the Champs-Élysées to watch victorious Allied soldiers march past. Less than two years ago, French troops had occupied Moscow. Now, tens of thousands of men from across Europe and Russia paraded through the unfinished Arc de Triomphe, a monument to Napoléon's hubristic glory. A few days later, crowds gathered in the Place Vendôme in the centre of Paris to watch as a statue of Napoléon was lowered from the colossal column that celebrated his famous victory over Austria and Russia at the Battle of Austerlitz.

Outside Paris, Napoléon reluctantly admitted defeat. On 11 April, he signed the Treaty of Fontainebleau, renouncing the throne and agreeing to exile on Elba, a small island off the Italian coast. In return, his family would receive generous financial compensation and keep much of their property in France. In Napoléon's place, the Allies imposed the Bourbons, which meant the enormously fat Louis XVIII, a younger brother of Louis XVI, became King of France. The title was significant: Napoléon had been Emperor of the French, of the people rather than the land. With royalists back in power, this was a dangerous time for those associated with the Empire, but Joséphine and Hortense had as their protector the man who had done most to bring about Napoléon's downfall: Tsar Alexander. Before Napoléon's second marriage, Joséphine had presided over France with magnetic elegance as empress. The tsar wanted to meet this celebrity at Malmaison.

He soon fell under Joséphine's spell, and while he was there, Hortense and her two children arrived. A few days before his sixth birthday, Louis-Napoléon was, therefore, surprised to find Malmaison full of Russian cavalry. His grandmother came out and introduced Hortense and her two sons to the tsar, before taking the children away. Self-conscious and awkward, Hortense did not know what to do. She decided that cold reserve was the best attitude to adopt in the face of Napoléon's nemesis, which resulted in a short and uncomfortable conversation, before Joséphine rejoined them with the children. Joséphine, a consummate survivor, was much warmer when talking to the tsar. Hortense watched on silently, noticing that the tsar constantly ruffled her children's hair. Then the ruler of Russia turned to her and said, 'What can I do for them? Allow me to be their chargé d'affaires.'[23]

Hortense thanked him, replying that her children needed nothing. Theoretically, she was right. Napoléon had made financial settlements for his family a condition of his abdication. But in practice, this was dependent on the goodwill of the French king and his royalist supporters, who loathed the Bonapartes. With the future precarious, Hortense realised that the tsar was an invaluable ally and struck up a friendship with the Russian sovereign.

He became a regular at Malmaison, playing with Louis-Napoléon and his brother, staying for dinner or going on excursions. All this attention made a great impression on the quiet and shy Louis-Napoléon. On one occasion when the tsar visited, the six-year-old crept up quietly to the Russian autocrat and silently placed a ring in his hand before fleeing the room. Hortense brought him back and asked him why he had given his ring. Blushing, lowering his head and avoiding eye contact, Louis-Napoléon replied, 'I only have this ring, it was my uncle Eugène who gave it to me, and I wanted to give it to the emperor because he is good to Maman.'[24] The tsar kissed Louis-Napoléon, put the ring on his watch chain and said he would always wear it.

Up to this point, the fall of Napoléon's Empire had been something of an adventure for Louis-Napoléon and his brother, but now their beloved grandmother Joséphine became sick. Her breathing was laboured and she suffered from excruciating throat and chest pains. On the evening of 28 May, a distraught Hortense brought Louis-Napoléon and his older brother to see their grandmother. Joséphine urged Hortense to take them away, worried that they might catch whatever she had. The next morning, she was dead.

Not long afterwards, Hortense risked losing her eldest son too; her husband demanded she give him custody. When Hortense remonstrated, the comte de Saint-Leu replied that she should be glad he did not want the youngest, Louis-Napoléon, whom she was welcome to keep. Though Napoléon had made an exception for his beloved Hortense, his legal reform, the Code Napoléon, gave fathers complete power over their children. Regardless, Hortense contested his wishes, but a court decided on 8 March 1815 that she must hand her eldest to his father. By then, however, Hortense had more to worry about than a custody battle. Days earlier, news had reached Paris that put the lives of her children in danger, and threatened to reignite war across Europe. After a mere ten months away, Napoléon was back.

———

On 1 March 1815, landing in south-eastern France with only a thousand men, Napoléon launched an outrageous bid to march on Paris and take back power from the Bourbon King Louis XVIII, who could call on 150,000 soldiers. On the road to Grenoble, troops barred Napoléon's way. According to Napoleonic legend, on dismounting, Napoléon walked towards ranks of infantrymen who had their muskets aimed at him. 'Here I am, soldiers, recognise me. If there is a soldier among you who wants to shoot his emperor,' he said, opening his greatcoat, 'he can do it.'[25] The front rank lowered their weapons, cries of '*Vive l'empereur!*' rang out, and Napoléon was mobbed. The gamble paid off, and his journey became a triumphant procession towards Paris.

By 20 March, he reached Fontainebleau, where he had abdicated less than a year earlier. In nearby Paris, Louis XVIII fled. In just over three weeks, Napoléon had chased away the divinely appointed king without firing a shot. Here was another legend for the imperial scrapbook: the journey soon took on magical qualities and became known as the Flight of the Eagle.

Before Napoléon reached Paris, Hortense, fearing a royalist backlash, had sent her children into hiding, which was terrific fun for the boys. Smuggled by their governess through the streets of Paris to nondescript rooms overlooking rue Montmartre, Louis-Napoléon delighted in the clandestine adventure, conspiracy and chance to see life beyond the closeted walls of palaces and sumptuous houses. Hortense, though, was terrified. Having openly flirted with Napoléon's great enemy, Tsar Alexander, she feared how the emperor, who had invited her to the Tuileries, would receive her.

On the evening of 20 March, Napoléon's carriage drove through an enormous cheering crowd and then into the main entrance of the Tuileries. The courtyard was so packed he had to alight long before the staircase leading into the palace. People swarmed around the emperor, jostling, pushing, almost crushing him. Once the excitement died down, Hortense, waiting nervously inside and dressed in mourning for Joséphine's death, made her way into a drawing room. There, Napoléon embraced her, but did not speak to her, conversing with others and walking straight past her when dinner was announced. Hortense waited until Napoléon re-entered after eating.

'Where are your children?' he asked.

'Sire, existing conditions obliged me to send them away from home. I ask your permission to bring them to you tomorrow.'

'I see by the papers', Napoléon replied, 'that you lost your case. I would have bet on it. Paternal authority is everything.' With that, the emperor went into his study to set about recreating his Empire. Already late, Hortense left, hoping for a more amicable meeting the next day with her children.

With Louis-Napoléon and his brother in tow, Hortense entered the Tuileries the next morning. Napoléon was at the window of a drawing room, revelling in cheers from the crowds outside. He received Hortense coldly, her children warmly. Napoléon made Hortense wait in silence as he paced the room before speaking.

'I should never have thought you would forsake my cause,' said Napoléon.

'Forsake your cause, Sire? Would I, or even could I, have done such a thing?' replied Hortense.

Napoléon was angry that Hortense had stayed in Paris during his exile, which he interpreted as tacit support for the Bourbons. Hortense explained that she had to stay with Joséphine and that, besides, she had nowhere else to go. After arguing, Napoléon said, 'What does it matter? You had no business to stay in France . . . You have behaved like a child. When one has shared in the elevation of a family, one must share in its misfortunes.' Hortense started crying. Moved, Napoléon said, 'Come, come, you have not a single good excuse to make, but you know I am an indulgent father. There! I forgive you. We won't speak more of it.'[26]

With her children, he had shown no coldness. Delighting in their presence when they came into the room, he caressed them, played with them and took great pride in showing them at the window to the rapturous people outside. As ever with Napoléon, this was family mixed with politics. He liked children, he especially liked Hortense's children, but with his wife and, more importantly, his son in Vienna, having two imperial princes on hand to display was a card worth playing. For her part, Hortense became the leading lady of imperial Paris, and Napoléon asked her to bring her children often to the Tuileries.

And so for Louis-Napoléon the imperial adventure with all its pomp and majesty started again. A thrilling moment for the young boy was watching his uncle review his troops in the gardens of the Tuileries. As much as the brilliantly uniformed officers and soldiers, the swords and the muskets, the boys were struck by the crowds – thousands lining the streets, people packed precariously onto roofs, hanging onto scaffolding – shouting delirious, deafening cries of '*Vive l'empereur!*'

The popular support was real, for in contrast to his previous incarnation, the returned Napoléon promised to rule constitutionally. His populist message was simple: foreigners had humiliated France, imposed the old kings and stolen the revolution with the connivance of French elites. Napoléon was the man of the people, the saviour of the revolution who would restore France to greatness. 'The cause today is that of the people against the nobles, peasants against the landlords, the French against the foreigner,' he wrote.[27]

On 1 June 1815, some two hundred thousand people turned out to watch Napoléon pledge his allegiance to a new liberal constitution. With what remained of the imperial family behind him, including Hortense and Louis-Napoléon in privileged positions, Napoléon addressed the crowds. Unfortunately, the emperor had decided to wear his old coronation robes from 1804, with a few Roman-inspired extras. But he was not the man he was ten years ago. It was one thing to figuratively recall past glories, quite another to force his now considerable paunch into clothes designed for a less corpulent emperor. After a rambling speech, he realised he was losing the day. Recapturing his elan, without warning he ran down the steps of the platform and, with confused officials chasing him, Napoléon made his way to a raised altar in the middle of the Champ-de-Mars, where thousands of troops formed a square around him. Now he harangued his soldiers to ever more dramatic acts of future bravery and distributed eagle standards to men whipped up into a martial frenzy.

For Napoléon knew that his future, his family's and France's would be decided on the battlefield. He positioned himself as a man of peace, claiming he represented the will of the French people and that foreign powers had no right to intervene in the internal affairs of France. The foreign powers did not share this view. They hated Napoléon. That he was a bellicose Corsican arriviste who felt he was equal to the royal houses of Europe and had plunged the continent into war was bad enough. But if now, as he claimed, he stood for liberty and democracy, that was even worse. For the conservative states of Europe, Britain, Austria, Prussia and Russia, this was a nightmare they had lived through before: revolution exported at the point of French bayonets. It had to be stopped. They would make war until he was dead or gone. So it was that on 12 June 1815, Louis-Napoléon and his brother saw the emperor at the Tuileries for a family dinner, as was Napoléon's custom before he went on campaign. Then Napoléon left to join his army.

———

Eight days later in Paris, Hortense was told by a high-ranking French military officer of an unfortunate engagement, which turned out to be a euphemism for Napoléon's defeat at the Battle of Waterloo against British and Prussian forces. Flying from the battlefield, Napoléon reached the capital the next day. Egypt, Russia, now Waterloo: he was an old hand at this game – the key was to get back quickly and spin the narrative. This time, however, he cut a dejected and, strangely for him, indecisive figure. As he often did at times of crisis, he had a bath, but it did not help. He swung between creating a military dictatorship and abdicating. In the end, politicians took the decision out of his hands, forcing him to step aside in favour of his son, who became known as Napoléon II, though he never officially reigned. This was a ruse to get Napoléon out of the way, for the

French political elite was not going down with Napoléon and schemed with foreign powers for a second restoration of the Bourbon king.

On 25 June, Napoléon retired to his personal place of safety, Malmaison, accompanied by Hortense; Louis-Napoléon and his brother were back hiding in Paris. At Malmaison, Napoléon vacillated, unsure whether to make for the coast and head into exile in the United States or wait for some improbable reversal of fortune. Instead of acting, he wandered the corridors and gardens of the chateau. He visited the room where Joséphine had died, telling Hortense that he expected her to appear at any moment. With rumours that troops were on their way to arrest him, he left after five days. Napoléon and his entourage clambered into carriages that took them to a port on the Atlantic coast. After days of indecision, the former emperor surrendered to a British ship blockading the port. Months later, he was transported into exile on the remote island of Saint Helena in the middle of the South Atlantic.

The end was distinctly underwhelming, but what became known as the Hundred Days – the period from Napoléon's return from Elba to his defeat at Waterloo – had an impact in France that far outweighed its short duration. It became part of a powerful myth: popular Bonapartism championed the people and raised France to such heights that it had to be struck down by the combined despotic powers of monarchical Europe. In Paris, this was the tale Hortense told her sons, and it was one Louis-Napoléon uncritically accepted. After Napoléon's defeat, however, Hortense's children were not safe. Royalists, determined there would be no third coming of Napoléon, were persecuting his supporters in what became known as the White Terror.

2

AN UNSENTIMENTAL EDUCATION

In Paris, they were shooting people for a crime of which many were guilty: rallying to Napoléon during the Hundred Days. After Waterloo, there was a royalist backlash from supporters of the Bourbon King Louis XVIII, and for those whose treason was considered especially grievous, execution was the remedy. More terrifying than the official crackdown was the licence given to armed bands of royalists across France who lynched those they deemed complicit with the imperial cause. And few were more complicit than Hortense, the unofficial first lady of the Hundred Days.

In the capital, royalist mobs insulted Hortense, threatening to ransack her home. She rented a house under a pseudonym and put Louis-Napoléon and his older brother once again into hiding, but the authorities claimed they could no longer guarantee her safety. One morning in July, she was ordered to leave Paris. That evening, with her two children in the carriage, she set out. Hortense hoped to find asylum in Switzerland, but to get there she had to pass through a country on the brink of civil war. Though terrified of royalist vigilantes, she had no fear of the people or French soldiers. The Bonapartist myth that Hortense bought into, and told to her children, was that Napoléon was immensely popular with both. The next stop on her journey proved otherwise.

In Dijon, three French officers came into the room where Hortense was staying and ordered her not to leave. When an Austrian aide-de-camp travelling with her to ensure her safety protested, the men withdrew and gathered a crowd around the inn. From their room, Hortense and her children heard angry shouts of 'Long live the king!' Much of France was under Allied occupation and the Austrian aide rounded up some troops who dispersed the crowd. The royalist soldiers remained. Their commander paced menacingly outside, his long sword rattling as he walked, while his men guarded Hortense's carriages. He watched on in disgust as Hortense and her children made their way downstairs between ranks of Austrian troops summoned to protect them.

For some in the French army, though, the Napoleonic flame still burned. At other stops on the journey veterans broke down and wept when they saw her and her children. One said to her, 'We must submit, but our day will come, and then it will be the awakening of the lion.'[1] The Bonapartist stab-in-the-back myth was already well founded among the rank and file of the army. It was not the genius Napoléon who had been defeated, rather it was the pusillanimous royalists – in league with self-serving politicians in Paris desperate to restore their *ancien régime* privileges – who had given over France to the humiliation of foreign occupation.

Hortense and her children's wanderings did not end when they made it to Switzerland. The Swiss authorities, under pressure from the French and the Allies, had no desire to become a centre of Bonapartist intrigue. The trio were refused permission to stay. Trailed by spies of various different powers, and with French agents intercepting Hortense's correspondence, they made for Aix-les-Bains – once French territory, but after Waterloo given by the Allies to the Italian kingdom of Piedmont-Sardinia. Here, Hortense rented a dilapidated house with a large courtyard, where Louis-Napoléon and his brother played. Their games fuelled rumours: when Louis-Napoléon and some other local children pretended to be soldiers, it was reported that Hortense was raising Bonapartist regiments.

Things got worse. Her husband sent an agent to Savoy to take custody of her oldest son, Napoléon-Louis. He would live with his father, who had fled to Italy. There was nothing Hortense could do. The comte de Saint-Leu had no interest in taking his younger son, who was catatonic at being separated from his brother. With his father all but absent for most of his life, his beloved grandmother dead and his uncle Napoléon prisoner, the one constant in Louis-Napoléon's life apart from his mother had been his brother. Sweet-natured, quiet, pensive, shy and speaking seldom, Louis-Napoléon had leaned heavily on his more outgoing sibling, who returned his affection and looked after his little brother. As he said goodbye, Louis-Napoléon, only seven years old, was inconsolable. Overwhelmed by misfortune, Hortense hugged her remaining son, repeating out loud a mantra unlikely to provide enormous reassurance to the young boy in her arms: 'No, no. I will not let myself die. I can still be of use!'[2]

Hortense's situation was unfortunate, but she had money and powerful connections. Her brother, Eugène, had stayed out of the Hundred Days. He was still on good terms with the tsar and was married to the daughter of the King of Bavaria. With his help, she secured permission to travel to Constance, a soporific town beside the beautiful lake of the same name on what is today the Swiss–German border. She reached Constance on 7 December 1815 – 'a lost corner of the world', as she described it, where she and Louis-Napoléon found refuge. In January 1816, the French government banished all members of the Bonaparte family from France on pain of death. Upon hearing the news, Louis-Napoléon asked, tears falling down his cheeks, 'Can it be, mamma, that we shall never see France again?'[3]

After a few years, Hortense found a permanent residence which gave Louis-Napoléon the stability and structure that had been lacking ever since the (first) collapse of his uncle's empire in 1814. Hortense bought the chateau of Arenenberg in 1817 and moved there in 1820. Perched atop hills rising steeply from Lake Constance and secluded among vineyards and tall trees, the chateau dated back to the sixteenth century and had superb views of the countryside and scattered villages below, with sombre dark woods, vestiges of the Black Forest, on the horizon.

Inside, Hortense quickly turned it into a museum to Napoléon. She had the ground floor draped in tents, an interior decor tip borrowed from Napoléon, who liked to mirror his campaign marquee at home. Walls were lined with portraits of Napoléon, Joséphine and Eugène, as well as assorted swords, pikes and muskets. Louis-Napoléon grew up among the relics of his uncle's glory. Obsessed, he marked the fallen emperor's place of exile, Saint Helena, on a globe.

Twelve years old when they moved to Arenenberg, Louis-Napoléon was a taciturn, shy, lackadaisical but sweet-natured boy who had developed a love of exercise, especially fencing, swimming and horse riding. The chateau was isolated. Hortense's ladies-in-waiting and occasional visits to the extended Bonaparte family were Louis-Napoléon's only chances of company. He spent much time on his own, daydreaming.

Family anecdotes from this time still remarked on Louis-Napoléon's kindness and empathy. Once, he came back home without shoes or a jacket: while out walking he had given them away to a poor family. On the other hand, a servant reminisced, with peculiar fondness, that when carrying heavy loads after working in the garden, Louis-Napoléon would wait until he was putting them down and then push him over. After one particularly nasty fall, the servant cried and Louis-Napoléon ran inside to get him some bread and came back to comfort him.

Despite the comte de Saint-Leu's absence, the erratic behaviour of his father affected Louis-Napoléon. The comte swung between trying to get his marriage annulled and desperately pleading with Hortense to get back together. He was, she concluded, a sick lunatic. Regardless, Louis-Napoléon revered his father, always looking for his approval. This was rarely forthcoming. What the comte de Saint-Leu cherished most in letters from his absent son was spelling, grammar and neat handwriting. 'You cannot give me a greater present', the comte de Saint-Leu wrote to Louis-Napoléon, 'than writing me a beautiful letter, <u>without a single mistake</u> [underlined in original], and without the help of your tutor.'[4]

Although the comte de Saint-Leu rarely saw his younger son, this did not stop him pontificating on how he was raised. Often he focused on petty details, insisting his son not have lunch too late and go for a walk afterwards. But his most important act, no doubt in part inspired by the hope of getting a well-written letter, was to demand improvements in his son's education. During their wanderings after leaving France, this had been woefully neglected. Louis-Napoléon's tutor was eccentric, good-natured and had a dry wit, but was not cut out for the life of a teacher, preferring late mornings and writing poetry to the strictures of pedagogy. Napoléon-Louis had been his ward before his father took him to Italy, and he knew that his younger brother had little formal schooling. Chastising Louis-Napoléon and his old tutor for not replying to his letters, Napoléon-Louis wrote, 'As for you, I excuse you because, as we well know, it is much more fun to play in the snow, to be *en garde* [fencing] . . . than to write to me.' His old tutor, however, 'would have easily been able to write to me. It is true that he has to look after you (which is not easy), and rouse himself from time to time to make the effort to walk to the window where, after taking a deep breath, he screams, "Prince Louis, come here, my child, *cave ne cadas* [careful not to fall in Latin], ah! ah!, *mon dieu*, how that child scares me!"[5]

Hortense wrote that the 'most delightful of my occupations was the education of my younger son, who spent most of his time with me'.[6] Delightful it may have been, effective it was not. The comte de Saint-Leu, who fancied himself as a man of letters, was shocked at the gaps in his youngest son's learning. Unless it improved, he threatened to take him from Hortense. There was nothing for it: Hortense had to hire a new tutor for Louis-Napoléon.

———

Fifty soldiers ran up the main staircase in the Hôtel de Ville, Paris's city hall, making as little noise as possible. It was around 2 a.m. on 28 July 1794, and they had come to arrest the architect of the Terror during the French Revolution, Maximilien Robespierre. He had gathered with his remaining supporters on the first floor of the building, hoping to make a stand against the *coup d'état* which had been launched against him the day before. Rushing into the room, the soldiers ended Robespierre's resistance. Whether a failed suicide or a shot from one of the attackers, a pistol ball tore off much of Robespierre's jaw, but he was still alive. Another man, Philippe Le Bas, was not. He lay dead on the floor, preferring suicide to life without Robespierre in power. Le Bas had been a father for less than six weeks. At the end of June, his wife and fellow Jacobin, Élisabeth Duplay, had given birth to a baby boy, also named Philippe.

The boy's mother brought him up as a republican who worshipped his Jacobin father. Like most Frenchmen of his generation, the young Le Bas was swept up in the Napoleonic wars and served in the imperial navy before fighting in the army during the campaigns of 1813 and 1814. After the wars, he entered the civil service, but his true calling was classics. With a wife to support, a position as a tutor to an illustrious family would provide financial security and allow Le Bas to pursue his own studies. Mutual acquaintances recommended him to Hortense, who was desperately looking for a tutor, and he was appointed in June 1820. So it was that Le Bas, an avowed republican and the son of a radical revolutionary martyr, came to be one of the most important influences on a nephew of the Emperor Napoléon.

His new tutor brought discipline to Louis-Napoléon's hitherto haphazard studies and a zeal for learning. It was said of Le Bas that 'he loves the Greeks to the point of madness, and their language to the point of rage'.[7] Hortense gave him almost complete control over Louis-Napoléon and they lived together in a small annexe to the chateau. A punishing timetable was soon devised which meant Louis-Napoléon spent nearly all his time with his tutor. Much to his horror, Le Bas found that the boy would sometimes get out of bed as late as 9 a.m. Under the new regime, they got up at 6 a.m. and walked in the hills until 7 a.m. Seven to 8.30 a.m. was dedicated to revising what they had learned the day before. There was half an hour for breakfast before study began with Latin until 10 a.m. Then on Mondays, Wednesdays and Fridays there were two hours of mathematics; on Tuesdays, Thursdays and Saturdays, French grammar, dictation and spelling. This latter skill, Le Bas lamented, as Louis-Napoléon's father had, was almost entirely absent. At midday, a spartan lunch – austerity necessary, so Le Bas felt, for what he called a 'weak and greedy' child. After lunch, a walk, then more study, including history, geography and German lessons, as well as homework. Dinner, together, was at 7 p.m. Even breaks took the form of didactic walks where Le Bas would hold forth on botany or astronomy.

As Le Bas noted, they were completely isolated and almost always alone together; however, Louis-Napoléon was allowed to spend his final hour before bed with his mother in her drawing room with her ladies-in-waiting and guests. 'I have not been able to refuse this,' complained Le Bas – 'but', he continued, 'this is the most dangerous hour of the day . . . How harmful is the idleness of such a place to the child!'[8] For Le Bas the conversation of these society women in Hortense's salon was pointless, rarely touching on interesting subjects such as Greek or Latin inscriptions. Indeed, Le Bas had been frustrated in his attempts to discuss his favourite topic, noting that when he tried to talk about Greek, the women uttered cries of protest. Despite the shocking lack of regard for ancient Greek in the salon, Le Bas realised he could not stop Hortense seeing her son for one hour a day.

Le Bas was right: these evening discussions were dangerous, but not for the reasons he thought. Hortense was a celebrity, and her position as a fallen Bonaparte queen only increased her allure, while her well-known passion for the arts made Arenenberg a stop-off point for many an artist or intellectual. Over the years, she would welcome such luminaries as the celebrated French writer Casimir Delavigne, the illustrious French Romantic and politician François-René de Chateaubriand and the novelist Alexandre Dumas *père*; however, it was the politics that worried the authorities. They were liberal, sometimes radical, always freely spoken. Spies watched Arenenberg, and were horrified at the revolving cast of fallen Bonapartes, former imperial politicians, generals and down-and-out adventurers, many of them on the run, that made up Hortense's entourage. Knowing her correspondence was read, Hortense delighted in sprinkling it with disinformation. For the young Louis-Napoléon, then, a loose relationship with the truth, conspiracy and imperial nostalgia were quotidian events.

Major Denis-Charles Parquin, for example, who married one of Hortense's ladies-in-waiting, was a man who had never let go of the Empire. A former cavalry officer and then a member of Napoléon's elite Imperial Guard, Parquin was the embodiment of the diehard Bonapartist officer class, cashiered under the Bourbons and put on half pay. Washed-up and slightly overweight, but with magnificently styled whiskers, the hard-drinking, hard-gambling former soldier was always ready to reminisce about the glory days, and equally happy to conspire to create new ones. He would tell tall tales of his escapades in the Napoleonic army to anyone who would listen, and in the teenage Louis-Napoléon he had a spellbound audience. In the summer, in his rare free moments, the emperor's nephew was often to be found under a tree with Parquin, who, smoking a cigar, regaled him with boy's own tales of bravery under the Empire.

At first, Louis-Napoléon showed less devotion to his studies than he did to memorising his uncle's history. It was hard work teaching his pupil, Le Bas wrote, because he had so many gaps in his knowledge and was not used to following such a rigorous timetable. Despite this, Le Bas found a gentle, passive child with 'an excellent heart' who was keen to please. With these qualities, he concluded, there was plenty to work with. He soon warmed to Louis-Napoléon, and the two developed a close bond. 'He is very attached to me,' wrote Le Bas, and 'for my part, I like him a lot already'. This was just as well because Louis-Napoléon spent more time with his tutor in six months than he had with his own father in twelve years. One day, Le Bas spoke to Louis-Napoléon about the happiness he had felt at the birth of his son, but tears soon filled his eyes as he remembered the death of this newborn. 'Console yourself, sir,' replied Louis-Napoléon, 'you no longer have a son, but I want to take his place.'[9] It was a well-meant if somewhat clumsily expressed thought, and Le Bas found it incredibly touching.

It helped their relationship that after a slow start, Louis-Napoléon made excellent progress, especially in classical studies, and soon Le Bas finally had someone he could talk to about ancient history. After less than a year together, he was pleased to report that his student could discuss the first-century philosopher Seneca. Most important of all for Le Bas, Louis-Napoléon was learning Greek verbs. His student was, therefore, 'becoming more interesting each day', and soon, wrote Le Bas with palpable excitement, it would be time to introduce him to the works of Plutarch.[10] To further Louis-Napoléon's learning, Le Bas had Hortense enrol her twelve-year-old son at school in Augsburg, Bavaria, where she owned a house. With the help of Le Bas, and desperate to please his mother, Louis-Napoléon did well in class, especially given lessons were in German, not French. His letters home delighted in recording his improving position within the class, while his school reports praised his 'quiet manner towards his fellow students' and picked up on his burgeoning Romanticism: 'this pupil possesses an ardent feeling for all that is elevated, good and beautiful'.[11]

Louis-Napoléon was at Augsburg when he received devastating news: Napoléon Bonaparte had died in exile on 5 May 1821. 'My dear Mother,' wrote Louis-Napoléon:

This death has caused me, as you can imagine, such a great grief . . . Happily, he is in a better world than ours, where he peacefully enjoys the fruits of his good works. What gives me so much sorrow is not to have seen him even once before his death because in Paris I was so young that it is almost only my heart alone that has a memory of him. When I do wrong, if I think of <u>this great man</u>, I seem to feel within me his spirit telling me to be worthy of the name Napoléon.

Finishing his letter, Louis-Napoléon said that if occasionally his youth meant he seemed happy, this did not mean that his heart was not sad, 'and that I do not have an eternal hatred against the English'.[12]

Le Bas was struck by how much the death affected Louis-Napoléon. Indeed, he was so moved he gave his student three days off, which, given Le Bas's horror at time spent not learning, was as much a tribute to the former emperor as the numerous valedictory poems from the pens of the Russian writer Alexander Pushkin, the French poet Alphonse de Lamartine and the English Percy Bysshe Shelley.

The range of poets, and there were many more, was testament to the seismic event that was the death of Napoléon. He was already the most famous man in Europe and the Americas, and the death of the former emperor further burnished his powerful legend – not least because Napoléon shaped it from beyond the grave. In 1823, *The Memorial of Saint Helena* was published and became one of the most read works of the nineteenth century. Napoléon may have lost the Battle of Waterloo, but in these self-serving reminiscences, awash with embellishments, half-truths and full lies dictated before death to a companion in exile, he won the propaganda war. In the gospel according to Napoléon, he was a far-sighted ruler who governed on the side of progress in the interests of the people and was only defeated by a reactionary coalition of foreign powers. This was the version of his uncle that became seared into the nephew's heart and mind. Memorising passages, Louis-Napoléon treated the book as a bible and it deepened the mystical awe in which he held his uncle.

More than his uncle, though, Louis-Napoléon missed his mother, writing achingly sad letters from school to Hortense about how much he loved her. Le Bas did what he could to offset this homesickness and treated him as his own son. They amused themselves with amateur dramatics, including one play in which Louis-Napoléon refused to act because the role required him to disrespect his tutor on stage, something he could not bring himself to do even in fiction. At public events, Le Bas would put Louis-Napoléon on his shoulders to get a better view of whatever was going on. And he made sure that there were parties on Louis-Napoléon's name day, which he shared with his absent father, organising magic shows, fireworks and inviting his classmates. Several times Le Bas wrote that in Louis-Napoléon he had found a 'friend for life'.[13] These years were happy ones for Louis-Napoléon, and his studies continued to improve.

But the comte de Saint-Leu made a proposal in 1823 that turned the carefully ordered world of Le Bas's pupil upside down. Louis-Napoléon and Hortense should winter in Italy. From now on, Louis-Napoléon spent months immersed in the sumptuousness decadence of Rome's aristocratic world and the revolutionary politics of Italian nationalism.

———

Many of the large Bonaparte clan had found refuge in Rome. Here, Napoléon's imperious mother, known as Madame Mère, reigned over her relatives in the eternal city with a despotic tyranny that would have made her dead son proud. Her Olympian disdain for those outside – and within – her family was made all the more awesome by the fact that she remained in mourning for her son. It was a large court. Napoléon's oldest brother, Joseph, lived in exile in the United States, but his three younger brothers, Lucien, the comte de Saint-Leu and Jérôme, all ended up in Rome. Lucien and Jérôme lived with their second wives – dynastic matches chosen by Napoléon – and their numerous children (by 1823, Lucien had nine, Jérôme three). One of Napoléon's sisters was also there, Pauline, whose scandalous affairs even Napoléon – generally tolerant of such things – had found embarrassing. They were an eccentric, ridiculous coterie who, despite their protestations of poverty, lived in opulent palaces after managing to extract money and titles from their brother's Empire which they had done nothing to earn. As worship of his uncle shone brightly in Louis-Napoléon's teenage mind, his relatives were fascinating to him on his visits to their Roman palaces.

For Louis-Napoléon, trips to Madame Mère's were especially mesmerising, if lugubrious. She rarely left her palazzo, and it was said the lack of sun on her face left it with a ghostly pallor that resembled the marble busts she surrounded herself with. When visiting, children were expected to be silent and follow arcane etiquette; everything was imbued with a mysterious scent of the past. Even the furniture had to be respected in the dimly lit, cavernous rooms. A large trunk that contained her most precious possessions was the object of especial speculation from her numerous nieces and nephews. With a mixture of fear and respect, they would ask what it was for. 'It is to lock you in if you are naughty,' she replied, 'but I will show it to you when better times return.'[14]

Le Bas, however, did not appreciate time in Rome. Like most people who met him, he had nothing but disdain for Louis-Napoléon's father, noting the comte de Saint-Leu's violent mood swings and paranoia. Or, as Napoléon Bonaparte put it in *The Memorial of Saint Helena*, the comte de Saint-Leu's mind 'naturally inclined towards the perverse and the bizarre. He was further spoiled by reading too much Jean-Jacques [Rousseau].'[15] Worse for Le Bas, there were, he complained, only three or four hours' study a day. Louis-Napoléon spent evenings with his father, returned home late and slept in the next day. 'Our life here', Le Bas wrote, 'is uniform in its dissipation.'[16] That was an exaggeration. Louis-Napoléon's time with his father was hardly riotous. The first on the comte de Saint-Leu's esoteric list of rules for his teenage son, 'only drink Bordeaux, no coffee, no liqueurs', was misleading. The others showed him as the obsessively controlling misanthrope that he was: 2. Wash your feet once a week, if necessary, the nails with lemon, hands with bran, never soap . . . 4. (a risk given 2) The use of eau de Cologne or any other scent is forbidden . . . 6. (sensible if following 2) We will make him large shoes that fit both feet; 7. Clean your head with a dry sponge, not water! . . . 10. Must obey even an unjust order; 11. Chocolate will be kept in a locked place, a quarter of a bar at most a day.[17]

Louis-Napoléon was freed from trying to wash his head with a dry sponge when the trip to Italy was cut short because news arrived that his Uncle Eugène had died. On the journey back to Arenenberg, he stopped to fill a bottle with water from the Rubicon river. His love of ancient history saw him increasingly fixate on the life of one of Napoléon's heroes, Julius Caesar, who, in crossing the Rubicon, had announced his intention to violate Roman law and seize power in the name, so Caesar argued, of the people.

Over the next few years, the winters in Rome continued. Here, Le Bas lamented, it was only with great difficulty that he could get his student to sit down and read passages of the Roman historian Tacitus. The long journey and the rich world of Italy took Louis-Napoléon away from his studies. The magnificent Roman carnival, for example, saw a week of feasts, celebrations and horse racing, as well as decadent masked balls at night. This was impossibly exciting for the teenage Louis-Napoléon. For Le Bas, though, this was a nightmarish time, as the libraries were closed.

Just before Louis-Napoléon's eighteenth birthday in 1826, therefore, Le Bas wrote that his pupil's character was always 'so good, so amiable. His spirit develops, his ideas mature' but 'his studies suffer'. It is necessary to resign oneself, he wrote sadly, 'to being only a superficial man when one leads a nomadic life too young'.[18] He consoled himself with the thought that whatever happened, he would keep the friendship of his student and the esteem of his mother for life.

One year later, in the summer of 1827, Le Bas was sacked. He felt, not unreasonably after dedicating seven years of his life to Louis-Napoléon, that this was unfair. But while for many parents complaints that their teenage son should spend more time studying and less going out would be met with sympathy, it was not so for Hortense. She wanted Louis-Napoléon to be educated, not a tediously boring academic. As a young Bonaparte prince, he should be accomplished in society, enjoy riding and hunting, attend balls and salons. He was now able to hold forth on a range of subjects: history, politics, literature and sciences. Moreover, the remoteness of Arenenberg combined with Le Bas's discipline turned Louis-Napoléon into an autodidact, content to while away hours reading and studying independently. There was, then, no need to keep a tutor. And in terms of preparing her son for high society, Hortense – her salons under the Empire had been famed for their elegance – was as accomplished a tutor as Le Bas was a classical scholar.

Freed from Le Bas's punishing timetable and moralising, Louis-Napoléon developed two lifelong passions: politics and women. The most important people in his upbringing were female: Hortense, her ladies-in-waiting, Joséphine, his nanny, with whom he remained friends into adulthood, and Hortense Cornu, a childhood playmate who was a daughter of one of his mother's ladies-in-waiting. Men – his father or the emperor, for example – loomed large in his imagination but, with the exception of Le Bas, not in his reality. He was, therefore, at ease around women. Moreover, Louis-Napoléon was a romantic. It was German literature, which he read in the original – he was particularly fond of the playwright, poet and philosopher Friedrich Schiller – as much as French that fired his imagination. It was with the melodramatic tropes of Romanticism firmly in mind that, aged fifteen, while out for a walk with female cousins, the subject turned to the declining standards of chivalry. Louis-Napoléon took umbrage. There was a time, remarked one of his cousins as they crossed a bridge, when a man would leap into a torrent to rescue a lady's glove. Louis-Napoléon then plunged into the river below, which demonstrated his prowess at swimming, if not common sense or a gift for retrieval, given that no one had lost a glove.

In Rome, he was on the outside of the intensely glamorous and often decadent beau monde. Hortense's salon became one of the most talked-about gatherings, but for any self-respecting blue-blooded French aristocrat she was the enemy. The French ambassador representing the Bourbon king in Rome refused to be seen with any Bonaparte and went to great lengths to avoid Hortense and her sons. It was, therefore, those marked by their liberal politics and love of the arts who embraced Hortense. The heart of Roman society in the 1820s was a crowd of rich and idle British aristocrats who passed slowly, with a studied air of ennui, from one salon to another. Their scandalous lives were documented by one of their number, Edward Henry Fox. He had a penchant for older women; Hortense had a penchant for younger men, some rumoured to be less platonic than others; and the two became friends. Fox found her conversation fascinating, and witty. Discussing the wife of the Emperor of Brazil, Hortense said she was a 'monster of ugliness', but the emperor had had five children and that 'at least shows courage'.[19]

As many were, Fox was struck by Hortense's closeness with her son. One day when he called to see her, he found Hortense close to tears. Louis-Napoléon had just left to stay with his father, who divided his time between Florence and Rome. Fox thought that something serious must have happened, or that at least he would be away for a long time, but was incredulous when Hortense told him that she would see her son before the end of the month. But when Fox was introduced to Louis-Napoléon, he was underwhelmed: 'an amiable, good-humoured young man, but his ugliness and the peculiarity of his position, which prevents his mixing in general society and gives him manners that from awkwardness are not *liant* [affable], prevent the first impression being agreeable'.[20]

Fox's family were notorious in England for their liberal and pro-Bonaparte politics; others Louis-Napoléon met were infamous for their sexual ones. Hortense became acquainted with Marguerite Gardiner, Countess of

Blessington, one of Byron's former mistresses, who now scandalised British and Roman society with her relationship with Alfred d'Orsay, the archangel of dandyism, as one French poet called him. The two lived together in a *ménage à trois* with Lady Blessington's rich husband, the Earl of Blessington, a set-up made even more scandalous when d'Orsay then married the earl's fifteen-year-old daughter from his first wife. By Bonapartist standards, though, such things were par for the course, and Hortense befriended Lady Blessington. In turn, Lady Blessington developed a fondness for Louis-Napoléon. He lives with his mother, she wrote, 'and never did I witness a more devoted attachment than subsists between them. He is a fine high-spirited youth, admirably well educated, and highly accomplished, uniting to the gallant bearing of a soldier all the politeness of a *preux chevalier*.'[21]

Louis-Napoléon was too young to play a role other than *preux chevalier* in the highly seductive and sexualised world of Roman high society; how-ever, there was plenty to catch his eye. Also a regular at Hortense's salons was Countess Teresa Guiccioli, another of Byron's former mistresses and Fox's current one, although it was a tempestuous relationship ('Poor Lord Byron! I do not wonder at his going to Greece,' wrote Fox).[22] These, then, were not the polite drawing rooms of genteel society – although Louis-Napoléon had plenty of experience of those with his more respectable relations – but subversive gatherings of politically radical, sexually liberated social misfits. They railed against the inequities of authoritarian politics as much as they revelled in transgressive societal ones.

It was within this milieu that Louis-Napoléon came of age. Lovers were fought over, lost, shared; fortunes were gambled away in long evenings of heavy drinking; disgraced Bonapartist adventurers, cashiered or on half pay and often part of Hortense's entourage, told embellished legends of their exploits during the Napoleonic wars. One evening Parquin, who some-times came with Hortense to Rome with his wife, managed to fleece a young French aristocrat out of ten thousand francs.

Unlike Fox, another British aristocrat, James Harris, later 3rd Earl of Malmesbury, took to Louis-Napoléon and the two became lifelong friends, Louis-Napoléon having forgotten his pledge of eternal hatred against the English. Malmesbury, a raffish scion of the British ruling class who, in the words of a contemporary, was someone who 'courted women, respectable and disrespectable: succeeded in the pursuit: and was somewhat promiscuous in his love affairs', was a man after Louis-Napoléon's own heart.[23] In 1829, Malmesbury recalled, Louis-Napoléon was 'a wild harum-scarum youth . . . riding at full gallop down the streets to the peril of the public, fencing, and pistol-shooting, and apparently without serious thoughts of any kind'. Malmesbury felt that he had 'no remarkable talent or any fixed idea' and added that he was 'short, but very active and muscular. His face was grave and dark, but redeemed by a singularly bright smile.'[24]

In 1829, the year he turned twenty-one, Louis-Napoléon was looking for adventure and confirmed Malmesbury's analysis that he had no fixed idea: he decided to volunteer for the Russian army that was then fighting against the Ottoman Empire, an Islamic power with extensive land in Europe as well as Turkey, the Middle East and North Africa. Hortense agreed to use her address book to pull the necessary strings, and all Louis-Napoléon needed was the consent of his father. 'Finally I will do something worthy of you,' he wrote to the comte de Saint-Leu in January 1829. 'I have taken up a great cause that I hope you will not disapprove of, it is too beautiful and too noble . . . Ah, my dear father, to think that you were not yet my age and you were already covered with glory.' If his father did not give permission, he claimed he would 'die of disappointment'.[25] The comte de Saint-Leu, however, had hated his time in the Army of Italy, which his son thought so glorious, and refused, replying, 'Only make war for your country, those that do otherwise are nothing more than adventurers, ambitious or villains.'[26] Reluctantly, Louis-Napoléon renounced the idea, which was, he wrote, proof of the deep respect he had for his father, because 'if I did not have it, I would not have been able to resist the desire of accomplishing it even without your consent'. He consoled himself, as he often did, with Napoléon's memoirs. 'The more I read him,' he wrote to his father, 'the more I admire his universal genius.'[27]

Instead of serving in the Russian army, determined to get a military education, Louis-Napoléon settled on the rather less belligerent Swiss militia, volunteering in 1830 for the artillery – the part of the army where Napoléon had made his name. A one-month summer training camp, however, was hardly the stuff of dreams, and Louis-Napoléon yearned for greater glory. In July 1830, astonishing events in Paris fuelled these reveries.

3

THE COLUMN

In Paris on 26 July 1830, some of the capital's finest writers and journalists were crammed into a stifling newspaper office. In the face of the increasingly reactionary policies of Charles X, the Bourbon king who succeeded his brother Louis XVIII in 1824, these journalists had championed liberalism, reform and freedom of speech in the press. Now they had gathered to defend something even more precious: their jobs.

That morning the official government paper had announced a *coup d'état* in print. Breaking with the constitution, the reactionary Charles X decreed that parliament was dissolved, the already highly restricted franchise was further narrowed and new elections would be held in September. The king also declared an end to freedom of the press. Unless they did something, the men now gathered in a hot newspaper office would be looking for work the next day. Preferring protest to job-hunting, they decided to resist. If the *coup d'état* was declared in print, so too should be the fightback. As might be expected when writers assemble, there was some debate over the exact wording, but they eventually agreed to end their protest on a less than revolutionary rallying cry: 'We will resist insofar as we are concerned; it is for France to judge how far its own resistance should go.'[1] It turned out France, or at least Paris, was willing to go further than the journalists.

Only four newspapers were bold enough to print the declaration in the next morning's edition, but it was enough. Workers – many of them printers who needed employment much more than bourgeois journalists – met in the garden of the Palais-Royal and read out the protest to the gathering crowds. The mood turned from resentment to anger, anti-government graffiti was chalked on nearby walls and shouts against Charles X became louder. Police cleared the gardens, but people kept coming to the square outside. Troops were ordered to disperse the crowds. Sabres drawn, cavalry thundered into the masses. Makeshift projectiles were thrown; panicked soldiers fired back. Memories of the revolution of 1789 loomed large – this was a drama Parisians knew how to perform. Barricades went up, and street fighting broke out. As the commander of the capital's armed forces wrote to the king: 'This is no longer a riot, this is a revolution.'[2]

He was right. Fuelled by hatred for the Bourbon kings, who had insisted on restoring the white flag of their family, the revolutionary tricolour was raised on the barricades, and people wore its colours while white flags with royal fleur-de-lys were torn down. Palaces were stormed; furniture, manuscripts and priceless books floated down the Seine after the looting of the archbishop's chateau. Royal authority melted away after three days of fighting. But what to replace it with? The revolution lacked leadership. The wealthy liberal opposition wanted reform through legal means and abhorred violence. What galvanised them into backing the revolution were the cries on the barricades. '*Vive Napoléon!*' was heard, but much louder were those voices calling for a republic.

This prospect terrified the reluctant revolutionary journalists and their backers into what amounted to their own *coup d'état*: they proclaimed the duc d'Orléans, Louis-Philippe, king. Louis-Philippe was their man because he had liberal credentials. His father, known as Philippe Égalité, had supported the 1789 revolution and voted for the death of his cousin, Louis XVI, before he was guillotined himself in 1793. His son had briefly fought under the tricolour flag, although he had gone into exile to avoid the fate of his father. Louis-Philippe had supported the restored Bourbons, who were also his cousins; however, he had been careful to position himself as a defender of the liberal charter that the Bourbons agreed to rule by, and that Charles X had just broken.

Even so, there was little popular support for Louis-Philippe. When he appeared before the crowd on the balcony at the Hôtel de Ville, he was met with a chorus of '*Vive la République!*' and 'Down with the duc d'Orléans!' It was only the popular marquis de Lafayette who saved him. Brandishing a tricolour flag, Lafayette, who had fought in the American Revolution and was a leader during the moderate phase of the first French one, embraced Louis-Philippe. The mood turned: there were cries of 'Long live the duc d'Orléans!' and 'Long live Lafayette!'[3]

Eugène Delacroix painted one of the most enduring images of what became known as the Three Glorious Days of the July Revolution. *Liberty Leading the People*, with its iconic bare-breasted Liberty guiding the heroic Parisians to victory, symbolised the hope of those who fought and died on the streets of Paris in the summer of 1830. What they were led to, however, was a very bourgeois and cautious liberty. Through the swift machinations of wealthy, elite politicians, Charles X was replaced with the third in line to the throne, Louis-Philippe. As king, he promised to rule constitutionally, restored freedom of the press and doubled the franchise from a restrictive 115,000 to a still restrictive 230,000. Fifty-two years old in 1830, he was a dull man who thought himself clever and whose jowly face so closely resembled a pear that a caricaturist argued in court that he was not insulting the king by pointing out the similarity.

In short, Louis-Philippe was not a revolutionary hero. This was a great comfort to the sovereigns of Europe, for whom recent events in Paris seemed like a recurring nightmare; they feared ideologically charged French armies once again exporting radical ideas across the continent. This was unlikely under Louis-Philippe, who preferred brandishing an umbrella to a marshal's baton. Despite the July Revolution's underwhelming denouement, disillusioned, romantic revolutionaries across Europe saw the Parisians who overthrew a tyrant as heroes. Radicals devoured news of events in Paris, and young men looking for action began plotting repeat performances. When these came, Louis-Napoléon was determined not to miss out.

———

While Parisians were fighting in the streets, Louis-Napoléon, twenty-two years old, was repairing fortifications near a somnolent medieval Swiss town. When he heard about what had happened in France, the contrast struck him. 'We are very quiet in our little corner,' he wrote to Hortense. 'At this moment the tricolour flag is flying in France, happy are those who were the first to restore it to its former glory.'[4] Brought up to despise the Bourbons, Louis-Napoléon was delighted at their fall. Moreover, he expected the law banishing his family would soon be revoked and he could return to France. As he read about the events of the July Revolution he was overwhelmed with patriotism. 'Oh, yes, Maman, it is so beautiful to be French.'[5] He hoped to spend the winter in Paris and dreamed of seeing French soldiers march under the tricolour and joining the army himself.

Louis-Napoléon's dreams went further: he saw a chance to promote the Bonapartist cause and see Napoléon's son, the Duke of Reichstadt, a virtual prisoner at court in Vienna, returned as Napoléon II. Against the wishes of his mother, Louis-Napoléon wanted to donate money to the families of the dead or wounded during the street fighting in Paris. This was not altruism, but an opportunity to promote the Bonapartist cause. 'You have often repeated to me', he argued with his mother in a letter, 'that one cannot create events, but once they have come it is necessary to profit by them. It seems to me that our goal must be to try always to associate ourselves somehow to what is done in France so as not to seem foreign to its fate.'[6]

But that was exactly how Louis-Philippe wanted Bonapartes to seem. He and his supporters were acutely aware that the throne they had hastily imposed on France was precarious. Republicans were already disappointed with the conservative nature of the regime that followed the radicalism of the street fighting, but Bonapartism also presented a challenge. With the family in exile, the movement was disorganised; however, there remained a deep well of support for Napoléon. Insofar as there was a Bonapartist political programme, it represented the moderate values of the 1789 revolution and social order: in short, the same platform as Louis-Philippe's, but with bayonets rather than umbrellas making it a more tantalising vision.

Having won the throne for his family, Louis-Philippe had no intention of letting his rivals return to France. On 11 September 1830, his government renewed the law banishing Bonapartes on pain of death. Louis-Napoléon would be spending the winter in Rome, not Paris. But having seen the July Revolution pass him by in France, he was determined not only to profit from events in Italy, but also help create them.

———

In his mother's comfortable Rome salons, Louis-Napoléon had listened as liberal-minded aristocrats breezily opined that Italy was oppressed by a patchwork of petty kingdoms and duchies. Worst were the repressive Catholic Papal States governed by the pope and the foreign subjugation of Lombardy and Venetia under Austrian rule. While people complained about this in Hortense's drawing room, Louis-Napoléon was secretly meeting men who were going to do something about it.

It was his brother who introduced him to the shadowy world of revolutionary Italian politics. Napoléon-Louis resented the control his father exerted over him. In part, he had agreed to marry his cousin, Charlotte, the daughter of Napoléon's eldest brother Joseph, to assert his independence. The choice had been his father's, more desperate for the dowry than his son's happiness. Perverse as ever, the comte de Saint-Leu wrote to Louis-Napoléon, 'Perhaps I am mistaken, but her figure recalls yours.'[7] But if marriage to a cousin who his father thought looked like his younger brother hardly screamed autonomy, it did at least mean Napoléon-Louis could move out of his father's home.

More outgoing than his younger brother, Napoléon-Louis had a passion – since the age of ten, he claimed – for Italian nationalism. In Florence, he surrounded himself with Italian patriots. But he went further than the refined company of respectable people: he joined a terrorist organisation known as the Carbonari. Borrowing symbols and rituals from the Freemasons, the Carbonari (literally charcoal makers) were made up of secret cells. Ironically, the group had begun in opposition to Napoléon's dominance of the Italian peninsula, but compared to what came after, many saw the Kingdom of Italy that the French emperor had created as a high-water mark for Italian unity.

The Carbonari wanted to overthrow the order imposed from abroad after 1815 and to create a new Italian kingdom; many in their ranks were former Bonapartists. Whether Louis-Napoléon was a member is an open question, but what is beyond doubt is that, inspired by his brother, in smoke-filled taverns he befriended many people who were, adopted their cause and carried out secret missions on their behalf. With the example of the Paris revolution fresh in their minds, the Carbonari thought it was time to act.

On 20 October 1830, Louis-Napoléon set out with Hortense on the journey from Arenenberg to Rome. They had with them Hortense's new lady-in-waiting, Valérie Masuyer. Thirty-two years old, Valérie was awed, as many of her generation were, by what she saw as the brilliance of the Napoleonic era and Hortense's place within it. 'To my eyes', she wrote,

Hortense 'represented what was most brilliant and most dazzling in the whole Empire.' She had been at the side of Napoléon, 'at all the ceremonies and all the parties . . . Placed in his confidence from beginning to end, she had known him in his greatest glory.'[8]

It was an exciting world to join, but when Valérie first met Louis-Napoléon he hardly gave the appearance of Napoleonic grandeur, enveloped in an oversize frock coat that made him look smaller than he was, which was not very tall – five feet four inches. Thin, handsome and with good features, including, according to Valérie, lovely hands, he improved in appearance when dressed for dinner. He was, Valérie thought, sentimental, melancholic, interesting.

When they reached Florence, Louis-Napoléon was reunited with his beloved brother for the first time since the revolution in France. Despite their separation, they were intensely close and excitedly discussed politics. Napoléon-Louis was a republican; Louis-Napoléon shared his brother's beliefs, but, Valérie noted, more out of youthful ardour than genuine conviction.

In mid-November, Louis-Napoléon began for Rome with his mother. Soon afterwards, the carriage of Louis-Napoléon's father, travelling in the other direction, pulled up alongside that of his mother. Neither Hortense nor the comte de Saint-Leu deigned to leave their carriages, but Louis-Napoléon's father coldly ordered Hortense to make sure their son stayed out of politics and made his son promise that he would.

This was not a promise Louis-Napoléon kept. Rumours spread that there was a conspiracy to place Napoléon's son on an Italian throne, reviving the Napoleonic Kingdom of Italy, and Louis-Napoléon's involvement with Rome's revolutionary underworld soon came to the attention of the authorities. Given that he ostentatiously rode through the streets with the seditious tricolour flag adorning his saddle, it did not require any great detective work to discover his sympathies.

On 12 December 1830, Louis-Napoléon was receiving a lecture from his mother. She knew that he was involved in a plot. As she was urging him to end his involvement, a colonel from the papal government was announced. He told Louis-Napoléon in front of Hortense that in one hour he would be escorted to the borders of the Papal States. As if this was not distressing enough for Hortense, when she embraced her son he whispered that he had given refuge that morning to a fugitive wanted by the police and the man was now hiding in the palazzo where they were staying. Displaying impressive calm, Hortense promised to take care of things. Then Louis-Napoléon was deported.

While hardly delighted with the prospect of having a political renegade foisted upon her, Hortense was pleased that Louis-Napoléon was out of Rome. Whatever he was planning, she reasoned, he was safer outside the city, where he could no longer take part in it. Under the watchful eye of his father in Florence, she thought, there was only so much trouble her son could get into.

———

While staying with his brother in Florence, Louis-Napoléon's biggest worry, he wrote to his mother, was that he had lost his dog, the unimaginatively named Fido. In fact, he was not having much luck with animals – his horse was also sick, but it was Fido's absence that hurt him the most. 'May God grant', he wrote to his mother, 'that I never have greater sorrows, and I will get over it easily.' Concluding his letter, he wrote, 'We are very calm here, I hope that nothing will come to trouble us.'[9] And nothing would have done, but Louis-Napoléon and his brother were going to cause trouble.

Towards the end of January 1831, Count Joseph Orsi, Italian patriot and scion of a banking family, hosted a secret meeting. At 9 p.m., Louis-Napoléon entered with his brother and a radical Italian nationalist, who was a member of the Carbonari. Louis-Napoléon listened on silently as his brother explained the plan. Inspired by the July Revolution in Paris, insurrection would sweep through Italy.

'It is hateful', replied Napoléon-Louis, dismissing Orsi's concerns that the plan was impractical, 'for my brother and myself to remain idle spectators of current events, and to shut ourselves out from the rest of the world.' Their name, he continued, and their beliefs, inspired them to join the insurgents and to 'fight with them the battle of independence, or to die in the struggle'. After Orsi tried to talk them out of it, Louis-Napoléon spoke for the first time. 'You lose sight of the engagements we have entered into, which we swore to perform.'[10] That closed the heated discussion.

In February 1831, the revolt began. A revolutionary provisional government was proclaimed in Bologna. Soon, other towns declared themselves for the cause. Knowing that an uprising was planned in Rome, the brothers had written to Hortense urging her to join them in Florence, which remained quiet during the tumultuous first weeks of February. Hortense came, managing to smuggle out the political refugee who had been palmed off on her, but when she reached Florence, her children were gone. Louis-Napoléon left a note: 'We have accepted engagements, and we cannot depart from them. The name that we bear obliges us to help a suffering people that calls us.'[11]

As the brothers walked through the streets of a rebel-held town decorated with tricolour flags and revolutionary cockades, Louis-Napoléon was struck by the popular enthusiasm. The illustrious name the brothers carried saw them welcomed as heroes and they were made officers in the revolutionary army. After giving his mother this rather disturbing news, Louis-Napoléon urged her not to worry: 'we are wonderful'. Closing his letter, he asked for their horses to be sent, before the time-honoured sign-off from wealthy children travelling away from home: send as much money as you can.[12]

The plan was for the insurgent army to march on Rome. Louis-Napoléon was given command of small group of men, but the revolt was not the trigger for a mass movement throughout the peninsula. The entire force was no more than 2,400 strong, far too few to take the city. The army halted about 100 kilometres north of its objective. Here, the rebels received an emissary from the Bonaparte family, who were horrified that the two young brothers had joined the rebels. They demanded that the siblings renounce their commissions. Instead, Napoléon-Louis scribbled a letter to the pope, insisting that if he wanted to stop the revolution, all he need do was grant a liberal constitution, a gesture as futile as asking the brothers to stand down.

Using contacts within the movement, the Bonaparte family pressured the minister of war to sack the brothers from the revolutionary army. The minister obliged. When they discovered what had happened, Napoléon-Louis penned a vitriolic letter to his father and Louis-Napoléon added a petulant postscript, insisting that he had decided to 'live or die for the cause that I have embraced' and certainly was not going to return to Florence to face his father's wrath. If he was not wanted in the Italian revolution, he would join a Polish one that had just broken out against Russian rule.[13]

Soon, however, the brothers had greater concerns than their father's anger. In an attempt to calm the comte de Saint-Leu's fears, Louis-Napoléon had written, 'We are so angry to learn that you are tormented by our position, and above all by the coming of the Austrians.' It seemed certain, he declared with confidence, that they would not enter rebel-held territory.[14] Two weeks after he wrote that, the Austrians entered rebel-held territory.

———

If he had been wrong about the Austrians, Louis-Napoléon was right to be worried about his father's reaction. The comte de Saint-Leu thought his hot-headed youngest son, raised on Hortense's potent brew of imperial nostalgia combined with vague thoughts of a glorious future, was exactly the kind of idiot who would get himself mixed up in an unpromising revolution. That his eldest, over whom he had exerted near-tyrannical control, would be so stupid was even worse.

When he read the letter that his beloved Napoléon-Louis had sent to the pope explaining the aims of the uprising, the comte de Saint-Leu – a fervent Catholic – became so angry that he had to have an emergency bloodletting with leeches. Then he sent courier after courier imploring his sons to come back, but once they refused, he fixated on the idea that Hortense should drag them home. She was reluctant, yet by the beginning of March it was clear that the insurgents' days were numbered. Austrian troops would soon mop up the rebels. If her children were captured, they might be executed, certainly imprisoned. It was, Hortense decided, up to her to rescue them.

The question was, though, what could she do even if she did find them? The authorities in Tuscany had made it clear that the brothers could not re-enter Florentine territory, let alone reside there. At first, she thought the plan of reaching the port of Ancona a good one: they could get a ship to Corfu and from there to the Ottoman Empire, where, she reasoned, they could live their lives in exile, but she soon worried that the Austrian navy patrolling the Adriatic would intercept them before they could reach safety.

Then she hit on a plan so outrageous no one would suspect it. She would find them and then travel in the opposite direction, overland across Italy into France and ultimately to Paris. Whatever the law might say about banishing Bonapartes on pain of death, she would throw herself at the mercy of Louis-Philippe as a mother doing the only thing she could to save her sons. After that, they would go to London.

There were several problems with this, not least how her sons could travel across Italy when they were wanted men. Hortense solved this by securing a false passport from a friend at the British consulate. She could travel on her own passport until she found her sons, and then she would use the British one issued to a Mrs Hamilton and her two adult children for the journey to France. Many male friends in Florence offered to accompany her when they learned that she would travel through rebel-held territory with only two servants and a lady-in-waiting, but Hortense refused. 'I had my plan,' she wrote confidently. 'I didn't need any man with me.'[15] She was most worried about Louis-Napoléon, whom she thought less prudent, and less lucky, than his older brother.

Hortense was well received as she travelled through the territory still held by the insurgents. There was no news, however, about her children's whereabouts, so she assumed that they too were making their way to Ancona and decided to do the same. Then, on the morning of 19 March, she received a message from Louis-Napoléon. They were at a small town called Forlì, and she must come quickly.

———

On 6 March, Louis-Napoléon and his brother had left Bologna with the remnants of the army to escape the advancing Austrians. They took lodgings in a poorly furnished tavern in Forlì, while Napoléon-Louis recovered from a bad cold. Soon, however, he was feverish, coughing up bile and complaining of chest pains. Louis-Napoléon stayed with his brother, who was too sick to leave, while the rest of the army kept moving.

To placate his father, Louis-Napoléon wrote a letter. 'Napoléon-Louis's sickness, from which he has been suffering lightly for the last three days, prevents him giving you his news himself, but he has charged me with telling you that he is almost entirely better.'[16] That was a lie. Napoléon-Louis had measles. On 17 March, delirious, very tired – he had not slept for days – Napoléon-Louis turned to one of his travelling companions and said, 'Maman is going to come.' She knew, he said, that he was seriously ill, 'and that's enough so that nothing will stop her'.

As the Austrians closed in, Louis-Napoléon sat up each night at his brother's bedside reading newspapers aloud to him. But after learning what the disease was, the doctor ordered Louis-Napoléon not to enter the room. Napoléon-Louis, in intense pain, was not able to close his eyes for three days and nights. 'Do you think that one can live long in such a state . . . I don't think so . . . Is it day? Is the window open? I see nothing.' The doctor told Napoléon-Louis not to worry. The patient was not convinced. Talking to an Italian revolutionary who had stayed with him, he spoke about his younger brother: 'We loved each other too much and I fear that he won't be able to live without me. As for me, I don't want to see him, it would hurt him too much, anyway, it could give him measles.'

Soon after he spoke these words, Napoléon-Louis's condition worsened; a priest was summoned. After agonising convulsions, he died in a cheap hotel in a small Italian town. When Louis-Napoléon learned his brother was dead, his world collapsed. 'So I no longer have any friends,' he said between violent sobs.[17] He could not, however, attend the funeral. The Austrians were only days away. Devastated, he fled in search of his mother.

As Hortense raced to Forlì, she heard rumours that her son was dead. She refused to believe it. Finally, though, a trusted messenger confirmed the news. 'Him too,' she said. 'My two children' – recalling the death of her firstborn in 1807.[18] Determined to save her surviving son, she continued her journey to Pesaro, where she was reunited with Louis-Napoléon. Running into her arms, crying, he told her that he had lost his brother, his best friend, and that without Hortense he would have died of grief on the corpse that he did not want to leave. Although raised a Catholic, Louis-Napoléon had little interest in religion, and Hortense's lady-in-waiting pitied him even more in his sorrow because he did not believe that he would see his brother again in the next world. There was no time to grieve. The Austrians were occupying nearby towns, including Forlì the week after Louis-Napoléon's brother died. Hortense, drawing strength from danger, ordered horses to be readied and made for Ancona, which the Austrians had not yet reached.

One advantage of the extended Bonaparte family was that it owned property across the peninsula, and Louis-Napoléon and Hortense found refuge in a palazzo belonging to her brother's family. As Hortense's British passport was for two children, they picked up a young Italian aristocrat who had fought with the rebels to pass off as her dead son, and planned to leave right away. But on the first day in Ancona, Louis-Napoléon came down with a terrible headache. Taking one glance at him, a doctor diagnosed measles. As he was too sick to move, Louis-Napoléon and Hortense would have to stay in Ancona.

To misdirect the Austrians, Hortense bought passage for Louis-Napoléon on a boat departing that evening. Then she spread word that her son had gone, but she had remained behind because she was sick. Having come of age in one of the most ruthless courts in Europe and then thrived in exile while under constant surveillance, Hortense was an expert in the arts of deception and misinformation; however, even her considerable skills were put to the test when the Austrian troops entered Ancona, for a disadvantage of owning some of the most desirable real estate in the city presented itself: Austrian officers requisitioned the villa where Louis-Napoléon was convalescing as their headquarters.

The Austrian commander took as his office the room adjoining the one where Louis-Napoléon was in his sick bed. Hortense warned her son not to speak. For days and nights, whenever he coughed, she held her hand tightly over his mouth to stifle the sound. The Austrian was good enough to apologise to Hortense for the inconvenience of having her villa full of troops. Then he asked if she was alone. She was, Hortense coolly replied, and she assured him that her son had left for Corfu days ago. The officer was so courteous that Hortense felt guilty for lying.

After a few days, Louis-Napoléon was well enough to travel. Of course, Hortense could not pass herself off as an Englishwoman travelling with her sons now that she had been recognised by the Austrians. Instead, she would travel on her passport and the two fugitives would disguise themselves as her servants. Wearing servants' clothes and with his head shaved and covered with a tight black cap, Louis-Napoléon was unrecognisable. At 4 a.m. on Easter Sunday, 3 April, they left their apartments and crept through the antechamber where Austrian soldiers lay sleeping. As they went downstairs, dawn was breaking, and in the dull early-morning light they slipped past incurious guards. The Austrians had given Hortense a pass to travel, and at the checkpoint leaving the port she and her 'servants' were not stopped.

The early start had been explained to the Austrians as necessary to get to the nearby hilltop Basilica della Santa Casa for Mass. Once they had made their way up the steep, winding roads overlooking the Adriatic, Louis-Napoléon showed his dedication to the role by walking three paces behind his mother and carrying her umbrella. Deliberately overperforming, he put on a silly face and ridiculous air so that as they entered the holy sanctuary Hortense's lady-in-waiting was giggling. Back on the road, they came across the less amusing sight of the fleeing remnants of the rebel army in which Louis-Napoléon had served.

When they passed Lake Trasimeno, Louis-Napoléon rallied sufficiently to explain in granular detail to Hortense's lady-in-waiting the battle that the Carthaginian general Hannibal had fought there against the Romans. Once they were beyond Austrian-controlled territory, Hortense became Mrs Hamilton and Louis-Napoléon changed into the clothes of an English gentleman. Though devastated over the death of his brother, on the journey Louis-Napoléon laughed and joked with the young Italian pretending to be his brother, often with a lewdness that Hortense's lady-in-waiting found uncomfortable. At one point, travelling in a second carriage far behind Hortense, Valérie noted with disgust that the two men had stopped at a bend in the road. She saw them 'chasing a woman and disappearing with her behind a rock'.[19]

———

For sixteen years, Louis-Napoléon had dreamed of returning to France. When he did, he was so overwhelmed he cried. On the way to Paris, he would talk to the strangers he encountered, wander the streets, frequent cafes. When they entered one to read the newspapers, French officers playing billiards looked up and stopped their game. The soldiers asked if they were foreigners travelling from Italy and, if so, did they have news about the two imperial princes? The men were distraught to hear of the death of the elder; delighted when they learned that Louis-Napoléon had escaped to Corfu.

Returning to the hotel that same day, an emotional Louis-Napoléon cried again, touched by the sentiments of the officers. He was so moved he penned a letter to Louis-Philippe that evening: 'I beg you to open the gates of France to me and allow me to serve as a simple soldier . . . Since nearly all the states of Europe are closed to me, France is the only one where it would not be a crime to have embraced the holy cause of a people's independence.' He wrote that after fighting for liberty in Italy and losing his brother, 'life would be insupportable' if 'I did not continue to hope that your Majesty will permit me to return as a simple citizen in the French ranks – happy if one day I may die fighting for my country'.[20] The letter was not sent. Hortense applauded the patriotic sentiment, but thought they should prioritise avoiding execution for breaking the law of banishment. 'Ah,' Louis-Napoléon sighed by way of reply, 'only serving France can bind me to life.'[21]

On 23 April, Louis-Napoléon saw Paris for the first time since he was seven. He was disappointed. Entering from the south, he thought the suburbs less impressive than Milan. Hortense, keen to show her son the best of the capital, made the driver turn towards the Jardin des Plantes and reach the centre via the grand boulevards. Now Louis-Napoléon could not contain his excitement, constantly standing up in the carriage, straining for a better view of the sights.

At 6 p.m., they arrived at the Hôtel de Hollande on rue de la Paix – formerly rue Napoléon – and took an apartment on the first floor. From here, Louis-Napoléon could see the Place Vendôme, a barometer of Bonapartist sentiment in Paris. The Bourbons had torn down the statue of Napoléon at the top, but the column remained. Indeed, Louis-Philippe's government, keen to bring some of the emperor's lustre to the regime, had just agreed to put a new statue of Napoléon on top of it.

The arrival of one of the great celebrities of the Napoleonic era along with her fugitive son, an imperial prince, was an intense embarrassment to Louis-Philippe – or it would be, if it got out that they were in Paris. More embarrassing, however, would be executing a mother and son on the run from the reactionary powers of Europe. After a secret meeting with Hortense, the king agreed to ignore the law banishing them as long as they left as soon as possible for London without making their presence in France known to anyone. He even agreed to let Louis-Napoléon serve in the French army at a later date, on the condition that he renounce his name. When Hortense told Louis-Napoléon this, he rose angrily from the sofa and paced the room. 'Give up my name!' he exclaimed. 'Who would dare make such a proposition? Think of this no more, let's return to our retreat. Ah, mother, you were right!'[22] Then, grabbing a newspaper hostile to the July Monarchy, he affected to be absorbed in reading it.

The generous treatment accorded to Hortense had been with the hope she and Louis-Napoléon would leave Paris before the anniversary of the death of Napoléon on 5 May, when demonstrations were expected at the Place Vendôme. The last thing the precariously established July Monarchy wanted during a pro-Bonapartist protest was for people to discover that the stepdaughter and nephew of the emperor were staying in an apartment above them.

Louis-Napoléon, however, fell sick again and the doctor pronounced him too ill to travel. The increasingly worried aide to the king regularly checked on the health of the patient, urging Hortense to leave. Hortense, though, was enjoying herself. Wandering the streets of Paris, she was delighted to find that portraits of herself were on sale. Moreover, she went out to see the latest attractions that were the talk of Paris. First a neorama – a panorama of an interior of a building – of Saint Peter's and Westminster Abbey. And then, ever the Bonaparte tourist, a diorama of the tomb of Napoléon on Saint Helena, in part so that she could describe it to her son, who was too ill to visit.

The diorama was the latest technological innovation of Louis Daguerre, who would go on to even greater fame when he invented the forerunner of the photograph, the daguerreotype. The diorama placed the viewer before a three-dimensional image, and on 4 May, the day before the anniversary of his death, Hortense stared in silent reverence at the grave of Napoléon, her stepfather and benefactor, on Saint Helena, surrounded by a simple iron fence, trees and the rays of the setting sun lighting up a distant mountain. Her reverie was interrupted when in the crowded room her eyes met with an officer who used to frequent her salon in Rome, and she fled in panic into the streets. Returning to the hotel via a circuitous route to avoid being followed, Hortense told Louis-Napoléon about the diorama.

His appetite whetted for imperial nostalgia, that evening Louis-Napoléon asked Hortense's lady-in-waiting to read to him the latest poem by France's most renowned poet, Victor Hugo, titled 'À la Colonne', one of his various odes to Napoléon. As she read, Louis-Napoléon listened in raptured silence. Then he rose from the sofa, emotionally pacing the room, lost in thought.

Despite having been urged to leave, Hortense and Louis-Napoléon were in Paris on 5 May. From their windows, they saw people make their way silently to the Place Vendôme to leave, with religious solemnity, splendid bouquets of flowers, floral crowns, handwritten notes and Bonapartist placards around the column that celebrated Napoléon's stunning victory. Then, thrillingly for the nephew, the crowd roared, *'Vive l'empereur!'* The square was illuminated at night, searing the vista below into Louis-Napoléon's mind. He had long believed that the memory of the emperor lived in the imagination of the French people and that he remained a popular hero. As he looked down on the square strewn with Napoleonic memorabilia, he had his proof.

———

They left the day after the anniversary and were soon in London, which Louis-Napoléon thought lacked the grandeur of Paris. Writing to his father, he offered the timeless insight that the weather was bad and the cost of living expensive. But he enjoyed his time in Britain. They arrived during a general election, a heated campaign in which the liberal Whig party won a majority to reform the archaic electoral system and extend the franchise. Louis-Napoléon, of course, declared himself in favour of the Whigs.

Hortense's connections ensured they were feted in society, although, as in Rome, usually only among the more transgressive members of the British aristocracy. On a journey back from one country estate, Hortense tried to amuse Louis-Napoléon and Valérie by reading Victor Hugo's latest novel, *Notre-Dame de Paris*, better known in English as *The Hunchback of Notre-Dame*, but they found it 'baroque, pretentious and boring'.[23] Louis-Napoléon, his imagination fired by what he had seen in the Place Vendôme, then entertained them by creating a cabinet for a fictional second Empire ruled by his cousin Napoléon II, the Duke of Reichstadt. They had filled all but two posts by the time they reached their lodgings near fashionable Hanover Square.

Louis-Napoléon went to see King William IV open parliament, although he got there late and missed much of the monarch's speech. He took in other sights too, including the Tower of London, the zoo at Regent's Park and the Thames Tunnel, then under construction and a marvel of modern engineering. What moved him most, however, was the stage. Showing his uncle's enduring appeal, there were two rival performances about the emperor's life in Covent Garden's theatres. When Louis-Napoléon returned late in the evening after attending one, his eyes were red with tears, his face full of emotion.

In London, Louis-Napoléon met shadowy intriguers who claimed they could bring his family back to power. For a mere 25,000 francs a month an imperial officer fallen on hard times told Louis-Napoléon he could put the Duke of Reichstadt on the French throne as Napoléon II. This was nonsense, but Louis-Napoléon took the offer seriously and corresponded with the conspiracist. Alarmed that this would compromise them while they were awaiting approval for their passports, Valérie warned Hortense. She did not care: her son was 'having fun'.[24] But Hortense's lady-in-waiting was less enamoured with Louis-Napoléon's constant plotting, and she held the purse strings. One morning, he asked her for money.

'Come on,' replied Valérie, 'admit that you are still conspiring and that this money is not for you, but for some political factotum.'

'Perhaps,' replied Louis-Napoléon.

'You will ruin yourself, for people who are deceiving you and only think of cheating you.'

'Wrong, wrong.'

But plots, Valérie argued, merely strengthened the government. 'Wrong,' answered Louis-Napoléon again; the government 'is close to death, and another party will replace it'.

'The republicans . . .'

'The republicans don't have the army; the army is Bonapartist,' Louis-Napoléon confidently asserted. 'All reports agree.' Of course, Louis-Napoléon had few, if any, reports to go on, but he was convinced. 'If I hadn't been ill on 5 May,' he declared, 'and if I had gone down into the

Place Vendôme shouting: "Long live Napoléon II!" everyone would have followed me. Louis-Philippe knew it, and that's why he made me leave. Being on the throne only by luck, he knows that a flick could overthrow him.'

'You see, Mademoiselle,' Louis-Napoléon said, returning to the point, 'that you would be wrong to take Louis-Philippe's side and refuse me money to fight him.' He insisted she give him some. 'Impossible,' replied Valérie. 'Adieu, then,' said Louis-Napoléon, turning to leave and adding, fairly good-naturedly, 'You are a villain.'[25]

Lack of money, though, did not stop Louis-Napoléon getting further drawn into the conspiracy. With the imperial officer now in prison, his wife begged Louis-Napoléon for funds and told him that France was on the point of a revolution in favour of the Bonapartes, a risible claim, but, wrote Valérie, because it came from 'the mouth of a pretty woman', Louis-Napoléon treated it as gospel. Valérie noted that 'still waters run deep': underneath his habitual calm, Louis-Napoléon hid plenty of passion. She concluded that 'he who has never loved for the sweetness of loving, is ready to fall in love with an adventuress for the pleasure of conspiring'.

Prone to deep infatuations, Louis-Napoléon had confessed to Valérie that he had never known love. Once, he told her, when he was fifteen, he had felt 'an infinite pleasure, the sweetest he had felt in his life, in looking at a young girl seated at the window, whom he never saw again and whom he will never forget'. He also related the time when, only twelve years old, he had spelled out the name of a neighbour with watercress seeds in a flowerbed at Arenenberg – a gesture his austere tutor, Philippe Le Bas, discouraged, destroying the floral tribute with a pickaxe.

Aware of this weakness for women, the conspiracists alighted on the tactic of having an attractive lady eye Louis-Napoléon at the theatre one evening. The next day, a note signed 'Laure' requested a date. The final straw for Hortense was when she spotted this 'Laure' in Hyde Park, following Louis-Napoléon. Turning to Valérie, she said with a mother's frankness that he 'is not attractive enough for women to run after him'.[26] She resolved to get her son out of London. It would be hard, Hortense thought, even for her son, to conspire against the French government from somewhere as genteel as Tunbridge Wells.

Louis-Napoléon did manage to fall in love in this Kent spa town. Miss Godfrey, who spoke French and seemed straight out of a Jane Austen novel, became an especial favourite. He let his moustache grow to impress her. She did not like it; he trimmed it. They stared at each other lovingly in the moonlight on chaperoned carriage drives and discussed literature. Louis-Napoléon lamented that as the nephew of the emperor he could never marry an Englishwoman and told her the story of a novel in which the characters killed each other because they could not wed. When it was time to return to London, they spent a long time whispering romantic nonsense to each other. Impatient at this lingering farewell, Valérie made a sign for the carriage to draw up, and Louis-Napoléon was forced to leave. She tried to talk to him on the journey, but he just let out loud, lovelorn sighs.

By the first week of August, their passports were ready, allowing them to travel through France home to Arenenberg. After Louis-Napoléon told Hortense that if he saw street fighting in Paris, he would join the insurgents, she decided it was best to avoid the capital. Instead, they went via Boulogne, where Napoléon had trained his army in preparation for an invasion of Britain. Hortense had spent time here with the emperor and delighted in showing her awestruck son the sights. They also made a pilgrimage to the tomb of the French *philosophe* Jean-Jacques Rousseau.

At the end of August, they reached Arenenberg. It was only ten months since they had set out from here for Italy, but Louis-Napoléon's life had changed for ever. It was only now that he began to work through the grief caused by his brother's death. 'I wanted to write to you every day,' he explained when finally penning a letter to his brother's widow, 'but every day I put off doing it.' It was too painful. Knowing she blamed him for dragging his brother into the rebellion, Louis-Napoléon wrote, 'you will never blame me as much as I blame myself' for the death of the person 'I loved best on this earth'. Without him, he was lost. 'I never conceived a wish, never formed a plan, in which my brother had not half of all my thoughts.'[27] Another death in the family, however, soon meant that Louis-Napoléon started planning for himself.

4

SOME NEW NAPOLÉON MIGHT ARISE

In the seclusion of his mother's chateau in the Swiss countryside, Louis-Napoléon sunk into depression. When he saw his brother's portrait on the wall at Arenenberg, or came across his things, he cried. His father offered little comfort. He was still furious at his sons, especially the surviving one. When he had met his father on the way to Rome in 1830, Louis-Napoléon had promised not to get involved in politics.

'You see what you failing to keep your word has cost us all,' his father wrote from Florence. 'Let this catastrophe be a lesson for you. Listen to me finally: you see if I am right. Forget politics . . . Above all,' he urged, 'in the name of God, make sure that in the future this cannot happen to you who are the only one left to us.'[1] Always keen to placate his father, with words at least, Louis-Napoléon reassured him. 'I am in a neutral country, occupied in politics only to the extent of reading the papers.' My part, he claimed, is an easy one to play: 'I remain a calm spectator of the drama that is acted before my eyes; and I only ask my father to give me back all his affection, and Fate to restore me to my country.'[2]

Some of this was true; Louis-Napoléon did read the newspapers, but he did so to be ready when the time came to act. Far from heeding his father's advice, he had written a letter to his uncle Joseph outlining how he envisaged returning the family to power in France. Explaining why his brother abandoned his wife, who was also Joseph's daughter, to take part in the Italian insurrection, he wrote that Napoléon-Louis 'believed, and I believe it also, that the great name he carried imposed on him the greatest obligations'. When they heard the cry of liberty resound in Italy, he added, 'we thought only of embracing a cause that we found noble and just'.[3] In France, he then explained, the name of the emperor was once again on the lips of the people. Moreover, there were many there working in the shadows – he meant the intriguers who had contacted him in London – to further the Bonapartist cause. The only thing preventing a second Empire, Louis-Napoléon explained, was a lack of funds.

This was not, then, the letter of a man who had renounced politics. Indeed, shortly after returning to Arenenberg, Louis-Napoléon agreed to join Polish rebels fighting against Russian occupation. Only the fact that the Russian army crushed the uprising before he could leave prevented him embarking on the kind of foreign adventure his father hated. Hopes of revolutionary action dashed, Louis-Napoléon further disregarded his father's warnings. He wrote a political manifesto.

Published in May 1832, *Rêveries politiques* was soaked in utopian thinking and eclectic influences and awash with fantasies about the Empire. Short, written in simple language and full of memorable aphorisms, it also contained ideas considered radical and dangerous. For a nation 'to be free', Louis-Napoléon wrote, the people must be the 'source from which all power emanates', and 'sovereignty resides in the people'.[4] Few elites in Europe, or anywhere in the world for that matter, agreed with this in the 1830s. In much of Europe, sovereignty resided in a divinely ordained autocratic monarch whose power derived from God, not the people. Even in liberal outliers like Britain and France where the ruling class reluctantly agreed that people should have some say in governing the country, it was also agreed that only wealthy people counted. Those who orchestrated the July Revolution thought extending the franchise to just over 200,000 was generous; the Great Reform Act of 1832 in Britain meant that some 650,000 people could vote; even in one of the most democratic countries in the world at the time, the United States, many states in the 1830s restricted the vote based on income or property, not to mention race. But Louis-Napoléon argued that any Frenchman – only a minuscule number of the already small proportion who believed in democracy in 1830s argued for women's right to vote – over the age of twenty-five could vote.

For Louis-Napoléon claimed that as emperor his uncle had represented everyone, especially the people; the Bourbon restoration after 1815 served only the aristocracy, and it fell in 1830 because it was overthrown by the bourgeoisie. It was because the July Monarchy only protected bourgeois interests, maintained Louis-Napoléon with the vehemence of a

Marxist – not that there were any in the 1830s – that class struggles would inevitably result in Louis-Philippe losing his throne. Writing to his mother, he put his case clearly: 'As long as universal suffrage will not be one of the fundamental laws of the state, the national representation will only be the representation of particular interests, the deputies will only be the mediators of a class and the chamber will have neither dignity nor influence.'[5]

By writing his manifesto, Louis-Napoléon hoped to resurrect Bonapartism as a rival to the three main political movements in France. Legitimists believed the Bourbons were divinely appointed kings. The staggeringly incompetent and reactionary Charles X, overthrown in 1830, had discredited them, but legitimists retained support among the traditional aristocracy combined with strong devotion in certain regions from pious Catholic peasants. Now in power, Orléanists who backed Louis-Philippe – head of the junior Orléans branch of the Bourbons – were liberals. At this point in the nineteenth century, however, liberalism looked very conservative. It placed great importance on constitutions and certain individual rights, but believed governments should do little if anything to help the poor and abhorred mass democracy. In France, only 0.3 per cent of the population had a vote in national elections.

Finally, there were the republicans. As often the case on the left, the movement was fractured into groups that often hated each other more than their oppressors in power. This broad church ranged from moderates who would have been happy with the July Monarchy if ruled by a president rather than a king to those who embraced the Terror of Maximilien Robespierre, peppered their thoughts with newfangled socialist ideas and preached revolution. These latter claimed to represent the people, but this came as a surprise to most of the people they claimed to represent. Republican support came mainly from workers and artisans in urban areas, but was limited among the rural population which made up the majority of the French nation. While some republicans did believe in universal male suffrage, others argued that giving what they saw as uneducated peasants the vote was the height of foolishness, not least because if they did vote, they would not vote for republicans. Instead, they organised in secret societies, launching regular plots to overthrow the July Monarchy and seize power.

Louis-Napoléon wanted to create a fourth movement that drew its strength from the deep nostalgia for Napoléon and the Empire and ploughed a middle way between royalists and republicans. As few but the most outré thinkers believed in popular sovereignty combined with universal male suffrage, Louis-Napoléon acknowledged in *Rêveries politiques* that his views aligned him with the most left-wing group in French politics, republicans. What set him apart, however, was that he believed France's customs and history meant that a monarch, not a president, should govern. Of course, republicans did not believe this, but many others did. Pushing himself out of the political wilderness and into territory possibly inhabited solely by himself, Louis-Napoléon insisted that the French king, or rather emperor, should be a member of the Bonaparte family, confirmed as the will of the people in a plebiscite.

Louis-Napoléon's manifesto was steeped in radical and Napoleonic tradition. The Empire alone, he maintained, could marry the principles of the French Revolution of 1789 with order; a republic meant the Terror; an unelected monarchy, reaction. Though the emperor would have considerable executive power, the Empire was on the side of progress. There were two parties in Europe, Louis-Napoléon wrote, 'one turning towards the future in pursuit of the useful, the other clinging to the past in order to preserve its abuses'.[6] Louis-Napoléon, of course, represented the former. Under the restored Empire, there would be an end to aristocratic privilege – it would be a meritocratic state open to all with talent – and a free press. His hatred for the Bourbon kings and his continued banishment from France, confirmed by the July Monarchy, gave an urgency to his anti-elitist rhetoric, which placed Louis-Napoléon, an imperial prince, on the side of the masses against the classes. He argued that under the Empire France had been magnificent, under the Bourbons it had sunk into malaise, and now under Louis-Philippe, who stole the 1830 Revolution from the people, it was in thrall to outrageously mediocre and petty bourgeois interests. To make France great again, a second Empire was needed, ruled by Napoléon II.

In theory, all this should have made for a potent platform. In reality, hardly anyone was interested in the musings of a little-known imperial prince and few read *Rêveries politiques*. Indeed, that Napoléon II should reign was not even a majority view held by those called Bonaparte, let alone by people in France. The first group, therefore, that Louis-Napoléon needed to convince of his quixotic beliefs was his own family. In the summer of 1832, the perfect opportunity presented itself. Joseph was coming to London.

———

But Louis-Napoléon's dreams were dealt a severe blow on 22 July 1832, when Napoléon's only legitimate son and heir, the Duke of Reichstadt, died of tuberculosis at the age of twenty-one. He had been held as a pawn in European power politics, sequestered in the Austrian court at Vienna. Louis-Napoléon, who had tried to smuggle letters to him declaring his support, was devastated at his cousin's demise. All his hopes now rested on the eldest surviving Bonaparte, Joseph.

Yet for Joseph the news came as something of a relief when he learned it upon arriving in Liverpool on 24 July 1832. Napoléon Bonaparte had read his brother correctly when discussing Joseph's exile to the United States: 'If I was in his place I would found a great empire of all Spanish America, but you will see that he will be a bourgeois American and spend his fortune making gardens.'[7] Out of deference to his dead brother, Joseph had paid lip service to the idea of another Empire while the Duke of Reichstadt was alive. With the death of the would-be Napoléon II, the tedious idea of restoring the Bonapartes could be dropped. Certainly, Joseph had no ambitions to put himself forward as an imperial pretender. Instead, he dreamed of an even more bourgeois life in France: the law that banished the family overturned, confiscated wealth given back.

Louis-Napoléon, however, had travelled to London for what he thought would be a discussion about how to overthrow the July Monarchy. To fuel his ardour, he took a detour via the Waterloo battlefield. 'You can understand', he wrote to his mother, 'all I felt in seeing the spot where the fate of France was decided, and where the star of the emperor set for ever.'[8]

After this, Joseph's limited horizons were a crushing disappointment. 'I thought to find a second father in you' but 'my first interview with you froze me . . . you received me as a stranger, and not as a nephew', wrote Louis-Napoléon.[9] He had been ready to sacrifice his life for a second

Bonapartist coming; instead, he found a bourgeois American gardener. For his part, Joseph thought Louis-Napoléon a reckless schemer liable to ruin any chance of a rich retirement in France.

So profound was Louis-Napoléon's disillusionment at what to him seemed a heretical lack of grandeur on Joseph's part that he fell into a deep melancholy. 'Since I have been here,' he wrote to Hortense, 'I feel down. I see everything in black and nothing makes me smile.' His usual source of solace, dreams of Napoleonic glory, depressed him, and Joseph's inaction had turned his name into a burden: 'When this obligation cannot be fulfilled then one has all the disagreements of having an elevated position without any of the advantages.'[10]

Having realised that there was nothing to be gained from Joseph, Louis-Napoléon decided to see more of England. In a sign that he had spent too long in Switzerland, he was amazed there were no mountains, though he did admit that hills, rivers and what he thought of as magnificent trees made up for it somewhat. What struck him most about the country was its industry and technology. His tour, unusual for a wealthy European at the time, was to the industrial heartlands of Manchester, Liverpool – both beautiful cities, according to him – and Birmingham. To get to Liverpool, he travelled on the recently opened railway. With childlike wonder, he described to his parents the extraordinary and then unknown speed the train travelled at: so fast, he wrote, that objects passed in a blur.

Obsessed with technology and convinced the future was steam-powered, he marvelled at textile machines in Lancashire cotton factories. In Birmingham, he looked on in amazement as the night sky was lit up with the fires of iron forges. He descended 300 feet below ground in a coal mine – the vast depths reminding him of the catacombs of Rome – where the air was ventilated by a 120-horsepower steam engine. Such was his obsession with steam engines that he wrote to his mother to reassure her that he had not been 'vaporised' by one.[11] He was back at Arenenberg by the spring of 1833. Time with Joseph had depressed him, but had also taught him that if the Empire were to be restored, he was going to have to do it himself.

———

While Louis-Napoléon was away, Alexandre Dumas *père*, author of *The Three Musketeers*, visited Hortense at Arenenberg. When they went for a walk in the gardens, the conversation turned to politics. 'Do you believe', asked Hortense, that 'if the Duke of Reichstadt had not died, he would have continued his father's work?'

'In my opinion,' replied Dumas, 'men like Napoléon have neither father nor sons. They are born like meteors in the twilight of the dawn, and light up the sky from one horizon to the other as they cross it before they are lost in the twilight of the night.'

'What you are saying is not consoling to those of his family who preserve some hope,' replied Hortense.

'It is as I say, Madame; for we have only given him a place in our heavens on condition that he did not leave any heir on the earth,' answered Dumas.

'But he bequeathed his sword to his son.'

'The gift was fatal, Madame, and God broke the bequest.'

'You terrify me, for his son, in turn, bequeathed it to mine,' said Hortense.

That, Dumas replied with some understatement, was a heavy sword for a mere junior officer in the Swiss militia to bear. As for a second Empire in France, there was no chance. What then, Hortense asked, would Dumas say to 'a member of the family' who was still dreaming of a 'resurrection of Napoleonic glory and power'?

'I should counsel him to wake up,' answered Dumas.[12]

This dreamer was, of course, Louis-Napoléon. In his view, he was awake – everyone else was asleep. With the death of the Duke of Reichstadt and Joseph's indifference, Louis-Napoléon believed that it fell to him to recreate his uncle's Empire. But if his belief that given the choice, French people would choose a legitimate son of Napoléon Bonaparte to reign was, to put it mildly, an optimistic one, the idea that if the French people were given the vote, they would elect a largely unknown, hot-headed and disgraced young nephew of Napoléon was nothing short of delusional. Not least because there was no chance that French people would get the vote. The July Monarchy faced frequent protests, riots and plots to overthrow it. But these were repressed – a republican insurrection that broke out into open revolt in June 1832 was crushed and then immortalised in prose (and later indelibly in song) by Victor Hugo's *Les Misérables*. For Louis-Napoléon, unsuccessful uprisings were proof of the regime's weaknesses; however, the king withstood all opposition.

There was little, then, for Louis-Napoléon to do but try to raise his profile. 'My life is so sad and boring here and I can only distract myself by occupying myself with serious things,' he wrote to his father.[13] Certainly the detailed analysis of Swiss politics and history that he wrote, *Considérations politiques et militaires sur la Suisse* – the title a nod to one of his main influences, the eighteenth-century philosopher Montesquieu – was serious. As Napoléon had imposed a political settlement on Switzerland when emperor, it also afforded him an opportunity to ruminate on his uncle's policy, and as it was positively reviewed in the Swiss press, it ingratiated him with the Swiss public.

With his penchant for radical politics well known locally – he frequently involved himself in charity events raising money for Polish refugees fleeing Russian persecution – he was dubbed the 'republican prince'. When well-lubricated members of a local shooting club learned that he was staying in their town, they marched late at night to his hotel and woke him up by serenading him with republican songs. Despite being rudely awakened, Louis-Napoléon welcomed the impromptu gathering with effortless charm. 'I should not be called Napoléon if I did not love freedom,' he told them.[14]

After his work on Switzerland, Louis-Napoléon wrote a manual on artillery. As Hortense noted, 'It would hardly be interesting to read.'[15] But even if it was not a page-turner, the topic was carefully chosen to publicise his name and associate himself with the branch of the army that had won Napoléon fame. 'Fate', he wrote grandiosely in the introduction, 'has denied me until now the happiness of serving my country.'[16] The 'until now' showed his belief that he was destined for more than the life of a Swiss country gentleman. For the moment, though, Louis-Napoléon was dangerously bored – so bored that he decided marriage might alleviate the soul-destroying monotony.

———

Louis-Napoléon's head had been turned, as it often was, by an attractive female visitor to Arenenberg, Mademoiselle de Reding. When she left, he told everyone he was going to a nearby town for the evening. Instead, he galloped to where he knew the young woman would stop for the night. Finding Mademoiselle de Reding there, he dined with her, walked through the picturesque lakeside town and relentlessly flirted. Thinking little of it, Mademoiselle de Reding retired to her room, locked the door and undressed for bed.

At that moment, Louis-Napoléon burst into her bedroom through a side door she thought no longer in use. Pale, emotional, Louis-Napoléon threw himself at her feet and begged her to have sex with him. It was no use, he continued, to cry for help. No one would come to her aid. He had paid off the servants at the inn. Mademoiselle de Reding was unmoved. All she had in this world, she said, was her virtue, and he would not want to take that from her. Finally, she talked him round and got rid of him.

This, at least, was the gossip among Hortense's ladies-in-waiting. By his mid-twenties, Louis-Napoléon had become a consummate charmer. And he was as democratic in his taste in women as he was in his politics, happy to seduce all social classes. There was not much nightlife in the nearest town, Constance, but Louis-Napoléon was a regular on the scene of what there was, attending the theatre, balls and public fetes, paying as much attention to the wives and daughters of the bourgeoisie as the tradesmen. His modus operandi, so it was alleged, was to rent a boat, row to the middle of Lake Constance and have sex with whatever young woman he had managed to coax to go with him.

He was impulsive, a romantic – dangerously ready to quote German poetry – and prone to becoming passionately infatuated after meeting women he found attractive. Once the crush passed he hardly gave them another thought. Hortense usually did not mind. Indeed, she encouraged flirtations, seeing them as a harmless part of nineteenth-century aristocratic life. Occasionally, she urged him to marry. Louis-Napoléon, bored and lonely, was not against the idea. 'At the moment, I have such a need for affection', he wrote to his father, perhaps hoping for some in return, 'that if I could find a woman that pleases me and is suitable to my family, I would not hesitate in marrying.'[17] Two years later, he wrote, 'I don't ask for anything more than marrying,' but, showing keen perspicacity, added that the difficulty was 'finding a woman'.[18]

This was indeed the problem. Louis-Napoléon's social circle in his Swiss hermitage was limited. Any marriage, therefore, would have to be arranged. Hortense and the comte de Saint-Leu thought Louis-Napoléon was in the upper echelons of the aristocratic elite, but this was not a view the aristocratic elite shared. Above all, one of their number noted, Bonapartes were outrageous parvenus. After Napoléon's death, they were merely 'ruined gamblers who still retain some remains of their borrowed magnificence'.[19] The illustrious families of Europe had no desire to tie their daughters to a Bonaparte, particularly one known, if he was known at all, for disreputable conspiracies and who gambled that the emperor's death was not the end of the family's fortunes. As for an actual fortune, Louis-Napoléon had none, which made him an even less attractive proposition.

There were half-hearted attempts to arrange a union, but none proved successful. When the Queen of Portugal's husband died, Louis-Napoléon was rumoured to be in the running as a replacement. Instead of pursuing the marriage, however, he denied it publicly and thereby skilfully got himself in the papers:

> Convinced that the great name I bear will not always be a title of exclusion in the eyes of my compatriots, since it reminds them of fifteen years of glory, I wait calmly . . . for the people to call back to their bosom those who were exiled [by] foreigners in 1815. This hope of one day serving France as a soldier strengthens my soul and in my eyes is worth all the thrones in the world.[20]

France, of course, was in a similar position to Mademoiselle de Reding, uninterested in his services, but he reminded readers of the greatness of Napoléon, the humiliation of Waterloo and himself all in a few carefully worded lines. That may have been good politics, but Louis-Napoléon still had no serious prospects of marriage. In the end, it was decided he should fall back on marrying a cousin, the teenage daughter of his uncle Jérôme, Mathilde. This had been a vague family scheme for some time, but it was revived in 1835. In the hope of securing the match for her son, Hortense invited Jérôme and his family to spend the winter at Arenenberg. Louis-Napoléon's initial interactions with Mathilde were not promising. He had spent some days with her after the death of her mother earlier that year. To cheer her up, he lectured her on the life of the emperor and discussed his favourite book, *The Memorial of Saint Helena*. He was shocked to discover that Mathilde had never heard of it, let alone read it. Writing to his mother on 5 December 1835, he told her that Mathilde was 'very charming, but do not think that I am in love with her, not at all'.[21]

That changed after Mathilde, only fifteen years old, spent time at Arenenberg. Lake Constance was frozen, and Mathilde watched admiringly as Louis-Napoléon skated or pushed Hortense across the ice on a sled. Mathilde thought her twenty-seven-year-old cousin great fun – he would do anything to make her laugh – and she enjoyed his rebellious nature. She had to go away for a few months, but was coming back to Arenenberg soon. After spending time with her, Louis-Napoléon had fallen into one of his romantic infatuations and was now desperate to marry her. Knowing his father was against it, he wrote to the comte de Saint-Leu that his happiness depended on him giving his consent, and money.

While he waited for a reply, he was anxious, writing that he was only calm when ice skating. Warming to his theme, he went into full-blown Romanticism: 'This frozen lake where the feet glide without encountering any obstacle contrast so much with life!' At one point, he felt he had to quote Dante. Concluding his letter, he said he had so many wishes: to be in Stuttgart (where Mathilde had gone); to be in Paris; to have in his hands the fingers of his cousin or the hilt of a sword. 'And of all of these wishes, which will be granted? Probably none.'[22]

But with Louis-Napoléon absence made the heart grow colder and he greeted Mathilde with indifference when she returned in the spring of 1836. She rekindled her cousin's interest with low-cut dresses that shocked her father but caught Louis-Napoléon's attention. As one of Hortense's ladies-in-waiting put it, he 'devoured her with his eyes. With him, the flesh is weak.'[23] Smitten once again, Louis-Napoléon, kneeling, told his bemused cousin that people were like letters: everyone saw the outside, the envelope, the address, but the soul – in this analogy, the letter – was only intended for, read and understood by one person. More excitingly for her, on another occasion, Louis-Napoléon detached his horses from his carriage and pushed it over a ravine because she wanted to see what would happen.

The potential lovers were given the chance to play up to the romantic tropes of the times because it seemed as though they would never be together: the comte de Saint-Leu refused permission. His main objection was that he hated his brother Jérôme, who he thought, not without reason, was a debauched wastrel. So it was decided that Mathilde and Jérôme, who was bored at Arenenberg and desperate to see his mistress, would travel to Florence to persuade Louis-Napoléon's father. Here, the comte de Saint-Leu was typically unpleasant. When Mathilde visited him, he spent most of the time insulting Hortense. Hardly providing evidence for his case, the comte de Saint-Leu said that Mathilde would be better off marrying him rather than his son, but he eventually relented. Joseph, still in London, gave his blessing, not least because he thought that marriage might cool the ardour of his rash nephew. In this belief, Joseph was mistaken. For while courting his cousin, Louis-Napoléon had been making other plans.

———

Louis-Napoléon was aware that his ambition – to emulate one of the most astonishing men in history – was not matched by his achievements. 'I know', he wrote to a confidante, 'that I am much through my name, nothing through myself.' He believed, however, that Napoléon shone brightly enough to illuminate the next generation; all Louis-Napoléon needed to do was force 'myself to such a height that the dying rays of the sun of Saint Helena may still light me'.[24] What was needed, therefore, was action.

For that, however, Louis-Napoléon needed people to act with him, and he did not have many friends, let alone ones devoted or mad enough to try to propel an unknown exile to power. But in the summer of 1835, he had met someone whose fanatical commitment to the cult of Bonapartism was even more deluded than his own. Born in 1808, the same year as Louis-Napoléon, Jean Gilbert Victor Fialin was a young man searching for a cause. Brought up by his mother after his father died in the Napoleonic wars, Fialin joined the French army in 1825 under the Bourbons but was discharged in 1831 after the July Revolution because of his republican sympathies.

He reinvented himself as a journalist, styling himself as Victor vicomte de Persigny, an aristocratic title he claimed had lapsed in the family. He was a mediocre hack, writing for whatever newspaper would pay him.

What Persigny did have, though, was anger. He was angry at being thrown out of the army, angry that he was not rich, angry at the July Monarchy and, above all, angry that what he considered his considerable talents were unrewarded.

His Damascene conversion to Bonapartism took place in Germany, where he was researching a story. While driving along in a carriage and enjoying the scenery, a cry of '*Vive Napoléon!*' jolted him out of his reveries. It came from his driver as they passed another carriage. 'Napoléon?' enquired Persigny. 'What do you mean?' Explaining, the driver replied, 'It's the son of King Jérôme. We drive him to college.'[25] The veneration of a German coachman for a nephew of the emperor was a revelation for Persigny. With the fervour of a religious convert, Persigny passed a restless night. By the morning he was convinced there was a middle way between the tyranny of monarchy and the revolutions of republicans: Bonapartism. And he dreamed of making this heaven a reality on earth.

Short-tempered, with dark hair violently parted to one side and a moustache reminiscent of Louis-Napoléon's, Persigny became an unquestioning acolyte of his moustachioed hero after he contrived to have himself introduced to Louis-Napoléon at Arenenberg in 1835. The two soon became friends, staying up late and excitedly discussing the future, conspiring, chain-smoking. Unlike Louis-Napoléon, Persigny was able to travel between Switzerland and France, and started to put their plans into action. The strategy was simple: the template came from the life of Napoléon, the Flight of the Eagle, the dramatic return from exile on the island of Elba in 1815, when the emperor had marched on Paris, picking up supporters on the way, before being carried into the Tuileries on a wave of popular enthusiasm.

Louis-Napoléon would enact his own version of this legendary moment, presenting himself before soldiers garrisoned at Strasbourg in eastern France, on the German border. Upon seeing the imperial eagle, the iconic standard of the French army under Napoléon, the troops would rally to the nephew of the great man. Just as in 1815, as Louis-Napoléon marched on Paris, garrisons would flock to his side, young men would enlist, old veterans would put down the plough and run to his side. Faced with an unstoppable popular movement, Louis-Philippe would be finished.

Louis-Napoléon and Persigny's plans took serious shape in 1836. The timing was propitious: the popular Napoleonic legend which had been growing in France since 1815 was reaching new heights. From the literature of the novelist Stendhal to the popular songs of Pierre-Jean de Béranger, Napoleonic nostalgia was everywhere. Hoping that some of the glory might rub off, the government even encouraged it. In 1836, decorations on a Napoleonic monument, the Arc de Triomphe, were finally completed, and for three years Napoléon's statue had once more sat atop the Vendôme column. Not only was the emperor staring down again on Paris, but his face was also staring out from everyday objects. Wallpaper, biscuits, cider bottles, inkwells and popular prints: if Napoléon could be put on it, someone had done it, and sold it.

'It is impossible', wrote the German poet Heinrich Heine, trying to explain this support for Napoléon, 'for anyone outside France to imagine the extent to which the French people still idolise Napoléon.'

> Napoléon is for the French a magical word which electrifies and dazzles them . . . Last night, passing through an obscure little street to return home, I saw a child, barely three years of age, sitting on the ground in front of a small illuminated tallow candle; he was mumbling a song to the glory of the Empire.[26]

If Louis-Napoléon could harness the reverence for his uncle behind a political programme that took advantage of widespread discontent with the July Monarchy and combined it with mass democracy, then he would have a phenomenally powerful movement. Unfortunately, few people in France knew who he was, certainly not those who mattered for his plan to work – namely, officers in the army. To rectify this, he did what many an author has done to promote their work: he sent copies of his book on artillery to anyone in the military he could think of. Unlike most writers, though, this had a political purpose: replies were scrutinised for pro-imperial sentiment.

During the summer of 1836, when he was supposedly pining for his cousin Mathilde, he was, in fact, courting disillusioned French army officers in German spa towns near the Rhine. Baden was his preferred location. As cover, he wrote to his mother that he was taking the waters there and a local doctor had recommended eating eels to improve his health.

Louis-Napoléon, however, was not the most inconspicuous of conspirers. He could be found walking around, arms behind his back in classic Napoleonic pose, claiming that he would be emperor. His method of seduction was also not subtle. He requested meetings with officers, or fortuitously bumped into them at social occasions he knew they would be at. As Louis-Napoléon assumed that the entire French army was loyal to the memory of his uncle, there was not much vetting.

'Captain,' he said to one potential recruit in July, 'you have courage and loyalty and I believe I can confide in you. You love the emperor too much not to love his family. A movement is about to break out, I count on you, and I will put myself at its head.' Unfortunately, the would-be emperor delivered this speech lying down while suffering from a cold and had most of his face covered with a handkerchief. This less-than-majestic appearance did not convince the shocked officer, who tried to talk Louis-Napoléon out of his plan and then reported the interview to his commanding officer when he returned to Strasbourg.[27]

Not that this would have bothered Louis-Napoléon. In seeking out adherents he had already gone to the top of the chain of command, the highest-ranking officer in Strasbourg, General Théophile Voirol. 'General,' he wrote on 14 August from Baden, 'my heart is torn, having had France before my eyes for the past month without being able to set foot there. Tomorrow is the emperor's birthday, and I will spend it with strangers. If you can give me an appointment in a few days . . . you will erase by your presence the sad impressions which oppress me.'[28] Voirol reported what amounted to an invitation to commit treason to the minister of war in Paris, but did not take it seriously and took no further action to crack down on the conspiracy.

But Louis-Napoléon was serious and did have adherents, a ragtag band of misfits, malcontents and adventurers, most of whom had a hint of madness about them. One of their number was a suicidally brave veteran of the Napoleonic wars, Denis-Charles Parquin. The cult of the emperor still shone brightly in this epitome of the gruff old soldier. He had sworn an oath to serve Napoléon in 1804 and, as he said, unlike the elite of France, who readily pledged allegiance to whatever regime was in power, he could not swear others. He was loyal only to the emperor, and now his nephew. His devotion was especially strong because he lived near Arenenberg and had watched Louis-Napoléon grow up, regaling the enraptured boy with tales of imperial heroism. Impressive though Parquin was, he was no longer in active service and had little influence with the army in Strasbourg. Louis-Napoléon needed another veteran on side.

Enter Colonel Claude-Nicolas Vaudrey. While he had fought at Waterloo, his record was nothing compared to Parquin's. He was, however, the commanding officer of the 4th regiment of artillery stationed at Strasbourg. Tall with short black curly hair, a high forehead, a bushy moustache and a wisp of a goatee, Vaudrey was an imposing man. He was also a disillusioned one, repeatedly passed over for promotion. Louis-Napoléon met him several times across the border, urging him to join the revolt, pouring out noble sentiments as to how they would save France. Vaudrey would be a hero and, more importantly, would be rewarded. 'I have never conspired in the common acceptation of the word,' Louis-Napoléon told Colonel Vaudrey as he tried to win over the officer to his conspiracy. 'Believe me,' said the imperial pretender, who in the last twenty-one years had spent only a few weeks in his country of birth, 'I know France well.' He then outlined the plan:

> My object is to come with a popular flag – the most popular, the most glorious of all – to serve as a rallying point for all that is most generous and national among the various parties . . . And to bring about such a result, what is necessary? Derive all your power and all your rights from the masses; for amid the masses are to be found reason and justice.[29]

Vaudrey, however, did not have a shrine to the emperor in his heart, nor was he won over by populist arguments or even promises of promotion. What he loved was women. Louis-Napoléon, therefore, introduced him to Eleonore Gordon, a strikingly beautiful singer who had received lessons from the Italian composer Gioachino Rossini. With two strands of her rich, dark hair enclosing an oval face and dimpled chin, the elegantly dressed twenty-eight-year-old did not have to work hard to attract the fifty-two-year-old Vaudrey's interest. Unlike her target, she had been brought up to revere the emperor, as the daughter of a soldier in the Imperial Guard, Napoléon's elite troops. She was as committed a Bonapartist as Louis-Napoléon, who many thought was her lover. He denied it, and so did she. She loved him politically, she claimed, but physically he reminded her of a woman. Whatever the truth of these rumours, she was so faithful to the imperial pretender that she gave herself body and soul, becoming Vaudrey's mistress on the condition that he back the *coup d'état*.

Persigny, a disgraced soldier; Parquin, the personification of imperial bravado; Vaudrey, a disillusioned officer willing to commit treason for his lover; Gordon, a sensual singer and fellow traveller; and, of course, Louis-Napoléon, the nephew of the emperor – such was the crew assembled to usher in a new golden age for France.

So confident was Louis-Napoléon of success that he organised a party in the ruins of a castle near Baden towards the end of August. Here, illuminated by candles and lanterns, young men involved in the plot sang songs, made speeches and gave toasts to the future Emperor of the French. So bright were the illuminations that in Baden some people wondered what was causing the glow rising out of the forest; many others knew that it was Louis-Napoléon's self-arranged coronation party.

In case his correspondence was intercepted, Louis-Napoléon added an 'e' to his first name and signed off his letters to Vaudrey 'Louise', pretending to be a suitor hopeful for marriage ('You alone, *monsieur*, unite in yourself everything that can make my heart vibrate, past, present, future!' was at least passable prose for a romantic missive);[30] however, this was hardly top-secret planning. Given that most of the officers in Strasbourg knew about Louis-Napoléon's plans, some confidants advised him to postpone, while others urged him on. In the end, he decided to go ahead at the end of October.

On 15 October, Louis-Napoléon said goodbye to Hortense, claiming he was going away for a hunting weekend. How much she knew of her son's plans is unclear, but if she did not know the specifics – and he may well have told her exactly what he was going to do – she knew her son was up to something. She urged him to be cautious, and placed on his finger Joséphine's wedding ring from her marriage to Napoléon.

———

On the evening of 29 October, in the cold, damp and dark streets of Strasbourg, near a deserted canal, two conspirators wrapped against the autumnal chill met. It was Louis-Napoléon and Colonel Vaudrey. The *coup d'état* was on, and would take place the next morning. After meeting Vaudrey, Louis-Napoléon dined on chicken and a bottle of wine at Persigny's, before retiring to a safe house with his co-conspirators. The night passed slowly; no one slept. Louis-Napoléon ran through the plan and checked over three proclamations: one for the army, one for the people of France and one for the Strasbourgeois.

The message was simple, populist, radically democratic and, naturally, heavy on Napoleonic nostalgia. The people of France, Louis-Napoléon declared, had been betrayed. After the glory of the July Revolution, a government had been imposed without consulting the people. 'Everything that has been done without you is illegitimate.' Now, Louis-Napoléon came before them as a 'representative of the sovereignty of the people':

> Faithful to the maxims of the emperor, I know of no other interests
> save yours, no other glory than that of being useful to France and
> humanity . . . I have devoted my existence to the accomplishment of
> a great mission. From the rock of Saint Helena, a ray of the setting
> sun has passed into my soul . . . Men of 1789, men of 20 March
> 1815, men of 1830, arise! See who governs you, and behold the eagle,
> sublime emblem, the symbol of liberty, and choose![31]

Just after 5 a.m., the early-morning silence was broken as trumpets echoed across the city; it was the sound of Vaudrey calling his men to arms in a nearby barracks – the signal for the uprising to begin. With his co-conspirators, Louis-Napoléon rushed into the freezing streets. 'Let's go, gentlemen,' he said. 'The moment has arrived. We shall see if France still remembers twenty years of glory.'

The young pretender looked the part. Dressed in a blue military tunic with a red collar, he had added the epaulettes of a colonel on his shoulders and the star of the *légion d'honneur* on his breast, as had his uncle, who often wore the uniform of a grenadier colonel. An officer's hat and cavalry sabre completed the outfit. As Louis-Napoléon was marching through the streets, Vaudrey readied his men. His confused regiment formed up in the courtyard of the barracks.

Louis-Napoléon entered and marched confidently towards Vaudrey in front of the troops. The soldiers presented arms. Then Vaudrey addressed his men: 'Soldiers of the 4th, a great revolution begins in this moment under the auspices of the nephew of the emperor. He is before you . . . he counts on your courage, your devotion and your patriotism . . . Soldiers, your colonel has answered for you; therefore repeat with him! *Vive Napoléon! Vive l'empereur!*' The men roared back these cries.

Louis-Napoléon gestured that he wanted to speak; the noise quietened. He told the soldiers that he was resolved to triumph or die for the glory and liberty of the French people. He had chosen the 4th artillery regiment carefully; it was steeped in Napoleonic legend. 'Soldiers, new destinies are reserved for you,' he harangued; 'to you the glory of beginning a new enterprise.' At this point, Louis-Napoléon seized an imperial eagle that one of his plotters had procured and held it aloft. 'Soldiers, here is the symbol of French glory . . . We march together against the oppressors of the country to cries of: *Vive la France! Vive la liberté!*'[32]

This was met with delirium from the men: sabres waved over heads, shakos thrown in the air, shouts of enthusiasm resounding. As planned, detachments of soldiers then fanned out through the streets of Strasbourg to take over key sites and arrest the prefect of the department and the highest-ranking officers.

Though the 4th regiment had rallied, there had been some confusion in the ranks about exactly who Louis-Napoléon was. A bewildered captain asked what was going on.

'It's the son of the emperor who is being proclaimed.'

But he's dead, replied the officer.

'His son, his grandson, an emperor, in fact,' said an artilleryman.[33]

Louis-Napoléon along with Vaudrey, Parquin and the largest detachment of soldiers went to find the highest-ranking officer in Strasbourg, General Voirol. As they made their way to his headquarters, curious Strasbourgeois came out onto the streets. Seeing a procession of soldiers marching behind the imperial eagle brought out the popular Bonapartism of the people. Many shouted, '*Vive Napoléon!*', others mobbed Louis-Napoléon and still more joined the march.

When they reached Voirol's headquarters, soldiers took control of the building, while Louis-Napoléon and a group of officers burst into his bedroom. This veteran of the Napoleonic wars had been caught – despite numerous warnings about the revolt – unawares and was still in his vest and underpants. 'General, I come to you as a friend. I should be sorry to raise our old tricolour banner without the aid of a brave soldier like you. The garrison is in my favour. Decide and follow me,' said Louis-Napoléon, before someone brandished the imperial eagle at the general.

'Prince, they have deceived you. The army knows its duties, as I will prove to you immediately,' replied General Voirol, before ranting at Vaudrey for his treachery.[34]

Louis-Napoléon was stunned. He could not believe that a veteran officer of the Napoleonic wars could look upon an imperial eagle and not be won over. Recovering, he ordered that Voirol be arrested and continued with the plan. This aside, it was going well. Persigny had detained the local officials, the printing and semaphore telegraph offices were in the hands of the conspirators, the people were behind them and junior officers were bringing more and more soldiers over to the *coup d'état*. The next obstacle was to convince the 46th infantry regiment in the nearby Finckmatt barracks to join the revolt.

Louis-Napoléon, therefore, left Voirol's headquarters to present himself before the 46th. In the confusion and excitement, however, he led his troops the wrong way. He should have marched to the ramparts that loomed over one side of the barracks, where, from the heights, he could deploy all his followers to intimidate the garrison below. Instead, he approached along a narrow lane, where there was a single entrance into a courtyard. There was no room to bring all his troops with him; half were left behind. Despite this, some four hundred men marched into the barracks, drums beating, and cried: '*Vive l'empereur!*'

Unlike the 4th, the 46th regiment had not been called to arms but was still in barrack rooms. Confused men ran to the windows, some down into the yard below. On seeing an old sergeant of the 46th, the conspiracists said, '*Voilà*, an old veteran. Shout: *vive l'empereur!*'

'I don't know your emperor. The emperor is dead, *vive le roi!*' replied the soldier.[35]

Then the sergeant heard that the rebels wanted to arrest his lieutenant. If anyone tries to arrest the lieutenant, the sergeant replied with impeccable sangfroid, they will not get out of here alive. The sergeant ran back upstairs to fetch his men and charge his musket. When he returned to the courtyard, a major told him that the men were rebels, and Vaudrey a traitor.

As this news spread, the yard descended into a chaotic shouting match, with Vaudrey and his regiment ordering the infantry to cry '*Vive l'empereur!*' and the infantry officers ordering their men to shout '*Vive le roi!*' An officer loyal to the king threatened to plunge his sabre into any soldier who went over to Louis-Napoléon. Then he rushed towards Louis-Napoléon, trying to seize him. Instead, the artillerymen grabbed him, but the officer shouted, 'Men of the 46th, to me!' and his own troops freed him. At that point, the commanding officer of the 46th arrived in the yard. 'Soldiers,' he shouted, 'you are being deceived: this is not the emperor's nephew.' Another officer added, 'It's the nephew of Colonel Vaudrey that is being presented to you as emperor.'[36]

Then the officers of the 46th closed the gates to the courtyard and began to form their men into line. The two sides faced off against each other, bayonets fixed, officers' swords drawn. Turning to Louis-Napoléon, some of those loyal to him suggested cutting a passage through the infantry; however, his uncle's return to France had been bloodless and so, reasoned the nephew, must his be.

Instead, he tried the distinctly Napoleonic tactic of rushing towards the undecided soldiers to rally them to his cause. They raised their muskets and pushed him back. Parrying bayonets with his sabre, Louis-Napoléon was surrounded. Artillerymen threw themselves in front of him, but Louis-Napoléon had been separated from his followers. He tried to seize a horse, but the infantry dragged him down and then pushed him against a wall in the courtyard. He was a prisoner.

People lined the ramparts where Louis-Napoléon should have led his men. They had been enjoying the spectacle and were furious that the infantry had taken him prisoner. They threw stones at the soldiers and shouted, '*Vive l'empereur!*' Had the order been given, perhaps Louis-Napoléon could have fought his way out; however, he was determined not to spill blood. Resistance ended, Vaudrey commanded his men to return to barracks and obey the law. He, Parquin and Louis-Napoléon were arrested.

Persigny had escaped and ran back to his safe house, where, along with Eleonore Gordon, he frantically burned as many compromising papers as he could. When the police knocked on the door, Eleonore drew on her talents as an artist and performatively fainted. This gave Persigny the chance to escape out of a window.

Louis-Napoléon had not been so lucky. Marched into the barracks' guardhouse, he found Parquin. 'We will be shot, but we will die well,' said Parquin.

'Yes,' replied Louis-Napoléon coolly, 'we have fallen in a beautiful and noble enterprise.'[37]

'My dear Maman,' he wrote the next day, 1 November 1836, 'you must have been so worried at not receiving my news . . . But your worry will be doubled when you learn that I attempted [an uprising] in Strasbourg that has failed. I am in prison.'[38]

5

CITIZEN OF NOWHERE

The punishment for treason was death. But Louis-Philippe had no intention of executing the nephew of Napoléon and turning him into a Bonapartist martyr. In fact, he did not even want him on trial. This would give Louis-Napoléon, self-appointed tribune of the people, the platform he craved. Instead, the king and his ministers decided to downplay the affair and paint it as a misguided and farcical pastiche of Napoléon carried out by an adventurer of little import and questionable motives. Given this largely matched what had happened, it was not a difficult narrative to push. What should have been another Flight of the Eagle went down as *l'échauffourée de Strasbourg* – the Strasbourg brawl.

As one of Louis-Philippe's ministers noted, Louis-Napoléon had 'an invincible confidence' and believed himself 'destined to be an emperor', but he was 'young, unknown to France, to the army, and to the people; no one had seen him; he had done nothing'.[1] To keep him in obscurity, it was decided to exile him to the United States. If there were any doubts as to the wisdom of sending Louis-Napoléon into exile, his responses to interrogation settled them:

'Did you want to establish a military government?'
'I wanted to found a government based on popular election.'[2]

Giving a nephew of the Emperor Napoléon a platform to argue for democracy in the decidedly undemocratic July Monarchy was exactly what Louis-Napoléon wanted. The prisoner was, then, furious when on 9 November he was taken from his cell and put in a carriage for Paris. He spent only a few hours in the capital, where the prefect of police informed him that King Louis-Philippe had interceded on his behalf. Then he was driven to Lorient and shut up in the citadel that guarded this Atlantic port until favourable winds allowed for his departure.

As well as genuine concern, it was the optics of leaving his friends that infuriated Louis-Napoléon. 'My enterprise having failed, my intentions being unknown, my fate being, in spite of my remonstrances, different from that of the men whose lives I have compromised, I shall pass in the eyes of everybody for a fool, a self-seeking man, a coward,' he wrote to a friend. He had been prepared for the first two, he explained, but the third was 'too cruel'.[3] There were also rumours that Hortense would join her son in exile, and Louis-Napoléon begged her not to come. He wrote to his mother that the shame of having 'dragged' her into a new exile would be unbearable for him.[4]

On 21 November, Louis-Napoléon boarded a French frigate and began his voyage. Once they reached the midpoint of the Atlantic, the captain opened sealed orders. The ship was going to New York via Rio de Janeiro, a deliberately circuitous route. The French king was determined that Louis-Napoléon be at sea during the trial, preventing him from commenting in the press. Instead, he penned achingly melancholic missives to his mother, occasionally wondered about Mathilde and cheered himself up thinking that the breeze in the South Atlantic blew from Saint Helena, carrying the dying words of Napoléon. Then Louis-Napoléon spent a month in the harbour of Rio de Janeiro, where he was not allowed to disembark, before the ship reached the United States in February 1837. Here, he learned what had happened at the trial.

———

Even without Louis-Napoléon, the trial of those who took part in his attempted *coup d'état* became a cause célèbre. While the pretender was off the coast of Rio de Janeiro under a hot sun, crowds were queuing in the dark, freezing cold streets at the height of the Alsace winter in Strasbourg to catch a glimpse of what promised to be scintillating political theatre.

The accused played their parts magnificently, particularly the three leads, Vaudrey, Parquin and, no stranger to the stage, Eleonore Gordon. Vaudrey was in uniform; Parquin wore a blue frock coat, the star of the *légion d'honneur* on his breast. Tall, broad-chested and stout, he looked every inch the Napoleonic hero. Gordon wore a white satin hat and a black silk dress with an embroidered collar. She gave her profession as artist, and when the charges against her were read out, she dramatically resorted to a bottle of smelling salts.

The case for the prosecution was simple: the men were caught weapons in hand, and had committed treason. Moreover, numerous letters – including, embarrassingly, one from 'Louise', aka Louis-Napoléon – and documents tied them and Gordon to the plot. She had not been haranguing the troops, but the police found her burning Louis-Napoléon's papers. To add insult to injury, she had then distracted them while Persigny made his escape. It would not require a legal genius to prove guilt. But the accused did not deny their culpability, they revelled in it – this was a trial before public opinion. The prosecution, therefore, painted the conspirators as men – and one woman – of low morals motivated by greed.

Yet when Vaudrey was asked what Louis-Napoléon had promised him, he replied, nothing, he could not be bought. And Parquin maintained that he had sworn an oath to the emperor thirty-one years ago, so when the nephew asked for help, he gave himself body and soul. Far from breaking oaths, he was keeping his. The attacks on Gordon were predictably low: she was a stage singer, paid for public performances, and what this implied was clear. The prosecution hardly helped portray itself as on the side of the people: when it summed up its case, the prosecutor claimed that Louis-Napoléon's proposed constitution was so democratic it would have plunged France into anarchy.

Vaudrey's lawyer turned the tables: he put the government on trial. One of the cornerstones of the July Revolution, he argued, was equality before the law. Yet the king had freed the ringleader, Louis-Napoléon, against his wishes, and now the government sought only to punish the men he had led. Brushing aside the attacks on Gordon's profession, her defence exclaimed, 'A singer! . . . In France we honour those who cultivate [the arts]; we pity those who look down on them and seek to demean them.'[5] By the end of the speech, Gordon was in floods of tears, grasping the hand of her lawyer.

Parquin was defended by his brother. His sibling ran through Parquin's long history fighting for France across Europe. As Parquin listened, the veteran of countless battles could not hold back the tears. In his final summing-up, Parquin's brother appealed to the jury: after spending restless days and sleepless nights, his eighty-two-year-old mother would ask him,

'What have you done with your brother?' He responded, 'Ah! My good, venerable mother, dry your tears. Your son? A jury of Alsace will return him to you.'[6] This time it was not merely Parquin in tears, but much of the courtroom.

After these marvellous histrionics, the jury was asked to deliver its verdict. As the jurors retired from the courtroom, spectators chanted, 'Acquit! Acquit!' It took only twenty-two minutes for the jurors to find the defendants not guilty. The men and one woman who had committed treason were mobbed, then feted in Strasbourg, where a banquet was organised that night in their honour. The government's humiliation was total, and the Bonapartist cause was reported in newspapers across France.

——

When Louis-Napoléon arrived in the United States, he cried after glancing one final time at the French tricolour that flew from the mast of the frigate. He was comforted when he learned that his friends had been acquitted. 'France', a veteran of the Napoleonic wars he met across the Atlantic reportedly said, 'now knows that the emperor has an heir.'[7] He was annoyed, however, that he had not received word from his uncle Joseph. Although Joseph was now in London, he had lived many years in the United States, and Louis-Napoléon was piqued that his uncle had done nothing to help him now he was exiled there. But Joseph was too angry with his nephew to do anything. 'This rascal', Joseph said of Louis-Napoléon after learning of his attempt at Strasbourg, 'has ruined everything.'[8]

The rascal was unapologetic. After learning that Joseph wanted nothing to do with him, he wrote to him that he would never change and his conscience was clear. What sustained him above all else, he wrote, was 'the belief that if the emperor looks down upon me from heaven he will be happy with me'. Then he turned on his uncle:

My enterprise has been defeated, this is true, but it has announced to France that the family of the emperor was not yet dead, that it counts still on devoted friends; finally, that its pretensions are not limited to reclaiming from the government some money, but to re-establish in favour of the people what foreigners and the Bourbons had destroyed. *Voilà*, what I have done; and for this you blame me?[9]

Louis-Napoléon was also furious that Mathilde had not contacted him. Despite receiving letters from his numerous cousins, there was no word from her. 'It's infamous!' he complained to his mother.[10] In fact, Jérôme, as angry as Joseph at Louis-Napoléon, broke off the engagement and forbade his daughter to write. She was not particularly distraught by this.

Louis-Napoléon headed to New York. There he was delighted to find his valet, Charles Thelin, who had crossed the Atlantic to join him in exile, as had an old friend, an Italian aristocrat and fellow conspirator. They took rooms at the Washington Hall hotel on Broadway, and Louis-Napoléon soon found himself courted by New York society. His name opened doors. Learning that he was in town, the owner and editor of a popular newspaper invited him to a dinner party where he met Winfield Scott, later Commanding General of the United States Army and a presidential candidate, as well as other luminaries of the political and social scenes. Soon, much of New York high society competed to add some old-world lustre to their soirées and balls, although Louis-Napoléon's moustache was considered outré. Overblown facial hair was soon to be de rigueur in the United States, but at this point it was considered subversive, dangerously European and, worst of all, the mark of a dandy. Louis-Napoléon was all these things, and he worried about the impact his moustache was having – forced shavings by vigilantes outraged at the affront caused by hirsute faces were not unknown.

Apart from his upper lip, three things struck American acquaintances about Louis-Napoléon. First, he was slightly mad. This was because, as one New York companion noted, he would frequently drop into conversation the phrase 'when I become emperor'. The second was that the normally thoughtful, serious and laconic man became alive around women. 'Louis Napoleon Bonaparte', reported the *New York Herald*, 'is carrying everything before him in fashionable life. He is a very Napoleon in the *beau monde* at present. The ladies are all dying to see him.' The paper described him as 'young, amiable and good looking' but 'perfectly innocent of any of the great talents or magnificent conceptions of his wonderful uncle'.[11]

A dissolute cousin, Pierre Bonaparte, also in New York, had even less Napoleonic grandeur about him. Pierre had been thrown into prison in Italy accused of murder, but had been released. After fleeing to the United

States, he earned a reputation as one of the most notorious brawlers in the bars of New York – quite an accolade given the levels of violence in the average New York bar. Louis-Napoléon claimed that he kept his distance from his degenerate cousin; Pierre claimed that he saved Louis-Napoléon from a drunken street fight with judicious use of his cane. Pierre was soon run out of New York after allegedly stabbing a dog.

Among politer society, Louis-Napoléon praised the United States, extolling its democratic virtues. In private, he was scathing. For Louis-Napoléon, as for many a romantically minded young Frenchman at the time, the United States was an obscure backwater and a vulgar country where people were only interested in money and the tyranny of public opinion was far more tedious than European despotism. It was, he complained to Hortense, difficult to adapt to the 'puritanical habits and mores of a prosaic people'.[12] He did note, however, that despite its profitability, some 'honest' people were beginning to question slavery, and that therefore, for the first time, 'the heart of the American has vibrated for an interest other than money'.[13]

Louis-Napoléon saw his time in the United States as more of a holiday than an exile and was already planning his return to Europe, perhaps as early as the autumn. He would first go to London, where Persigny was reorganising a cadre of loyal Bonapartists – mainly debauched and disillusioned young men. In the meantime, Louis-Napoléon asked his mother to provide a pension to help his disciple.

The third thing US acquaintances noted about Louis-Napoléon was how much he idolised his mother. When Louis-Napoléon's thoughts turned to her, recalled one New York friend, 'the intonations of his voice and his whole manner were often as gentle and feminine as those of a woman'.[14] Louis-Napoléon was desperately worried about Hortense because news had reached him that she was sick. Then he had no letters for weeks. On 3 June 1837, he received one while dining. Recognising the handwriting, he hastily broke the seal. His mother was dying.

Ignoring his exile, Louis-Napoléon booked passage on the next ship to London, leaving on 12 June. Always with one eye on publicity, however, he found time to write, unsolicited, to the president of the United States. Despite not having been invited, he apologised for not making it to

Washington to meet the president because filial duty to an ill mother called him back to Europe. Keeping his personal antipathy towards the United States to himself, he praised a country 'intimately bound up with memory of our French glory'. In France, the July Monarchy had spread the rumour that he had promised never to return to Europe as a condition of his exile. This, he told the president, was a lie. It was unlikely the president was wondering, but just in case he was, Louis-Napoléon added that 'with the name I bear' it was 'impossible' to 'stray one moment from the path which my conscience, my honour, and my duty trace'.[15]

The letter read like one head of state apologising to another; it was not, of course, for the benefit of the president, but for Louis-Napoléon. His newfound friends in the American press made sure it found its way into the newspapers, where it not only made Louis-Napoléon seem much more important than he was, but also acted as a public defence for his decision to return to Europe less than eight months after leaving France.

After his ship docked at Liverpool, Louis-Napoléon immediately made for London, arriving on 10 July. So determined was Joseph to avoid contact with his wayward nephew that he left the capital for the countryside. But he wrote his nephew an excoriating letter, accusing him of wanting to take his and the comte de Saint-Leu's place as the next in line to the Bonapartist succession. 'What would become of the world', complained Joseph, 'if children and nephews did not wait for the death of their parents before occupying their place!! Neither the imagination of Milton, nor the brush of Michelangelo would be capable of representing the horrible scene of this disorder.' Joseph now considered Louis-Napoléon 'separated from the four brothers of the emperor . . . Time,' he continued, and 'the wishes of your father, of your uncles, may one day perhaps change my resolution', but 'as for today, I desire that you leave me in peace in my retreat; that's enough bitterness with which you have so far poisoned the days of your family, who had the right to count on more confidence and moderation on your part.'[16]

It was, complained Louis-Napoléon to his mother, 'a ridiculous letter' and he was saddened to be shunned by his relatives.[17] But he remained unapologetic. 'What, then, have I done to be the pariah of Europe and of my family?' he wrote to his father. 'I have raised for a moment in a French town the flag of Austerlitz, and I have offered myself as a holocaust to the memory of the prisoner of Saint Helena.'[18] Showing that he had little understanding of his nephew, Joseph counselled Louis-Napoléon that he would find happiness only in repentance. 'I do not reproach myself at all,' replied Louis-Napoléon, 'because I have acted out of conviction; the motive of my actions is the intimate knowledge of what I must do for the name that I carry and an almost fanatical veneration for everything that the emperor has done.' In language unlikely to dissuade Joseph from the view that his nephew was of unsound mind, Louis-Napoléon explained that 'I have a religion that guides me'. With the fire of a prophet, he concluded his diatribe: 'Yes . . . I appeal to the Emperor Napoléon! He reads my heart, he will deliver me justice, he watches over me [and] he will not abandon me!'[19]

In London, Louis-Napoléon begged for a passport to travel to Switzerland to see his sick mother. The goal of his journey, he reasoned, was so legitimate that permission could not be refused. He was wrong. The French government placed him under surveillance and insisted that all countries deny him permission to travel. Not having the right documents, however, was no obstacle for a man used to operating in the shadows. He procured a false passport, gave French secret agents the slip and left Britain at the end of July. Within a week, he was at Arenenberg.

Hortense had stomach cancer, and by October it was clear that she did not have long to live. Louis-Napoléon was constantly at her side. On the night of 4 October, he knelt beside her bed. He covered her hands and face with kisses. The voice of her beloved son gave Hortense some comfort. 'My dear Maman, my dear Maman,' he said, choking with emotion, 'I will follow you into the better world where you are going. You will find your mother, my brother!' These moments were horrific, with Hortense moving between agony, delirium and occasional moments of lucidity. It was difficult for her to speak; her son would not let go of her hand. By the early hours of the morning, Hortense's voice had become weaker. Louis-Napoléon, on his knees by his mother's bed, broke down in tears. 'Bless me, Maman,' he cried. 'Maman, I am here, can you hear me?'[20] She could not. She died at 5 a.m. in Louis-Napoléon's arms. He had to be forcibly torn away from her body.

Among her things, Louis-Napoléon found a letter she had written to him but never sent months earlier, when she thought she would have to undergo a dangerous operation while he was in the United States. Now he read it.

> We shall meet again, shall we not, in a better world where you will come and join me as late as possible. And you will remember that in leaving this one I regret only you, only your good tenderness, which alone has made me find some happiness here. It will be a consolation for you, my dear friend, to think that, by your cares, you have made your mother as happy as she could be. You will recall all my tenderness for you and you will have courage . . . I press you to my heart.[21]

———

Hortense came of age in the cut-throat world of Napoléon Bonaparte's court and she had seen at first hand how he had gained, ruled and lost an empire. In short, she knew a thing or two about politics. In her will, however, she wrote that 'I have no political advice to give to my son'. This was because she had already given it. Louis-Napoléon had learned from someone whose worldview was almost as Machiavellian as the emperor. Be a friend to everyone, she had told him, but pay especial attention to the people, for it was from them that Bonapartism drew its strength. Opportunistic, she cautioned secrecy until the moment came to act. Time and again, she urged her son not to rely on the luck of his birth, but to develop his talents. Crucially, Hortense, unlike most other Bonaparte family members, believed Bonapartism had a political future as well as a glorious past. This she instilled in her son until it became an article of faith. As she also wrote in her will, her son 'understands his position and all the duties that his name imposes on him'.[22]

For the moment, though, Louis-Napoléon was too devastated to do anything but grieve. The bond between mother and son had been intense. Except perhaps for the reverence in which he held his uncle and the feelings he had for his dead brother, nothing came close to the love Louis-Napoléon felt for his mother, a relationship that was forged in a lonely seclusion where they were almost always in each other's company. Unlike the rest of his family, Hortense rarely reproached him, always loved him, and encouraged his ambitions rather than ridiculing them. In a short note, Louis-Napoléon informed his father that Hortense had died in his arms, adding, in handwriting unsteady from emotion, that he did not have the strength to write more.

'After the tenderness you have just lost,' wrote the comte de Saint-Leu in a rare show of compassion, 'you still have mine, which will never fail you.'[23] Signing off his letter, he gave his son his blessing. This was a comfort for Louis-Napoléon, who thought his father had disowned him after Strasbourg. But he did not want his father's approval enough to do the one thing that would have earned it: renounce politics. In November 1837, the comte de Saint-Leu urged, as he had many times before, his son to do exactly that. Yet by January 1838, Louis-Napoléon was again conspiring.

History, Napoléon Bonaparte remarked when in exile on Saint Helena, is but a fable agreed upon, and his nephew was determined that people agree on a different story to the one the government had told about his Strasbourg insurrection. After the death of his mother, he edited an incendiary pamphlet that gave his version of what happened. Rather than a derisory brawl, Louis-Napoléon's narrative was of an epic enterprise narrowly defeated. Moreover, in outlining his democratic principles and attacking the king, his fable was as much a future call to arms as it was a defence of the past. As Louis-Napoléon knew, when published it would be treasonous and its named author, a young lieutenant called Armand Laity who took part in the failed revolt, would be prosecuted.

After rattling round a nearby crumbling medieval castle for a few months because he found it too sad at Arenenberg, Louis-Napoléon's irrepressible confidence overcame his self-pity. In the summer of 1838, he decided it was time to act. In June, he sent Laity to Paris to publish the pamphlet they had written together defending his actions at Strasbourg. Laity printed ten thousand copies before he was arrested. The French government was determined to make an example of Laity and put him on trial for inciting rebellion, which was what Louis-Napoléon wanted. Laity, aware that the maximum penalty for his offence was twenty years in prison, was a willing martyr, and one Louis-Napoléon was happy to sacrifice.

With his remarkable talent for self-deception and his unique definition of the word 'conspire', Louis-Napoléon wrote to Laity in prison: 'They say your pamphlet is a fresh conspiracy; while, on the contrary, it relieves me from the reproach of ever having conspired.' Then he explained that he had 'no other support in the world than public opinion'. Hoping to turn the trial into another sensation, Louis-Napoléon coached Laity from Arenenberg, feeding him lines: the Bonapartist party 'has partisans everywhere, from the workshop of the mechanic to the council chamber of the king, from the soldiers' barracks to the palace of the marshal of France . . . All these, I say, are [Bonapartists].' The 'imperial system', he added, embodied the principles of the revolution of 1789: 'hierarchy in a democracy, equality before the law, reward for merit; it is, in short, a colossal pyramid with a broad base and a high head'.[24]

But there was little evidence of this broad base at the trial. Rather than risk going before a jury again, the government prosecuted Laity in the Chambre des pairs, the French equivalent of the House of Lords. Unlike at Strasbourg, there were no queues for the public galleries, no histrionics and no crowds shouting for acquittal. Laity was found guilty and condemned to five years in prison and a ten-thousand-franc fine. This made the government look repressive but had little impact beyond a few columns in the press.

For the comte de Saint-Leu, however, his son's actions were outrageous, proving his claims to have renounced politics were lies. 'If the Great Man whose name you bear saw from on high your conduct . . . how sad he must be,' he wrote in exasperation. 'How', he continued, 'can you lower yourself to the role of adventurer, intriguer, usurper, dare I even say conspirator?' Cruelly, his father then reminded his son of his first 'astonishing escapade' in 1831, which resulted in 'the loss of your brother', whom Louis-Napoléon's 'secret intrigues tore from my arms with as much speed as cruelty'. That was bad enough, the failed *coup d'état* at Strasbourg was worse, and now the Laity affair demonstrated that Louis-Napoléon had learned nothing. How dare he speak, his father thundered, on behalf of the family? 'Do not let yourself be blinded by the example of your immortal uncle,' he warned, before, not unreasonably, pointing out that his son had done nothing comparable to Napoléon. When he came to power, he had saved France at Toulon, conquered Italy and then Egypt. 'On what basis, then, would you establish your parallel?' The comte de Saint-Leu claimed to have 'served our country for fifteen years, more and better than you ever could'. Tired of being deceived by his 'incorrigible' son whose 'base ambition' was 'dishonest' and 'worthy of the streets', these would be his last warnings. 'Listen to them, or fear the terrible misfortunes you gratuitously bring upon yourself. I fulfil my duty by speaking frankly . . . My age and my health prevent me from returning to a subject that is killing me in a thousand ways.'[25]

But if the trial failed to put Louis-Napoléon in the spotlight, what happened next made him notorious across Europe. Just as it had to his father, the Laity affair proved to the French government what it already knew: Louis-Napoléon had no intention of renouncing his ambitions to restore his uncle's empire. In August 1838, therefore, the government demanded his expulsion from Switzerland. But Louis-Napoléon had courted Swiss opinion. He and Hortense had funded schools and charities; he had served in the Swiss militia and written a flattering analysis of the country's political institutions. In the kind of thing that happened to Louis-Napoléon, he had also galloped after a runaway carriage and saved a mother and child who otherwise would have plunged to their deaths. In short, he was a local hero. Swiss public opinion backed Louis-Napoléon, and the Swiss government refused to yield. Desperate to avoid another humiliation akin to the Strasbourg trial, the French moved twenty-five thousand soldiers to the border in an unsubtle attempt to force the issue.

Now, Louis-Napoléon played his part superbly. He wrote an open letter thanking the Swiss for their support and was brazen in his denial of any wrongdoing. 'They [the French government] pretend that the house in which my mother lately died, and where I am living almost alone, is the centre of intrigues. Let them prove it, if they can. For myself, I deny the accusation in the most formal manner.'[26] This was untrue, but it made excellent copy, which, in Louis-Napoléon's worldview, gave it a truth greater than fact.

As war seemed imminent, Louis-Napoléon artfully manipulated public opinion. Not wishing to be the cause of conflict, he wrote in another open letter, he would leave voluntarily. That should have settled the matter;

however, much to the delight of Louis-Napoléon, even this proved inadequate for the French government, which, in a move of unfathomable stupidity, demanded that he be formally expelled. France was on the precipice of war to remove an individual from a small country where, by the time an invasion was under way, he would no longer be. Finally, calmer heads in the French cabinet prevailed, but not before making France look absurd while turning Louis-Napoléon into a celebrity.

He even managed to dominate editorials in *The Times* for three days in a row. The paper speculated that the only reason France had backed down was because it could not count on the loyalty of its army if pitted against a Bonaparte. This was giving far more importance to Louis-Napoléon than he merited, but it was exactly the narrative he wanted printed. Indeed, the article read like Bonapartist propaganda: there were 'tempestuous elements in action which might have blown the loosely soldered crown from the temples' of Louis-Philippe.[27]

Less than two years ago, Louis-Napoléon had been humiliated as a farcical adventurer; now the French government had transformed him into a popular hero. In October 1838, he left Arenenberg. The streets of Constance were lined with cheering crowds, the town decked out as if for a military triumph; women waved handkerchiefs from windows, while men cheered and shouted '*Vive Napoléon!*' in the street. These scenes were repeated in the towns and cities he passed through on the way into exile in Britain. Here, another editorial in *The Times* described him as 'a restless intriguer, the organ and instrument of a military, predatory, revolutionary faction'.[28] This mad, bad and dangerous man, however, soon made himself at home in British high society.

———

Hundreds of burning candles suspended in chandeliers reflected off steel armour in an enormous ballroom in Eglinton Castle, Scotland. Under a canopy with curtains lined with silver thread and plumed coronets on the corners, British aristocrats dressed in period costume at a faux-medieval tournament sat waiting for the hand-to-hand combat to begin. Wearing a polished steel cuirass over a leather jacket trimmed with crimson satin, white silk stockings and russet boots, Louis-Napoléon entered the ballroom. From beneath his steel-visored helmet he stared at his opponent. Trumpets blasted; battle commenced. The two armoured knights closed and the sound of their broadswords colliding rang out. For nearly an hour, they kept up the fight. Athletic and a talented fencer, Louis-Napoléon parried, feinted and returned blows.

The heavy broadsword, however, was not the ideal weapon for a man only five feet four inches tall, and Louis-Napoléon began to tire. At the end of each round, he lifted his visor, his face dripping with sweat; his loyal squire, Persigny, attended him. In the end, Louis-Napoléon was defeated. He fared better the next day at the ball that closed the tournament. Donning his white stockings again, but this time with a short, dark green velvet cassock with crimson sleeves and rich gold trimming, offset with a matching cap adorned with a yellow feather, Louis-Napoléon waltzed around the ballroom with the British elite.

The whole affair was ridiculous conspicuous consumption to entertain the wastrel youth of a British aristocracy caught up in a craze of medieval revivalism, the result of having too much money and too much time, and reading too much Walter Scott. The tournament was immensely popular, attracting some twenty thousand people to watch posh people play out medieval fantasies, although the Scottish weather meant that the opening procession saw most of the knights wield little more deadly than umbrellas. Lampooned in the liberal British and French press, it was a rare public relations misstep for Louis-Napoléon, a man convinced he was on the side of progress. Yet as he waltzed his way through the daughters of Britain's most illustrious families, it showed how quickly the nephew of the country's great nemesis had integrated into the upper echelons of British society.

On 25 October 1838, Louis-Napoléon had checked into the fashionable Fenton Hotel on St James's Street. From here, he picked up where he'd left off with his London acquaintances, frequenting fashionable soirées with prominent Whig families at Holland House. Through his old friend James Harris, later 3rd Earl of Malmesbury, he also befriended Tories. Hortense's connections as well as the ever-expanding Bonaparte family, which had married into the British aristocracy, meant he was never short of invitations. At one party, he even bumped into Napoléon's vanquisher at Waterloo, the Duke of Wellington. Most British people he met liked him, mainly because he did not seem French. Taciturn and laconic, he possessed, according to the writer and politician Benjamin Disraeli, who later became prime minister, 'that calm which is rather unusual with foreigners, and which is always pleasing to an English aristocrat' – or at least that is how he described a character based on Louis-Napoléon in one of his novels.[29]

Louis-Napoléon was not short of French company because the usual suspects were with him in London: his loyal valet, Charles Thelin; Colonel Vaudrey; and his devoted consigliere, Persigny, who acted as his confidant, gatekeeper and conspirator-in-chief. When out in London, Louis-Napoléon made sure he was noticed. His carriage had the imperial coat of arms emblazoned on the side; when formally dressed for dinner, he fastened his black satin neckerchief with a diamond-studded eagle clutching a thunderbolt of rubies. At the theatre, he took a box, with Vaudrey and Persigny standing either side throughout the performance. Not that everyone was impressed. Another French exile thought it all preposterous, Louis-Napoléon surrounded, as he was, by men of dubious quality and with peculiar names, 'borrowed from novels of long ago'. She was scathing about his chances of one day becoming emperor: 'How deplorable it is', she wrote, 'to persist in playing a part for which one is not suited.'[30]

But Louis-Napoléon did not believe he was playing a part, and the money he inherited from Hortense allowed him to set up in a style befitting an imperial pretender. He took a year's lease at 17 Carlton House Terrace. Designed by Britain's most sought-after architect, John Nash, these newly built mansions were an ostentatious display of wealth and power. Towering over the Mall, Louis-Napoléon's residence matched his ambition and he adorned the interior with his considerable collection of imperial memorabilia – down to towels emblazoned with 'N' for Napoléon. Persigny vetted visitors, leading those granted an audience into a salon. While they waited, eyes fell upon celebrated works of art: a bust of Napoléon; a portrait of Joséphine; and another of Hortense. In the middle of the room was a large table. On it, conspicuously arranged to give the impression of a serious and learned man, were collections of newspapers, journals, maps and works on science, politics and finance.

Thirty years old, single and rich, Louis-Napoléon had plenty of time for less lofty pursuits, although he took these seriously too. As a friend later reminisced, 'he had his full share of the fashionable vices'. Chief among these were horse racing, gambling and women. Indeed, his interest in the theatre had little to do with the performances, which usually ended with him propositioning the female leads. In this he was not always successful – the celebrated ballerina Marie Taglioni turned him down – but 'if he was dissipated', one friend wrote, it was, at least, 'amongst gentlemen'.[31]

That said, there was often nothing very gentlemanly about the company he kept. London had yet to give way to Victorian prudishness, and St James's Street had one of the most notorious gambling dens in the city, Crockford's, which catered to the great and the good who were happy to lose staggering amounts of money. One of its most infamous clients, Alfred d'Orsay, was a firm friend of Louis-Napoléon's, as was his mother-in-law, and lover, Lady Blessington. She had been a confidante of Hortense's in Rome and knew Louis-Napoléon. In London, she took him under her wing, and he became part of a literary and political set that centred around Gore House in then very unfashionable Kensington. Here, the likes of Charles Dickens, Edward Bulwer-Lytton and Benjamin Disraeli could be found. Once, Louis-Napoléon managed to strand Disraeli and his wife on a mudbank in the Thames after taking a rowing boat out. 'You should not undertake things you cannot accomplish,' Disraeli's wife admonished him. 'You are always too adventurous.'[32] Impetuous and elegant as he was – 'gorgeously arrayed in the dandy evening costume of the period', as one guest at Gore House noted[33] – his conversation did not shine. 'He was quiet, silent and inoffensive,' noted another guest after an evening with him, 'but he does not impress one with the idea that he had inherited his uncle's talents.'[34]

Frequently at Louis-Napoléon's side in London was the dandy of dandies, d'Orsay, a man who thought six gloves the minimum one needed to get through the day. He was a London celebrity, an 1830s influencer – shops paid him for his custom; clubs gave him free credit to park his carriage outside. Extremely tall, with a shock of black hair and excessively tight trousers, he towered above Louis-Napoléon, though the imperial pretender matched him in sartorial elegance. When they drove dangerously fast around town, they made a striking pair. In a customised hooded cabriolet, with d'Orsay 'half standing on the footboard, half swinging in the air, clinging on to the straps . . . with clear-cut features and raven hair, the king of the dandies', the Bonaparte pretender, exile and would-be emperor added more colour to the spectacle.[35] As d'Orsay was not only Lady Blessington's live-in lover but also rumoured to sleep with men, he was considered impossibly debauched.

Louis-Napoléon solely focused on women, but his penchant for 'shady society', as one teenage girl who knew him later recalled, ensured that he was 'not altogether to the taste of young ladies' mothers . . . for they were rather afraid of him'. His appearance, she noted, 'could not be called handsome or imposing', but when he wanted to be, he was 'exceedingly amusing, and would frequently make my sister and I laugh very much . . . Though not perhaps exceptionally brilliant, [he] was amusing and agreeable enough, and my sister and I saw a good deal of him, enjoying his society – so much so, indeed, that we were often told to see less of him.'[36]

What struck British acquaintances was what had also astonished New Yorkers: Louis-Napoléon had absolute faith that he would rule France. Bemused interlocutors were stunned when at some point in the conversation Louis-Napoléon explained what he would do once he became emperor. No one took these utterances seriously, passing them off as the kind of eccentricity that one might expect of a foreigner and a Bonaparte. But Louis-Napoléon was serious, impervious to ridicule and fixed on his goal. To further this, he wrote *Des idées Napoléoniennes* in the reading room of the British Museum.

It was an astonishing work – not for its prose, or for its political philosophy, but for its esoteric interpretation of Napoléon and his Empire. What, asked Louis-Napoléon, was the emperor's ultimate goal? It was, he wrote in an answer that would have surprised keen students of Napoleonic France, 'liberty'. Aware that this might require repetition, he added, 'Yes, liberty, and the more one studies the history of Napoléon, the more one will be convinced of this truth.' It was the case, the nephew admitted, that 'liberty was not . . . placed at the head of every law or posted at every public square', but that was because Napoléon did not have time to get round to it.[37] If he had stayed in power, France would have enjoyed freedom and democracy.

And the emperor had plans for Europe too. Perhaps even more surprising than the notion that Napoléon was working ceaselessly in the name of liberty was the conclusion that he was a man of peace. Although he had unleashed chaos and death across the continent on a colossal scale, Louis-Napoléon maintained that he was 'not the aggressor'. If sometimes 'he seemed to get the start on his enemies, it was because taking the initiative in war is the guarantor of success'. What might on the surface, then, have looked bellicose – invading Russia, for example – was, in fact, part of a plan to 'establish a solid European peace'. This was the goal towards which Napoléon was working and which, the nephew added, without irony, he was 'so close to achieving'.[38]

Had he achieved it, he would have gone further: the creation of a European Union. National rivalries would have disappeared; instead, there would have been a European legal code, a European court, a single currency, conformity of weights and measurements and uniformity in legislation. It was Britain, not for the last time, that ruined this dream of a federal Europe.

Des idées Napoléoniennes was, then, an uncritical commentary on Napoléon's words as dictated in exile on Saint Helena – 'the review of a loving, zealous and undoubted believer in the Divinity he worships', as one literary magazine put it.[39] It was, however, not meant to be read as history, but as a political manifesto. A restored Empire, the work made clear, would be a democratic and liberal regime tempered with authority that guaranteed order. In this updated and more in-depth version of his earlier *Rêveries politiques*, popular sovereignty and universal male suffrage remained at the heart of the programme, but this time radical ideas were fused with a stronger dose of militarism and conservatism. The mix was designed to appeal across the political spectrum, positioning Bonapartism as a serious opposition to the July Monarchy and a popular alternative to republicanism.

The work was not critically acclaimed. 'In a country where so many political quacks have had their day,' wrote a reviewer in *The Times*, not missing an opportunity to ridicule France, Louis-Napoléon 'thought he might renew the imperial quackery, [and] why should he not?' But, concluded the writer, 'We know not whether the present work is an apology for himself as well as for his uncle; it seems to us, however, to be entirely insufficient to prove his uncle's case, and much more so therefore to prove his own.'[40]

A leading French newspaper lampooned the disjuncture between the reality of Napoléon's Empire and the version that existed in Louis-Napoléon's head. Soldiers, the reviewer asked, 'do you know why your blood was spilled in torrents on all the battlefields of Europe? It's because Napoléon wanted to seat public happiness on the throne of general and perpetual peace.' While waiting for Louis-Napoléon to bring back the heavy censorship of the Empire, the article concluded, he exploits the free press of the July Monarchy. 'It is his right . . . I would add that it would be desirable if all pretenders . . . made use of it as perfectly harmlessly as [Louis-Napoléon] has just done.'[41]

Regardless of the critical reception, *Des idées Napoléoniennes* caught people's attention. Written in Louis-Napoléon's accessible style and sold cheaply, it went through countless editions and was translated into numerous languages. Scorn from government-supporting elite Parisian newspapers only helped Louis-Napoléon's cause, marking him out as a man of the people, publicising his political views and reiterating the contempt in which he held the current regime.

To further that image, Louis-Napoléon reached out to the republican left – men who were responsible for even more conspiracies against the French king than he was. As long as they replaced the monarchy with a system based on universal male suffrage, Louis-Napoléon reasoned, then the Bonapartist cause would triumph at the ballot box, and he was hopeful of forging an alliance. A revolving cast from the fringes of society passed through Carlton Terrace, including one man who offered, in return for 250,000 francs, to kidnap the French king and put Louis-Napoléon on the throne. The imperial pretender also held a series of meetings with the proto-communist thinker Étienne Cabet. For a man whose utopia included a state-sanctioned cookery book issued to every family, the idea of a second Empire did not seem ridiculous, though Cabet baulked at associating himself with Bonapartism.

These connections to known radicals combined with his perennial love for intrigue meant that when a republican uprising broke out in Paris in May 1839, and was swiftly crushed, Louis-Napoléon was accused of involvement. 'If I were the soul of a conspiracy,' he wrote grandiosely to *The Times* in a letter disavowing any connection to the failed plot, 'I should also be its leader on the day of danger.'[42]

This was exactly the kind of romantic revolutionary nonsense Joseph hated, and even after three years had passed, he had still not forgiven

Louis-Napoléon for Strasbourg, refusing to see his nephew in London. This annoyed Louis-Napoléon. Somewhat overestimating the interest people took in the Bonaparte soap opera, he thought it of great import that there should appear to be no rupture between him and Joseph. To that end, he sought a reconciliation. Louis-Napoléon's go-between, Persigny, did little to improve matters. Like many, Joseph considered Persigny to be a jumped-up, irascible con artist with the mad glint of the devoted in his eye who constantly urged Louis-Napoléon on to ever greater folly: a view easily arrived at, given it was largely true. Joseph banned Persigny from his sight, but by December 1839 anger towards his nephew had subsided sufficiently for him to agree to discussions.

After a mistrustful start, Joseph extracted the price of reconciliation: 'I promise you, Uncle,' insisted Louis-Napoléon, 'everything that people say about me is exaggerated. As for me, I have decided never to get involved in political plots again.'[43] This was enough for Joseph, who organised a full-dress banquet to celebrate. With much merriment and even more opulence, surviving Napoleonic grandees – the emperor's oldest and youngest brothers, Joseph and Jérôme, were present alongside nephews, former ministers and generals – toasted the compromise between old and new generations.

For the next few months, Louis-Napoléon continued his fashionable dandy existence, attending the theatre, riding in Hyde Park and fighting a duel. The challenger belied harmony between Bonapartes for he was an illegitimate son of the Emperor Napoléon who was insulted that Louis-Napoléon refused to see him. So it was that Louis-Napoléon found himself on Wimbledon Common at 7 a.m. on 3 March 1840, with d'Orsay and Parquin acting as his seconds. As the participants were arguing over their choice of weapon, the police arrived and arrested everyone. After appearing before a magistrate at Bow Street, both parties were released on bail.

On 26 July 1840, Louis-Napoléon boarded a steamer anchored on the Thames. He had come to say goodbye to Joseph, whose doctors recommended he take the waters in Germany for his health. His secretary and doctor supported the frail, seventy-two-year-old Joseph while he stood on the quarterdeck. As the bell sounded for visitors to leave before the steamer departed, Joseph took Louis-Napoléon's hand.

'No conspiracies, you hear,' he said.

'Don't worry, Uncle,' replied Louis-Napoléon, 'you can count on me.'

'Really?'

With one hand on his heart, Louis-Napoléon replied: 'My word of honour.'[44]

This was not a promise he intended to keep.

6

THE EAGLE HAS LANDED

The Emperor Napoléon was coming home. In 1840, the French government secured permission from the British to bring his corpse from Saint Helena to France. After Louis-Napoléon heard the news, excited discussions took place at his London mansion over what to do – the conclusion, what better welcome for the dead emperor than for his Empire to be restored before he arrived? There was talk of hijacking the French frigate carrying the remains; however, in the end Louis-Napoléon decided to channel, again, what his uncle had done in 1815: a second Flight of the Eagle, or a third if you counted the 1836 one in Strasbourg that failed to take off.

To prepare public opinion, Persigny wrote an absurd work of propaganda where his inventiveness reached its most creative heights when discussing the nephew's relationship with Napoléon. The story of how the seven-year-old Louis-Napoléon, sobbing, ran into his uncle's room with the prescient warning not to fight the Battle of Waterloo was touching, but fabricated – as was Napoléon's response, now also moved to tears and hugging his nephew, that one day this little boy might be the saviour of his family. To further the cause of Bonapartism, however, Persigny was happy to say anything. He even wrote that emperor and nephew resembled each other.

One man who knew that was untrue was General Charles Tristan, marquis de Montholon. He had been a staff officer during the Napoleonic wars and had gone into exile with Napoléon on Saint Helena, something the former emperor likely appreciated more for the company of his attractive wife than for the general's conversation. In spite of his mediocrity, Montholon was there to the last. In his own words, he received the dying breath of the emperor. Napoléon's will made him rich, but after his return to France, Montholon lost this fortune. Fleeing creditors, he found himself destitute in London, where Louis-Napoléon offered him a way out of bankruptcy: restore the Empire. Montholon accepted, as did a few other officers disgruntled with their treatment under the July Monarchy.

Montholon's closeness to the dead emperor added a veneer of Napoleonic sheen to the ranks of Louis-Napoléon's outcasts. Chief among these were Persigny and Parquin, as well as several more who had taken part in the failed 1836 uprising. There were also new additions to the cult, including Henri Conneau, Hortense's doctor. He was not the only disciple of Hortense's helping with the plot. In Paris, women from her inner circle were doing all they could to further the Bonapartist cause, while the irrepressible Eleonore Gordon was said to be preaching to the people and to revolutionary republicans. Louis-Napoléon used an English mistress as a courier to communicate with supporters across the Channel.

The plan was to land at Boulogne with some sixty men, march on the barracks and rally the regiment stationed there, the 42nd, another steeped in Napoleonic history. Again, Louis-Napoléon had a man on the inside, Lieutenant Jean-Baptiste-Charles Aladenize, who would help turn the soldiers. He needed men, though, to make the force that landed at the town appear intimidating. He managed to convince some French and Polish mercenaries to join, but the rest of his 'army' was less impressive, recruited, as it was, from an agency that hired out domestic servants.

By early August, everything was ready. Joseph Orsi, Italian banker and Louis-Napoléon's friend from his days in Italy, helped raise finances. He procured £20,000 from a corrupt treasury official who speculated on the success of the *coup d'état*. Orsi also hired a steamer, the *Edinburgh Castle*, ostensibly for a pleasure cruise to Germany. Early in the morning of 4 August, a beautiful, clear day, the steamer was loaded by London Bridge. Crates stamped 'Hamburg' were brought on board with everything required for insurrection, including weapons, nine horses, a carriage and, crucially, hundreds of bottles of wine, porter, punch, ginger beer and soda water.

At 6 a.m., the steamer made its way downriver. To allay suspicions, men were picked up in stages, first at Greenwich, then Blackwall, before they reached Gravesend at 2 p.m., where Louis-Napoléon would rendezvous with the ship. By 3.30 p.m., however, there was no sign of the imperial pretender. Fifteen minutes later, the captain came to tell Orsi that a customs boat had rowed out alongside them.

'What are you doing here in the middle of the river?' the customs officer asked.

'I am waiting for the party who should have arrived by this time,' replied a nervous Orsi, terrified that the ship would be inspected and its incriminating cargo discovered. After hearing that the steamer was chartered for a pleasure cruise, the officer said, 'I suppose you have ladies on board?'

'None as yet,' replied Orsi, 'but I fancy there will be a few engaged to join the party at Ramsgate.' Clearly Ramsgate was the right answer because the officer said, 'Ha! Ha! That's the place! I wish you a good passage; but be off sharp.' Yet with no sign of Louis-Napoléon, the steamer could not leave. Parquin, already aboard, was getting impatient. 'I want to go on shore to buy a few good cigars. Those we have on board are detestable, I cannot smoke them.'

Orsi was stunned. He had orders that no one should leave the steamer lest they arouse suspicion. It would, however, take more than an Italian banker to stop a veteran of countless Napoleonic battles. Eventually, Orsi acquiesced, on the condition that he went too. They rowed to the pier, and as they were walking to the cigar shop, Parquin spotted a young boy sitting on a log and feeding a chained eagle. The lure of having an imperial bird on board for the restoration of the Empire was too much for the Napoleonic warrior. Parquin went up to the boy and said, '*Est-il à vendre?*' A pointless question, given that the boy did not speak French. Parquin demanded Orsi ask the boy in English; Orsi refused. Parquin, his Bonapartist heart set on the eagle, then resorted to the well-worn strategy of the linguistically challenged: he asked again, louder this time, in French. The confused boy shrugged his shoulders. Summoning all his talent for languages, Parquin tried, in a thick French accent, 'How mooch?'[1] It turned out that the price of an eagle was only a pound, which also procured the services of the boy to chain it to the mainmast of the ship.

While they had managed to get good cigars and a bird, there was still no sign of Louis-Napoléon by 6 p.m. Worried that suspicious-looking Frenchmen soliciting eagles on the banks of the Thames might draw unwanted attention, Orsi once again went ashore and took a fast carriage to the next stop, Ramsgate, in the hope of finding Louis-Napoléon there. When he arrived at the hotel where Montholon and other conspirators were waiting, there was no sign of Louis-Napoléon. Finally, in the early hours of 5 August, Orsi heard the steamer coming downriver. Then a messenger appeared announcing that Louis-Napoléon had boarded at Gravesend. He had been tailed by French agents and had been criss-crossing London to give them the slip. Orsi and Montholon joined him on board.

At 5 a.m., the ship set off, its captain oblivious as to the real purpose of the voyage. It came as something of a surprise, therefore, when Orsi told Captain James Crow of the Commercial Steam Packet Company that they were not, as he thought, heading to Hamburg on a pleasure cruise, but rather to a 'political demonstration, which, if successful, will probably cause great changes to take place in France'.[2] Before the captain had the chance to digest this news, Louis-Napoléon bounded in and explained that the ship had been commandeered. Now uniforms and weapons were issued, proclamations were read out and, no doubt helped by the enormous quantities of alcohol on board, there was great enthusiasm as Louis-Napoléon addressed the men, explaining that they were about to make history.

———

Only the occasional smuggler broke the monotony of the graveyard shift for customs officers in the impoverished fishing village of Wimereux, a few miles north of Boulogne. That changed on the morning of 6 August, when men wearing French army uniform approached. They told the customs officials that they were members of the 40th regiment and that their steamer had broken down en route to Cherbourg from Dunkirk. Then an officer asked to be guided to Boulogne. The customs officer refused, stating that he was on duty and could not leave his post. Parquin, putting his hand on his sword, made clear that this excuse did not hold water.

The customs officer reluctantly led the band of men over the cliffs and through cornfields towards Boulogne. On the way, they passed the Column of the Grande Armée, which had been intended to celebrate Napoléon's unrealised invasion of Britain. This was too much for the Bonapartists, who cried, '*Vive la colonne! Vive Napoléon!*' When they arrived on the edge of town, one of the men turned to the customs officer and said, 'Do you know who you are escorting? It's Prince Louis-Napoléon.'

The response was not one of unbridled Bonapartist enthusiasm. Customs work may not have been glamorous but it was a steady job and the man did not want to lose it, no matter how illustrious the rebel he had unwittingly aided. 'One doesn't dismiss those who are under duress, don't worry,' replied a conspirator. 'The family of the prince is rich; they will not abandon you.'[3] Despite the offer of a pension for life, all the man asked for was to be allowed to return to his post. Louis-Napoléon granted his wish on the condition he tell no one about their arrival.

Lieutenant Aladenize, their inside man, met them on the outskirts of Boulogne. It was his job to get them past the town's sentries and win over the troops. As they approached a guard post, Aladenize shouted, 'To arms!', and then, '*Voilà, le prince!*' But again, the effect was less than hoped. Aladenize ordered the men to join them; however, as he was only a junior officer, the sergeant insisted that he would not quit his post unless he received a direct order from his commander. 'Tomorrow', Parquin snarled, pointing his finger at the sergeant, 'you will be punished.'[4] Then Louis-Napoléon marched his men towards the barracks.

———

At around 5.30 a.m. on 6 August, Second Lieutenant Ernest-Louis-Marie de Maussion was on his way to conduct a survey of the forests near Boulogne. As he walked through the town, he was surprised to come across a group of armed men in military uniform. An officer approached him and asked, 'Have you seen the prince?' Taken aback, and somewhat confused as to which prince it might be, Maussion replied that he had not. Then the officer said, 'Come, I am going to introduce you to him.'

'I hope that you will join us,' said Louis-Napoléon. 'I have come here to restore to humiliated France the rank that it deserves.' A slightly rambling speech followed, but instead of joining the glorious Bonapartist future, Maussion hurried off to warn his commanding officer, Captain Pierre Col-Puygellier. Maussion found him at his house getting dressed and informed him he had been introduced to none other than Louis-Napoléon in the streets. Now Col-Puygellier knew that Boulogne was the centre of insurrection. He rushed to the barracks. Two men stopped him outside. No one can pass, they told him. Col-Puygellier walked round them, saying they had no authority. Approaching the barracks, he found it guarded. A man wearing an officer's uniform said, 'Captain, join us. Prince Louis is here, your fortune is made.' Col-Puygellier drew his sword and, waving it threateningly, said, 'You will break it, or I will use it.' Dodging left and right, Col-Puygellier managed to get to the door of the barracks.[5]

Inside, Lieutenant Aladenize, sword in hand, told the sentry, 'Soldier, shout "to arms". Here comes the prince.' The man did as he was told, and the confused men of the garrison gathered in their quarters. Then Louis-Napoléon addressed them. He was a nervous public speaker who spoke French with the hint of a foreign accent; some could not hear what he said. The gist, though, was clear: first we take Boulogne, then we take Paris. More immediately, he promised promotion, medals and money to those who joined. Aladenize pointed out soldiers he deemed worthy of rapid advancement. Then there was a commotion on the other side of the room; Maussion had managed to force his way into the barracks. Aladenize walked up to him, embraced him and told him to shout, '*Vive l'empereur!*'

'No, never! Long live the king always!'

Persigny, furious, thrust a bayonet at the lieutenant, who parried it with his sabre. At this moment, Louis-Napoléon saw Col-Puygellier at the door and said, 'Join us and you will have whatever you want.' Cutting him off, Col-Puygellier replied, 'I don't know you. I see nothing more than a usurper.' Given the tension in the barracks, Col-Puygellier then took the bold step of arguing Napoleonic doctrine, claiming that as the first Napoléon had destroyed royalty it was foolish for the nephew to try to restore it. Whether shocked because he thought all officers were devoted to his cause, or confused at this attempt to discuss the contradictory nature of Bonapartism, Louis-Napoléon was stunned into silence. Col-Puygellier tried to move away from the door and join his men. The conspirators grabbed him. 'Kill me,' shouted Col-Puygellier, 'but I will do my duty!' He managed to take a few steps towards his men, whereupon a tug of war over him ensued between his soldiers and the conspirators. The soldiers won.[6]

————

This was not the stuff of Napoleonic legend. There had been none of this scuffling when Napoléon had presented himself before the army as he marched on Paris in 1815. Demoralised, Louis-Napoléon and his troops retreated a few steps to confer and regroup. Col-Puygellier took the opportunity to stiffen the resolve of his troops, explaining that the intruders were traitors and that they must remain loyal to the king. While he was doing this, Louis-Napoléon, pistol in hand, returned to make another attempt to win over the captain, who told him to leave the barracks, or suffer the consequences.

Then a shot was fired. The pistol Louis-Napoléon had been waving had gone off. The bullet ricocheted against a wall and into the face of a soldier. If there had been any sympathy for Louis-Napoléon among the troops, now it evaporated. Seeing that the situation was hopeless, the conspirators rushed into the streets. It was hastily decided to march on the old town. Here, they could storm the castle, seize weapons and arm the population for a popular uprising. The gates to the old town, however, were locked. After a brief attempt to break down the door, Louis-Napoléon realised it was pointless. The town was on the alert, the National Guard – local militia – was pouring into the streets and the army regiment was in pursuit.

At this point, a Napoleonic homing instinct kicked in and the men made their way to the column built in memory of Napoléon's Grande Armée. By the time they reached it, some 150 members of the National Guard were approaching. A hurried argument ensued. Louis-Napoléon was determined to make a last stand beneath the monument to his uncle; his supporters urged him to make a run for it. In the small paved area below the column, Louis-Napoléon clung on to the iron railings that surrounded it, screaming that he would die where he stood. His men had other ideas. They manhandled him out of one side as the National Guard entered from the other. The flagbearer clumsily tied the imperial colours to the railings with a blue scarf and a red handkerchief, then did his best to hold up the pursuers while the rest of the conspirators made a dash for the beach to try to get back to the *Edinburgh Castle* anchored in port.

Finding a small rowing boat in the harbour, Louis-Napoléon, Persigny and a few others dragged it into the surf. Just as they got it into water deep enough for it to float, the National Guard arrived. Seeing the rebels getting away, they took aim and fired. Two men were hit and fell overboard. The boat capsized, throwing Louis-Napoléon into the water. This probably saved his life – more bullets smashed into the hull. But Louis-Napoléon surfaced. A strong swimmer, he headed for the steamer.

Before Louis-Napoléon could get to it, men in a boat came alongside and fished him out of the sea. It was the port authorities. He was rowed ashore. Then, in front of the National Guard, the men of the 42nd regiment and the townspeople of Boulogne who had been enjoying the show, the nephew of the emperor, soaking wet, shivering, humiliated, was placed under arrest. Someone took pity and gave him an overcoat, but this was one of only two things Napoleonic about an adventure that had turned out to be beyond farcical.

The second was discovered on board the *Edinburgh Castle* by the authorities. In among the horses, carriages, splendid uniforms for a celebratory ball planned that evening, cases of excellent wines, a lady's dressing case, Louis-Napoléon's sketches of Arenenberg and some poetry he had written was found one live eagle. The bird had remained on board, sensibly deciding not to associate itself with the imperial pantomime unfolding onshore.

———

At a stroke, Louis-Napoléon had undone all the careful work of rebuilding his reputation since his previous fiasco at Strasbourg in 1836. 'A madman', ran one government proclamation, 'attempted to incite insurrection . . . by invoking a great man whose name he prostitutes.'[7] The failure was so great – and the attempt so absurdly pathetic – that the king and his entourage found it amusing. 'The poor fool . . . came to Boulogne to be arrested,' wrote one of the king's ministers. 'I have just been shown his proclamations, appointments, decrees, etc. It is perfectly stupid.'[8]

The French press had enormous fun writing about the nephew's lamentable attempt to recreate his uncle's glory. 'We do not believe', ran one editorial, 'that history records an enterprise more crazily conceived, ridiculously conducted, miserably terminated.' Bonapartism was now dead, continued the writer, employing journalistic licence to make the pastiche all the more riotously enjoyable: 'Where was Monsieur Louis Bonaparte arrested? At the foot of this column raised to the Grande Armée and its leader! Bonapartism came to expire there.'[9] As several thousand pounds in Bank of England notes were found on the steamer, the rumour soon started that Louis-Napoléon was in the pay of the British government. 'He thinks he is heroic,' opined a French daily, 'but is only sadly ridiculous; he calls himself a patriot, but he serves – very poorly, it is true – the cause of the most mortal enemies of the country.'[10] *The Times*'s correspondent in Boulogne was more prosaic: 'Had Bonaparte been shot, it would have been the proper end of so mischievous a blockhead.'[11]

Although one or two managed to escape, everyone else was imprisoned, including the unfortunate Captain James Crow. He was released after satisfying the authorities that he had acted under duress. When questioned, he told his interrogator that on the voyage over the conspirators had consumed prodigious amounts of alcohol: 'I never saw people drink more than they did.'[12] The statement, a local report noted, no doubt with knowledge of drinking habits across the Channel, was all the more remarkable when it was taken into account that it was an Englishman who used this language.

After a couple of days locked up in the castle of Boulogne, Louis-Napoléon was taken to another prison. As he was put into a carriage, Parquin cried out from a window above, 'The spirit of Napoléon will protect you.'[13] When he got to his new cell, Louis-Napoléon consoled himself with scrawling on the wall with a piece of charcoal, 'The Napoleonic cause is the cause of the interests of the people, it is the European cause. Sooner or later it will triumph.'[14]

That seemed far from the case on 12 August, shortly after midnight, when the disgraced pretender arrived in Paris. Here, he met, for the second time after a failed *coup d'état*, the prefect of police, who noted that his prisoner was dejected and depressed. Locked up in the Conciergerie, the infamous prison on the banks of the Seine that counted Marie Antoinette among its former guests, Louis-Napoléon's mood did not improve as he awaited his fate.

He knew, at least, that death was unlikely. With his uncle's corpse due to arrive shortly in France, where it would be interred at the Invalides in Paris to great fanfare, executing a nephew would be too embarrassing. That was as far as the government's leniency would go. After entering France illegally in 1831 and treason in 1836, this was the third capital offence the imperial pretender had committed. This time, Louis-Napoléon would be tried, and not before a jury, but before the Chambre des pairs, the French House of Lords.

Louis-Napoléon drew some comfort when he learned that his father had written a public letter protesting against the supposed ill treatment of his son. Always desperate to gain his father's affection, although never doing anything to get it, Louis-Napoléon was moved and penned a letter:

> My dear father, I have not written to you yet because I was afraid of upsetting you. But now that I have learned of the interest you have shown in me, I come to thank you and ask for your blessing . . . In my misfortune my sweetest consolation is to hope that your thoughts turn sometimes towards me . . . Proud of the mission which I imposed upon myself, I will always show myself worthy of the name I bear and of your affection.[15]

His father's thoughts did turn towards him, but not in the way Louis-Napoléon hoped. 'After what he has just done,' the comte de Saint-Leu wrote to Joseph, 'I regard myself as having no obligation towards him and I repeat to myself often: I no longer have a son.'[16]

In fact, Louis-Napoléon was treated perfectly well. He was allowed visitors, pen and paper and books. To pass the time, he translated Schiller's *Die Ideale* into French. He also put his affairs in order. Having staked his fortune on success, he was forced to auction his London possessions, his beloved Napoleonic memorabilia, furniture, even his linen and tableware. This gave him cash to pay for the best legal defence. With no jury, acquittal was unlikely, but Louis-Napoléon wanted to turn the trial into a public sensation. To this end, he hired, at great cost, one of France's most famous lawyers, Pierre-Antoine Berryer. He had made his name defending former Napoleonic generals after Waterloo, including Marshal Ney, condemned to death before the Chambre des pairs in 1815. The optics, then, perfectly fitted Louis-Napoléon's obsession with all things imperial; however, Berryer was also a legitimist who believed that Louis-Philippe had usurped the throne from the rightful Bourbon kings. He was, therefore, no friend of the government and could be relied upon for an incendiary evisceration of what he saw as an illegitimate regime.

The trial began on Monday 28 September. At 12.30, wearing black trousers, boots, dress coat with a white waistcoat underneath and the star of the *légion d'honneur*, Louis-Napoléon, escorted by two gendarmes, calmly made his way to the place allotted for prisoners. In front of him, sitting in a hemicycle, were the peers of France, many of whom owed their titles to his uncle. After a roll call of peers, nearly half of whom absented themselves from the trial because they thought condemning a Bonaparte would embarrass them, the prisoners were asked to give their age, name and profession. Louis-Napoléon stated that he was born in Paris and was an exiled French prince. After the prosecution made its case, he read a statement to the court:

> For the first time in my life, I am finally permitted to raise my voice in France, and speak freely to the French . . . As I find myself within these walls of the senate, full of memories from my childhood, among you whom I know, gentlemen, I cannot believe that I have here the hope of justifying myself, nor that you can be my judges.

But justify himself he did. He had acted not out of self-interest, but for France, to save the country from the abyss into which he claimed it had sunk. 'One final word, gentlemen,' he concluded. 'I stand before you representing a principle, a cause, a defeat. The principle is the sovereignty of the people; the cause is the Empire; the defeat, Waterloo. The principle, you have recognised it; the cause, you have served it; the defeat, you want to avenge it.' This was rousing stuff. Louis-Napoléon divided the world into those who had fought for Napoléon and France at Waterloo – the vanquished – and those who had served a foreign cause and accepted the defeat – the vanquishers. 'If you are the men of the vanquishers, I don't expect justice from you, and I don't want your generosity.'[17]

The rest of his defence, however, was less stirring. He was a talented writer, and his written statement was powerful, but he was a nervous speaker. When questioned further, his answers were often monosyllabic, sometimes inaudible – elderly, hard-of-hearing peers had to ask court officers to repeat them – or he simply referred to previous responses under interrogation.

The fact that the defence of his co-conspirators was laughable hardly helped the trial reach the grandeur which Louis-Napoléon hoped for. To try to lessen their sentences, Louis-Napoléon claimed he was the sole arbiter of the plot. While a noble sentiment, this meant maintaining the fiction that men with known Bonapartist sympathies and connections had boarded a steamer for an unlikely pleasure cruise, oblivious to the true purpose of the voyage, and yet, strangely for a holiday, they had packed their uniforms and weapons.

General Montholon's defence was particularly risible. When asked why his uniform was on board, the general said he had no idea that it was. Louis-Napoléon had told him that they were attending a full-dress ball in London. He had, therefore, left his clothes at Louis-Napoléon's house so he could get changed there before the party, and the pretender had used this ruse to secretly pack them onto the ship. When he got on the steamer, Montholon claimed, he thought they were going to Belgium. In the end, the best Montholon's defence could do was invoke Napoléon. The general had received the last breath of the emperor. That was explanation enough for his conduct.

On the other hand, Louis-Napoléon's most devoted acolytes refused to plead ignorance. Persigny said he knew the plan. 'I belong to the prince, I am his soldier; I obeyed him in everything that he ordered me to do.'[18] Later, he launched into a soliloquy defending Bonapartism. The Napoleonic idea, Persigny explained, was 'the most sublime expression of the French Revolution' and would replace an aristocracy of eight hundred years with a society open to all. This would be, Persigny insisted, 'the greatest social organisation that man has ever known'.[19] His rhetoric captured what was radical and exciting about Bonapartism, but his demagogic rant was cut off just as he was warming up. When Persigny asked the court to imagine how great France would be if Napoléon had never been defeated, the judge could bear it no longer. He questioned the relevance of historical counterfactuals about Waterloo to Persigny's defence, before insisting the accused stop talking.

Berryer was more effective in embarrassing the government. Like Louis-Napoléon, he believed that the July Monarchy was an unlawful regime. Why, he asked, was overthrowing the government a crime in 1840, when ten years earlier, in the July Revolution of 1830, it had been justified? Besides, the Napoleonic claim to rule in the name of the people based on universal male suffrage was much more convincing than Louis-Philippe's regime, which abhorred democracy. Berryer then said that in actively promoting the memory of Napoléon, not least in bringing back his body, the government had encouraged Bonapartists. As Louis-Napoléon intended, the speech was splashed across French newspapers and read the next morning over breakfast.

It had no impact on the judges, however. On the afternoon of Tuesday 6 October, Louis-Napoléon was condemned to life imprisonment. The guilty men were not present at the sentencing. Court officers entered Louis-Napoléon's cell and informed him that he would spend the rest of his life in prison. 'At least, sir,' he reportedly replied, 'I shall die in France.'[20]

7

THE PRISONER

Hundreds of thousands of people lined the streets of Paris on the morning of 15 December 1840. Many were Parisians; many more had journeyed from across France. The roads into the capital were blocked, with pedestrians weaving their way through vehicles of every description; others came by train. Once there, they jostled for the best positions in the streets, climbed trees or stood on balconies, even rooftops. The luckiest had tickets to stands holding some thirty thousand people that flanked the way to the Invalides, a palatial complex of buildings originally designed as a military hospital. It was the power of Napoléon Bonaparte that drew the crowd. They had come to watch his funeral procession. Louis-Napoléon had been right about one thing: his uncle was enormously popular.

At 6 a.m., Napoléon's coffin was unloaded from the steamer that had brought it up the River Seine. Twenty-four sailors carried the coffin to a funeral carriage of immense proportions which mirrored the magisterial bombast of Napoléon's Empire. Resting on four huge gilt wheels, it was twenty-five feet long and fifty feet high. At the front was a semicircular platform where, amid cannons, statues held up the crown of the medieval Emperor Charlemagne. Hung from each side, a velvet drape in imperial purple emblazoned with the Napoleonic 'N' covered the wagon. In the centre, fourteen caryatids supported with their heads and their hands a vast shield upon which rested the sarcophagus, which had a cushion with the imperial crown nestled on top. It took sixteen black horses, liveried in medieval costume replete with gold cloth, and with white plumes in their manes, to drag this behemoth through Paris.

Along the route to the final destination, the funeral carriage was met with rapturous cheers. Cries of '*Vive l'empereur!*' resounded throughout the capital and artillery punctuated the cacophony. Flanking the carriage and in its wake was an enormous escort of soldiers, cavalrymen, officers, marshals of France, dignitaries, university students and, most striking of all, veterans of Napoléon's armies. The debris of this once mighty force in antiquated military attire was an incredible sight; there were former members of the Imperial Guard, Polish lancers, Egyptian Mamelukes. The cortège paused as it went through the Arc de Triomphe, then onto the Champs-Élysées, the road lined with flags, columns and large vases with flammable material, which was ignited shortly before the procession so that plumes of smoke drifted languidly into the sky.

Inside the domed church of the Invalides, thousands of wax candles and lanterns burned, so many and so tightly packed together that the high walls looked like they were on fire. At the bottom of the cavernous building was the catafalque where the coffin was to rest. The lower walls of the church were decorated in black drapes with imperial emblems. Spectators in mourning dress looked on, suitably awed, as the coffin was carried in and laid in its resting place while an immense orchestra with four hundred singers performed Mozart's 'Requiem'. The sublime music announced the beginning of the service. After nineteen years, Napoléon Bonaparte's wish to be buried by the Seine had come to pass.

A hundred miles away, in a damp medieval fortress, Louis-Napoléon sat at a desk to pen a letter to his dead uncle. 'Sire, you return to your capital and crowds of people salute you, but I, from the depths of my dungeon, can only see a ray of the sun which lights your funeral.' The nephew went on to lament the current state of France, that no member of his family could welcome his uncle's remains and that no one today understood his ideas. Concluding, he wrote, 'From your sumptuous cortège, you cast your eyes for a moment on my dark rooms and, remembering the caresses you lavished on me as a child, you said to me: "You suffer for me, friend, I am proud of you!"'[1]

As with much of what Louis-Napoléon wrote, this was intended for a wider audience. But it also reflected his innermost thoughts. It is unlikely that Napoléon would have looked on his nephew being fished out of the sea after the Boulogne farce with anything other than contempt. Yet despite the fact that he would spend the rest of his life in jail, Louis-Napoléon's confidence burned as brightly as ever, convinced, as he was, that he was carrying out his uncle's holy mission on earth and would one day triumph.

———

On 7 October, Louis-Napoléon had been transferred from the Conciergerie to the Fortress of Ham on the River Somme, north-east of Paris. In the winter, the wet, cold climate – prone to frequent fog – gave this medieval stronghold a lugubrious air, but Louis-Napoléon was not in a dungeon. He occupied two rooms on the first floor and he soon comfortably furnished his living quarters with a table, some wooden chairs and a lamp. On one side shelves, which Louis-Napoléon put up himself, ran up to the ceiling and were crammed full of books. Engravings and small family portraits decorated the walls.

To share his captivity, Louis-Napoléon had been allowed to choose from two of those convicted alongside him, though not Persigny, as the authorities felt that locking up these arch-conspirators together would be unwise. Louis-Napoléon, then, went with his friend Dr Henri Conneau and General Charles Tristan, marquis de Montholon. The latter was not chosen for his company, but rather for the optics of having the man who had shared Napoléon's exile on Saint Helena in captivity with the nephew.

Despite these companions, Louis-Napoléon's life was dull. He rose early and worked on literary pursuits until breakfast was served at 10 a.m. After this, he donned a red kepi and took what exercise he could. He was permitted to walk a section of the walls, forty yards long by twenty wide. There was a garrison of four hundred men, but he was always accompanied by a guard. Then he dedicated himself to caring for a small garden he had created on the ramparts.

Returning to his rooms, he spent the rest of the afternoon reading or at correspondence. Dinner, which he took with Montholon and Conneau, was at 5 p.m., and after that he passed the time with these two fellow inmates. In the evenings, they played cards. The convivial commandant of the prison joined them after his rounds, before he locked up their wing of the fortress for the night. Louis-Napoléon's ever-faithful *valet de chambre*, Charles Thelin, who had shared his exile to the United States, chose to join him. Soon, Thelin was given permission to come and go freely from the fortress, which meant that Louis-Napoléon could smuggle out uncensored letters. Completing his society was a dog, named Ham after the fortress.

Louis-Napoléon, as far as anyone can be, was suited to life in prison. Years as a teenager with his austere tutor had accustomed him to studying independently for long hours. Moreover, in semi-seclusion at Arenenberg, he had toiled alone in his small study researching and writing his various works of history, politics and Bonapartist propaganda. As he put it, 'Happiness lies much more in the imagination than in the real world, and as I carry my imaginary world with me, composed of memories and hopes, I feel as strong in solitude as in the crowd.'[2] A keen autodidact, Louis-Napoléon resolved to use his time productively.

Fascinated with technology, he set up a small laboratory and conducted electromagnetic experiments, but it was writing that occupied him most. Initially, he attempted a history of Charlemagne, who loomed large in the Bonapartist worldview. 'History seems to me,' wrote Louis-Napoléon, 'after religion, all that is most sacred in the world. Because the one and the other are the principal guides of our existence. Religion shows us the future; history shows us the past.'[3] But after a historian he corresponded with insisted that one had to start earlier, with the Roman Emperor Augustus, and to work through eight hundred years before starting on Charlemagne, Louis-Napoléon abandoned the idea.

Instead, he decided to write a history of artillery. This was serious scholarship. For years, Louis-Napoléon buried himself in French, German and Italian works on firearms, medieval chronicles and manuscripts. Of course, being in prison somewhat limited the research he could undertake, but Louis-Napoléon rekindled an old friendship with someone who became his researcher, political adviser, therapist, personal assistant and platonic lover.

Hortense Cornu was the daughter of a lady-in-waiting of Louis-Napoléon's mother, after whom she was named. She grew up to be intelligent and sophisticated, a talented writer and translator; politically, she was a republican. And alongside her husband, an artist, she was a regular Parisian socialite on the fashionable moderate-left circuit. A year younger than Louis-Napoléon, she had been his childhood playmate. As adults they had not seen each other for years, but once Hortense heard that

Louis-Napoléon was in prison in Paris before his trial in 1840 she came to visit him. After that, they were devoted friends.

Louis-Napoléon wrote to her frequently, almost obsessively, as though she replaced the space in his life – and in his correspondence – left by his mother. Like a jealous lover, if she did not write, he was worried. 'Are you sick? Are you angry with me?' he began one typical letter after not hearing from her. 'I need your letters.'[4] She was special to him, he explained, because it was rare to find someone who shared so intimately all one's thoughts and feelings. In a particularly confused attempt to explain these feelings, Louis-Napoléon began one letter by saying that he wished Hortense was a man.

> You understand things so well, and, except for some details, I think like you. However, I find that you are very good as you are, and it would be a shame to change; our relations would lose their charm, because the sentiment that I have for you is worth more than love, it is more durable, it is worth more than friendship, it is more tender.[5]

Despite his belief in his destiny, Louis-Napoléon was prone to melancholy. 'The uniformity of days turns you into a machine,' he complained in a letter to Hortense, 'and the machine is a being little intellectual and little sensible; it stops or it works, that's all.'[6] Some days he was so depressed he could not even bring himself to discuss the history of artillery. Hortense eased his life in prison, sending him jams, cakes and, crucially for a chain-smoker, tobacco, but there was another woman who gave even more. While Louis-Napoléon often wrote to Hortense with the passion of a lover, he was not sleeping with her. He was sleeping with someone else.

———

On paper, recruiting General Charles Tristan, marquis de Montholon, to take part in the attempted *coup d'état* at Boulogne added Napoleonic lustre. In fact, Montholon merely compounded the parody. Upon landing at Boulogne and seeing that there were no cheering crowds to greet the conspirators, he put his head in his hands and wailed, 'My God, how mistaken and betrayed we are!'[7] Fifty-seven years old and with a weak chest, he could not keep up with Louis-Napoléon's supporters. Lost, out of breath and wheezing, he was arrested, in his general's uniform, on the streets of Boulogne.

Montholon was not even a good raconteur in prison. There was nothing Louis-Napoléon liked to hear more than stories about Napoléon, whose exile Montholon had shared. The nephew complained, however, that getting Napoleonic tales out of Montholon was like getting blood from a stone. And even then, Louis-Napoléon grumbled, what he got was vague generalisations and clichés that were hard to verify, which, given his liberal relationship with the truth, especially when it came to imperial legends, was quite the criticism.

Once in prison, though, Montholon proved his worth in another respect. Given his ill health, his wife, a countess, was permitted to live with him. After Montholon's son-in-law visited his father, the relative brought interesting information to the attention of the authorities. Montholon was not living with his wife, nor, indeed, a countess. Rather, she was an Irish nurse whom Montholon had met in London and who became his mistress. After the deception was uncovered, she was forced to leave.

The woman she had employed as a servant continued working for Montholon. This was Éléonore Vergeot – striking in appearance, twenty years old and the daughter of a local weaver. In May 1841, she was given permission to take care of Louis-Napoléon's laundry. Within a year, she was taking care of his child. To avoid scandal, Éléonore went to Paris to have the baby, Eugène, born in February 1843. The father paid for him to be brought up in the capital under the care of Hortense Cornu. As far as one can be from prison, Louis-Napoléon was an attentive father. 'It is a chagrin for me not to see him,' he wrote to Hortense, referring to his son.[8] In 1844, Éléonore was pregnant once more. Again, she went to Paris to have the baby. A month before, Louis-Napoléon joked in a letter to Hortense that 'if I had to do it again I would take a vow of celibacy, but it is too late now; I must carry my cross'.[9] But he made sure that his two children were well looked after, and though Éléonore stayed in Ham, he arranged for her to visit them regularly.

A family, however, was merely a distraction; what drove Louis-Napoléon in prison was his belief that he was the providential heir of Napoléon. This passion lit up his otherwise anodyne missives. Defeat at Waterloo, he wrote to Hortense, is celebrated by the men in power today because it made their government possible. But 'for me, as for the people of France, Waterloo is a poignant memory which still makes my hair stand on end because this defeat was the signal of the fall of French power . . . It is this conformity of interests with the French people that is my strength and it exists not only in my spirit and my heart, but in my blood, in my flesh, in my bones.' The impact of this impassioned cry was somewhat lessened by its bathetic end: 'We pass now onto a sweeter subject: I thank you for your jams.'[10] The anger was palpable, though, and Louis-Napoléon consoled himself with the thought that 'happily one day the people, the true people, and the army will bring to justice all these filthy animals who owe [their position] only to corruption'.[11]

Prison had not dimmed his conviction. 'I have seen for myself the most frightening shipwrecks,' he wrote to Hortense, 'without fear and without despair for the future, because deep in my heart I have the only support, the only certain guide in exceptional situations: faith in my mission.'

> I believe there are certain men who are born to serve as a means for the progress of the human race . . . I wait with resignation, but with confidence, the moment either to live my providential life or to die my fatal death, persuaded either way I will be useful to France first, and then to humanity.[12]

Indeed, far from seeing himself as a failure, despite much evidence to the contrary, Louis-Napoléon believed he had been fantastically successful. 'In 1833 the emperor and his son were dead,' he wrote to another friend; 'there was no heir of the imperial cause. France knew none . . . Well, I retied the thread. I resuscitated myself alone, and with my own strength, and I am today, within twenty leagues of Paris, a sword of Damocles over the government.'[13] Being closer, if only geographically, to power was a marvellously positive spin to put on his predicament.

To edge closer, Louis-Napoléon, believing in the power of the written word to shift opinion, penned articles for the *Progrès du Pas-de-Calais*, a left-leaning provincial republican newspaper. Like any good columnist, he proved adept at inserting himself into controversial issues and excoriating the government at every opportunity: give the people education, comfort, property – what only belonged to the few should be the right of all was a typically populist message concluding one piece.

Aside from articles, he also published pamphlets on topical subjects. His first work, *Historical Fragments, 1688–1830*, a treatise on English history, seemed far from relevant. But it was a riposte to an idea popular at the time, not shared by Louis-Napoléon of course, that the July Revolution of 1830 marked the end of political instability in France. The work concluded with the kind of memorable aphorism that came easily to him: 'March at the head of the ideas of your century, and these ideas will follow and support you; march behind them, and they will drag you along; march against them, and they will overthrow you.'[14]

Louis-Napoléon had a high opinion of his literary output. He admitted that there were a hundred writers more talented than him, but he regularly moved his readership to tears. 'Why? It is because', he explained, answering his own question, 'the Napoleonic cause goes to the soul; it moves, it awakens palpitating memories – and it is always through the heart, and never through cold reason, that the masses are stirred.'[15]

Unless his readers became emotional over tariffs on sugar imports, it is unlikely that his next work, a polemic on that topic, moved his readers to tears; however, the one after that, *The Extinction of Pauperism*, was much more effective in positioning him as a man of the people. In a series of articles, Louis-Napoléon argued that to alleviate the plight of the unemployed the state should create agricultural colonies. To acquire and develop land, the government should take out loans, which would soon be paid back, once these idyllic rural communes became profitable. The result: millions of happy and healthy French people saved from misery who would become a bulwark of a government based on mass democracy. Finishing with his usual rhetorical flourish, Louis-Napoléon wrote that once his scheme had been implemented, it would be said: 'The triumph of Christianity has destroyed slavery; the triumph of the French Revolution has destroyed servitude; and the triumph of democracy has destroyed pauperism.'[16]

There was little, if any, original thought in Louis-Napoléon's vision; such impractical utopias were a genre beloved of those on the left in France, who were fascinated and horrified by the plight of the desperately impoverished people who made up most of the nation. Louis-Napoléon knew nothing about farming, little about French workers or, for that matter, setting up such an ambitious scheme. But that was irrelevant. Aside from genuine, if vague, paternalist sentiment, the point of the work was less about helping poor people and more about helping Louis-Napoléon. As he wrote to Hortense Cornu on 2 February 1843, it was 'a work which cannot fail to do me a lot of good'.[17]

The articles were then published as a single volume and, in no small part because he paid for most of them, the work went through various editions and helped place Louis-Napoléon, an imperial prince, on the side of the poorest in society. A prominent French socialist, Louis Blanc, was so intrigued by the pretender with a conscience that he visited him in prison. After his attempt at Boulogne, wrote Blanc, 'Who does not remember' that Louis-Napoléon 'was made the laughing stock of Europe?' Blanc wanted to find out whether Louis-Napoléon was serious or not.

When they met towards the end of 1844, they agreed that Louis-Philippe was a terrible king, but they disagreed on what should replace him. Louis-Napoléon said he was a true democrat who believed in universal male suffrage; Blanc took the view that giving what he saw as ignorant peasants the vote was the last thing France needed. 'Do you mean to say,' replied Louis-Napoléon, 'that the national will is to be disregarded, and that you have a right, if powerful enough to do so, to impose your political creed . . . upon an unwilling majority?' That was exactly what Blanc meant. In his own words, giving peasants the vote was akin to putting a 'loaded pistol in the hands of a child'. They then fell out further over Louis-Napoléon's insistence that the Empire was the model for France, which meant hereditary monarchy.

After this, though, the two men turned to social reforms, and Blanc was astonished to find Louis-Napoléon in agreement with his own views. 'I felt amazed', recorded Blanc, at his readiness to adopt 'the principles of socialism'. This was not perhaps as radical as it sounds. At the time, socialism was an embryonic, heterogeneous movement, and given liberals' insistence that governments should rarely intervene in the economy, even moderate measures to help the poorest were branded socialist. Nonetheless, Louis-Napoléon's interest in these ideas marked him out from those in power.

But then he and Blanc, as men often do, got into a heated argument over whether the first Roman emperors were tyrants.

Regardless of their differences, the meetings made an impression on Blanc. 'When I took my leave of him,' he recalled, 'his eyes were moistened with tears, and he clasped me in his arms so eagerly that I could not help being moved.'[18] Both men held deep political convictions, and neither persuaded the other of the righteousness of their cause, but the meeting demonstrated that Louis-Napoléon had restored some credibility. Blanc was not the only luminary drawn to his newfound love for social reform. The novelist George Sand – a woman known for her radical politics, smoking in public and dressing as a man – was one of the writers Louis-Napoléon admitted was more talented than him. She read his works and found his name and his progressive ideas an intoxicating if terrifying mix. Though hoping he never came to power, she wrote that 'he has the gift of making himself loved, it is impossible not to love him'.[19] If Blanc and Sand proved immune to the merits of Bonapartism, other republicans were swayed and Louis-Napoléon developed from prison a network of converts. This required some dissimulation on his part. All he wanted, he told one left-leaning acolyte when discussing his failed *coups d'état*, was to 'let the entire people choose the form of government that would suit them best'. This was as far as his ambition went, he lied. 'I was not crazy enough to have the pretension of founding a dynasty on a ground littered with all the debris of past dynasties.'[20]

Through his writings, Louis-Napoléon curated an image that appealed across the political spectrum. He believed that in politics power was shifting towards the people. There was, he argued, a floating mass in the country that would rally to something and someone. To bind people to him, his writings aimed at turning nostalgia for the legend of Napoléon into a political programme. After five years, he was cutting through and was no longer quite the ridiculous figure he had been after his arrest at Boulogne in 1840. The government, however, took a different view. When a publisher began to collect his works into a single volume, the authorities made it clear there was no need to censor this because his words were 'miserable fantasies' from a 'sick mind' that could not 'exert any influence on public opinion'.[21]

After five years of ignoring his son, another person with a troubled mind, his father, wrote him a letter. The comte de Saint-Leu was dying, a fact he made clear his son's actions had played no small part in bringing about. Regardless, before he died, he wrote, he wanted to see his only surviving son. 'My dear father,' replied Louis-Napoléon, 'I felt yesterday the first joy I have known for the last five years on receiving the friendly letter which you have been kind enough to write to me.'[22] Given the ice-cold tone of his father's words, this was a generous – or wishful – interpretation on the son's part. Nevertheless, Louis-Napoléon, who had not seen his father since 1831, when he promised not to do anything rash before embarking on an adventure that saw his brother die, was determined to fulfil his father's wishes.

Over the next few months, there were pleas on his behalf, and letters to ministers; Louis-Napoléon even deigned to write to King Louis-Philippe, begging permission to visit his dying father and giving his word he would return to prison afterwards. The government offered more: freedom. All he had to do was ask for a pardon. Louis-Napoléon refused. 'I would rather stay all my life in prison than debase myself,' he wrote angrily.[23] To ask for forgiveness meant admitting guilt, and Louis-Napoléon believed he had done nothing wrong. That left only one way out: escape.

———

In May 1846, repairs began on the wing of the fortress where Louis-Napoléon's rooms were. For eight days, the prisoner carefully observed the movements of the workmen charged with carrying out the job. Security was tight. At dawn the men filed into the fortress. Once they were inside the gate, a sergeant and prison officer carefully inspected each one. At the end of the day the same rigorous check was employed before they left. Louis-Napoléon noticed, however, that once inside the fortress individual workmen could come and go freely, pick up tools, make deliveries, whatever was needed for the day's work. This provided an opportunity. Louis-Napoléon, who had already demonstrated a skill for dressing up when he had disguised himself as his mother's servant and an English gentleman to get out of Italy in 1831, would, in the clothes of a workman, walk out of the prison's front door. His valet Thelin, who could come and go as he pleased, procured the necessary outfit.

Early on Monday morning, 25 May 1846, Louis-Napoléon, Thelin and Conneau, wearing no shoes so as not to make a noise, looked anxiously at the courtyard below from behind drawn curtains on the first floor. The only sound in the stillness of the dawn was the footsteps of the sentries marching in the yard. Louis-Napoléon was not yet in disguise. To look the part, he planned to shave off his beloved moustache and beard, but such was his attachment to his facial hair that if, for whatever reason, the workmen did not come today and he was found clean shaven, he thought the commandant would guess something was up.

Then, just after 5 a.m., daylight breaking, the workmen came through the prison gate. Taking a razor, Louis-Napoléon started shaving – the Rubicon had been crossed. Next, he put on his usual grey trousers and boots, shirt and waistcoat. Over them, he wore a coarse linen shirt cut off at the waist. Then dirty trousers over his clean ones and that most ubiquitous signifier of the French working class at the time: a well-worn and stained blouse, a voluminous garment that billowed down to just above the knees. Round his neck, he tied a cotton handkerchief and added an old blue apron for good measure. Getting into the role, he covered his face and hands with dirt, and put on a long black wig and a worker's cap.

Once dressed, he downed a cup of coffee and put clogs on. These had been specially made with high heels, giving him an extra four inches of height. Then he grabbed a cheap clay pipe – the kind preferred by workmen – and picked up a plank of wood which had served as a bookshelf and put it over his shoulder. Thus attired, so stepped out, in his own mind at least, the providential saviour of France.

On the staircase leading from Louis-Napoléon's rooms to the courtyard, Thelin offered all the men working there a drink in one of his master's rooms. With the coast clear, Louis-Napoléon descended. When he reached the bottom of the staircase, he came face to face with one of the guards. The guard did not recognise him. Louis-Napoléon positioned the plank to hide his face and went into the courtyard.

Then, just as he walked past a soldier on duty, Louis-Napoléon dropped his pipe. The sentinel stared at the prisoner as he stooped to pick it up, but there was no flicker of recognition. Louis-Napoléon kept going, past soldiers basking in the morning sun who glanced at him with disinterest. Walking behind Louis-Napoléon now, Thelin had his dog, Ham, a firm favourite with the prisoner warders, on a leash to provide more diversion.

As he approached the main gate, the sergeant who guarded it looked straight at Louis-Napoléon. With a deft movement of the plank, the prisoner once again obscured his face and waited. The sergeant opened the gate. Louis-Napoléon walked out. Thelin, wishing the gatekeeper a good day, followed. While making his way across a drawbridge, Louis-Napoléon passed two workmen. Worried that they would speak to him, he passed the ever-useful plank from one shoulder to the other. After they went past, he heard them say, 'Oh! It's Bertou.'[24]

Louis-Napoléon walked quickly, terrified he would be discovered, along the road towards the spot where Thelin would meet him in a carriage. It was near a cemetery, and seeing a crucifix in the middle of the burial ground Louis-Napoléon – hardly a man of deep faith – threw himself prostrate before it and prayed.

Back at the fortress, Conneau – whose devotion was such that he had volunteered to stay in prison after his sentence ended to be with Louis-Napoléon – was a sacrificial pawn. To delay discovery of the escape, he let it be known that the prisoner was sick and could not see anyone. He even tried to make himself vomit, thinking the smell would give authenticity to the ruse. Failing in this, he mixed together coffee, chunks of bread, milk, eau de cologne and nitric acid. He had also created a fake Louis-Napoléon out of straw, laying it down on the prisoner's bed, head resting on the pillow, handkerchief over its face.

When the commandant came later that day, Conneau said that Louis-Napoléon was ill and asleep. This put the governor off for a few hours, but by evening, the officer was worried and demanded to see the prisoner. Conneau, drawing on skills developed as an actor in long evenings at Arenenberg performing Hortense's plays, opened the bedroom door, called out and, receiving no answer, tiptoed back to the commandant and said Louis-Napoléon was still sleeping. Where was Thelin? asked the commandant. Conneau told him that he had hired a carriage and was out running errands. Now the governor was worried. Creeping into Louis-Napoléon's dark room, he listened at the bedside. Unable to hear any breathing, he grabbed the figure and shook it. 'He has escaped then?' enquired the commandant with resignation. 'Yes,' replied Conneau.[25]

———

On 27 May 1846, James Howard Harris, 3rd Earl of Malmesbury, was returning home from his London club. A short man with a few days' stubble on his face ran across the street and stopped him. The Earl of Malmesbury stared in confused outrage at the stranger before realising it was Louis-Napoléon, whom he had visited in prison a year earlier. At dinner that evening, Malmesbury was sitting opposite an attaché from the French embassy.

'Have you seen him?' asked the earl.

'Who?' replied the French diplomat.

'Louis-Napoléon,' replied Malmesbury coolly. 'He is in London, having just escaped.' The Frenchman left the lady on his arm and ran out of the room. 'I never saw a man look more frightened,' remarked the earl.[26]

The French diplomat need not have been frightened – not yet at least. Louis-Napoléon was sincere in his desire to see his dying father. He wrote to the French ambassador that this was the sole reason he had escaped and that he had no intention of launching another attempt against the July Monarchy. The French government, which had seen this play before when Louis-Napoléon had promised he had no ambition other than to see his dying mother in 1837, was unconvinced. He was refused a passport. Louis-Napoléon lobbied everyone in his extensive network to intercede on his behalf.

While he waited for an answer, he picked up in London society where he had left off in 1840. The first evening back, he went to his old Gore House haunt for a dinner party hosted by Lady Blessington and attended by comte Alfred d'Orsay and a few other guests. He regaled them with the story of his flight from prison, although as one attendee noted, he did it 'in his usual un-French way without warmth or excitement'.[27] Among polite company, it was hard to know which of Louis-Napoléon's two conversational gambits was more absurd: he was soliciting investment on behalf of a company with the dubious idea of building a canal through Nicaragua, and he repeated his claims that he would be emperor.

To further his imperial dream, Louis-Napoléon ensured that a letter outlining his daring escape – and the noble reason behind it – was published in the French press. And within days of arriving in London, he had d'Orsay use his extensive contacts to get favourable coverage in the British press. A few months later, a puff piece was rushed out which detailed his time in prison and sensationalised his escape, the nineteenth-century equivalent of a Sunday supplement – in prison with the prince – and the type of self-promotion Louis-Napoléon excelled at.

Not everyone bought into the narrative. One newspaper wrote that 'Louis Napoleon is really making himself a greater noodle than people even thought him'. The book ostensibly about his time at Ham was in fact about his 'claims' to be the 'imperial successor of his relative'. It was, continued the writer, 'to be pitied that he spends his money indulging so ridiculous a delusion; for strange to say, however eager this would-be Emperor may be to govern the French, they have never shown the least anxiety to become his subjects'.[28]

It was this ridiculous delusion that meant that Louis-Napoléon was refused permission to travel. On 25 July 1846, aged sixty-seven, the comte de Saint-Leu died, embittered and alone in his dilapidated Florentine palazzo. Louis-Napoléon had not seen him in over fifteen years; their correspondence was intermittent, brief and, on his father's side, cold, angry and disapproving. Indeed, the comte de Saint-Leu had all but disowned his son after the Boulogne attempt. Nonetheless, Louis-Napoléon was obsessed with his family and held his father in an idealised and sentimental reverence that the cantankerous and paranoid old man did not deserve.

Despite being perennially disappointed in him, the comte de Saint-Leu's will left his son nearly everything, making Louis-Napoléon rich. Almost as important as money, he inherited his father's collection of Napoleonic memorabilia, which went some way to replacing what had been auctioned after Boulogne. The estate, however, was mainly in property and Louis-Napoléon remained short of cash. Providing for his followers was expensive, and the pretender frequently lost what money he had at the races. He was forced to borrow from his British bankers – Barings, the Rothschilds – and other less respectable sources, including, it was rumoured, vast sums from mistresses, to fund his lifestyle among London's beau monde.

It showed Louis-Napoléon's eye for self-promotion that he saw his father's death as a chance to profit politically too. He made sure that part of the will was published in the press. This put a stop to the belief – at one point true – of a rupture between father and son. It also gave credence to his reason for escaping and made the French government – which had denied a son the chance to see his father before he died – look bad. Finally, it publicised the fact that with the death of his father – his uncle Joseph had died two years previously – Louis-Napoléon, according to Napoléon's act of succession, was the official Bonaparte heir.

Despite this, most of his relatives wanted nothing to do with him. However, there was one cousin mad enough to be drawn into his circle: Prince Napoléon-Jérôme Bonaparte, or Plon-Plon as he was known because of the difficulty he had in pronouncing 'Napoléon' as a child. He was the second son of Napoléon's youngest brother, Jérôme. Vain, venal and mercurial, Plon-Plon, unlike Louis-Napoléon, bore a striking resemblance to the emperor. What he did share with his cousin, however, was political ambition, although he placed himself much further on the republican left.

Louis-Napoléon took the family connection seriously; in a letter to his cousin the imperial pretender complained, somewhat forgetfully for a father of two, that it was 'so sad that neither you nor I have children. There will be no more Bonapartes other than Lucien's unfortunate branch.'[29] Louis-Napoléon took Plon-Plon under his wing, as much to keep an eye on him as for the somewhat dubious merits of his company. Rarely troubled by conscience, untrustworthy and erratic, Plon-Plon was a potential rival. While in prison, Louis-Napoléon heard alarming reports about his cousin's political activity, so, to bind him to his cause, he promised, with confident certainty, that when he came to power, 'be sure that my first thought . . . would be to intimately tie your destiny to mine'.[30]

Plon-Plon was intrigued by his renegade cousin and delighted when he heard that Louis-Napoléon had escaped, soon joining him in London. Over the next few months, they became inseparable. They talked politics into the early hours, Plon-Plon more radical than Louis-Napoléon, but while they waited for providence to turn in their direction, they enjoyed themselves in London and travelled round England, even taking up the very English pursuit of fox hunting. On one trip, dressed in riding boots, red coats and top hats, the two cousins discussed the likelihood of a general European war amid the barking of hounds and the noise of horses.

With no close family, Louis-Napoléon desperately hoped that Plon-Plon might become a trusted confidant, but he never knew what to make of his unpredictable cousin. Sometimes 'his heart seems to speak of glory, to suffer and beat with you; sometimes he expresses hardness, trickery', wrote Louis-Napoléon. 'What are we to believe?' he asked rhetorically. 'I always think the best until I have positive proofs to the contrary.'[31]

One of the first things that Louis-Napoléon had done after arriving in London was to inform his lover in prison and the mother of his two children, Éléonore Vergeot, through an intermediary, that their relationship was over. 'I hope she consoles herself well,' he wrote optimistically.[32] As a wealthy, fashionable and single man in London, Louis-Napoléon was not short of other opportunities, often pursued through his love of the theatre, or rather the female cast. He regularly frequented the St James's Theatre, which put on French plays. Here, he saw the great celebrity French thespian, and a woman whose performances that summer were so sensational that Queen Victoria and her husband, Prince Albert, were often in attendance, Eliza Rachel Félix, better known by her stage name of Rachel.

Louis-Napoléon was, in his own words, 'enchanted'. He thought her a 'French woman' of 'genius' who had revived interest in 'our great classical authors'.[33] Beyond his genuine enthusiasm for her merits as an actress and services to France, he found her extremely attractive and the two became lovers. Soon, however, she returned to France, allowing Louis-Napoléon to pursue an interest in ballet, or rather ballerinas. He was friends with the director of Her Majesty's Theatre, who threw lavish garden parties in Fulham where society met with the stars of the day. Louis-Napoléon was often there, one afternoon dancing with three of the most celebrated ballerinas in one quadrille, Carlotta Grisi, Fanny Cerrito and Marie Taglioni.

At the beginning of 1847, Louis-Napoléon moved into a rented house on King Street, off St James's Street. 'For the first time in seven years,' he wrote to a friend, 'I am enjoying the pleasure of being at home.' As was his custom, he decorated it with Napoleonic memorabilia, paintings and family portraits – all the precious objects that had escaped 'the shipwreck', his euphemism for the Boulogne catastrophe.[34] As a satirical London newspaper quipped, Louis-Napoléon has taken 'possession of a permanent residence' but he 'has not yet quite decided on his selection of a *mistress* for his new mansion'.[35] That, as it turned out, was not true.

———

The daughter of a bootmaker, Elizabeth Ann Haryett was born on 13 August 1823 in Brighton. Growing up amid the tedium of lower-middle-class respectability, she yearned for stardom, shocking her parents with a desire to become an actress, a profession which for many self-respecting people was little better than prostitution, and for some, worse. Undeterred by her parents' disapproval, she ran away and found work in some stables. There, she met a jockey who went on to win the first ever Grand National in 1839 and became a famous dandy. Still only a teenager, she lived with him in London, changed her name to Harriet Howard and pursued her dream of becoming a celebrity on the stage.

Seventeen years old, she made her debut in 1840. 'Her figure is commanding and graceful,' wrote London's foremost theatrical journal, 'her features expressive and full of playful beauty.' The audience loudly applauded when she came back on stage after the show and the review concluded that 'Miss Howard's performance was a charm not likely ever to be forgotten by those who were present . . . We believe she will achieve lofty triumphs in her profession.'[36] In fact, her performance was soon forgotten. After her debut, she got only minor parts, and two years later she went on stage for the last time as Third Apparition in *Macbeth*, a role that has five lines.

Her 'lofty triumphs', it turned out, were as a courtesan. For the daughter of a bootmaker to shine in the class-conscious, cut-throat world of London society, those required no less skill as an actor. But those who knew her described 'an exquisite figure, at once stately and graceful, with a head and features such as only one of the great Greek sculptors could have chiselled'.[37] And she used this to work her way up the London social scene.

The jockey was ditched, and she became the lover of an army officer, Francis Mountjoy Martyn. He was already married, but Harriet became his mistress and gave birth to his illegitimate son in 1842. The diminutive Martyn was a social climber whose expensive clothes and good looks took him into fashionable society. No doubt his wealth helped too – he lent d'Orsay £10,000 – and this took him to Gore House. Harriet came with him. It was likely here that Louis-Napoléon first met her in 1846. Tall, elegant and considered strikingly beautiful, she soon left Martyn for him.

Not that Louis-Napoléon stopped sleeping with other women. Rachel returned to Britain in the summer of 1847. Louis-Napoléon and Plon-Plon accompanied her on her northern tour. Sharing a train carriage, Louis-Napoléon fell asleep, only to wake and find his cousin and Rachel in a compromising embrace on the seats opposite. Rather than make a scene, Louis-Napoléon closed his eyes and pretended to be asleep. Seducing his mistress while he slept would have been, for many, the 'positive proof' of bad character that Louis-Napoléon said he would wait for before coming to a definitive judgement on his cousin. Showing remarkable discretion, however, he left his cousin and Rachel to it, returning to London alone the next day. There he enjoyed himself. In the month of July 1847 alone, Louis-Napoléon could be found at the Duchess of Glasgow's *fête dansante*, the Duchess of Bedford's *fêtes champêtres* – there were three that month – and a christening for the son of the Marquis and Marchioness of Douglas.

That autumn there was a more solemn occasion which he could not attend, the funeral of his father. It took place in a small church in the countryside near Paris that was decorated as though Napoléon's Empire had never ended. Tricolours, eagles and drapes with the letter 'N' embroidered on them were lit by candles. In the middle where the choir sat were two coffins, those of the comte de Saint-Leu and Louis-Napoléon's beloved older brother, whose body had been taken from Italy to be interred alongside his father's.

Louis-Napoléon was deemed too dangerous to be allowed to go, but his uncle Jérôme and Plon-Plon were among the mourners. The French government had given them permission to return to France despite the law banishing Bonapartes. There were also veterans of the imperial armies, Italians, Poles and French in eclectic, vintage uniforms. Two former members of the imperial guard flanked the coffins. When Jérôme entered, they presented arms. After the ceremony, as the mourners went out into the streets, crowds shouted, '*Vive l'empereur!*'

'Those who believe', wrote the *Times* correspondent who covered the funeral, 'that Napoléon and his family are forgotten in France would had they witnessed all I did today doubt the accuracy of the impression.' There was never clearer evidence, he continued, of 'attachment and respect' for Napoléon than 'indicated on this day'. It was, he concluded, a day of sadness, 'but every eye riveted' on Napoléon's relatives and 'the decaying remnants of the Grand Army who surrounded them'.[38]

———

The Napoleonic memorabilia charting the incredible history of Louis-Napoléon's uncle which furnished his modest lodgings in King Street – drab blue damask curtains hanging in the drawing room – contrasted acutely with the nephew's own listless, frivolous life. One print on the wall, *The Court of Napoléon*, depicted Louis-Napoléon's grandmother, Joséphine, and his mother, Hortense, front and centre among the most important men and women of the regime, dressed with conspicuous opulence. The point of the image was that they looked born to rule, but if history had followed its traditional eighteenth-century trajectory, many of them should have been nowhere near the French throne. That they were was because of the incredible disruption wrought by the frontman, Napoléon Bonaparte, standing in the image at the apogee of his power, thirty-eight years old.

By that age, Napoléon's Promethean rise had seen the forces of old Europe defeated in stunning victories across the continent; he had seized control of France in a *coup d'état* and, in 1804, done what an obscure Corsican should never have been able to do: crown himself emperor. From childhood, Louis-Napoléon had idolised this unlikely legend and fantasised about emulating his uncle. As a romantic young conspirator raised by his mother to worship the miraculous power of Napoléon, that was understandable, but for a man turning forty in 1848, these were not reasonable dreams. As his father had pointed out, his uncle had achieved extraordinary things before he came to power; Louis-Napoléon, with two derisory *coups d'état* behind him, was a joke to the French political class.

Louis-Napoléon did not see himself as a failure because he clung to his providential mission, but this time in London it had become more understated. Unlike his first exile, there was little urgency to his actions, nor the self-important court. Indeed, rather than orchestrating conspiracies, Louis-Napoléon's main preoccupation was at the British Museum, working on his history of artillery. With Harriet Howard moving to lodgings closer to his own, the next year, 1848, held little more for him than romance, writing and the dull rhythms of London high society.

But if Louis-Napoléon's Bonapartist dreams had become less feverish in Britain, in France the flame shone as brightly as ever for Persigny. Prison had affected his health, and from 1847 he was recuperating in a medical facility near Versailles. Whereas Louis-Napoléon had focused on politics when locked up, Persigny, as well as developing a cheese addiction, had used his time to publish the as-yet-unproved theory that the pyramids were built to prevent sand blowing into the Nile and silting up the river. To contemporaries, his judgement on Egyptology was less bizarre than his political views. For he was telling anyone who would listen – and many who would not – that a restoration of Napoléon's Empire was imminent. Persigny's predictions were met with derision: exactly the kind of thing to be expected from a hot-headed crackpot who thought the pyramids were giant windshields. After all, Louis-Philippe had provided nearly two decades of strong and stable leadership, and unless something extraordinary happened, nothing was going to change.

PART II

THE WORLD IS A STRANGE THEATRE

8

NAPOLÉON'S GHOST

Few politicians in France worried about a revolution in January 1848. But the celebrated author of *Democracy in America*, Alexis de Tocqueville, did. 'I believe', he warned during a parliamentary debate, 'that we are at this moment sleeping on a volcano.' There was, Tocqueville continued, 'a gale of revolution in the air', and 'the earth is quaking once again in Europe'.[1]

These mixed metaphors were certainly not going to move Louis-Philippe and his chief minister, François Guizot, into conceding to opposition demands that the narrow franchise be extended. In parliament, Guizot had made his view clear: 'The principle of universal suffrage is so absurd that none of its partisans dare accept or support it completely,' he said in a statement which suggested Louis-Napoléon's writings did not loom large in his life. 'The day of universal suffrage will never dawn. There will never be a time when all human beings, whoever they are, will be called upon to exercise political rights.'[2]

Repression, therefore, was the order of the day. Despite rising political discontent, exacerbated by an awful economic downturn, Guizot and his ministers were confident. They had thirty-one thousand troops, four thousand armed police and nearly a hundred thousand National Guards – civilian militia, the backbone of the regime. When protests broke out on 22 February, these men were called to arms. It soon became clear, however, that few National Guards were willing to defend the government. The streets of Paris were increasingly chaotic, and the government was losing control. But events the following day turned protest into revolution.

On the evening of 23 February, a march took crowds demanding reforms and an extension of the franchise to the foreign ministry. As Guizot had been foreign minister for nearly eight years, the building was associated with Louis-Philippe's detested creature. On the streets outside, soldiers and

135

their commanding officer had orders not to let anyone pass. An officer on horseback met the protesters. They took the reins of his horse, urging him to stand his men down. The officer refused. With that, he turned his horse around and placed himself behind his soldiers, who lowered their weapons. The demonstrators at the front of the crowd were being pushed towards the bayonets by those at the back. Amid the shouting, jostling and confusion, shots rang out from the panicked troops, followed by a more devasting volley straight into the chests of the largely unarmed crowd.

The screams of the dying and wounded mixed with the shouts of stampeding people. Soon the folk memory of previous revolutions kicked in. This massacre – for that is what it was being called – awoke the people. A nearby cart was requisitioned and sixteen corpses, including, always helpful for the revolutionary imagination, a dead woman, were placed in it. A cortège of rage illuminated by torchlight then rumbled through the streets of Paris. The people knew what to do: barricades went up, weapons were looted, the revolutionary volcano erupted.

This time the people were determined the revolution would not be stolen, as many said it had been in 1830, when another king came to power. On 24 February, an armed mob invaded parliament. Tocqueville was in the chamber watching the poet and opposition politician Alphonse de Lamartine struggling to seize the initiative, 'for in a rebellion, as in a novel, the most difficult part to invent is the end. When, therefore, someone took it into his head to cry, "To the Hôtel de Ville!", Lamartine echoed, "Yes, to the Hôtel de Ville."'[3] Whereupon most people rushed to the city hall to be present at the birth of the new government.

King Louis-Philippe abdicated and fled Paris; Lamartine and a few others formed the provisional government. Alongside Lamartine there was Louis Blanc, who had visited Louis-Napoléon in prison and was a socialist better known as a historian, and editors and journalists from Paris's left-wing newspapers, as well as a token worker. They then issued hurried decrees. Lamartine hung on to the tricolour against calls for the red flag of socialism, but plenty of other radical concessions were made – that one revolutionary punctuated his demands with the sound of his musket butt hitting the floor concentrated the mind. Restrictions on the press ended, political prisoners were released and the right to work was guaranteed.

Crucially, a republic was declared, and it would be based on what Guizot had called 'absurd', universal male suffrage – the electorate went from 246,000 to 9.4 million.

What Louis-Napoléon had long dreamed of had arrived: the French Second Republic, as it became known, would be the greatest democratic experiment ever tried thus far in European history. And as Louis-Napoléon wrote to his cousin from London, 'I must be its master.'[4]

———

For that to happen, he had to be there. Like republicans, Louis-Napoléon believed that the 1830 Revolution had been a missed opportunity for the French people, but also for himself. The absence of family members in Paris, he argued, meant that events had not turned in a Bonapartist direction. He was determined not to make the same mistake in February 1848.

Summoned to King Street, Joseph Orsi, Italian banker, long-time friend and co-conspirator of Louis-Napoléon, arrived at midnight. On entering, he found Louis-Napoléon pacing the room. 'My dear Orsi! It is marvellous to see how well things look in France. I must start for Paris without losing a moment.'[5] The two men left the next morning, catching a steamer. Louis-Napoléon, still banished from France, hid below deck. When they reached Calais, he wrapped a thick scarf round his face to cover his distinctive moustache. He was travelling, again, on a false British passport. Upon disembarking, he was asked whether he was an Englishman. He replied nonchalantly that he was. Passports inspected without comment, they made their way to Paris.

'Gentlemen,' Louis-Napoléon grandiosely declared in a letter to the provisional government after entering the capital on 28 February, 'I hasten back from exile to place myself under the flag of the Republic . . . Without other ambition than that of serving my country, I announce my arrival to the provisional government.'[6] The provisional government was swift in its reply. Louis-Napoléon would best serve his country by leaving it. They asked him to return to London.

Persigny, with customary impetuosity, urged Louis-Napoléon to defy the request. Better, he argued, to force the government to deport him, capitalise on the publicity, play the martyr. But Louis-Napoléon calculated that presenting himself as a loyal citizen at the Republic's inauguration would gain him greater political capital. Replying to the government, he wrote, 'after thirty-three years of exile and persecution, I believed I had earned the right to return to my homeland. You think that my presence in Paris at this time would be an embarrassment; I therefore retire for now. You will see in this sacrifice the purity of my intentions and my patriotism.'[7] Soon he was back in London.

Despite his best efforts, Louis-Napoléon's arrival in Paris barely registered in the French newspapers, but his appearance was the first step in a longer-term strategy. He had no intention of repeating his two previous catastrophic attempts at seizing power. He would present himself before the French people, but as a candidate in elections rather than as a usurper. Few had thought more about how to manipulate the world of mass democracy than Louis-Napoléon, and if he could marshal nostalgic Napoleonic fervour behind his name and ideas, he would have unrivalled popular support.

Yet he decided not to stand as a candidate in elections held on 23 April for a constituent assembly tasked with creating a new constitution for France. A nervous speaker with no public debating experience, Louis-Napoléon knew he would not shine in a chamber containing some of the most elegant rhetoricians in recent French history. Better, he reasoned, to watch French politics unfold from across the Channel and enter the stage at the apposite moment.

By April, many in London were worried that the continental fad of revolutions – uprisings were taking place in most major capitals now – would spread to Britain. The Chartists, a workers' movement that campaigned for universal male suffrage and political rights, organised a mass demonstration that would take place on 10 April 1848, before presenting a petition to parliament. In the paranoid minds of the establishment this was turned into a revolutionary threat on the Parisian model. To ensure any insurrection met its Waterloo, the Duke of Wellington was put in charge of the army, ready to crush rebellion. Thousands of special constables were enrolled to police the capital, and Louis-Napoléon volunteered as a performative gesture to present himself as on the side of order. On 10 April, tens of thousands of Chartists met on Kennington Common; however, the protest was peaceful. Louis-Napoléon, diligently serving on the beat in central London, had little to do except wave his truncheon.

A few weeks later, France went to the polls. In siding with order, Louis-Napoléon had astutely judged the direction French politics was moving in, for the people were far more conservative than the radicals in Paris who claimed to represent them. In the Assembly, out of 851 representatives, a mere 285 were republicans and only 55 of those radicals or socialists. Lamartine's revolutionary government of 1848, then, had to try and rule with a chamber predominantly made up of conservatives and monarchists.

To do this, a five-man Executive Commission was set up, but as it consisted of those who had led the uprising against Louis-Philippe, it was far more left-wing than the majority in parliament. Yet the February 1848 Revolution, not to mention recent French history, had shown that an elected assembly was powerless in the face of those who controlled the streets. For radicals, socialists and revolutionaries – who saw even the moderate left Executive Commission, let alone the Assembly, as counter-revolutionary – anything that thwarted the will of the people would be swept aside as easily as the July Monarchy had been.

———

The will of the people, or so the radical left in Paris argued, and they tended to conflate their desires with the nation's, was war. On the morning of 15 May, thousands gathered to present a petition to the Assembly demanding that the French army leave immediately for Poland, where, as was often the case in the nineteenth century, a revolt was being crushed. The plan was for a legal demonstration, but when they reached the Palais Bourbon, where the Assembly sat, they found it barely guarded. With people pushing from the back, those at the front were shoved inside the grounds of the palace.

Here, some protesters encountered Lamartine, poet, member of the Executive Commission and self-proclaimed leader of the revolution. He tried to stop them illegally entering the Assembly. 'We admire you as a poet,' replied one of the demonstrators generously, before adding, 'but not as a politician'. An older man was less polite: 'Vote for the freedom of Poland, or you are lost.' Unmoved, Lamartine insisted that they would enter the chamber over his dead body. Brushing aside the poet's words, the protester replied, 'We are the masters here; we belong to the sovereign people. You are nothing more than our clerks.'[8]

And so, only eleven days after its first sitting, the Assembly was invaded. In the chamber, it was anarchy: confused shouts, people manhandling representatives, others fighting over the speaker's podium, where a proclamation about Poland was eventually read, although few heard it above the commotion. Armand Barbès mounted the tribune. He was a revolutionary caricature, a veteran of secret societies, defeated uprisings and prison – like Louis-Napoléon he had tried to overthrow Louis-Philippe. Released as part of an amnesty in February, he led a faction of the extreme left. Today, Barbès had promised that he would be moderate. When he fought his way to the tribune, however, he felt the revolution coursing through him. Speaking to France, he went big. 'The Assembly must vote immediately . . . the departure of the army for Poland, a tax of a billion francs on the rich . . . it must force troops to leave Paris: if not, the representatives will be declared traitors to the fatherland.'[9] This led demonstrators below to debate, often violently, the finer points of this impromptu political programme. Outside, drums were beating, calling the National Guard onto the streets. Amid the panic inside, one man leapt on to the podium and declared the Assembly dissolved. The February 1848 hand was played again. Names of a provisional government were read out, and its members and supporters rushed to the Hôtel de Ville.

Here, Barbès and some three hundred others took over the building. They shut themselves up in the same rooms that Lamartine and his revolutionaries had occupied a few months beforehand, and began issuing decrees. Then National Guards entered the room. Barbès looked up with the irritated air of one interrupted in the middle of important business. The guardsman asked him who he was. A member of the provisional government, he replied. This turned out not to be true; he was arrested and sent back to prison.

Although the Republic had not fallen on 15 May, it nearly had. This did nothing to inspire confidence in those who had never supported the revolution and who feared a second republic would unleash a new terror to rival the thirty thousand guillotined under the First Republic in the 1790s.

From the perspective of Parisians who considered themselves 'respectable', the people who overthrew the July Monarchy, and those who invaded the Assembly, were not heroes, but rather escaped convicts, vagabonds and other scum 'vomited up from the depths of hell', as one bourgeois memorably put it. If calm occasionally reigned in the capital, this was only, and quite literally, a stay of execution. Paris, wrote one nervous bourgeois woman, resembled 'a cursed city, a threatened Gomorrah, having received in secret the warning of its impending destruction'.[10]

Socialists had replaced Jacobins in the nightmares of the bourgeoisie. Few, if any, of these fears were based on an understanding of what socialism was, but respectable people were certain of one thing: it was an attack on what was most sacred, their own property. As many of the rural and Catholic population often owned their land and shared this paranoia about left-wing revolutionaries, there was an enormous constituency to be won for the man who could present himself as the defender of society against the barbarism of socialism.

It was amid this uneasy stand-off between radicals in Paris and much of the rest of the country that by-elections to the Assembly took place in June. Louis-Napoléon's name was thrown into the contest. It resonated with voters, and the Bonapartist message did too: a heady dose of nostalgia for the past and glory for the future, with an emphasis on the people and concern for the poor. Louis-Napoléon had long believed his name was popular in France. Now he had proof. The electoral system allowed for multiple candidacies in departments – the administrative divisions of the country – and Louis-Napoléon was returned for three different seats.

To the political elite, who had taken no notice of him, this was a tremendous shock. To the horror of republican newspapers, Louis-Napoléon's message appealed to workers in Paris as much as it did to people in the countryside; everywhere, the magical name of Napoléon seemed to reverberate. The triumph was all the more astonishing because the campaign was a largely uncoordinated grassroots movement, especially in rural areas, where he was elected without newspaper backing, posters or even printed ballots, meaning voters had to write his name themselves.

Political leaders, republican or monarchist, were forced to take note. When the names of the newly elected representatives were read out from the Hôtel de Ville, Louis-Napoléon's was cheered the loudest. As was so often the case in French politics, the fear surrounding this was as much informed by the past as the present. Any self-respecting politician knew their history: in 1799, Napoléon Bonaparte had launched a *coup d'état* – known after the date in the revolutionary calendar as 18 Brumaire – which was the first step from Republic to Empire.

There was, however, a way to stop history repeating itself: prevent Louis-Napoléon taking his seat in the Assembly. The law banishing the Bonaparte family had never been repealed. True, three of his cousins, including Plon-Plon, had been elected to the Assembly and taken their seats, but Louis-Napoléon was a special case. He had twice conspired against the French government. Many thought he was doing so again because, to add to the confusion in the Paris streets, Bonapartist crowds assembled, crying his name and shouting, '*Vive l'empereur!*' Surely, many argued, this was a result of Bonapartist agents distributing money from the pretender's fortune. In the Assembly, therefore, the government argued that he should be barred from entering.

On 13 June, Bonapartist crowds protested, determined to intimidate the Assembly into admitting Louis-Napoléon. In the Place de la Concorde, a young well-dressed woman harangued her audience; they were there to support Louis-Napoléon not as a pretender, she insisted, but as a representative of the people. Others disagreed, one asking how anyone could be stupid enough to support a man who had made two remarkably absurd attempts to revive his uncle's despotism. Another citizen took off his hat and shouted, '*Vive la République!*', but few repeated his cry. A bolder soul insulted Louis-Napoléon; a worker punched him.

Inside the Assembly, Louis-Napoléon was the topic of debate. Jules Favre, a republican, argued that he must be admitted. This was not out of love for Louis-Napoléon. By trying to exclude him, the Executive Commission had, Favre argued, given him popularity and importance he did not merit. It had let people think that the Republic 'could be overthrown by the breath of a pygmy'. Louis Blanc, one of the few men in French politics who had spent time with Louis-Napoléon, was similarly not worried about him entering the fray. 'Let the emperor's nephew draw near the sun of our Republic. I am sure he will disappear in its rays.' An imperial restoration was ridiculous, maintained Blanc confidently, because 'the time of emperors and kings has forever passed'.[11]

With the matter still unresolved, a Bonapartist committee with Persigny at its heart did everything it could to impose Louis-Napoléon into the imagination of the French. His image was ubiquitous: street hawkers sold matchboxes with his face, medallions with his slogans, miniature imperial eagles with red ribbons. Music and poetry were yoked to imperial propaganda, stretching rhyme in the service of the Bonapartist cause: 'I am a true republican / I say it to you for certain / It is necessary a Napoléon.'[12]

Several Bonapartist journals sprang up, often pasted onto street corners where they could be read for free. Playing heavily on imperial longing, a preferred tactic of these rags was to give Parisians the opportunity to hear Napoléon speak from beyond the grave. In *L'Aigle républicaine*, with the air of an irascible elderly uncle Napoléon's ghost complained that he was waiting for his nephew in Paris, but 'you remain *provisionally* in London'. Then the ghost became bogged down in travel logistics, explaining that if he wanted, he could go to London, but he chose to stay in France. Just in case the idea of the dead Napoléon sending a letter from Paris to London came across as absurd, his uncle explained that it was being sent via a trustworthy eagle.

Part of the reason he had not come to London, clarified Napoléon's spectre, was because he preferred Paris. Each night he would set up his headquarters atop the Vendôme column and look down, but the tumultuous street politics below worried him. Not missing a chance for self-promotion, Napoléon's ghost reminded his nephew about his memoirs. With suspicious precision, he urged him to open volume six at page fifty. Just in case Louis-Napoléon did not have it to hand, the ghost helpfully quoted the relevant passage (death must have affected his memory, because the reference was incorrect): when society is in danger, Napoléon had said, 'it seems to look for a man who can save it'.[13] For those who feared an imperial restoration, this was not reassuring: it was Napoléon's justification for launching the *coup d'état* in 1799 that saw him become dictator.

The government was worried. It ramped up attempts to exclude Louis-Napoléon, claiming the Republic was in danger, a Bonapartist plot imminent. Persigny was locked up, to be on the safe side. The day of the vote on whether he should be excluded, many predicted, would turn into a street battle between supporters of the pretender and the Republic. When Louis-Napoléon heard in London about the sensation he was causing in Paris, he hurriedly penned a letter, handing it to his secretary, who arrived in Paris hours before the debate began. 'I desire order,' wrote Louis-Napoléon, 'and the maintenance of a wise, great republic; and since, involuntarily, I am the excuse for disorder, I place, not without deep regret, my resignation in your hands.'[14]

It was a masterstroke. His opponents weakly protested that as he had never taken his seat, he could not resign, but Louis-Napoléon had out-manoeuvred his enemies. The more the government had tried to prevent him taking his seat, the more he became the people's champion. Now he could once again play the wrongly persecuted loyal citizen. Staying in London proved serendipitous for another reason. Days afterwards, violence broke out in Paris on a scale far beyond anything that had happened during the February Revolution.

———

The first barricades went up on Friday morning, 23 June. Workers, the poor, the unemployed, women as well as men, many very young, were determined to resist the government, which had announced that the National Workshops were to be wound down. The right to work had been a cornerstone of the February Revolution and the workshops provided jobs, but they were inefficient and expensive. For many in Paris, though, they were the only source of income. For weeks, rumours of royalist plots, deliberate plans to starve the people and politicians in the pay of Russia or, worse, Britain had resounded through the streets. Closing the workshops was proof: the reaction had begun and, it seemed to the dispossessed of Paris, the revolution had been stolen, again.

At one barricade, National Guardsmen rushed the defenders. They were met with a volley of bullets; the cobblestones were strewn with the blood and bodies of the attackers. They prepared to take the barricade a second time. Then, Victor Hugo recorded, 'a woman appeared on the top of the barricade, a young, beautiful, dishevelled woman. This woman, who was a streetwalker, raised her dress up to the waist and shouted at the National

Guards in the horrible brothel-language that has to be translated: Cowards. Fire, if you dare, at the belly of a woman!'

As Hugo noted with understatement, 'here the story gets ghastly'. The guardsmen did not hesitate. Bullets smashed into the woman, who fell, screaming. Silence. Then 'a second woman appeared. She was younger and even more beautiful . . . barely seventeen years old . . . It was another streetwalker. She raised her dress, showed her belly and cried: Fire away brigands!' They fired and she fell, riddled with bullets, on the body of the first woman. 'That is how the war began.'

Or *possibly* began; the line between fiction and reality was a fine one for Hugo, frequently crossed, and his account of attractive sex workers heroically, if rather ineffectually, defying the forces of order is likely to have been embellished. But France's greatest poet and novelist witnessed first hand the desperate fighting between the government and the rebels. He had been voted into the Assembly in the same by-elections as Louis-Napoléon. Unlike Louis-Napoléon, he had taken his seat, and now he was crushing the people who had elected him.

On Saturday 24 June, at about 2 p.m., Hugo was leading the National Guard into battle. 'Let's get it over boys,' cried Hugo. 'We'll lose fewer men if we march bravely toward the danger. Forward!' Unarmed, Hugo advanced down the middle of the street. His men were less brave, or more sensible, and took cover as they moved. One of them tugged at Hugo's sleeve and shouted, 'You'll get yourself killed!'

'That is why I am here,' Hugo cheerfully replied, before shouting, 'Forward!' The barricade was taken; pretty 'streetwalkers' were noticeable by their absence.[15]

Known as the June Days, the struggle saw the government repress the uprising and kill some three thousand Parisians, leaving an indelible mark on French politics. Across the Channel, Louis-Napoléon's absence from the scene meant he was well placed to exploit the controversies that arose from the slaughter, but the fighting eclipsed the furore over his election to the Assembly earlier in the month. Indeed, once the streets of Paris returned to what passed for normal in the febrile post-revolutionary atmosphere, his dramatic arrival on the political scene was followed by an almost as dramatic silence.

For political elites, this vanishing act proved that the Bonapartists' demonstrations were conjured up by gold; Louis-Napoléon was an idiot who had shone brightly but, happily, briefly. What they knew of him, they did not like. 'His stature is hardly suitable for the part that he is expected to play,' wrote one French monarchist who knew Louis-Napoléon in London. 'Imagine a little man of four and a half feet, ugly and vulgar, with large moustaches and the eyes of a pig!' This tiny porcine man also had loose morals, explained the Frenchman: 'He lives openly . . . with a fifteenth-rate actress, very beautiful admittedly, named Miss Howard; this behaviour, which has slowly closed the doors of London high society to him, casts him out and pushes him into the world of low-class actors.' Worse, continued the observer, if by some freakish accident he came to play a role in French politics, 'he would lean on the Socialist Communist Party, perhaps even on the Red Republicans'.[16] Another leading monarchist put his view more succinctly, if more damningly: 'What dominates in him is insignificance.'[17]

In London, where Louis-Napoléon was biding his time for his re-entry into French public life, it was not just 'low-class actors'; there were society engagements as well as riding in the park and trips to theatres – public appearances kept up in part to disprove rumours that he was incognito in Paris. In the evening, he would take his dog Ham for a walk before picking up the latest editions of the newspapers from Burlington Arcade, Piccadilly. Here, he sat, read, analysed. Fresh by-elections for the Assembly in September, he decided, were the time to throw his name back into French politics.

Once again, Louis-Napoléon had no national newspaper backing him and his low-key campaign relied on his friends writing short manifestos, publishing his ideas and putting up posters. These promised all things to all men: Louis-Napoléon would revive the economy, improve the lot of workers and reduce the burdens of taxation and army conscription. The glory of his uncle was front and centre: 'by the application of Napoleonic ideas', he would 'make France as rich and as great by its commerce and industry as it was powerful by its arms forty years ago'.[18] In short, the repeated refrain was that he would make France great again.

This repetitive message worked. In the September elections, Louis-Napoléon was returned in five regions, most strikingly in Paris. Here, untainted by involvement in the June Days, to some he represented order, while to others he was a radical. He was elected in first place, receiving 110,752 out of 262,000 votes. When the result was read out at the Hôtel de Ville, National Guardsmen played an old imperial song – that the chorus demanded 'liberty' and warned all tyrants to tremble showed that this was revolutionary, popular Bonapartism – and crowds cheered, shouting, '*Vive l'empereur!*'[19]

When news of his election reached him in London, Louis-Napoléon immediately departed for Paris with such haste, so his landlord claimed, that he left the water in his bath and his bed unmade. He arrived quietly and took up residence in the palatial Hôtel du Rhin, near the Place Vendôme, where his uncle's statue, if not his ghost, watched over him.

———

On 26 September, there was great anticipation for Louis-Napoléon's first public appearance in the Assembly. As he entered the chamber from a side door during a speech, all eyes turned to him. Showing no emotion, he walked in with an old friend, also a representative, and sat down alongside moderate republicans. Hushed conversations drowned the words of the speaker – nobly ploughing on – as fascinated deputies nudged each other and pointed out the infamous imperial pretender whom the government had so feared that it had tried to prevent him taking his seat months earlier.

After the formality of his election was confirmed, Louis-Napoléon asked to speak. The president indicated the tribune, and calmly, as all stared at him, he walked to the platform. Taking a piece of paper from his pocket, he read a banal speech in an unplaceable foreign accent declaring his loyalty to the Republic, which was met with polite applause. The only thing remarkable about the whole affair was how unremarkable it was. 'He is a man of ordinary height, with a slightly awkward gait, an impassive face and no other distinction than a pair of long, abundantly furnished moustaches,' opined one newspaper. Another reported that he has 'a modest attitude, and he has no resemblance to the emperor whatsoever', before wondering what all the fuss had been about. For republicans and monarchists fearing the Empire would be restored, it was a relief. 'The so-called imperialist party', concluded one article, 'was dissolved today. Disavowed by its leader, it cannot raise its head without being shattered by the most odious, bloody reproach of hypocrisy.'[20] The effect of Louis-Napoléon's entry into French politics was, a British editorial declared, 'flatter than the flattest of flat beer'. Rumours 'of the approaching doom of the Republic, and dreams of the speedy proclamation of NAPOLEON III, by the grace of GOD, and the will of the people, Emperor of the French' had been greatly exaggerated.[21]

If Louis-Napoléon's first foray into parliamentary politics had merely been underwhelming, his second was disastrous. He had one eye on the presidential elections scheduled for December, and on 9 October, a representative put forward a motion before the Assembly that would end Louis-Napoléon's political ambitions if it passed. It stated that no one whose family had previously ruled France could be elected president. During the debate, one speaker pointed at Louis-Napoléon and questioned his loyalty to the Republic. At this, all eyes turned towards Louis-Napoléon, who stood up and mounted the tribune to shouts of 'Speak! Speak!'

In a faltering voice, nerves making his accent more pronounced, Louis-Napoléon stumbled through a few words, not, as he said, to speak against the amendment, but to reject the word 'pretender' that 'people always throw at me'.[22] With this, he abruptly finished, casting an anxious eye around the Assembly like a schoolboy before his classmates, not quite sure whether he has read out the right paragraph, before returning – the chamber in stunned silence at this underwhelming, petulant performance – to his seat. With a mocking tone, the man who had proposed the amendment now announced to the Assembly that after witnessing Louis-Napoléon speak, he realised it was unnecessary and withdrew the motion, much to the amusement of the chamber. As he left the Assembly, one former member of the provisional government was overheard muttering, 'What an imbecile, he is sunk!'[23]

The press enormously enjoyed this public humiliation, particularly the opprobrium – familiar to any tourist who has tried to speak French in Paris – that his Swiss German-accented French provoked. One newspaper wrote that Louis-Napoléon 'barely said a few words, and yet his voice failed him more than once . . . [It was] a laborious speech, delivered with a foreign accent.' Before printing his words, the article joked, 'We are forced to translate, because it was not precisely in French that he spoke.' With less than sincere concern, the newspaper continued, 'We do not want to be too cruel towards a man' condemned to this contradiction: 'such inadequacy and such a name'.[24]

Yet as Louis-Napoléon well understood – and more illustrious rhetoricians did not – there was much more to mass democratic politics than parliamentary speeches. This was especially the case given that it had been decided that the president would be directly elected. Pre-empting this decision, Louis-Napoléon met with political leaders to prepare the way for running. He started on the far left, speaking with, among others, the bête noire of the bourgeoisie, Pierre-Joseph Proudhon, of 'property is theft' fame.[25] The conversation was amiable and, as was his wont, Louis-Napoléon said little and listened much. After the meeting, Proudhon noted in his diary that Louis-Napoléon 'appears well intentioned, chivalrous head and heart; more filled with the glory of his uncle than with a strong ambition. At the same time, a mediocre intellect.'[26] Proudhon remained suspicious, but his doubts over Louis-Napoléon's republican convictions were somewhat allayed.

Not long afterwards, Louis-Napoléon met with a newspaper proprietor who so identified with the middle classes that he titled his autobiography *Memoirs of a Bourgeois*. A pot-bellied scrofulous eccentric, Louis-Désiré Véron had done everything from hawking medical ointments to directing the Paris opera. Now he owned an influential conservative daily. Over dinner, Louis-Napoléon reassured Véron, who was alarmed at his supposed socialist leanings, that before social reform could be attempted it was necessary to reseat society on its 'eternal bases' and revive in all hearts 'respect for the law, order, property, [and] family'.[27] That the man who thought property was theft, Proudhon, and the man who thought property was sacred, Véron, came away charmed by Louis-Napoléon was testament to his skill as a politician.

He also secured an endorsement from the one man in France whose celebrity rivalled the name Napoléon. A year earlier, before the revolution, Victor Hugo, speaking in the French parliament, had fanned the embers of Napoleonic memory, saying: 'When seeing the misery of the present, I think about the great things of the past and, now and then, I'm tempted to say to the Chamber, to the press, to all of France: Look, let's talk about the emperor, it will do us some good!'[28] Hugo, whose political journey had taken him from ultra-royalist to moderate republican and would soon see him join the radical left, had supported every regime in France, from the Bourbons to the Second Republic. Now he adopted Louis-Napoléon in almost spiritual terms, because 'since 1815 the people have waited for Napoléon. Plunged into ignorance and suffering, they need an ideal, a vision, a love: this ideal, this vision, this love is the emperor . . . The city and countryside eternally dream of the great things of the Empire.'[29]

Hugo, though, was in a minority. Most republicans were intensely suspicious of Louis-Napoléon. But they could not scrutinise him in the Assembly because he rarely attended sessions, which, aside from shielding him from making speeches, ensured he did not alienate voters by coming down on one side in controversial issues. When necessary, he relied on the more eloquent Plon-Plon to defend him in the chamber. For committed republicans, this contempt for parliament was unacceptable. In the Assembly during a session in late October, one of their number remarked on Louis-Napoléon's absence, noting it was not the first time he was not there – 'He is never here!' shouted another politician from the floor, which was met with laughter. With Plon-Plon and the few other Bonapartists in the chamber shouting at him, the republican pressed on. Since his cousin seems to respond here for Louis-Napoléon, said the representative, 'I will ask him if it is not true that official agents [of Louis-Napoléon] travel through . . . France . . . to put forward his cousin's candidature, by addressing to the least enlightened part of the population and supporting his candidature on the most absurd promises.'[30] At this point all semblance of order broke down, not least because another of Louis-Napoléon's cousins, Pierre Bonaparte, once New York's finest bar brawler and an alleged dog killer, joined Plon-Plon to shout abuse from the foot of the tribune.

Such a sensation required a response, and the next day, Louis-Napoléon did come and speak to the Assembly. Prepared this time, he read from a piece of paper. He said that the regrettable scenes of yesterday had forced him to appear. 'Of what am I accused?' he asked. 'Of accepting from the popular sentiment a candidature which I did not seek? Well, yes, I accept this candidature which does me honour; I accept it because . . . France regards the name I bear as one able to serve the consolidation of society shaken to its foundations.' Though it had long been rumoured, Louis-Napoléon had until now held back from publicly confirming that he would stand for president. The announcement caused a commotion. After the president of the Assembly calmed the noise, Louis-Napoléon continued. 'How little those who accuse me of ambition know my heart! If an imperious duty did not keep me here, if the sympathy of my fellow citizens did not console me for the animosity with which I am attacked . . . I would long ago have regretted my return from exile.' He then told the Assembly he would not deviate from the path he had traced for himself, nor would he respond to personal attacks; he would not speak when he wanted to remain silent. 'I have but one object – it is to deserve the esteem of the Assembly.'[31]

The Assembly, however, was far from holding him in esteem, and its members certainly did not believe him when he said he lacked ambition. After his speech, a republican accosted him. We cannot support you, he said, because 'you will march towards a monarchy; for what impels you forward is the ignorance of the country people'.

'But Monsieur,' replied Louis-Napoléon, 'must not attention be paid to the majority?'

No, not if they could not be trusted to vote the right way, responded the republican. 'Look at the poor country people,' he continued, 'on whose votes you reckon':

> They have in their humble cottages plaster busts and coloured
> prints . . . and the . . . prints which are now hawked about from village
> to village, and from workshop to workshop, paid for by I know not
> whom, what period of the life of your uncle do they represent? . . . It is
> the grey greatcoat of the emperor . . . That, Sir, is why no sincere and
> enlightened Republican will vote for you.[32]

At that, Louis-Napoléon turned and walked away without replying.

Louis-Napoléon's declaration announced what people had known for weeks: the presidential race would be between two main candidates, the nephew of Napoléon Bonaparte and the son of a radical republican revolutionary, General Louis-Eugène Cavaignac, a military man who masterminded the crushing of the June Days uprising and was appointed head of state afterwards. The election was set for 10 December. The battle for who would govern France had begun.

————

When exiled in London, Louis-Napoléon took hot chocolate in bed before rousing himself at midday. Then, dressing himself in the most expensive and luxurious clothes money could buy, he went to study the poses of the archangel of dandies, the comte d'Orsay, before going to Newmarket racecourse to gamble. Back in the city, he had dinner with a dancer of questionable morals picked up from a cheap theatre. Later, he opened the dancing at one of the Duke of Wellington's soirées. Was this, asked one anti-Bonapartist tract whose parody of his daily routine in London was surprisingly accurate, the man whom France would elect as its president? 'Yes, if France, like a prostitute, unties her belt of virtue and tramples ten centuries of immortality under its feet.'[33]

'There is in this world an adventurer without spirit, without talent, without merit of any kind,' ran a newspaper editorial similarly unenamoured with Louis-Napoléon, 'so foreign to France that he can barely stutter its language.' In his forty years, opined another article, Louis-Napoléon has shown only 'levity, incompetence and stupidity'.[34] A fellow representative was equally horrified: 'You are the most negligent and the most inept member of the Assembly.' But perhaps worst of all, Louis-Napoléon had lived the 'effeminate life of an English aristocrat'.[35]

This was but a small sample of the hysterical deluge of vitriol, outrage and disbelief that poured from the pens of French writers and politicians in the national and regional press after Louis-Napoléon announced his candidature. British newspapers were similarly incredulous. *The Times*, such a respected commentator that even French readers took it seriously, asked in an editorial who would be the president of France. 'We will venture to predict that whoever this historical personage may turn out to be, his name will most assuredly not be Louis Napoleon,' trumpeted the paper.[36]

This was a view many French observers shared. As one satirical paper pointed out, Louis-Napoléon's only virtue was that he was his uncle's nephew, something he shared with all nephews who had uncles. The comparison with Napoléon was caricatured relentlessly in political cartoons.

Louis-Napoléon was drawn with a conspicuous nose and moustache, head slouched into his shoulders and small in stature. He was dressed in clothes symbolic of his uncle, the bicorne hat, greatcoat and military boots invariably too big, reinforcing the idea that he was a mannequin unworthy of the imperial mantle he claimed. People were constantly reminded of the failed *coups d'état*, especially the 1840 Boulogne one – the accompanying eagle became a minor celebrity. Also featuring prominently were Louis-Napoléon's participation in the faux-medieval tournament in Scotland and his service as a special constable in London, two vignettes from his life that seemed especially bizarre to a French audience. On one poster urging people to vote for him, someone had scrawled 'ex-London policeman'.

The nephew's exploits were juxtaposed with his uncle's glorious deeds, but in doing so the attacks revealed something about the French political landscape. The derision poured on Louis-Napoléon required the Napoleonic legend to be burnished. Such was the emperor's pull, and the allure of an empire gone for over thirty years, that even Louis-Napoléon's bitterest opponents could not escape its gravity.

For while educated elites were laughing at Louis-Napoléon, far more people were enjoying the Bonapartist propaganda that flooded every city, town, village and cottage. He was adopted as the anti-establishment candidate. After all, regardless of whether he had been or not, many believed Napoléon had been on the side of the people, and so his nephew probably was too. Furthermore, there was little love for Cavaignac. There had been a deeply unpopular tax rise, and Cavaignac had played a key role in the massacre that was the June Days – there was little positive voters could point to after the February Revolution. Cavaignac was continuity; Louis-Napoléon was change.

Grassroots support for Louis-Napoléon began to swell. He may not have been an impressive speaker, but he got others to do the demagoguery for him. 'Every moment of his life has been devoted to progress,' one Bonapartist declared in a speech at a packed meeting in a working-class district of Paris. It had been 'the ambitious and the incapable' who plunged France into chaos. 'Citizens! let us restore this beautiful country to its splendour . . . What do we need for this? A man around whom we can rally.'

Another rabble-rousing speech gave a much more positive spin on his life than the one beloved of republican satirists. In Italy, he had put himself at the head of revolution and 'paid his debt to the holy cause of oppressed peoples'; he had wanted to fight for Poland, 'another debt paid to the cause of people struggling with their tyrants'. This was met with ecstatic applause. The Bonapartes, the speaker continued, 'emerged like all of us from the ranks of the people, [and] have never forgotten their origin'. More, 'the most exquisite goodness reigns among them: no arrogance, no pride, always affable, always compassionate', a characterisation of the family that would have surprised its members. As for Strasbourg and Boulogne, these were glorious attempts. 'Did he present himself as emperor? No . . . read his proclamations. Is this the language of a pretender? Is it not that of a committed democrat?'

'Yes! Yes!' shouted the crowd in response.

'Universal suffrage was proclaimed by him in 1836 and 1840. The men of 1848 were only his imitators.' At this point, cheers broke out. 'It's true! It's true!' bellowed the audience. After running through his time in prison, and making much of his work *The Extinction of Pauperism*, the speaker asked his audience, 'Will you still doubt, citizens, the feelings and sympathies of our candidate in favour of the people?'

'No! No! Long live Louis-Napoléon!' came the inevitable response.[37]

———

Yet apart from Hugo, Louis-Napoléon had few well-known names behind him. As his campaign gathered grassroots momentum, it gained more prominent backers. These included one of France's most influential politicians, Adolphe Thiers. He conducted the conservative monarchist majority in the Assembly, which had become known as the 'Party of Order'. Thiers had played a leading role in Louis-Philippe's ascent to the throne during the 1830 Revolution. In 1848, he hoped to perform the role of kingmaker once again, though this time with a president.

It was not, however, his positive qualities that attracted Thiers to Louis-Napoléon; rather, it was his perceived stupidity. The word 'cretin', frequently attributed to Thiers, may never have been uttered, but it certainly reflected what he thought of the presidential candidate. Thiers believed Louis-Napoléon was a playboy who could be distracted with women while Thiers and his backers ran the country. Louis-Napoléon was, therefore, a useful idiot, his presidency a stepping stone to a royalist restoration. On 15 November, Thiers's influential newspaper came out in his favour.

Thiers and his friends then set about moulding their candidate, but discovered he was not a man to bend to the will of others. Louis-Napoléon had been working on his manifesto and read it out to Thiers. Shocked at what he thought were nods to socialism, and at what he perceived as inelegant French, Thiers demanded changes. The finest minds of the Party of Order rewrote it and sent it to Louis-Napoléon for approval. A few days later, Thiers came to see Louis-Napoléon and asked to hear the new manifesto. Taking the document out of his drawer, Louis-Napoléon read it. Bar a few words, it was exactly the same as the one Thiers found so objectionable.

'This is unacceptable!' cried Thiers. If Louis-Napoléon presented France with such projects, Thiers warned, then he would need to find another party to support him. 'France does not know you. Your nomination is, or will be, due to the name that you carry,' said Thiers. 'Let's cut to the chase, people consider you incapable,' and, he warned, if Louis-Napoléon published the manifesto he had just read, he would do nothing to disabuse them of that notion.[38] Thiers had decades of experience, he had advised Louis-Philippe, he had been a minister, and now he was stunned that this imbecile was defying his political judgement. But Louis-Napoléon had already defied Thiers over a recommendation to shave his moustache, and when the manifesto was published, it was Louis-Napoléon's words, not those of the Party of Order.

Louis-Napoléon's version was a much more concise, simple and effective document than the verbose one Thiers recommended. First, Louis-Napoléon drew attention to his name, which was a 'symbol of order and security', before acknowledging that it was his uncle, 'the emperor', who inspired the people's votes and protected him. 'I am not an ambitious man,' Louis-Napoléon claimed, somewhat insincerely, 'who sometimes dreams of the Empire and war and sometimes of the application of subversive theories.' Rather, he would dedicate himself to preserving society – a reference to the June Days and showing voters he would deal firmly with any similar insurrection – and to the consolidation of the Republic. To soothe worries about an imperial restoration, he added, 'I should consider it a point of honour leaving, after four years, to my successor, power strengthened; freedom intact, real progress accomplished.'

His vision was to reconcile the parties of France and defend the sacred principles of religion, family and property, but he also promised reforms to improve people's lives. In terms of foreign policy, he proclaimed peace, while warning that France would not be weak. The army, so long neglected, he wrote, would be respected. 'The Republic', he continued, 'ought to be generous,' and he yearned for the day when there would be no persecutions, which dangled the possibility of an amnesty for the thousands of political prisoners locked up or deported after the June Days.

With the conclusion of his manifesto Louis-Napoléon showed his popular political instincts were better calibrated than those of his new conservative friends. Thiers's version concluded on the anodyne note that if he lost the election, Louis-Napoléon would serve the Republic in a lesser role. Louis-Napoléon, however, went for a far more inspiring denouement: 'I am aware the task is difficult and the mission immense,' but, he continued, 'when one has the honour of being placed at the head of the French people, there is an infallible way to do good: it is to will it'.[39]

Published on 27 November, this optimistic and patriotic manifesto was a political masterclass that had something for everyone. Outside Louis-Napoléon's hotel, huge crowds gathered – many in shabby clothes, showing his appeal to the poor – to catch a glimpse of the man of the people. At 1 p.m., when his carriage appeared, there was a surge forward. The people blocked the way, and the driver was forced to go the long way round the Vendôme column as the throng shouted, '*Vive Napoléon!* We must have him and no other!'[40]

His electoral committee was relentless. For Persigny, the presidential campaign was akin to ushering in the Second Coming and he stopped at nothing to will his dream into reality. He ensured that Bonapartist agents pounded the streets in Paris, visited political clubs and cafes, and preached to the poor in hard-drinking cabarets. Outrageous promises were made, and rumours were not denied – one was that Louis-Napoléon was so wealthy that he would personally pay the national debt. Persigny also oversaw the distribution of campaign material, had new editions of *The Extinction of Pauperism* printed, raised money and ensured that what he was doing in Paris was repeated across France.

In the week before the election, though, it was still not clear who would win – not least because the constitution stipulated that the president must get over half of the votes cast. If no candidate secured the required majority, then the choice would go to the Assembly, which would vote for Cavaignac. Turnout was expected to be around four to five million, meaning that to win outright Louis-Napoléon would need to get more than two million votes, a huge figure most believed impossible, especially as, besides Cavaignac, there were numerous other candidates who would split the vote.

———

On Sunday 10 December, the weather was unseasonably warm as the largest experiment in democracy thus far in history took place. Trouble had been expected, especially in Paris, which had attracted British tourists hoping to see revolutionary violence. But as one foreign correspondent remarked with disappointment, 'We continue here in a most uninteresting state of tranquillity.'[41] There was plenty of drinking, though, which provided an unscientific exit poll in the capital: the raucous songs, unsteady, rambling street orations and alcohol-fuelled chants were almost all for Louis-Napoléon.

In villages across France, people were having tremendous fun exercising their newfound democratic right. Many dressed up as the Emperor Napoléon, with bicorne hat, riding boots and greatcoat, and then marched in procession to cast their vote. In a small provincial town, others carried a bust of the emperor before them and, fearful of disturbances, a local official called for a squadron of cavalry to police the procession. It arrived as the people were crying, '*Vive Louis-Napoléon!*'[42] To the dismay of the authorities, the cavalrymen joined in the shouts.

Scenes like this were repeated across the country, as the French people in their droves vented their anger at the political class, be it republican or monarchist. The government, local notables, much of the press had urged people to vote for Cavaignac, but as they went to the polls many shouted, 'Down with Caviagnac!' and 'Down with the rich!'[43] Louis-Napoléon, born into imperial splendour, with wealth beyond the imagination of most of the people who voted for him, a man who had lived the high life of the English dandy through the recent awful winters in France when many faced starvation, had successfully positioned himself as the anti-establishment candidate.

As soon as the polls closed, it was clear to even the staunchest republican that Louis-Napoléon would not only win, but also get the majority required to prevent the decision reverting to the Assembly, the last-ditch hope for an elite stitch-up. Even so, when the official results were confirmed, the enormity of Louis-Napoléon's victory was astonishing.

On the metric of recorded votes, Louis-Napoléon was the most popular man in history up to 1848, receiving more than 5.5 million. In terms of votes for an individual, it would not be surpassed until the 1892 US presidential election. Cavaignac managed just under 1.5 million; Lamartine, the hero in February, a humiliating 17,914. It was a sensational victory: 75 per cent of those who voted did so for Louis-Napoléon. 'It is not an election,' wrote one French commentator, 'it is an acclamation.'[44]

But for many elites, right and left, this was the outpouring of irrational, poorly educated public opinion. Given the centrality of universal male suffrage to French politics in 1848, no politician could openly state it, but most would have agreed with *The Times*'s analysis: 'The very existence of Louis Napoleon as a candidate is in itself proof of the uses to which popular ignorance, invested with full political rights, may be turned.'[45]

For Louis-Napoléon, who at the beginning of the year had looked forward to little more than finishing his history of artillery in London, it was a remarkable change in fortune. It was also, at least partially, the fulfilment of what he had long believed – and been oft ridiculed for: that it was his destiny to rule France. Thirty-three years after his uncle had been defeated at Waterloo, another Bonaparte was the French head of state.

But as the country was beset with enormous challenges, and Paris with endemic political violence, many expected his fall to be as spectacularly swift as his rise. Not only that, but even if he was not overthrown and made it to the end of his term, panicked at the prospect of Louis-Napoléon winning the election, the Assembly had passed a law limiting his power: the president could not be re-elected and elections for a new president would take place in 1852. Louis-Napoléon's victory, therefore, announced the beginning of a three-way power struggle between republicans, monarchists and Louis-Napoléon over who would control France.

9

THE CHOSEN ONE

At 4 p.m. on Thursday 20 December 1848, as darkness was falling over Paris and the chandeliers were lowered in the Palais Bourbon, where the Assembly sat, the newly elected president walked into the chamber. Silence transformed into hushed whispers as some nine hundred representatives muttered their opinions on Louis-Napoléon. One of them, Victor Hugo, noted with an eye for melodrama that it 'was the future that was entering, an unknown future'.[1] After swearing to uphold the Republic's constitution, the unknown future took a piece of paper from his pocket and promised to be a lawful president. 'The suffrages of the nation, and the oath I have just taken, command my future conduct . . . I will see as the enemies of the country any who seek to change, by illegal means, that which all France has established.'[2]

There were many in the Assembly who doubted his sincerity. After all, Louis-Napoléon had made it his life's mission to restore his uncle's Empire, a hereditary monarchy. Persigny had already urged Louis-Napoléon to do exactly that; however, the new president had no desire to begin his presidency with a *coup d'état*. He was content to rule France as the elect of some 5.5 million Frenchmen, for the time being. For a veteran politician, this would be an enormous challenge. For Louis-Napoléon, who had no experience of government, let alone France, it was even harder. The left distrusted him; the right wanted to see the Republic fail and hoped for a monarchist restoration.

The people who voted for him were more optimistic. At the Bonapartist and Democratic Banquet, organised at a restaurant in a working-class district of Paris, hundreds of workers, bourgeois and even some peasants had gathered to celebrate the election of their man. During the banquet, a veteran of the Napoleonic wars, at least sixty years old and wearing his archaic Napoleonic uniform, was holding court. His hair was a brilliant white, his face as lined as the map of Europe he had fought over as a young man. Eyes black and sparkling, he told larger-than-life tales of his time in the French army.

After he had eaten, he stood to speak and proposed a toast to Louis-Napoléon, but 'without forgetting the other one'. The other one, needless to say, was the Emperor Napoléon. Then he reeled off a perfect military salute, which was greeted with delighted applause. The band played the 'Marseillaise' three times, and there was much discussion of Louis-Napoléon's determination to ensure free primary education, followed by more toasts to the president. As one journalist noted, however, though they toasted the Republic, they were 'equally, perhaps more, desirous of a government which will present a hope of durability'.[3]

In this snapshot of the president's supporters were all the contradictions of his appeal. The 'Marseillaise', a subversive and revolutionary song for which Louis-Napoléon had little love, was sung after paeans to the authoritarian Empire of Napoléon. Popular policies were discussed, democracy was celebrated, but the theories of socialism and communism were denounced. And Louis-Napoléon was championed as the president of the Republic, but the Republic itself engendered little enthusiasm. In their political eclecticism and wide demographic, the banqueters reflected Bonapartism itself, a heterogeneous and contradictory mix of ideas with an even more disparate constituency that spanned militaristic reactionaries and radical democrats.

These latter were disappointed when Louis-Napoléon appointed his cabinet. Unable to choose men from the Assembly devoted to his cause because there were none, he drew on those from the Party of Order, which dominated in the Assembly and took its lead from Thiers. The man who headed Louis-Napoléon's government also had Thiers's backing: Odilon Barrot, a man of moderate liberal views who had led the opposition in parliament against King Louis-Philippe. The rest of the ministers were there as much to keep an eye on Louis-Napoléon as to serve him – jailers, as one contemporary called them. Barrot, his fellow ministers and Thiers, however, found that Louis-Napoléon was far from the pliable pleasure seeker they had hoped to manipulate. One of his first demands as president was to read secret files relating to his two failed *coups d'état*. The minister of the interior refused. Louis-Napoléon insisted and the minister resigned.

Willing to dispense with ministers if they got in his way, Louis-Napoléon showed incredible loyalty to those close to him, refusing to discard family and friends regardless of the embarrassment they caused. Few were more embarrassing than his uncle Jérôme and his cousin Plon-Plon, but Louis-Napoléon appointed Jérôme to the honorific and well-paid position of governor of the Invalides; Plon-Plon became ambassador to Spain; the president's former fiancée, Mathilde, hosted balls and receptions.

Even worse for the French political establishment, at the Élysée Palace, the presidential residence, Louis-Napoléon surrounded himself with men who should never have been close to power, let alone in it. These were his devoted followers, those misfits who had dedicated themselves to his conspiracies in exile. Persigny, Armand Laity – both of whom had served time in prison – and Claude-Nicolas Vaudrey, who as an officer had committed treason at Strasbourg on Louis-Napoléon's behalf in 1836, were appointed as aides-de-camp and given the *légion d'honneur*. The rarefied world of elite Parisian politics had nothing but contempt for what Alexis de Tocqueville described as Louis-Napoléon's penchant for the 'footman class'. It was just about understandable that, *faute de mieux*, in his twenty years of conspiring the president had surrounded himself with 'low-class adventurers, men of ruined fortunes or blemished reputations, and young debauchees'. But, continued Tocqueville, disdain dripping from his pen, that he 'continued to take pleasure in this inferior company after he was no longer obliged to live in it' was contemptible.[4] Thiers described the Élysée as smothered in a 'cloud of vice, cigar smoke and debauchery'.[5]

Most shockingly, Louis-Napoléon had brought his English lover, Harriet Howard, to Paris. Inaugurating a tradition many subsequent French presidents have honoured, Louis-Napoléon kept his mistress close to the Élysée: a gate from the palace's garden opened onto the rue de Cirque, where Harriet had a house. Even more scandalously, when Louis-Napoléon toured France, she came with him. One outraged civil servant complained he had to provide lodgings for the presidential mistress. 'I admit myself culpable of seeking, in an illegitimate liaison, the love my heart needs,' wrote an angry Louis-Napoléon, responding to the complaint. 'I may well, I believe, be pardoned an affection which does no one any harm and which I make no attempt to proclaim.' He then turned his ire on the civil servant. 'If he believes, as he says, that his house is polluted by the presence of a woman who is not married, I pray you let him know that, for my part, I regret intensely that a person capable of such pure devotion, and of so high a character, should have by chance fallen upon a house where, under the mask of religion, reigns only the ostentation of self-righteous virtue without Christian charity.'[6]

In Paris, the president's routine was far from that of a workaholic. Rising at a leisurely hour, he took his time getting ready before attending to government business from noon. If his ministers are to be believed, and they did not like him much, he presided over cabinet meetings, but rarely contributed to discussions. Instead, he busied himself by folding paper into intricate shapes or doodling on state documents. Then in the afternoon he went out riding, or took a drive with Harriet in the Bois de Boulogne, after which they would have a rum in a cafe. He would retire to her house on the rue de Cirque in the evenings with a few close friends, cigarette in one hand, cup of tea or coffee in the other and beloved black dog at his feet. Evenings not spent with her were passed at official functions, at the theatre or wooing other women.

Surrounded by his coterie of eccentrics, spending time with an English mistress yet still far too involved in the governing of France and surrounded by his feckless relatives, Louis-Napoléon's first few weeks in office had done little to convince Thiers and his conservative backers that he was the man who should head the majesty of the French state. Given a choice between Louis-Napoléon and revolution, however, they rallied behind the president – and on Monday 29 January 1849, these men, in their terror, looked to the president to save them.

————

The Mountain – the group of radical representatives in the Assembly – saw Louis-Napoléon's cabinet of conservative monarchists as the counter-revolution. This fear was confirmed for them when a bill was introduced in January 1849 to dissolve the Assembly. As this was still the constituent assembly mostly elected the previous year for the purpose of creating a new constitution, this was not unreasonable. The Mountain, however, saw the dissolution as a prelude to a *coup d'état*, though whether it would be a royalist or a Bonapartist one was unclear. On Saturday 27 January, therefore, the socialist Pierre-Joseph Proudhon issued a call to arms: the president 'posed the question of the dissolution of the Assembly', harangued Proudhon in print, and 'this Monday, the Assembly will pose the question of the resignation of the President'.[7]

On Monday, Parisians awoke to rain, and the sound of drums beating, calling the National Guard out onto the streets. The man in charge of Paris's military forces, General Nicolas Changarnier, was taking no chances. Thousands of cavalry lined the Champs-Élysées; artillery covered the Place de la Concorde and cannonballs were stacked into pyramids; National Guardsmen were picketed on street corners; at the Palais Bourbon, where the Assembly sat, a thicket of steel bayonets surrounded the building. At 2 p.m., the expected mob appeared; however, the people were unarmed and few in number. The overwhelming display of force had worked. After a few cavalry charges, the crowd dispersed.

In the Élysée, Louis-Napoléon displayed sangfroid and leadership. At 2.30 p.m., he rode through the streets of Paris. With an escort of twelve cavalrymen and some aides-de-camp, he trotted along the boulevards. When the people heard that he was on the streets, an immense crowd gathered, cries of '*Vive Napoléon!*' louder than those of '*Vive la République!*'.

Changarnier, however, wanted more. He was a man of the right – he once quipped he hated fraternity so much that if he had a brother, he would call him 'cousin' – and he would have preferred a monarchy to a republic. He believed now was the time to crush the left and launch a *coup d'état*. In a secret meeting with Louis-Napoléon and Thiers that same day, this was discussed. Much to Changarnier's displeasure, Louis-Napoléon was against it. Turning to Thiers and indicating the president, Changarnier said, 'He's a . . .'[8] The person who recorded the conversation politely left out the word, but it likely began with a 'c' in English and in French. Changarnier felt that Louis-Napoléon had missed the moment to make himself emperor.

But Louis-Napoléon was happy, for now, as president. As his triumphal ride through the streets of Paris showed, Changarnier's low opinion was not widely shared; Louis-Napoléon's striking appearance cheered his supporters and showed him as a popular man of action. In more good news for the president, on the same day, the Assembly narrowly voted for dissolution. Elections for a new chamber would be held in May. With the Mountain on its way out, and calls for insurrection, at least for now, over, Louis-Napoléon could focus on consolidating his position.

In part, this was done through society events at the Élysée, where Louis-Napoléon relied on his one-time fiancée, Mathilde, to host. For the first, she shone in a ball gown and diamond-encrusted jewellery, while Louis-Napoléon wore his usual National Guard uniform with the grand cordon of the *légion d'honneur*. True to Bonapartist philosophy, he wanted to unite all factions in France, and republicans rubbed shoulders with royalist aristocrats. Louis-Napoléon, with his impeccable manners, took time to meet the great and good from all political parties.

Dazzling high society was important, but courting public opinion even more so, and Louis-Napoléon instinctively knew how to play the role. He visited hospitals, schools and workshops. When cholera broke out in the capital, he showed leadership, visiting the sick and comforting the dying. On one visit to a hospital set up for poor women, Louis-Napoléon was mobbed. When he had barely set foot in the first courtyard, a crowd of old women rushed towards him, trying to grab his hand or coat. Those who could not reach him blew kisses and cried out Napoleonic slogans. The president struggled through the throng, visited patients and distributed money as he went.

After another such visit, Louis-Napoléon found a scrap of paper in his carriage. On it was scrawled an appeal from a destitute widow, the daughter of an old soldier and mother of five children, whose husband had been killed on the barricades. The next day a carriage pulled up outside the run-down apartment block where the woman lived and out stepped a well-dressed gentleman. He climbed the steps to the impoverished attic. Upon seeing the widow, he said, 'I bring you assistance in the name of the President of the Republic.' He gave her two hundred-franc notes and left a calling card, telling her to visit whenever she needed help. When she read the card, she burst into tears. It read, 'President of the Republic'.[9] Of course, Louis-Napoléon was not a man to let his charity work go unnoticed. This vignette found its way into the press, as did other similar stories with the kind of Napoleonic flourishes that people expected from the nephew of the emperor.

Indeed, on a drive home after another brilliant ball, *The Times*'s correspondent, in middle-class fashion, sounded out the views of his cab driver. All he wanted to talk about was the president. 'What a good man he is. You see, my bourgeois, how I love him – but how I love him!' Compared to those in the provisional government, Louis-Napoléon was a real man. 'President for life!' was the cab driver's view.[10]

———

One man not won over by Louis-Napoléon's charm offensive was his cousin, Plon-Plon. He remained true to his radical principles and was increasingly critical of Louis-Napoléon's presidency. Louis-Napoléon was increasingly critical of his cousin, who had moved into the Invalides with his father. Here, if gossip was to be believed, he brought shame upon veterans by entertaining prostitutes and hosting orgies. Louis-Napoléon appointed him ambassador to Spain, but if he hoped that a posting far from Paris would remove an embarrassing problem, he was to be disappointed. As he made his way to Spain, Plon-Plon met with opponents of the president, openly criticised his government and urged voters to reject his preferred candidates in the upcoming elections. This was not, then, a man with a gift for diplomacy. He lasted less than two weeks in Madrid. Before he could be sacked, he left his post without permission. The cousins who had once shared a mistress were no longer on speaking terms.

Plon-Plon had left Madrid to take part in the elections, and he was not the only confidant of the president causing embarrassment. As part of Louis-Napoléon's alliance with the Party of Order, Persigny had been allowed into secretive meetings where elites hoped to manipulate the country into returning a conservative majority. For the refined men in whose company he now found himself, Persigny was not an equal but an absurdly comic figure, 'as much like a gentleman as chicory is to coffee'.[11] Now forty-one years old, with his hair receding and a bushy moustache tapered and waxed at the ends, Persigny found that his faith in Louis-Napoléon shone even brighter after the object of his reverence was elected president. Persigny was tolerated in the meetings because his endorsement for electoral candidates added Bonapartist gloss, and because they thought that in the presence of such distinguished company he would behave. In this, they were mistaken.

He tried to be respectful, but when he was asked to recommend to voters a man who had been hostile to Louis-Napoléon he could contain himself no longer. 'You probably believe', he lectured the room, 'that in my amazement at finding myself as the colleague of the most eminent men in the country my satisfied vanity makes me forget what I owe to the cause I represent . . . Think again, gentlemen.' Then he said the unsayable. 'I'm no more republican than you. The Republic is a scourge for France . . . Each of you has your own ready-made remedy . . . Well! I also have mine, it's the Empire.' After this, as was his wont, he began a long soliloquy on recent French history, explaining to the men who had served either the Bourbon restoration or Louis-Philippe that their politics, which represented only one class, were doomed to failure, whereas Bonapartism, which represented all classes, would triumph. He finished with a warning: 'If you rally to [Louis-Napoléon] you will be welcomed; if you become an obstacle . . . you will be discarded.'[12]

Persigny claimed that his aim was not to found a new party, but to rally honest men around the president. He exceeded his own expectations in the first part of the plan: Bonapartists did badly in the elections. That Louis-Napoléon was all things to all men was an advantage when electing one man to a presidency; it proved a disadvantage when electing many men to a parliament. After all, there were only so many people with the name Bonaparte one could vote for, and as the dispute between Louis-Napoléon and Plon-Plon showed, there was even disagreement in the family over what its politics should be. Riven by factionalism, few supporters of the president were returned.

In contrast, the Party of Order had admirable message discipline: the election was fought to save civilisation against socialists. Huge sums were spent on propaganda distributed to peasants and workers. From the pulpit, priests warned of the danger from the left: 'The Mountain', ran one sermon, 'are monsters vomited up from hell who want to overthrow the social order.' Should they come to power, they would destroy family, property and religion, even marriages would be annulled: 'Your husbands will no longer be your property, and you will no longer be theirs.'[13] Against this message of fear, the left forged an alliance between republicans, socialists and democrats, known as *démoc-socs*, and preached a far more hopeful sermon, including wealth redistribution, fairer taxation, shorter military service, jobs and education.

Fear proved much more popular than hope: when the votes were counted it was a crushing victory for the Party of Order. It won some 450 seats. The *démoc-socs* won only 220, but such was the paranoia of conservatives that their imaginations turned triumph into defeat. The red republic, as they called it, was rising, perhaps in reach by the next election in 1852. The Party of Order, therefore, resolved to stifle it before it could become a reality, passing repressive laws to suppress the left, creating a strange Republic where republicans were persecuted.

Despite their shared fear of the left, the alliance between the right and the president was precarious. Insofar as Louis-Napoléon served its interests, the Party of Order rallied around him, but only 'until things are sufficiently stable to move to a definitive form of government', wrote one of its number, 'which will most certainly not be his'.[14] Until then, the party had to make do with Louis-Napoléon. After the election, there was a cabinet reshuffle, which saw the patrician Alexis de Tocqueville – a man more willing than most of his class to tolerate the Republic – appointed foreign minister. He worked closely with Louis-Napoléon, and Tocqueville thought him 'vastly superior to what his preceding career and his mad enterprises' might have led one to believe.

Tocqueville, though, believed that the president had 'the deep dissimulation of a man who has spent his life in plots'. Moreover, 'generally, it was difficult to come into long and very close contact with him without discovering a little vein of madness'. It was this 'madness' that Tocqueville believed was behind Louis-Napoléon's meteoric rise, for 'the world is a strange theatre. There are moments in it when the worst plays are those which succeed best. If Louis-Napoléon had been a wise man, or a man of genius, he would never have become president.' For Tocqueville, Louis-Napoléon's fanatical belief that he was an 'instrument of destiny' was the most obvious symptom of the president's madness and the key to his success.

Yet Tocqueville, one of the great minds of nineteenth-century France, had little time for Louis-Napoléon's political thought: 'His intelligence was incoherent, confused, filled with great but ill-assorted thoughts, which he borrowed now from the examples of Napoléon, now from socialistic theories, sometimes from recollections of England . . . far removed from the contact of men and facts, for he was naturally a dreamer and a visionary.' The president, Tocqueville believed, was especially inept when it came to foreign affairs. 'I was sometimes frightened', he wrote, at 'how much there was in his plans that was vast, chimerical, unscrupulous, and confused'.[15] This analysis appeared to be confirmed within days of Tocqueville becoming foreign minister. The Mountain again called for the impeachment of the president and once more urged the people of Paris to take to the streets – all because Louis-Napoléon had sent a small military force to Rome.

——

In the spring of 1849, a coalition of reactionary forces was fighting a crusade against the last vestiges of the revolutions that had swept through Europe the year before. Russia was poised to intervene in Hungary to crush liberal nationalists; Prussia was leading the counter-revolution in Germany; and in northern Italy, Austria was reasserting control. That left Rome, where the pope, Pius IX, had been driven from his seat of temporal power, from which he ruled despotically, and a republic had been proclaimed. All eyes turned to the eternal city, which, as one of the last holdouts, drew in renowned revolutionaries determined to make a stand.

There were other luminaries in Rome, but Giuseppe Garibaldi was the foremost revolutionary celebrity. Broad-shouldered, square-chested, with long chestnut-brown hair falling over his shoulders, Garibaldi was a veteran of wars in Latin America fought in the name of liberty, and had come to make his mark in Europe. He looked the part, wearing a red tunic, a black felt hat with ostrich feathers, sabre on one side, carbine on the other and cartridge bag slung across a shoulder. He commanded the Italian Legion, men determined to fight for democracy and unify the many Italian states. But for the pope, these were not heroes: 'The city of Rome, the principal seat of the Church, has now become, alas, a forest of roaring beasts, overflowing with men of every nation, apostates, or heretics, or leaders of communism and socialism.'[16] In March 1849, he appealed to the Catholic powers to crush the unholy republicans and restore his rule.

This was language that the Party of Order, which represented traditional Catholicism in France, well understood, but it put Louis-Napoléon and the French Republic in a difficult position. Restoring the pope would mean destroying a sister republic and alienating the left in France. On the other hand, if the president did nothing, not only would this offend the far larger French Catholic constituency, but also another power, likely Austria – France's traditional rival for influence in the region – would march on Rome, brutally repress the resistance and return the pope to absolute power. For Louis-Napoléon, it was even more confusing. He had long supported Italian nationalism, fighting for it in 1831, when his brother died in the last serious attempt to end autocratic rule and unite the Italian states.

He came up with a beautiful idea, a Bonapartist middle path. Convinced, as he was, that the Roman Republic was a minority oppressing a silent majority, France would intervene not as aggressor, but as liberator. In a triumphal march, the French army would be welcomed into the city, a grateful pope would grant a liberal constitution and Louis-Napoléon would be feted by jubilant Catholics and delighted republicans alike. As well as achieving the long-held foreign policy aim of denying Austria influence in Italy, the successful French army would once again bask in Bonapartist glory.

General Charles Oudinot was confident when he led his small army from the port of Civitavecchia to Rome on 30 April 1849. Nonetheless, he had a plan just in case what he saw as the socialist scum in the city had the temerity to resist. Rome was surrounded by walls. Having studied maps of the city, Oudinot identified a weak spot, the Porta Pertusa. Here, French soldiers carrying sacks of gunpowder would blow open the medieval gate, allowing the army to pour in.

An old watchtower loomed above the gate and acted as a guide for the approaching French soldiers. As a hot sun shone down, a shower of grapeshot from the walls disabused the attackers of the notion that they were liberators. The infantrymen dashed for cover while the French artillery returned fire, covering their men running towards the tower, where they would blow up the gate. It came as a surprise, then, to the brave men who rushed into the gunfire to discover that there was no gate. A few years earlier, it had been walled up, something not marked on Oudinot's outdated map.

There then followed a dash to find other ways into the city that would have been comical if it had not been across difficult terrain under fire. Of course, these gates were well defended and the French were driven back. Oudinot sent a further thousand men forward to help the hapless attackers. Roman troops streamed out of the city to engage them. Under umbrella pines in the beautiful gardens of a villa, and amid the arches of a Roman aqueduct with Saint Peter's visible in the background, the soldiers of the French Republic fought those of the Roman one. The French professionals bested the inexperienced volunteers. Then, thundering through the gardens came the Italian Legion, with Garibaldi on horseback, white poncho flowing in the breeze. They crashed into the French army and forced them into a desperate retreat.

When this was over, numerous French corpses lay among rose bushes, and still more French had surrendered. It was a humiliating defeat. The prisoners were well treated, however. Indeed, they were given a political education. They were reminded of clause five of their own constitution, which stated that the French Republic 'respects the nationality of foreign states . . . It undertakes no wars with a view of conquest, and never employs its power against the liberty of any people.'[17] What the French soldiers had done, their kindly captors explained, was unconstitutional, but of course it was not their fault: the error was their president's. And their republican brethren in Paris were going to bring him down.

—

Back in Paris, Louis-Napoléon was in a state of fatalistic disbelief, not quite able to reconcile the fact that he, a supporter of Italian nationalism, was somehow crushing the last hope of Italian unity. 'This unfortunate Roman business', he wrote to a friend, 'must be ended with cannon shot. I deplore it, but what can be done?'[18] That was indeed how the business would end. Reinforcements were sent and Rome was bombarded. Yet Louis-Napoléon's sorrow was of little import to the republican left in France, which wanted him to pay for the slaughter of revolutionary heroes.

On 11 June, Alexandre Auguste Ledru-Rollin, one of the leaders of the Mountain – 'a very sensual and sanguine heavy fellow, quite without principles and almost without brains', according to Alexis de Tocqueville – stood at the tribune in the Assembly and declared: 'The constitution has been violated; we will defend it by any means possible, even by arms!' The Assembly erupted. After bringing some order to the chaos, the shocked president of the Assembly said, 'This is a call to civil war!'[19] That was the point. It would be fair to say that Louis-Napoléon's first foray into foreign policy had not gone well.

'PEOPLE! THE MOMENT IS SUPREME!' ran a proclamation posted up on the streets of Paris on the morning of 13 June – the moment so supreme it required capital letters. 'All these acts' – referring to those of the president and his ministers – 'reveal one grand system of monarchical conspiracy against the Republic . . . In this struggle between peoples and kings, the government has ranged itself on the side of kings against peoples.'[20] Some twenty-five thousand marched on central Paris, or, as one journalist put it more colourfully, making clear where his loyalties lay, 'loathsome reptiles who lurk in the cellars and obscene haunts of the capital skulked forth from their slimy lairs' and down the boulevards of Paris.[21]

Cavalry lay in ambush. As the demonstration passed the corner of rue de la Paix, horses charged, breaking the crowd in two before the people fled to arm themselves. Gun shops were looted. Barricades were hastily assembled, using whatever was to hand, mainly chairs and tables from cafes lining the streets. Meanwhile, Ledru-Rollin and sixty or so representatives of the people made their way, under the protection of sympathetic National Guardsmen, to the Conservatoire national des arts et métiers, a large building near the centre of Paris. Arriving just after 2 p.m., they forced their way in, went upstairs and began the now familiar business of forming a provisional government.

Outside in the courtyards, barricades were being thrown together when soldiers arrived. After a brief exchange of fire, the soldiers rushed the defences, surrounded the National Guardsmen loyal to Ledru-Rollin and took them prisoner. Not for the first time, the politicians inside found that they were not, as they thought, the new government of France, but rather criminals about to be arrested. Some escaped by breaking the glass in the windows at the back of the hall and squeezing themselves through the apertures, which for the corpulent Ledru-Rollin was not easy.

In the streets, barricades were dismantled, largely by waiters annoyed that their tables and chairs had been taken. Once again, the forces of order reigned supreme. And once again, in the Élysée, Louis-Napoléon was preternaturally calm. Despite the prospect of revolution, not to mention rumours that the mob planned to march on the palace, Tocqueville noted that the only thing different about Louis-Napoléon was that he was in military uniform. Otherwise he 'was exactly the same man as on the day before: the same rather dejected air . . . his eyes no less dull'.[22] That afternoon, the president rode out in the streets of Paris to another ecstatic reception. For while his conduct over the Roman Republic was controversial, there were plenty who welcomed restoring the pope, or, even if they did not, were not going to die in the streets over it.

Louis-Napoléon's statement after the attempted insurrection showed he was as much a man of order as a man of the people: 'A few factious people have dared to raise the standard of revolt.' Such demonstrations, warned the declaration, must end. Now, it was time for the 'good' to be reassured and the 'wicked to tremble'.[23] The politicians who led the uprising were tried, and their newspapers shut down. Paris and other departments were placed under martial law, while anything that was vaguely progressive was denounced as socialism. Astutely, Louis-Napoléon let his ministers and the Assembly take the lead. For, having faced down the revolutionary left, he now turned his attention to undermining the powerful conservative elites who dominated French politics.

———

Positioning himself as the people's champion, Louis-Napoléon distanced himself from his own government and complained that his ministers only paid lip service to his visionary reforms: agricultural colonies, credit for the poor, legal aid – all were politely discussed, then put to one side. His ministers thought these ideas dangerously left-wing. Worse, the president kept trying to free political prisoners. 'It was with the utmost difficulty', lamented Thiers, 'that we could prevent his granting indiscriminate amnesties to the most ferocious of the socialist rebels.'[24]

The Roman expedition gave Louis-Napoléon an opportunity to demonstrate his independence from his right-wing backers. After the city was taken, the pope's forces presided over a crackdown on those who supported the Republic. Louis-Napoléon's dreams of a liberal intervention proved disastrously naive. To pressure the pope into concessions, he wrote a letter to the man commanding French forces in Rome. 'The French Republic', he wrote, in spite of the evidence, 'did not send an army to Rome to stifle Italian liberty.' Instead, Louis-Napoléon wanted political prisoners pardoned and a liberal government. 'When our armies made the tour of Europe,' concluded his letter – 'tour' being a novel euphemism for his uncle's conquest of much of the continent – 'they left everywhere . . . the destruction of the abuses of feudalism and the germs of liberty; it shall not be said that in 1849 a French army could act otherwise.'[25]

When he showed this letter to his ministers, they made the usual indulgent noises one gives to the deluded, but thought nothing of it. Most of them were delighted that the Roman Republic had been crushed and papal absolutism restored, which was another victory in the existential struggle of civilisation against barbarism. For them, what the president thought was of little consequence, and anyway, he had assured his ministers his letter was a private one. This was a lie. Louis-Napoléon put it in the newspapers without informing his cabinet, happy to drop his ministers in a scandal to boost his popularity. This leak was a shocking manoeuvre at the time, causing a sensation, as Louis-Napoléon knew it would. Karl Marx saw through the ruse. 'With studied indiscretion,' he wrote, Louis-Napoléon 'raised the curtain on his cabinet in order to expose himself to the eyes of the gallery as a benevolent genius who was, however, misunderstood and shackled in his own house.'[26]

That was only part of the calculation. Louis-Napoléon genuinely wanted his policy pursued and defended. He urged Barrot to do this in the Assembly, but when the Roman expedition was debated in mid-October there was no mention of the president's letter. Seeing him afterwards, Barrot recalled that it was 'perhaps the only time that I have seen Louis-Napoléon animated by something resembling passion'.[27] He was angry. On 31 October 1849, he sacked Barrot and his fellow ministers.

———

'An entire system triumphed on 10 December,' Louis-Napoléon declared in a message read out to the Assembly, 'for the name of Napoléon is itself a programme.' At home, it meant 'order, authority, religion and the welfare of the people'; abroad, it meant 'national dignity'. And, declared the president, 'It is this policy inaugurated by my election that I want to see triumph with the support of the Assembly and that of the people.'[28] The implication was, of course, that it had yet to triumph – hence Louis-Napoléon had sacked his ministers. The replacements were young, capable, ambitious but largely unknown. They were his men; they were not, as some of his former ministers had been, working behind his back to bring about a monarchist restoration, nor were they, like Tocqueville, so Olympian as to look on Louis-Napoléon with contempt.

The rumours in the salons, cafes and press were that this *coup de théâtre* would be followed by a *coup d'état*. When asked whether she would tour Russia, the great celebrity of the French stage, Rachel, still friendly with Louis-Napoléon – and more than friendly with Plon-Plon – joked that if she wanted to see an empire, she could just stay in Paris.

Gossip about the president seizing power was given further credence because Louis-Napoléon groomed the army, frequently holding military reviews, handing out medals and making speeches praising their courage before liberally dispensing wine and garlic sausages. Invariably, these performances were met with cries of '*Vive Louis-Napoléon!*' This was a worry for republicans, who, not unreasonably, expected the army to be loyal to the Republic rather than an individual. It also caused the Party of Order great anxiety, for when the moment came to decide the future of France, the army would be key.

When that showdown came, Louis-Napoléon also wanted to have the edge in street politics. To that end, a Bonapartist society had been set up, known as the Société du Dix-Décembre. To get around laws Louis-Napoléon's government had passed banning political clubs, it was billed as a philanthropic organisation. Its charity work, however, involved beating up opponents of the president, a benevolent service its hard-drinking and violent members were called upon to regularly perform. This was ripe for satire, and the characters of Ratapoil (literally in English, 'skinned rat') and his sidekick, Casmajou ('break my jaw'), became famous in the republican press for carrying out the president's charity work across the country.

Reports of *coups d'état* were ever present because Louis-Napoléon's long-held dream to become emperor was well known, but also because men in his entourage, especially Persigny, urged him on. Unlike his acolyte, however, one of Louis-Napoléon's virtues was patience. Instead of a *coup d'état*, the president wanted to legally revise the constitution that prohibited his re-election. To do that, he needed to undermine the Party of Order. It soon gave him the perfect opportunity.

Despite their comfortable majority in the Assembly, Thiers and his fellow travellers were terrified of the republican left. Their fears were seemingly confirmed when radicals – including, humiliatingly, a novelist with socialist sympathies – defeated conservatives in by-elections. Electing left-leaning writers to the Assembly proved to conservatives that the people could not be trusted. Party of Order representatives drove through yet more repressive legislation. Tighter press laws were introduced, but this was mere tinkering; what was required was major surgery – ending universal male suffrage. On 24 May 1850, Thiers stood up in the Assembly and argued that some three million people should be struck off the electoral roll, for they were, in his phrase, 'the vile multitude'.[29] And true republicans, Thiers claimed, should be afraid of this 'multitude' because in return for bread and circuses it had delivered Rome to Caesar.

This was problematic for Louis-Napoléon, a great admirer of Caesar. After all, many of Thiers's 'vile multitude' had elected him president. Moreover, he had long argued for universal male suffrage. But the president gave lukewarm support to the law, although he was careful to distance himself from it as far as he could. After it was passed, it reduced the electorate from 9.5 million to 6.8 million, but Louis-Napoléon, unlike Thiers, was thinking further ahead. It was not the people he worried about, but the Assembly. To undermine it, he had drip-fed into public discourse the idea that the Assembly was thwarting the will of the people. Thiers's characterisation of the people as the vile multitude and the franchise restriction were, then, a gift for him.

'You, a child of universal suffrage,' asked a disbelieving Hortense Cornu, the president's friend and a committed republican, 'do you support a limited suffrage?'

'You understand nothing about it,' replied Louis-Napoléon. 'I am preparing the ruin of the Assembly.'

'But', she answered, 'you will perish with the Assembly.'

'Not in the least. When the Assembly goes over the precipice, I shall cut the rope.'[30]

10

COUNTDOWN

At the beginning of 1851, there were many obstacles to Louis-Napoléon holding on to power, not least the constitution that barred him from a second term as president. The most immediate was also the one Louis-Napoléon found most annoying: General Nicolas Changarnier. This man buttoned his uniform so tightly that people thought he wore a corset underneath. Diminutive, arrogant and vain, Changarnier wore a wig to hide his baldness and was nicknamed 'General Bergamot' due to his penchant for pungent perfume. One British aristocrat memorably described him as having a 'shrivelled puckered-up face like a monkey' combined with 'a short snappish way of talking and every now and then a sort of little hyena laugh'.[1]

But this sweet-smelling, small, wrinkled man was the only person whose power rivalled the president's. He had command over the army in Paris as well as the capital's National Guard. Given his control of the armed forces, which side Changarnier backed when the political crisis everyone expected arrived would determine the future of France. And one thing was certain: Changarnier would not back Louis-Napoléon.

Changarnier held the president in such contempt that seditious talk took place in the Tuileries, Changarnier's official residence, where the general liked to mock the president over dinner, referring to him as Thomas Diafoirus, a maladroit social climber and charlatan with terrible hair from a Molière play. One officer, recently arrived in Paris and dining at Changarnier's, was astonished at such disrespect, but an aide-de-camp reassured him that the general 'need only lift a finger' to have Louis-Napoléon arrested.[2] Changarnier was emboldened because in the Assembly, where he was also a deputy, the monarchist majority courted him. Thiers and the Party of Order hoped that when the time came, the commander of Paris's armed forces would help them restore French royalty. To do that, Changarnier and his supporters had to stop Louis-Napoléon's own ambitions.

For his part, Louis-Napoléon had wanted to sack Changarnier months ago, but lacked the political capital. Instead, he had contented himself with removing one of Changarnier's subordinates. Not only did this infuriate Changarnier, it also confirmed what he thought: the president was too weak to move against him. The general was not worried, therefore, about a showdown. During a heated exchange, Changarnier threatened the president: 'One cannot insult me with impunity!'[3]

This was a sentiment the president shared, but his half-brother Charles de Morny had cautioned against moving too soon. The president had a complicated relationship with Morny, who was the son of Louis-Napoléon's mother, Hortense, and her lover, the dashing comte de Flahaut, once an aide-de-camp to Napoléon. Hortense had given birth to Morny in great secrecy and he was raised in Paris by parents who adopted him. It was not until after his mother's death that Louis-Napoléon learned he had a half-brother. When he found out he was so upset he cried.

The best course of action, Louis-Napoléon reasoned, was to pretend his half-sibling did not exist. As an exile, this had been easy; as president, however, it was harder. Not only was Morny an important political figure in Paris, but, more crucially, he was now also useful. Unlike his half-brother, Morny had long experience of French politics. Urbane, debonair and impeccably dressed, as a parliamentarian under Louis-Philippe's monarchy Morny had built up a list of contacts almost unrivalled in French politics. He had also amassed an enormous fortune as an industrialist and speculator using insider knowledge. It was not, therefore, his critics maintained, filial devotion that brought Morny into the Bonapartist camp, but lust for money and power. Victor Hugo described him as 'possessing the manners of the world and the habits of the roulette table . . . well dressed . . . without conscience, irreproachably elegant, infamous and amiable'[4] – in short, a character straight out of a Balzac novel and the perfect man to orchestrate Louis-Napoléon's hold on the presidency.

But in his long time in French politics, Morny had rarely been as shocked as he was on 3 January 1851, when he left the Palais Bourbon, meeting place of the Assembly. Changarnier had just mounted the tribune and outlined the constitutional right of the Assembly to requisition troops to protect itself in case of danger. Morny interpreted this as a prelude to what Changarnier had so often boasted about: arresting the president. Morny ran from the chamber and hurried to the nearby Élysée in the company of another of Louis-Napoléon's loyal lieutenants, Persigny. Morny turned to him and said, 'Either General Changarnier must be sacked immediately, or we will no longer have power.'[5] Convinced that Changarnier would take action that evening, Persigny stayed at the palace all night, sending out agents to gather information. He soon realised, however, that fears had been exaggerated. This was not the prelude to a military attack on the president, merely a parliamentary one.

This was only marginally less serious. Louis-Napoléon wanted to sack Changarnier, using his speech as a pretext. But there was a problem: he needed ministers to countersign the order for it to be constitutional. Yet Louis-Napoléon's ministers were not willing to back a presidential whim opposed by the majority in the Assembly. Instead, they resigned, plunging the Republic into crisis. After a few days Persigny went to the Palais Bourbon, where angry deputies accosted him, asking how could the president dare to sack Changarnier. Then, learning of Persigny's presence, some of the most powerful men in the country came to remonstrate with him. 'Young man,' one elder statesman said, 'you will push [the president] into the abyss, him and the country. Do you want civil war?'

Persigny lost his short temper, insisting it was not Louis-Napoléon who wanted war, but the conservatives in the Assembly who were backing Changarnier. And since they wanted civil war, they could have it. The bloodshed would fall on their heads, continued Persigny, getting carried away, because between cries of *'Vive l'Assemblée nationale!'* and *'Vive Napoléon!'* it was obvious on which side the people and the army would be. 'As for me,' Persigny added, unable to control his zeal, 'I have nothing to lose, neither a fine house in Paris, nor a chateau in the countryside.' Stunned silence met this diatribe. The great dignitaries of France's former monarchies were shocked at this unsubtle threat of revolution. One of their number, aged sixty-nine, remembered the guillotining of his father during the first revolution. Adding to the histrionics, he turned, walked slowly away and buried his face in his hands, groaning, 'Oh, unhappy France! Unhappy country!'[6]

The crisis continued for days. Louis-Napoléon summoned Persigny to the Élysée. It was 4 a.m., and the president was still in his dressing gown. 'I have thought about my situation,' he said to Persigny. 'It demands a heroic remedy.' He had wasted too much time, he explained; every day lost strengthened his enemies. The solution was simple. If he could not find ministers from inside the Assembly to sack Changarnier, he would appoint men from outside this body. This would be constitutional, but highly unconventional, and Louis-Napoléon concluded by saying that he stood 'ready to draw the sword, if the Assembly draws its own'. Then he showed a list to Persigny, whose name was on it as minister of the interior.

Persigny agreed, but first summoned the old cabinet to a meeting. He explained what Louis-Napoléon had planned. 'With the name of Napoléon, we will shake this nation down to its foundations and do in one day the work of half a century.' But, added Persigny, he preferred a less 'perilous solution'. If, he continued threateningly, they wanted to resolve the impasse '*peacefully*', then he gave them until midday. If they had not signed off on Changarnier's dismissal by then, he concluded, 'at 12.15 p.m. I shall have taken possession of the ministry'.[7] With that, Persigny walked out. It is not clear what the ministers thought was worse: Persigny as a minister, or civil war. Either way, with forced gaiety, the ministers presented themselves at the Élysée at 11.45 a.m. The necessary decrees were signed. Louis-Napoléon then handed his aide-de-camp, military adviser and fixer Colonel Émile Félix Fleury a letter dismissing Changarnier. Worried the general might resist, Louis-Napoléon insisted it be hand-delivered 'just as he is getting out of bed, before he has time to think'.[8]

When the Assembly heard the news, there was outrage. A motion was passed that created a commission with extraordinary powers to reinstate Changarnier or remove the president from office. One Bonapartist shouted, 'These are revolutionary measures!' while another deputy exclaimed, 'It's a committee of public safety!'[9] It was not. It was parliamentary procedure, and the men on the commission knew that while they might command a majority in the Assembly, they could not compete with Louis-Napoléon's popularity in the country. They censured the president's conduct, but agreed he had acted constitutionally and contented themselves with a motion of no confidence in his farcical ministers, who had resigned in protest against a measure they now backed.

This was a conclusion far short of what Changarnier and his supporters had hoped for; nonetheless, they made the most of it to embarrass the president. During the debate on the no confidence motion, Changarnier made another none-too-subtle threat. 'Gentlemen,' he said, 'my sword is condemned to rest, at least momentarily, but it is not broken, and,' he continued, his voice tremulous with emotion, 'if one day the country has need of it, it will find it completely devoted, loyal only to the inspiration of a patriotic heart and a firm spirit, and very disdainful towards the tinsel of false grandeur.' The Assembly erupted into applause and cheers as Changarnier made his way back to his seat, representatives shaking his hand as he passed.

Soon afterwards, Thiers lent his rhetorical weight to the anti-Bonapartist tirades. Speaking from the tribune, he said that 'there are not more than two powers today in the state, the executive power and the legislative power. If the Assembly backs down, there will not be more than one.' In this case, he argued, the form of government will have changed even if its name has not. If the Assembly gave in to Louis-Napoléon today, he said, 'the Empire is made'.[10] Uproar broke out; Thiers, who had gone from backing Louis-Napoléon to identifying him as a national threat, was mobbed by his colleagues, and applause mixed with shocked murmurs filled the chamber. The next day, the Assembly passed a vote of no confidence in the ministry, bringing down the government, and with it, they hoped, the president.

Losing the confidence of the Assembly and having no ministers might have forced a conventional man to resign, but Louis-Napoléon cared little for convention. After the grandees of French politics had shown themselves united in refusing to serve under him, or in some cases unwilling to work alongside rivals, the president simply ignored them. Instead, he appointed, as Persigny had threatened he would, a ministry made up of non-entities and civil servants. In the first few weeks of January 1851, Louis-Napoléon had removed Changarnier and faced down Thiers and his right-wing cabal in the Assembly.

What would the president do next was the question everyone was asking, including Odilon Barrot, Louis-Napoléon's prime minister in 1849.

He had been called to the Élysée in the hope that he might help form a cabinet. 'What do you want?' asked Barrot. 'The extension of your powers as a result of re-election made possible through revising the constitution, is that enough for you?'

After a long pause, Louis-Napoléon replied, 'That is enough for me.'[11]

———

In northern France in 1358, some French peasants were drinking wine and discussing politics. The Hundred Years' War against England had dev-astated the region, times were tough and the more the men drank, the more they blamed their problems on the nobility. Excited by this talk, they decided to exact revenge. Armed with pitchforks and scythes, the men ransacked a nearby castle, killing the husband, wife and children who lived in it. Inspired by this easy victory, peasants from the nearby village joined them to pillage another castle. Presently, the entire region was in revolt. The attacks grew worse: 'They skewered a gentleman alive and roasted him in front of his wife, and then, ten or twelve of them, after having raped her, compelled her to eat [her husband's cooked flesh], and finally tore her to pieces and fed her to the dogs.'

This was the Jacquerie of 1358 – a French peasants' revolt – and accord-ing to a former civil servant who now penned apocalyptic, hysterical sketches on the future of French society, Auguste Romieu, it was not only civil war that awaited France in 1852; it was 'the Jacquerie'.[12] The phrase was enough to strike terror into the heart of any self-respecting French bourgeois, but in case their memories needed refreshing, Romieu's short work, *The Red Spectre of 1852*, brought his wildly inaccurate version of French history quoted above into the comfortable drawing rooms of his middle-class readership.

Although more prone to outrageous hyperbole than most, Romieu rep-resented a popular – his work went through three editions in 1851 – view among the propertied classes: 1852 would be a socialist armageddon to rival any revolt or revolution in French history, which, to their minds, was a very high bar. Whether through the election of a left-wing president, a socialist majority in the Assembly, an old-fashioned revolution or all three, France was on the precipice of a red abyss. As one Parisian bourgeois noted, people looked towards 1852 as those in medieval times awaited the year 1000, expecting the world to end. The simplest way to avoid this nightmare, Louis-Napoléon and his supporters argued, would be to allow him to stand for an election he would undoubtedly win in 1852. This would put an end to the so-called red republic, or 'save society' in the preferred euphemism of Bonapartists, but before society could be saved the constitution had to be revised.

Louis-Napoléon made this point to the representatives in the Assembly. 'I consider as great criminals', his message to politicians read when opening the session for 1851, 'those who by personal ambition would compromise the small amount of stability guaranteed by the constitution . . . bound by my oath, I confine myself within the strict limits which that constitution has laid down for me.'[13] So far, so constitutional, but the address pointed out that he was the elect of the people and that the Assembly could revise the constitution in his favour. If it did not, then there would be uncertainty, but whatever happened, he claimed, he would work ceaselessly in the time he had left in office to prevent the decision about who would govern France descending into violence.

Though more elegantly put than Persigny's threat of civil war, the message amounted to the same thing: we have a nice country, what a shame if bloody revolution broke it, again. Moreover, analysts did not have to read too hard between the lines to see that Louis-Napoléon considered his mandate from the people more important than the Assembly, or the law. And the people, so he claimed, wanted the constitution revised. Many did. Bonapartists had relentlessly pushed the message: the president was the elect of six million (they rounded up the 5.5 million), and it was the people and the president versus an elite, out-of-touch Assembly with its own agenda.

This narrative was enormously helped by the fact that many in the Assembly were out-of-touch elites with their own agenda. Thiers may have named Louis-Napoléon as the Republic's number-one enemy, but Thiers, fairly openly, was working to restore the monarchy. Besides, few people outside the political elite cared about his parliamentary speeches, which were often three hours long. If they had bothered to read them, Thiers's hatred for the people – he had, after all, called them the 'vile multitude' – would have stood out more than his wit, rhetorical flourishes and newfound love for the Republic.[14] If it was a showdown between Thiers and Louis-Napoléon as the people's champion, there was only one winner. Thiers had published *The Rights of Property*, a rehash of old arguments and highly critical of left-wing ideas. Louis-Napoléon, on the other hand, had written *The Extinction of Pauperism*. Although critics quipped that he had only meant his own, voters needed merely to read the titles to see who was more likely to take their interests into account.

Presenting himself as a man of order to the right, and a man of the people to the left, was a difficult tightrope for Louis-Napoléon to walk; however, if he could do it, he might scrape together the three-quarters majority he needed in the Assembly to revise the constitution and allow him to stand for re-election. On the other hand, he might not. In that case, he would need a back-up plan.

———

On 8 May 1851, a burning sun shone on a small French army outside the Algerian town of Milah. This was an ancient settlement, and from ruined Byzantine walls local inhabitants watched on as the latest invaders marched south – drums beating, music playing – towards nearby mountains. The final destination was a town on the Algerian coast under French control, but first the soldiers had to make their way through the hostile, rugged region known as Petite Kabylie, which had yet to submit to French imperialism. As a lumbering convoy of twelve hundred beasts carrying supplies for some ten thousand men traversed a narrow pass between a ravine and woods, they were attacked by Algerians. After a vicious struggle, the French fought off the enemy and the convoy eventually reached an open space where it set up a defensive camp. The wounded were laid out on the grass, while those who had escaped injury relaxed. A regimental band started playing tunes from a popular *opéra comique*, while soldiers milled past, listening and talking as though they were *flâneurs* strolling along the Champs-Élysées.

Uneasy at such repose, General Armand-Jacques Leroy de Saint-Arnaud, the commander of the expedition, ordered his men to start moving. Just as he did, shots rang out from a nearby thicket. A guide fell dead at Saint-Arnaud's side, and another soldier had his horse shot from underneath him. Then French cavalry charged the ambushers, scattering them. The officer leading that charge was none other than Louis-Napoléon's confidant and military fixer Fleury.

Like many of Louis-Napoléon's supporters, Fleury had had a dissolute youth. After wasting an inherited fortune, he ended up in London in 1837, where he met Persigny and then Louis-Napoléon. From that moment, he was hooked on the cult of Bonapartism. Unlike most Bonapartists, he practised entryism, joining the army and working his way up. He was a man of good judgement and strong loyalty. As one contemporary noted, Louis-Napoléon was the man who laid the mine, but Fleury was the one who lit the fuse.

Although he was now on a military campaign, Fleury's mission was political. While Louis-Napoléon hoped to retain power legally, his close aides were less sanguine. And if there were a showdown between the president and the Assembly, the loyalty of the army would be the deciding factor. Changarnier had been removed, but as Fleury pointed out months earlier when discussing the situation with the president in Paris, the highest-ranking generals in France were either monarchists or republicans. 'Believe me,' Fleury told him, 'the time has come . . . to find new men, energetic, ambitious.'[15] These men were to be found in Algeria, where French generals, including Changarnier, had made their name overseeing ferocious colonial warfare since the region had been invaded in 1830. Saint-Arnaud was the ambitious man singled out.

Saint-Arnaud had lived a storied life. He had been thrown out of the army, twice – the second time for desertion, which landed him in prison. Broke upon release, he made money giving language lessons, although his main source of income was gambling and, thanks to his good looks, living off women. Indeed, he travelled round Europe in the company of a married woman whom he passed off as his wife. Building on his dashing appearance and talent for deception, he then became an actor and musician. On returning to Paris, he was a regular at the capital's seedier theatres. But after 1830, France was so desperate for men to fight in Algeria that even his peripatetic life did not disbar him from once again rejoining the army and making a name for himself as a brutal soldier, perfectly happy to massacre civilians and burn down villages.

'*Voilà*,' said Fleury to Louis-Napoléon, tactfully leaving out some of the more colourful parts of Saint-Arnaud's past, 'the man whom I propose to you to become, in six months, your minister of war and the instrument of a *coup d'état*.'[16] There were two problems. First, Saint-Arnaud was not of sufficiently high rank to be appointed a minister. Second, he was not a Bonapartist. The second was easily solved: mercenary, without scruples but with a flair for dissimulation that rivalled Louis-Napoléon's, Saint-Arnaud was an ideal accomplice to the president's plans – Fleury just needed to persuade him. He could do this while addressing the first problem; all Saint-Arnaud needed was a military campaign that could be passed off as a dazzling success. Then Louis-Napoléon could promote him, recall him to Paris and shower him with honours. Combining conspiracy, military glory and personal aggrandisement, it was a plan after Louis-Napoléon's own heart and the president told Fleury to light the fuse.

Once in Algeria, Fleury sounded out Saint-Arnaud, who proved amenable, and a deal was quickly hammered out. 'My dear Fleury,' Saint-Arnaud said while shaking Fleury's hand, 'as of today, [the president] can count on me. If he makes me *général de division* as soon as possible, I'll take care of the rest. We can talk about it while on campaign.'[17]

The campaign, though hard and bloody, was something of an afterthought, for the French at least. As Saint-Arnaud wrote to his wife while in the field, he would easily defeat the Algerians defending their homes. Later that day, he added a postscript: 'From my tent, as I write to you, I see the Arab villages burning. I hope the lesson will be a good one and benefits them.'[18] But the only people who would benefit were Saint-Arnaud and Louis-Napoléon. The dead Algerians, the crops and olive groves deliberately destroyed, the villages in flames – these were sacrifices to the altar of Louis-Napoléon's ambition.

———

At 2.30 p.m. on 1 June 1851, a train carrying the president pulled into Dijon station. Here, on a stage, sat the bishop of Dijon, flanked by his clergy, with an altar behind them, the canopy of a richly decorated tent shielding the priests from the strong sun. On the other side of the railway track, huge crowds had gathered to see Louis-Napoléon, and enormous semicircular marquees provided shade. The president had come to Dijon to open a new stretch of railway, which in mid-nineteenth-century France was as much a religious occasion as a triumph of engineering. Thus Louis-Napoléon had to sit through a sermon, before the bishop – cross in hand, mitre on head – made his way in great solemnity towards a steam engine decorated with flowers and flags. Standing before this symbol of modernity, the bishop blessed the engine.

Once the service was over, Louis-Napoléon could focus on the more important task of promoting himself. When he theatrically mounted a horse, the crowds roared their enthusiasm. The president looked good on a horse. His short legs made him underwhelming on foot, but his long torso and talent for riding ensured that even his opponents admitted he sat well mounted. As he went through the streets – specially asphalted for the occasion – the people cried, '*Vive Napoléon!*'[19]

The set piece of the day was a banquet for 250 people at the town hall, and, after everyone had been wined and dined, the president's speech. Having taken elocution lessons to smooth out his accented French, Louis-Napoléon was a more confident speaker now than when his risible first attempts in 1848 had been widely mocked. In a firm, emphatic voice he said, 'How I wish those who entertain doubts for the future had accompanied me' on this journey. For they would have seen that the intrigues, attacks and passions of party politics in Paris did not reflect popular sentiment in the country. 'France does not want', he continued, 'a return to the old regime under whatever form it may be disguised, nor the attempt of disastrous and unworkable utopias. It is because I am the most natural adversary of both that [France] has placed its confidence in me.'

This was a thinly veiled attack on the monarchists and radical republicans in the Assembly, but Louis-Napoléon soon dispensed with any veil whatsoever. 'For three years,' he claimed, 'I have always been supported when it has been a question of combating disorder by repressive measures. But when I have wanted to do good . . . [and] take measures to improve the lives of the people, I have only found apathy.'[20] Now, across France, he noted, petitions were arriving in Paris pleading for the constitution to be revised. The battle lines were clear: the people and the president versus the self-interested elites in the Assembly. The audience broke out into rapturous applause.

Louis-Napoléon was now keener than ever to paint the Assembly as the bastion of an out-of-touch minority because the parliamentary machinery required to revise the constitution had slowly been turning. Finally, in early July, France's foremost expert on political systems, Alexis de Tocqueville, as head of a committee charged with reporting on the issue, had recommended revision to the Assembly. The debate that followed would determine the future of France, and Louis-Napoléon needed a majority of three-quarters in favour of revision at the end of it.

To get this, the president mobilised supporters across France to pressure undecided deputies. Petitions with some two million signatures arrived in the capital. Critics alleged that these were of dubious origin – extracted under pressure from government officials or Bonapartist thugs – but as his welcome at Dijon showed, Louis-Napoléon remained immensely popular: certainly more so than a somewhat arbitrary clause in a constitution hastily cobbled together only three years earlier. Few people had much faith in the Republic, least of all many of the monarchist representatives in the Assembly, whose defence of it was more out of contempt for the president than reverence for the constitution. An editorial in *The Times* argued the president's line as eloquently as any of his publicists: 'No attempt could be more hopeless than to uphold and defend a constitution which nobody approves, simply because it renders ineligible the man whom nine-tenths of the community desire to elect.'[21]

From his first year in office, Louis-Napoléon had adroitly used provincial tours to cement his popularity. The president had shown himself to be a politician far superior in manipulating public opinion in an age of mass democracy than his enemies. Now the pageantry at Dijon was repeated in numerous towns to pressure the Assembly into revising the constitution. Using France's burgeoning railway network, Louis-Napoléon moved fast and stopped at local stations, where National Guardsmen and crowds came out to meet him, bands played, flags waved, platitudinous speeches were read out. Other heavily choreographed moments included finding local veterans of the Napoleonic wars to greet the president, preferably in old uniforms, tears welling in the eyes. Charity was bestowed on the unfortunate, respect was paid to the church and clergy and, of course, cries of '*Vive Napoléon!*' were strongly encouraged – and '*Vive l'empereur!*' even more so.

Louis-Napoléon mastered the art of making banal speeches about the locality. He would praise an aspect of the region, mention some local history, throw in a tendentious reference to his uncle's relationship with the people and finish by saying that the area was the very embodiment of the greatness of France. The novelty of such remarks for the time, combined with a sprinkling of Napoleonic grandeur, meant these trite soliloquies were enthusiastically received, extending his appeal across the country. Not everyone was welcoming, though, and cries of '*Vive la république!*' – an oddly subversive slogan when shouted at the president of a republic – were protests. In Dijon, a gang of boys ran alongside Louis-Napoléon repeating this. That was as far as it was safe to go. When insults against the president were heard, the police arrested those who shouted them.

With his skill for popular politics whipping up a crescendo of support during this summer tour, and the threat of violence hanging over the 1852 presidential election if he were not allowed to stand for president, Louis-Napoléon hoped to force the Assembly into backing revision; however, in this body there were those whose implacable hatred meant they were determined to resist. Thiers and Changarnier were two examples from the right, but there were many more on the left who had a visceral loathing for a president they blamed for turning a republic they envisaged as a socialist paradise into a reactionary dystopia.

When the debate on the constitution came, it was expected to be tempestuous, but it began calmly. Louis-Napoléon had won over key politicians on the right who saw his re-election as a bulwark against a socialist Jacquerie and a means to buy time until a king could be put on the throne. Soon, however, France's most famous writer ended the civilised discourse. Victor Hugo had once been a zealous supporter of Louis-Napoléon, but Bonapartism turned out to be merely one of the many stops on his political journey from ultra-royalist to radical republican.

Beginning his speech, Hugo was not going to allow the topic of the debate stop him from delivering a lecture on his esoteric interpretation of French history. He declared that the French Revolution of 1789 was the 'ideal of great philosophers realised by a great people' and an education for all nations. Its sacred goal was the universal well-being of humanity. So far, this was relatively demure by the standards of republican rhetoric, but Hugo went further. The Revolution was a kind of providential human redemption. 'It is the era foreseen by Socrates, and for which he drank hemlock; it is the work done by Jesus, and for which he was put on the cross.' If Socrates and Jesus as proto-French republicans seemed outlandish to his audience, what Hugo said next they found even more extraordinary. He claimed that the French people 'had carved in indestructible granite and laid in the middle of the old monarchical continent the first foundation of this immense edifice which will one day be called the United States of Europe!' Showing that some things in politics are timeless, this provoked laughter from the right.

Hugo was merely warming up, however, before turning his ire on Bonapartism. Where was its glory? he asked rhetorically. Hugo's father had been a general under the Empire, and so one representative quipped, 'Ask your father.' Undeterred, Hugo then lambasted Louis-Napoléon's domestic and foreign policies, which, he argued, were repressive at home and abroad. Hugo said there was no comparison with the first Napoléon, whom he admired, but the dead emperor would be turning in his grave to see the modern parody 'and five or six thousand scoundrels shouting: *Vive l'empereur!*' He then exalted Napoléon's genius to demean the nephew: 'What!' he cried. 'Because we have had Napoléon the Great we must have Napoléon the Little!' The chamber descended into raucous chaos, but Hugo was not done. 'Let him finish, for the love of God,' exhorted the president. 'For the love of dinner,' remarked one politician.[22] Finally, Hugo got to his closing sentence: 'I vote against revision.'[23] This obvious conclusion drew ironic laughs from the right, ecstatic cheers from the left.

Two days after Hugo's performance, on 19 July 1851, the debate closed: 446 had voted for revision; 278 against. Louis-Napoléon had won; however, he was ninety-seven short of the three-quarters required. Hugo's insults hurt Louis-Napoléon, but what annoyed the president far more was that Thiers and Changarnier had cobbled together enough votes on the right to deny him the necessary majority.

———

Soon after the vote, Louis-Napoléon was walking in the gardens of the Élysée with Morny. 'I don't know how you see the future,' Morny asked his half-brother, 'but I see only one thing in your interest and that of the country: a *coup d'état*.'

'I am of your opinion,' replied the president, 'and I am considering it.'

'Finally!' exclaimed Morny.

In fact, Louis-Napoléon had begun preparing already. To maintain secrecy, only a few others were in on the conspiracy, including the Paris prefect of police; Fleury; Persigny; Saint-Arnaud, who had returned to France in August after being promoted to *général de division* as planned; and now Morny, whose recent speculations had nearly ruined him financially and who gambled that his chances of solvency were better with his half-brother in power.

A few days after this conversation, Louis-Napoléon talked with Morny again. Casually he said, 'Well then, we will launch the *coup d'état* next week. Come tomorrow to dinner at Saint-Cloud; we will hunt rabbits and after dining . . . I will examine all the plans.'[24] Here, after two hours killing rabbits, the first democratically elected president of France sat down with fellow plotters to discuss ending a republic that only three years earlier he had sworn to protect. Morny thought it badly planned, but Louis-Napoléon wanted to press ahead: the *coup d'état* would take place on 22 September. Just before this date, however, Saint-Arnaud refused to take part.

'It is an abominable betrayal!' exclaimed Louis-Napoléon. In a rare show of emotion, the president was still angry that evening when he made his way to the theatre. He poured out invective against Saint-Arnaud to Fleury and Persigny, who accompanied him. The president told Fleury, 'I will become a general. I will mount a horse and then present myself before the troops!'[25] Fleury managed to talk him down. Unlike his uncle, Fleury told the president, he did not have the support of the army.

After eight days, Louis-Napoléon's sangfroid returned. Fleury judged his temper sufficiently cooled to see if a rapprochement could be brought about between Saint-Arnaud and the president. It could: Saint-Arnaud was committed to the *coup d'état*, just not the timing. He argued that the blow against the Republic must be struck while the Assembly was sitting in Paris. With the politicians in the city, it would be easier to arrest troublemakers than if they were dispersed across France, where they could rally resistance.

If the president waited for a more opportune moment, said Saint-Arnaud, then he could still count on his support.

With Saint-Arnaud back on board, Morny now took the lead. As there were reports circulating in every Paris salon about the *coup d'état*, he was worried that the Assembly might move first and impeach the president, and then, he warned Louis-Napoléon, 'God knows what can happen!'[26] Two things were needed, Morny explained. First, exasperated at the inept planning thus far, Morny wanted complete control. He did not claim to be more capable than everyone else, but what he did have was a very particular set of skills that made him ideally suited to carrying out a *coup d'état*: unwavering self-control, a relentless ability to pursue ends and no qualms about means. The second thing needed, Morny explained, was an audacious plan that put the Assembly on the back foot and whipped the people up to new levels of outrage against their elected representatives.

———

On a cold autumn evening, small groups of men made their way along Paris's dark, muddy lanes, sodden with filthy water, before reaching a hall nestled among ramshackle hovels straight out of one of Victor Hugo's novels. The men climbed an uneven narrow wooden staircase to the second floor. Only those known to the doormen were admitted into the hall, which was usually a theatre. Heavy iron lamps suspended from the ceiling dimly lit the room, where, at the far end, there was a badly built stage. Here, four tallow candles burned on a table, casting a sallow light onto the audience, made up of furtive men talking in hushed tones. They were dressed in workers' clothes, had thick beards and were sitting on hard oak benches in this damp, cold room. The spartan setting in one of Paris's poorest districts was fitting, as was the secrecy. For this was a meeting of democratic socialists, France's much-persecuted far left.

Beforehand, in the time-honoured tradition of the left, the audience began by criticising the left. Conversations among small groups rambled, always prefixed with the word 'citizen': the Mountain in the Assembly was hopeless – why, the people had as much faith in them as they did in the right-wing majority, said one. Still, at least they were better than the left-leaning newspapers. *La Presse* had sold itself, body and soul, to the Élysée; and if

La République had not sold itself yet, that was only because it could find no one to sell itself to. The regular fines for *L'Événement* – Victor Hugo's paper – and the imprisonment of its journalists were publicity stunts. *La Siècle* was bourgeois; *La National* beneath contempt; *La Révolution* too stupid to bother with.

Discussions finally turned to the reason the meeting had been called: electoral strategy. The committee wanted to boycott an upcoming by-election in the department of the Seine. These boycotts were now commonplace on the left, a way of protesting against the 31 May 1850 law which had seen some three million of the poorest Frenchmen denied the right to vote. Talk also turned to the elections of 1852. For these, the hated law would simply be ignored: men would vote whether it allowed them to or not. This put the most radically progressive political group in France – the *démoc-socs* – in the strange position of supporting Louis-Napoléon. For as they discussed the inequities of restricting the franchise in a dank, second-floor theatre, the president was trying to have the law they hated overturned in the Assembly.

This was part of Morny's plan. For the upcoming legislative session, Louis-Napoléon would tack left, proposing that the restrictive 31 May law be overturned. Morny, correctly, calculated that this would outrage the right-wing majority, who had pushed for the law and saw it as crucial in the fight against socialism. Meanwhile, Morny pointed out, the left would be embarrassed because they would be placed in the awkward position of supporting Louis-Napoléon or arguing against democracy. It all played out exactly as predicted. After yet another debate in which speakers claimed the future of France was in the balance – and Louis-Napoléon enjoyed the rare spectacle of the Mountain arguing in his favour – the Assembly voted 353 to 347 to keep the law. It was a gift to Louis-Napoléon. The most skilled propagandist could never have made the Bonapartist claim that the elect of the nation was frustrated by the elites in the Assembly more eloquently persuasive than a narrow conservative majority voting down the president's motion to give power back to the people.

Louis-Napoléon now arranged his pieces on the board. Saint-Arnaud became minister of war, and there was another change: Louis-Napoléon appointed a largely unknown civil servant, Charlemagne de Maupas, as prefect of police. Maupas had come to the president's attention earlier that year, when he had recommended the arrest of republicans known for opposition to Louis-Napoléon. When his superior asked what the charges were, Maupas exploded. 'Charges! . . . What need is there for charges against notorious enemies? It is enough to know their thoughts. However, if evidence is as necessary as you say it is, it will be found at the homes of the accused on such a day and at such a time: I will get my agents to plant it.'[27] While Maupas was unlikely to win awards as a detective, Louis-Napoléon thought his approach deserved 'nothing but praise'.[28]

But while the president was preparing, his opponents were making their own plans, insisting on the Assembly's constitutional right to call on the army to defend it in case of danger and reminding troops not to obey illegal orders to shut down parliament. Saint-Arnaud, on the other hand, issued a circular, stressing to officers and soldiers what he saw as much more important than the law: blind obedience. Yet Louis-Napoléon's politicking had worked so well that many republicans saw the Assembly's measures as a prelude to a royalist *coup d'état* led by Thiers and Changarnier. Given a choice between a Bonaparte who wanted to restore the vote to millions and those on the monarchist right who had removed it, the left would take their chances with the president. Even Victor Hugo, a man who now rarely gave Louis-Napoléon the benefit of the doubt, scribbled in his notebook that he was not particularly alarmed by the Élysée but was worried about the conservative majority.

Hugo should have been alarmed by the Élysée. Here, Louis-Napoléon was preparing public opinion before he moved. On 24 November, an article in a sympathetic newspaper caused a sensation, writing of conspiracies hatched 'in the higher circles of society and among the old parties'. Referring to a motion for defending the Assembly, the journalist commented, 'On Monday last, a week today, we were within a hair's breadth of civil war.'[29] Changarnier, the article insisted, was poised to become dictator, supported by Thiers. Against the will of the people, monarchists wanted to plunge France into chaos on behalf of exiled French royals. By midday, thousands of copies had been bought on the streets of Paris. In a prize-giving ceremony not long after, which the president turned into a political rally, Louis-Napoléon presented himself as a bulwark against the machinations of politicians. France was caught, he claimed, between 'demagogic ideas' and 'monarchical hallucinations'. But 'have no fears for the future', he reassured the crowd. 'A government based on the whole mass of the nation . . . this government, I say, will know how to fulfil its mission because it has in it the right that comes from the people, and the strength that comes from God!'[30]

Despite reports of imminent violence, the Assembly continued to debate other business, including a proposal members found even more absurd than the restoration of a Napoleonic empire: female suffrage. As politicians collapsed into laughter, some representatives cried that you might as well let children vote. Trying to make himself heard over the derision, the man arguing for women's right to vote pointed out that what seems strange and bizarre today will not be so tomorrow.[31] This was a sentiment one fervent republican might have taken into consideration when he had labelled any threat to the Assembly as absurd only days before its members were doubled over laughing at the prospect of women voting. Dismissing a Bonapartist power grab, he said there was no danger and, even if there were, 'there is an invisible sentinel who guards you – this sentinel, I don't need to name it', though he did anyway: 'It is the people.'[32] That theory was about to be put to the test.

———

On the evening of Monday 1 December 1851, Louis-Napoléon was holding his regular Monday soirée at the Élysée, but the most glamorous show that night was at the Opéra-Comique, where the great, the good and the not so good gathered. Morny was there, as was Changarnier, watching a performance of *Le Château de la Barbe-Bleue* (*Bluebeard's Castle*). Even by the standards of comic opera, the plot was preposterous – much of it set in India, where the deposed English King James II had put in motion a plot to restore himself to the throne – but the drama was dull and the audience's minds turned to conspiracy closer to home. 'It was said earlier', remarked one woman to Morny, 'that the president is going to sweep out the Assembly.' If he does, 'what will you do?' In that case, Madame, Morny quipped, 'I shall be on the side of the broom.'[33]

Just after 10 p.m. at the Élysée, Louis-Napoléon gathered with Maupas, Saint-Arnaud, Persigny and Morny – straight from the theatre – in the

Salon d'Argent, a private room where Napoléon Bonaparte had signed his abdication after Waterloo. They were all immaculately dressed in their finest evening wear or, in Saint-Arnaud's case, military uniform. Standing behind a desk, Louis-Napoléon took a key from his watch chain, unlocked a drawer and removed a dossier, on which he had scrawled a not particularly subtle code word: 'Rubicon'. The conspirators ran through their plan one more time. As they were leaving, Morny remarked that if they failed, they would be executed. 'I am confident of success,' said Louis-Napoléon. 'I have always on my finger my mother's ring, which bears the motto: hope!'[34] Then he shook the hand of each man before they went their separate ways, all with specific tasks to accomplish.

Morny, though, had nothing to do until the morning, so went to play cards at his club. As he made his way through Paris late at night, there were still a few carriages rolling along the streets, some restaurants with lights on and men out for late strolls, humming ariettas as they smoked cigars, little suspecting that the next morning, 2 December – the anniversary of Napoléon Bonaparte crowning himself emperor in 1804, and then winning the Battle of Austerlitz one year later – was the date planned for what its backers hoped would become another Napoleonic landmark.

11

HISTORY OF A CRIME

At 6 a.m. on 2 December 1851, police found General Nicolas Changarnier outside his apartment. Having been woken by the sound of heavy footsteps in the courtyard, he was waiting barefoot in his nightshirt, two pistols in his hands. 'I had expected the *coup d'état*,' he said, 'and here it is.'[1] Adolphe Thiers was asleep when the police entered his room. An officer opened his crimson damask curtains lined with white muslin. 'What's this about?' asked Thiers, jolting awake and pushing a white cotton hat out of his eyes.

'Remain calm, we mean you no harm,' replied the officer.

'But what do you intend to do? Don't you know that I'm a representative of the people?'

'Yes, but I cannot discuss my orders.'

A reluctant Thiers slowly got out of bed and continued his remonstrances while getting dressed. Then he said, 'What if I blew your brains out?'

'I believe you incapable of such an act, Monsieur Thiers.'[2]

Thiers resigned himself to arrest. Across Paris, others did the same, and soon most of those who could organise resistance to defend the Republic were in prison. Arresting unsuspecting generals and politicians in their homes at dawn was easy; occupying the Palais Bourbon where the Assembly sat was another matter. Before daylight, soldiers commanded by Colonel Charles-Marie-Esprit Espinasse marched to the seat of French democracy. When they arrived, they disarmed soldiers guarding the entrance.

Inside, the quaestors, representatives charged with the Assembly's defence, slept soundly in government-provided accommodation. An abrupt knock on the door woke one of them, a former general and now a representative of the people. 'I have come to fulfil a duty,' announced an officer. 'I understand,' replied the general, 'you are a traitor.' The officer mumbled that there was a plot against the state and produced some papers, which the general knocked out of his hands. A hero of France's Algerian wars, he pointedly dressed himself in military uniform, then hugged his wife, while his seven-year-old son, still in pyjamas, burst into tears. Recognising Espinasse, the general said, 'You are a villain, and I hope to live long enough to tear the buttons from your uniform.' But his words had no effect. A major shouted, 'We have had enough of lawyer generals.' Then he was bundled outside into a carriage, where a lieutenant walked up to him, looked into his eyes and said, 'Scum.'[3]

Soon, the palace where the Assembly sat resembled a military camp, with soldiers lounging around in the courtyard. Yet the building was cavernous, and one entrance remained unguarded. Through here some sixty representatives who had arrived for the morning's parliamentary business found their way inside. Determined to resist, they took their seats in the debating chamber.

Then the symbolic moment they had been waiting for arrived: soldiers burst in. '*Vive la République!*' shouted the politicians. Next, one of them read out articles from the constitution to the bewildered soldiers, notably article sixty-eight, which deposed the president should he act illegally. Another deputy shouted, 'Soldiers, your very presence here is treason. Leave the hall!'[4] The troops wavered, but then a second column marched in with Espinasse at their head. He demanded that the politicians leave; they refused. The soldiers then began hauling out resistant representatives. One particularly recalcitrant individual declined to get out of his seat, insisting that a soldier force him. 'Is that your last word?' replied an infantryman. It was, and so the soldier hit him with a blow that knocked the man to the ground, before he was carried out of the chamber.

Having cleared the Assembly, Espinasse discovered representatives outside the palace now trying to rally his soldiers to defend the Republic, as well as a crowd of curious onlookers. Espinasse had had enough, and addressing the politicians he said: 'In my eyes you are no longer representatives of the people, but merely insurgents who are stirring up the people to revolt.' If they continued, he warned, 'I will have you instantly shot.'[5] This had the desired effect: those not under arrest hurried off.

———

Still in his dressing gown, but with riding trousers and spurs underneath, at 6 a.m. Louis-Napoléon was drinking coffee in the Élysée. The last couple of hours he had spent at his desk writing invitations; now, the president was going for a ride. Before that, though, he instructed Fleury to make sure that Paris was occupied militarily; some fifty thousand troops would secure the streets. Bread, wine and money were distributed. Well-lubricated, bribed soldiers were tasked with what was euphemistically termed 'saving society', and might better be described as terrifying Paris into submission.

That morning, however, the people were more confused than scared. In the early hours, the national printing office had been occupied. Workers, each given only parts of the text to maintain secrecy, had toiled through the night to ready proclamations that a motley crew of street-fighting Bonapartists plastered over the city. As Parisians went about their morning business, they read the president's appeal:

> The present situation cannot last much longer. Each day increases
> the danger to the country. The Assembly which should be the firmest
> support of order has become a hotbed of conspiracy . . . Instead of
> framing laws for public welfare it forges arms for civil war, it attacks
> the power I hold directly from the nation . . . I have dissolved it, and I
> call upon the whole of the people to judge between it and me.[6]

This was a succinct rendering of the message which had been drip-fed for years; however, the genius lay in Louis-Napoléon's second act, which declared universal male suffrage restored. Not only was treason dressed up as a blow against an elite conspiracy, it was also done to give back control to the people. Of course, those who supported Louis-Napoléon – and there were many – were delighted he had acted. But with prominent leaders of the left and right in prison, the army on the streets and enough people sufficiently confused by the proclamations, there was no popular uprising that morning. Louis-Napoléon could go riding.

At 8 a.m., a man dressed in the uniform of a marshal of France arrived at the Élysée. It was Jérôme Bonaparte, sixty-seven years old and the last surviving brother of Emperor Napoléon. He was not the only remnant of the First Empire: there was also Morny's father, Charles Joseph, comte de Flahaut, an aide-de-camp to the emperor at Waterloo; Edgar Ney, a son of Napoléon's great marshal; and Prince Lucien Murat, son of the legendary cavalry commander from the Napoleonic wars. These apparitions from the old Empire mounted their horses to ride out into Paris. Louis-Napoléon led them, dressed in National Guard uniform, black trousers with a red stripe down each side, black tunic tightly cinched at the waist, grand cordon of the *légion d'honneur* affixed to his left breast and a tricorn hat with tricolour feathers.

As he rode along the Champs-Élysées, he raised his hat to the soldiers who cried '*Vive l'empereur!*' More troops acclaimed the cavalcade as it rode into the Place de la Concorde and then made its way through the Tuileries gardens and crossed the Seine, before returning via the Left Bank. Not all the cries were welcoming. Plenty shouted, '*Vive la République!*'; one brave soul cried, 'Down with the dictator! Down with the Praetorians!' Fearing classical allusions to the Roman emperor's bodyguards were too highbrow, he then went with 'Down with Bonaparte!' which caused a stir in the crowd, but Louis-Napoléon rode on.[7] As he went past the Quai d'Orsay an officer galloped up to Fleury, telling him that hundreds of deputies were meeting in the tenth arrondissement. Worse, they had just named one of their number commander-in-chief of the army, and the National Guard was supporting him.

———

After they were thrown out of the Assembly, many of the deputies made their way to the tenth arrondissement. Here, a sympathetic detachment of the National Guard guaranteed their safety. The strategy of right-leaning deputies, and some from the left who got swept along for want of a better plan, was to hold an impromptu parliament, depose Louis-Napoléon, appoint a general to lead the armed forces and then defeat the *coup d'état*.

By 11 a.m., there were some three hundred deputies at the local town hall, gathering in a rectangular room on the first floor. Mostly royalists and conservatives, these were unlikely saviours of the Republic. They were predominantly men of letters, not of action. Alexis de Tocqueville was there, pale, ill and leaning on a windowsill. Opposite the door was a long table covered with an ink-stained green cloth and piles of paper, with presiding officers sitting behind it. Nervous and excited politicians milled about; some stood on benches to get a better view as the conservative majority tried to decree the *coup d'état* out of existence.

First, a resolution was passed deposing the president. Then there was uproar as men rushed to put their signatures to hastily copied-out documents, shouts of '*Vive la République*', proposals, counter-proposals, many self-congratulatory cheers and applause. But what to do next? Members from the left argued that the people must be called to arms. This was worse than a *coup d'état* for those on the right, who shouted, 'The law, the law, no revolution!' Several motions later, the deputies got round to naming a commander for the army, which they had already decreed was now under their orders.

Just as a general accepted this rapid promotion, soldiers appeared at the door, putting his appointment to the test. A pantomime ensued in the hallway outside, with the politicians claiming that they had the law and the constitution on their side, and soldiers insisting they had orders. But their superior hesitated. These politicians seemed certain they were right and debating the niceties of constitutional law with some of the finest legal minds in France was above his pay grade. He decided to await orders.

They soon arrived: disperse the deputies or arrest them if they refuse. When these were read out to the politicians in the hall, several of them cried, 'Well! Arrest us.'[8] Soldiers obligingly swarmed in and roughly dragged the leaders of the Assembly downstairs. One representative dared to insult the hard-drinking Bonapartist officer in charge. 'If you are insolent,' replied the officer, 'I'll hit you with the butt of my rifle.'[9] Showing that an avalanche of decrees was no match for brute force, the representatives of the people accepted their fate.

Just after 3 p.m., they were taken to the nearby Quai d'Orsay barracks and locked up. Rarely has there been such an illustrious roll call of prisoners; some of the most celebrated names in France now shuffled about in a freezing cold courtyard. Generals and admirals rubbed shoulders with Louis-Napoléon's former ministers, including Odilon Barrot and Alexis de Tocqueville. 'It was an act of brutal tyranny,' wrote one of the jailed luminaries, such as France 'had never known' or would 'ever forget'.[10]

But the Bastille this was not. Two hundred bottles of wine soon arrived, which the prisoners drank to wash down the soup, bread, legs of lamb, veal kidneys, roast beef and vegetable side dishes. Naturally, there was a cheese course. Publicly, they claimed that the food was meagre, but if it was, that was the fault of the nearby Café d'Orsay, where they spent 587 francs on this feast. As one wit quipped, it was like a ballroom supper. Tocqueville had a fine time, 'the gayest that I ever passed . . . The elite of France in education, birth, and in talents of society, was collected within the walls of that barrack.' Some hired mattresses from the soldiers, others laid out cloaks on the floor, but instead of sleeping they spent the night talking: 'anecdotes, repartees, jokes, and pleasantries' from the masters of the bon mot. Howls of laughter greeted one man as he exclaimed with great solemnity, looking at the floor, strewn with mattresses and statesmen, and lighted by two tallow candles, 'So, this is what the famous Party of Order is reduced to.'[11]

The barracks was a holding pen and throughout the night the politicians were bundled into whatever transport could be found – police vans, post wagons and public omnibuses – to take them to prison. By the time Odilon Barrot was driven through the faubourg of Saint-Antoine, famed for its revolutionary radicalism, men were leaving for work. When they discovered who was inside the heavily escorted carriages, Barrot heard them say, 'Ah! They are going to lock up the twenty-five francs! That's well done.'[12] Twenty-five francs was the daily stipend given to each member of the Assembly, an enormous sum to an ordinary worker.

The half-hearted resistance from the right ended in prison cells and had been met with indifference by the people. At least Tocqueville and his friends had an enjoyable soirée. If the leaders of the left were captured, they were unlikely to have such a fun evening, and while the men of the right were drowning what sorrows they had – few would mourn the Republic if it fell – the Parisian left was beginning to organise.

———

Victor Hugo was in bed when he learned that the *coup d'état* had begun. While he quickly dressed, a man entered, an unemployed cabinetmaker who had a room in Hugo's house. 'Well,' Hugo enquired, 'what do the people say?'

'People are dazed,' replied the cabinetmaker. 'Workmen read the placards, say nothing and go to work. Only one in a hundred speaks. It is to say, "Good!" This is how it appears to them. The law of 31 May is abrogated – "Well done!" Universal suffrage is re-established – "Also well done!" The reactionary majority has been driven away – "Admirable!" Thiers is arrested – "Capital!" Changarnier is seized – "Bravo!'"

Undeterred, Hugo took the tricolour sash of office worn by representatives of the people, determined to rendezvous with his fellow Mountain politicians and resist. 'What are you going to do?' his wife asked before he left. 'My duty,' replied Hugo.[13] But first he had breakfast, a cutlet he devoured in two mouthfuls before heading out. Meeting with like-minded deputies, Hugo wanted them to march wearing their sashes of office and to shout, '*Vive la République!*' If the troops fired on them, they should call the people of Paris to arms.

Cooler heads talked him down. The mood in Paris ranged from outright support through confusion and indifference to mild anger. Before an appeal could be made, others argued, public opinion needed to be prepared, proclamations explaining that the constitution had been violated printed, loyal National Guardsmen mobilised and barricades constructed.

A meeting at a nearby house was called to organise this. Walking in, Hugo found about sixty members of the left standing in a room and talking excitedly. He took charge and began dictating a proclamation: Louis-Napoléon was a traitor. Twelve copies were made, and men hurriedly left to find a printer, but it soon became apparent that all were shut and troops were guarding them. Fearful that police were on their trail, the deputies fled, promising to reunite at another location.

Hugo went onto the streets. It was too far, and too dangerous, to go home. Instead, he took an omnibus in the direction of the Bastille. As the wagon passed through the Porte Saint-Martin, a regiment of cavalry came the other way and stopped opposite the omnibus. Hugo lowered the window, stuck out his considerably sized head and shouted, 'Down with Louis Bonaparte! Those who serve traitors are traitors!'

Emboldened, Hugo's companions joined in the cries, as did one young man they did not know. The rest of the passengers, however, were less sympathetic at having their commute hijacked for the revolution. 'Hold your tongues,' they told Hugo. 'You will cause us all to be massacred.' Either through Bonapartist sympathy or from a keenness to demonstrate that this bus was not the vanguard of the republican fightback, another passenger started shouting, '*Vive l'empereur!*'[14] The cavalry trotted off; the omnibus moved on.

After meandering through the streets of Paris, despairing at the apathy of the people and eating chocolate cake, Hugo found himself at 8 p.m. on the fourth floor of a tall house, which, he noted, would have been an ideal place to watch the storming of the Bastille in 1789. In 1851, however, revolutionary action seemed far off. The deputies had still found no one to print their proclamations.

While they waited, they got down to the important business of forming a committee, initially of insurrection, and then, at Hugo's insistence, renamed the Committee of Resistance. This, of course, necessitated the forming of a sub-committee. While working through the details for this, word reached them that one of France's most notorious socialists wanted to meet at the Place de la Bastille. Pierre-Joseph Proudhon had been imprisoned for sedition, but it just so happened that he had a furlough day that coincided with Louis-Napoléon's *coup d'état*, and he had asked to speak with Hugo.

Soldiers bivouacked in the gloomy square. Reflecting the moonlight, their bayonets gave off showers of silver sparks, and above the murk rose the Column of July, celebrating the Revolution of 1830. Leaning against a wall in a particularly dark corner and wearing a broad-brimmed hat was Proudhon. 'I come to give you a friendly warning,' he said. 'You are entertaining illusions. The people are ensnared in this affair. They will not stir. Bonaparte will carry them with him. This rubbish, the restitution of universal suffrage, entraps the simpletons . . . He will succeed and you will fail . . . We must wait; but at this moment fighting would be madness. What do you hope for?'

'Nothing,' said Hugo.

'And what are you going to do?'

'Everything.'

Realising that Hugo and the Mountain were resolved to resist, Proudhon disappeared into the darkness.

Only two things remained standing, Hugo declared grandiosely at yet another furtive meeting later that evening, 'the *coup d'état* and ourselves. Ourselves! And who are we? We are Truth and Justice! We are the supreme sovereign power, the people incarnate.' Tired of hurried conferences in the surprisingly extensive real estate of the Parisian left, Hugo wanted action. He urged all present to meet tomorrow morning in the faubourg Saint-Antoine, at the Salle Roysin, a celebrated left-wing cafe. Here, they would put on their sashes of office, march through the streets and call the people to arms. Hugo gave a rousing speech: 'On the one side an army and a Crime; on the other a handful of men and Right! Such is the struggle. Do you accept it?'[15] The cheers and applause indicated that they did. Proudhon's prediction that the people would not rise was about to be put to the test.

Hair dishevelled, boots covered in mud, Hugo found refuge that night on a sofa in a friend's apartment. Unable to sleep, he paced the room, occasionally peering out at the starless night from behind the muslin curtains, watching the clouds race past and counting down the church bells until dawn. It was unlikely this behaviour endeared him to his host family. He shared the room with a two-year-old girl, but she slept soundly in her cot as France's greatest poet and would-be freedom fighter thought about his day of destiny.

———

Early next morning, at the Salle Roysin, amid the cafe's marble-topped tables and velvet-covered benches, left-wing radicals were already gathering. Hugo's rhetoric the night before had electrified his audience, galvanising resistance, but there was one drawback to the brilliance of his speech. In the euphoric cheers that greeted his call to arms, the exact time for the rendezvous had been drowned out. Hugo thought it was 9 a.m., others 8 a.m. By 8.30, impatient republicans who thought their comrades were late wanted to get the revolution started.

Although there were no more than fifteen of them, the men decided to act. They marched into the street with their tricolour sashes, crying: 'To arms! To the barricades! *Vive la constitution!*' From windows and half-opened shop fronts came occasional cries of '*Vive la République!*', although only a few joined the procession. As soon as they came to a crossroads, they started to build barricades. A manure cart was overturned, then one carrying milk. Seeing what was happening, a baker spurred his horse to a gallop so he could escape with his bread wagon, but it was chased down and soon formed part of the Republic's first line of defence. Finally, an omnibus hove into view, and its driver and passengers graciously allowed it to complete the makeshift ramparts among the manure, milk and bread.

The representatives had disarmed nearby guard posts. Now they had muskets and ammunition. From a military point of view, the situation was hopeless; however, they hoped to win soldiers over to their side and make a symbolic stand that would galvanise the people. But the only people out in force at this point were Bonapartists, who came to shout at the deputies. 'Down with the twenty-five francs!' they yelled. Alphonse Baudin, a deputy standing on the barricade, stared them down and reportedly replied, 'You shall see how one can die for twenty-five francs!'[16]

At about 9.30 a.m., the deputies saw troops marching; some locals who had joined the resistance fled. As three companies of soldiers and a mounted officer approached at a funereal pace, eight deputies climbed onto the overturned wagons to face them. The politicians insisted the troops halt; the soldiers continued. Then seven of the deputies clambered down from the wagons and walked towards the oncoming soldiers. The soldiers stopped.

'We are representatives of the people,' the politicians argued. 'You are deceived. It is the constitution you attack.'[17] They urged the soldiers to join their ranks.

'Retire, or I will order the men to fire,' responded the officer.

'You may kill us, but you will not make us fall back; our bodies must protect the people!' came the response.

'Fix bayonets,' ordered the captain, and turning towards his men, he shouted, 'Charge!'[18]

The soldiers surged towards the deputies, but passed them like water flowing around stones in a stream. As they did so, a musket shot came from one of the panicked defenders manning the barricade. In the street below, between two of the deputies, a young soldier fell to the ground. Volleys of gunfire were now exchanged. Three musket balls tore into the head of Alphonse Baudin, who was standing on a wagon. He fell to his death before the soldiers rushed the barricade, dispersing the remaining defenders and chasing them down alleyways. On the now silent street, the stunned deputies looked down as the pale wintry sun shone on the corpse of the young soldier dead at their feet. His eyes were closed, and blood streaked down his face from his mouth and his nose, staining his uniform and spreading on the ground around his lifeless body.

Only a few streets away, Hugo heard the gunfire as a cab drove him towards the cafe. He soon learned that despite the fact that the resistance had its first martyr in Baudin, the people had not risen. Disillusioned, Hugo decided there was only one thing left to do: hold another meeting.

———

In the Élysée, confidence was waning. Numerous reports reached Louis-Napoléon that the situation in Paris was worsening, panic was spreading, resistance rising. Out reconnoitring with a squad of cavalry, Fleury had been met with a furious mob. Waving their hats in the air and shaking their fists at the troops, the men cried, '*Vive la République!*' A general with Fleury who had taken the Bonapartist line that they were saving the Republic at face value asked whether his men should also shout '*Vive la République!*' 'No, a thousand times no!' replied Fleury, before turning towards the cavalrymen and roaring, '*Vive Napoléon!*' Fleury rode on, ignoring the crowds. Then a shot rang out. He was flung forwards onto his horse. Instinctively, he put his hand behind his head and saw it was covered with blood. His uniform stained with red, head bandaged, Fleury returned to the Élysée. 'My poor Fleury!' a startled Louis-Napoléon exclaimed, taking him by the hand.[19]

Louis-Napoléon's prefect of police, Maupas, who had drunk deep from the well of rabidly anti-socialist propaganda, was especially worried. His frequent and increasingly hysterical briefings included rumours that the most feared revolutionaries of Europe were converging on Paris. 'We should be under no illusions, it is the great struggle of 1852 that we have to fight in December 1851,' he wrote to Morny. Worse, 'I do not believe that popular sympathy is with us.'[20]

Underground networks began to co-ordinate and barricades were springing up across central Paris. Threatening crowds gathered, insulted troops and then ran off, tiring the army out with forced marches while experienced street fighters built defences more formidable than the hastily constructed one Baudin had died on.

Maupas believed that this resistance must be crushed as it formed, but Saint-Arnaud and Morny preferred to employ other brutal strategies learned from urban warfare and previous insurrections. Prior attempts to crush uprisings, Saint-Arnaud and Morny argued, had failed because soldiers became worn down by frequent raids, rushing from place to place to put down rebellion. Tired, demoralised and poorly supplied, many troops then defected. The solution was simple: pull the soldiers back and allow opponents to concentrate. Then send in the army, using artillery to smash the barricades and infantry to kill anyone left standing. Morny and Saint-Arnaud's arguments won over Louis-Napoléon. But this, Maupas warned, was the tactic that led to the victory of the people over the army in 1830 and 1848.

———

Victor Hugo's meetings, proclamations and committees were finally having an impact. The Mountain managed to get a decree that deposed Louis-Napoléon printed. Copies were hurriedly distributed and posted in the streets under cover of darkness. People gathered in cafes, read them and then cried, 'Down with Soulouque!' – a pejorative comparison to the president of Haiti, who had declared himself emperor in 1849.[21] When the names of the deputies who signed the decrees were read out, people cheered. Insults were shouted at the few troops still on the streets.

On the boulevard Saint-Martin and boulevard du Temple, people gathered. From the gloom of these dimly lit streets, the crowds could see people with torches moving towards them. Then they heard singing. It was the 'Marseillaise', and it was being sung as part of a funeral procession. Two dead bodies, victims of earlier fighting and covered in blood, were being carried on improvised stretchers. The crowd parted to let them through. At each chorus the cortège stopped and people raised their torches, the flames reflected against the unlit windows along the street as the words rang out: '*Aux armes, citoyens! Formez vos bataillons!*' This is exactly what many did through the night of 3 December.

On the morning of 4 December, Victor Hugo and the Mountain met in another house – the seventeenth since the *coup d'état* began, Hugo noted. After proclamations were finalised, he and his companions went out to inspect the streets. What they saw cheered them. As Hugo wrote, 'Our voice was reaching the people, [and] a certain confidence was springing up.'

So were barricades, more than seventy in total, some as high as two-storey buildings. These were constructed with whatever was at hand – paving stones, wagons, furniture, buckets. Bottles had been smashed, lining the streets with broken glass to impede cavalry. Hugo wrote that central Paris resembled 'a labyrinth of streets which appears to be made for a labyrinth of riots'.

The defenders of this labyrinth grabbed whatever weapons they could. One woman was seen armed with a sabre; wearing a red dress and a black lace bonnet with red ribbons, a flower seller swapped her roses for an iron bar. Disarming National Guard units proved more effective: some eight hundred muskets were taken. Spirits were high, and one hitherto pessimistic republican exclaimed that tomorrow they would have Louis-Napoléon's head. Sensing a teachable moment, if slightly dampening the revolutionary fire, Hugo said that if they defeated Louis-Napoléon, they would not have his head because the first thing they would do was abolish the death penalty.

But outside the centre, the self-appointed saviours of society were organising as well. Noticing the military build-up, a passer-by asked an officer, 'Up to what point are you going?'

'To the end,' came the reply.[22]

———

Among the soldiers poised to strike, the *coup d'état* was popular. Many had voted for Louis-Napoléon, or, if they were too young to vote in December 1848, their parents had. Either way, the president was their man, not least because he made sure they were well garrisoned, well fed and, crucially, well lubricated during the cold December days. Most had little time for sophisticated elite republicans like Victor Hugo, or the radical Parisian artisans whose progressive politics were absurd to those with the deeply conservative and Catholic convictions held by many French people.

If some cared little for who was in charge, they did care about staying alive. And the major obstacle to that was the mythical revolutionaries now holding the centre of Paris. Tales about these fighters from previous clashes bred hatred among the rank and file: snipers shooting from windows, paving stones pushed from barricades crushing unsuspecting infantrymen or, more simply, the taunts and insults crowds had subjected them to since 2 December. In short, tens of thousands of loyal, heavily armed, albeit nervous and slightly drunk men were about to descend on the capital. At midday on 4 December, the troops marched from their garrisons. 'Turn back, don't go,' cautioned an old man. 'It's teeming with the mob. You and your troops are going to be slaughtered.'[23]

Central Paris, however, was not quite the hellish throng of angry men ready to destroy the soldiers that the old man had painted. If the capital stopped every time violence seemed imminent, then little business would ever get done. Gentlemen were out for strolls, cafes were open and women and children peered into shop windows to see the New Year's Day displays, a more important gift-giving occasion than Christmas in nineteenth-century France. The sweetshops were particularly magnificent, each trying to outdo the other for delicious, eye-catching mountains of bonbons or sugar sculptures as beautiful as works of art. It was a child's paradise, and martial law or not, people came to see it.

Even when troops marched in early that afternoon, among more affluent Parisians the mood was one of curiosity rather than fear. Barricades were not unusual, barely more irritating than roadworks, the military was a regular sight on the streets and political violence, or its threat at least, had been common in the last few years. Moreover, reasoned 'respectable' members of society, if the army were here to crush the socialist 'scum', then so much the better, but that was hardly a reason to stop shopping. In fact, it was a spectacle worth watching, and men and women came out onto the balconies of their apartments.

One such onlooker was a British officer and his wife, on a balcony overlooking rue Montmartre. The whole street as far as the eye could see was covered with soldiers as well as pockets of artillery. The mounted officers, noted the British army captain with disapproval, were smoking cigars. Then, from the distance came the sound of gunfire. 'In a few moments it spread' and 'came down the boulevard in a waving sheet of flame'. In vain, the officer strained to see what they were firing at. Then he realised. They were aiming at the windows.[24]

As the soldiers below raised their muskets, he pushed his wife inside and they sheltered behind the small section of wall that divided the window. A shot smashed into the ceiling above them, showering them with dust and broken plaster. A second volley crashed into the room, shattering every pane of glass but one, breaking a mirror behind them, and a bullet ricocheted into a clock. As the soldiers reloaded, the British man grabbed his wife and ran into a back room.

Below, there was carnage. Panicked soldiers who thought they were under attack had opened fire; terrified, young, inexperienced troops joined in. There were fifteen minutes of indiscriminate shooting, in which artillery demolished a building suspected of sheltering insurrectionists. The men, women and children who moments before had been peaceably walking along pavements were now screaming, running for cover wherever they could find it. Many could not, and their bloodied corpses were left in the street.

Not long after this random fire was brought under control, the targeted killing began. Hugo described it as a 'furnace' and the sound as like a 'thunderstorm'. Determined to resist, he walked towards the fighting, 'this butchery, this tragedy. I saw the rain of blind death, I saw the distracted victims fall around me in crowds.'[25] As a light drizzle fell, barricades and houses were blasted with artillery, then rushed with infantrymen who cut down any who resisted, and many who did not. After witnessing it, Hugo reported back to his committee, which was sitting in a nearby house. As he relayed what he had seen, the sound of gunfire drew closer, and he and his fellow politicians made a run for it, mingling with frightened groups fleeing advancing troops. The deputies with Hugo found (yet) another house and resolved to continue the struggle.

There were, however, few people left willing to resist. After wolfing down some bread and chocolate, Hugo ventured out again at 9 p.m. A guide led him stumbling through the dark. He came upon poorly manned barricades, one with only two defenders, before reaching a half-demolished building on a barricaded street. Here, it was hoped, reinforcements would gather. Inside, lit by one candle, a woman and child tended two wounded men. His guide could not understand where everyone else was and decided to find out what had happened, leaving Hugo to talk to the wounded and listen to ever-closer gunfire. When the guide returned, he said they should go home, for no one would come. As a dejected Hugo planned how to escape Paris, he walked past a bivouac. Soldiers were laughing, warming themselves around a fire fuelled by wagons that hours earlier had formed barricades. In the capital, the fight was over. Louis-Napoléon had won.

————

Now, Louis-Napoléon could turn his attention to securing his future. As he had pledged, this would be decided by the people. This promise had done much to undermine resistance in Paris. Few Parisians had responded to the calls of Hugo and his fellow deputies, which was reflected in the number of soldiers killed: only twenty-seven. The four hundred or so dead civilians were a testament to the effectiveness, and brutality, of Saint-Arnaud's tactics; however, this was not insurrection on the scale of the 1848 June Days, when some three thousand civilians and sixteen hundred soldiers had died.

On 6 December, with what resistance there had been crushed, Louis-Napoléon felt confident enough to go to a ball. Having made his way through streets still littered with the debris of battle, he alighted from his carriage just before 10 p.m. in the Place Vendôme. Far above him, left hand tucked into his waistcoat, telescope in the other and wearing his distinctive bicorne hat and military overcoat, was the statue of his uncle atop the column cast from captured cannons after the Battle of Austerlitz on 2 December 1805.

Inside the Hôtel Bristol was a collection of aristocrats gathered to welcome the new British ambassador to France, Henry Wellesley, known as Lord Cowley. Louis-Napoléon danced a quadrille before talking serenely with guests, making sure to pay especial attention to Cowley. At midnight, the president left, the Duke of Hamilton seeing him out. When the duke returned to the party, he remarked, as Louis-Napoléon must have known he would, that the president was unaccompanied by a military escort. He returned to the Élysée in a simple one-horse carriage.

Having courted foreign opinion, which would be key to giving whatever regime emerged from the *coup d'état* legitimacy, Louis-Napoléon turned to the French people. All Frenchmen over the age of twenty-one would vote yes or no to the questions: did they want Louis-Napoléon to stay in office and would they delegate him powers to draw up a new constitution?

He had been silent since 2 December – testament to how worried he had been – but on 8 December he issued a proclamation: 'The troubles are over. Whatever the decision of the people, society is saved. The first part of my task is accomplished . . . Why should the people rise against me? If I did not possess your confidence, if your opinions have changed, there is no need to spill precious blood. It is sufficient to put a "no" vote in the ballot box. I will always respect the will of the people.'[26]

The question 'Why should the people rise against me?' had been a rhetorical one, but beyond Paris it was anything but. It turned out tens of thousands of people were not going to wait for the vote due to take place on 20 December, and they were happy to spill blood. It seemed as though the *coup d'état* had conjured into existence the Jacquerie it had been designed to prevent. Paris was calm, but the country seemed on the brink of civil war.

12

VOX POPULI, VOX DEI

'The Jacquerie in the provinces', Louis-Napoléon told the Austrian ambassador, 'supports my words.' Rather than a crisis, it was an opportunity. 'People will be forced to rally around me to avoid disorder.'[1] As Louis-Napoléon realised, the uprisings outside Paris proved to many wavering conservatives that the social war long prophesied was real. Indeed, in the minds of those terrified by the Jacquerie, the revolt conjured up apocalyptic scenes. 'Gendarmes are butchered; their barracks set on fire; children are killed; they even try to burn one alive; he succeeds in escaping the flames, but is thrown back' – or so believed Louis-Napoléon's chief of police, who claimed a soundtrack of revolutionary songs accompanied this orgy of violence.[2]

To the stolid bourgeoisie who read salacious reports like this in the newspapers, Louis-Napoléon had indeed saved society from the horror. In fact, the uprising was remarkably peaceful: only nine gendarmes, nine soldiers and four civilians were killed as a result of some hundred thousand men taking up arms. The gendarmes and soldiers were more violent in response to the badly organised and swiftly crushed uprising, although even then there were only about a hundred deaths.

What was more ferocious was the repression that followed. Morny instructed the authorities to arrest anyone considered dangerous, even if the courts had already released them for lack of evidence. Over-zealous officials saw a once-in-a-lifetime opportunity to cleanse the country of socialism, and in the largest crackdown against political activism thus far in nineteenth-century France, twenty-seven thousand people went through what passed for justice – the numbers so high special courts were hastily convened. Some managed to get off, one peasant ingeniously arguing that he had joined a march only because he thought it was in celebration of Louis-Napoléon's birthday. Others were less successful; ten thousand were deported to Algeria. Indeed, the enthusiasm to punish became an embarrassment for Louis-Napoléon and he pardoned many of those sentenced. Though more lenient than those who carried out his orders, he was in no doubt that he had 'saved society' and that people would thank him for it, which is why he wanted to legitimate his actions through direct democracy. On 20 and 21 December 1851, the people of France were asked in a plebiscite whether they backed his illegal *coup d'état*.

Unlike when he was elected president on 10 December 1848, this would not be a free and fair vote. Opponents could not publish newspapers, nor meet to organise; there would not be a 'no' campaign. Furthermore, most departments were under a state of siege, a legal term which meant that martial law reigned. With criticism in France impossible, it was left to the British press to wonder, 'If the people were really disposed spontaneously to place unlimited power in the hands of Louis Napoleon Bonaparte, would it be necessary to drive and cudgel them like beasts to the slaughterhouse?'[3]

'The French people', ran the carefully worded plebiscite, 'want the authority of Louis-Napoléon Bonaparte to be maintained, and delegate to him the necessary powers to establish a constitution.'[4] And given that the choice was between yes and no, it was a referendum on the known versus the unknown, or, as supporters of the president framed it, between civilisation and chaos. Certainly, many conservatives, some begrudgingly, agreed that the only option was to vote yes – as did the Catholic Church, which brought its considerable weight behind the president.

Others were more enthusiastic, and if voting was not quite the day of 'downright national rejoicing' that the obsequious police prefect presented it as, where each elector 'gaily went to the poll to deposit the voting paper which would ensure his deliverance', the result was nonetheless a crushing victory for the president.[5] More than 7.4 million Frenchmen voted yes; only 640,000 no. There were around 1.5 million abstentions, and the margin of victory was much smaller in Paris and other large urban areas; still, it was a stunning triumph. Though the result had never been in doubt, for Louis-Napoléon was not stupid enough to call a vote on a question he might lose, the endorsement of the president's *coup d'état* was astonishing.

For some, however, it did not matter how many votes there were: Louis-Napoléon would never be the legitimate ruler of France. In a work that was part polemic, part therapy, Victor Hugo likened the plebiscite to a criminal stopping a stagecoach, killing those who resist, robbing the survivors and then saying: 'Now, I have written on a piece of paper that you acknowledge that everything I took from you belonged to me and that you grant it to me of your own free will.' Tossing his head, the brigand says, 'I have 7.5 million votes.'[6]

But the yes votes were not robbery under law. Another republican novelist, George Sand, gave a more honest appraisal. 'How can one respond to 6 or 7 million votes?' she mused. 'They were a bit extorted it is true . . . But, after all, no one was forced to vote yes . . . One does not buy or intimidate 6 to 7 million votes.'[7] Sand was right: though opposition had not been permitted, the vote had not been rigged, nor fraudulently counted.

Whatever his opponents thought, Louis-Napoléon believed himself vindicated when presented with the landslide result on 31 December 1851. 'I only left legality to return to the law,' he said. 'More than seven million votes have just absolved me,' he added, a statement which, as people commented, revealed that he thought he had sinned.[8]

On New Year's Day 1852, Notre-Dame was decked out in splendour for a Te Deum – a celebratory Catholic Mass – to demonstrate that God too had voted yes. Over the main entrance to the cathedral, just about visible through the thick January murk, the number '7.5 million' was emblazoned in gold numerals three feet high. As the president entered the cathedral, the orchestra and choir played music by the official composer to Emperor Napoléon Bonaparte. After the service, the choir sang '*Domine salvam fac Rempublicam et Napoleonem*' – 'God save the Republic and Napoléon'. That afterwards Louis-Napoléon returned not to the Élysée, the presidential palace, but to the Tuileries, the traditional residence of kings, suggested that God would soon have to choose between the two. For this was a celebration fit for an emperor, not a president. Certainly, the extraordinary powers Louis-Napoléon granted himself were suited more for an absolute monarch than a democratically elected president.

———

'The dictatorship which the people entrusted to me ceases today,' Louis-Napoléon told dignitaries assembled in the Tuileries on 29 March 1852.[9]

It was fortunate he announced the end of his dictatorship because it would have been hard to notice otherwise. Based on the constitution Napoléon Bonaparte adopted after his *coup d'état* in 1799, Louis-Napoléon's updated version was innovative and created a regime unlike any other in history. It was an extraordinary system that blended authoritarian rule with mass democracy. Contrasting with most constitutions, but as his uncle had done, the document made clear the person in charge: 'The government of the French Republic is confided for ten years to Prince Louis-Napoléon Bonaparte.'[10] But his power came from the people, or so he said. 'Society', the president told his audience in the Tuileries as he explained the new order, 'had too long been like a pyramid resting upside down; I replaced it on its base. Universal suffrage, the only source of power under such circumstances, was immediately re-established.'

Louis-Napoléon boasted that deputies in the Corps législatif, the lower chamber of the new French parliament, were elected under the 'most liberal law in the world'; however, there was very little liberal about the rest of the regime.[11] The Corps législatif was composed of 261 deputies (the National Assembly of the Republic had 750) – the reduced number, the preamble to the constitution noted, was 'a guarantee of calm deliberations' – and had extremely limited powers.[12] It could not propose or amend legislation, the only public record of its debates was an official precis, the president could dissolve it at will and it sat only for short periods. Ministers were not drawn from it, nor were they responsible to it, only to the president, who could appoint and dismiss them as he pleased. There was an upper chamber, an appointed Senate, but this was even more servile to the president than the lower one. The primary function of these assemblies was to wave through legislation drawn up in the Council of State, 'the first cog in our organisation', made up of 'practical men' who drafted laws behind closed doors and without 'ostentatious oratory'. The hope was that the state would be 'free in its movements, and enlightened in its progress'.[13] Technocratic in conception, the idea was to apply scientific principles to government, focusing on economic development and allowing policy to be far removed from the vicissitudes of party politics.

The central idea of the regime was that Louis-Napoléon represented the indivisible will of the people, and if the eagle was the most prominent imperial symbol, the constitution was inspired by another Napoleonic emblem: the bee. Party politics, the press, anything that was believed to sow division or represent private interests was discouraged or banned. Draconian censorship laws, therefore, were introduced, which all but ended press freedom in France. Another key provision of the constitution was that the president reserved the right to directly consult the French people through plebiscites, as with the December 1851 vote after the *coup d'état*.

The constitution, then, was a mixture of Napoleonic influences and Louis-Napoléon's political thinking from the 1830s and 1840s; however, many of his ideas from that time were radical, whereas this document was decidedly authoritarian. This was a reaction to the Second Republic. As its president, Louis-Napoléon had developed contempt for parliament and a free press. Though he admired these institutions in Britain, he believed that France's history of political volatility showed that it was not ready for them. Stability and order were preferred to liberty, and voting was carefully managed. It was an illiberal democracy. Nonetheless, Louis-Napoléon took its populist base seriously. 'Former governments tried to reign by the support of perhaps one million of the educated classes,' he said. 'I have tried to lay hold of the other twenty nine.'[14]

At least now there was a constitution. Prior to 29 March, Louis-Napoléon had ruled by issuing decrees, many of which were designed to bury the Republic, though France nominally still was one. Marianne, the republican symbol, was replaced by Louis-Napoléon. The revolutionary legend '*Liberté, Égalité, Fraternité*' was effaced from public buildings and documents – although, sadly for the police, new stationery was not ordered in time and those reporting suspected republicans after the *coup d'état* were, humiliatingly, required to write on paper still headed with the motto; the most diligent carefully put a line through it.

The usual right-wing pillars, the Catholic Church and the army, were now front and centre. In churches, prayers were offered to Louis-Napoléon, as they had been for French royalty in the past. In return, the Church was given a prominent role in public life. The Panthéon, a barometer of any French government's stance on religion, had swung between being a church and a temple to liberty ever since the Revolution of 1789. Under Louis-Philippe and the Second Republic, it had been a temple; now it was restored to the Church. As for the army, in a grand ceremony where the figure '7.5 million' was visible everywhere alongside the inscription '*Vox Populi, Vox Dei*' – 'The voice of the people is the voice of God' – Louis-Napoléon distributed imperial eagles to troops, binding soldiers to him personally and recalling past Napoleonic triumphs.

And every opportunity was taken to celebrate the glory of his uncle. The most important public holiday was designated as 15 August, Napoléon's birthday and the saint day for Saint Napoléon, who had been invented under the First Empire. It was commemorated with especial elan in Paris that year, 1852. The crescendo was a fireworks display on the banks of the Seine that recreated Jacques-Louis David's painting of Napoléon crossing the Alps on a magnificent white horse, cloak billowing. If transporting an army across inhospitable terrain had been a triumph over the elements, the nephew was less fortunate. Strong winds blew away much of the wood and canvas mountain that served as a backdrop, leaving Napoléon and his horse eerily suspended in mid-air as fireworks burst in the sky. In an illustrated weekly newspaper, Parisians were given a taste of the regime's approach to the truth. The sketch of the display showed the Alps scene as it was intended, mountain intact, rather than Napoléon floating – the official narrative thus starkly different from what Parisians had seen with their eyes. Of course, since Napoléon had never ridden a white charger over the Alps in the first place, the nephew was merely channelling his uncle's imaginative relationship with reality.

What upset monarchists more than this, and much more than the arrest and deportation of thousands of Frenchmen, was one of Louis-Napoléon's first acts. He confiscated property belonging to the former king, Louis-Philippe. This was denounced as vindictive, which it was, or worse, as socialism, which it was not. The French people were less concerned. Much of the money raised went on popular causes, mutual aid societies, affordable housing and a pension fund for the poorest. This seizure of royal wealth was spun to show that Bonapartism was on the side of the people.

These flourishes showed that if Louis-Napoléon leaned heavily to the right at his regime's inception, he remained a quixotic dreamer in his political thinking, with a genuine, if patrician, concern for the people. He decreed better pay for the rank and file in the army, generous pensions for military veterans and free funeral rites for the poor, among other measures. Moreover, Louis-Napoléon wanted to provide cheap credit to the masses, a long-held vision, which led to the creation of the Crédit Foncier de France, a mortgage bank with branches across the country. Further impetus was given to the economy and grand construction projects commissioned in Paris provided work, while the building of railways, canals and telegraph lines was promoted: in short, a whirlwind of measures with the distinctly modern idea behind them of getting the economy booming.

As to elections for the Corps législatif, the government designated official candidates to ensure supporters were returned. 'If a man has made his fortune by hard work in industry or agriculture,' wrote Morny in a job description for these men, 'if he has taken care to improve the conditions of his workers, if he has made himself popular by a noble use of his fortune, he is preferable to what is generally termed a politician.'[15] The ideal official candidate was thus the complete opposite of Morny; less politics, more government was the mantra. Once a candidate was selected, to help voters make the right choice, everyone received a ballot paper with the correct name printed on it. If that was not enough, civil servants campaigned for them and kindly mayors – rewarded with government handouts for particularly impressive results – talked misguided voters round to the right choice. Without a free press, or the right to hold political meetings, there was little opposition politicians could do. Out of 261 deputies elected, only eight were not government-backed men, including three republicans from Paris and Lyon. As they refused to swear the required oath of allegiance to Louis-Napoléon, they resigned their seats.

Victor Hugo saw the electoral landslide as proof of Louis-Napoléon's rigged system, but the results were not falsified. What left-wing critics like Hugo missed was that the president was authoritarian *and* popular. He had married mass democracy with conservatism in a way that no one in modern history had. Unlike his uncle, under whose reign elections and plebiscites were rigged, the nephew embraced the ballot box to give legitimacy to his regime. It was buttressed with repression, especially in the aftermath of the *coup d'état*, but if there was tyranny, it was that of the majority; those who opposed Louis-Napoléon were branded enemies of the people.

More perceptive, though not more generous, in his analysis than Hugo was Karl Marx. In his excoriating essay on the failure of the French political class, right and left, to stop Louis-Napoléon's rise, he developed his theory of the lumpenproletariat to explain the president's popularity. Marx described this class as 'vagabonds, discharged soldiers, discharged jailbirds, escaped galley slaves, swindlers, mountebanks, lazzarone [vagrants], pickpockets, tricksters, gamblers, maquereaux [pimps], brothel keepers, porters, literati, organ grinders, ragpickers, knife grinders, tinkers, beggars – in short, the whole indefinite, disintegrated mass, thrown hither and thither, which the French call la bohème'.[16] In other words, people.

'Do not fear the people. They are more conservative than you!' was an aphorism attributed to Louis-Napoléon.[17] Whether he said it or not, in politics he believed and acted on it. Harnessing the masses behind him was where his originality lay. For his progressive opponents, what they saw as his Mephistophelian insight had become a terrifying revelation: conservativism could be popular in a world of democratic politics. With this premiss, he built an edifice with him at the top, making him one of the most powerful men in the world. But Louis-Napoléon could rise higher still.

———

'A little cadet from nowhere,' wrote an observer from the Parisian beau monde sketching Persigny, with a 'real scoundrel's face, without candour in his eyes nor sureness in his words; counsellor of violent means, vain as a lackey, hateful as a verger, believing in the quickest and most crooked means to achieve a goal . . . In short, a bad melodrama actor.'[18] There were many who shared this view of Louis-Napoléon's friend. Certainly, they thought he should be nowhere near a great French office of state and were appalled that he was appointed minister of the interior in 1852.

Persigny, however, was not content with being a minister in a republic. Knowing this, after dinner, a friend asked him when the Empire was going to be restored. 'You don't know what's holding the Empire back?' replied Persigny. 'It's the emperor and the emperor alone . . . He takes his ten years seriously,' he said incredulously, referring to the constitution, which stipulated that Louis-Napoléon would be president for this period of time.[19]

Persigny, however, spotted a chance to hurry things along during an upcoming presidential tour. Showing his confidence in winning people over, Louis-Napoléon planned to travel to the regions where resistance had been greatest in the aftermath of his *coup d'état*. At a cabinet meeting, Persigny remarked that people 'freed from the nightmare of anarchy will probably express their feelings very openly. Now, what attitude should we recommend to the prefects in these delicate circumstances?'

'What attitude? What circumstances?' asked several voices.

'What circumstances?' replied Persigny. 'But what if they shout, "Long live the emperor!"'[20] This caused a sensation. Men stood up, shouted, gesticulated, and when they had calmed down, they asked Persigny, not for the first time in his life, if he wanted civil war. Louis-Napoléon, watching, his expression unchanged, waited for silence before rebuking Persigny. He rejected the idea of changing the system he had just created. When announcing the end of his dictatorship, Louis-Napoléon had publicly declared, 'Let us preserve the Republic, it threatens nobody, it can reassure everyone.'[21]

Worried that the president would demand his resignation, Persigny fell into restless depression – 'My anxiety was terrible,' he complained. Then he had a brilliant idea. He would ignore Louis-Napoléon. He summoned the relevant prefects to Paris. When the prefect for the Cher arrived, Persigny told him the plan. There was a train leaving in an hour. 'Return to your post,' he said, 'without seeing anyone here and without making known to a living soul the secret instructions.' Then, the excitement almost too much, he continued, 'Here are the instructions: The Empire! Long live the emperor!'

Realising this was a bit vague, Persigny went into more detail. 'Without wasting a moment, have flags distributed to everyone . . . On one side: "*Vive l'empereur!*" And on the other: "*Vive Napoléon III!*"' For good measure, he instructed the prefect to make sure crowds of people shouted '*Vive Napoléon III!*' at the president when he arrived and that triumphal arches were put up with this legend inscribed on them.

'Let's not kid ourselves,' Persigny said, feeling he had to account for the number III, 'the Duke of Reichstadt, Napoléon II, did not reign, but the people knew him by this name for a long time. He was proclaimed by his father. Let us pay this tribute.'[22] That was why, he explained, they were going with Napoléon III. Getting slightly carried away, Persigny added that this would make things easier for Napoléon IV and Napoléon V in due course. Coming back to what was, for him at least, reality, Persigny reiterated that these preparations were to be done secretly.

Once again, Persigny's anxiety rocketed. He was nervously counting down the days until Louis-Napoléon left, lest his plans be discovered and stopped. Then his inner demons preyed on his mind. What if he had misjudged the popular mood? Did the French people really want to restore the Empire? Rather than joyous ovations, might not these shouts lead to violent clashes in the streets? But with the calm that belongs only to men of true faith, Persigny composed himself. Of course people wanted the Empire, he told himself. He would soon find out if he was right.

———

On 14 September 1852, Louis-Napoléon left with a large entourage for central and southern France, regions where only a few months earlier tens of thousands had revolted against the *coup d'état*. Yet when he arrived at the capital of the department of the Cher, he was met by the prefect whom Persigny had briefed in Paris, and the official had surpassed even Persigny's expectations. As soon as the president got off the train, he was met with a thunderous '*Vive Napoléon!*'[23]

This marked the beginning of an imperial progress. Moving to another town the next day, 'Napoléon III' made its first appearance, and it soon became ubiquitous throughout the tour: on flags, arches, shouted by the crowds or, in the case of the especially devoted, written on paper and pinned to hats. As he walked or rode through streets adorned with the Napoleonic symbols of eagles and bees, his path strewn with flowers, petitions were thrust into his hands imploring the restoration of the Empire, and Louis-Napoléon's reticence was worn down.

The month-long imperial bandwagon was accompanied by official journalists who sent back dispatches to Paris. In the nineteenth-century equivalent of live updates, readers of the official newspaper followed time-stamped information detailing by the hour the ovations Louis-Napoléon received wherever he was. Towards the end of the tour, overworked hacks ran out of superlatives, merely stating that enthusiasm for Louis-Napoléon and the Empire was indescribable.

For others, though, it was describable, and it was far removed from the carefully curated image painted in the official press. In one city, a republican recorded in his diary, 'If we go behind the scenes of this new sort of theatre . . . it was pure comedy.' Crowds were numerous, but local officials ordered them to attend and cheers of '*Vive l'empereur!*' were rare. The prefect 'on foot and in the mud ran' before the carriage, 'crying, "Long live the emperor!"', and urging, unsuccessfully, the people to do likewise. Throughout the tour, those who shouted seditious cries, which included – though France was nominally a republic – '*Vive la République!*', were seized by gendarmes or beaten up by Bonapartists.[24]

Regardless of whether it was genuine or not, the enthusiasm impressed Louis-Napoléon. Less than three weeks after a timid speech at Lyon in which he claimed he had no ambition other than that of being president, Louis-Napoléon told France and the world what he really thought about the Empire at Bordeaux on 9 October 1852, where some hundred thousand people came to enjoy the pomp and pageantry.

The country, Louis-Napoléon said, speaking after dinner, wanted the Empire. Tired of 'absurd theories' and ideologues, France desired 'confidence for the present, security for the future'. There was, however, one point he had to address. When Louis-Napoléon thought of his uncle, he saw a pacifist bent on world peace. However, 'some people', he said unbelievingly, 'say the Empire means war. I say, the Empire means peace. It is peace, because France desires it and, when France is satisfied, the world is tranquil.' Loud cheers stopped the president from speaking. When they died down, he continued, 'I confess, however, that, like the emperor, I have conquests to make.' He wanted to reconcile hostile parties, restore religion and improve conditions for people who were struggling to meet their everyday needs. There was land to cultivate, roads to open, canals to dig, railways to build. 'These are the conquests I think about, and all you who surround me who, like me, want the good of our country, you are my soldiers!'[25]

If he stopped short of saying 'The Empire is made' – Thiers's famous phrase when struggling to stop exactly that happening just over a year ago – this was how it was interpreted. Indeed, in Paris, imperial stamps for official documents were ordered, imperial uniforms were designed for Louis-Napoléon's servants and preparations began for a triumphal return worthy of an emperor. Arches were hastily erected, delegations from various municipal bodies were strongly encouraged to join the festivities and flags were distributed. Police instructed those living along the grand boulevards to open their windows for the procession and illuminate their houses at night. This was no time for understatement. 'To Napoléon III, Emperor. Saviour of Modern Civilisation', proclaimed one inscription on an arch above the entrance to the Tuileries.[26]

Dressed in military uniform, Louis-Napoléon rode through the streets of Paris on 16 October. The weather was fine and large crowds came to witness the proto-imperial procession. Riding fifteen paces in front of his entourage, hat in hand, Louis-Napoléon basked in the adulation of the people. Occasionally women managed to break through the cordon – Louis-Napoléon waving away the guards – and present him with bouquets of flowers. Strewn on the ground, like a carpet of crushed purple, were violets – a Napoleonic symbol – that people had thrown in front of him.

In Paris as in the provinces, there was plenty of indifference. Many of the hundreds of thousands who lined the streets were merely curious to see the spectacle. As for delegations of peasants and workers, most depended on the government for work, which helped when cajoling people to cheer for the Empire. Even then, wrote one patriotic British journalist, 'The cheering of any kind was so feeble as to astonish some of our countrymen who are accustomed to the hearty shouts of an English crowd.' The Empire, he continued, was seen as a necessity, but not something to rejoice at. Then, however, he betrayed his prejudices: 'If there is enthusiasm in favour of Louis Napoleon at all, it is only among the lowest and most ignorant classes.'[27]

In fact, the reality lay between the fantastical government propaganda, which expressed Bonapartist devotion probably only Persigny felt, and the cynicism of opponents who thought it was all confected. These critics missed something essential: it was not enough for Louis-Napoléon to be popular; he had to be the undisputed embodiment of the will of the people. If he had stood for re-election as president in 1852, he would have won, just as he would have won the plebiscite after the *coup d'état* without repressive measures, but he would not have won by such a large margin. The police state, the propaganda, the choreographed spectacle were not intended to fabricate support for Louis-Napoléon – he had enough supporters – but to crush alternatives. And they had worked so well that Louis-Napoléon had become emperor in all but name.

That soon changed, for a few days after Louis-Napoléon returned to the capital, the Senate issued a proposal re-establishing the Empire, a hereditary monarchy under Napoléon III. Once again, this was put to the people and 7.8 million voted in favour; only 253,000 were against, an increase in the yes count of around 400,000 from the year before. The fact that there were some two million abstentions showed there was more opposition than those who decided to state it actively; however, it was another sensational victory.

On 2 December 1852, a day now heavier still with significance for Bonapartists, Louis-Napoléon signed the decree establishing what he had long dreamed of – and had long been ridiculed for: the Second Empire. Unlike other regimes, he declared when accepting the throne, his did not have its origin in violence, conquest or trickery – a statement that even his supporters might have found hard to take at face value – but was rather 'the legal result of the will of an entire people'.[28]

If at the beginning of 1848, observed one British journalist, someone had predicted that in under five years Louis-Napoléon would become emperor, they would have been sectioned. Recent history, however, had shown how precarious French regimes were. To consolidate his hold on power, the emperor's supporters decided, it was necessary to have an empress. Louis-Napoléon must marry.

13

THE IMPERIAL CLOAK

From the backstreets of Brighton to the bedroom of a French president, Harriet Howard had come a long way, but she wanted to go further. As Louis-Napoléon's preferred – though by no means only – sexual partner, she had been happy to stay out of the limelight when he was president, but as he edged towards the throne, she dreamed of sharing his imperial splendour. In January 1852, therefore, striking, tall and dressed like an immaculate duchess, she swept imperiously into an official ball on the arm of one of Louis-Napoléon's close associates. Most of those present took her for a beautiful English aristocrat recently arrived from London, but those in the know, especially Louis-Napoléon's inner circle, were scandalised. As Fleury noted, 'From that evening on, Miss Howard appeared to us in her true light, that of a great courtesan whose ambitious plans had to be foiled at all costs.'[1]

Fleury took it upon himself to solve what he saw as an embarrassing problem for Louis-Napoléon. Yet the president did not see it that way. Harriet was not only the president's lover, but also a friend and a confidante. Despite the rising scandal, she continued to appear with him in public. In fact, he found her rooms in the palace of Saint-Cloud, where he spent much of the summer of 1852, and where she attended more soirées. That October, in the president's box at the opera, covered in diamonds, Harriet sat in full view of Parisian high society.

There was only one thing for it, Fleury reasoned: Louis-Napoléon would have to get married. Knowing that the president had strong feelings for Harriet, when the Empire was established Fleury painted a terrifying scenario: if Louis-Napoléon died, he would be succeeded by his cousin, Plon-Plon. Louis-Napoléon agreed reluctantly to consider marriage. After trawling through the *Almanach de Gotha*, a directory of royalty and aristocracy which doubled up as a mail-order bride catalogue, candidates were found. Unfortunately, though, the royal houses of Europe had imposed a matrimonial blockade on Louis-Napoléon: no reigning family was willing to marry off their daughter to what they saw as a parvenu adventurer. In desperation, proposals were sent to ever more obscure princesses. In the meantime, Louis-Napoléon fell in love.

———

In March 1849, Eugenia Ignacia Agustina de Palafox y Kirkpatrick, a young Spanish aristocrat chaperoned by her mother, was presented to the recently elected president of France. 'We have often spoken about you to a lady who is absolutely devoted to your interests,' said Eugenia. 'And pray what is her name?' enquired Louis-Napoléon. 'Madame Gordon,' was the reply.

Louis-Napoléon stared at Eugenia. Eleonore Gordon, cabaret singer, fervent Bonapartist and co-conspirator, was a woman from the president's past whom he had not expected to be reminded of in the salubrious surroundings of the Élysée. Bemused, Louis-Napoléon moved on. Eugenia had made an impression, though. A few months later, she and her mother were invited to dine at Saint-Cloud. Dressed in their evening finery for what they expected to be a banquet with numerous guests, Eugenia and her mother were astonished to discover that the dinner was with Louis-Napoléon and only one of his friends. Afterwards, Louis-Napoléon suggested a walk in the grounds of the chateau. Suspecting this invitation would afford her a more intimate acquaintance with the grounds and the president than she wanted, Eugenia said, 'My mother is here,' and quickly stepped aside to avoid taking his arm.[2]

But Eugenia remained devoted to the Bonapartist cause, for like Eleonore Gordon, she was raised on tales of Napoleonic legend. She worshipped her father, Don Cipriano de Guzmán Palafox y Portocarrero, who was from one of the most aristocratic and wealthy families in Spain. In 1808, French armies invaded his country and overthrew the monarchy, and Napoléon installed his brother, Joseph, on the throne. At first, Cipriano fought against the French, but in 1810 he switched sides. When the French army was chased out, he took part in the retreat. Ending up in Paris, he defended the city until its capitulation in March 1814. After Napoléon returned from Elba in 1815, Cipriano again took up his sword for the Empire, until its collapse after the Battle of Waterloo.

While Cipriano was from the highest ranks of Spain's aristocracy, his wife was not. María Manuela Kirkpatrick de Closeburn y Grivegnée was the daughter of a Scottish fruit and wine merchant, who was rumoured to have gone bankrupt. Outgoing, well read and outrageously flirtatious, María Manuela was educated in Paris, where she met Cipriano and married him in 1817. They returned to Spain and had two daughters, the youngest, Eugenia, born on 5 May 1826 during, as family legend had it, an earthquake. 'What would the ancients have thought of such an omen?' Eugenia later reminisced. 'Surely they would have said I was destined to unsettle the world.'[3]

After the eight-year-old Eugenia saw from her window a monk have his throat slit, blood drenching the dying man's robes, the family decided that Paris was a place of greater safety than politically unstable Spain. Here, the girls were educated at a very fashionable, and very Catholic, convent, where the nuns instilled in Eugenia a deep sense of religion which never left her. Their father, whom Eugenia adored and to whom she had listened in rapture as he recounted tales of heroism fighting for the French emperor, remained in Spain. But in an approach to parenting that Louis-Napoléon would have applauded, he encouraged his young girls to educate themselves about Napoléon. 'Dear Daddy, you tell us to read Napoléon and learn his history, it made me cry a lot,' was Eugenia's analysis.[4]

In Paris, Eugenia and her older sister, Francisca, known as Paca, became further indoctrinated in the Bonapartist cult. Their mother moved in literary circles, and one of her friends came every Thursday to regale the sisters with legends about Napoléon. Whether he was resplendent under the sun of Austerlitz, pale in the Russian snows or dying on Saint Helena, each episode ended on a cliffhanger and the girls would wait impatiently for their storyteller to return the next week. The girls were utterly captivated, for their narrator was one of nineteenth-century France's great novelists, who wrote under the name of Stendhal. He was so enamoured with the sisters that he put a cryptic footnote into his book *The Charterhouse of Parma*,

'Para v. P. y E.', abbreviated Spanish which translates as 'For you, Paca and Eugenia'.

Not long after Stendhal wrote that, Eugenia's father died. Returning to Spain, she was devastated, shutting herself in her room for two days. Her mother, however, recovered quickly, and decided that the family would stay in Madrid. With the death of her husband, she inherited his wealth and titles and set up one of the most splendid houses in the Spanish capital. Their home became a centre for parties, political intrigue and love affairs. Eugenia liked to shock. At one soirée, she burst into the room and, as the gentlemen bowed to greet her, jumped onto a billiard table. Laughing and kicking the balls away, she broke into a traditional Spanish dance, 'bouncing her hips, thrusting her chest forward, snapping her fingers, lifting her skirt . . . her head bowed, her eyes half-closed', as the men stared in disbelief.[5]

If her behaviour was hardly that of an archetypal young female aristocrat, she was considered to be stunningly attractive, 'the most beautiful and gracious person one could see', according to yet another enchanted author, this time Alexandre Dumas *fils*.[6] Slender, petite, with bright blue eyes, long dark lashes and luxuriant auburn hair – which observers usually insisted on saying Titian would have loved to paint – Eugenia shone at the never-ending society events she attended in Madrid. There was, then, no shortage of admirers for this wealthy, arresting and patrician woman, but Eugenia refused them all. By 1852, she had turned twenty-six and her mother was desperate to find a match. So María Manuela decided to try their luck in Paris.

———

Here, it was not long before Eugenia, again, caught Louis-Napoléon's eye, exercising on him, as he recalled, 'all the attractions of her beauty, of her *spirit*, and of the supreme nobility of her sentiments'.[7] That was a polite way of saying that he wanted to have sex with her. Eugenia, though, refused to sleep with him. In the autumn of 1852, therefore, Louis-Napoléon deployed the majesty of the French state to get what he wanted. He invited Eugenia to balls at Saint-Cloud and hunting parties at the palace of Fontainebleau, and in December, just after he had been proclaimed emperor, he brought her and her mother to a select gathering at the magnificent chateau of Compiègne.

None of this got Louis-Napoléon what he wanted. Eugenia was not immune to his charms, which, at the age of forty-four, were not physical. As one contemporary described him, he had 'a long face and heavy features, a grey and sickly complexion, a large parrot nose . . . small eyes, the colour of the cheeks, and whose wrinkles give no expression other than a soupçon of lechery'.[8] This was combined with a head too large for its body, and a body too long for its legs, which gave him a shuffling, awkward gait. To give his face elan, he had taken to waxing his long moustache so it tapered at the ends and to growing out his goatee, a style that became known as 'the imperial'. He dragged his feet with one hand behind a stooped back, twirling the ends of his moustache and uttering absurd phrases – or at least that was how novelist Gustave Flaubert performed his impression of the emperor. Regardless of these less than stunning physical attributes, he was kind, gentle and charming. It also helped that he was one of the most powerful men in the world. Eugenia was drawn to him. Yet as a pious Catholic, or, as others alleged, a smart woman, she made it clear that there was no sex before marriage.

One December morning, as they walked on the terrace outside the chateau of Compiègne overlooking gardens that stretched into the distance, Louis-Napoléon and Fleury talked about Eugenia. 'Ah,' the emperor confided to his friend, 'I am really in love with her.'

'I know it, Sire,' replied Fleury. 'But then there is only one thing for it: marry her.'

'I'm seriously thinking about it,' answered Louis-Napoléon.[9]

Yet the marriage of the emperor was not merely an affair of the heart, but a matter of state, and many of Louis-Napoléon's closest advisers were horrified at the choice. When he heard, his foreign minister, determined to secure a royal alliance, threatened to resign. The ever-charming Plon-Plon said that while one certainly slept with women like Eugenia, one did not marry them. Persigny was appalled. 'We didn't create the Empire so that he could marry her,' he said in disgust. Such was his sacral veneration for the emperor, it was unlikely that in Persigny's eyes any woman was worthy of marrying Louis-Napoléon, certainly not Eugenia. He could not even bring himself to say her name, referring to her as the 'foreigner' or 'that Spanish woman'. Eugenia thought Persigny was jealous. 'I was honoured with his hatred,' she recalled, 'a venomous and besmirching hatred.'[10]

Ignoring his friend, Louis-Napoléon continued his pursuit, inviting her to a ball on New Year's Day 1853. As Eugenia was going into supper, the spouse of one of Louis-Napoléon's ministers asked in an ostentatiously loud voice why a Spanish countess thought she could enter the room ahead of the wife of a French minister. Stepping back, Eugenia said, 'Pass, Madame.' Upon entering the grand hall, she found herself sitting at the imperial table, still distressed. Louis-Napoléon stood behind her. 'What is the matter?' he said. 'Oh, Sire, I beg you – do not ask me now – everyone is watching us,' replied Eugenia. But after supper, Louis-Napoléon insisted. 'Sire,' Eugenia told him, 'I have been insulted tonight, but I shall not be insulted a second time.'

'Tomorrow,' said the emperor, 'nobody will dare insult you.'[11]

Not long afterwards, Eugenia's mother received a proposal for her daughter's hand in marriage. Eugenia was still not sure. She sent a telegram to another suitor in Spain. One of the benefits of running a police state was that Louis-Napoléon could read his prospective wife's correspondence, but he let the message reach its recipient, who replied congratulating Eugenia. She interpreted this as a sign that her former paramour had lost interest, and with that news, she decided to marry Louis-Napoléon.

For the British ambassador, there was nothing romantic about any of this. 'I cannot conceal from myself', he wrote about his time at court, 'that all inside is rotten and that, with few exceptions, we are living in a society of adventurers. The greatest one of all has been captured by an adventuress.' She had played her game so well, the ambassador continued, that Louis-Napoléon 'can get her in no other way but marriage, and it is to gratify his passions that he marries her. People are already speculating on their divorce.'[12] Another court wit put it more crudely: Louis-Napoléon became emperor by election; Eugenia became empress 'by erection'.[13]

The British ambassador was not the only statesman interested in the marriage. George Villiers, 4th Earl of Clarendon, soon to be appointed British foreign secretary, had been a lover of Eugenia's mother and was widely rumoured to be her father. Someone tipped off Louis-Napoléon and, worried that he might accidentally marry the daughter of an Englishman, he confronted María Manuela. 'Sire,' she replied, 'the dates do not match.'[14]

——

'When, before Old Europe, one is carried by the force of a new principal to the height of ancient dynasties,' Louis-Napoléon told the Senate when announcing his marriage,

> it is not by ageing one's coat of arms or by seeking to introduce oneself at all costs into the family of kings, that one is accepted. It is rather by always remembering one's origins, by preserving one's own character and by openly taking towards Europe the title of parvenu, a glorious title when one arrives at it through the free votes of a great people.

Thus Louis-Napoléon turned the humiliation of not securing a royal bride into a political virtue, while at the same time taking a shot at the reigning houses of Europe. Unlike their relationships, his was a free choice, democratic, sentimentally bourgeois. 'I preferred to have for a wife', he continued, 'a woman whom I love and respect, rather than a woman unknown to me . . . In placing independence, the qualities of the heart and family happiness over and above dynastic prejudices and the calculations of ambition, I will not be less strong.'[15]

'I have just this moment arrived at the Élysée,' Eugenia wrote to her sister on 22 January 1853. 'Today is the first time that people have cried, "Long live the empress!"' The enormity of her situation began to sink in. 'Today I still look with fear at the responsibility that will weigh heavily on me.' She was, however, determined to fulfil what she called her 'destiny'. It helped that she was now enamoured with her fiancé. 'I love him,' she wrote, which is 'a guarantee for our happiness'. She added that 'he is noble of heart and devoted' and 'you have to know him in his intimate life to know how much he should be esteemed' – the latter statement suggesting she did not know much about his intimate life.[16]

The last act recorded in the official register from the First Empire was the birth of Napoléon's son, the Duke of Reichstadt, on 20 March 1811 and, on the evening of 29 January 1853, showing continuity between the two empires, another was added to the same ledger: the marriage between

Louis-Napoléon and Eugenia. The next day, the pageantry of the imperial revival act was further ramped up for the public ceremony. Just after noon, the same carriage that Napoléon had used for his second wedding in 1810 slinked its way along the route from the Tuileries to Notre-Dame, pulled by eight cream-coloured horses with headdresses of white feathers. On top of this baroque, gaudily decorated vehicle was an oversized imperial crown; large windows afforded onlookers a glimpse of the emperor and empress as they passed immense crowds.

Inside the cathedral was the usual array of velvet drapes embroidered with large 'N's; gilded eagles were, of course, on show, glittering in the chandelier light. As the imperial couple entered at 1 p.m., the orchestra struck up the wedding march. Neither Louis-Napoléon nor Eugenia had much interest in music and the choice fell to Persigny. He played it safe and opted for classics rather than the magnificent Te Deum that Hector Berlioz, France's greatest living composer, hoped would be chosen. Eugenia looked resplendent in the finest gown money could buy. After more imperial spectacle, the newlyweds retired to a small house near Saint-Cloud for a few days' honeymoon. The Spanish Eugenia was now the French Eugénie, though she never got over the fact that her adopted people could not pronounce her name.

One person not invited who also had a name French people struggled with was Harriet Howard. Before the announcement of his engagement, Louis-Napoléon had ordered his secretary to get his mistress out of Paris. She had been told an invented story: compromising letters from a former lover had surfaced and she had to go to England to get them. On 22 January, she was at Le Havre, waiting for a ship to cross the Channel. Unfortunately for Louis-Napoléon, a storm delayed her departure. The next morning, she opened the newspaper and read about her lover's imminent marriage. Furious, she demanded that Louis-Napoléon's secretary drive her to Paris. When she returned to her apartment, she found it had been ransacked. Furniture was broken, drawers open and emptied. While she was out of town, Louis-Napoléon had sent men to destroy all his letters to her.

She refused to fade away, though, and in the weeks after the marriage she placed herself ostentatiously on the route of the newlyweds when they came to Paris, conspicuously saluting the emperor. In the end, she was bought off for an outrageous price. Louis-Napoléon gave Harriet the title comtesse de Beauregard, a vast chateau and a financial settlement that came to 5,449,000 francs, over £36 million in today's money. She had been born the daughter of a Brighton bootmaker, and this was exactly the kind of revolutionary social mobility that was at the heart of Bonapartist rhetoric, the Extinction of Pauperism in action, if not exactly in the manner Louis-Napoléon had theorised while in prison.

All this, and with the added bonus that she no longer had to sleep with Louis-Napoléon. Having said that, her chateau was close to Saint-Cloud and the gossip was that she retained this dubious prize. After all, Louis-Napoléon had not remained faithful to his last solemnly sworn oath – to uphold the constitution of the Second Republic – and most people expected him to be similarly unscrupulous when it came to his marriage vows.

———

A few weeks after his marriage, Louis-Napoléon invited James Harris, 3rd Earl of Malmesbury to dine at the Tuileries. Greeting him warmly, the emperor introduced him to generals and ministers as an old friend who had visited him while a prisoner – a background Malmesbury thought it brave to refer to, given the illustrious company. At dinner he sat next to the empress, admiring her 'beautiful bust and shoulders, and small hands and feet'. She spoke to him in English and used the language with her husband when she did not want to be understood by those around her, laughing when she remembered who was next to her.

Although the dinner was splendid, Malmesbury believed the performance of the drama was lacking, for the actors had not 'perfectly learnt their parts'. As he had known Louis-Napoléon for over twenty years, his present position 'looked like a dream or a play', but 'when each actor becomes acclimatised by time, it will be a magnificent court with a Sovereign who will command the attention of all Europe'.[17] Initially, though, the court did not seem especially magnificent, not least because to cement power, Louis-Napoléon needed his family at the heart of it. After all, taking the title Napoléon III was part of making the reign seem more legitimate, and not, as some alleged, a result of government officials mistaking exclamation marks for Roman numerals when instructed to encourage cries of

'*Vive Napoléon!!!*' Unfortunately for the emperor, this emphasis on the Bonaparte dynasty meant giving Jérôme and his two children, Plon-Plon and Mathilde, important roles.

The best that could be said about Jérôme Bonaparte was that he was consistent: he was as embarrassing under the Second Empire as he had been under the First, 'an old debauchee who would lose all respect today if he ever had any', as even a Bonapartist put it.[18] Vain, pompous and venal, he was sixty-eight when Louis-Napoléon became emperor, and had done nothing to help his nephew's rise. But he was appointed president of the Senate in 1852. On top of this, he was given an enormous annual sum from the civil list. But for Jérôme it was not enough; he resigned from his position in November 1852 because he felt that he and his family had not been sufficiently favoured.

This was an odd conclusion to come to given that his son, Plon-Plon, was designated as Louis-Napoléon's heir. Louis-Napoléon's cousin had undermined him when president and opposed the *coup d'état*, even meeting with Victor Hugo in the days after it. Plon-Plon claimed that he was a republican, but his principles did not stop him seeking money and power when Louis-Napoléon was on the throne. He was made an imperial prince, put on the civil list and given the right to sit in the Senate. Moreover, he had a place of honour at ceremonies. He was not, however, a decorous ornament for the throne, enduring the innumerable imperial displays with ostentatious ennui. Furthermore, among the brightly coloured, beautiful uniforms he stood out by wearing a black suit which, in his own mind at least, marked him as a simple republican amid the extravagance of monarchy; given his heavy frame and indulgent living, it gave him the grace of a worn-out opera singer. Despite the wealth and honours heaped on him, Plon-Plon frequently criticised the emperor behind his back and argued with him to his face. During one tempestuous exchange, knowing how hurtful Louis-Napoléon found the rumours that he was not his father's son, a furious Plon-Plon reportedly shouted, 'You have nothing of the Emperor Napoléon about you!'

'You are mistaken,' Louis-Napoléon replied serenely, 'I have his family.'[19]

The nepotism at the heart of the regime did not stop there. The court needed nobility, but most of the old aristocracy remained loyal to exiled

French royals and refused to join the extravaganza. Instead, there was an unexpected pay day for survivors or descendants of those prominent under the First Empire, and parvenu names many hoped had been consigned to history – Murats and Neys, for example – joined the imperial revival.

Court life, then, was contemptible to France's old aristocracy. Made up of stolen titles, hustlers and arrivistes, wrote one critic, it was a court where 'nothing was respected or esteemed except the four things that a court must scorn: diamonds, youth, beauty and a dress'.[20] Of course, that may not have been classy, but it did make it sound fun. In reality, it was intensely dull, even for the emperor. The court was depicted in clandestine opposition pamphlets as decadent, little better than a network formed to organise high-class orgies; Louis-Napoléon said that the best punishment for these slanderers would be for the writers to spend an evening there.

It was less the ghosts of the First Empire that led the British ambassador to conclude that he was surrounded by adventurers than the emperor's close entourage, whose fortunes had risen with his own. Persigny was now a minister, while Fleury was *premier écuyer*, a court position that meant he was close adviser, confidant and (well-paid) friend. Saint-Arnaud, a marshal of France and a minister, using his insider information to speculate on the stock market and incurring enormous losses, was especially distrusted. Morny did the same, though he had the knack of making money, which made him slightly more respectable. Intensely loyal, Louis-Napoléon made sure he looked after his friends, finding places for all the misfits who had conspired with him during his years in exile. For the Empire's enemies, this furthered the image of a crooked upstart regime.

For many, that Eugénie was not a royal confirmed this impression. She had her coterie, which the most famous court painter of the day captured on canvas. In an idyllic rural setting, with radiant light breaking through languid, luxuriant trees, Eugénie was surrounded by her elegant ladies. For many, these women were style icons and impossibly glamorous. For others, though, they were the epitome of frivolity and, as outrageously expensive court dresses could never be worn twice in public by the same person, symbolised waste at the heart of the Empire.

It did not take a particularly skilful propagandist to caricature all this. 'These individuals', wrote Victor Hugo, 'are in possession of immense, incomparable, absolute, unlimited power, sufficient, we repeat, to change the whole face of Europe. They make use of it only for amusement.' It was easy to paint them as dissolute: 'They drink, they eat, they laugh, they feast; banquet . . . they swim in all sorts of abundance and intoxication.' All this, of course, while the poor went hungry.[21] The reality was less dramatic. Louis-Napoléon's court was intended as a ceremonial backdrop against which he and the empress could shine, but not one that had any meaningful political role. Louis-Napoléon was determined to govern France as he pleased. Hugo was correct that the regime had the power to change the face of Europe, but this was in the emperor's hands, not those of his friends.

It was not even in the hands of his ministers, who were mere political instruments; the emperor often overruled majority opinion in ministerial councils. He made decisions without their knowledge, leaving them to learn government policy from the newspapers. Foreign affairs especially the emperor considered his private domain. 'What am I doing here?' lamented one foreign minister. 'I am ignorant of the emperor's political plans. I work in the dark, without objectives, without plans, advancing, retreating, playing a double game which is never explained.'[22]

Ignorance about the emperor's ideas was heightened because Louis-Napoléon's impassive nature was legendary. Once at dinner a waiter accidentally sprayed water from a seltzer bottle into the emperor's face. His expression remained unchanged despite water dripping from his waxed moustache as he reassured the unfortunate servant that the levers on such bottles were indeed treacherous. Given this self-control, ministers had no idea whether their advice had any impact. 'The words one addressed to him were like stones thrown down a well,' recalled Tocqueville of his time as Louis-Napoléon's minister. 'Their sound was heard, but one never knew what became of them.'[23]

Likely little when he was emperor, as Louis-Napoléon wrote to Plon-Plon: 'No one must take policy decisions without consulting me, however sensible they may be.' The emperor made this clear to ministers whenever they showed signs of independence. 'I invariably welcome your observations,' he wrote to one, 'but I will never accept that the Minister of State should adopt practices and policies of his own.' As one astute observer noted, the emperor was the state. 'Good or bad, everything comes from him . . . His gentle and deep smile, his vague and veiled gaze, the slowness of his speech and that of his walk, indicate a man who talks more with himself than with those around him.'[24]

That said, Louis-Napoléon disliked change, and over time his ministers built up experience and – with it – power. Yet few, except Persigny, were Bonapartists. Most were rich, bourgeois men who had come of age under the July Monarchy, and often in its service. As long as they accepted his rule, Louis-Napoléon was largely indifferent to previous allegiances. 'There is in every man, unless he is an idiot, a truth to be put to good use,' he said; 'real politics consists in discovering this truth.'[25]

With immense power in his hands, capable if not outstanding ministers and no meaningful opposition, Louis-Napoléon could embark on ambitious, long-held plans for transforming France. Railways, cheap credit for the masses, industrialisation and freer trade were at the heart of his technocratic and economic programme. Most ambitious of all were his plans to turn Paris into a model city of modernity, which required destroying the medieval warrens at its heart. This project had long been dear to the emperor, who had already spent much time drawing lines across a map of the city, planning new roads and parks. But it was foreign affairs that came to dominate the early years of the Empire.

———

London surrendered without much of a fight, although the beefeaters sold their lives dearly, if futilely, defending the Tower of London. After the French army stormed the medieval fortress, they set up artillery on the ramparts, amusing themselves by taking potshots at boats on the river. Having defeated the British army on the plains of Reigate, French forces now occupied the capital. Soon the sack began, prisons were opened and, adding to the confusion and terror, animals from the zoo were released into the streets of the capital; robbery and murder were universal. Perhaps the cruellest of the atrocities committed occurred at Smithfield, where London's aldermen were boiled alive in huge vats of bubbling turtle soup while delighted French soldiers looked on. The queen managed to escape, but London lay at the feet of 'the murderers' of 2 December.[26]

Or at least that is how a fictional French attack unfolded in one of the many invasion pamphlets that flourished across the Channel after the restoration of the Empire. Showing a wonderfully Anglocentric perspective, the destruction of Britain as revenge for Waterloo was the only reason Louis-Napoléon had come to power, or so claimed the author of 'A History of the Sudden and Terrible Invasion of England by the French'. That Louis-Napoléon must be an apocalyptic reincarnation of his uncle was a popular view across the Channel, where the name Napoléon still conjured awe and fear, something Alfred Lord Tennyson cashed in on, publishing a terrible poem that included the line: 'We love not this French God, the child of hell.'[27] Like Tennyson, much of the British press reviled Louis-Napoléon. *The Times* was relentlessly hostile, its editorials lamenting the absurdity of allowing poor people the vote and the fact that thus 'a thousand bumpkins' were worth more than one wise sage.[28]

This knockabout stuff annoyed Louis-Napoléon, but far more important was what British and European governments thought because, in theory at least, the major powers were united in stopping him becoming emperor. Determined to end the recurring Napoleonic nightmare, Britain, Austria, Prussia and Russia had signed a treaty in 1815 forever excluding Napoléon Bonaparte and his family from the French throne. Indeed, Louis-Napoléon's reticence to become emperor was as much to do with fear of the international reaction as the domestic; his 'Empire means peace' speech at Bordeaux was designed to reassure European royals as well as the French people.

Much of the ruling class in Britain, however, was aware he was not a facsimile of his uncle bent on world domination because they had known Louis-Napoléon as a foppish dandy from his time in London. On the other hand, many thought he was either an adventurer or an idiot, or both – he 'had never ceased to be obscure except by bringing upon himself the laughter of the world', as one man who knew him in London wrote, although he slightly undermined this judgement with the implausible claim that 'his skin, when he was in a state of alarm, was liable to be suffused with a greenish hue'.[29] Prince Albert, Queen Victoria's husband, hated him. Louis-Napoléon was 'a walking lie' and 'once a conspirator, always a conspirator'.[30]

Yet Louis-Napoléon received support from an unlikely advocate, the British foreign secretary Henry John Temple, 3rd Viscount Palmerston. No friend of the French, he hated former King Louis-Philippe's family even more and was delighted at Louis-Napoléon's *coup d'état*, seeing it as ending machinations to restore the French monarchy. Moreover, he had little time for the Second Republic or its constitution, referring to it as 'day-before-yesterday tomfoolery' which the scatterbrain head of 'Tocqueville invented for the torment and perplexity of the French nation'. It was therefore, he reasoned, 'high time to get rid of such childish nonsense'.[31] For her part, Queen Victoria thought the illegal seizure of power 'wonderful . . . like a story in a book or a play', but she was unamused when she read the emperor's speech about his wedding, in which he celebrated parvenus, thinking it in bad taste and somewhat proving a point about parvenus.[32]

Nonetheless, Britain was the first major power to recognise the Empire. The other powers followed its lead, albeit reluctantly. After all, that a monarch claimed legitimacy from the votes of his subjects was hardly a principle that the reactionary governments of Prussia, Austria and Russia wanted to encourage. It was too much for Tsar Nicholas I. God, not people, appointed emperors. Nicholas could not bring himself to address Louis-Napoléon as a fellow emperor with the customary salutation of 'brother'; instead, he signed off as a 'good friend'.[33]

Such an insult, Persigny argued, meant war. Louis-Napoléon was more diplomatic. Just as with his marriage, he turned a slight to his advantage. It was an honour to be called a friend, he insisted, because, as Louis-Napoléon well knew, one cannot choose one's family but one can choose one's friends. Anyway, reasoned the emperor, it would be absurd to go to war over what he called 'a personal matter'. True to his word, he did not go to war over a personal matter. He invaded Russia for another reason.

14

WAR AND PEACE

On 10 April 1846, candlelight shone through thick clouds of incense in the Church of the Holy Sepulchre, the centuries-old place of worship built on the ground where Jesus was said to have been crucified in Jerusalem. Isabella Frances Romer, a British travel writer, was watching a Catholic service on Easter Friday in one of the holiest buildings in Christendom. As priests carried an effigy of the crucified Christ towards the altar, the French consul, traditionally the protector of Catholics in the Holy Places, looked on. It was a Greek Orthodox diplomat, however, who caught Isabella's eye. He was dressed in magnificent Albanian costume, and the snowy white fustanella – a pleated kilt – of the Greek consul fluttered elegantly as he moved through the church. Less graceful was the sound of his weapons, and those of his followers, clanking against the marble floor.

As the Catholic priests approached the altar, they warily eyed the Greek Orthodox ones who flanked it like sentinels. To the horror of the Catholics, an Orthodox cloth had been laid upon the altar. The Catholics tried to remove it; the Orthodox priests remonstrated. Then the fighting began. Orthodox priests pulled down a chandelier and broke pieces of wood into makeshift poles, bludgeoning the Catholic priests, who used their enormous ceremonial candles to defend themselves. Chaos ensued as supporters from both religions rushed into the melee. Crucifixes, candlesticks and chalices became lethal weapons – almost as lethal as the knives and pistols people had smuggled in. Blood flowed, the wounded screamed, women and children fled, some were trampled in the carnage. Isabella thought she was going to die.

A regiment of Ottoman soldiers, bayonets fixed, quelled the riot after some forty people died. The arguing did not stop, though. The Catholic priests insisted that their service must be completed; the Orthodox ones refused. In the end, the Ottoman governor removed the offending Orthodox cloth from the altar and the Catholic ceremony concluded under armed guard. The fact that the officiating priest was 'trembling in every limb . . . his magnificent robes torn and soiled' somewhat undermined the sense of the numinous.

'It cannot be holy ground,' remarked the Ottoman governor in perfect French. 'If it were, God would not permit it to be desecrated by such disgraceful scenes.' Isabella agreed it was shameful. 'I blushed for the name of Christian . . . The only actors in it who exhibited good sense, moderation and decorum, were *the Turks*.'[1] Conducted with the visceral hatred of a neighbourhood planning dispute turbocharged with religious fanaticism, the argument about who had rights over the Holy Places in Jerusalem sparked the first major European conflict since the Napoleonic wars.

Not that Louis-Napoléon had much interest in the issue. As he cheerfully admitted to his foreign minister, he had little understanding about the dispute between Catholic and Orthodox Christians in the Middle East. His faith was not deep, though he had become more religious with age, and as emperor he understood the importance of the Catholic constituency to his popularity. France was traditionally the defender of Catholic claims, and he was, therefore, happy to appoint a hawkish ambassador to the Ottoman Empire to push them. In November 1852, the French secured a major victory: the Ottomans granted Catholics the right to have their own key to the Church of the Nativity in Bethlehem. In response, Tsar Nicholas mobilised Russian troops.

Nicholas did not see the issue as some obscure and arcane dispute. He dreamed of driving the moribund Ottoman Empire out of its European lands – the sick man of Europe, as he called it – and, like many a Russian leader, of uniting Orthodox Christians under Russian tutelage, even taking Constantinople. This was an ambitious geopolitical dream, but it was inseparable from his deeply held conviction that Russia was a third Rome and that he was the divine instrument in a holy mission to force Ottoman Muslims out of what he saw as Christian Europe.

Nicholas was not going to have his sacred vision ruined by an upstart parvenu calling himself 'emperor' whose only interest in the affair was to give a bit of popular Catholic lustre to his reign. To make this clear to the Ottomans, he demanded the recent ruling in favour of Catholics be overturned. The ultimatum, however, went much further, requiring a new treaty that would make the Ottoman Empire little more than a Russian vassal state. If the sultan refused, it would be war.

'Turkey's last hour has struck,' said Louis-Napoléon's foreign minister in a meeting convened to discuss the crisis. Louis-Napoléon thought of sending the French fleet to the Eastern Mediterranean to stop Russian aggression, but, argued his foreign minister, this would be a mistake. If France stood up to Russia alone, another coalition of European powers would form against it, as had been the case in the Napoleonic wars, which ended in defeat and the overthrow of the First Empire. Speaking in turn, other ministers agreed; Louis-Napoléon seemed convinced.

'I am tempted to wonder in which country and under what government we live,' said Persigny, barely able to contain his fury. If the emperor was weak now, 'Do you know what will happen? The first time you review the troops, you will find saddened faces, silent ranks, and you will feel the ground shaking beneath your feet.' It was necessary to act boldly, Persigny maintained, as he usually did. As for a coalition, the ministers understood nothing of international relations, for Britain would support France against Russia. 'Persigny is right,' said Louis-Napoléon, interrupting his friend. 'If we send our fleet . . . England will do the same, and the union of the two navies will bring about the union of the two peoples against Russia.' With that, the emperor gave the order to dispatch the fleet.

Louis-Napoléon and Persigny were correct: this action pushed the British into sending their navy. Emboldened, the Ottomans rejected Russian demands and, in October 1853, declared war on Russia. The tsar then ordered the invasion of the Danubian Principalities, roughly modern-day Moldova and Romania, a region then loosely under Ottoman control. What took British Russophobia to new heights of jingoism, however, was what happened at sea. On 30 November, technologically and numerically superior Russian ships annihilated the Ottoman navy. British opinion – presumably on the basis that only the Royal Navy should massacre opponents in one-sided battles – was outraged; a rabid press exhorted the government to support the plucky Ottoman underdog.

Although hatred of Russia ran deep in the French imagination, it was not the cause célèbre that it was in Britain and Louis-Napoléon was less bellicose. Whereas Palmerston dreamed of redrawing the map in a once-in-a-lifetime opportunity to break Russian power in Europe, the emperor's aim in backing the Ottomans had been to shore up Catholic support at home and secure an alliance with Britain. At a stroke, this latter goal would end the isolation imposed on France after Waterloo at the Congress of Vienna in 1815. Moreover, Louis-Napoléon believed that British sea power combined with the might of the French army would make the two countries supreme in Europe and around the globe. For Louis-Napoléon to achieve this, war was not necessary.

So, on the brink of hostilities, and against the wishes of the British government, Louis-Napoléon sent a last-ditch peace offering, suggesting an armistice. The tsar refused and, adding insult to injury, wrote to Louis-Napoléon that he would find Russia the same in 1854 as it had been in 1812, when his uncle launched his disastrous invasion. By 28 March 1854, Britain and France were at war with Russia.

———

Louis-Napoléon needed someone to lead the French army against Russia. Saint-Arnaud, the man he chose, had three virtues to recommend him: he spoke passable English, which would help co-ordination with British generals; he was an experienced military commander; and he was devoted to the imperial cause. It was how he had acquired his English that made France's new allies wary: his dissolute youth in London, where, it was alleged, he found work variously as a fencing coach, dance instructor, poet, violinist, singer and billiards hustler. This background did not endear him to highborn British officers. They also believed rumours that he was an incorrigible gambler, which he certainly was on the stock exchange – Louis-Napoléon had recently bailed him out after enormous losses.

Saint-Arnaud's reputation did not impress the traditional aristocrat in charge of the British forces: FitzRoy Somerset, better known as Lord Raglan. He was a general of the old school. So old, in fact, that he had last seen combat at the Battle of Waterloo, where he lost an arm serving as an aide-de-camp to the Duke of Wellington. Turning sixty-five in 1854, he distrusted the French; in forgetful moments he referred to them as the enemy.

Given this, it must have been a terrifying moment for Raglan in April 1854, when, on the way to take up his command in the East, he was confronted with twenty thousand French soldiers at a military review in Paris. In a moment that showed just how far things had changed since the First Empire, when Britain had been France's mortal enemy, Louis-Napoléon rode with British generals through the streets and they were feted with the ubiquitous cries of 'Long live the emperor!', alongside ones rarely heard in Paris, 'Long live the English!' – though someone in the crowd could not resist shouting 'We tore that arm off at Waterloo' when Raglan rode past. Afterwards, there were soirées, trips to the opera and dinners. At these, 'God Save the Queen' was played and then 'Partant pour la Syrie' ('Leaving for Syria'), the tune written by Louis-Napoléon's mother and preferred to the dangerously revolutionary 'Marseillaise' as the Empire's anthem.

With his British allies in Paris, Louis-Napoléon discussed strategy for the campaign. There were differences between what France and Britain wanted to achieve and over where the fighting should take place. Some thought the war should be purely defensive, reinforcing the Ottomans to stop the Russian advance towards Constantinople; others favoured an attack in Eastern Europe, driving the Russians back. Then there were those who argued for a campaign in Crimea and an immediate assault on the Russian naval base of Sevastopol, which commanded the Black Sea.

To ensure there was no rupture in the fragile alliance, however, these important questions were not decided in Paris. French and British forces sailed for the East with no idea what their military objectives were. Everyone was sure of one thing, though: the troops would be home for Christmas. The memory of Napoléon's disastrous invasion in 1812 – when his retreat through the brutally cold Russian winter had destroyed his ill-provisioned army – dominated thinking for Russia as much as it did for Britain and France, but not, strangely, to the extent of the allies packing winter uniforms.

Compared to the British, and the Russians for that matter, the French army was a modern, professional force. It was, however, an astonishingly low bar. Many British officers were gentlemen who had bought their commissions or owed their position to nepotism. They had little or no military training, let alone combat experience. This made for a sharp contrast with their French counterparts, educated at officer schools or promoted from the ranks, and veterans of fighting in Algeria.

Yet by giving his cousin Plon-Plon a command, Louis-Napoléon did his best to bring the French army down to the level of British incompetence. Aged thirty-two at the time of his appointment in 1854, Plon-Plon was annoyed that he had not been given command of the entire French army in the East. Although there had been rumours that the emperor might do this, Louis-Napoléon was not stupid enough to entrust his wayward cousin with such an awesome responsibility. He was, however, foolish enough to give him an important role. Louis-Napoléon soon regretted it. Saint-Arnaud and his fellow officers loathed Plon-Plon, who, despite having no military knowledge whatsoever, explained to anyone who would listen that the coming campaign should become a pan-European and revolutionary war which aimed at liberating Poland. The British were not impressed either: as Prince Albert wrote of Plon-Plon, he was 'the greatest scamp in all of France', had 'conspired with socialists' and was 'not trusted by his cousin'. In short, he had lived a 'life of profligacy which has even disgusted the French'.[2] Like many in Britain, Albert was suspicious of an alliance with the nation's traditional enemy. France, Victoria's husband believed, needed to be 'licked once every fifty years' in the interests of 'civilisation'.[3]

With these inauspicious beginnings for the new Anglo-French world order, allied forces set sail for the East towards the end of April 1854. The more he reflected on the situation, Louis-Napoléon wrote to Saint-Arnaud on 9 May, the more he was persuaded of two things. First, if the Russians advance on Constantinople, give battle. Second, 'If they do not advance, take Crimea.' With that there was little more the emperor could do but wait for news.

———

On the evening of 14 September 1854, Saint-Arnaud was sitting on a camp stool in the late autumn sun, reading a newspaper on a Crimean beach. The landing of French troops had been conducted with precision; Plon-Plon's only concern was where he could find a stove of sufficient size to cook his dinner. He suggested a nearby village might have one, but when it was pointed out that the tsar's Cossack cavalry might ambush them there, he decided to make do with what could be provided behind the security of French lines.

As Saint-Arnaud glanced up from his newspaper, he was less pleased with the progress of his British allies. Things were going badly for them. When the sea was calm, the British landed their infantry, but without tents, and only later did the cavalry disembark. The sea was now rough; men and horses struggled in the surf. That night, soldiers slept in the open, drenched by rain. 'The English are not ready and have made me lose precious time,' Saint-Arnaud complained to his wife.[4]

The French commander was impatient. Speed was essential to surprise the Russians and take the key Black Sea naval base of Sevastopol. Months of campaigning had already been lost. After arriving in the East at the beginning of May, the French and British armies had achieved nothing. The vague Franco-British war aims saw allied forces landing at Gallipoli to defend Constantinople from Russian attack, but it soon became apparent that no attack was imminent and the area was a poor place to supply the armies.

Moreover, with nothing to do, the soldiers soon took to heavy drinking and sex with prostitutes. This did not endear them to their Muslim Ottoman allies. As one British officer recorded, French soldiers 'lounged in the mosques during prayers, ogled licentiously veiled ladies, poisoned the street dogs . . . shot the gulls in the harbour and the pigeons in the streets'. Worse, they mocked the Muslim call to prayer. 'The Turks had heard of [European] civilization,' continued the officer, and 'they now saw it . . . Robbery, drunkenness, gambling, and prostitution revelled under the glare of an eastern sun.'[5]

They moved on to Varna, a port in modern-day Bulgaria but then in the Ottoman Empire, where the allied navies could better restock the troops. Here, a cholera epidemic decimated the British and French armies. To increase the despair, fire broke out and flames burned Varna's wooden buildings; supplies were destroyed, and in the confusion, allied soldiers looted much of what remained. In short, though there had been little fighting, the war was not going well. Then it nearly ended. The Ottomans proved much tougher soldiers than any of the European powers expected. They held up the Russian advance. Soon, under Austrian diplomatic pressure, the Russians withdrew. With the Russian invasion over, Britain and France could have made peace.

But Louis-Napoléon had not sent his army east to get drunk, have sex and die of cholera – it could have done that in France. A striking victory was required to give his regime military glory. The plan to attack Sevastopol was revived. The immense Franco-British forces set sail on 7 September. The transportation of some sixty thousand men, at the time the largest naval invasion in history, was an awesome sight: the sea was covered with steam-powered ships, smokestacks rising like a floating industrial city.

In what was becoming a tradition for the French army, they had no up-to-date maps. Worse, Saint-Arnaud had been suffering from stomach pains which turned out to be cancer. As the fleet sailed towards Sevastopol, he was fading fast, prone to fevers, agony leading to insomnia. With super-human effort, when the fleet reached its landing site, Saint-Arnaud rode his horse along the beach, supervising the disembarkation of the French troops. Having managed to get the French army ashore and ready to move in twenty-four hours, he was understandably annoyed that it was not until five days later that the British were ready too.

The next day, 20 September, they came before the Russian forces defending the heights across the River Alma, blocking the way to Sevastopol. Saint-Arnaud's plan was for a co-ordinated attack. The French and a contingent of Ottoman troops would launch a diversionary assault on the Russian left flank, drawing the enemy forces away, then the main French army would smash through the centre while the British advanced on their right. It was an excellent strategy with only one drawback – it required the British army to be awake. The 7 a.m. start proved too early for Raglan to get everyone out of bed. The French troops, however, were in position, and this made it clear to the Russian commander that the attack on their left was a sideshow.

But the French general leading this sideshow had different ideas. As he waited impatiently for the British to wake up, he surveyed the heights across the Alma river where it met the sea. These rose sharply to nearly fifty metres and were only lightly defended because the Russian commander thought them impossible to scale. The French officer believed otherwise. He ordered his men to wade across the river and then climb.

Looking down on them from the high ground, a Russian officer thought the ascent hopeless. He ironically held out his arm as if to help up the French. A Zouave – battle-hardened veterans of Algeria and the elite of the French army – bounded over rocks, aimed his rifle and fired. Hit in the leg, the Russian officer slipped and slid down the rocks, landing wounded at the Frenchman's feet. 'Well,' said the Zouave, lifting up the Russian and carrying him to a tree, 'you wanted to help me and it's me who helps you.'[6]

Elsewhere, in their billowing red trousers and blue tunics, Frenchmen swarmed up the hills. Helping each other, clinging on to overhangs and vegetation, they advanced. On the plateau at the top, they met a platoon of Cossack cavalry, which charged them before it was cut down with well-aimed volleys. The men cheered as more of their comrades reached them and formed a defensive position. The Russian commanding on the heights did his best to match Raglan's incompetence. Bottle of champagne in one hand, he ordered his men to attack, but the alcohol had not sharpened his senses – he launched them against another Russian regiment. With the allied fleet bombarding their positions, the Russians began to lose morale.

Watching from below, officers around Saint-Arnaud could not believe that the Zouaves had taken the high ground. 'But no,' cried Saint-Arnaud, 'I can see the red trousers!' Then, with the elegance of the actor he had once been, he took his fine white-plumed feather hat and turned to his men. 'Gentlemen,' he said, sensing victory, 'this battle will be called the Battle of Alma.'[7]

Saint-Arnaud was right. Once the British engaged the Russians, albeit with Raglan's flair for chaos and ineptitude, and the French advanced in the centre, the Russians panicked, fleeing in all directions. By late afternoon, the battle was over. The French even captured the carriage of the Russian commander-in-chief, finding pornographic novels and ladies' underwear. 'Your majesty's cannons have spoken,' wrote Saint-Arnaud to Louis-Napoléon from the battlefield; 'we have gained a complete victory. It is a great day, Sire, to add to the military festivals of France.'[8]

But Saint-Arnaud was wrong, it was not a complete victory. The Russian army was defeated, not annihilated, and it staggered back to defend

Sevastopol as thick, smouldering smoke rolled lazily across the plains. Saint-Arnaud wanted to pursue it; Raglan refused. Once they finally made it to the Russian port, however, it was the French, fearing heavy casualties, who persuaded the British not to storm the city. Instead, they resolved upon a siege. Forty-two years after Napoléon's infamous invasion, another French army was going to spend the winter in Russia.

———

This was not something the army's commanding officers were prepared for, least of all Plon-Plon. As winter approached, he had no intention of staying on the inhospitable heights around Sevastopol. Pleading sickness, in November he retired to the luxuries of Constantinople and wrote to Louis-Napoléon begging for permission to return to France.

'It pained me greatly to learn that you were sick,' the emperor replied, but 'I implore you as soon as you can to return to the army'. Having a Bonaparte enjoying comfort while the French soldiers suffered was disastrous for public opinion and military morale. In case his cousin was not getting the point, Louis-Napoléon repeated it: 'If you are sick, stay at Constantinople until you are better, but I strongly repeat that you are going to return to the army as soon as you can.'[9]

It was a surprise, then, when Plon-Plon arrived in Paris. Most put his unexpected reappearance down to cowardice, and 'Craint-Plomb' – literally 'fears lead' – became a common wordplay on his nickname. In fact, it was not lack of courage but lack of comfort that compelled Louis-Napoléon's debonair cousin to return. He could not face the hunger, the cold and the lice that were quotidian nightmares for the French and British troops stranded in Crimea. His father Jérôme – who had, sensibly as it turned out, run away in the early days of Napoléon's invasion of Russia in 1812 – was more sympathetic. 'How wonderful the French are,' he complained, 'already throwing stones at this poor child who has not seen his mistress in months.'[10]

Meanwhile, the French army suffered. Saint-Arnaud was too sick to command. He took a ship for Paris, but he died on the way. As a former wastrel with a debauched past, a talent for acting and a penchant for wild speculation – and a highly effective killer untroubled by scruples – Saint-Arnaud was in many ways the epitome of a Second Empire man. He represented something else about the regime too, though. Louis-Napoléon required talent and loyalty. The first had taken Saint-Arnaud to the upper echelons of the French army; the second got him to the apex, where he acquitted himself admirably, organised a vast expeditionary force and, at the Battle of the Alma, orchestrated a much-craved French victory, the first major one since Waterloo.

His ability shone all the brighter in comparison to what came after. During the Battle of Balaclava in October, Lord Raglan managed to exceed even his own high standards of buffoonery; he found immortal infamy after giving such a vague order that it resulted in the suicidal Charge of the Light Brigade through the so-called Valley of Death. 'It's magnificent, but it's not war,' was the view of one French general. The allies soon fought another battle at Inkerman in early November, which they won; neither side, however, could strike a decisive blow. With French losses mounting, the war became increasingly unpopular in France. As the emperor knew, 'the success of armies, however brilliant they may be, is only transitory. In reality, it is public opinion that wins the last victory.'[11] Louis-Napoléon resolved to break the impasse: he would go to Crimea and take personal command.

Apart from Eugénie, everyone thought this insane. His ministers threatened to resign; the British were appalled; but Louis-Napoléon insisted. In a last desperate bid to forestall a Bonaparte becoming commander-in-chief of British armed forces, Queen Victoria reluctantly put country before self and agreed to grant the parvenus Louis-Napoléon and Eugénie a state visit to England. It was hoped that royal charm would persuade the French emperor to give up his madcap plan.

———

Prior to the emperor and empress's arrival, Bonapartemania hit London. Union Jacks vied with tricolour flags in the streets; suspended from the roof of a house in the churchyard of St Paul's Cathedral a banner fluttered with the eagle embroidered on it, the imperial crown atop, complete with Napoleonic bees and the letters 'N' and 'E'; tickets for stands or on balconies in private houses sold out; one correspondent was moved to write to the *Morning Post* and suggest that Marble Arch be renamed the Arch of Napoléon.

On Monday morning, 16 April 1855, Albert stared out into the Dover fog which covered the Channel. Finally, later than expected, a dark shape glided out of the murk, its slowly appearing masts flying the French and British flags. Artillery boomed onshore, adding its fire to that of the escorting French vessels. As the ship carrying Louis-Napoléon came alongside the pier, he took off his hat in salute to Albert. Upon stepping onto British soil, the emperor and empress – she was wearing a red and green tartan silk dress to emphasise her Scottish ancestry – were greeted with wild cheers, hats thrown in the air, handkerchiefs waved. In return, Louis-Napoléon bowed several times. It was a wondrous reception showing how quickly the wartime alliance had become popular in Britain, only slightly diminished by the fact that local workers charged with preparing an imperial welcome, unaccustomed to producing oversized ceremonial eagles, had attached the bird's wings upside down.

After taking the train to London, the imperial couple were driven across the capital in open carriages in what resembled a triumphal procession. When they passed King Street, Louis-Napoléon pointed out his old bachelor pad to Eugénie. The crowd, realising what he was doing, went wild. By 6 p.m., they had reached Paddington, where another train took them to Windsor Castle. Here, Queen Victoria, wearing a light blue dress and a pearl necklace, waited nervously. She heard cheers as Louis-Napoléon and Eugénie made the short journey from station to castle. As the carriages approached the entrance, Victoria stepped outside, children in tow, and a band struck up 'Partant pour la Syrie'. Louis-Napoléon kissed Victoria's hand; she embraced him, 'giving him 2 salutes on either cheek'. Albert escorted an anxious Eugénie, who was overawed by the occasion. After the imperial couple was shown five other children not deemed important enough to be in the initial welcome party, Louis-Napoléon and Eugénie were taken to their rooms. 'Everything had gone off beautifully,' gushed Victoria.

In Eugénie's room, things were going less well. She had lost her luggage. Worse, she had lost her hairdresser, who was delayed on the way from London. After much panic, and contemplating pleading tiredness instead of facing the queen of England with less than perfect hair, Eugénie borrowed a grey dress trimmed with black lace from one of her ladies and got her attendants to do her styling. 'The profile, and line of the throat and shoulders are quite beautiful,' wrote an enraptured Victoria about Eugénie at dinner that night, 'the expression, charming, and gentle – quite delightful'.

'The Emperor is extremely short, but with a head and bust, which ought to belong to a much taller man,' was Victoria's less rapturous verdict on Louis-Napoléon. But they got on, as she put it, 'extremely well at dinner'. Louis-Napoléon's charming manners meant conversation flowed easily. And he had done his homework: he threw into conversations vignettes about Victoria's reign, as well as mentioning that he had seen her in parliament when she was eighteen. He also pointed out to her that he had been a special constable in 1848. 'The emperor is so very quiet, his voice low, and soft,' she wrote happily in her journal about their first dinner.[12]

Over the next few days, Louis-Napoléon applied a thick veneer of charm. His chief weapons were flirtation, playing with Victoria's children and Anglophilia – he even stopped to admire the grass and said, 'You could never get that on the continent' – which left Victoria smitten.[13] The emperor 'made love to her', the foreign secretary told a confidant, speaking figuratively, 'which he did with a tact that proved quite successful'. The queen was 'mighty tickled by it, for she had never been made love to in her life, and never had she conversed with a man of the world on a footing of equality; and as his love-making was of a character to flatter her vanity without alarming her virtue . . . she enjoyed the novelty of it'.[14]

One evening, there was a ball in the unfortunately named Waterloo Chamber. Portraits of the architects of Napoléon's defeat, the Duke of Wellington and Tsar Alexander I among others, looked down as the man who had restored his uncle's Empire opened the dancing with Victoria. 'Really,' recorded an overwhelmed queen, 'to think of a Gd Daughter of George IIIrd, dancing with the nephew of our great enemy, the Empr Napoleon now my most firm Ally, in the Waterloo Gallery – is incredible! And this Ally was only 6 years ago, an exile in England, poor, and not at all thought of!'[15]

The next day was more extraordinary still. Louis-Napoléon was awarded the Order of the Garter, a medieval honour founded by Edward III in

1348. Looking uncomfortable in white stockings, he half knelt before the queen while she 'fumbled ostensibly, as she always does, to show her unfamiliarity with the slightly indiscreet article of male attire'.[16] Then he kissed her hand, and she embraced him. Given that Louis-Napoléon had to swear allegiance to the queen, there was some doubt as to whether the emperor would accept the honour, but as he had shown with his *coup d'état* of 2 December, he was not a man to let oaths trouble him. 'At last,' he said, leaving the ceremony, 'I am a gentleman.'[17]

At dinner that evening, Eugénie and Victoria tried to outdo each other with the brilliance of their diamonds; but there was only ever going to be one winner. Queen Victoria wore the Koh-i-Noor, recently purloined from India. Over dinner, Louis-Napoléon complained about French republican exiles in London who wanted to assassinate him. He also lamented that Victor Hugo had once supported him and dined at his table, but was now one of his most implacable enemies, in exile on the Channel Islands.

When they got a chance, Louis-Napoléon's entourage urged the queen to persuade the emperor not to go to Crimea. After dinner, the French minister of war, equally keen to keep the emperor away from the front line, asked if she had made any progress. 'I dared to make some observations,' replied the queen. '*Mon dieu*, dare!' said the exasperated minister, explaining that she needed to do a lot more than that. Fleury told her the same, warning that the regime was not sufficiently consolidated for the emperor to be away from France for a long time.[18]

The next morning, Louis-Napoléon was getting ready for a reception at the Guildhall in the City of London. Reading out his speech in English, he asked Victoria to correct his pronunciation, 'though it required but little', according to the queen.[19] From Buckingham Palace, Louis-Napoléon and Eugénie were driven in state through the streets of London. Crowds, bunting and flags were all along the route, and the ovations were ecstatic. Outside a bookshop there was a poster advertising a Victor Hugo pamphlet criticising Louis-Napoléon and his visit to England. Having somehow secured a boathook, a particularly irate member of the public tore it down and the bookseller's window was smashed. Hugo would have been pleased, though, to have learned that a dwarf dressed in the style of the original Napoléon and chain-smoking cigars drew considerable attention outside a shop in Ludgate. At the Guildhall, Louis-Napoléon's speech went down well, frequently interrupted with cheers. Journalists reporting on it commented that his English was perfect, if accented, which was a much kinder reception than the one he received from the French press when he made his maiden speech in the Assembly in 1848.

The next day was Louis-Napoléon's birthday, not that he told anyone, but Victoria found out and gave him a pencil case as a present. Then they went to see the monumental iron and glass hall, the Crystal Palace, built for the Great Exhibition held in 1851. As they made their way, cries of '*Vive l'empereur*' and '*Vive l'impératrice*' rang out, and much to Victoria's delight, 'sometimes even "*Vive le Hempereur*", in cockney English!' That evening was their last together, and Victoria spent most of it talking with Louis-Napoléon. She gently tried, again, to persuade him not to go to Crimea, but he insisted, lamenting only that he did not have an heir to leave behind. Victoria asked whether he could rely on Plon-Plon. 'Oh my God, no,' replied the emperor.

Recording her thoughts in her journal, Victoria wrote:

Albert gets on famously with the Empress, and so do I, with the Emperor, who is very fascinating. He is so quiet and gentle, and has such a soft pleasant voice – is so simple and plain spoken, in all he says – so devoid of all phrases, and has besides a poetical and romantic turn of mind, which makes him particularly attractive.[20]

Before he left Buckingham Palace, the emperor invited Victoria to Paris in the summer. Then there were affectionate, tearful goodbyes. As the imperial couple and their followers got into their carriages, 'Partant pour la Syrie' was played – an anthem, Victoria noted, she had heard fourteen times on Thursday. At least it would be the last time she heard it for a while, for it was not one the emperor particularly enjoyed, either. 'Ah!' he had remarked of the hymn that followed him wherever he went. 'My poor mother did not foresee what she would inflict on me, when she composed that tune.'[21]

Victoria missed Louis-Napoléon. She consoled herself with the fact that the visit had been a triumph, 'a brilliant, successful and pleasant dream, the recollection of which will always be firmly fixed in my mind'. And she was 'very glad to know this wonderful and remarkable man, whom it is certainly impossible not to like'. The wonderful and remarkable man was in a hurry to get back to Paris. He wanted everything to be ready for the Exposition universelle in May. This international exhibition was designed to show the world that Paris and the Empire were the epicentre of modern civilisation, for the capital was undergoing the most transformative experiment in urban planning yet undertaken in modern history.[22]

———

If mid-nineteenth-century London was known for its smog, Paris was known for its smell. Human and animal excrement, rubbish and other filth piled up in the streets; what sewers there were deposited raw waste into the Seine, poisoning water many still used for washing and drinking; cholera epidemics were frequent. In the summer, malodorous miasmas wafted up from unknown depths and made passers-by retch. There were fine apartments, mansions and monuments, but often within spitting distance of medieval houses, shacks and hovels. Soiled, insalubrious, ridden with vice and crime, Paris was not a shining beacon of modernity.

But Louis-Napoléon wanted it to be, and as president, he had a bold vision for remodelling the capital. Progress, however, had been painfully slow. The need to balance the city's budget meant there was little money to invest in construction. Even when funds were available, there was tortuous bureaucracy, confused jurisdictions and little co-ordinated strategy. As emperor, one of Louis-Napoléon's first priorities was to put his plans into action. He simplified compulsory purchase orders, pushed aside local government and revolutionised the city's finances. Instead of balancing its budget, the city of Paris would borrow money, on the rationale that urban development would provide employment, increase rents and raise land values. A new bank, Crédit Mobilier, had been set up to invest in high-risk ventures and new technologies where more traditional financial houses feared to tread. The capital the bank raised was the lifeblood of the Second Empire, pumping money into everything from railways and gas lighting to the Crimean War and the development of Paris. All Louis-Napoléon needed to realise the latter was someone monomaniacally obsessed with making his vision a reality.

Enter Georges-Eugène Haussmann, whose huge frame – he was six feet three inches – matched his ambition. 'With a visible self-satisfaction,' Persigny wrote after interviewing him, 'he explained to me the achievements of his administrative career, sparing me nothing; he would have talked for six hours without stopping, provided it was about his favourite subject, himself.' Persigny was fascinated, as much, he admitted, by the defects in Haussmann's character as by his obvious intelligence. When Haussmann went blow by blow through the various power struggles he had had to deal with as a civil servant and how he had triumphed, Persigny thought it wonderful: 'While this absorbing personality spread out before me with a sort of brutal cynicism, I could not contain my keen satisfaction.' Haussmann was the man to break old economic orthodoxies, smash through red tape and get things done. This 'broad-shouldered, bull-necked man, full of audacity and cunning . . . setting trap for trap would certainly succeed'. Persigny, the disruptor par excellence *avant la lettre*, enjoyed the thought 'of throwing this tall tigerish animal among the pack of foxes and wolves combining to thwart the generous aspirations of the Empire'.[23]

At their first meeting after Haussmann's appointment on 29 June 1853, Louis-Napoléon showed his new prefect of the Seine a map of Paris. The emperor had sketched out routes, colour coded in order of priority, and explained plans for new parks – especially the Bois de Boulogne, where the emperor took time marking out walks and water features himself – to rival those he had enjoyed in London. Soon monumental, cathedral-like train stations were envisaged. There were grand state-of-the-art sewers planned, as well as distinctive rows of modern, uniform apartments and thousands of gas lamps lighting the streets at night. Louis-Napoléon wanted his capital to be a majestic imperial centre from which his power radiated across France and Europe. Haussmann, a workaholic obsessed with digestion and with no regard for the feelings of others, least of all those who lived in the areas marked for demolition, set about razing the charming if insalubrious quarters of medieval Paris with all the zeal of a gastroenterologist. The city became one of the largest building sites on earth.

Though the work was far from finished, the Exposition universelle opening in May 1855 was, in part, intended to show off the emperor's capital. This fair, inspired by the success of the Great Exhibition of 1851 in

London, would also showcase the world's technology, industry and art, with numerous nations sending exhibitors. In opposition to French industrialists, who were not keen on promoting competition from other nations, Louis-Napoléon had used his powers to decree the event into existence. An estimated six million people had visited the 1851 exhibition in London and so the Paris one was an unrivalled opportunity to blind the French people with the glare of another elaborate spectacle. More than that, at the heart of the project was a fetishisation of social progress through knowledge – a chance to demonstrate the regime's embrace of the white heat of technology, and for the emperor to flaunt his esoteric interpretation of socialism, which, given the opulence of his court, was very much of the champagne variety.

There was, then, idealism at the heart of the programme, which drew on the utopianism much in vogue in 1840s France and which Louis-Napoléon, and even Eugénie, had read about. In this new dawn, technology, expertise and free markets would boost commerce and industry across the globe, resulting in prosperity for all, thereby reconciling workers to liberal capitalism. At the same time, mass production would reduce costs, boosting consumerism and quality of life. Everything that would revolutionise people's lives was on display: lawnmowers, baby's bottles and Colt revolvers.

And Louis-Napoléon wanted to show off the extravaganza to his new friends, Victoria and Albert, who came to Paris in August. The arches, banners, flags, illuminations, plaster statues and faux-marble columns, illuminations and anatomically correct eagles dwarfed anything in London or Windsor. The people and soldiers shouted, 'Long live the Queen of England!', something of a first on the streets of Paris, and military bands played 'God Save the Queen' as the royal couple made their way through newly opened grand boulevards in the capital and then on to the palace of Saint-Cloud. 'One can give but a faint notion of what was a veritable Triumph,' recorded Victoria.

Over a stifling dinner, with plentiful candles adding to the warm Parisian air, Victoria renewed her platonic love affair with Louis-Napoléon, whom she found as charming as before. She was less kind about Plon-Plon. He 'made himself very disagreeable, disagreeing with everybody, and being thoroughly rude' when, in the stuffy Paris heat, he showed Victoria around the exhibition's art gallery, which he curated.

His family aside, Victoria got on famously with the emperor, 'whom I become more and more fond of', and the empress. Louis-Napoléon led Victoria and Albert on a sightseeing tour, proudly showing new boulevards and buildings that were either finished or in development. When they passed the Conciergerie, Louis-Napoléon pointed to it and, with breezy charm, said, '*Voilà*, where I was in prison,' referring to the time he was held there after his failed *coup d'état* in 1840. Then they took in Notre-Dame – 'There is nothing particularly to admire in the interior,' was the queen's verdict. She liked the Tuileries, though, where Louis-Napoléon showed Victoria and Albert his private rooms, including his sacred Napoleonic relics that helped keep his faith burning while exiled in London.

The Louvre she especially enjoyed, bustling about with the determination of a tourist intent on making every second count, much to the dismay of the foreign secretary, Lord Clarendon, who was forced to trail along behind her, perspiring in the Paris summer. 'No royal person ever yet known . . . comes up to her in indefatigability,' he complained.[24] As they went round the gallery, the emperor began to flag. At this point, Clarendon asked hopefully if the queen was not perhaps more tired than she looked, but the monarch, splendidly oblivious to the suffering of those around her, replied that she was not in the least fatigued.

All the coming and going meant long carriage drives. During one of these, Louis-Napoléon revealed that he had abandoned his idea to personally command the army in Crimea. He could not trust anyone to govern in his absence, a revelation that showed how precarious his regime was. His uncle Jérôme – who was sulking and refused to be in Paris during the visit of an English monarch – was a coward, Louis-Napoléon told Victoria; and Plon-Plon was dangerous.

Of course, there were balls; one at Versailles was the most sumptuous. At the top of the main staircase, Eugénie greeted Victoria and Albert, 'looking really like a Fairy Queen', wrote Victoria, 'in white, with bunches of grass & diamonds, & a beautiful diamond "tour de corsage", round the top of the dress, all "en rivière" – the same round her waist and a corresponding coiffure'. When Louis-Napoléon saw her, he said, 'How beautiful you are.'[25] Then, in a blaze of reflected light, he walked down the Hall of Mirrors with the queen leaning against his arm, Eugénie and

Albert following behind. The emperor led them to seats of honour at a window. Explosions filled the night sky, the ladies' diamonds refracting the light of the moon and the colourful bursts of fireworks, which ended in explosions that outlined Windsor Castle in the dark above Versailles. Louis-Napoléon then waltzed with Victoria. Later, there was a chandelier-lit supper for four hundred people which Victoria thought one of the finest she had ever witnessed.

There was also a visit to Britain's mortal enemy, Napoléon, in the enormous domed church of the Invalides, where his tomb was housed. It looks like a 'large pool', said Louis-Napoléon, referring to the open circular vault below. 'One comes in and asks oneself, where is the Emperor's tomb? One expects to see water.' In fact, the coffin was not yet at the bottom of this crypt but in a side chapel. Louis-Napoléon led Victoria to it, and 'there I stood on the arm of Napoleon III, before the coffin of his Uncle, our bitterest foe!' an incredulous Victoria wrote.[26] 'God Save the Queen' soundtracked this visit, played slowly and lugubriously on the church's organ.

For Victoria's eldest son, the Prince of Wales – known as Bertie – Paris and the emperor were anything but lugubrious. For a prince brought up on a strict diet of Victorian repression and loneliness as per his father's wishes, the dynamic eclecticism of Paris alongside Louis-Napoléon's worldly bonhomie turned a dull world into colour. As part of his upbringing he had been shielded from people of dubious character, like Louis-Napoléon. Now, cigarette dangling out of the corner of his mouth, the emperor took him for a fast-paced carriage drive through the bustling boulevards of Paris. On another occasion, as they strolled in palace grounds, Louis-Napoléon threw his cigarette to the ground and said they should get back. 'You have a nice country,' Bertie blurted out. 'I would like to be your son.'[27]

On their way back to Britain, Louis-Napoléon accompanied the royal party on the train to Boulogne. Under a dazzling moon, with band playing, fireworks exploding in the sky and illuminations in the town, Victoria and Albert boarded their royal yacht. Louis-Napoléon sailed out of the harbour with them. When it was finally time to leave, Victoria embraced the emperor and kissed him twice; he shook Albert's hand warmly. But the queen could not bear to part: she followed him to the ladder at the side of the yacht, squeezed his hand and embraced him again, 'Once again, adieu, Sire!' she exclaimed. As Louis-Napoléon got into the barge below, he called out, 'Adieu, Madame, au revoir.'

'I really hope so,' replied a slightly too eager Victoria.

And then it was all over, 'like a brilliant dream, never to be forgotten'. If she had warmed to Louis-Napoléon when he came to England, Victoria was enraptured now. She maintained that physically he was not much to look at – 'I like his face though,' she conceded – rather, it was his personality she found beguiling: 'His society is particularly agreeable and pleasant; there is something fascinating, melancholy, and engaging, which draws you to him.' More than that, she found his calmness appealing. 'He is so quiet, so simple, naif even . . . so gentle, so full of tact, dignity and modesty, so full of respect and kind attention towards us, never saying a word, or doing a thing, which could put me out or embarrass me.' With all the warmth and confusion of a lover, she wrote, 'I felt – I do not know how to express it – safe with him.'[28]

––––––

Through the bitter winter and then into the blistering summer months, British, French and Ottoman troops laid siege to Sevastopol. Yet the Russians held out. A new offensive was planned for September 1855, and a major bombardment preceded it: fifty thousand artillery rounds a day battered the already shattered city. At night, shells screamed through the air, tracing fiery arcs through the black sky before immense explosions as they landed in the town, followed by the screams of the wounded and dying.

On 8 September, the attack began. It was a cold day, and a strong wind blew clouds of dust into the smoke from the burning port, which covered the advance of the soldiers as they made their way silently to the front of the trenches. The target was the Malakoff, a fort on high ground that was key to the defence of the city. At midday, the commanding officers cried, 'Soldiers! Forward! *Vive l'empereur!*' – a shout the soldiers roared as they rose up from behind the trenches, which appeared to the Russian defenders as though the earth was spitting out thousands of men. Drums, trumpets, artillery, bullets, yells filled the air as the French attackers dashed the thirty yards that separated the two armies, Zouaves leading the way.

The first wave threw themselves into the ditch below the fortifications. The ladders had not arrived, but the Zouaves climbed up the rockface or made improvised ladders by placing rifles over their backs, allowing their comrades to clamber onto the Russian defences. Hand-to-hand fighting ensued. Finally, ladders arrived and French reinforcements stormed the redoubt. Despite Russian counterattacks, the tricolour continued to fly from the ramparts.

Though the fighting elsewhere was less successful, taking the Malakoff proved decisive. Without it, Sevastopol could not be defended and the Russians began to evacuate the city. The echo of Napoléon's invasion had terrified and inspired both sides, and to complete the comparison, the Russians rendered Sevastopol a second Moscow, setting the city on fire. Flames engulfed what remained of the shell-shattered town and burned uncontrollably for the next few days, while the allies occupied the port as black velvet smoke sluggishly rose into the sky.

In 1812, Napoléon had taken Moscow and still was unable to dictate peace terms, but in 1855 Russia was in a far worse situation. Whereas Napoléon's army had been cut off deep in enemy territory, the British and French at Sevastopol could be resupplied and reinforced by sea before campaigning in Crimea, which they would likely occupy. Moreover, their naval forces were preparing for a Baltic campaign, threatening St Petersburg. Finally, diplomacy brought Austria in on the allied side, which meant that if Russia continued to fight, it might face a land invasion on its European frontier. Besides, Tsar Nicholas had died a few months earlier and the new tsar, Alexander II, wanted peace. This was much to the disappointment of the British press and Palmerston, who clamoured for a punitive war that would break Russia for ever.

The bulk of the fighting and losses had been borne by France, however. There, the war was not popular, and, obsessed with public opinion, Louis-Napoléon was keen to end it. So, in February 1856, the representatives of the European powers gathered at the Quai d'Orsay, newly built to house the French foreign ministry. With a bust of the current Emperor of the French placed in the conference room and, in a fine piece of diplomatic trolling, a portrait of the previous one, Napoléon Bonaparte, looking down on diplomats from the powers that had consigned France to isolation in 1815, a treaty was hammered out.

In terms of the map of Europe, the Crimean War changed little; however, no one was under any illusion that this was anything other than a seismic shift in international relations. With the Paris Exhibition, France had shown itself to be a world leader in industry, trade, science and art. Now, with the peace conference, it was, once again, the centre of European diplomatic and military power.

In just over three years, Louis-Napoléon had spectacularly consolidated his regime. With the construction in Paris matched by a boom in building railways, which in turn fuelled manufacturing, the economy was roaring. Abroad, Louis-Napoléon's armies had won stunning victories, the humiliating Congress of Vienna which had isolated France after 1815 had been overturned and the emperor had succeeded where his uncle failed: invading Russia. Louis-Napoléon's fervent belief that the Empire would make France great again seemed more like demonstrable reality than deluded dream. Yet the dynasty was still only precariously established. 'If, by misfortune, something should happen to the emperor,' one of Louis-Napoléon's generals had candidly told Queen Victoria during her stay in Paris, 'there is absolutely nothing after him.' That was about to change. Eugénie was pregnant.

15

THE BEGINNING OF THE AFFAIRS

Eugénie did not much enjoy sex with Louis-Napoléon. 'After the first night,' she said, giving advice about marriage, 'it doesn't matter whether a man is good looking or ugly. After a week, it's all the same.'[1] Yet in public they were affectionate, holding hands in company. When they were apart, Louis-Napoléon's letters were loving, if banal. 'My dear and much-loved Eugénie,' ran a typical one he wrote when she was away, 'my first thought when waking is to think of you.' His missives were usually signed '*tout à toi*', but they were no more – perhaps less – passionate than his letters to Hortense Cornu when he was in prison in the 1840s, or, indeed, to his mother while she was alive.[2]

This was not, then, the obsessive, sensuous relationship of Napoléon and Joséphine. Nonetheless, Eugénie respected him. 'They say no man appears great to his valet,' she wrote, and this 'applies even more to his wife; well, as for me, I admire him more every day'.[3] But everyone from Eugénie to the French people understood that regardless of Louis-Napoléon making a virtue of the fact that this was no dynastic alliance, the primary purpose of the union was to produce heirs. There was hope mixed with anxiety, then, when in 1855 she became pregnant.

On 15 March 1856, Eugénie went into labour. It was agony. In a letter to Queen Victoria, Louis-Napoléon wrote, 'Not only was the pain intolerable for more than twelve hours, but the doctors were worried for a long time about the fate of the mother and child. Finally, they decided to use forceps, which is what saved everything.'[4] The next day, 101 cannons boomed from the Tuileries, and then across France, to announce the arrival of a baby boy, named Napoléon Eugène Louis Jean Joseph, known as the prince imperial. Eugénie recovered from her ordeal, and the baby was healthy, fat and happy, soon babbling and dribbling away in the luxury of court life.

Louis-Napoléon had immense love for his son. In the first few weeks, he came at all hours to the baby's cradle, anxiously and tenderly watching over him. He took great interest in his development, astonished, and no doubt disappointed, to learn from the baby's doctor that teething could discomfort a child for up to two and a half years. This led him to ruminate on his own poor teeth, wondering why nature had not provided for replacement ones. After all, he noted, 'the deer in the park at Saint-Cloud lose their antlers every year' and then grow new ones.[5]

The birth of an heir, and the perpetuation of the regime, was another occasion for spectacular pageantry, culminating in the prince imperial's baptism on 14 June 1856 in Notre-Dame. Crowds surged forward and cheers burst out as the emperor and empress's carriage drove from the Tuileries to the cathedral. Men strained to catch a glimpse, children clambered onto parents' shoulders and some women wept with joy. Inside the carriage, the emperor waved and Eugénie reminded herself that it was through her son 'that the dynasty of the Napoleons will take final root in the soil of France'.[6] She could not silence another inner voice which told her that the heirs of Louis XVI, Napoléon and the last French king, Louis-Philippe, had all undergone the same ceremony, yet none had reigned.

This was something that Louis-Napoléon had already addressed. Replying to a vote of thanks from the Senate and the Corps législatif, he said, 'If I hope that his fate will be a happier one' than that of recent royal heirs, 'it is because, relying on Providence, I cannot doubt of its protection.' Just in case providence was not enough, Louis-Napoléon claimed he had also learned lessons from history: 'A dynasty has a chance of stability only while it remains faithful to its origin, and has a care for the popular interests for which has been created.' Referring to a telegram from the Vatican, he also noted that the pope carried his blessing 'by electricity'.[7]

Not that the pope bothered with the baptism. In another snub to Louis-Napoléon – he had refused to come to Paris to crown him emperor and there had never been a coronation – the pope did not deign to perform the ceremony and sent a cardinal in his place. Still, more than five thousand guests crammed into the cathedral, ruining many a crinoline dress crushed in the cramped space, and they were illuminated by ten thousand candles that set the interior ablaze and made the jewels of the finely dressed women shimmer. The cardinal performed the religious ceremony, then the baby was handed to Eugénie as the master of ceremonies marched to the centre of the cathedral, shouting three times, '*Vive le prince impérial!*'[8] Now Louis-Napoléon took the child, holding him up to wild cheers as an orchestra played, a choir sang and bells rang. The next day, bonbons were thrown from three hundred balloons, sparking huge scrambles below for the sweets.

Later that summer, Eugénie and Louis-Napoléon took the prince imperial to Biarritz, a favoured place where, in a lavish villa built in the shape of an 'E', strict court etiquette was relaxed. Louis-Napoléon threw himself comically into the evening entertainments. He had the endearing habit of laughing, sometimes close to tears, at his own jokes. Tone deaf, he enjoyed singing raucously and badly in French and German while someone played piano, or embracing terrible and exaggerated dad dancing, much to the amusement of onlookers. There were also violent parlour games that Eugénie organised, involving variations on women hitting men with napkins, with Louis-Napoléon gamely clambering over chairs, tables and sofas to escape the blows.

For the most part, though, he was his usual quiet, contemplative self, which contrasted with the more impetuous Eugénie. She dominated conversations, opined on any topic, often without much knowledge, and enjoyed practical jokes. At times, one guest commented, it was very unladylike, a fault the disgruntled person put down to her not being French. But Eugénie especially shone in the evenings, holding court and radiant in her oversized crinoline dresses, wearing a different one every time.

When announcing his marriage, Louis-Napoléon had said that Eugénie would be an ornament for the throne. Soon she gravitated from ornament to fashion icon, and a few years after becoming empress, Eugénie, shockingly, chose a male British designer, Charles Frederick Worth, as her personal couturier. The House of Worth became one of the first and most sought-after trailblazers for haute couture; a certain Louis Vuitton did her luggage. Whether in beautiful white state ball gowns with red velvet trains, historical costumes for masked balls or oversized crinoline dresses, Eugénie set trends that were copied in Paris, and then across the Western world — fashion magazines as far afield as Philadelphia explained how women could get the imperial look.

Unfortunately, the look Eugénie championed was crinoline. By the mid-1850s, new technology, steel wiring, meant the penchant for voluminous dresses reached extremes. Though many wearers found it preferable to the layers of uncomfortable, stiff petticoats previously required to get the wide style, and the amount of colourful fabric looked spectacular, the dress was deliberately impractical. Literally caging women, it required what was considered at the time a suitably feminine, stiff gait. This lack of manoeuvrability was problematic: whether catching fire after going unwittingly close to a flame, being blown into the street and then run down by carriages or simply falling downstairs after tripping over the hem, the crinoline found ingenious ways straight out of a horror story to kill its wearer.

Eugénie's conspicuous sartorial consumption often drew criticism, but it was her increasing involvement in government that made her hated among the political class. In choosing Marie Antoinette as a role model she hardly helped herself. Eugénie became obsessed with a woman whom she saw as an example of a foreign-born queen admirably serving her country, but for most Marie Antoinette represented the worst excesses of the *ancien régime*. Like her heroine, Eugénie became the target of misogynistic pornographic pamphlets that told fabricated tales of sexual debauchery. In reality, she was entirely faithful to her marriage.

Despite this, Eugénie stopped sleeping with her husband after the birth of their son, fearing another dangerous labour. By then, it turned out Louis-Napoléon had been a faithful president of the Republic longer than he had been a loyal husband. It was nearly three years before he broke his oath to uphold the constitution, whereas he managed only six months of fidelity before indulging in what he called 'little distractions', his euphemism for affairs.[9] Months after his wedding, it was rumoured that he was sleeping with Harriet Howard again. Whether the stories were true is unclear, but not long after Eugénie gave birth to their son, he definitely was sleeping with an eighteen-year-old countess who happened to be a secret agent of a foreign power.

———

Virginia Oldoini, Countess of Castiglione, was born in 1837 and married at seventeen. She was not loyal to her husband for long; gossip had it that she became the mistress of the King of Piedmont-Sardinia, Victor Emmanuel II. Piedmont, a kingdom that spanned north-west Italy and Sardinia, was a rising power which had ambitions of harnessing Italian nationalism behind its king and unifying the peninsula under his rule. Camillo Benso, Count of Cavour, Virginia's distant cousin, was at the heart of this project. Cavour thought that one way of furthering it was for his cousin to have sex with Louis-Napoléon; as he wrote to his foreign minister, 'I have enlisted in the diplomatic service the very beautiful countess, inviting her to flirt with the emperor and to seduce him if she gets the chance.'[10]

She did get the chance. Virginia became an overnight sensation when she crashed onto the Parisian scene in January 1856. She had no time for huge crinoline dresses. Instead, she wore, without a corset, risqué ones that clung to her figure. As one eagle-eyed witness pruriently observed, a zephyr gauze barely covered her décolletage and 'the eye followed the outline and the smallest details, finally the part that the gauze itself left completely exposed extended to the end of the breast'. That was not all he had to say on the subject. 'The two breasts seem to pose a challenge to all women,' he concluded.[11]

At a ball in February 1856, Virginia caused a furore in an audacious queen of hearts costume. Tousled hair fell over plunging neckline and the dress not only revealed a shocking amount of ankle, but also had hearts in what nineteenth-century decorum described as 'decidedly unexpected' places. Congratulating her on the outfit, Eugénie is said to have coolly remarked, 'But your heart seems a little low down.'[12]

Louis-Napoléon was infatuated. He invited her to a small party in a villa in the grounds of Saint-Cloud. As Eugénie danced with other guests, the emperor took the Italian countess on a night-time boat ride to an island in the middle of a lake. Soon they returned to the party; Virginia's dress was somewhat creased. Eugénie made her disdain clear for all to see. But Louis-Napoléon did not bother to hide his affair. That autumn, Virginia was invited to the chateau at Compiègne, where she spent time with the court. At a theatre performance, she not so quietly slipped out of the audience; Louis-Napoléon followed.

Virginia reported the emperor's pillow talk to Piedmont, but the emperor tired of her after about a year – 'undoubtedly very beautiful', he said of her, but 'insipid, she overwhelms me'.[13] He quickly moved on. As the imperial train made its way to Compiègne for the autumn court season there in 1857, Eugénie and Mathilde were talking in one of the carriages. The jolting train caused the door to the adjoining carriage to swing open and Mathilde saw 'my dear cousin straddling' another woman's knees, 'kissing her on the mouth and plunging a hand onto her breast'.[14] The woman in question, Marie-Anne Walewska, was none other than the wife of the emperor's foreign minister, who was an illegitimate son of Napoléon, Alexandre Colonna-Walewski, which gave an added frisson to discussion of foreign affairs.

Not that Louis-Napoléon's liaisons with women were any more exclusive than his marriage. He seduced women where and when he could, which was often. One woman with whom the emperor had flirted at court described a later rendezvous she had arranged with him in the early hours of the morning. The emperor appeared in her bedroom at 1.30 a.m. in billowing purple silk pyjamas. He clumsily approached her bed, stumbling over furniture in the near darkness. By 2 a.m., the emperor, waxed moustache now dripping and drooping from the heat of the encounter, put his arms in front of him and used the furniture to guide him out of the room. 'It had only taken half an hour to make me an empress,' noted the woman.[15]

While the emperor was having affairs, Gustave Flaubert was on trial in January 1857 for portraying adultery as an enjoyable pastime in the novel *Madame Bovary*. 'Ah! How proud one is to be French! / When one looks at the column!' Flaubert wrote to his brother, ironically quoting a famous song celebrating the legend of Napoléon.[16] Even though he was acquitted, Flaubert, who quite enjoyed his day in court, where his defence called his book 'a masterpiece', was disgusted by the hypocrisy of it all. 'Poor Bovary,' he wrote to a friend, 'dragged by her hair like a whore before the correctional police.'[17]

Reactionary Catholic opinion, which such policing of morals was designed to please, was outraged that Flaubert was not more severely dealt with. To help placate it, a few months later, another trial was launched against the poet Charles Baudelaire. Six poems were found to be obscenely sexual; the poet was fined three hundred francs. These trials were a reminder that the Second Empire monitored the morals of the

French nation as it did its politics. How effective it was at this latter pursuit was about to be put to the test, for elections to the Corps législatif were scheduled for June 1857.

———

'A small number of persons', ran an incredulous circular from the minister of the interior to prefects across France, have set themselves up in opposition to 'a government established on the most democratic basis which ever existed'. On the eve of elections, the minister added in outraged disbelief and without irony, these men 'thought [it] proper to commence a contest'. He urged his prefects to remind voters in their departments of their duty to return official candidates, not republicans and socialists who wished to revive the chaos of 1848. 'They will not succeed; their efforts will be shattered against those electoral masses whose good sense and patriotism founded the Empire.'[18]

The full machinery of the French state was geared towards this: political meetings were banned, the press was heavily censored and national dailies did not dare publish anything critical of the regime. Nonetheless, opposition candidates were free to stand, and in Paris and the major cities where support for the Empire was weakest they thought they had a chance of winning. On top of the legal barriers, therefore, government officials employed less subtle methods. Posters were torn down, ballot papers with names of non-government candidates were seized and those distributing them were beaten up.

Despite this, five republicans were returned and the opposition vote did especially well in Paris. If across the country more than five million votes for official candidates to just under six hundred thousand for opposition ones meant the elections were, once again, billed as the masses crushing a small minority of malcontents, there were nearly 3.5 million abstentions, which many interpreted as protests. Worse, unlike in 1852, some anti-government candidates put their scruples to one side and swore the oath of allegiance to the emperor, which meant republicans took seats in the Corps législatif. 'I am really annoyed with the Paris elections,' Louis-Napoléon wrote to Eugénie. 'There are in this capital twenty thousand incorrigible men and the others who follow them are just sheep.'[19]

Louis-Napoléon consoled himself with his summer holiday, first to the spa town of Plombières and then, in August, to the Isle of Wight. When he entered a yacht club in Cowes, everyone carried on sitting, chatting or reading without paying the emperor the slightest regard. Fleury was outraged at this lack of respect, but Louis-Napoléon, veteran of many a London club, made a virtue of it. 'I was part of this circle once,' he told Fleury, 'and I am sure that they affect this indifference, which shocks you, to make me understand that they still consider me as one of them.'[20]

The purpose of the trip was to spend more time with Victoria and Albert and smooth over cracks appearing in the *entente cordiale*. Louis-Napoléon, therefore, spent hours indoors discussing international relations with Albert or Lord Palmerston, which was just as well because it rained a lot. Victoria enjoyed the dinners, and the dances, ending up 'with Sir Roger de Coverley, which the Empress had particularly wished to dance'. She also met Persigny, whom Louis-Napoléon had appointed his ambassador in London. Victoria thought it funny how intimate the two friends were, still speaking to each other with the informal French *tu*. Once again, she was charmed with her imperial guest; once again, Louis-Napoléon laid it on thick, telling her 'it's lucky we're not staying in England longer or we'd end up forgetting France altogether'.[21]

On the Isle of Wight, Louis-Napoléon had spoken to Victoria enthusiastically about the craze of table-turning. A nineteenth-century form of spiritualism, it derived its name from the fact that the dead spoke to the living through the eminently practical means of tapping out messages on tables or moving them. The greatest practitioner of the art was Daniel Dunglas Home, who performed seances at the Tuileries. He had, wrote the British ambassador to the foreign secretary, 'complete hold over the emperor and empress who both believe in his supernatural powers'. At one seance, the ambassador reported, Louis-Napoléon asked to speak to his uncle Napoléon and the dead French king Louis-Philippe. On being told they were present, the emperor replied that he could not hear them. 'Wait a little,' said Home, 'and Your Majesty will feel their presence.' Soon afterwards, the ambassador cheerfully related, Louis-Napoléon 'experienced a violent kick on an unmentionable part of his sacred person, but could never ascertain which of his predecessors had applied it'.[22]

After the Isle of Wight and then time at Biarritz, Louis-Napoléon went to inaugurate a vast military training camp with room for some forty thousand soldiers near Châlons-sur-Marne, about a hundred miles due east of Paris. It was an immense engineering project: a railway was built, as were barracks, mess halls, magazine dumps and theatres capable of holding two thousand, as well as space for twenty thousand men to celebrate Mass every Sunday. Much of the terrain was reclaimed wasteland and the camp was the embodiment of Louis-Napoléon harnessing state power to turn his dreams into a reality, even down to insisting that soldiers cultivate plots of land, an idea inspired by the pamphlet he wrote in prison, *The Extinction of Pauperism*.

The propaganda value of such a military installation was obvious, and Louis-Napoléon liked to bring foreign dignitaries to witness the power of the French army. Moreover, the emperor, who had enjoyed Swiss militia summer camp when younger, felt at home here, and a trip to Châlons became an annual event in the imperial calendar. As you know, he wrote to his wife, 'I am a soldier in my soul.'[23] That said, he was deeply traumatised when a cannon misfired and he saw two veterans of the Crimean War disfigured, one losing an arm, the other an eye and a finger. 'I unfortunately saw the sad spectacle of war,' he wrote as only someone who had never seen the sad spectacle of war could.[24]

The emperor did not neglect the navy, either. From an early age, steam technology had fascinated him and he committed sixty-five million francs to an ambitious modernisation of the French fleet. With steam-powered ships rendering older ones obsolete, this meant that the French might rival British sea power. Through cutting-edge armed forces, Louis-Napoléon was making France into a superpower that could bestride the globe. Indeed, the scale of the emperor's vision meant that the British alliance was becoming parochial. His visit to the Isle of Wight was not what people were talking about in 1857, for just as Louis-Napoléon was seeing other women, he was also seeing other monarchs.

After Châlons, the French emperor went to Stuttgart, and on 25 September he met the new Russian tsar, Alexander II, as well as numerous other European royals. As befitted such an illustrious gathering, far outstripping the rain-drenched humdrum of the Isle of Wight, elaborate illuminations celebrated the occasion. These were not to the liking of *The Times*'s correspondent, who complained that the smell of the fat burning in the lamps mixed unpleasantly with local tobacco and beer to create a most unpleasant sensation. The initials blazing at night on the side of a villa to celebrate King William of Württemberg, Alexander II, Napoléon III and Crown Prince Karl of Württemberg may have further undermined the majesty of the occasion, for an English reader at least. The legend 'W.A.N.K.' lit up the side of the building.

For observers, the obvious comparison for the meetings that followed between the French emperor and the Russian tsar was when Napoléon and Alexander I met at Tilsit in 1807. The talks at Stuttgart were far from that famous occasion, which resulted in a Franco-Russian alliance, but were useful to Louis-Napoléon. First, it confirmed him as a leading light on the diplomatic stage, equal to the tsar, and thus publicly effaced the snub he received from Alexander's predecessor, who had once refused to recognise him as a brother emperor.

Second, Louis-Napoléon was not done revising the post-1815 settlement. Virginia di Castiglione need not have troubled herself sleeping with the emperor, for he was determined to drive Austria out of northern Italy and fulfil the dreams that he and his brother had fought for in their youth. Peace was Louis-Napoléon's preferred option, but if negotiation failed, then he was happy to continue his policy by other means. In the event of war against Austria, Russian neutrality would be key. There was a cost to this manoeuvring, though, for British statesmen and public opinion were deeply suspicious of Louis-Napoléon courting a power only recently defeated in the Crimean War. Yet it was not his secretive diplomacy that nearly shattered the alliance between Britain and France, but something far more dramatic.

———

On 28 November 1857, a striking, well-dressed gentleman with robust whiskers and flowing, greying locks left London for Paris via Brussels, travelling on a British passport under the name of Thomas Allsop. There was ostensibly little unusual about him, although if anyone had observed him closely, they might have noticed the reverential care he took with a paper parcel. They would have seen him regularly unwrapping it and furtively sprinkling the contents with water. It was important he did so: the package contained enough mercury fulminate, a volatile explosive, that if it dried out and was left at room temperature, it could blow the ship out of the water.

In Brussels, he met up with the man who had the bomb cases for the explosive. They knew the weapon worked – it was an ingenious new design manufactured specially in Birmingham, a large grenade that detonated on impact – because a prototype had blown up a shed in Putney. With their deadly luggage, they made their way by train to Paris. Thomas Allsop was a real person, and he had ordered the bombs to be made, but the man travelling on his passport was an Italian called Felice Orsini.

Like Louis-Napoléon, Orsini had been involved in secret societies engaged in revolutionary activity to bring about the unification of Italy. He was a politician in the Roman Republic before French soldiers crushed it in 1849. Afterwards, he continued to work for the cause of Italian unification, for which Austrian forces arrested him in 1855 and locked him up in a medieval fortress. Also like Louis-Napoléon, he escaped, tying bedsheets together and abseiling down the side of the castle. After many an adventure, he made his way to London, where he became a minor celebrity, publishing a bestselling book on his time in prison as well as giving public lectures. In between these activities, he found time to plan the assassination of Louis-Napoléon with British, French and Italian co-conspirators. They thought Louis-Napoléon must die not only because he had destroyed the Roman Republic in 1849, but also because French troops still occupied Rome, where they propped up the pope. If the French emperor were killed, reasoned Orsini and his fellow travellers, then Italy would be free.

By January 1858, Orsini had rendezvoused with accomplices in Paris. On 13 January, he read the Paris papers and learned that the next day, at the opera on rue Le Peletier, Louis-Napoléon and Eugénie would be in the audience. No doubt with some apprehension, Orsini dried out the explosive powder in front of a fire and primed the bombs. On the evening of 14 January, the assassins lost themselves in the crowd that had assembled outside the opera house in the hope of capturing a glimpse of the emperor and empress as they arrived.

The future Napoléon III sits on the lap of his uncle, Napoléon Bonaparte.

Josephine, Hortense, Louis-Napoléon and his brother meet Tsar Alexander I.

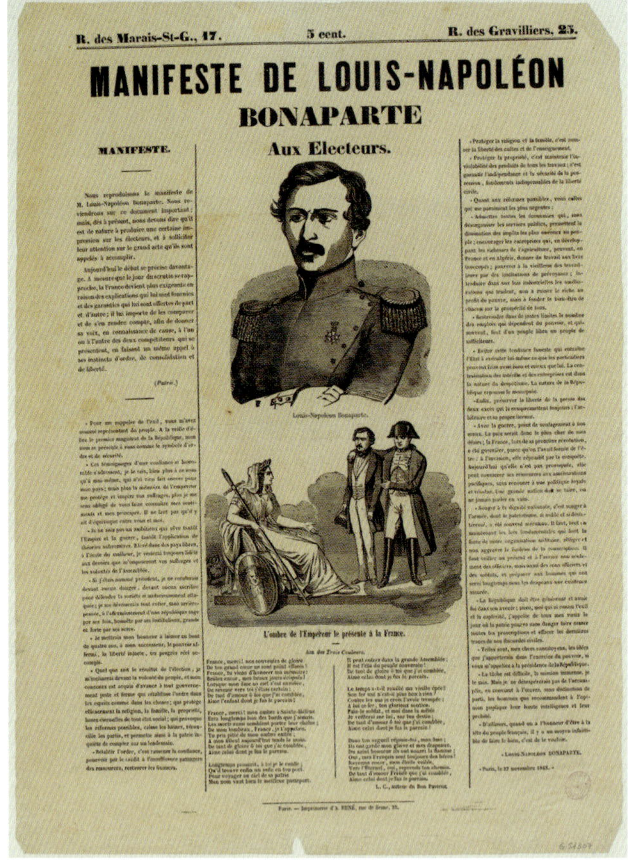

After his second farcical attempt to seize power, Louis-Napoléon is arrested.

Louis-Napoléon's manifesto was a political masterclass.

For a time, Harriet Howard was Louis-Napoléon's preferred mistress.

Louis-Napoléon in 1852.

For Louis-Napoléon, the plebiscite legitimised his 2 December *coup d'état*.

For Victor Hugo, the illegal seizure of power was an unforgivable crime.

In 1852, Louis-Napoléon achieved the dream many had ridiculed him for: becoming emperor. His uncle's statue looms behind him in this print.

The Empress Eugénie praying, which she did a lot.

Plon-Plon lived a 'life of profligacy' which 'even disgusted the French'.

The emperor on horseback and in mental and physical agony at Sedan.

The Franco-Prussian War destroyed Napoléon III's reputation.

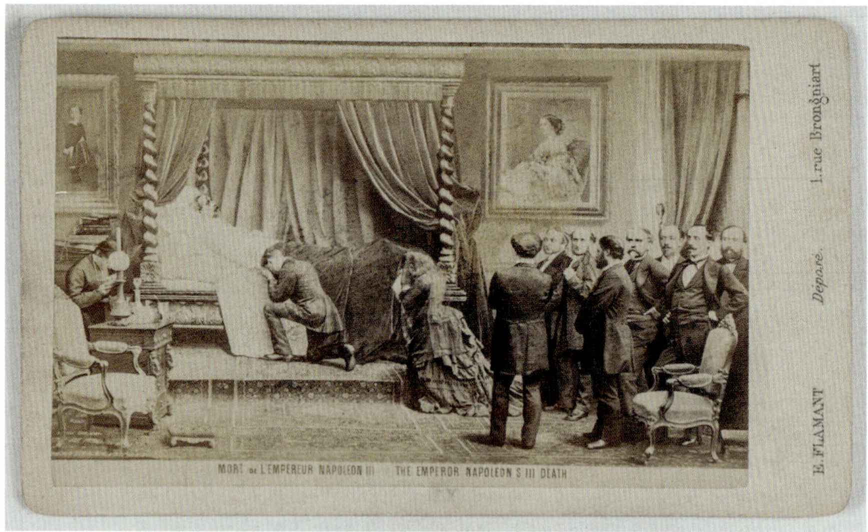

The exiled imperial family at home in Chislehurst, Kent.

Napoléon III died on 9 January 1873. His son arrived after his father's death.

Earlier that day, Louis-Napoléon had come up with a brilliant idea to make train travel cheaper: a single-price ticket, like a postage stamp, he explained. Pleased with himself, that evening he did some paperwork in the Tuileries, then dined and dressed for a night at the opera. With Eugénie, he climbed into the imperial carriage with an aide-de-camp and, escorted by cavalry, they were driven to the theatre. At 8.35 p.m., they pulled into rue Le Peletier.

At a sign from Orsini, the assassins threw their bombs. Two explosions as loud as artillery fire burst near the cavalry escort, rocking the imperial carriage. The blast knocked out the gas lighting, plunging the street into darkness. Screams from the wounded blended with the hideous cries of injured horses. Just as those thrown to the ground staggered to their feet, another bomb detonated right by the carriage, killing two horses that pulled it. Inside, splinters and bomb fragments flew through the air, smashing the windows. Two pieces pierced the emperor's hat, flying glass cut his face and a small piece went into the empress's eye. Something lodged in the neck of Louis-Napoléon's aide, splashing blood over Eugénie's white dress.

After the explosions, a police officer wrenched open the carriage door. Louis-Napoléon and Eugénie descended into the panicked streets. Outside it was chaos, with shouts from the wounded, and blood and debris on the street, but the imperial couple stepped down from the carriage calmly, Louis-Napoléon offering Eugénie his hand. In the street, the empress told terrified officials not to worry about them but to look after the wounded instead. 'It's our business to be shot at,' she said. Having shown themselves to the people to demonstrate they were unhurt, Louis-Napoléon wanted to go back and help the injured. 'Don't be so stupid!' Eugénie told him, suspecting the assassins might still be at large.[25] Instead, they attended the opera, the crowd cheering them when they appeared. It was not until they returned to the Tuileries and stood over their infant son's cradle late at night that they burst into tears and cried in each other's arms.

———

The attempt on the emperor's life became the occasion for another crackdown. Press censorship was tightened, police were told to ramp up surveillance and a law was passed that allowed for the deportation of anyone convicted since June 1848 if it were deemed in the public interest. Moreover, Louis-Napoléon appointed a military general to the ministry of the interior, a position normally occupied by a civilian. The general was an authoritarian Bonapartist, and Louis-Napoléon left him in no doubt as to what he expected. 'Society is being eaten away by vermin that must be eliminated at all costs,' he wrote. This was not a time for moderation, warned the emperor. 'You must be feared.'[26] To that end, the minister insisted that hundreds of radicals and socialists were rounded up and deported on little or no evidence, even though the assassins were not French, nor had they planned the attack in France.

Louis-Napoléon also, therefore, demanded action was taken against his enemies across the Channel, and in London, the French ambassador, Persigny, a man about as stable as mercury fulminate, did not help calm Anglo-French relations. At the Foreign Office, in full court dress, hand on the hilt of his sword, he shouted, 'It's war! It's war!' During this outburst, the foreign secretary recorded, 'I sat perfectly silently and unmoved, till he was blown over, which is the best way of meeting such explosions from foreigners.'[27]

Though Persigny's histrionics could be ignored, the not unreasonable demand to take action over a terrorist attack planned on British soil could not. To avoid a diplomatic crisis, the British government decided that it did not matter what was done, merely that something was seen to be done, and a Conspiracy to Murder Bill was hurriedly drawn up. As it was seen as a response to French pressure, and not only that but from a French emperor who had spent much time conspiring in London, it was a gift for opposition MPs. 'The people of England are a brave people,' thundered one politician; 'they put down one Napoleon and they are not afraid of another.'[28] On the second reading, the Bill was defeated and Palmerston's government fell.

In official British circles, it was, therefore, hoped that the trial of a man who had helped plan the Orsini attack would be more successful in calming French anger. The prosecution had put together a watertight case. The defence barrister's peroration, however, did not bother with the facts. 'Tell him', the lawyer said, summing up to the jury – 'him' being Louis-Napoléon – 'that the jury box is the sanctuary of English liberty . . . Tell him that . . . though 600,000 French bayonets glittered in your sight . . . your verdict will be firmly and courageously given – careless whether that verdict pleases or displeases a French despot.'[29] Predictably after such a performance, the jury returned a verdict of not guilty to wild cheers from the galleries.

In Paris, Louis-Napoléon was furious when he learned this. Malmesbury, foreign secretary at the time, excused his friend's anger, knowing that the emperor had been greatly shaken by the ferocity of this attack, which had killed and wounded bystanders. His sympathy, however, only went so far. Soft living, he felt, meant that Louis-Napoléon 'does not stand being shot at as well as he used to do'.[30] Eugénie was even more outraged than her husband about the court case. That 'a presumably impartial jury deemed it necessary to satisfy a frenziedly applauding mob with a verdict which can only teach that "killing is not murder"' was, complained the empress to the British ambassador, worse than 'the daily fear of seeing my husband and my son struck down in my arms by an assassin'.[31]

The trial of Orsini in Paris should have been a simpler affair, but if anything its drama turned out to be greater than that across the Channel. Jules Favre was experienced in defending conspirators. He had been on Louis-Napoléon's defence team in 1840 after his attempted *coup d'état*. But Favre was no Bonapartist. He was a republican, one of Louis-Napoléon's most outspoken critics. Favre knew that the tightly controlled legal system and press meant that the trial could not be turned into a cause célèbre; however, he also knew Louis-Napoléon was prone to personal appeals and that he had been a youthful supporter of Italian nationalism.

Favre, therefore, suggested that Orsini write a letter to the emperor explaining his actions. This Orsini did. Moved, as Favre hoped he would be, the emperor gave permission for it to be read at Orsini's trial. 'May your Majesty remember that the Italians', said Favre, reading Orsini's letter, 'shed their blood for Napoléon the Great . . . May he remember that, as long as Italy is not independent, the tranquillity of Europe and that of your Majesty will be only a chimera.' Writing that it was the last wish of a man condemned to die, Orsini's letter concluded by asking Louis-Napoléon to liberate Italy.[32]

Not only did Louis-Napoléon allow the letter to be read, but he also had it published in the government newspaper. It caused a sensation. Though Orsini was, of course, found guilty, the emperor and empress were so moved they now wanted to pardon him. Astonished, Louis-Napoléon's ministers urged him not to show leniency towards someone who had tried to assassinate him. In the end, a Bonapartist middle ground was found. Two of the assassins were sentenced to hard labour in a French penal colony and the other two, including Orsini, to execution. That Louis-Napoléon allowed Orsini's plea for French intervention to be published was emblematic of his penchant to turn a crisis to his advantage. For he was preparing public opinion for his next foreign policy gamble.

———

Orsini was not the only Italian who travelled to France on a false passport in 1858. The prime minister of Piedmont, Camillo Benso, Count of Cavour, did so too, taking a circuitous route by train to the spa town of Plombières to see Louis-Napoléon. The clandestine summit was the result of months of back-channel communications and Cavour was coming for a secret meeting to redraw the map of Italy. He was nervous. He had dedicated his life – and the sex life of Virginia di Castiglione – to bringing France into an alliance with Piedmont to drive the Austrians out of Italy. Now was the moment when, he hoped, the sphinx-like Louis-Napoléon would reveal his intentions.

At 11 a.m. on 21 July, Cavour was ushered into the emperor's private study. Louis-Napoléon put him at ease, telling him he would back Piedmont in a war against Austria. There was, however, a problem. There was no reason to go to war with Austria, and Louis-Napoléon, mindful of domestic and international opinion, did not want to be seen as the aggressor. Cavour was embarrassed: he could not come up with a good excuse. Louis-Napoléon decided to help. They could foment a liberal revolt in one of the tiny states on the peninsula, which would force Austria to send troops and crush it, exactly as had happened in 1831, when Louis-Napoléon and his brother were part of the rebellion. But unlike that failed insurrection, during which his brother had died, this time France would come to the rescue as the defender of Italy.

Having concocted a pretext for conflict, Cavour asked a not unimportant question: what was the point? First, Louis-Napoléon replied, to chase the Austrians out of northern Italy, where they ruled the province of

Lombardy–Venetia. As for what came afterwards, the emperor envisaged Italian kingdoms uniting in a loose confederation, with the pope at its head. This, Cavour thought, would be acceptable because Piedmont would control the north, the richest part of Italy, and therefore dominate the rest of the peninsula even if it did not rule it. In return for his help, Louis-Napoléon asked for Nice and Savoy, areas that had been taken from France after 1815.

After these discussions, he took Cavour on a drive, during which the emperor made a request that seemed to Cavour much more outrageous than secretly arranging a European war. As they passed through the valleys and forests of this picturesque corner of France, the emperor made a suggestion: Plon-Plon should marry the fifteen-year-old daughter of Piedmont's king, Victor Emmanuel II. In a character assessment that would have surprised his cousin, Louis-Napoléon tried to assuage Cavour's fears over Plon-Plon. He 'is much better than his reputation', claimed the emperor. Admittedly, 'he is rebellious, loves to be contrary, but he has a lot of spirit, not bad judgement, and a very good heart'.

It was not easy to find examples of his very good heart, though, and when Cavour tried to sell the marriage to his king, he had to scrape the barrel, assuring his master that Plon-Plon had shown great care for a former lover. 'A heartless man', he wrote, 'would not have left Paris amid the pleasures of carnival to pay a last visit to Rachel, who was dying in Cannes.' The time he dragged Rachel from his bedroom by the hair, locked the door and left her crying outside all night is perhaps more illustrative of his nature, but regardless of Plon-Plon's character, Cavour argued that it was worth sacrificing the king's daughter for the glory of Piedmont.[33]

Louis-Napoléon had carved up Italy in a secret meeting without the knowledge of his foreign minister. International affairs were conducted as outrageously as marital ones. That summer, outside a hotel room, his long-suffering foreign minister waited for an audience. The emperor's secretary entered the room without knocking, then stepped back, stunned. It had happened again. 'Through the open door', gossiped the secretary, 'I was able to see' the foreign minister's wife 'in the arms of the emperor', and the foreign minister, 'next to me, must have seen everything'.[34]

But to engineer the war he craved in Italy, Louis-Napoléon had to be better at hiding what he was doing from other European powers. To sound out British views, Lord Palmerston and Lord Clarendon were invited to Compiègne in November. Clarendon had a fine time. When rain called off a hunt, he wrote that 'the day was got through by such pastimes as *conversation sprituelle*, kept up by thirty people, football in the gallery and quadrilles on horseback'.[35] When the weather was slightly better, Palmerston, who had as keen an eye for his public image as Louis-Napoléon, refused to don the imperial hunting livery, preferring a red British hunting jacket without a waterproof over it. When the emperor warned him he would get wet, Palmerston imperiously replied, 'Nothing pierces a red coat.'[36]

More important than sartorial patriotism were British views on what would happen if France went to war. When asked, Palmerston answered that it would depend on the cause. Clarendon was clearer: it would be a disaster that would lead to a European-wide conflict. But it was Louis-Napoléon's friend Malmesbury who was in charge of British foreign policy at the time. It shows just how far outside the norms of rarefied mid-nineteenth-century diplomacy Louis-Napoléon's clandestine and Machiavellian scheme was that Malmesbury, who knew the emperor's character better than anyone in Britain, could not bring himself to believe that his friend was secretly manoeuvring to bring about a conflagration. Malmesbury's denial ran against mounting evidence. Articles in the French press were not subtle. 'We do not like war, and we hope someday it will disappear from the surface of the earth,' wrote a journalist, 'but we would like to see one more, directed against Austria.'[37]

Another clue was the marriage between Plon-Plon and the King of Piedmont's daughter, Princess Maria Clotilde of Savoy, which took place in January 1859. An Italian diplomat had only recently informed Cavour that Plon-Plon had been conducting 'almost public orgies, accompanied by the band of the Imperial Guard', but Clotilde, not yet sixteen, became the first casualty of Louis-Napoléon's Italian policy.[38] She was a petite, pious, conservative teenager, Plon-Plon a militant atheist, veteran of some of the most infamous courtesans in Europe and, in his late thirties, a large, heavy man. The marriage was compared to that of an elephant with a gazelle. Meanwhile, in high society, the British ambassador spoke for many when he said, 'It is positively horrible . . . to see that poor frail creature by the side of that brute.'[39] The brute did not stay at his wife's side for long: within days he was back with his mistress.

Alongside the dynastic alliance, there was a secret military one which committed France to war if Austria attacked Piedmont. In the end, Louis-Napoléon got his war, though his elaborately constructed plan to goad Austria proved unnecessary. Instead, as tensions increased, Piedmont moved troops to the border. Austria demanded they stand down. The Italian kingdom rejected this ultimatum and the Austrian emperor, Franz Joseph, declared war on 26 April 1859. Though technically Austria was the aggressor, for most observers it was clear that Louis-Napoléon was at the heart of it. If it had not been known in Britain beforehand, this was because, as an editorial in *The Times* put it, 'English politicians cannot fathom the depths of duplicity' that existed across the Channel. 'The very fact that Englishmen cannot comprehend the unscrupulousness of Continental Potentates does honour to their character,' but now Louis-Napoléon had shown his hand, and proved what many had long believed. He was not to be trusted and endangered the peace of Europe by 'making preparations for a gigantic war'.[40]

This was Louis-Napoléon's second gigantic war. His declaration seven years ago that the Empire meant peace had aged about as well as his oath to defend the French Republic or his marriage vows. Seen from European capitals, the Second Empire, repeatedly shaking the continent's tranquillity, now looked a lot like the first one. To add to the sense of history repeating itself, Louis-Napoléon appointed himself commander-in-chief for the campaign in Italy, and would lead his army across the same territory where his uncle had won so many historic victories.

16

WAR AND PEACE REVISITED

The campaign in Italy against the Austrians was going so well that Louis-Napoléon decided to split his forces. The French and their Piedmontese allies were pushing the retreating Austrian army across the picturesque Italian plains west of Milan. The terrain was cut by fast-flowing rivers bringing water down from the Alps, which framed the horizon to the north. Through fields soaked with heavy rain and especially at bottlenecks over river crossings, the French and Piedmontese armies were reduced to a crawl. As his forces converged on the small village of Magenta, commanding the main road and railway to Milan, therefore, Louis-Napoléon decided to speed things up and sent some of his men north to cross the river upstream, reducing traffic on the main road. Although he was not sure where the Austrian army was, its commander had shown no desire to fight, and so the emperor was not worried about dividing his army.

It came as a surprise, then, to find forty thousand Austrians blocking his depleted forces before Magenta on 4 June. With two corps some miles north and the rest of his army delayed behind, Louis-Napoléon dispatched riders to bring reinforcements. The few regiments he had to hand were sent into the fray towards two bridges. Then the emperor fell into a pensive silence, desperately hoping that his generals would arrive and relieve his outnumbered men. Initially, the shock of the French attack at a key bridge drove the unprepared Austrians back. Before it could be blown up, a French soldier bayoneted an Austrian engineer standing over the charge, and the French pushed barrels of gunpowder into the water below.

It might have been better if the bridge had exploded. Though the French held it, the Austrians had far more men to throw into the fight. The counterattack was relentless: the French general commanding the defence was killed, his men were barely able to hold their positions and one of their artillery pieces was captured. Not far behind the fighting, an officer galloped towards Louis-Napoléon and his staff, asking him to send more men. 'I don't have anyone,' the emperor replied, the fighting so close that shells were landing nearby.[1]

Though this was his first time on a battlefield, Louis-Napoléon knew enough about warfare to understand that Austrian numbers would be decisive at the bridge. Unless his other commanders arrived, the battle was lost. So worried was the chain-smoking emperor that he forgot about his cigarettes. The Austrian commander-in-chief also knew a triumph was close; he sent a telegram to Vienna announcing victory.

————

Four weeks earlier at Genoa on 12 May 1859, Louis-Napoléon set foot on Italian soil for the first time since his brother's death in 1831. He was welcomed as a popular hero, for Louis-Napoléon had come to liberate Italy. 'Soldiers,' ran his proclamation to the French army posted throughout Genoa, 'we will second the struggle of a people demanding their independence, and rescue them from foreign oppression. It is a sacred cause which has the sympathies of the civilised world.'

The tradition of Napoléon weighed like a dream, or a nightmare, depending on what side you were on, for everyone involved in the campaign. 'Already from one end of France to the other', concluded the emperor's proclamation, 'these words of happy omen are resounding: "The new army of Italy will be worthy of its older sister."'[2] To push the analogy as far as possible, Louis-Napoléon visited the site of the Battle of Marengo, where his uncle had crushed the Austrians at the beginning of the century. And in something of a novelty for the French army, this time they had maps, including one Napoléon had used to plan his 1800 campaign.

The Austrian strategy relied on speed. If the Habsburg army could mobilise quickly, then it could crush the much smaller Piedmontese forces, take the capital Turin and compel King Victor Emmanuel II to surrender before the French arrived in the peninsula. In this, they failed. By the time Louis-Napoléon was at Genoa, more than seventy thousand Frenchmen had been shipped to the port, while others had crossed the Alps on foot. The Austrians could not take the offensive. Instead, the Habsburg army retreated towards Milan, planning to defeat the advancing allies before this city at a place of their choosing. The French followed.

'You must not have any worries for me,' Louis-Napoléon wrote on 14 May to Eugénie, who was acting as regent in Paris, for 'commanders-in-chief are rarely in real danger.'[3] He also told her that he had not seen any truly beautiful women in Genoa, which he put down to the fact that her memory was imprinted on his heart, a less than reassuring message that might well have caused his wife worries of another sort. Despite his protests, Eugénie was right to be anxious. After all, Louis-Napoléon had never commanded an army before. Fleury was also concerned. 'The task is very heavy for a sovereign who begins war at fifty and who, thanks to the telegraph and the railways, does not have an hour, not a minute of rest,' he wrote. 'I sincerely pity him and do not believe that he can continue the profession of general and emperor for long in these modern conditions.'[4]

Though Louis-Napoléon knew his uncle's military campaigns by heart, he did not intend to imitate his style of leadership. Having celebrated his fifty-first birthday by the time war was declared, the emperor was not a dashing general; rather, he saw himself as a mediator between seasoned commanders. He reviewed their plans, adopted the ones he thought best and made sure the army had what it needed to carry them out.

At first, this did not go well. 'We sent an army of 120,000 men to Italy before gathering supplies there,' he wrote to the minister of war, and, showing he had grasped the basics of command, added: 'This is the opposite of what we should have done.'[5] Nonetheless, within a few days the most outrageous mistakes were corrected and, steeped in history combined with a politician's eye for the present, the emperor excelled at looking like a commander. Never far from the front line, he made sure that he was visible to his troops, speaking to them informally and asking how he could improve conditions. Soon the army was pursuing the enemy and the Austrians were bested in a skirmish. 'It is a good start,' wrote the emperor to his wife on 31 May. It was not, however, bloodless. 'What a sad thing', he thought, 'to see the wounded and the dying.'[6] He was about to see a lot more.

———

'I do not yet know the enemy's position,' the French General Patrice de Mac Mahon, the man Louis-Napoléon had sent to cross the river a few miles north of Magenta, scribbled in reply to the desperate messages for reinforcements. 'I cannot therefore give you any indication of what I will do, but', he concluded, 'may the emperor be calm about the arrangements I will take.'[7] A general of the old school, Mac Mahon was going to march to the sound of the guns.

As evening was falling, just as it looked like the men fighting on the bridge could hold it no longer, Mac Mahon's artillery opened fire on the village of Magenta. With reinforcements arriving, it was now the Austrians who were on the defensive, falling back into the town to fight house by house. French heavy guns turned the streets into blood-soaked chaos, strewn with the dead and wounded. The fresh French troops proved decisive and the Austrians were forced to retreat. The Austrian commander's triumphant telegram having proved somewhat premature, at 11.30 p.m. Louis-Napoléon dashed one off to Eugénie: 'a great victory but dearly bought'.[8] Though broken with tiredness after the battle, he showed that his serenity had been restored when he asked for cigarettes and started smoking again.

With nearly five thousand French killed, wounded or missing, to the Austrians' ten thousand, the Battle of Magenta was a French victory, though not a crushing one; the colour magenta, invented in the same year and named after the battle in a patriotic marketing move, proved far more enduring than the clash itself. But for Louis-Napoléon, in the thick of the action, it had felt like a close-run thing. The emperor was so grateful to Mac Mahon for his timely arrival, which covered his blundering into the Austrians, that he made the general duc de Magenta and a marshal of France there and then. And what joy Louis-Napoléon felt at success was tempered the next day as he watched the heart-rending procession of French wounded, uniforms torn, covered in dust and powder and blood, being taken away from the front line.

Nevertheless, the road to Milan lay open and the Austrians abandoned the city, much to the delight of the inhabitants, who loathed them as foreign occupiers. Yet Louis-Napoléon felt that since the war was not won, it would be embarrassing if his entry to the city resembled a triumph. He decided to ride into Milan early on the morning of 8 June alongside King Victor Emmanuel II, with only a small cavalry escort and without advance notice. But the people of Milan were determined to make it an event to remember – Mac Mahon had entered the day before to carnival-like celebrations. When word spread that the two sovereigns were coming, thousands of people, many brushing hangovers to one side, rushed to catch a glimpse of the victors. From balconies, hurriedly dressed in their best clothes, people waved French and Italian tricolour flags and hurled flowers onto the roads, which soon became carpeted with crushed petals. In the streets, men, women and children dropped to their knees or threw themselves at the emperor as he rode, grabbing his hands, kissing his legs and hailing him as the liberator of Italy.

'It was not enthusiasm but delirium,' Louis-Napoléon wrote to Eugénie.[9] He was now what he dreamed he and his brother would be in 1831, when they took up arms: the saviours of Italy. The British poet and supporter of Italian nationalism Elizabeth Browning was so caught up in the mood that she wrote 'Napoleon III. In Italy', a nineteen-verse poem that would have made the regime's propagandists blush: 'For this he fought in his youth, / Of this he dreamed in the past; / The lines of the resolute mouth / Tremble a little at last. / Cry, he has done it all! / Emperor / Evermore.'

'He came to deliver Italy,' wrote Browning in her concluding verse, yet Louis-Napoléon was far from achieving that.[10] One man determined to stop him was the Austrian emperor, Franz Joseph. After the defeat at Magenta, he took command of the 130,000 troops facing the combined forces of France and Piedmont, which numbered about the same. The next showdown was going to be personal, emperor against emperor.

———

The French army slowly trailed the Austrians. Louis-Napoléon dined well on the way, eating beef or chicken cooked in myriad different ways and with elaborate sauces; cheese and fruit followed. He wheeled out his preferred joke in these situations: he had never eaten so well. His army was less comfortable. Long marches in the hot Italian sun, difficult river crossings and far from plentiful supplies combined with the increasing number of sick men were turning the advance into a slog.

On 24 June, the army prepared to move in the early hours of the morning to avoid the midday heat. On the vast plains extending from the Alps to the River Po, weary soldiers woke, the dull light towards the east showing that morning was approaching. They quickly washed, folded away tents, packed bags and brewed coffee before columns formed up. As they moved off, a fiery red sun rose in the direction of Venice. Soon the advanced guard saw a cloud of dust from which emerged steel bayonets glittering in the morning light. It was the Austrian army. An officer dashed off to warn the emperor. When the messenger was ushered into his quarters, the emperor was sitting on his bed putting his socks on. 'It is not possible,' he said in reply to the news that the Austrian army had been spotted. 'It is the rearguard.'

'No, Sire, it is the entire army; I saw it: it stretches as far as the eye can see,' replied the officer. 'You can already hear the cannon.'[11] The decisive moment had come. Louis-Napoléon finished dressing and made for a village near the action. Calmer than he was at Magenta, the emperor climbed the bell tower of a church and surveyed the battlefield with a telescope.

The panorama below was of an epic struggle developing over a ten-mile front, the view framed to the north by the beautiful blue waters of Lake Garda sparkling in the morning sun beneath plunging hills, and to the south by the church spires of the town of Mantua. With 250,000 men at arms this was the largest engagement since the Battle of Nations fought outside Leipzig in 1813, a cataclysmic defeat for Napoléon which paved the way for the invasion of France and the end of the First Empire. Thinking about how to save his own regime, the nephew's gaze stopped at Solferino.

A small village perched on hillsides, Solferino commanded heights overlooking the centre of the two armies. Here, Louis-Napoléon concluded, was where the battle would be decided. Whoever held Solferino would split the enemy's forces in two and rain artillery fire on the ranks below. The French had to take it. That required storming steep terrain with fortified defences that loomed over the road to the village.

After issuing orders, Louis-Napoléon took up position with some artillery on heights about a mile and a half from Solferino. This put him in range of the Austrian guns, whose shells crashed into the ground around the emperor and his staff. Louis-Napoléon remained impassive, helping to direct return fire. From his position, the emperor watched as waves of French infantry attacked the high ground in front of Solferino. Through vineyards and mulberry trees and thick smoke, men launched themselves at well-defended positions. Artillery shells exploded around them, grapeshot decimated their ranks and musket fire cut down officers waving their swords and urging men on. As a standard bearer struggled towards the Austrians, a cannonball smashed the golden imperial eagle he was carrying, before he too was hit and fell dead. Another soldier picked up the broken standard and a shell blew his head off, blood drenching the fallen eagle. Just as an Austrian seized the standard, a Frenchman bayoneted him and took it back.

After three hours watching the slaughter, Louis-Napoléon now had only his Guards in reserve, an elite military corps modelled on his uncle's famous soldiers from the Napoleonic wars. As ever, history hung heavily over the battlefield. At Borodino, the battle his uncle fought before Moscow in 1812, Napoléon had refused to commit his Guard, resulting in catastrophic losses for his main army. 'Sire,' said Fleury in a low voice so as not be overheard, 'don't do as your uncle did. Send in your Guard. Sire, please believe me, there is no reason to hesitate.'[12]

Without answering, Louis-Napoléon turned to a general and ordered his last reserves into the struggle. Though the French attacks had been driven off all morning, they had allowed the artillery to get within a few hundred yards of the enemy. Grapeshot poured into the Austrian defenders, while shells blew holes in the walled defences. A cloud of smoke obscured the enemy, but the screams of the Austrians told the French what devastation the barrage had wrought. Then, to cries of *'Vive l'empereur!'*, the tired French, bolstered by the arrival of the Guard, swarmed up the crevices and slopes. The hills were soon covered with the dead. It was hand-to-hand fighting now as the French tried with one final effort to overrun the Austrians.

The Austrians broke, retreating in panic through the village and into the plains on the other side, with French artillery killing more as they fled. In Solferino, the French took guns, flags and prisoners. Though fighting continued across the front until 5 p.m., the battle had been decided here, as Louis-Napoléon had said it would be. Seeing his men streaming past him, Franz Joseph broke down in tears. It could have been worse; a storm prevented the French pursuing the Austrians and turning a defeat into a rout.

'Great battle and great victory,' Louis-Napoléon wrote that evening in a telegram – a form of communication that lent itself to the emperor's laconic style.[13] Though the Austrian army had not been annihilated, it was a major battle and Louis-Napoléon had played his part. The emperor's obsession with technology and artillery meant he was instrumental in getting the army to adopt rifled heavy guns, which could fire further and more accurately than the enemy's. It was, therefore, a triumph for an emperor taking command of his army on campaign for the first time, made all the more striking given the victory over his fellow emperor, Franz Joseph. Indeed, a Prussian general who witnessed the war first hand and knew a thing or two about strategy, Helmuth von Moltke the Elder, praised Louis-Napoléon's leadership.

But as Louis-Napoléon fell asleep on the night of the battle, he heard the heartbreaking cries of the wounded and dying calling for help. When the sun came up the next day, it revealed mutilated corpses, some with limbs or heads missing, or deep wounds from bullets or shells. The dead were luckier than the dying ones, delirious through suffering, faces contorted in agony and often asking comrades to shoot them rather than prolong the struggle. One observer, a Swiss businessman called Henry Dunant, found the aftermath of the carnage so moving that he later founded the Red Cross and helped bring about the signing of the first Geneva Convention.

The first Napoléon would not have blinked at such scenes – by Napoleonic standards Solferino was not an especially bloody battle. But the nephew proved that he was not his uncle. The reality of war was far removed from the sanitised version that Louis-Napoléon had reified ever since he was a child memorising his uncle's campaigns. The duty he found most difficult was visiting the wounded, which overwhelmed him with sadness, compassion and guilt because he had sent these men into the horror. And there would be plenty more horror, for the Austrian army retreated into a formidable network of fortresses. To dislodge them would require a long campaign, which, even if successful, would result in appalling casualties. Louis-Napoléon wondered if Italian independence was worth the sacrifice of so many Frenchmen, especially as few people in France cared about Italy.

———

In Paris, Eugénie, thirty-three years old, ruled as regent. Louis-Napoléon had gradually involved her in politics, but it was not a role to which she was suited. She had had a haphazard education with the occasional tutor, and her most formal schooling at a French convent had imbued her with a deep respect for religion, but was light on history, politics or economics. She spent a lot of time praying and visiting churches in disguise before her husband left for the front.

The Second Empire was a personal regime, set up to revolve around the emperor; however, Louis-Napoléon's ministers were competent and the machinery of state continued in his absence, with Eugénie a passable imperial mannequin. There were three cabinet meetings a week, but she was asked to preside over only one. The focus of these was the Italian war, which terrified her, for if the emperor lost a battle, or was captured or killed, she feared the collapse of the Empire.

Even if all went well, Louis-Napoléon's Italian campaign was an extraordinary political gamble. Few understood what he was trying to achieve, and many of those who did failed to see why French troops should die to force Austria out of northern Italy and create a confederation of Italian states – not the catchiest of war cries. The emperor's normally clear prose struggled to put his vague ideas into words. 'The aim of this war', ran his proclamation to the French people, is 'to restore Italy to itself', and therefore France 'will have a friendly people on our borders, who will owe us their independence'.[14]

For conservative supporters of the regime, the emperor was playing with what they saw as a subversive nationalism across the Alps. Indeed, the Corps législatif was treated to the rare spectacle of a deputy criticising the government. 'One cannot be revolutionary in Italy,' warned the speaker, 'and conservative in France,' before concluding that while it was easy to see what France might lose by going to war in Italy, it was hard to see what it could gain.[15]

What backing there was for the campaign came from normally hostile republicans, especially in the notoriously radical faubourg Saint-Antoine.

Here, when the emperor left Paris for the front, flags were waved and revolutionary songs were sung – the police decided that the popular enthusiasm outweighed the seditious chants and slogans. Indeed, nothing showed the contradiction in Louis-Napoléon's foreign policy more than the fact that the great revolutionary hero of Italian nationalism, Giuseppe Garibaldi, who had fought the French army when defending the Roman Republic in 1849, now raised men to fight alongside it against Austria.

Fleury neatly put the problem of supporting radicals like Garibaldi: 'The revolution that we do not want will replace the revolution that we do want.'[16] He was right: the successes at Magenta and Solferino emboldened nationalists in Italy and revolts broke out across the peninsula. When the empress told her three-year-old son that his father had won a battle, he replied, 'Only one? My uncle [Napoléon] won a great many more!' – but Eugénie did not want her husband to fight any more.[17] Her dispatches were increasingly fraught, haunted by the spectre of revolution spreading. They became even more panicked when Prussia threatened to involve itself in the conflict to save Austria, mobilising its army and menacing France while much of its forces were across the Alps.

Yet in his proclamation to the French people, Louis-Napoléon had promised to free Italy from the Alps to the Adriatic. This was one slogan that was easy to understand. After Solferino there were still about a hundred miles to go – not to mention an Austrian army now safely garrisoned in vast fortresses – before the emperor reached the Adriatic and made good on his pledge. With the peninsula on the brink of revolution and France on the point of invasion if Prussia backed Austria, Louis-Napoléon had a decision to make.

———

After Solferino, the weather in Italy was unbearably hot. Louis-Napoléon sweated copiously, resorting to wearing a dressing gown. It was much worse for his army: tens of thousands of men in close proximity led to suffering and disease. As the emperor struggled with the heat, he was bombarded with messages urging him to end the war. Persigny remained bellicose, penning warlike missives from the comfort of London, where he was ambassador, insisting Louis-Napoléon fight to the end. Most of the emperor's other advisers, however, encouraged him to sue for peace.

Faced with domestic opposition, a Europe-wide war and his own deep aversion to further losses, Louis-Napoléon wrote to Franz Joseph on 5 July 1859 suggesting an armistice. Charging Fleury with the mission to deliver the letter to the Austrian emperor in nearby Verona, Louis-Napoléon waited for a reply with trepidation. It came the next day. 'Good news,' Fleury told a visibly relieved Louis-Napoléon, handing him Franz Joseph's answer, which agreed to an armistice and requested a meeting between the two emperors to discuss terms.[18] And so on 11 July, the Italian War of 1859 ended as it started: with two men sitting in a smoke-filled room deciding the future of Italy, this time in the Italian town of Villafranca di Verona. Unlike at Plombières, however, there was no Italian present. The peninsula's fate was determined by a Frenchman and an Austrian.

It fell far short of what had been agreed with Cavour, prime minister of Piedmont. Though Franz Joseph gave up Lombardy, he refused to cede unconquered Venetia – Italy was, therefore, not free from the Alps to the Adriatic. Furthermore, while it was agreed that an Italian confederation would be set up with the reactionary pope as its head, for many Italian nationalists this was little better than insulting because the pontiff hated the idea of a united Italy. Worst of all, there were rumours that Plon-Plon might be given a kingdom in Italy, with Florence as his capital. 'He would make our beautiful Tuscany a brothel,' lamented one patriot.[19] Having his cousin on a throne was not part of Louis-Napoléon's plan; however, when he heard the peace terms, Cavour was furious at what he saw as betrayal, and resigned as prime minister.

'I have been miserable about public affairs,' wrote a similarly distressed Elizabeth Browning when the peace terms were publicised, 'couldn't keep the tears from my eyes for days and days, wasn't fit to write or sleep or eat or do anything.' As the alternative was a European war, Browning thought that Louis-Napoléon 'did what he could' and that 'his sagacity will save Italy'; however, British Italophile poets were about the only constituency satisfied with what the French emperor had done.[20]

'Phew! He's gone,' was reportedly King Victor Emmanuel II's comment when watching Louis-Napoléon depart for France.[21] The king spoke for

Italy. French flags were removed from the streets and cafes; portraits of Orsini, the man who tried to assassinate Louis-Napoléon, appeared in shops and sold well. At Milan, the emperor was coolly received; in Turin, crowds met him with silence and the occasional hiss. Liberator a month earlier, now Louis-Napoléon was a traitor to Italy who had gone back on his word.

Louis-Napoléon, therefore, did not linger and travelled quickly back to France, quietly slipping into Saint-Cloud on 17 July without fanfare. Aware that French opinion was mixed at best as to what, if anything, had been achieved, the emperor insisted that there were no public events to mark his return. Instead, Eugénie and his son, dressed in the uniform of the Imperial Guard, greeted him at the palace; Louis-Napoléon hugged the boy tightly to his chest. Despite winning two battles, the emperor had not enjoyed the experience of war, nor had the campaign achieved what he wanted.

Indeed, the whole venture had been an extraordinarily naive miscalculation, a Bonapartist middle way that pleased no one. Louis-Napoléon's understanding of Italy was outdated and based on what he and his brother had fought for in 1831. Then, the various states of Italy grouped together in a confederation might have worked, but in 1859 Italian nationalism had moved far beyond this limited goal. Men like Garibaldi dreamed of an Italian republic, Cavour of an Italy unified under Piedmont's King Victor Emmanuel II. No one, except Louis-Napoléon, wanted his ill-defined confederation, which never came into existence.

In France, except insofar as there was jubilation when peace was announced, the war had been unpopular. Obsessed with what the French people were thinking, Louis-Napoléon had his *procureurs généraux* – regional magistrates – write detailed reports analysing local opinion from a cross-section of society. These revealed that the emperor had alienated right and left: the clergy and staunch Catholics were alarmed that the Italian campaign encouraged revolution and undermined papal authority; whereas many radicals and republicans were furious that he had betrayed Italian nationalists by signing an early peace. As he had not driven Austria out of Italy, France did not even get Nice and Savoy. As Eugénie wrote, 'The job of saviour is a job for fools.' The emperor, she continued, had taken France to war 'against the feelings of his own country'.[22] In return, he had got nothing.

In spite of the antipathy, or perhaps because of it, much was made of the military parade to celebrate the returning French troops on 14 August. Regardless of their thoughts on war and peace, people crammed the streets for the victorious army. Special trains had been put on to bring spectators from across France, and that Sunday everywhere was packed with people in trees, windows, balconies – places on the best ones were said to be going for two thousand francs – clinging to chimneys on rooftops, some up to their waists in fountains, anywhere to get a view of the spectacle. The parade ended at Place Vendôme, which was covered with the usual Napoleonic paraphernalia. Here, Eugénie and the prince imperial sat on a raised platform. On seeing his father enter the square, the little boy stood up, drew a miniature sword and saluted, resulting in wild cheers from the crowds.

The party in Paris continued. The next day was the national holiday to celebrate the birthday of the first Napoléon. Theatres gave free performances during the day. At night there were fireworks; illuminations using the new technologies of gas and electricity were especially dazzling. When hungover Parisians emerged the next morning, they read in the papers that Louis-Napoléon had issued a general pardon for all political crimes. In between affairs with servants, coming up with a new religion and writing poetry, Victor Hugo melodramatically refused this amnesty, preferring exile. 'When freedom returns,' he declared grandiosely, 'so shall I.' For France's greatest poet, the pardon was merely the murderer forgiving 'his victims'.[23]

For the emperor, it was a sincere move but also political theatre. He needed to bring fresh elan to his regime, for his hurriedly stitched-together peace treaty was unravelling. Indeed, even as they watched the French army parading through Paris, French officers sensed this. 'We felt in a confused way', recorded one, 'that the emperor no longer had his hand on the tiller of Europe.'[24]

———

'The battle of Michael and his hosts against Lucifer and his rebellious legions', wrote the Bishop of Poitiers in a punchier-than-usual circular to priests in his diocese, 'is the history of the struggle that is now taking place.' The struggle that the bishop put up there with defeating the devil was a battle fought near Rome on 18 September 1860 against what he called 'the cohorts of the revolution and of hell'.[25] In fact, the cohorts were not from hell, but from Piedmont; the defenders were not angels, but rather the pope's army, which consisted of many French volunteers and was led by a French general. Nothing showed how quickly Louis-Napoléon's interfering in Italian affairs had backfired than the fact that his allies from the year before were killing pious French Catholics in central Italy.

The nationalist fervour that Louis-Napoléon had hoped to harness in Italy for his own ends proved impossible to control. In violation of the peace treaty of Villafranca, Louis-Napoléon backed Piedmont annexing Italian states in revolt against their reactionary rulers. In return France finally got Nice and Savoy, as had been agreed at Plombières. Now it was not just Austria that had reason to mistrust France; the world knew there had been secret agreements between Piedmont and France. Louis-Napoléon's intervention in the peninsula was not only, as he had claimed, to liberate an oppressed people.

'The Emperor has alas! behaved with great duplicity. It is quite shocking,' recorded a disappointed Queen Victoria, lamenting his 'hypocrisy'.[26] Palmerston, now prime minister, told the queen he had ceased to have any trust in the French emperor. The more emollient Lord Clarendon put Palmerston's bluster down to the fact that the prime minister's 'rage now knows no bounds at finding that Louis-Napoléon is a more artful dodger than himself'.[27] Why did people doubt the sincerity of his intentions, a hurt Louis-Napoléon complained to the British ambassador when news of this opprobrium reached him. 'People who knew nothing of His Majesty personally, could only judge him by his acts,' replied the ambassador, adding with diplomatic decorum that these 'tended to create alarm'.[28] Back in London, things had become so bad that Persigny threatened war, but as this was something of a go-to position for the French ambassador, few took him seriously.

Ignoring British protests, Louis-Napoléon pushed on, presenting the acquisition of Nice and Savoy as the will of the people. Plebiscites were hastily arranged and the inhabitants overwhelmingly voted for the regions to become part of France. If it upset international opinion, especially in Britain, the annexation was popular in France, securing what patriotic French people considered the country's natural borders and overturning the despised 1815 settlement imposed after Waterloo; however, a man born in Nice was about to further show just how ill-thought-out Louis-Napoléon's Italian policy was, revolutionising Italy and turning clerical opinion in France against the emperor.

In a feat worthy of the first Napoléon, Giuseppe Garibaldi set sail for Sicily with just over a thousand men. By September 1860, he had occupied not only the island, but also Naples, and had overthrown the tyrannical king who had ruled southern Italy. Coming from the north, Piedmont invaded the Papal States, hoping to prevent Garibaldi's revolt from turning Italy into a radical republic. The Piedmontese defeated the pope's army, which included thousands of devoted French Catholic volunteers fighting a holy war to preserve the leader of their faith. Now, the pope controlled little more than Rome. That he still did was down to the French garrison that had been there since 1849, but this did little to placate Catholic opinion in France.

In Italy, it infuriated nationalists. In a deal hammered out with Garibaldi – talk of a confederation notable by its absence – Victor Emmanuel II became King of Italy on 17 March 1861. Yet he was not king of all Italy, for Rome, which many saw as the new country's natural capital, and Venetia remained outside it – the former because French troops propped up the pope, and the latter because Louis-Napoléon had reneged on his promise to free the country from the Alps to the Adriatic. Meanwhile, strident Catholics in Italy and France reviled him for a policy that further weakened the pope. The outcome of the emperor's Italian campaign was a shambolic disaster, Nice and Savoy little compensation.

———

While Louis-Napoléon was trying to reassure an alarmed Europe that he had no intention of emulating his uncle's wars after Nice and Savoy, the last living brother of Napoléon, Jérôme, died in June 1860. Plon-Plon asked the doctor if he could see his father on his deathbed. 'Don't disturb your father's rest,' replied the doctor; 'it would be pointless anyway because he won't recognise you.' Ignoring the doctor's orders, Plon-Plon approached. At the sound of footsteps, Jérôme stirred. 'Is it you, my good man?' came a weak voice.

'You see,' said the doctor to Plon-Plon, 'your father doesn't recognise you.'[29]

At least, that was the joke which went around the salons of Paris, showing the contempt in which Plon-Plon was held. After overseeing the funeral arrangements, Louis-Napoléon and Eugénie, with the prince imperial in tow, toured their newly acquired territory in Nice and Savoy towards the end of August. Events were meticulously prepared, including detailed notes on local notables, which meant that with a few kind words the emperor or empress could further bind these people to the regime. The emperor excelled in the banal but charming chatter beloved of politicians visiting places they know nothing about. 'This is the most beautiful country I have ever seen,' said Louis-Napoléon, admiring magnificent views from a steep hill overlooking the port of Nice.[30] For her part, Eugénie, a fashion icon, brought the kind of glamour to the provinces oft yearned for in many a nineteenth-century French novel. 'I saw some of them cry with emotion,' wrote Fleury, 'when, in these great provincial balls, on the arm of the emperor, the empress, radiant, elegant, noble, beautiful as well as pretty, walked through the crowd.'[31]

As for people not invited to balls, the visit gave them something to celebrate, perhaps a day off, and ties to the popular First Empire were emphasised – when Louis-Napoléon visited Nice, a local newspaper article claimed to have overheard hundreds of people born under the First Empire expressing their joy at now being able to die under the second one. Whatever the truth of that, the emperor's announcements of new railways, roads and schools meant that investment and employment would at least allow many to live slightly richer lives before dying French.

The imperial bandwagon then sailed overseas, first to Ajaccio in Corsica, where Louis-Napoléon held back tears as he went through the house in which his grandparents, father, uncles and aunts had been born, then to the French colony of Algeria. On the morning of 17 September, the imperial flotilla sailed into Algiers, the first visit by a reigning French monarch. After landing on African soil, Louis-Napoléon and Eugénie were driven through the streets, with crowds cheering and waving. Berber leaders wrapped in red cloaks and mounted on richly ornate saddles were alongside a deputation, dressed in flowing robes and carrying long rifles, from the Kabylia – the area where Saint-Arnaud had campaigned in 1851 to give him the quick victory required for his promotion, and only recently subjugated after more French repression.

Though he paid respect to European immigrants, the French army and officials, Louis-Napoléon had shown himself more interested in the non-European population. At a dinner, the emperor gave a speech that unsettled colonists, for he had long thought about transforming French policy to favour not Europeans, but Algerians. 'Our first duty', Louis-Napoléon declared in a speech, 'is to take care of the happiness of the millions of Arabs whom the fate of arms has brought under our domination.' He then spoke of the benefits of civilisation, a standard trope in European colonialism that was usually a euphemism for exploitation, but Louis-Napoléon defined what he meant: it was 'raising the Arabs to the dignity of free men, spreading education among them, while respecting their religion, improving their existence by bringing out from this land all the treasures that Providence has buried there'.[32]

Later, Louis-Napoléon would declare that 'Algeria is not a colony properly so called, but an Arab kingdom'. This, he clarified, meant that 'the *indigènes* as well as the *colons* have an equal right to my protection and I am just as much Emperor of the Arabs as Emperor of the French'.[33] It was an eminently reasonable statement, but one that caused much controversy, for the powerful French colonial lobby, which wanted more European settlement and more Algerian land, did not think that the local populace should have any protection, let alone one equal to that of French subjects. Despite the lofty rhetoric, there was little that Louis-Napoléon could do for the moment to change how Algeria was governed, not least because news about the empress's sister meant they had to cut short their trip.

Eugénie's sister had been ill for some time. They were extremely close, and the empress had been wary of travelling while her beloved sibling was sick, but knowing that outside Paris Eugénie was a political asset, her husband had cajoled her into it. On the evening of 19 September, Louis-Napoléon received a cable informing him that Eugénie's sister had died.

But he hated difficult conversations and did not want to jeopardise the set-piece moment that was his speech on Algeria. He withheld the news. Even after the dinner, rather than telling the truth, he told Eugénie that her sister was in a dangerous condition and they should leave for France.

It was not until a stormy crossing that Louis-Napoléon, suffering from seasickness, told Eugénie what had happened. She was devastated, and furious that her husband had kept it from her. When she returned to Paris, she fell into a depression. It was so bad she went away from her husband, child and role as empress, which had kept her from her sister's sickbed, travelling to Scotland and England in November. Officially, people were told she had gone away for her health, though as many pointed out, Scotland in November was a strange choice for a curative tour, and so there was plenty of gossip: a furious row over a mistress was deemed the most likely cause of the separation.

Her absence put Louis-Napoléon in contemplative mood. 'I hope to find you again well in body and mind,' he mused, but 'unfortunately you are going to fall back into a life that is little made to distract you and this is a true sorrow for me to think that you are tied by fate to a laborious life of abnegation that I myself imposed'.[34] This was hardly a missive to make one's partner hurry back, but Eugénie replied that she preferred sharing his troubles to an independent life. Louis-Napoléon was grateful for this, though slightly undermined the impact by saying that their 'little one' was sitting next to him and wanted his mother to bring back an axe. 'A bizarre idea', he continued, showing excellent parenting skills, 'that I beg you not to realise.'[35]

Louis-Napoléon enjoyed being a father. Just as his mother had been with him, the emperor was affectionate, spending hours playing with his child. Much to the astonishment of his ministers, he sometimes let his little boy run around during meetings. He doted on him, procuring the world's first recorded model railway as a toy. It was set up alongside a campaign tent in the grounds of Saint-Cloud. Being strict, however, was not his strong point. While playing with a small orange, the boy put it in his mouth. 'Take it from him!' shouted the emperor to a courtier. 'He will choke himself.' Orange removed, the courtier asked why Louis-Napoléon had not done it himself. 'I could not,' he replied: 'he would not love me.' Eugénie was more severe, annoyed at the ease with which her husband gave in to their son's whims. 'Mama always says no,' the little boy told a lady-in-waiting, 'but then Papa always says yes.'[36]

He had not forgotten his illegitimate children, either. In a typically bizarre Bonaparte alliance, he married the son of his foster nurse, who had been a close friend since childhood and had a position at court, to his lover when imprisoned at Ham, Éléonore Vergeot. They were happy enough, and Louis-Napoléon made sure his two sons with Éléonore – seventeen and fifteen in 1860 – were provided for, materially at any rate.

Eugénie had travelled incognito, but she was soon recognised and was cheered in Glasgow, Edinburgh, Manchester and places not usually visited by empresses – but which certainly would have been the change of scene from Paris she was looking for – such as Bolton and Preston. She was on more familiar territory when visiting Queen Victoria at Windsor Castle on 4 December. When Eugénie spoke to the queen about the return voyage from Algeria, however, she started crying and said that it was only since coming to Britain that she had been able to sleep and eat again.

Though she had gone to get away from the cares of being an empress, Louis-Napoléon thought it politic to have news of her favourable reception published in the French press. Eugénie's welcome was all the more striking because of the popular Francophobia which had been whipped up after the annexation of Nice and Savoy. Yet if Louis-Napoléon's foreign policy in Europe angered the British, France was acting alongside Britain on the world stage as a global superpower. In China, French soldiers were, once more, fighting with Queen Victoria's.

———

The Garden of Perfect Brightness, Yuanmingyuan in Chinese, known to Westerners as the Summer Palace, was a paradise created for the emperors of China. Built in the eighteenth century, inside its high walls were serene gardens with ornate ponds. The branches of tall, elegant trees languidly reached down to the water, where lilies and white lotus flowers floated. Beyond the vast audience hall – the ceiling twenty feet high, the marble floor finely cut in geometric patterns that fitted together so neatly it looked like a carpet – were more extravagant palaces, the emperor's apartments and a large library containing irreplaceable literary treasures, including what was at the time the largest encyclopedia compiled in history.

On 7 October 1860, this paradise was lost to the Emperor of China when three thousand French soldiers entered the complex. An expeditionary force had fought its way up to modern-day Beijing in the culmination of the Second Opium War, a conflict in which British and French troops united to humiliate China and force its closed economic system to open to European commerce. France joined Britain ostensibly to avenge the death of a Catholic missionary, which played well domestically. For Louis-Napoléon, however, there were more important reasons: a distant expedition was a relatively cheap way to maintain British support, while at the same time showing France as a powerful actor on the global stage and pushing French commerce and influence.

The French general leading soldiers into the Summer Palace gave orders that there be no looting and placed guards at the various buildings to ensure discipline. What would be the harm, though, he reasoned, if officers helped themselves to one or two souvenirs to take back to France? Within minutes, French soldiers were playing boules with priceless Ming vases; rare porcelain was smashed on the floor; French peasants squeezed themselves into elegant imperial dresses. As the Frenchmen dashed frenziedly from room to room looking to loot what they could carry and smash what they could not, the palaces echoed to the sound of precious jewels being crushed into the floor; scrolls from the library were set on fire and used to light pipes; potshots were taken against chandeliers and mirrors. 'For two days I walked over more than thirty million francs' worth of silks, jewellery, porcelain, bronzes, sculptures and infinite treasures,' wrote one French soldier. 'I don't think we've seen anything like this since the sack of Rome by the barbarians,' he concluded.[37] Finally, the French army pulled out, leaving with three hundred wagons laden with stolen treasure. Some entrepreneurial looters had press-ganged locals into helping them carry their load. To stop the Chinese escaping, their long braided hair was leashed to French soldiers.

Much of what had not been destroyed, sold or kept as souvenirs was sent back to Eugénie. After it went on public display at the Tuileries, she created a museum at Fontainebleau to house these artefacts, along with other exhibits from Siam (today Thailand), Vietnam and, showing a typically imperial view of geography, North Africa. The museum was designed to showcase what was seen as exotic and demonstrate France's global power. More prosaically, it was a good conversation piece – Eugénie never failed to show it off to visitors. Lest anyone forget the real star of the show, Eugénie hung a portrait of herself with her ladies-in-waiting in the museum ante-chamber, conspicuously looking down on the plunder.

The British were outraged at the looting of the Summer Palace. Not only had the French got there first and taken all the best stuff, but they had done so with all the impetuous flamboyance that a British officer expected of a Frenchman. Far better, reasoned the British, to organise it properly. They auctioned what they had stolen, and they had stolen so much it took three days to complete the sale.

Then the British burned the palaces and gardens to ashes. The French general refused to take part, writing that 'this vengeance is worthy of a people more barbarous than the Chinese'.[38] The British, however, were determined on revenge. During aborted peace negotiations, the Chinese had taken thirty-nine hostages, torturing some to death. One of the men who died was a journalist for *The Times*. 'What would *The Times* say of me', the British commander reportedly told a French general, 'if I did not avenge its correspondent?'[39]

So it was that on the morning of 18 October 1860, British soldiers marched through the elegiac beauty of the ransacked imperial paradise. The buildings were mostly wooden, and soon crackling fire roared through the palaces and temples, destroying what treasures had not been robbed or smashed. Thick, black smoke lurched skywards, blocking out the sun. The red flames, noted one British observer, 'gleaming on the faces of the troops' made them look 'like demons glorying in the destruction of what they could not replace'.[40]

Louis-Napoléon did not lose too much sleep over what amounted to war crimes in China. After the burning of the Summer Palace, a treaty was imposed that further opened China up to European trade. 'Our flag,' Louis-Napoléon declared when opening the new legislative session in February 1861, 'united with that of Great Britain, flew victorious' over the Chinese, alongside, he added, without irony, 'the cross, the emblem of Christian civilisation'.[41]

As for the British alliance, it gained some goodwill. 'I rejoice with your Majesty at the glorious successes that our allied armies have just obtained in China,' wrote a happy Queen Victoria to the French emperor. It would benefit not only Britain and France, added the queen, but also 'these bizarre people' – she meant the Chinese – 'whom we have forced into relations with the rest of the world'.[42]

Further Anglo-French co-operation resulted from a commercial treaty which caused outrage in France. Louis-Napoléon went against fiercely protectionist domestic opinion and lowered tariffs on British manufactured goods and French luxuries. Signed in 1860, the treaty only came into existence because the French emperor willed it – it would never have been passed in a free French parliament. It was labelled an economic *coup d'état*. Though the French emperor was far from a free-trade radical, it was a landmark agreement and the first of similar treaties that France signed with its European neighbours, leading to what some have called Europe's first common market. It was part of a commonly held belief, which Louis-Napoléon shared, that trade led not only to prosperity, but also to co-operation between nations. The treaty, he claimed, would usher in a new era of peace.

With increasing industrialisation, booming commerce and now freer trade, backed with a powerful navy and gunship diplomacy, across the globe, France was a world power second only to Britain. In fact, for those who believed in the British alliance, like Louis-Napoléon, it was not a question of being second. Rather, the 1850s had resembled an Anglo-French condominium. With the two nations supporting each other, their combined influence radiated across Europe and the world, checking Russian expansion, lowering trade barriers across Europe and extending their influence in Asia and the Pacific.

French influence was growing significantly in these regions, because China was not the only venture Louis-Napoléon had undertaken. In 1858, French troops intervened in Vietnam; a year later they took Saigon, and soon most of south Vietnam was under French control. 'We have conquered a position', Louis-Napoléon boasted, 'which . . . will allow us to exploit the immense resources of these regions and to civilise them through commerce.'[43]

In Syria, too, French arms had again responded to the call of 'civilisation'. After a massacre of the Christian population in Damascus, then under Ottoman control, Louis-Napoléon, in agreement with other European powers, had sent the French army to protect lives and restore order. In August 1860, he had personally seen off these troops from the military camp at Châlons-sur-Marne. 'You are leaving for Syria,' the emperor helpfully told his troops, 'and France happily welcomes an expedition which has only one goal, that of ensuring the triumph of the rights of justice and humanity.'[44] Many observers thought they had heard that line before: this was a prelude to a land grab like the one that had come after the supposedly disinterested intervention in Italy, but French troops returned to France a year later having helped set up an autonomous region in Lebanon under an Ottoman-appointed Christian governor and with safeguards for Christian lives. Rather than a colonial conquest, it was a forerunner of later humanitarian interventions.

By the early 1860s, then, Louis-Napoléon's foreign policy had gone some way to offsetting the shambles in Italy. The emperor had placed France in a position of prestige it had not enjoyed since the reign of his uncle. Indeed, as Napoléon Bonaparte had spectacularly failed in North Africa and the Middle East, and had never reached East or South-East Asia, the nephew could claim to have raised France to heights that it had not enjoyed since the reign of Louis XIV in the eighteenth century. Confident, the emperor now turned his attention to domestic reforms that, much to the shock of his ministers and closest advisers, began to unpick the system behind this stunning elevation and gave away some of his dictatorial powers.

PART III

TRAGEDY AND FARCE

17

BLOOD AND IRON

At a routine cabinet meeting in November 1860, the emperor explained to unsuspecting ministers that governments which do not make concessions – the reference to previous French regimes was obvious to his audience – were doomed to fall. Rising from his seat and pacing the room, he read out proposals. Some of his closest political allies soon rose too, in bewilderment, shocked at what they saw as dangerous plans to liberalise the authoritarian Empire founded in 1852. 'Liberty', Louis-Napoléon had then declared after he proclaimed himself emperor, 'has never helped to found a lasting political edifice: it crowns it when time has consolidated it.'[1] Many thought this mere rhetoric to veil autocracy, but Louis-Napoléon was sincere. And by the end of 1860, he felt his reign secure enough to bring a bit more liberty to the people. As he wrote to Eugénie, his ministers hated the idea, but 'as always, I followed my thoughts'.[2]

These thoughts meant that the assemblies, the Senate and Corps législatif, could debate Louis-Napoléon's annual address from the throne. Furthermore, ministers without portfolio would answer questions and defend policy before these bodies. Finally, whereas previously newspapers had only been given a precis of parliamentary proceedings, they now received transcripts and were allowed to publish them. Shortly afterwards, another law conceded parliamentary scrutiny over the budget. In short, French foreign and domestic policy could be attacked, government ministers would have to explain themselves before the assemblies and all this would appear in the press.

Nonetheless, this was not a return to a parliamentary regime. The assemblies could discuss policies, the emperor explained; however, if they rejected them, it was merely a warning that the government would take into account; it would not make him change course or sack his ministers.

But what was more striking than the substance of the reforms was what they signalled. Louis-Napoléon had long argued that his authoritarian Empire was a necessity of birth amid what he saw as revolutionary turmoil and that its constitution would adapt to circumstances. In the 1850s, few had believed him. 'Well,' said Morny, discussing the reforms with Émile Ollivier, one of five republicans who had taken their seats in the Corps législatif, 'I hope you're happy now.'

'Yes,' replied Ollivier, 'only allow me to say this: if it is an end, you are lost, but if it is a beginning, you are secure.'[3] That remained to be seen. Yet if these political reforms were cautious, in other areas the Second Empire had been radically bold.

It is perhaps fitting that the school of thought that influenced Louis-Napoléon's economic policy was best known for its scandalous past as a sex cult. Henri de Saint-Simon was one of the more striking class traitors that the French Revolution of 1789 threw up. Born an aristocrat, he became an eclectic, provocative and radical polemicist who espoused shocking ideas. A single European government was one, but more immediately influential was his belief that class conflict could be resolved by technocratic rule and that science would usher in a world of universal peace, while state-led economic intervention would create prosperity. Even by the standards of later French utopianists, this was risqué, not least because Saint-Simon saw priests, kings and lawyers as useless parasites.

After his death, his followers, known as Saint-Simonians, developed his ideas. To their credit, they wanted to break down boundaries, including that of gender. Unfortunately, they first focused on breaking down taboos about sex, without worrying too much about staunchly conservative and Catholic French society. Free love, wrote none other than Louis-Napoléon's later economic adviser, Michel Chevalier, would result in a world without jealousy, envy and boredom: 'The nuptial bed, liberated from the rigorous policing of the married couple, will no longer be a prison for the wife.'[4]

French society did not agree and the government of the day threw Saint-Simonians in an actual prison for offences against public morality. After this, the group broke up, but many remained imbued with the movement's ideas and went on to have important careers. Chevalier, for example, became one of France's leading economists and financial journalists. A supporter of Louis-Napoléon, he was a close adviser to the emperor and a member of his Council of State whose zeal for free love morphed into a slightly less exciting passion for free trade. Though he failed to revolutionise sexual relations, he did manage to significantly lower British tariffs on French silks and wines, negotiating the landmark free trade agreement of 1860, known as the Cobden–Chevalier Treaty.

Louis-Napoléon had independently arrived at the conclusion he should be allowed to sleep around without the help of Saint-Simonians, but their ideas informed his economic policy. For Louis-Napoléon was one of the first political leaders to put economic growth at the heart of state policy, seeing it as crucial to avoiding revolution. For him, government was not, as it was for laissez-faire liberals, a 'necessary ulcer' but rather the 'beneficent engine' of society.[5] With this mantra, banking was reformed, credit coursed through the French economy and the 1850s were boom years. By 1859, the nation's railway network had tripled. Now railways connected the major cities of France to Paris, where colossal train stations were gateways of modernity. The coal mines of the north expanded to fuel this, as did iron and steel production; industrial growth averaged over 4 per cent annually in the 1850s. Telegraph poles stretched across the country and the network was opened to the public. Canals were dug, roads built, wasteland reclaimed.

Furthermore, this immense infrastructural undertaking was funded through an innovative approach to finance: investing to make money rather than raising taxes. This was done not only through creating new financial institutions that challenged the old orthodoxy, but also through raising huge loans, especially to finance wars, to which ordinary people subscribed. The universal suffrage of capital, as it was soon dubbed, further tied people to the regime.

Though other cities and towns underwent ambitious programmes of modernisation, Paris remained the centrepiece. Here, Louis-Napoléon's prefect of the Seine, Baron Haussmann, continued to preside with tyrannical power over a frenetic pace of change, turning Paris into a gargantuan building site. Train stations, bridges, schools, hospitals, sewers and department stores were constructed. To make way, medieval lanes and houses were razed to the ground and replaced with uniform apartment blocks running along spacious tree-lined boulevards.

The emperor enjoyed opening these as much as a military parade. Indeed, the two were elided. Troops lined the boulevard Malesherbes for its inauguration on 13 August 1861, stone and iron skeletons of unfinished housing blocks stretched down the long street and boisterous crowds enjoyed themselves before the emperor's speech. As Louis-Napoléon noted when he spoke, such occasions were now familiar in Paris, but what would have struck a foreign listener were the emperor's policies. Cheaper water for Parisians, lower prices for meat and bread as well as tax relief for the lowest rent payers were all examples of 'the incessant solicitude for those who suffer' and who were 'the true heart of France which beats with her for its glory and its prosperity'.[6] Few other sovereigns went onto the streets of their capital to outline the minutiae of what they were doing to bring down the cost of living.

Les Halles, a new central market, was part of that project and one Louis-Napoléon played a leading role in creating. He rejected initial plans for the market as too conventional. Instead, he sketched his own vision for Haussmann in pencil. From this, an architect designed immense pavilions made from materials symbolic of the new industrial age: iron and glass. The eastern section was completed in 1858, and the market became known as 'the belly of Paris' (the title of an Émile Zola novel), with a huge arcade, a giant 'gaping gateway', as Zola described it, 'a metal Babylon, with a Hindu lightness, crossed by suspended terraces, aerial corridors, flying bridges thrown over the void'.[7] Here, the produce of France, and the world, poured in every morning to sate the needs of Paris's growing population. For Paris had physically expanded. On 1 January 1860, it doubled in size: its outskirts were formally annexed and the city went from twelve arrondissements to twenty.

All the change in the capital was not to everyone's taste. Some found the new boulevards too straight, 'without adventures and perspectives, implacable straight lines'. Quite frankly, it was disturbing, and Paris 'no longer felt like the world of Balzac' but more 'like London, or some Babylon of the future'. For others, it was even worse: it reminded them of Philadelphia.[8] But Paris soon became the model for other cities across the globe.

There were problems with an economic boom built on cheap credit – the regime soon became associated with financial scandal. Louis-Napoléon had little interest in accumulating money for himself, and Haussmann, whose Paris revolution relied upon sharp financial practice, was similarly uninterested in hoarding personal wealth. Others, however, were less scrupulous – or, in Morny's case, without scruple – and many politicians and officials saw it as a perk of office to engage in insider trading. Indeed, the phrase 'Morny is in on it' came to mean that an investment would pay out. Louis-Napoléon did his best to curb the avarice of those close to him, or at least cover up their involvement, but for his critics nearly a decade in power meant that his entourage had merely graduated from adventurers to fabulously rich speculators.

The emperor himself was sensitive to the charge that capitalism unchained had got out of hand. In November 1861, he appointed a finance minister who abhorred government spending and saw balanced budgets as sacred. This, and reforms allowing the assemblies to scrutinise the budget, were as much to calm the money markets as they were political. This fiscal conservatism was sold in the selfless language of patriotism that would have appealed to a British chancellor of the exchequer and marked a departure from the 1850s. Regardless, the Empire's economy remained dynamic compared to that of previous French regimes and its politics were revitalising, but its emperor was far from well.

———

By the early 1860s, Louis-Napoléon was aged beyond his years, his face lined, the skin sagging, his drooping eyelids more pronounced and accentuating his somnolent, impassive expression. His swollen joints ached and he had gout. Chain-smoking had left him short of breath. Moreover, he suffered from excruciating neuralgia, bouts of which lasted from minutes to days. He had little appetite, and after he did eat, he often experienced uncomfortable bowels and constipation. Haemorrhoids added to his distress. Louis-Napoléon slept badly, too. Even sex, which normally helped him sleep, was no longer the panacea it had once been. Most disturbingly for a serial philanderer, there were times when he did not want to have sex or, more alarmingly, could not.

These complaints were nothing compared to the agony when urinating. The pain began in 1863 and was caused by bladder stones, though given the statistical probability, many gossiped that it must have been venereal disease. At this point in the nineteenth century, bladder stones was a case of the cure being at least as bad if not worse than the disease; his good friend Henri Conneau occasionally inserted a catheter in an attempt to widen the urethra. There were other cures, but these were far from pleasant. One saw a wire inserted into the penis in an attempt to catch and crush the stones. After his doctor recommended this, Louis-Napoléon stopped inviting him to dinner. Instead of submitting to torturous surgery, he put his faith, as his mother and father had done, in spa towns. This may have helped his mental well-being but did little for his physical one, and he became increasingly lethargic. Moreover, his doctors gave him chloral, a sedative that made him more tired still.

This hardly enlivened court life, especially in the evenings at the Tuileries, where etiquette was the most formal. Dinners were short because Louis-Napoléon did not enjoy long ones. After less than an hour, everyone decamped to the Salon d'Apollon, where coffee was served; Louis-Napoléon took his standing, with several cigarettes. He did not stay long, retiring to his study when tea was served at 10 p.m. Eugénie stayed longer, until about 11.30 p.m. As she left, male courtiers agonisingly watched the last fold of her long dress trail out of the door and then, with sighs of relief, threw themselves onto sofas – they were not allowed to sit while she was in the room.

At Saint-Cloud, Fontainebleau and Compiègne, things were slightly more relaxed, although, as one courtier noted with dread, the evening entertainment relied heavily on conversation. Louis-Napoléon was a good raconteur, but only when he wanted to be, and increasingly his health meant he was not in the mood. As a result, conservation, noted a usually generous observer, 'often flagged', with the emperor 'benevolent but silent'.[9] There were games, but the ones Eugénie most enjoyed involved hitting people with napkins, and these were deemed suitable only for the less strict rules enjoyed at Biarritz. Instead, there was blind man's bluff, which Eugénie liked; Louis-Napoléon preferred the French version of shove ha'penny.

Most lugubrious of all, at Compiègne there was the mechanical piano in the evening. Either to save money on musicians or, as some claimed, because Louis-Napoléon did not trust them to keep secrets, whenever the empress wanted to dance, someone had to turn the handle of this awful instrument. Often the tone-deaf emperor took it upon himself, invariably resulting in tunes being woefully out of time.[10] Nonetheless, invitations to Compiègne, where the court retired every autumn, were highly prized. This was democratisation, or rather the embourgeoisement of the court. Each week a new set replaced departing invitees and the guest list was eclectic, including people celebrated in science, business or the arts. They had to endure a lot of hunting: Louis-Napoléon killed 343 rabbits in just one year. For rainy days, there were parlour games or an infamously hard dictation test where people could show off their command of the French language, or lack thereof.

Despite the mechanical piano and spelling test, people tended to have a good time. 'The bourgeois of Rouen', wrote the novelist Gustave Flaubert after he stayed at Compiègne in November 1864, having presumably forgiven the Empire for prosecuting him over *Madame Bovary*, 'will be even more amazed than they are if they knew of my success in Compiègne.' The writer had expected to be bored. Instead, he wrote, 'I had a lot of fun. But the hard part is the costume changes and the exactitude of the timings.'[11] The fun stopped one evening, however, when someone insulted Victor Hugo. 'Stop this!' interjected Flaubert. 'He is the master of all of us.'

'Nevertheless you will agree, sir,' replied an aspiring literary critic, 'that the man who wrote *Les Châtiments* . . .'

'*Les Châtiments!*' exclaimed Flaubert, cutting off the reply and rolling his eyes. These 'are magnificent verses; I will recite them to you if you want'.[12] Luckily, someone moved the conversation on before he could launch into them; *Les Châtiments* was Hugo's masterpiece of vitriol against Louis-Napoléon, poem after poem excoriating the emperor.

After coffee or tea was taken in the evenings, Louis-Napoléon retired to his rooms to conduct business with his private secretary. 'What that business was, on too frequent occasions, had better not be too closely examined,' wrote a courtier, aware that late at night the emperor usually tended to affairs other than those of state; however, from 1860, he was often engaged in a more innocent project.[13] After changing into his dressing gown and slippers, Louis-Napoléon would work long into the night researching and writing a biography of a man who had also illegally seized power and paved the way for a republic to be replaced by an empire: Julius Caesar.

'I could understand', exclaimed an incredulous Persigny, 'a general book of thoughts that one writes in spare moments, but a scholarly book! Instead of telling the story of a great man, it would be better to have a great reign.'[14] Yet whenever he could, Louis-Napoléon shut himself away and worked on his biography, lost in classical texts, ignoring government papers. As far as possible, he wanted to recreate the way he researched when in prison at Ham, and he reached out to the staunchly republican Hortense Cornu, who had cut off contact after the *coup d'état*, to once again be his research assistant. In March 1863, she relented. When the emperor saw her in the Tuileries, he forgot all etiquette, ran towards her, embraced her, kissed her and then everyone began to cry, including Eugénie.

'Wicked woman,' teased the emperor, 'for twelve years you've been holding it against me.' The 'it' was the *coup d'état*. Then there was an awkward silence, broken only when the seven-year-old prince imperial was brought in. Louis-Napoléon took the boy between his knees and told him to recite one of the stories he had been learning.

'I have forgotten', the boy said, 'the ends of all of them.'

'Then tell us the beginning of one of them,' replied his father.

'I have forgotten the beginnings.'

'Then let us have the middle.'

'But Papa, where does the middle begin?'

Presented with this imponderable, Louis-Napoléon decided it would be better if his son went off to play. The moment broke the ice, though, and soon he and Hortense were talking as familiarly as ever. 'I hope', pleaded Louis-Napoléon as she said goodbye, 'that you will not leave me for another twelve years.' She did not, and saw him most weeks to discuss his biography and reminisce about old times. Hortense, however, had not forgiven him. Sometimes, she said, she forgot all that had passed since 2 December 1851, when he was still an 'innocent man'. At other times she remembered 'the destruction of our liberties, the massacres of 1851, the deportations of 1852 and the cruelties which revenged' the Orsini assassination. Then she shrank 'from the embrace of a man stained with the blood of so many of my friends'.

Hortense was also struck by the emperor's physical decline: 'He rides little, walks less and is getting fat.' Moreover, he more and more 'hated' the detail of government, but was afraid to entrust it to his ministers. His life of Caesar, however, 'absorbs and consoles him'. In fact, he had finished the first volume, but his publishers had told him they would sell more copies if they waited for the completion of the second, and 'as even emperors must submit to booksellers, he waits till the second is finished'.[15]

On 1 March 1865, the publishing sensation that was *The History of Julius Caesar* arrived, and was said to have sold forty thousand copies in the first three hours. Of course, the emperor had an advantage over most authors: he controlled the press and published excerpts in the official paper. Though he had given instructions that it should be reviewed free from censorship, most literary editors read the runes and French newspapers were awash with sycophantic praise. That said, the republican novelist George Sand, no friend of the Empire, thought the book had merit, 'so I owed my unbiased praise to the talent, which is real'.[16] An obituary in *La France*, however, was taken as veiled criticism: 'On Thursday evening M. de Brotonne was engaged up to a late hour in reading the *History of Julius Caesar*; next morning, at eight o'clock, he was found dead in his bed.'[17]

The second volume of the life of Caesar came out a year later, in 1866, but now that it was apparent it was a serious and deep dive into Roman history it caused less of a sensation. The third volume was never written, for by that time Louis-Napoléon had more to worry about than bad reviews and, despite his ill health, sex remained a rival to Caesar for the emperor's attention.

His latest affair was his most scandalous yet. Like Harriet Howard, Justine Marie Leboeuf was a girl from a humble background who dreamed of more. She worked as a chambermaid, but soon abandoned a life of provincial drudgery to run away to Paris, where she became an actress, changing her name to Marguerite Bellanger. In the capital, Marguerite threw herself into the bohemian life of the Parisian demi-monde. Vivacious, lively and arresting, she liked to dress up in men's clothes and soon became a favourite on the scene, with numerous wealthy lovers.

How she became Louis-Napoléon's mistress remains a mystery; some said he spotted her sheltering in the rain in the gardens at Saint-Cloud and gave her a shawl to cover herself with; others that she was invited to dine at the legendary Café Anglais with three men from the imperial household. As she wolfed down delicious spiced prawns, quails stuffed thickly with truffles served on buttered toast with asparagus, pheasant and Russian salad – all with fine wine and champagne flowing until coffee – she wondered which of the men was interested in her. None, as it turned out: they were recruiting her for the position of imperial mistress.

However they met, Louis-Napoléon soon became infatuated, and Marguerite with him, calling him 'Dear Lord'. Part of the emperor's obsession, it was alleged, was Marguerite's past as an acrobat – it was said that she could go from lying on her back to upright in one spring, skills for which she found use despite no longer being a performer, on stage at least. She went everywhere with the emperor – Plombières, Biarritz and Compiègne – and Louis-Napoléon got her a conveniently located apartment in Paris.

It was not a discreet affair, and Eugénie soon discovered it, not least because the emperor was carried back one night from Marguerite's apartment after over-exerting himself. Because of Marguerite's humble origins, Eugénie, who did not share her husband's democratic tastes, especially loathed Louis-Napoléon's new mistress, calling her the 'scum of the earth'. She had tolerated his past infidelities, but 'now that he has condescended to this scoundrel I can stand it no longer!' she complained to none other than Madame Walewska, an aristocrat and her husband's former mistress, who, in Eugénie's view, at least had class.[18] So desperate was Eugénie to be rid of Marguerite that she went to see her and offered her a large sum of money, which she refused.

Painfully humiliating for Eugénie, this incident was widely gossiped about in elite circles, as was another scandal. Marguerite had given birth to a son, rumoured, not least because she encouraged the rumours, to be the emperor's. To dispel this hearsay, one of Louis-Napoléon's acolytes tracked down Marguerite, who had gone into hiding on her parents' farm to avoid the furore. A far cry from luxurious decadence in Paris, Marguerite was dressed in peasant clothes, clogs instead of fine shoes, and sitting before a pot of cabbage stew, surrounded by jugs of cider.

'Dear Lord,' wrote Marguerite, 'I have not written to you since my departure, fearing to upset you,' but after the visit of Louis-Napoléon's man, she felt it was her duty to put the record straight over the paternity of the child. She acknowledged that she was guilty of spreading misleading rumours, 'but I assure you I had my doubts'. She begged forgiveness, claiming she was ready to make any sacrifice. 'My heart is so full of gratitude for all you have done . . . I do not wish you to doubt . . . the sincerity and depth of my love for you.'[19] Marguerite was right to be grateful; the emperor made her rich enough to buy a fine chateau and live out the rest of her days in luxury few French peasant girls could dream of.

———

There were those who thought that a sex-crazed ancient historian with failing health was not the best person to be running France, if only because these traits meant his attention often wandered. And international affairs in the 1860s were tumultuous, requiring the kind of statesmanship and focus of which many thought Louis-Napoléon no longer capable. A month after the creation of the Kingdom of Italy in March 1861 changed the balance of power in Europe, civil war broke out in the United States. That summer, on the run from what was even for him an unusually high number of scandals, Plon-Plon arrived in New York. Soon, he was invited to meet President Abraham Lincoln at the White House in Washington.

Though he was ostensibly a republican, there was no one more important in Plon-Plon's life than himself, certainly not the President of the United States, and the imperial prince was shocked that there was no reception committee to welcome him and his entourage. 'One walks straight in, like a cafe,' noted a disgusted Plon-Plon.[20] In fact, it was worse than a cafe because no one arrived to seat them. For fifteen minutes, Plon-Plon waited impatiently. Just as he was about to storm out, Lincoln's secretary of state arrived.

A few minutes later, Lincoln loped in. This was one of the great bodily mismatches in history. Still angry and dressed in a tailcoat, the short, corpulent Plon-Plon resembled an irritated penguin. Lincoln, by contrast, was incredibly tall, with an angular face and gangly limbs – a wiry giant looming over his guest. Sensing all was not well, he shook Plon-Plon's hand and then invited everyone to sit. Plon-Plon, who was long practised at upsetting people on diplomatic missions when annoyed, sat opposite the president, deliberately not saying a word.

With the awkwardness increasing by the minute, Lincoln tried small talk and enquired about Plon-Plon's father, Lucien. Unfortunately, the president had got the extensive Bonaparte clan confused: Lucien was Plon-Plon's uncle. Horrified at his faux pas, Lincoln tried everything in the repertoire of those desperately trying to salvage conversation: he mentioned the weather, complained about the rain and asked about the voyage from Europe. For any of this to work it would have required a willing interlocutor, but Plon-Plon responded with only a word or two. Finally, giving up, Lincoln resorted to painfully slow handshakes with Plon-Plon and his entourage to fill the minimum time expected of an audience.

Though the meeting was unofficial, it was important. Lincoln was desperate to forestall any European intervention in the civil war between the separatist rebel Confederacy and the Union. No matter how rude Plon-Plon was, Lincoln knew his thoughts would be transmitted back to the emperor. Despite this frosty meeting, therefore, Plon-Plon was invited to dinner at the White House, where things were slightly more cordial.

Though his critics, and he had many, accused him of virtue signalling, posing as what today would be called the 'woke' Bonaparte, in politics though certainly not in his personal life, Plon-Plon's progressive convictions were fairly firmly held. When he returned to France, he was openly pro-Union and told Louis-Napoléon that the North would win the war. Louis-Napoléon, however, saw the conflict as an opportunity to put into place an outrageously audacious scheme. With Washington distracted, he invaded Mexico.

Before the start of the conflict between the Union and the Confederacy, there had been another civil war in North America. Between 1858 and 1861, the Liberal and Conservative parties fought for control of Mexico. Under their inspirational president, Benito Juárez, the Liberals won, confirming a series of secular reforms that stripped the Catholic Church of much of its property and power. Conservative exiles then arrived in Paris, lobbying the imperial government for regime change: they sought to overthrow the Mexican republic and replace it with an empire modelled on the French one. Liberals, they argued, were a radical minority oppressing the silent majority who yearned for monarchy. All that was needed, they insisted, was a small European force, who would be welcomed as liberators. In the pious and Spanish Eugénie, outraged at Liberal attacks on the Church, they found a sympathiser who got them in a room with Louis-Napoléon.

After a dinner at Biarritz, a Mexican exile came into the emperor's study. Louis-Napoléon stood up, lit a cigarette and looked expectantly. The Mexican then explained that the time had come 'to annihilate the demagogues and proclaim a monarchy, which alone can save the country'.[21] With the United States in the midst of civil war, he added, now was the time to act. The emperor agreed. And so in his Biarritz villa, cigarette smoke swirling in the air, without the knowledge of the French foreign minister, the decision was taken to send French troops to the New World.

The emperor had his reasons. Rather than an expensive conquest such as France had undertaken in Algeria, a small force would create a regime that relied on European capital and expertise to develop the supposedly fabulous wealth of Mexico. In short, this would provide the benefits of colonialism at a fraction of the cost: empire and glory on the cheap. Moreover, Louis-Napoléon bought into an idea fashionable at the time: pan-Latinism. In mid-1850s Paris, the term 'Latin America' was invented. The doctrine of pan-Latinism argued that just as there were Latin nations in Europe, the Americas south of the United States border were culturally Latin because of shared history, language and religion. Many thought that the United States, which had already annexed over half of Mexico's territory after victory in the US–Mexican War, was poised to absorb the rest of the country unless something was done. The regeneration of the so-called Latin races, then, was another intoxicating idea which at a stroke placed France as a leading nation in the New World. At the same time, French intervention would stop rising US power. 'Jealous of Europe, enemies of the old world,' one adviser noted, discussing the United States, 'it would be capable of trying to enslave the universe.' Stopping this was the 'boldest [idea] of our century, I would say further, of modern times'.[22]

But these typically ambitious, visionary and vague notions were hard to sell to the French people. The explanation that did stick, however, was that the emperor's half-brother Morny was in on the affair. During the civil war, the Mexican Conservative party took out a loan on outrageous terms with a Swiss banking house, J. B. Jecker and Sons. In return for $750,000 upfront the party would pay back $15 million. When he came to power, Benito Juárez refused to honour his enemy's one-sided contract. The issue should have ended there, but Morny saw a profit to be made. In return for 30 per cent, he agreed to make the Jecker claim part of the French intervention. This was not the reason why France invaded Mexico, but that Morny wanted to make money, and that Louis-Napoléon was conducting French foreign policy to help him do so, seemed to many a much better explanation for why French soldiers were dying across the Atlantic than the nebulous cause of Latin regeneration.

Once again, therefore, French soldiers had little idea of what they were fighting for, nor, predictably, did the army have maps. There were more problems to overcome before the French geopolitical new world order was realised, not least who would rule the as yet imaginary Mexican Empire. Eugénie thought that Archduke Ferdinand Maximilian, a younger brother of the Austrian emperor, might be interested. Not that Louis-Napoléon waited to find out; French forces sailed to Mexico before Maximilian accepted the offer, and by March 1862 there were about six thousand troops across the Atlantic. The French emperor expected his soldiers to easily defeat the Mexican army, but they were not welcomed as liberators. Instead, Mexicans rallied behind their president and the Mexican army made a heroic stand at the city of Puebla, blocking the route to the capital. Here, on 5 May 1862, they defeated veterans of victories over Russia and Austria. The day went down in history as Cinco de Mayo.

Rather than end the intervention, Louis-Napoléon sent thirty thousand reinforcements. With superior numbers, and a map borrowed from the emperor's private collection, the French took Puebla, but only after a year-long siege, and they occupied Mexico City in the summer of 1863. A sham assembly supposedly representing the will of the people was set up and called for Maximilian to reign over Mexico as emperor. Even then, Maximilian and his wife Charlotte did not reach their new kingdom until May 1864, almost three years after the idea of a Mexican monarchy had been agreed.

Maximilian and Charlotte had been told that the country was pacified. When they arrived, they found it torn apart by civil war. Juárez retreated northwards into the vastness of Mexico using guerrilla measures to continue the struggle. In response, the French employed brutal counter-insurgency tactics. What an 'atrocious war' I have waged, wrote the French officer put in charge of this to his niece. He was an old imperial hand who had made a fortune selling loot plundered from the Summer Palace in Beijing. Now, he tortured, executed and burned down villages in the name of civilisation. 'If I were Mexican,' he wrote, 'what hatred I would have for these French, and how much I would make them suffer.'[23] As more French soldiers died, the intervention became increasingly unpopular at home. Louis-Napoléon's political reforms meant foreign policy blunders like Mexico were a gift to opposition deputies in the Corps législatif. The emperor's bête noire, Jules Favre, excoriated this personal foreign policy in set-piece speeches that were splashed in the next day's papers for Frenchmen and -women to read over breakfast.

In January 1863, another crisis erupted which afforded Louis-Napoléon an opportunity to disappoint the French people: Poland rose up, again, against Russian rule. The regime's Catholic base lamented the oppression of their co-religionists by Russian Orthodox Christians; for the left, it was a case of Russian despotism crushing liberty. Nothing showed the issue's power to unite strange bedfellows more than the fact that Eugénie and Plon-Plon, who loathed each other, both wanted Louis-Napoléon to act to prevent Russian repression.

As news of Russian atrocities reached France – cutting off prisoners' ears and noses and then making them eat them was one accusation – and petitions to help the Poles flooded into the assemblies, Plon-Plon spoke in the Senate. Privately, he had urged Louis-Napoléon to march his army through Germany, create an independent Polish kingdom and redraw the map of Europe – a policy that, if followed, would engulf Europe in war. In public, Plon-Plon was more circumspect, but only just. With the Empire at the height of its power, and even if it meant war, he declaimed, the time had come to do something for the great cause of Poland. Tapping into the popular mood, the speech caused a sensation.

Louis-Napoléon, however, did not want more wars and was furious at this public criticism. 'Since the day after I was elected President of the Republic,' he wrote to his cousin, 'you have never ceased to be, by your words and your actions, hostile to my politics.'[24] The letter turned into a form of therapy for the emperor, listing all he had done for his cousin and how his cousin had repaid him with failure and disloyalty. Concluding his diatribe, Louis-Napoléon gave Plon-Plon an ultimatum: support the government, or break with it.

'What would be the use of me responding to the numerous reproaches that your Majesty makes?' asked Plon-Plon, before responding at length to the numerous reproaches.[25] Rather than Louis-Napoléon's two options, Plon-Plon suggested a third. He would go to Egypt, where he would no longer be an embarrassment. Seeing that this was the best he was going to get from his cousin, Louis-Napoléon agreed and Plon-Plon absented himself from French politics for a few months, which meant he was out of the country while the latest rounds of elections were held in June and July 1863.

To compensate for foreign policy miscalculations, Louis-Napoléon wanted an unambiguous triumph for official candidates at the polls. With Persigny now minister of the interior, not a man who lost sleep over nefarious means to achieve his beloved emperor's goals, corruption was spectacular. As well as the usual manoeuvres, outrageous lies were spread. If one opposition candidate was elected, so government-backed propaganda ran – getting straight to the heart of French political culture – then workers would not be allowed to drink wine. Almost as bad, wages would be cut, there would be war over Poland and all men aged between eighteen and forty would be conscripted into the army.

If these tactics failed, there was always violence and, as a last resort, electoral fraud. Many voters across what passed for the democratic world in the nineteenth century would have been disappointed to have an election without violence, and fraud was endemic too, so there was nothing particularly unusual about these in France. Here, in fact, miscounting votes was frowned upon. If the emperor represented the will of the people, in a regime that revered universal suffrage, then being caught falsifying the vote upset the cornerstone of the political narrative; however, in 1863 there were examples of the practice.

In past elections, the government had rigged a game it was going to win easily. Now, there was more organised opposition. In Paris, nearly twice as many people voted against government candidates as for them, and despite Persigny's efforts, thirty-three opposition men were elected across the country, a significant increase from the last elections in 1857. There were some famous names from the past, including Adolphe Thiers, which meant that the previously somnolent chamber that had defined the first decade of the Empire became more lively. The result combined with the extent of the corruption cost Persigny his job.

As for Poland, nothing was done. With no end to the Mexican imbroglio in sight and pained by what happened after he invaded Italy in 1859, Louis-Napoléon was done with interventions. 'No matter how much sympathy one has for this or that people,' he explained, 'it is revolution . . . which spoils everything, it is the revolution that loses the best causes . . . which makes Italy odious to me and disgusts me with Poland.'[26]

Louis-Napoléon did write to the sovereigns of Europe in November 1863, calling for a congress to settle the matter. Its remit would extend beyond Poland, leading to the resolution of other areas of conflict and ushering in a golden era of European peace. The letter was published in the government newspaper. In its grandiosity, it was a typical Bonapartist *coup de théâtre*, and in its vision, typical of Louis-Napoléon's impractical utopianism; however, the other powers no longer trusted the playwright and, much to Louis-Napoléon's chagrin, refused. By 1864, Russia had savagely repressed the uprising. The emperor hoped to have more luck arranging affairs in Algeria during a visit planned for the next year, but his absence from Paris merely provided the occasion for yet more attacks on the government.

———

In May 1865, Louis-Napoléon sat down to dinner in a Moorish palace in Algiers for a banquet of North African delicacies – tortoise soup, porcupine garnished with antelope kidneys, gazelle and wild boar to start. Ostriches fared badly: there were roasted ones accompanied by ostrich eggs for the main course. Finally, there was a seemingly endless array of regional pastries for the emperor's delight, not that he took much pleasure in eating these days. This was part of a weeks-long visit that gossip in Paris put down to Louis-Napoléon wanting to be away from Eugénie, who was furious at his incessant affairs.

In fact, the trip to Algeria was the culmination of Louis-Napoléon's increasing fascination for this French colony and his determination to put into practice his idea for an Arab kingdom. Already, much to the annoyance of European colonists, he had decreed that the lands occupied by the various peoples in Algeria prior to the French conquest were theirs legally. Now he wanted to tour the region before enacting further legislation. Louis-Napoléon's visit was designed to bind the peoples of Algeria to France through association, not coercion. Rather than exploitation, his vision for Algeria was one of different peoples living together, their cultures respected and perhaps even one day an autonomous Algerian state – the Algerian kingdom. He also believed that Algerians could be assimilated peacefully into French culture, and, shockingly at the time, that Arabs, Berbers and Jews from Algeria could be French citizens. After he returned from his visit, the Senate decreed a law to that effect. Algerians would, however, have to renounce rights already held, whereby certain legal cases were tried under Islamic or Jewish law. Few took advantage of the new law. That did not stop republicans like Jules Favre ridiculing the emperor's plans, which Favre argued in racist terms might one day lead to Algerians sitting in a French parliament.

In 1860s France, many shared Favre's prejudices and few wanted to see Louis-Napoléon's Arab kingdom become a reality. Louis-Napoléon may have declared that the Islamic population enjoyed his protection, but in the late 1860s, after decades of pernicious colonialism, there was little evidence of that. The emperor's well-intentioned measures were counterproductive. Enshrining property rights in law made land easier for colonists to buy from locals, and European-owned land increased sixfold under the Empire, while rising birth rates and migration saw the European population double in the same period. Meanwhile, it is estimated that up to a quarter of the pre-conquest Algerian population died as a result of famine triggered by natural causes, but exacerbated by land expropriation, the collapse of traditional agriculture and colonial neglect.

While Louis-Napoléon was touring Algeria, Eugénie was acting as regent in Paris. From conviction, she was reactionary. She argued against reform, which put her at odds with those in the emperor's entourage who urged further liberalisation. In the case of Plon-Plon, by Bonapartist standards a radical, it merely added another reason for her to hate him. She eyed him with suspicion one day while the prince imperial bounced on his knee, and Plon-Plon told those around him, 'She thinks I've got arsenic in my pocket.'[27]

After their falling-out over Poland, Plon-Plon had managed to get back into Louis-Napoléon's favour, as he somehow always did. Before leaving for Algeria, the emperor asked him to support his wife as regent, but also asked him to attend an official engagement – the unveiling in May 1865 of a statue of Napoléon Bonaparte and his four brothers at their birthplace in Ajaccio, Corsica. There, Plon-Plon explained to his audience that Napoléon was not a tyrant, but a lover of liberty, freedom of the press and democracy. 'For long years past,' said the emperor's cousin as he soared to the climax of his speech, 'my mind has been haunted by the false interpretations given of Napoléon by those who only see in him the agent of a reaction of alarmed interests – of paltry passions to be satisfied; whereas he is the initiator of all the great ideas and of progress.' The mission of Napoléon, he insisted, 'was to make the dictatorship the means of emancipation'.[28]

This was not, then, the usual fare served up by minor royals unveiling statues; it was a manifesto for liberal Bonapartism and an explicit criticism of Louis-Napoléon for not further reforming his Empire. When Eugénie read the speech, she was furious, as were supporters of the government, wanting to know if 'the revolutionary theory' that Plon-Plon had traced in Ajaccio was government policy, for if it was, it would be 'nothing less than the banner of insurrection and civil war unfurled by a prince of the Imperial family'.[29]

'Well then,' Plon-Plon said to the empress when he arrived back in Paris, 'are you going to put me' in prison? 'Certainly,' Eugénie replied, 'if the emperor orders me to do it, but I await his decision.'[30]

'I cannot help but express to you the painful impression that the speech you gave at Ajaccio has caused me,' wrote a once more disappointed Louis-Napoléon after reading Plon-Plon's words. The speech 'can only serve the enemies of my government'. To know how to apply the ideas of Napoléon to the present, he continued, in a cutting aside, 'one must have gone through the harsh tests of responsibility and power'. But even then, 'can we really, pygmies that we are, truly appreciate' Napoléon? he asked rhetorically and somewhat worryingly, since much of his political career had been based on reinterpreting the life and work of his uncle.[31]

Louis-Napoléon summoned his wayward cousin to the Tuileries and, lighting a cigarette, said to Plon-Plon, 'I'm sorry about what happened . . . but I've been unhappy with the embarrassment you've been causing me for a long time.' Plon-Plon maintained, with some justification, that what he said about their uncle was only what Louis-Napoléon had written many times before he came to power. The emperor, however, explained that while he did not object to the content of the speech, what he could not have was anyone outlining a political programme other than himself.

There followed an acrimonious discussion, with Plon-Plon refusing to renounce his radical interpretation of Bonapartism while doing his best to hurt Louis-Napoléon, turning the conversation to Morny, who had died a few months earlier. Plon-Plon claimed that Louis-Napoléon indulged him because of an 'origin that I do not want to remind you of', thereby reminding Louis-Napoléon of it, namely his mother's infidelity. Morny 'used his influence to line his pockets', Plon-Plon said, before adding, somewhat against the evidence, 'I am an honest man.'[32] After arguing for an hour and a half, Louis-Napoléon agreed that Plon-Plon should absent himself, again, from Paris. Asking if his cousin would take leave of the empress, Plon-Plon said, bluntly, no, he would not.

Louis-Napoléon's farewell to Morny had been more tender. Holding back tears, the emperor had embraced his half-brother on his deathbed. Unlike Plon-Plon's departure, his death was a political loss, too. Morny had been an accomplished politician who had played a pivotal role in the 2 December *coup d'état*. Fabulously corrupt, he was often an embarrassment, but for all his sarcastic cynicism he was, unlike Plon-Plon, useful and loyal. From 1854, he had presided over the Corps législatif with skill, his charm doing much to win over deputies critical of government policy and making inroads to bring republican opposition on board. The loss of this trusted confidant, then, was a blow, especially as Louis-Napoléon needed sage counsel in the summer of 1865. He had to decide how to deal with a looming clash between two European heavyweights, Prussia and Austria.

––––––

The first thing he would do when in power, the Prussian politician Otto von Bismarck told Benjamin Disraeli when speaking to him in 1862, was reorganise the Prussian army. After that, he would 'seize the first best pretext to declare war against Austria', then he would subdue the minor German states and 'give national unity to Germany under Prussian leadership'. This was not the first time that Disraeli had heard foreigners tell him their grandiose ideas. With kindly patience, he had often listened to Louis-Napoléon's plans for when he was emperor during his time in exile in London. In contrast to the disbelief with which he met this talk, after speaking to Bismarck, Disraeli said to an Austrian diplomat, 'Take care of that man; he means what he says.'

Indeed he did, and not long after talking to Disraeli, Bismarck made this clear in a parliamentary speech: 'Prussia must build up and preserve her strength for the advantageous moment . . . For the great questions of the day will not be settled by speeches and majority decisions . . . but by blood and iron.'[33] Bismarck wanted to bring the German Confederation, a loose collection of independent states, under Prussian leadership and then forge them through war into a united Germany.

The first step in Prussian aggrandisement was an arcane crisis. It was famously said of the Schleswig-Holstein question that only three people understood it. One was Prince Albert, who was dead; the second a Danish statesman, who had gone mad; and the third was the British prime minister, Lord Palmerston, who had forgotten all about it. At its simplest, it was a dispute over who ruled two territories that bordered Germany and Denmark. The Danish king said he did; Prussia and Austria went to war to uphold claims of German rulers. Britain wanted to support Denmark, but needed French backing, which Louis-Napoléon refused in the hope he might get something from Austria and Prussia. He did not, and without allies, Denmark soon surrendered after a one-sided fight.

For Bismarck, Schleswig-Holstein was merely the means to do what he told Disraeli he would: find a pretext to declare war against Austria. In an arrangement of Byzantine intricacy, Austria and Prussia agreed to jointly administer Schleswig-Holstein, but so complex was the agreement that it would be easy to engineer a rupture at Bismarck's leisure. Towards the end of 1865, the Prussian minister-president saw that the moment was not far off, but he needed French neutrality. With that singular goal in mind, Bismarck headed to Biarritz in October 1865 to meet Louis-Napoléon.

While Bismarck was scheming, Louis-Napoléon was helping to plan a practical joke. One of Eugénie's ladies-in-waiting took a shine to the Prussian during his stay and the rest of the court tormented her with tales of Bismarck's boldness when it came to women. At Eugénie's suggestion, a replica of Bismarck's head was made and put on the pillow of her lady-in-waiting's bed. Then a handkerchief was placed on the head to resemble a nightcap, cushions were to pass for the body, and in the half-light of the room the illusion was complete. Before she went to bed, the lady-in-waiting was detained in conversation while Louis-Napoléon and Eugénie hid themselves down the corridor. The lady-in-waiting entered her room and soon came flying out. Frantically knocking on the door of another courtier, she exclaimed, 'There is a man in my bed!' At the end of the corridor, the empress could not stop laughing.[34]

When not watching practical jokes, Louis-Napoléon was meeting with Bismarck to discuss the future of Europe. Compared to Bismarck's clarity, Louis-Napoléon's thinking was clouded, a muddled mix of idealism and opportunism. Unlike Bismarck, he thought that the great questions of the day should be settled not by blood and iron but by speeches and majority decisions. This is why he endlessly proposed congresses that would reorganise the continent along national principles and settle disputes peacefully. As no one else was interested in this system, in practice Louis-Napoléon vaguely supported peoples who were aspiring to liberal nationalism; however, the contradictory caveat was that this should be moderate and monarchical rather than revolutionary and republican. As Italy and Mexico had shown, that was easy to proclaim, hard to make a reality.

But the emperor was also a revisionist, obsessed with overturning the Vienna Treaties imposed after the defeat of Napoléon in 1815. As this settlement was designed to restore as much of the *ancien régime* in Europe as possible and stem the tide of nationalism, this revisionism was linked to national principles. Yet Louis-Napoléon was also fanatical about raising French prestige and securing territory lost after the Napoleonic wars. To achieve this, he was intensely relaxed about putting national principles to one side.

These competing ideas made Louis-Napoléon's foreign policy confused, and Prussia was an especially confusing case. Its borders, Bismarck said in a less quoted line from his blood and iron speech, 'under the treaties of Vienna are not favourable for the healthy existence of the state'.[35] Louis-Napoléon, then, saw Bismarck as a fellow disruptor who might not only help end the hated settlement of 1815, but, if supported, might also acquiesce to French expansion in Belgium or Luxembourg. Bismarck had further leverage. The emperor was monomaniacally focused on fulfilling his promise made in 1859 to free Italy from the Alps to the Adriatic. This would mean ending Austrian control of its Venetian province, which, if Prussia defeated Austria in war, Bismarck could bring about.

In short, there was plenty that Bismarck could offer France and, confident in his ability as the master conspirator of European diplomacy, Louis-Napoléon thought he could outwit him. Walking along the beach, and over meals which the hulking, gluttonous Prussian enjoyed much more than the abstemious, diminutive emperor, Louis-Napoléon and Bismarck discussed the future. Bismarck kept his views opaque. Anything was possible; he mentioned revising the 1815 treaties in France's favour, securing Venetia for Italy and close Franco-Prussian collaboration. 'He talked a lot,' Louis-Napoléon recalled afterwards, 'but in general and vague terms; I couldn't figure out exactly what he wanted, and he made me no formal proposal.'[36] What Bismarck wanted, however, was simple: French neutrality. And he got it, for without promising anything he could be held to, Bismarck left Louis-Napoléon with the vague impression that there would be much to gain if Prussia defeated Austria.

Though many close advisers, including Eugénie, supported an alliance with Austria, Louis-Napoléon could not countenance one. He represented the new; Austria was the bastion of the old. That said, he had played both sides. In a secret treaty, in the event of victory, Austria, in return for French neutrality, agreed to cede Venetia, which the emperor would then give to Italy. Whatever happened, Louis-Napoléon hoped, France would gain something.

But he was not sure. As war between Austria and Prussia seemed days away in the spring of 1866, a worried Louis-Napoléon presided over a cabinet meeting and received contradictory advice over what to do. Then the emperor turned to someone who had been silent throughout the debate and said, 'And you, Persigny, why don't you say anything?' The future of

Europe hung in the balance, but Persigny did not miss an opportunity to insult those at the meeting: 'Because I don't know how to talk and say nothing, like we've been doing for two hours.'

Then he turned his ire on Louis-Napoléon. Ironically, it was the arch-Bonapartist Persigny who got to the heart of the problem with the way the emperor conducted foreign policy. 'We know nothing of the conditions, the resolutions, the stipulations that you had to agree to in Biarritz with Bismarck.' If Louis-Napoléon had received clear commitments from Bismarck that favoured France, then Persigny could comprehend the emperor's policy of not backing Austria. If not, 'I don't understand why your government hasn't armed the country to the teeth, and why it wastes a day, an hour,' not readying for war, because a militaristic Prussian backed by the German people posed an existential threat to France.[37]

In the end, though, Louis-Napoléon decided that the coming conflict between the two Central European behemoths would be a long one, weakening Austria and Prussia. Then France could step in, mediate peace and emerge more powerful than ever. This plan was about to be put to the test. That summer, Austria and Prussia fought a war that would determine the future of Europe.

18

THE EMPIRE IN THE PILLORY

At the Battle of Königgrätz on 3 July 1866, or Sadowa as it was known in France at the time, the Prussian army annihilated the Austrians. In a matter of weeks, Prussia had smashed Austrian power in Germany for good. If the speed of the Prussian victory was a shock, it at first seemed as though Louis-Napoléon's policy of neutrality had been a masterstroke. Desperate for France to mediate the peace, Franz Joseph offered Louis-Napoléon what he had long coveted: Venetia, which was transferred to Italy. On 5 July, the government newspaper announced this diplomatic success and painted Louis-Napoléon as the arbiter of Europe. There was rejoicing in Paris, flags were flown, buildings were illuminated at night and the stock market rose.

The emperor, however, knew he was not the arbiter of Europe. That was Bismarck, and Prussia's striking triumph placed a hostile power on France's border – or, as a French newspaper put it, 'Prussia supreme in Germany would be so great a danger to France that no government could accept it.'[1] What Louis-Napoléon's government would do was to be decided at an emergency cabinet meeting, where long, agonised discussion followed over whether France should prepare for war or accept the Prussian fait accompli. The minister of war declared the army ready, but others hoped that if France acquiesced in Prussia's rise, it would receive territorial compensation. At this, Eugénie leapt up, exclaiming, 'When the Prussian armies are no longer tied up in Bohemia and can turn back against ourselves, Bismarck will simply laugh at our claims.'[2] The road to Berlin, she said, lay open; it was time to act. Won over, Louis-Napoléon resolved to send a threatening note to Berlin, convene the assemblies to vote for war credits and place fifty thousand men on the Rhine frontier.

Yet in the evening, those who favoured peace worked on Louis-Napoléon. The French army, they argued, was not ready and, as the devastating effectiveness of the Prussian war machine had just shown, likely inferior to its prospective enemy. Moreover, nearly a third of French troops were tied down in Mexico, Algeria and Indochina. On top of that, public opinion favoured peace. Louis-Napoléon finally agreed: there would be no war. 'It is us', the minister of war cried bitterly when he heard that the decision had been reversed, 'who were beaten at Sadowa.'[3] That night, a storm broke out over Paris. In the morning, the streets were strewn with the half-broken lanterns that had lit up the buildings the night before, soaked flags lay on the ground, wet streamers were trodden into the pavement. Rejoicing at peace turned into anxiety as to what would come next.

Difficult decisions and intricate diplomacy were unwelcome to Louis-Napoléon because his health was suffering a crisis. To counter rumours about his condition, he kept up appearances at public events, but it was said that before entering a ballroom, he would hold his arm to the flame of a candle, hoping that a different pain might take his mind off his chronic ones. When an Austrian diplomat urged Louis-Napoléon to show more firmness towards Prussia, the emperor was in visible discomfort. 'I am not ready for war,' he repeatedly muttered.[4] The Austrian ambassador was even less impressed: after an interview, he wrote to Vienna that the emperor 'is very pale, very undone, and has the air of a man whose willpower had given way to general exhaustion'. Next, the ambassador saw Eugénie, who had long argued for a pro-Austrian policy. 'She is very uneasy about the emperor's health,' he recorded, 'and about his physical and moral decay, about which she gave me the most convincing evidence.' The moral decay was, of course, her husband's affairs. Not doing much for the grandeur of France, or her husband's reputation, Eugénie told a foreign diplomat that for years, Louis-Napoléon had 'fallen into complete prostration, no longer bothering himself with government, writing on Julius Caesar and giving it the little strength he had left'.[5]

This was an exaggeration, but Louis-Napoléon slept badly, hardly ate and found it difficult to preside over long cabinet meetings. Discussions of foreign affairs that summer were especially painful because they showed in detail how the emperor's opportunistic policy of staying neutral had backfired. After peace negotiations between Prussia and Austria concluded in August 1866, Prussia became the dominant power in Germany and France received nothing. This was a failure of Louis-Napoléon's foreign policy, one that was made all the more painful as he was reminded of another unfolding disaster that same month.

———

On 11 August 1866, the Empress of Mexico, Maximilian's wife Charlotte, left the Grand Hôtel for Saint-Cloud. Eugénie had opened the hotel, an opulent symbol of Georges-Eugène Haussmann's Paris, in June 1862, when the French Second Empire appeared to be an unstoppable global power. Charlotte and her kingdom in Mexico showed the limits of French ambition. After the US Civil War ended, Washington was free to pressurise the French into withdrawing their troops from Mexico. Maximilian was not worried. 'It seems to me impossible', he wrote, 'that the wisest monarch of the century and the most powerful nation in the world should give in to the Yankees.'[6]

'It is not without painful emotion', Louis-Napoléon began a letter to Maximilian on 15 January 1866 in which he gave in to the Yankees, 'that I am writing to your Majesty.' Using Maximilian's inability to honour financial engagements to which he was treaty bound as the pretext, Louis-Napoléon explained that he had no choice but 'to fix a definitive limit to the French occupation'.[7] It would take weeks for Maximilian to receive this letter in Mexico, but Louis-Napoléon did not afford him the courtesy of waiting before he announced his intentions publicly. At the opening of the new legislative session a week later, the French emperor told his audience that as far as Mexico was concerned, it was mission accomplished: 'The government founded by the will of the people is consolidated . . . our expedition is coming to an end.'[8]

But Maximilian's throne was far from consolidated. The thirty thousand French troops that had occupied Mexico were insufficient to end resistance to his rule. As one French officer noted, our 'army spent itself gloriously in the immensity of space', and 'our troops traversing Mexico resembled a ship gliding through the water, leaving behind no traces of its track'.[9] Moreover, in a model of imperialism that resembled a highly leveraged hostile takeover, the cost of this failed French occupation fell on Maximilian's treasury. As the Mexican Empire had no money, Louis-Napoléon had organised enormous loans so that Maximilian could make the payments. These loaded the near-bankrupt Mexican government with levels of debt that proved impossible to repay. Furthermore, because, as Maximilian insisted, they were friends, the Mexican emperor agreed to pay the scandalous Jecker claims.

When he received news that his 'friend' planned to abandon him, Maximilian decided to abdicate and return to Europe. His wife was made of sterner stuff. She berated him, writing a furious ten-page memorandum accusing him of cowardice, stupidity and dishonouring the Habsburg name. Instead of fleeing, she would go to Paris and change the emperor's mind, for before they had left for Mexico, Louis-Napoléon had written, 'You may be sure that my support will not fail you.'[10]

On 7 August, Maximilian wrote to his wife that 'you will find Europe very changed', but because of France's neutrality during the Austro-Prussian War, 'wise Napoléon [is] in a better position than ever', which showed the Mexican emperor was no better at analysing foreign policy than his French counterpart. Concluding his letter to Charlotte, he added, 'It would be deplorable for the country and for yourself if you leave Europe with promises, but without achieving results.'[11]

Yet 'wise Napoléon', having committed what many people, including his wife, saw as a catastrophic blunder over Prussia, did everything he could to avoid meeting Charlotte. 'He is on edge and irritated,' wrote a courtier. 'A day of good weather will put him right. But instead of good weather, he has the Empress of Mexico on his back.'[12] But Charlotte would not be denied an audience. She would come to Saint-Cloud, she insisted, and break in if she were not invited. Louis-Napoléon reluctantly granted her an audience on 11 August.

Wearing a striking long black silk dress which still had creases from packing, a black lace mantle and, completing the look, a white hat, Charlotte met Louis-Napoléon and Eugénie at the palace. As she remonstrated with them, she thought how visibly the emperor had aged. After listening in silence to Charlotte's lecture, Louis-Napoléon turned towards his wife and began to cry. Composing himself, he explained that there was nothing he could do for Maximilian. Charlotte had accomplished nothing, but the emperor agreed to another meeting. This time, she gave the emperor the letter in which Louis-Napoléon had pledged Maximilian his support whatever happened. Moved, Louis-Napoléon nonetheless refused more help. Seeing the distress that Charlotte was causing her husband, Eugénie ushered her out of the room. Louis-Napoléon found the meeting unbearably painful, and was 'nearly crushed, I remember, by the sight of such anguish which nothing could appease', he later recalled.[13]

The failure of her mission was too much for Charlotte. Her mind began to unravel. Writing to Maximilian, she told her husband that Louis-Napoléon 'means to commit a long premeditated and evil deed . . . because he is the evil principle upon earth and wants to get rid of the good, only humanity does not see that his deeds are evil and they adore him'. The French emperor 'has never loved you from beginning to end, for he neither loves nor is capable of loving; he fascinated you like the serpent, his tears were as false as his words, all his deeds are treachery'. She claimed the meeting reminded her of the apocalypse and Paris of Babylon, and added that 'it is enough to make any unbeliever believe in God to see this devil so near'.[14]

Charlotte journeyed to Rome, where she hoped to persuade the pope to support Maximilian. Instead of political talks, she broke down in the corridors of the Vatican, sobbing and screaming that Louis-Napoléon was trying to murder her. He was not; she had lost her mind. Eventually bundled out of the papal palace, Charlotte ended up so paranoid about poison that she locked herself in her rooms, where she insisted her servant obtain a small stove, a basket of eggs and two live chickens, which had to be killed, prepared and cooked in front of her. When even these measures struck her as insufficient, she somehow procured a cat, which she pressed into service as her personal taster before eating anything. As one of her entourage noted, she was 'haggard, the cheeks sunken and flushed; her eyes had a wild expression and, when her attention was not fixed, roamed vaguely and uncertainly as though in search of absent figures or far-away scenes'.[15]

With French power crumbling in Mexico, a mad empress convinced that Louis-Napoléon was a murderer in league with the devil and a hostile European superpower on France's border, 1866 had not been a good year for the emperor's foreign policy. Desperate for a success to show the French people, Louis-Napoléon tried to buy the Grand Duchy of Luxembourg in March 1867. Here, too, Prussia thwarted his ambitions, humiliating

France. With all these failures, Louis-Napoléon urgently needed to find another way to revitalise his regime.

————

On 19 January 1867, 'the Napoleonic regime struck out on a new path', Eugénie explained. 'On that day the curtain fell irrevocably on the "authoritarian Empire" which had given France fifteen years of greatness and prosperity.' For the empress, this was not a happy day: 'I was deeply hurt by this,' she said.[16] She was also deeply shocked, as were most people, that once again Louis-Napoléon had, with his usual theatricality, unleashed further liberalisation on unsuspecting ministers and the public.

One man who did know what was coming was Émile Ollivier. Born in Marseilles in 1825, Ollivier was the son of a radical republican. Politics and conspiracy meant his father spent months away from home, occasionally in prison. The son was raised on that familiar diet of Jean-Jacques Rousseau, glorious tales of the first French Revolution and, as Italian revolutionaries often came to stay, liberal nationalism. Enemies of French monarchs, an austere republican education and Italian sympathies – Ollivier's upbringing had much in common with Louis-Napoléon's.

After the 1848 Revolution, Ollivier joined the French civil service. He did well in the tumultuous, ever-shifting world of post-1848 politics, rising to become a prefect, but a jealous local rival engineered his downfall. He went to Paris, where he practised law and moved in republican high society, which included Plon-Plon, and the two became friends. In 1857, Ollivier returned to the political fray as one of the few republican deputies elected to the Corps législatif. An urbane dresser, with hair parted geometrically to one side and a lazy eye behind small, round, tight spectacles, Ollivier was an emollient and thoughtful man as well as a fine rhetorician. Though republican, he preached compromise rather than revolution.

'When you have known all the sadnesses and all the joys, there remains to taste only one pleasure which surpasses all the others,' he said in a speech in the Corps législatif after Louis-Napoléon's first series of reforms years earlier: 'to be the one who courageously and voluntarily initiates a great people into liberty.'[17] Liberal Bonapartists such as Morny and Plon-Plon assiduously courted Ollivier, hoping to co-opt his powers of oratory and his republican base for the Empire. Ollivier had been coy, but in January 1867, Louis-Napoléon felt the moment had come to win him over. He invited Ollivier to the Tuileries.

Shaking the republican by the hand, Louis-Napoléon asked him what he thought of the political situation. Not good, was Ollivier's reply. Apart from the rising opposition at home and an alarming international horizon, Ollivier told him, people were worried about the emperor's health. There was a sense of drift. 'It is urgent', the republican deputy said, 'that you assert your initiative with a determined act. You cannot do it through war – do it through audacious, liberal measures.'

Louis-Napoléon agreed with the gloomy diagnosis and the cure, but he was worried about the timing. 'Wouldn't I seem as though I were trying to make up for my failures in Mexico and Germany?' the emperor candidly asked. 'In this situation, wouldn't concessions weaken me?' Ollivier replied that on the contrary, it would 'in the eyes of public opinion be like an awakening'. After an hour of increasingly friendly discussion, the emperor seemed reanimated. 'I only want the good,' he said. 'If I didn't think I was useful to this country, I would leave without hesitation.'[18] As he always thought a Bonapartist empire useful to France, this was a slightly less dramatic revelation than it might seem, but it captured his belief that his government was a positive force. Louis-Napoléon then sounded out Ollivier. Would he be willing to serve as a minister?

Ollivier declined, claiming his support would be more useful if it were independently given; nonetheless, Louis-Napoléon was delighted with the meeting and the man. 'Our conversation left me with the sweetest feelings,' he wrote to Ollivier the next day. 'It is a great pleasure for me to talk with a man whose elevated and patriotic feelings rise above the petty interests of individuals and parties.'[19] Indeed, the co-operation with Ollivier was Louis-Napoléon's politics at its best. He had a talent for reaching out to talented individuals regardless of political background and forging a middle way between radicalism and reaction. The problem, however, was that the emperor had not run his new liberal programme past his ministers.

The most important of these men was Eugène Rouher. Like Ollivier, his background was in law, but that was where the comparisons ended. Heavily built and with a prominent forehead, Rouher was the epitome of the stolid bourgeoisie that rallied to Louis-Napoléon after he was elected president in 1848 to stem what it saw as the rising tide of socialism. Under the Empire, Rouher had become indispensable, especially in the 1860s, after reforms made debate in the Corps législatif more heated. He was the master of defending the indefensible whether he believed it or not, but one thing he was firmly against was further liberalisation.

At a cabinet meeting on 17 January 1867, Louis-Napoléon presented Rouher and his ministers with his fait accompli. They were outraged, threatening to resign. The emperor, who hated conflict, said they would discuss it another time. Instead, Louis-Napoléon acted. Two days later, he summoned his ministers, thanked them for their service and asked for their resignations. They gave them. Then the emperor sent a letter for publication in the official newspaper, outlining his programme:

> I said last year that my government wanted to walk on firm ground, capable of supporting authority and freedom. By the measures I have just indicated my words have come true. I am not shaking the ground that fifteen years of calm and prosperity have consolidated, I am strengthening it further . . . by finally completing the crowning achievement of the edifice erected by the national will.[20]

The reforms gave the Corps législatif the right to formally question ministers, loosened restrictions on holding public meetings and lessened press censorship. Though the rhetoric was of striking change, these were cautious measures. Woefully misjudging the intent, one prefect congratulated the emperor and said he looked forward to parliamentary freedom. 'As long as I live, you will not have this government,' replied Louis-Napoléon.[21]

Louis-Napoléon had addressed his letter to Rouher to bind him to the reforms regardless of whether he supported them. Unwilling to break with the emperor, Rouher came back into the ministry a few days after his resignation, but he hated the reforms. Though he backed them in public, he worked behind the scenes to weaken them, with the empress's tacit approval.

Disgusted at this campaign of obstruction, Ollivier was furious. Mocking Rouher, he claimed that he was not a prime minister, a grand vizier or a mayor of the palace, 'but a vice-emperor without responsibility'. Instead of putting Louis-Napoléon's programme into action, Rouher had accepted it with bad grace, prevaricated about implementing it and opposed it any way he could. The opposition piled in on Rouher – Favre and Thiers, among others, attacked him too – and Louis-Napoléon felt he had to back his man. The day after the speech, he sent Rouher the Grand Cross of the *légion d'honneur*, which was encrusted with diamonds, along with a letter which was published: 'In the middle of the unjust attacks of which you are the object, this friendly gesture will make you forget, I hope, the troubles inseparable from your position.'[22]

These were not the only reforms where Louis-Napoléon failed to impose his will. Victor Duruy was a celebrated historian whom the emperor found so helpful when writing his biography of Julius Caesar that he made him education minister. 'How could your Majesty have thought of making me a minister?' asked Duruy after his appointment. 'It'll be fine,' replied Louis-Napoléon. Duruy claimed this was all the guidance he ever received. Given the freedom to develop and implement his ideas, he liked working for the emperor, 'an affable and gentle man who, demanding neither baseness nor servility from those around him, allowed the most complete freedom of speech'.[23] It helped that their views on education were similar. Both wanted free, compulsory education at primary level, improved secondary schooling and much more female education. To achieve this latter goal, Duruy hit upon the idea of creating public courses for girls aged fourteen to seventeen. He was excited by an idea he thought inexpensive and unobjectionable.

When it was launched in October 1867, the backlash was immediate. Even if young women could be taught advanced studies – something the Bishop of Orléans, who penned a vitriolic series of pamphlets against Duruy's innovation, seriously doubted – then they would be corrupted and ruined. Duruy wanted to create what the bishop called with disgust 'free thinkers', and that ended only one way, with the destruction of religion itself.[24] It soon became a culture war, which the pope fuelled, agreeing that this kind of education – a course on vegetable physiology in Chartres, one in Bordeaux on mineralogy, for example – was indeed a plot not only against Catholicism, but also against women. With the pope on board, the Catholic press in France became hysterical in its condemnation, emboldening those opposed to the courses to heckle and threaten students. Duruy remained in place, but in 1869 Louis-Napoléon sacrificed him to appease Catholic opinion, and much of what they both wanted to achieve remained undone.

With Prussia more powerful than ever, the main priority for Louis-Napoléon was army reform. 'The influence of a nation', he said in a speech opening the new legislative session in February 1867, 'depends on the number of men it can put under the arms.' The emperor was acutely aware that by that metric, Prussia was almost twice as powerful as France. Despite having a population nearly double that of its German rival, France could put only 420,000 men into combat compared to Prussia's 750,000. That did not even include the contribution of Prussia's German allies, nor did it factor in the sixty thousand or so French troops stationed in Algeria. If he had not wanted to believe it in 1866, Louis-Napoléon now understood that the rise of Prussia was an existential threat. The only way to counter it was through astute diplomacy, bringing other European nations into alliance with France, and transforming French conscription to put more men into the army.

Almost immediately after the Prussian victory over Austria, the emperor put in train a process which he hoped would result in an army that could call on a million men. The military establishment, however, was deeply opposed to change, arguing that what the French army lacked in quantity it made up for in quality. Besides, the army had won every major military engagement it had fought in since the beginning of the Second Empire – why change a winning system? It was not just the military who hated the idea. Republicans and liberals were opposed to it – arguing that a large standing army increased despotism and taxes – as were middle-class parents, who could buy their children out of serving. Peasants and the poorest in society also preferred the current system of conscription, which was drawn by lot and gave them an almost one in two chance of avoiding call-up.

'Do not forget', Louis-Napoléon warned the Corps législatif, 'that neighbouring states accept much heavier sacrifices . . . and their eyes are fixed on you to see whether by your decisions the influence of France should increase or diminish in the world.'[25] This attempt to shame the legislature failed. When the new recruitment law was voted on in January 1868, it had been watered down so much that it bore no resemblance to what the emperor envisaged. This was in striking contrast to Prussia, where military reforms had been pushed through unconstitutionally against the wishes of parliament. In France, after nearly a year and a half of debate, there was still no meaningful reserve and the nation would be massively outnumbered should war with Prussia break out.

Thwarted in his attempts to overhaul the army, with Rouher blocking his political reforms and traditional Catholics stopping changes to education, the emperor was no longer able to exert his will on the Empire, let alone Europe. One area where the regime remained a world leader, however, was in putting on a spectacular show.

———

The American writer Mark Twain was impressed with the Empire. In Paris during the Exposition universelle of 1867, he rushed from the world's fair to see Louis-Napoléon review his troops. Standing on a board spread over two barrels and hastily erected by an intrepid street entrepreneur, Twain watched on as the emperor came into view: a 'long-bodied, short-legged man', wrote the American, 'fiercely moustached, old, wrinkled, with eyes half closed, and such a deep, crafty, scheming expression about them!'

Watching him, Twain ruminated upon the extraordinary rise from obscure exile to absolute power. 'Surrounded by shouting thousands, by military pomp, by the splendors of his capital city, and companioned by kings and princes – this is the man who was sneered at and reviled,' he wrote. 'Who talks of the marvels of fiction?' asked Twain rhetorically. 'Who speaks of the wonders of romance? Who prates of the tame achievements of Aladdin and the Magii [*sic*] of Arabia?' For Twain, the emperor had increased 'the commercial prosperity of France in ten years to such a degree that figures can hardly compute it', he had rebuilt Paris, but 'above all things, he has taken the sole control of the empire of France into his hands and made it a tolerably free land'.[26]

This was a case of one master storyteller talking to another, for the tale Twain told was precisely the narrative that Louis-Napoléon spun. And within all its glorious, extravagant hubris, the Exposition universelle was the apotheosis of projecting Paris, France and the Empire as the greatest show on earth. The publicity for the event made this clear. The Paris Exposition, as it was known, was bigger, better and more expensive than anything previously. Before entering the specially constructed Palais du Champ-de-Mars, where the main exhibition was, visitors wandered in a park where a marvellous clash of architectural styles could be endured. There were replicas of Egyptian pyramids and, a somewhat unfortunate reminder of Mexico from the French point of view, Aztec ones, alongside a Tunisian palace, a Gothic cathedral and an extremely underwhelming English cottage, which, as many disappointed British noted, did not even look much like an English cottage.

The exhibition hall was an immense iron and glass oval with concentric circular corridors that acted as galleries. For those who were not lovers of art or exhibitions, it was the architectural equivalent of Dante's circles of hell – the outermost ring dedicated to food and drink, with everything in between from perfume to heavy machinery, before finally arriving at the innermost gallery of fine art. Though art was the centrepiece, the real focus was on technology, displaying the awesome confidence of Europe and the United States in material progress. Visitors could marvel at the wonders of reinforced concrete, electric lighthouses and the modern-day fad of elevators. There was even a mechanical swan that mimicked eating a fish.

Indeed, so great was the spectacle that the officially commissioned guide to Paris included an introduction by Louis-Napoléon's great enemy, Victor Hugo. The guide was billed as written by the greatest French writers of the age, and the regime could not have got away with that claim without including him, while, for all his hatred of the Empire, the global event of the decade was a stage that Hugo's ego required him to perform upon.

Of course, as far as he could get away with it, the introduction was subversive, but it was also a paean to Paris and to international co-operation. The 'universe', wrote Hugo, 'was tilting in the right direction', for 'the immense winds of the future blow peace' and 'there was nothing that could stand in the way of this hurricane of fraternity and joy'. It was heady stuff, capturing the optimistic mood that the Paris Exposition embodied – the sense of science, commerce and collaboration creating a new age of harmony. Trolling this sentiment magnificently, and standing in the way of Hugo's hurricane of joy, the main Prussian exhibit was a gargantuan steel cannon weighing fifteen thousand kilograms – so heavy that no railway wagon was strong enough to move it and one had to be specially built to transport it to Paris. 'These enormous shells', wrote Hugo somewhat optimistically, 'are no more effective against progress than bubbles of soap blown through a straw by the mouth of a child.'[27]

For all its pomp and grandeur, the opening was underwhelming and perhaps better captured the true state of France. On 1 April 1867, Louis-Napoléon and Eugénie arrived at the Palais du Champ-de-Mars to inaugurate the Exposition, but little was ready. The various international displays were in chaos, with packing boxes strewn on the floor. Undeterred, the imperial couple made a tour of the concentric galleries. When they reached the British section, more finished than most, they were greeted with loud hurrahs in English. Eugénie smiled at two sailors who were particularly vociferous in their cheers. 'Ah, Bill,' said one, turning to the other, 'she guv me such a look.'[28]

Once it got going, the Exposition was enormous fun. A series of international restaurants ringed the entrance to the Palais du Champ-de-Mars. Pink champagne and vodka could be enjoyed in the Russian restaurant, but the speciality was the finest tea from China. If nothing else comes of the Exposition, one British journalist wrote, it might introduce a taste for tea among Parisians and, he added hopefully, 'they might even learn how to prepare it'.[29]

It was generally agreed that the only place vying with the Russian restaurant was the American one. Much to the relief of many British and American travellers, here you could get steaks that were cooked alongside green corn, stewed oysters and succotash. As much as the food, though, it was the drinks that attracted visitors. Making an early bid to become a global leader in sugary beverages, the US restaurant did a fast trade in soda water with a spoonful of ice cream and then generously laced with strawberry, lemon or vanilla syrup. For those looking for something harder, there were cocktails, or 'eye openers', 'moustache twisters' and 'corpse revivers', as they were known.

You did not need to go to the Exposition to enjoy fine food: Paris was the culinary capital of the world. On 7 June 1867, Tsar Alexander II, his son and King William I of Prussia with Otto von Bismarck – all in Paris for the Exposition – gorged themselves at the famed Café Anglais. It took eight hours for them to get through the sixteen courses, which were paired with Roederer champagne and the finest wines known to humanity.

The tsar needed a drink. The day before, someone had tried to assassinate him. After attending a military review, Louis-Napoléon, Alexander II and his two sons were being driven back through the crowds in an open carriage. At 4.30 p.m., a young Pole emerged from among the people lining the streets. He had two pistols; one exploded on firing, but the other shot hit a horse, splattering the carriage with blood. Once they realised no one had been hurt, Louis-Napoléon, who was used to this kind of thing, brushed it off with his customary sangfroid. 'Sire,' he said to the tsar, 'we have been under fire together.'[30] The tsar, however, was understandably upset that his two sons were covered in the horse's blood.

One royal who did enjoy the trip was the Prince of Wales. His mother, Queen Victoria, had decidedly cooled in her view of Louis-Napoléon, putting him back in the disreputable category, not least because she felt that her son, Bertie, had been corrupted by Paris, where he hung out with actresses, ballerinas and courtesans. This was certainly the view of Émile Zola, who caricatured the British royal in a novel under the not-so-subtle name of the Prince of Scotland.

But it was not just royalty that enjoyed the industrial pleasure complex that was Paris. Two and a half million foreign visitors poured into the city, which over the last fifteen years had been transformed. Much of the construction work had finished, though the gloriously flamboyant and gaudy opera house was not yet complete. 'What is this style? It's not style at all. It's neither Greek, nor Louis XVI, not even Louis XV,' complained the Pooterish Eugénie when reviewing the plans of the obscure architect whose winning designs were being built. 'No!' retorted the architect. 'Those styles have had their day . . . This is the style of Napoléon III.'[31] Indeed it was, and scaffolding was removed from the now famous facade in the summer of 1867 so visitors could gawp at its opulent magnificence.

Tourists also marvelled at Paris's wide boulevards, dined in its famed restaurants, ogled luxuries in massive department stores and, taking their lead from the emperor, threw themselves into the debauched opportunities the city offered. Everything was for sale, including sex. There were licensed brothels and Paris was said to have thirty-four thousand prostitutes, with numerous names to describe their status, from the so-called *grandes hori-zontales*, high-class courtesans who received fortunes to be on the arm – and more – of the rich, through to *comédiennes*, *lorettes*, *grisettes* and *cocodettes*. Unsurprisingly, cases of syphilis in the city were said to match the number of sex workers.

That there were so many who relied on sex work for income was symptomatic of the abject poverty that existed in Paris. Haussmann's intricately symmetrical apartment buildings stretching like endless wallpaper down leafy boulevards, punctuated with uniform street furniture including cast-iron public urinals, replaced medieval shacks, but these were places only the wealthy could afford. Louis-Napoléon's vision to remodel Paris had, in part, been predicated on the idea that building his dream would provide employment. Yet living costs rose faster than wages, and workers were pushed out from the centre of Paris into ghettos that were every bit as insalubrious as where they had once lived, and where seething resentment grew about the luxury on display elsewhere.

But to outside observers the show was spectacular, as was the culmination of the Exposition, a prize-giving ceremony on 1 July 1867. Twenty thousand people were packed into the Palace of Industry. There were a few false starts: the crowd stood and then, with the awkward embarrassment of those who are forced to admit their mistake, half sat down again upon realising that the imperial couple had not yet entered. Finally, all eyes were on Louis-Napoléon and Eugénie, wearing full court dress and glittering diamond tiara, as they slowly walked up the steps onto the platform.

After everyone was in place, an orchestra performed a new work written by the Italian composer Gioachino Rossini, entitled 'Napoléon III and His Valiant People'. Those in the audience complained that it was a little quiet, except for the end, when musical subtlety gave way to the beating of drums, ringing of bells and shouts of '*Vive l'empereur!*' Cannons also marked time – or rather failed to; they were out of synch with the music, adding to the cacophony. 'Nothing but Rossini's name can prevent this musical abortion from passing into the Hades of music,' wrote one unimpressed audience member.[32]

Few heard the emperor's speech in such a vast hall, but it was punctuated with cheers. In its utopian view of universal prosperity and global peace, it was a far less verbose and shorter version of Hugo's introduction to the official guide. 'The Exposition of 1867 will mark, I hope, a new era of harmony and progress,' said Louis-Napoléon. Given his deep anxiety over Prussia, 'hope' was doing a lot of work here. After that, the event had all the tedium of a school prize-giving, albeit one of the largest and most expensive in history. The only moment of interest was when the emperor won a prize. He had entered a design for affordable workers' housing in one of the categories and, to nobody's surprise, came first.

'I believe', Louis-Napoléon said, closing his speech, 'in the definitive triumph of the great principles of morality and justice which . . . alone consolidate thrones, elevate peoples and ennoble humanity.' Only hours before speaking these words, he had received shocking news from Mexico, where Maximilian's throne was anything but consolidated.[33]

———

When Maximilian heard the news of his wife's breakdown, he decided, again, to abdicate. But again he was talked out of it, this time by his Mexican allies, who argued that with the hated French departing, the nation would unite behind Maximilian's Empire. This was not the view of an aide-de-camp sent by Louis-Napoléon in September 1866 to report back on the situation in Mexico. Maximilian's abdication was, Louis-Napoléon's man concluded, the most urgent necessity, 'no less for the interests of France than for those of Mexico'.[34]

Having done everything in his power to get Maximilian to go to Mexico when he prevaricated in 1864, Louis-Napoléon now desperately wanted him to abdicate and come back, which would at least save the embarrassment of a Habsburg falling into the hands of his republican enemies. When his aide failed to persuade Maximilian to renounce his throne, Louis-Napoléon nonetheless insisted that all French troops evacuate Mexico. On 5 February 1867, the tricolour was lowered from above the French headquarters in Mexico City. As Mexicans watched silently, and Maximilian peered out from behind a curtain in his palace, French troops marched out of the capital they had occupied for nearly four years. In their wake came those who supported them, refugees desperate to escape the wrath of Benito Juárez's advancing forces.

A week later, despite never having commanded an army before, Maximilian led his troops to Querétaro, a provincial city north-west of his capital. Here, he rendezvoused with his depleted forces. They were soon outnumbered, put under siege and, despite heroic if foolhardy resistance, defeated. On 15 May 1867, the Archduke Ferdinand Maximilian, born at the Habsburg Palace of Schönbrunn, surrendered his sword to a republican general, once a farm labourer from the harsh sierras of northern Mexico.

While imprisoned in a former convent, Maximilian spoke with a Prussian diplomat. There, he received news of the diplomatic stand-off between France and Prussia over Luxembourg. Maximilian asked whether war was likely. According to the information he had, replied the diplomat, it seemed that peace had been agreed. 'But the war has only been postponed,' answered Maximilian. Such was his hatred for Louis-Napoléon, he added that 'if I return alive to Europe I will ask your king for permission to take part in the war against the French'.[35] That soon became something of a moot point. The courts of Europe interceded on Maximilian's behalf. Unlikely to listen to the monarchs of Europe, Juárez also received appeals from the United States and famous republicans, including Giuseppe Garibaldi and Victor Hugo, to pardon the Mexican emperor, but at a hastily convened court martial, Maximilian was sentenced to execution.

On 19 June 1867, Maximilian walked through the dust on a hill overlooking Querétaro towards an uneven adobe wall. Turning to face his executioners, he spoke in clear, loud Spanish: 'I forgive everybody, I pray that everyone may also forgive me, and I wish that my blood, which is now to be shed, may be for the good of the country. Long live Mexico, long live independence.'[36] The shots rang out, Maximilian collapsed, and a Habsburg archduke died in the dirt of a provincial Mexican town.

Louis-Napoléon 'must be satisfied with his work', ran an article in the Mexican government newspaper. 'The victims of the murderer of 2 December are incessantly multiplying and the flag of France continues to be covered with filth and blood wherever it flies. The death of the archduke . . . must weigh heavily on the fraud who seeks to govern the world from the imperial throne of France.'[37]

———

The death of Maximilian, one of the most famous men in Europe and the Americas, sent shockwaves through these continents. This was especially the case in France, where the tightly controlled press had kept people in the dark as to just how catastrophic Louis-Napoléon's intervention in Mexico had become. The savage struggle there and its bloody denouement now made a mockery of the hifalutin rhetoric of the Paris Exposition. 'Why did this explosion of Shakespearean tragedy come to mix with the ideas, habits and morals of our century, fundamentally rationalist and positive?' wondered an editorial in an influential journal. 'Who would have thought that in our time invisible witches could still drag an honest Macbeth into the abyss under the guise of chivalrous seduction by saying: You will be king?'[38]

The regime's opponents, notably Thiers and Favre in the Corps légis-latif, had an answer to these questions: Louis-Napoléon. This was not an unreasonable conclusion, and was one the French artist Édouard Manet, shunned during the Second Empire, shared. In his magnificent painting *The Execution of Maximilian*, the man preparing Maximilian's *coup de grâce* had the conspicuous features and imperial facial hair of the French emperor. The implication was clear: Louis-Napoléon had blood on his hands. Indeed, the execution of a Habsburg archduke was one of the more cataclysmic failures of foreign policy in the nineteenth century, and French foreign policy was the sole preserve of the emperor. The Mexico debacle seriously undermined people's confidence in the emperor's ability to guide France in international affairs, especially as thousands of middle-class savers had invested in Mexican loans, now worthless. On the other hand, the spurious Jecker claims, which many believed were the real reason for France invading Mexico, had been paid back.

Louis-Napoléon thought his role in the death of the Austrian emperor's brother necessitated offering condolences in person. Franz Joseph thought that he would rather see anyone else than a man whom he had long loathed and now blamed for Maximilian's death; however, fear of Prussia meant Franz Joseph could not afford to alienate France.

That summer, the imperial train rolled through southern Germany on its way to Austria. It stopped at Augsburg, where Louis-Napoléon had been at school, but rising German nationalism meant that many saw the

French emperor as an enemy. When he and Eugénie arrived, there were a few friendly shouts, but these were soon drowned in hisses and yells and cries of 'Hurrah for Germany!'[39] Having braved this opprobrium, Louis-Napoléon showed Eugénie his old school. With evident amusement, he pointed out a windowsill in a classroom where he had graffitied his name and the date, 1823. In the school grounds, he broke a twig from a tree to take back with him as a souvenir.

Given that Louis-Napoléon was in no small part responsible for the death of Franz Joseph's brother, the meeting with the Austrian emperor went remarkably well. When they had met in 1859, Louis-Napoléon was at the height of his power. After the French defeated Franz Joseph in war, the two men hammered out a deal that would redraw the map of Italy. Within months, that deal had unravelled, and eight years later, with numerous foreign policy mistakes behind him, Louis-Napoléon was in no position to dictate anything. Nonetheless, it was a suitably spectacular occasion for two emperors: the hills round Salzburg were lit up at night, people spent much time debating which empress was more glamorous, Eugénie or Franz Joseph's wife Elisabeth, and the Austrian emperor even found himself talked into returning the visit in October. In diplomatic terms, however, Louis-Napoléon achieved nothing. Franz Joseph would not form an alliance with a man he considered entirely untrustworthy.

Austria was not the only power the emperor had permanently alienated. Louis-Napoléon thought, not for the first time, that he had finally rid himself of the problem of keeping French troops in Rome with an agreement that would see the pope keep his temporal power in return for French troops leaving. In September 1867, though, Garibaldi saw this as a chance to seize the eternal city and make it the nation's capital. With the slogan 'Rome or death!', he recruited a legion to seize it. Eugénie was reported to have said they could have death but never Rome. 'I feel the pulse of France twice a day,' said the emperor. 'I know her temperament and I will not abandon the pope.'[40] French troops were sent back. Alongside the pope's forces, the French massacred Garibaldi's men at the Battle of Mentana on 3 November 1867.

The French army had deployed a new weapon, the chassepot, a bolt-action breech-loading rifle designed to counter a Prussian one that had been so devastating against the Austrians. To reassure the French public that the army was a match for Prussia, an account from the battle was published in the government newspaper. Some six hundred of the enemy were dead, more wounded. 'Our chassepot rifles worked wonders,' wrote the French general, an unfortunate phrase which, when picked up in Italy, created an even more furious backlash against Louis-Napoléon among all but the most piously Catholic.[41]

———

It played badly among republicans in France, too, where opposition was steadily increasing. Whether it was liberal reforms or foreign policy, Louis-Napoléon seemed trapped by his own regime. Not only was he unable to push through what he wanted, but also men like Rouher seized the initiative to pursue their own agenda. Defending the Empire's policy in Italy in the Corps législatif on 5 December 1867, Rouher painted it as a clash between order and revolutionary chaos. 'Well, we declare, in the name of the French government, Italy will not seize Rome! Never . . . Never will France support this violence against its honour and against Catholicism.' Chants of 'Never! Never!' echoed from the majority in the chamber.[42]

Louis-Napoléon was less enraptured. After congratulating Rouher on the speech in a cabinet meeting, he said in a soft voice, 'In politics you should never say never.'[43] Silence followed a reprimand which by the emperor's standards was severe. Yet regardless of his displeasure, Rouher's unequivocal public statement further entrenched Louis-Napoléon's position as the last obstacle to Italian unification. Led by Rouher, Bonapartists who had rallied to the president and then the emperor as a man of order decided they needed to save Louis-Napoléon from himself. They formed a vocal reactionary bloc in the Corps législatif opposed to all reform, especially a freer press. This had been a key part of the liberal project announced in January 1867, but with Rouher conducting the Bonapartist majority, discussion of the legislation had been postponed.

When it finally came up for debate in January 1868, it became clear that without Rouher's support the bill would not pass. Frantic discussions followed. Persigny, always helpful in a crisis, suggested a *coup d'état*. Louis-Napoléon changed his mind several times, but decided he could not go back on his reforms. Refusing to carry them out, Rouher resigned, again. Louis-Napoléon said sadly to his minister, 'So, you want to abandon me as well.'[44] Rouher, devoted to the Empire and the emperor, was shamed into backing the law. With Rouher eloquently defending something he hated, the law passed and came into force in May 1868. The new law was not intended to unleash an era of free, rambunctious discussion in the press and left plenty of restrictions in place, but just as ministers had warned, it emboldened opposition journalists.

A small magazine with a striking red cover and the legend *La Lanterne* emblazoned in spidery black font caused a sensation. Written by Henri Rochefort, an aristocrat turned radical who had written vaudevilles before becoming a journalist, the provocative magazine satirised the Empire. Rochefort wanted the government to know that the 'lantern may serve both to lighten the way of honest men and to hang wrongdoers'.[45]

'I have been accused', ran an article in the first edition, 'of being an enemy of the state.' Far from it, Rochefort insisted: 'I am deeply Bonapartist . . . but permit me to choose my hero . . . I prefer Napoléon II.' Readers, of course, knew that the son of Napoléon had never reigned. 'No one will deny that he occupied the throne, since his successor is called Napoléon III.' But 'what a reign my friends, what a reign, no taxes, no useless wars . . . none of these distant expeditions', no expensive civil lists or highly paid ministers. 'Oh yes, Napoléon II, I love him . . . Who will deny now that I am not a sincere Bonapartist?'[46] It was knockabout stuff, ridiculing the Empire with what felt like the sharp eye of an insider. It was so good it was read as much in the streets as in the corridors of power – even, it was said, by Louis-Napoléon, though he did not find the attacks on his mother and the empress, which had more than a hint of misogyny about them, or questions about his paternity funny or original.

At times, the Empire satirised itself. In June 1868, it was announced in the government press that Louis-Napoléon had lost his best friend. Readers were anxious to discover who had died. Persigny? Conneau? Fleury? It was, in fact, his dog, the unfortunately named Nero. Louis-Napoléon loved Nero. It was, therefore, a sad day when he was buried in the Tuileries garden, an event that filled many pages in *La Lanterne*, with Rochefort suggesting that, in a last desperate act, a plebiscite might be organised to save the dog.

It was not long before the authorities cracked down, first by banning the sale of the magazine at kiosks, which only increased its distribution by subscription, said to have reached ninety thousand (the leading Bonapartist paper had only fifteen thousand subscribers). After that, the printer was shut down and Rochefort was prosecuted. He fled to Brussels, where he continued to write *La Lanterne* and from where, with Victor Hugo's backing, the magazine was smuggled into France.

Louis-Napoléon's other liberal initiatives similarly backfired. Some restrictions on public meetings were lifted. This led, unsurprisingly, to an increase in the number of public meetings criticising the regime and, worse, advocating revolutionary ideas. Taking their cue from the more radical position adopted at the International Workingmen's Association meeting in Lausanne in 1867 where Karl Marx was in attendance, radical French workers now agitated not only for an improvement in material conditions, but also for political change.

In this, Louis-Napoléon further helped them, for as part of his reforming agenda he had legalised strikes. This led, unsurprisingly, to an increase in their number, particularly in the northern coal fields, where pay cuts had immiserated miners, throwing them and their families into awful, squalid poverty. From these desolate wastelands, the economic miracle of the Second Empire, with its fast and loose finance, its corruption, its sumptuous, extravagant court and public spectacles, no longer seemed – if it ever had – the solution to France's problems. Bankruptcies, ruined workshops, starving families and often, despite the law, the violent repression of strikers all contributed to rising levels of resentment. The Empire was tottering, after nearly two decades in power. Many in France and abroad thought that the fate seemingly reserved for all French governments was fast approaching: revolution.

19

THE LIBERAL EMPIRE

In November 1868, it was not the emperor's dead dog Nero causing a sensation, but a long-dead person, namely an obscure, forgotten politician, Jean-Baptiste Baudin, who had died in December 1851 on the barricades opposing Louis-Napoléon's *coup d'état*. Now, Baudin's grave in Montmartre cemetery became a rallying point for the increasing number of Parisians opposed to the regime. They organised through left-wing newspapers to put up a statue to Baudin. It was not only the subscription that annoyed Louis-Napoléon, but also the attacks against his *coup d'état* of 2 December – both, he made clear to his ministers, must stop. Always highly sensitive to the press, the emperor insisted on pursuing the editors and journalists behind the campaign in court.

Instead of stopping the attacks, it provided the perfect platform for them. An ambitious thirty-one-year-old lawyer, Léon Gambetta, turned the trial on its head and accused the emperor. 'On 2 December men gathered around a pretender . . . who had neither talent, nor honour, nor rank.' These men, Gambetta said, were 'the eternal rejects of regular societies . . . a pile of men lost in debt and crime'. Men like these, he argued, in a speech that could have been written by Victor Hugo, had been undermining institutions for centuries, crushing what was right under 'the boot of a soldier'.[1] Gambetta's eloquence did not save those on trial. It did, however, win in the court of public opinion.

Momentum and youth were with the opposition. Another up-and-coming critic of the regime, the journalist Jules Ferry, who had made a name for himself with a sensational pamphlet attacking the regime's electoral practices in 1863, published another bestseller, *Haussmann's Fantastic Accounts*. It was a collection of articles in which he railed against Georges-Eugène Haussmann's sharp financial practices and accused the all-powerful prefect of the Seine of bankrupting Paris. One accusation was true: the city had borrowed extraordinary sums of money without any democratic oversight. Another book, a pro-republican account of the *coup d'état* that eviscerated the Bonapartist argument and lauded the men who, like Baudin, had fought against it in 1851, had come out in September 1868 and quickly ran through three editions.

From the origins of the Empire to its leaders, everything was under attack, and therefore the big upcoming test was elections held in May and June 1869. Yet against the barrage of criticism Louis-Napoléon and his government had little to offer. There was humiliation abroad; limited liberal reforms, weakly pursued, interspersed with moments of repression, such as the prosecutions against Rochefort or the Baudin subscribers, were merely politics as usual; support was oozing away.

Someone who might have injected drama into the regime, Persigny, had been exiled from power. As was often the case, it was his own doing. He had always hated the empress, a hatred that turned into loathing the more she became involved in politics, attending cabinet meetings and advising her husband. Ruminating on the Empire's mistakes, he found one constant at the centre of them: Eugénie. Persigny had done his best to explain to Louis-Napoléon that the root cause of the nation's problems was his wife, but for reasons that he could not understand, the emperor did not listen. There was nothing for it, Persigny reasoned: he would have to put his thoughts in a memorandum – crucially, for the emperor's eyes only.

Suffering from a cold and rheumatism, Louis-Napoléon was in bed with his wife looking after him when he received the letter. 'I'm sure this is more recrimination from Persigny! How wearisome he is!' said the emperor. 'Look,' he continued, 'read me this letter: I haven't the strength today.' As Eugénie herself said, it was not so much a letter as 'a long diatribe against myself, against my presence at the Council of Ministers, against the detestable ideas which I personified in the government, and which were leading the Empire to its ruin'. She did not take it well. 'Calm yourself!' said her husband. 'This new foolishness of Persigny is of no importance. It is my opinion that your place is at the Council of Ministers, and you will not cease to sit there. It is I who am master.'[2] Persigny never appeared at court again, which was a loss, for though he was volatile, angry and often wrong, Persigny was nonetheless a brilliant propagandist for the Empire who understood that it must rejuvenate itself to survive.

But Louis-Napoléon, who turned sixty-one in 1869, went into the elections with listless fatality, suffering from ill health, the political situation weighing heavily on his mind. All that he asked, he wrote to Eugénie at a particularly low moment, was that he retained the strength to 'die with honour and not in my bed'.[3] In public, he was not much more inspiring. 'Soon the nation', he declared wearily in a speech opening the last legislative session before the vote, 'will sanction the policy we have followed; it will proclaim once again . . . that it does not want revolutions, but that it wants to base the destiny of France on the intimate alliance of power and freedom.'[4]

———

In the weeks leading up to the May elections, the thousands marching while singing the 'Marseillaise' in the streets of Paris suggested that people were not as averse to revolutions as the emperor thought. 'Long live *La Lanterne*! Long live Rochefort! Long live the Republic!' – these were the shouts heard everywhere people congregated.[5] Insults and, more painfully, stones were hurled at the police, who, hopelessly outnumbered, were engaged in a futile attempt to contain the crowds. Alongside the name of Henri Rochefort, the now renowned writer of *La Lanterne* and a candidate in the elections, there were shouts for the old revolutionaries of 1848. France had not seen politics as heated, violent and passionate since the days of the Second Republic.

France, and Paris especially, had election fever. Instead of peering through the windows of the shops in the Palais Royal, people were buried deep in their newspapers trying to make sense of the new political world. It was a confusing one. In Paris, there were nine seats for the Corps législatif and 333 candidates. Much to the delight of the government, the left had, predictably, split, with socialists attacking moderates even more viciously than they did Bonapartists (not only were these internecine struggles more fun, but the moderate left could not lock up radicals, which made it safer than going after the government). Every day when newspapers arrived at kiosks, people surged towards them, and the papers soon sold out. The walls of Paris were decorated with brightly coloured election posters, and everyone from workers to women with hatboxes stopped to read them.

Despite the usual tricks and chicanery, this time the result was close. The government scraped 4.4 million votes, the opposition 3.3 million. Though there was some comfort in the fact that the opposition was divided, for a regime that claimed to represent the will of the people, it was an appalling result – 40 per cent of voters had rejected the Empire.

Though the regime remained popular in the countryside, Paris, where abject poverty lived alongside outrageous affluence, had especially turned against the government. From 7 June there were riots every evening. Amid the singing of the 'Marseillaise' and shouts of 'Long live Rochefort!' – who lost in the election to the republican Jules Favre – shops were broken into, wine was plundered, street lighting was smashed and police were attacked. In one cafe, an enterprising protester collected newspapers that backed the government and created a bonfire around which people danced and chanted political slogans. There were running battles between police and students. It was not just Paris where there was trouble. There were serious disturbances in Nantes, Bordeaux and Saint-Étienne. Industrial action continued, and at one strike soldiers opened fire on workers, killing eleven men. Foreign journalists thought they had seen this performance before: the overture to revolution.

Then, on 11 June, Louis-Napoléon went for a drive through the centre of Paris to reassure people. He was well received and pro-government newspapers put the end of the disturbances down to the emperor's courage; others thought that it might have had more to do with the vast numbers of infantry and cavalry that had been deployed to reinforce the police. Either way, an uneasy calm returned to the streets of the capital, though strikes, often turning violent, remained endemic throughout much of the country.

Bold political action was required. With his typical elan, the out-of-favour Persigny did what he could. No liberal, he interpreted the election results for what they were – a defeat of the authoritarian Empire he had done so much to create. 'The emperor', he wrote, 'only has to continue on the liberal path . . . by calling to him a whole new generation that is young, strong, intelligent and above all courageous and determined. As for the men of 2 December, like me . . . our role is over.'[6]

Louis-Napoléon thought Persigny's letter unhelpful, but the disastrous election results had demonstrated to him that hanging on was not enough. He agreed the Empire urgently needed revitalisation, an injection of youth and dynamism. The new Corps législatif was not due to meet until November, but a newly energised Louis-Napoléon convoked an extraordinary session where his intentions would be set out publicly. Beforehand, he held a cabinet meeting and asked for Rouher's resignation. The so-called vice-emperor and conservative bulwark had to go, though his departure was sweetened with a seat in the Senate.

At the meeting, Louis-Napoléon outlined reforms that went further than anything previously. Though he hated what he called 'parliamentarianism', which he associated with the chaos of the Second Republic, the changes, if enacted, would create a liberal Empire where the assemblies would have real power, as would ministers. For Rouher's final service, he made him read out reforms Rouher hated on a stiflingly hot summer's day, 12 July 1869, to deputies as they wiped sweat from their brows during an emergency session of the Corps législatif.

Political reforms did not solve the problems of France overnight, but the emperor realised that the elections had been a victory for the moderate centre ground, and he was willing to work with these politicians. Only twenty-five irreconcilable republicans had been elected, and eight diehard reactionary Bonapartists. The rest were broadly liberal and willing to support the emperor as long as he rejected authoritarianism. And not only was the liberal programme significant this time; unlike in 1867, Rouher's downfall also showed that it would be implemented.

But just as the task of transforming the regime began, in August the emperor suffered from the worst flare-up yet of his bladder stones. He was in torturous pain for weeks, rarely able to sleep. He could preside over meetings for only a few minutes, and soon he was too sick to do even that. By September, he was writhing and convulsing and screaming with pain. All the doctors could do was give him opium. This relieved the suffering, but he spent most of his days in a stupor, falling asleep in his chair and seeming impossibly old to worried friends. It also made him delirious. Several times he asked for news of Marshal Saint-Arnaud, dead for fifteen years. It was so serious that he thought he might die, and in his lucid moments he drew up plans for a regency to govern until his son came of age.

Regardless of secrecy, word soon got out that the emperor was ill, though the full extent was never revealed. Despite some appearances in public, heroic ones given the circumstances – Eugénie insisted that he be wheeled into a cabinet meeting on 7 September, but barely had he arrived when he fainted and had to be wheeled out – rumours that he was dying undermined political confidence at this most crucial of times, and the financial markets went down with each piece of gossip about his health. He was forced to miss other events he would have enjoyed, including celebrations at Ajaccio for the hundredth anniversary of the birth of his uncle. There were few things in this world that Louis-Napoléon would have enjoyed more than that, but he was also forced to miss something even more exciting: the opening of a canal.

———

Louis-Napoléon loved canals. In 1846, he had even published a pamphlet arguing for one to be built through Nicaragua. In his famous 'Empire means peace' speech at Bordeaux in 1852, canals featured prominently among the conquests he wanted to make. But even if you did not share this enthusiasm for human-made waterways, the opening planned for October 1869 was exciting, for it inaugurated the largest, most important one yet dug: the Suez Canal.

That it had been brought into existence was down to Louis-Napoléon. In many ways, it was the epitome of the Second Empire: a grand, global vision – many said a delusion – that required outrageously speculative finance and an international network of dubious actors to get it off the ground. Then there was local politics in Egypt to contend with, not to mention crashing through some extremely sensitive geopolitical issues, ranging from Ottoman sensibilities over Egypt to British hostility to a scheme seen as a threat to India.

'It shall not be made, it cannot be made, it will not be made,' thundered Palmerston when asked about the canal.[7] 'Totally impossible to be carried out,' was Disraeli's verdict.[8] 'The British Government can in no case', opined another British prime minister and foreign secretary, Lord John

Russell, 'promote or favour the Suez canal, which they would wish to see abandoned.'[9] Those were the views of the greatest British statesmen of the age, but if Louis-Napoléon had listened to them when he knew them in London, he would never have become emperor. And if he had listened to them now, the Suez Canal would never have been built.

Under the leadership of a French diplomat, the Compagnie universelle du canal maritime de Suez had been set up in 1858. Work began the next year, but the extent of the opposition was as much a hindrance as enormous technical challenges. Three times Louis-Napoléon saved the scheme. First, when a new ruler in Egypt came to power and threatened, under British pressure, to revoke permission for construction. Second, when he strongarmed the Ottoman sultan, who had nominal control of Egypt, to back the project. Third, in 1868, when he supported a loan to bail out the French company, which was about to go bankrupt.

Given the emperor's personal involvement, the opening ceremony was an occasion to show that Louis-Napoléon could still bend the world to his vision. It would be a glorious celebration of French ingenuity, perseverance and capital, demonstrating that France was a global superpower whatever the pretensions of Prussia to European hegemony. But Louis-Napoléon was too ill to travel. He sent Eugénie instead, who took one hundred dresses inside two hundred packed Louis Vuitton trunks and her pet turtle, La Reine, with her.

The empress went by way of Constantinople, where she met the sultan. He took her to see his harem in a palace where, in a dark corridor, they met his mother, 'a great fat woman, rolling as she walked, wearing loose baggy trousers'. Not recognising the empress, the mother was furious to see a European woman on the arm of her son. She punched Eugénie in the stomach, knocking her back. A heated exchange in Turkish between mother and son followed, before the sultan explained to Eugénie what had happened. They laughed about it. At least, that is how Eugénie, who loved a good story, told it to Queen Victoria.[10]

Then she sailed to Egypt, where she took a cruise up the Nile. She was worried about the situation in Paris, but despite her antipathy to liberal reform, she urged her husband to stay the course now that he had embarked upon it. Even after all his affairs, there remained a tender affection and, of course, she loved her son, whose imperial future depended on the Empire's survival. As she sailed down the Nile, she was in philosophical mood. 'My heart is near you both; and if, on peaceful days, my truant mind loves to wander off into space, it is with the two of you I want to be when trouble and anxiety near.'[11]

At Port Said on 16 November, dressed in a low-cut lavender dress with dazzling white trimming and a hat with a large black feather, Eugénie stood on a platform and chatted with the Austrian Emperor Franz Joseph as she waited for the ceremony inaugurating the canal to begin. Surrounded by sand and nearby ramshackle wooden huts – not unlike a large Aldershot though with a little more bustle, was the view of a British traveller – the simplicity of the newly constructed town made a sharp contrast to the masts of ships from European navies that dominated the horizon. Taking her hat off respectfully, she listened to a Muslim prayer, before a Catholic service began. Then she walked through the sandy docks to board the imperial yacht.

After a volcanic sunset, the fireworks and illuminations began. The stillness of the water turned it into a perfect mirror, brilliantly reflecting back a kaleidoscope of colours from the explosions in the sky. Because of the role of the French in constructing the canal, the honour of leading the procession of European ships and their royals fell to the imperial yacht. With Eugénie on deck, at 8.30 a.m. the next day it left Port Said and entered the canal. The vessels and royals of other European states, among them Franz Joseph and the Crown Prince of Prussia, who might lay claim to European suzerainty, sailed symbolically behind the only nation that could claim to be powerful both on the European continent and across the globe.

At Ismailia, halfway along the canal, the flotilla stopped. Here, on the fringes of the Sahara desert, where the only break in the endless stretch of sand was the new waterway, that most European of events had been organised: a ball. The already crowded town was further swelled by local tribes who came from far and wide so as not to miss the absurd sight of European men and women finding surreptitious corners to squeeze into extravagant ball gowns and evening dress. There were six thousand guests and many more travellers, transforming a town that had been founded only six years ago into the place to be for high, and low, society. Many piled into the party uninvited: in one of the food tents a British MP, a French colonel and a Portuguese nobleman shared a table with coatless canal workers.

The inauguration of the canal was the outward manifestation of the triumph of French leadership in the region. Egypt had long been an area of French interest. Now French engineers overcame the technical challenges many thought impossible to build the canal (it was not French people who built the canal: tens of thousands of locals were employed under appalling conditions and thousands died). French capital largely financed the project and French shareholders now predominantly owned the canal. This nexus of technology, investment and trade, all promoted under the imperial protection of the emperor, drew Egypt into France's informal influence, binding the region much more closely than Napoléon Bonaparte's disastrous expedition of conquest some seventy years earlier.

After sailing on to Suez, the imperial yacht retraced its route before bringing Eugénie back to France, though not her pet turtle, which had wandered off during the opening ceremony and made a new life for itself in Egypt. In Paris, though his health was improved, Louis-Napoléon was desperately worried about the political situation. 'The winter', he wrote to his wife, 'will not pass without gunfire.'[12]

Back in the capital, there was much anticipation before the new legislative session opened on 29 November 1869. Political observers watched anxiously to see whether Louis-Napoléon would make good on his promised overhaul of the Empire, and whom he would appoint to his cabinet. Most were willing to give him the benefit of the doubt and see what emerged. There was a problem remaining, though, namely Henri Rochefort. In the earlier elections, he had been defeated by another famous opponent of the regime, Jules Favre. For supporters of the government, this had been a rare bright spot as a deliciously bitter campaign – Rochefort conducting his from exile in Belgium – developed between two eloquent men who found something they hated more than the Empire: each other.

Rochefort, however, stood in a November by-election in Paris. This time, he decided to campaign in person. As there was an arrest warrant against him, he looked forward to the sensation that his detention would cause when he returned. But Louis-Napoléon enjoyed a pardon, especially one that embarrassed his opponents, and ordered Rochefort's release when he was picked up on the border. Tall, angular, rakishly thin, with pronounced cheekbones and deliberately dishevelled, Rochefort was the poster boy of the radical left in Paris, as chants of his name during riots had shown. Receiving more than eighteen thousand votes to the two thousand of the official candidate, Rochefort was elected to the Corps législatif, much to the annoyance of the emperor.

'It is not easy to establish in France', declared a world-weary Louis-Napoléon when opening the legislative session, 'regular and peaceful enjoyment of liberty.' Though there had been, he admitted, disturbances recently, the country was returning to the right path. 'France wants liberty, but with order,' he continued with more passion, emphasising every word. 'I will take care of order. Help me, gentlemen, to save liberty.'[13] This was the kind of pithy aphorism Louis-Napoléon excelled at; it was also excellent politics. Though the substance of the message was what he had been saying for forty years, that Bonapartism was a middle way between revolution and reaction, the accent this time was on liberty. It was what the deputies, and the country, wanted to hear. At the end of the speech there were rapturous cheers.

Then the names of the deputies were read out. Rochefort was not present, and after his name there was an awkward silence. Someone started laughing, and soon the chamber was in hysterics; Louis-Napoléon could not help joining in. The outburst was reported in the press, and it turned out that while happy to ridicule others, the satirist did not like being laughed at himself. 'If I am ridiculous,' he said, 'I shall never equal in that way the gentleman who walked on the sands of Boulogne with an eagle on his shoulder and a bit of fat in his hands.'[14] This was a repetition of the much-loved, though sadly untrue, rumour that Louis-Napoléon had trained an eagle to eat out of his hand in preparation for his failed 1840 *coup d'état*. Referring to something that had happened nearly thirty years ago was not much of a comeback from Rochefort. However ridiculous the republican left thought Louis-Napoléon, he had, once again, outmanoeuvred them politically. Nothing showed this more than his co-option of one of their number to help him found the liberal Empire.

On 27 December, Émile Ollivier received a letter from the emperor. It asked him to form a cabinet to implement in 'letter and spirit' Louis-Napoléon's liberal reforms.[15] This phrase was important for Ollivier, a recognition that these were not the half-hearted, tepid changes that Rouher had deliberately mishandled in 1867, but a transformation of the Empire. In fact, Louis-Napoléon had already sounded out Ollivier, inviting him to secret discussions at Compiègne. Having lost none of his love for conspiracy, the emperor asked Ollivier to come at night and in disguise so that the meeting would not end up in the papers. Glasses removed and face obscured with a large scarf, Ollivier caught the evening train from the Gare du Nord. On arriving, he was ushered into a carriage waiting in the shadows and driven into the chateau via the back way.

In the emperor's study, over tea – Ollivier serving the tea, Louis-Napoléon taking care of the sugar – they spoke long into the night. They covered everything: the unrest in Paris; what to do about Prussia; Rouher, and his mistakes; Plon-Plon, and his many more mistakes. Finally, the emperor came to the point: 'And you, have you decided to give me your support?'[16] Ollivier said he had, though he would not enter into a ministry with certain personnel. Louis-Napoléon replied that it would take time to reshuffle the cabinet. By the end of December, that time had come and Louis-Napoléon assured Ollivier his confidence in him was absolute. As well as his confidence, the emperor gave more power to Ollivier, a former republican, than any politician had wielded in France since Odilon Barrot, when Louis-Napoléon had asked him to form his first ministry as president after his election in December 1848. Though the emperor reserved the right to appoint the minister of war and the minister of the navy, the rest were Ollivier's picks. The minister for foreign affairs, for example, was a former representative of the people in the Assembly under the Second Republic who had been briefly locked up for his opposition to the 2 December *coup d'état*.

Times had changed. And nothing showed this more than the dismissal of Haussmann as prefect of the Seine. Louis-Napoléon wanted to keep him. Ollivier insisted that this symbol of the old authoritarian order be removed. The emperor, therefore, reluctantly asked for Haussmann's resignation, but the prefect of the Seine did not want to make it easy and refused, forcing Louis-Napoléon to sack a man with whom he had worked closely for nearly seventeen years and who had helped transform Paris into one of the most elegant, modern and magnificent cities in the world.

'We are honest men,' the new foreign minister told the Senate on 7 January 1870. 'What we have said, we will do.'[17] If the language was slightly unfortunate, implying, as it did, that those who came before were not honest men, the phrase fit the new ministry, especially Ollivier. As befitted the son of an austere republican, he lived a simple life. With a sharp eye for his image, he played this up for the newspapers, inviting journalists to his home to give pen portraits for readers. Unlike many of those close to Louis-Napoléon in the past, the only disorder in Ollivier's home life was the clutter on his desk, which was strewn with books and papers. Readers were told that he received friends only at breakfast, went to bed early and rose at 6 a.m. On top of that, he drank just water, never smoked and seldom went to the theatre, and then only to listen to music. It was outrageously bourgeois, and dull – an at home with Persigny or Morny would have been a much more entertaining piece. But after the excesses of the Empire, the simplicity of Ollivier caught the public mood. The simplicity, though, was not to everyone's taste. In the end, political considerations forced Ollivier to host dinner parties. After one, Plon-Plon, whose radical politics sat uneasily alongside a rapacious appetite and love of all things debauched, took the arm of another guest in the street. 'Come, come with me,' he urged 'and we'll re-dine.' But, replied the bewildered man, 'have we not done pretty well already?' 'No, no; we have merely dined to please Ollivier. Come with me and we'll dine again to please ourselves.'[18]

With the exception of the far left and reactionary right, the press was delighted at the liberal Empire – as was Louis-Napoléon; Ollivier, he believed, was the tenor that had been lacking in the orchestra. Formerly implacable opponents came out in support of Louis-Napoléon, some even accepting government positions. If anything, the British press was more enthusiastic than its French counterpart. 'Probably nothing', wrote *The Times*'s Paris correspondent, 'that has occurred in France since the election of Louis Napoleon as President of the Republic has produced so good an effect.' Two days later, an editorial championed the Ollivier ministry and argued that if voters had not turned to the radical republican left during the uncertain last few years, 'are they likely to be more easily seduced now, when, under the Ministry of such men as M. Ollivier and his colleagues . . . the Empire is not unlikely to be hailed as "the best of Republics"?'[19]

For a man who had been the sole arbiter of French politics since his *coup d'état* in 1851, Louis-Napoléon found letting go of power easy. 'Why not try it?' he said to a friend. 'If it succeeds, people can only be grateful to me. If it fails, I will have proved my good faith by not rejecting it in advance.'[20] In the days after Ollivier's ministry was announced, Louis-Napoléon had the air of a man who had had a heavy burden lifted from him.

Apart from bowing to collective ministerial decisions, and even allowing ministers to meet without him, Louis-Napoléon agreed that Eugénie should no longer attend cabinet discussions. The opposition – and Persigny – had long attacked the empress's political role, painting her as a reactionary villain. With rising hysteria, Rochefort had been especially vocal in caricaturing her as an enemy of the people. Eugénie, as she always did, went along with her husband's decisions once made. But she was not happy. Ollivier's asceticism was far removed from her world of glamour and she had little time for the man of the moment. Ollivier's young wife, Marie-Thérèse Gravier, returned Eugénie's disdain. She refused to attend the empress's soirées and found court women haughty, the luxury decadent. When she had to go to state occasions with her husband, she studiously rejected the fashion for plunging necklines and bare shoulders. A Second Empire woman she was not.

Sidelining the empress was a popular move, and in the first week of January anything seemed possible. In return for liberalisation, Louis-Napoléon demanded social reforms and was sketching out a co-operative plan for mining which would see workers share profits with owners. Ollivier envisaged a permanent council of workers, employers and experts to arbitrate on industrial unrest and end strikes peacefully. Popular, dynamic, brimming with ideas, the Empire was back. Only an extraordinarily stupid mistake could use up this goodwill. Unfortunately, Louis-Napoléon had an extraordinarily stupid family.

———

Subjecting the volatile soap opera that was the extended Bonaparte family to a freer, more riotous press was not so much playing with fire as giving matches to an arsonist and leaving them next to a highly combustible building. Even so, few thought that the inferno would be quite so explosive as it turned out to be. Pierre Bonaparte, the third son of Lucien Bonaparte, liked a fight. While resisting arrest in 1836, he had killed one of the guards. He was sentenced to death, but this was commuted to exile and he went to New York, where his cousin, Louis-Napoléon, also happened to be. In the New World, Pierre found fame as a bar brawler and alleged dog murderer, before returning to Europe and living on a farm in Belgium deep in the Ardennes forest. Riding the wave of popular Bonapartism after the 1848 Revolution, he was elected as representative for Corsica. His politics were radical republican; his way of doing politics, New York bar style.

The restoration of the Empire had required an elevation of the Bonapartes. Jérôme and Plon-Plon were the best around, a shocking indictment of the shallowness of the pool. Pierre was beyond the pale. He was given no position, was not invited to court and, in return for the huge sum of a hundred thousand francs, Louis-Napoléon hoped he would never hear from him again. That was not the case. Pierre demanded money and a seat in the Corps législatif, which Louis-Napoléon refused.

That was irritating, but so were most of Louis-Napoléon's relatives. It was what Pierre did at the start of the liberal Empire that was the problem. He threw himself into a quarrel between republican and conservative newspapers that had been trading insults over a very Second Empire debate: the merits, or otherwise, of Napoléon Bonaparte. Wading into the controversy, Pierre wrote a letter to a conservative newspaper in December 1869 criticising the editors of the republican one. Elegant exegesis on the life of Napoléon this was not. He called the republican editors 'cowardly Judases, traitors to their country, whose own relatives in earlier days would have put them in bags and tossed them into the sea'. In response, the republican newspaper published an article saying that Pierre, who had been a radical in 1848, had betrayed his principles, calling him a liar. Naturally, this meant one thing to Pierre: a duel. For many men, one duel would have been enough. Not for Pierre.

Rochefort had founded a newspaper, *La Marseillaise*, a platform with which to continue his assault on the Empire. Always with an eye for publicity and scandal, he piled in on Pierre. 'In the Bonaparte family there are some strange individuals whose wild ambitions cannot be satisfied . . . Let us rank Pierre Napoléon Bonaparte in this category of lame unfortunates.'[21]

'I ask', Pierre wrote to Rochefort, 'if your pen is backed up by your chest.' If it was, 'I live simply at no. 59, rue d'Auteuil, and promise you, if you call upon me, that you won't be told that I am out.'[22] That was duel number two.

At this point things got confusing. Pierre was not a man to have a meticulously organised filing system to keep track of his duels. On the day he challenged Rochefort, 10 January 1870, the seconds from the first duel arrived at his house. Suffering from a cold, he read their calling cards and put on a jacket, in the pocket of which he, of course, had a revolver. Then he met the men who had come to his house.

It was understandable that Pierre became muddled. The two men at his house were journalists from the *Marseillaise* who had come to arrange the first duel, not Rochefort's representatives. This nuance was lost on Pierre. He suspected a trick. 'I am going to fight with Rochefort,' he shouted in bewilderment after reading their letter, 'not with one of his hacks!'[23] Insulted, one of the journalists, Victor Noir, struck him across the face. Pierre stumbled back, drew his revolver and fired, hitting Noir in the chest. Noir staggered out of the house. The other journalist drew his own pistol and aimed at Pierre. The gun misfired. Pierre shot back, and missed. The journalist fled into the street, where he found Noir collapsed on the pavement, groaning, in a pool of blood. Soon he bled to death. Pierre thought he had done nothing wrong.

When Louis-Napoléon was informed, however, that his cousin had killed a man who worked for a radical newspaper, he knew there would be a political storm. Returning from a hunting party, he was met at the station by his aides. The news was such a blow, they had to help him into his carriage. When Ollivier saw him that afternoon in the Tuileries, he had tears in his eyes.

His anxiety proved correct: the literary battle between Rochefort and the Empire had become a violently personal one. And Rochefort was determined to make the violence revolutionary. 'I have been so weak as to believe', wrote the journalist, 'that a Bonaparte could be something other than a murderer.'

Today we mourn the loss of our friend Victor Noir, assassinated by the bandit Pierre-Napoléon Bonaparte. For eighteen years, France has been in the bloody hands of these cut-throats, who, not content with shooting down republicans in the streets, entice them into iniquitous snares in their homes and murder them. People of France, have we not had enough?[24]

Printed in large type, two and a half pages of the newspaper were dedicated to the Pierre Bonaparte affair. Kiosks were mobbed for copies of *La Marseillaise*, with enterprising individuals buying several and selling them for six times the price. Everyone was talking about the murder, not least because on the same day the paper hit the streets, Rochefort called for civil war in the Corps législatif.

'Victor Noir was a child of the people,' he said. 'We are all children of the people,' shouted some, and one particularly quick deputy replied, 'We are more of the people than you, Count Rochefort!' Undeterred, Rochefort ploughed on through the heckles. And then he said it, the sacred phrase of revolution: 'As for me, I declare that I invite all citizens to . . .' At this point, shouts drowned out his words. 'He is preaching civil war!' exclaimed a deputy.[25] Indeed he was. He had invited all citizens to arm themselves. 'Tomorrow,' he said to a packed crowd at a political meeting that evening, 'we have a serious duty to fulfil. I beg you all to assemble at 2 p.m. . . . Do not fail to be at this rendezvous, which will decide, I hope, the future of democracy.'[26]

They did not fail. From early morning, soaked in heavy January rain, streams of workers and students made their way to the house in Neuilly where Victor Noir's body lay. From the Place de la Concorde, along the Champs-Élysées and away to the west, the streets were lined with shuffling masses dressed in black mourning clothes. By 2 p.m., there were as many as fifty thousand people waiting to escort the funeral procession.

But there was a problem. Inside the house were radical journalists and politicians, including Rochefort. There was only one way such a gathering of left-wing intelligentsia could end: an argument. Who did the body belong to? The people or the family? Where should the procession go? To Père-Lachaise, which would mean going through Paris, turning the affair into an insurrectionary demonstration, or to a nearby cemetery? Victor

Noir's brother begged to be allowed to go to the local one. With he and Rochefort seated on the hearse behind the coffin, an uneasy, simmering cortège lumbered off. It had not gone far before men started shouting that the body was being stolen from the people, cries of 'To Père-Lachaise!' rang out, the 'Marseillaise' was sung, and someone grabbed the reins of the horse, trying to guide it down the street towards Paris. At this point, Rochefort, who had not slept or eaten for days, fainted.

When he came to, the corpse had already been interred in the local cemetery, but with the funeral over, the people marched on Paris. Rochefort, revived, joined them. As they walked back down the Champs-Élysées, they ran into squadrons of cavalry, swords drawn. The crowd was ordered to disperse. If it had not after three warnings, the troops would charge. At the first roll of the drum, the horses trotted into position. At the second, there was panic. At the third, the crowd fled. The revolutionary moment passed.

In fact, though much of Paris pulsated with anger over Victor Noir's murder, the demonstration, despite Rochefort's incendiary rhetoric to the contrary the day before, was a peaceful one; the mourners were unarmed. Unlike in February 1848, when barricades went up and disillusioned Parisians overthrew Louis-Philippe after he had been in power for almost exactly the same amount of time, Louis-Napoléon remained secure on the throne. Ollivier had acted swiftly, deploying the army in massive force. But it was also testament to enthusiasm for the liberal experiment. The edifice the emperor had constructed, now crowned with liberty as he always said it would be, was strong enough to weather the scandal.

———

As one crisis receded, another loomed. The liberal Empire was such a radical departure from what was established in 1852 that many insisted it be sanctified by the will of the people in a plebiscite. Initially sceptical, Louis-Napoléon allowed himself to be convinced. When asked what he thought, Ollivier said that he believed a vote essential but pointed out there was no risk for him. If the result went against them, he would go home, but what, he asked, 'would your Majesty do?' After a long pause, Louis-Napoléon replied, 'Nothing ventured, nothing gained.'[27]

So it was that on 8 May 1870, Frenchmen, once again, went to the polls. The political atmosphere, though, was very different to what it had been in 1851 and 1852, when the Empire had won an overwhelming number of yes votes. Now there was a much freer press, combined with a well-organised and confident opposition – the Pierre Bonaparte scandal fresh in the mind – that was determined to end the Empire. Moreover, the emperor was old, and he had been in power for over twenty years, including his time as president. It was hard for any government, democratic or authoritarian, to remain in power for that long without losing popularity.

The question was carefully worded: 'The people approve the liberal reforms made to the constitution since 1860 by the emperor.'[28] To vote against the proposition was to vote against the reforms. That did not bother Victor Hugo. In what was not his most subtle work, Hugo wrote that if Louis-Napoléon asked the question 'Should I leave the Tuileries, go to prison and face trial?', then he would vote yes. As for the current question, it was a no from Hugo.

When the results started to come in on the evening of 8 May, the court gathered nervously at the Tuileries. The first counts were from Paris, where the no votes were winning. The mood darkened. 'Parisians have always been rebellious,' said the emperor, smiling. 'They vote against me . . . it is their right.'[29] Soon results from further afield came in. The mood went from nervous to reassured to triumphant. By midnight, there had been three million yes votes, only seven hundred thousand against. Louis-Napoléon was so confident that he went to bed. When he woke up, the news was better still: 7.3 million yes; 1.5 million no. Once again, Frenchmen had delivered a mighty endorsement of the regime. Turning to his son, the emperor said, 'You are crowned by this plebiscite.'[30]

Though there was some unrest in Paris in the following days, the opposition was devastated, resigned to defeat. 'It's a pounding, the emperor is stronger than ever,' said Léon Gambetta, the young lawyer turned politician whose attack on Louis-Napoléon had seemed so damaging only months before. 'There is nothing more to do in politics,' said Jules Favre, who had railed against Louis-Napoléon since 1848. The radical republican press, including Rochefort's *Marseillaise*, dusted off old arguments to explain what had happened. 'We prefer our fate to that of the Empire . . .

first because one must always prefer the applause of ten intelligent men to the applause of twenty imbeciles; then because the opinion of imbeciles ends always by yielding to people of intellect.'[31]

Yet after twenty years, the 'imbeciles', by which was meant the electorate, had again backed the Empire. Despite the long years in power, the mistakes, the scandals, the ill health, the vote was a testament to Louis-Napoléon's political skill in mobilising nearly 70 per cent of the electorate behind him. He had done what no other leader in France had managed since 1815: face down revolution and revitalise his regime.

Louis-Napoléon now presided over one of the most liberal and democratic countries in the world – the Bonapartist rhetoric of liberty tempered with order had been made good. What he had created, the British ambassador noted, was 'a Constitutional form of Government, more democratic than that which exists in England'.[32] Merely governing France for so long was an extraordinary feat of political dexterity. The last ruler to have reigned longer was Louis XV, who had died in 1774. Ollivier boasted that the liberal Empire would be Louis-Napoléon's retirement home. After his death, his son would be Napoléon IV. For as Ollivier made clear in the Corps législatif on 30 June 1870, the plebiscite was the French political equivalent of the Battle of Sadowa, where the Prussians had annihilated the Austrians. As for foreign affairs, 'The government has no uneasiness whatsoever,' he said cheerfully, for 'at no time has the peace of Europe seemed more assured'.[33] That, as it turned out, proved to be one of the more spectacular misjudgements in history.

20

WAR OR PEACE

Shortly before 9 p.m. on 23 February 1870, crowds of beautifully dressed men and women jostled forwards under blazing lights in the grand entrance to the Tuileries to gain admittance to a ball. Once inside, guests walked up an opulent staircase lined with soaring, impassive, motionless cent-gardes, the emperor's personal squadron, dressed in brilliant blue and gold uniforms with polished steel breastplates. After dancing, supper followed. The finest cuisine in France was laid out for thousands to fight over: plates piled high with iced vegetables, foie gras and chicken; pyramids of cakes; and pools of hot punch, though free-flowing champagne was the preferred drink.

The Empire may have been liberal, but it was still an empire, and it partied like one at the height of its power. The imperial couple worked the rooms. Eugénie sparkled in a white dress garlanded with flowers, hair blended with a double circle of diamonds that shone like a diadem. Louis-Napoléon was less inspiring. He gave the impression, recorded the Prussian military attaché in Paris, of an overweight, frail old gentleman. Though always ready with an affably banal comment, he spoke slowly and moved even slower, his eyelids drooping so much it seemed his eyes were permanently closed.

The Prussian military attaché had been told to stay to the end; it was in the early hours of the morning when the fun started. Drunk French officers, their once pristine uniforms now creased and haphazardly unbuttoned, danced the can-can riotously with what the Prussian called 'ladies of highly dubious character'. Even the cent-gardes were not safe. Women were reported to have propositioned them by slipping letters into their boots. For the Prussian military attaché, however, this display of conspicuous decadence and debauchery awash with sex and alcohol was not fun – it was 'as hideous as could be'.[1]

The view of the French Second Empire as a corrupt, degenerate and frivolous regime that, in the emperor, was rotting from the head down was one the minister-president of Prussia, Otto von Bismarck, shared. But it sat alongside another commonly held view: the French were a belligerent, warlike people who for centuries had been invading Germany. The French Revolution of 1789 had mainlined ideological fanaticism into Gallic bellicosity and the mere threat of a French attack was enough to send normally parochial men and women, from Baden to Bavaria, into throes of pan-German ecstasy.

As Bismarck knew, there was little love for the Protestant, militaristic Prussia in these remaining Catholic, independent southern German states. He also knew that the terror French aggression inspired would sweep away all the complex local loyalties and prejudices that stood in the way of Bismarck's lifelong goal of making the King of Prussia the Emperor of Germany. If French honour could be insulted loudly enough so that its pleasure-seeking, champagne-drenched elite heard it over the music of Jacques Offenbach, then a clash with the far more sonorous sounds of Richard Wagner might ensue. And in July 1870, Bismarck thought he had found just such a moment.

———

On Sunday 3 July, Émile Ollivier had his first day off in six months. He spent it attending a ceremony for a new church bell which his wife had sponsored in a small village near Paris. This was the kind of activity that passed for relaxation for the Olliviers. When he returned to the capital, he received a note that abruptly ended any repose he may have been enjoying. The news that sent Ollivier into despair, and soon had all of France in uproar, was that a member of the Hohenzollern family, the Prussian ruling dynasty, was to become King of Spain.

The French foreign minister, Agénor de Gramont, was an irascible man prone to tantrums. Side whiskers met retreating curls atop a large forehead, which meant that, when angry, which he often was, Gramont's puffy, red, sweaty face was perfectly bordered by a ring of dark oval hair and punctuated with a moustache tapered at either end in imperial style. Gramont was now so angry that he resorted to scribbled exclamations in his note to

Ollivier: 'I came to inform you that [Spain] has offered the crown to the Prince of Hohenzollern, who has accepted it. It's very serious! A Prussian prince at Madrid!'[2]

It was serious. Eugénie said the news exploded like a bomb; Louis-Napoléon, too, was greatly disturbed. For in the cold war between Prussia and France, which threatened to become hot, Bismarck had engineered a brilliant manoeuvre. With a Prussian royal on the Spanish throne, Spain's neutrality could not be guaranteed in any future conflict. Worse, if war with Prussia broke out, France would have to leave forces near the Pyrenees to protect its rear. As Louis-Napoléon understood, it was a plot against France.

Bismarck had been working for months to put this scheme in place. The Spanish throne had been vacant ever since Queen Isabella II had been overthrown in autumn 1868. For nearly two years various candidates had been proposed, but none had stuck, until Bismarck strong-armed Spanish politicians and Wilhelm I, King of Prussia, into thinking that what was needed was a Hohenzollern royal, Prince Leopold, ruling Spain. To the not unreasonable objection of Spanish politicians and King Wilhelm that it might lead to war with France, Bismarck cheerily downplayed the affair. It was a dynastic concern, he said, not a state one that could lead to conflict. Besides, if the Spanish parliament wanted Leopold, then that was the free expression of the national will, a Bonapartist solution if ever there was one. What possible objection, then, could the French emperor have against a Prussian prince in Madrid?

Plenty, as Bismarck well knew. At hastily convened cabinet meetings, Gramont, Ollivier and Louis-Napoléon planned to stop it. The press, most of which was virulently anti-Prussian anyway, would be briefed against the candidacy, the French ambassadors in Madrid and Berlin were instructed to protest, and the Corps législatif, and by extension France and Europe, would be informed that France would never accept a Hohenzollern on the Spanish throne.

On the afternoon of 6 July, Gramont and Ollivier entered the chamber. Silence reigned among the deputies as they fixed their attention on the foreign minister, who read a statement the emperor had edited that morning. Gramont confirmed what everyone knew: a Prussian prince had accepted an offer to become King of Spain. Gramont said that he hoped the matter would be resolved peacefully. If not, 'strong in your support, gentlemen, and that of the nation . . .' – 'It will not fail you!' shouted one especially enthusiastic deputy – 'we would know', Gramont concluded, 'how to fulfil our duty without hesitation and without weakness'. At this, the chamber was transported in patriotic delirium; deputies mobbed Gramont, shaking his hand and congratulating him.[3]

For Gramont had declared what Louis-Napoléon had put more concisely that morning when dictating a note for his old confidant Fleury, now ambassador to Russia: 'If Prussia insists upon the accession of the Prince of Hohenzollern to the throne of Spain, it will mean war.'[4] Now, the only way to prevent conflict between two European behemoths was for Prussia to withdraw the Hohenzollern candidacy. That put a lot of pressure on Count Vincent Benedetti, the French ambassador to Prussia charged with extracting this concession from King Wilhelm.

———

Wilhelm was looking forward to his stay at the sleepy German spa town of Bad Ems, where the River Lahn rolled languidly past picturesque townhouses lining the banks and gentle hills in the background. The rich and the famous and the sickly flocked here in the summer, none more celebrated than the King of Prussia. After he arrived, there were military reviews in the mornings, concerts in the afternoons and soirées to fill the evenings: the perfect way for a seventy-three-year-old monarch to relax far from the cares of state.

It would be anything but relaxing for the French ambassador to Prussia, Benedetti. The antithesis of Gramont, Benedetti was an emollient, reflective and thoughtful man, though the instructions he received from the foreign secretary tried his patience. 'It is absolutely vital', wrote Gramont on 7 July, that Benedetti obtain a statement from the king which declared that 'his Majesty . . . no longer approves of the candidacy and disavows it'. Forced to cut short his own holiday, Benedetti arrived at Bad Ems on 8 July. If he was in doubt as to the importance of his mission, Gramont made it clear: 'In case of a refusal, it's war.'[5]

As head of the Hohenzollern family, Wilhelm could order Leopold not to accept the Spanish throne, and it was, therefore, an astute move on Gramont's part to appeal to the Prussian king. Gramont's confrontational statement to the Corps législatif had been less intelligent, however. Predictably, it inflamed anti-French opinion throughout Germany, including in the independent southern states not under Prussian control. In the charged atmosphere, Benedetti realised that Gramont's demands would be seen as insulting. Instead, he alighted on the more diplomatic course of pointing out the dangers of Leopold taking the notoriously unstable Spanish throne, which, he hoped, would persuade Wilhelm to quietly drop the matter.

Wilhelm, too, was keen for the issue to go away. Though he had approved the idea, he had only done so because Bismarck had bullied him. Now, far from the influence of his minister, the king baulked at the idea of pushing Europe into war. When he met Benedetti, he told the French ambassador that though he would not order Leopold, he was doing everything he could to persuade his relation to reject the Spanish offer. It was, Benedetti thought, a good start to negotiations. In Paris, however, the lack of a clear answer was seen as a Prussian ploy, delaying tactics to allow their military to secretly prepare for war. Yet Benedetti was making progress, and Wilhelm was hiding nothing. Leopold had gone on a walking holiday in the Alps and no one knew where he was. Finally, on 12 July, a telegram arrived that gave everyone their answer.

———

While Benedetti was negotiating at Ems, in Paris war fever infected the press, and then the streets. French journalists hastily scribbled anti-Prussian articles, each trying to outdo the other. For too long, ran one, France had been humiliated by the evil machinations of Bismarck. With a Hohenzollern on the throne in Spain and Germany to the east, opined another, France would become a nation of thirty-eight million prisoners. 'We believe that the French government could not, without betraying France, tolerate Prussian actions one more day,' thundered a yet more jingoist writer.[6] Even the opposition press was furious. 'The Hohenzollerns', wrote Victor Hugo's son in a radical republican newspaper, 'dare to contemplate this monstrous project of universal domination of which . . . Napoléon vainly dreamed. It is no longer enough for them to have conquered Germany. They long to dominate Europe!'[7] It was perhaps the *Gaulois*, though, that got to the heart of the matter which no effusion of blood would be too great to prevent: if the Prussian affront were tolerated, there would not be a woman in the world who would accept 'the arm of a Frenchman'.[8]

In the streets, crowds gathered. Journalists and deputies were cheered if they supported war, booed if they argued for peace. These demonstrations took on a threatening, seditious air. The old revolutionary song, the 'Marseillaise' – composed during the first French Revolution in response to invading Prussian and Austrian armies and banned under the Second Empire – was sung. Rather than disperse people, the police let crowds grow. 'Never at any time', wrote one British journalist with long experience of reporting on Paris, including during the Crimean War of 1854 and the Italian one of 1859, 'have I seen the war feeling here so rampant.'[9] Among all the uncertainty, wrote a correspondent for *The Times*, one thing was certain: 'France is not only ready, but eager for war with Prussia. And not the whole strength of the Ollivier Government could . . . keep the people and the army back.'[10]

That was exactly what Ollivier hoped he could do, but he was barely six months into his position as France's leading minister, and had no experience of conducting foreign affairs. The strain was enormous. He became paranoid and anxious, and suffered from insomnia. Gramont was little help. He had been foreign minister for less than two months and, as a career diplomat, had little understanding of politics. With France's two most important ministers lacking experience – and, in Gramont's case, common sense – Louis-Napoléon needed to show leadership.

He, however, was undecided. On the one hand, whatever the quality of the French army, he knew better than anyone – for he had tried, and failed, to reform French conscription – that it would be outnumbered in a war against Prussia and its German allies. Moreover, seeing the awful casualties on the battlefields of Italy in 1859 had disabused him of any romanticised notions about the nature of conflict. For these reasons, if it could be obtained without humiliation, he preferred peace.

On the other hand, he was under tremendous pressure. Right-wing Bonapartists and many of his courtiers were determined to have a war that would, they reasoned, be glorious, sweep away the remaining opposition and perhaps even end what they saw as the disastrously liberal experiment under Ollivier. Eugénie, rabidly anti-Prussian, anti-liberal and anti-Ollivier, shared this view. Furthermore, public opinion in Paris seemed near unanimous in its desire to confront Prussia. The emperor embodied the national will, and the nation wanted war – how, then, could he refuse the people what they wanted?

Contributing to Louis-Napoléon's indecision that summer was another crisis of health, which impacted his judgement. He had piles with 'considerable haemorrhoidal flux', as one doctor put it, shooting pains, aching kidneys and, worst of all, suffered torture when trying to urinate because of the bladder stones, which now regularly flared into a crescendo of agony.[11] This made it hard to concentrate, which explains why the man who had single-handedly, albeit haphazardly, directed French foreign policy for over twenty years seemed to fade into the background, variously swayed by his ministers, his courtiers, his wife, his generals, public opinion.

After Gramont's explosive declaration on 6 July, and with talks at Ems producing nothing new, the mood in Paris was ever more febrile – though a hippopotamus escaping from the zoo and taking a leisurely swim in the Seine provided some distraction. Gramont, the diplomatic equivalent of an angry hippopotamus finding freedom, fired off ever more furious missives to Benedetti by the hour; public opinion became more bellicose; and Louis-Napoléon increasingly, if reluctantly, resigned himself to war.

Then, on 12 July, sensational news reached Paris. On behalf of his son, Leopold's father had withdrawn the Hohenzollern candidacy. Ollivier rushed to the Tuileries to speak with the emperor. 'It is a vast relief,' said Louis-Napoléon when he saw Ollivier. 'I am very happy that it has all ended thus. A war is always a great risk.' Speaking to the Italian ambassador, who happened to be there, he declared, 'It is peace . . . I know that some elements of public opinion in France would have preferred . . . war but I see in the renunciation a satisfactory solution that deprives us of any pretext for it.'[12]

Better than that, it was a stunning diplomatic victory. Louis-Napoléon and his ministers had played a dangerous game. They had taken the country to the brink of war, issuing an ultimatum, and Prussia had just performed a humiliating climbdown. As François Guizot, a former prime minister of France and the man who had dominated French politics under the July

Monarchy, exclaimed, 'Those fellows have insolent good luck: it's the greatest diplomatic victory I have ever seen in my life.'[13] After the triumph of the plebiscite at home, the emperor could add an astonishing foreign affairs success to his achievements in 1870. As he had noted, though, those clamouring on the streets of the capital to thrash the insolent Prussians would be profoundly disappointed.

———

The disappointment of belligerent Parisians was nothing compared to the devastation that Bismarck felt when he learned about the Prussian capitulation. While he waited for the crisis he had engineered to boil over, Bismarck went to his country estate in Pomerania. With gluttonous abandon, he devoured terrifying quantities of beef and ham, washed down with black velvet, his preferred cocktail of stout and champagne, and enjoyed the unfolding drama. Gramont had played the part of Gallic blusterer better than if Bismarck had written it himself: the French foreign minister had not so much fallen into the trap as dived in head first with gay abandon. But now word reached him that the King of Prussia was ruining everything, negotiating with Benedetti and upsetting Bismarck's plot to bring about German unification through war.

On 12 July, Bismarck started out for Bad Ems to stiffen his faltering monarch's backbone. Upon arriving in Berlin, however, a wad of papers was thrust into his arms which made the onward journey pointless – the Prussian candidacy had been withdrawn. Depressed, Bismarck resolved to resign. He thought 'this humiliation before France and her swaggering demonstrations' one of the most shameful in recent Prussian history – 'We had got our slap in the face from France,' he complained. The king's wife was to blame, he reasoned. Her 'feminine timidity and lack of national feeling' had worked away at Wilhelm and forced him, in Bismarck's view, into the unmanly and un-German course of not fighting France.[14]

There was only one thing for it: a dinner with copious amounts of beef, hams, wine and champagne with fellow disappointed war enthusiasts. One of Bismarck's guests, the Prussian army's commander-in-chief, Helmuth von Moltke the Elder, was especially sad. Sixty-nine years old, Moltke had long dreamed of invading France. Bismarck tried to cheer everyone up with new schemes for goading the French, but the magic had gone, the moment had passed, peace was assured. Unless, that is, France did something extraordinarily stupid.

———

Gramont did not share Louis-Napoléon's or Ollivier's delight about the withdrawal of the Prussian candidacy. He was worried about the politics. In the Corps législatif, militant Bonapartists had demanded to know what guarantees the government had to prevent the same crisis breaking out in future. Thus far, the foreign minister had none. On the evening of 12 July, therefore, Gramont raised his concerns with Louis-Napoléon. They were shared by others who made their views known, not least Eugénie. The withdrawal was a 'merely ridiculous solution, and would not satisfy French opinion', she said. 'If we do not secure these indispensable guarantees, then France is humiliated and affronted in the eyes of Europe; in the heart of every Frenchman there will be an explosion of wrath against the emperor; and that means the end of the Empire.'[15]

Forgetting, or not caring, that he was now a constitutional monarch, without consulting Ollivier or the cabinet the emperor and his foreign minister drafted another dispatch to the long-suffering Benedetti which was telegrammed at 6.15 p.m. The King of Prussia must 'give us the assurance that he would not authorise this candidacy again'. As Gramont made clear, politics, not diplomacy, dictated this new demand: public opinion was so inflamed, he wrote, that we 'do not know if we will succeed in controlling it' without further guarantees. War or peace depended on what happened between Benedetti and the King of Prussia at Ems the next day.

Benedetti was basking in the afterglow of having performed an exceptionally fine piece of high-wire diplomacy. Softening Gramont's bombast from Paris, tactfully manoeuvring the King of Prussia into a place where, as Benedetti knew, Bismarck did not want him to be, this was the kind of thing diplomats fantasised about. It came as a blow, then, when Benedetti received Gramont's new demands and realised that far from mission accomplished, it was mission difficult. On the morning of 13 July, he set out once more for the leafy promenades of Bad Ems for a high-stakes game of hide and seek, hoping to catch Wilhelm on his morning walk.

Spying Benedetti lurking in the trees, it was the king who went over to talk to him, and he spoke happily about the denouement of the crisis. Benedetti saw his chance. Given that it was all settled, might not the king 'communicate to us that you undertake never to allow Prince Leopold to accept the crown in the event that it were offered to him again?' Unable to hide his astonishment at this further demand, the king was visibly irritated. 'You are asking me for a statement that I am unable to make,' he replied. Benedetti tried again. Wilhelm refused. Benedetti put the question once more. Exasperated at the ambassador's persistence, the king stepped back a few paces and in a firm tone said, 'It seems to me, Monsieur Ambassador, that I have explained myself so clearly and so distinctly that I could never make such a statement that I have nothing more to add.' With that, he doffed his hat and walked away.[16]

France had its answer: no guarantee for the future. Moreover, Wilhelm now took Bismarck's advice: negotiations were over. That was not all the king did; with an aide he briefly sketched out the events of the day and telegrammed Bismarck in Berlin. Concluding the dispatch with the frustration of a man whose holiday has been thoroughly ruined by work, the king suggested that it might be a good idea to inform the press of France's impudence.

———

It was a morose dinner party that evening in Berlin, where Bismarck once again dined with the Prussian minister of war and Moltke, who was so upset that he would not get his war he had lost his appetite. As the three sullen men discussed Bismarck's plan to resign in protest over the capitulation to France, the telegram from Ems arrived. Bismarck read it aloud. It did nothing to improve Moltke's mood. It sounded like the king was entangled in more tedious diplomatic nonsense.

Bismarck, however, saw his chance. After sounding out Moltke as to whether Prussia was ready for war – of course it was, replied Moltke – Bismarck took a pen and began crossing out lines from the dispatch. Then he read his edited version. Now the meeting between Wilhelm and Benedetti lost all nuance. Benedetti had made new demands. In response, 'his Majesty the king thereupon decided not to receive the French ambassador again and sent the aide-de-camp on duty to tell him that his Majesty had nothing further to communicate'.

Moltke was delighted. Whereas before it had sounded like a genteel conversation, now it read as though the French ambassador had been insulted. That was the point, Bismarck explained to his guests. When he sent his version to the press, he continued, it 'will have the effect of a red rag upon the Gallic bull'. The mood lifted, appetite for food and drink restored. Moltke was ebullient. Beating his chest with one arm, he declared, 'If I may but live to lead our armies in such a war, then the devil may come directly afterwards and fetch away the old carcass.'[17]

———

In Paris, the Gallic bull was preparing for the charge before it saw Bismarck's red rag. The minister of war, Edmond Le Boeuf, was near hysterical when he found out on the morning of 13 July that far from a peaceful resolution, the new demand made war likely. Before a cabinet meeting at Saint-Cloud, he burst into the room and asked Ollivier and Gramont a series of increasingly irate questions. 'What's all this? What are these guarantees? Has the quarrel begun again, and I know nothing of it?' Not waiting for their replies, he shouted, 'You don't realise what a terrible responsibility rests on me! This state of things cannot go on: I must know absolutely, this morning, whether it's peace or war!'

He had good reason to be worried. If it came to war, the country that got its army to the front and ready to fight first would have the advantage. To ensure that this was France, the minister of war wanted the reserves called up immediately. 'Every day that you force me to lose', he cried, 'endangers the destiny of the country!'[18] That was true, but calling up the reserves and mobilising the army was as good as declaring war, for such an act could only be interpreted one way and Prussia would have to respond in kind. At the council that followed, the call-up was put to the vote, and with Ollivier arguing against it, the motion was defeated.

Le Boeuf was incensed. After the meeting, he spoke privately with Louis-Napoléon. Then, a wild glint in his eye, breathing heavily, his face purple with rage, he stormed back into the room and flung his briefcase down on the table. 'If it weren't for the emperor,' he shouted, 'I wouldn't remain for five minutes a member of such a cabinet.' Then, as he left the room, he barked, 'The emperor is betrayed, and' – pointing at Ollivier – 'there is the man who has betrayed him!'[19] At lunch, Eugénie, sitting next to Ollivier and outraged at what she saw as cowardice, ostentatiously turned her back on him. Finally, Ollivier and Gramont went to the Corps législatif, where the foreign minister stalled in the face of rabid demands for action against Prussia, insisting that negotiations were ongoing.

This did not go down well in the capital. People took to the streets, singing war songs and insisting France's honour be avenged; reporters ratcheted up the frenzy. 'The retreat is complete,' howled one journalist in print after listening to Gramont's prevarications that afternoon. 'This ministry will now have a new name: the ministry of shame!' Peace was unacceptable: 'Everywhere, in the chamber and on the street, people are saying: "This is the downfall of the cabinet, and it is war!"'[20]

On the morning of 14 July, though, Ollivier was still convinced he could stop war. While he was working in his office, an usher announced the foreign minister. Gramont strode into the room. '*Mon cher*,' he said with customary hauteur, 'you see before you a man who has just been slapped in the face.' He handed Ollivier a copy of Bismarck's edited telegram – the red rag – which had appeared in the evening editions of the German press the night before. For a few moments, Ollivier was silent, stupefied. 'We can no longer delude ourselves,' he said. 'They want to force us into war.'[21]

Louis-Napoléon convened an emergency cabinet meeting at the Tuileries for 12.30 p.m. As he made his way from Saint-Cloud, he passed through seething, angry mobs protesting against negotiation. They wanted war. Gramont agreed with them. 'After what has happened,' he said after another briefcase, his own, was thrown on a table, 'a minister for foreign affairs who could not decide on war would not be worthy of retaining his office.'[22] But there were still those who argued for peace. During a lull in the debate, one minister sidled up to Louis-Napoléon and whispered. 'Sire, between King Wilhelm and you, the game is not equal. The king can lose several battles. For your Majesty, defeat means revolution.'

'Ah, Monsieur,' replied the emperor, 'you are thinking about such sad things, but I thank you for your frankness.'[23]

In the end, it was military matters that won the debate. The minister of war insisted that the French army was ready – he reportedly boasted it had everything it needed, down to the last button – but must strike quickly. And to do that, the reserves must be called up, and the army mobilised. At 4 p.m., a vote was taken, and this time it passed. The minister of war left to give orders. Yet the council continued, and the men, realising the enormity of a decision which meant war, had doubts. Scenarios were played out, ideas put forward. Louis-Napoléon listened on, depressed, passive, silent. Might they not, someone suggested, convene the great powers of Europe to hold a congress and resolve the question?

At this, the emperor revived. 'That's it! That's it!' he cried. Ollivier proposed a way to phrase the call for a peace conference. Putting his hand on Ollivier's arm, Louis-Napoléon said, 'Go at once to my study and put that in writing.' As he spoke, two tears rolled down his cheeks.[24] The emperor wanted Ollivier's note read to the Corps législatif that day; however, it was past 6 p.m., and it was no longer in session. The council broke up, therefore, having mobilised the army and called for a peace conference.

The idea for a congress did not stand scrutiny. When he returned to Saint-Cloud and told his wife that it might avert war, Louis-Napoléon was ridiculed. 'I doubt', Eugénie said with imperious contempt, 'whether this accords with the sentiment of the chamber and the country.' That same evening, Louis-Napoléon summoned Ollivier. 'On reflection,' he said, greeting his minister at the palace, 'I find the statement that we agreed earlier far from satisfactory.'

'I agree, Sire,' replied Ollivier, whose wife had also told him that the idea for a congress was absurd. 'If we brought it to the chamber, people would throw mud at our carriages and we would be jeered.' After a long silence, the emperor said, 'You see in what a situation a government can sometimes find itself. Even if we had no legitimate reason for war, we would nevertheless be obliged to decide on it so as to obey the will of the country.'[25]

———

Ollivier had been on a long political journey: from republican opposition to the Empire's first minister. Now, on 15 July, at 1 p.m. in the Corps législatif, a pacifist by temperament, he was about to announce that France was at war. All that stood between Ollivier and history was the reading of the minutes from yesterday's debate on public works. With impatient tension rising in the chamber, these finally came to an end. 'Are there any observations about the minutes?' asked the president of the chamber, a necessary formality. With such momentous news about to be delivered, no one expected the agony to be prolonged.

'I request the floor,' said an obscure deputy, with the relish of a man who knows that the Friday-afternoon work meeting has overrun, but is determined to make his point now that the chair has called for any other business. Gasps of astonished irritation came from the politicians. The deputy continued, affecting obliviousness to his colleagues' complaints. There were, he said, some inaccuracies in the minutes and they needed rectification. This provoked more murmurs of outrage. 'Yes, gentlemen, inexactitudes, erroneous figures.' When discussing the construction of a canal, the minutes had the deputy down as saying that 2,500 mules had carried 1,000 tonnes of earth. 'It was 500 tonnes that I said.'

'Enough! Enough!' came shouts from the chamber. With admirable patience, the president said that the record would be amended. 'If there are no other observations on the minutes . . .' he added nervously, before quickly stating that they were adopted and handing the floor to Ollivier.

The first minister ran through the diplomatic spat with Prussia as the French government saw it, making much of the supposed insult – which never happened – delivered to the French ambassador by the Prussian king. France had done everything, he claimed, somewhat disingenuously, to avoid conflict; however, the country was determined to fight a war it had not sought. Riotous cheers and applause drowned out Ollivier's words. '*Vive l'empereur!*' shouted deputies. '*Vive la France!*'

When order was restored, Adolphe Thiers rose to speak. No one loved France more than him, he explained; but with the Prussian climbdown the country had got what it wanted. 'Well, gentlemen, do you want people to say', his voice rising to be heard over ever-increasing insults, 'that for a question of form, you decided to spill torrents of blood?' This was met with more outrage. 'You are the anti-patriotic trumpet of disaster!' yelled one particularly insistent heckler, which was the nineteenth-century equivalent of shouting, 'Why do you hate France?'

Feeling that 'the anti-patriotic trumpet of disaster' was insufficient rebuttal for a man of Thiers's standing, Ollivier returned to the tribune. Speaking off the cuff, he said that France had been insulted, and honour was at stake. As his rhetoric climbed, so too did his imagination. He forgot Thiers and the deputies. Instead, he saw the brave young soldiers who were about to sacrifice their lives for the nation. With the fire and brimstone of an Old Testament preacher, he reached for biblical allusions. Unfortunately, the biblical moment that came to him in his rapture was a rather obscure and convoluted one which admonished the impious for having heavy hearts. And so it was that Ollivier told the chamber that he and the government accepted war with a 'light heart'.

'Your heart is light yet the blood of nations is about to flow!' shouted one deputy with a malicious snarl which brought Ollivier back to reality. He had meant a heart unburdened with guilt, a clean conscience, he explained, qualifying what he had said. Of course, that nuance was lost and the phrase stuck: the government had committed the nation to war with a 'light heart'.

The debate rumbled on, with more dissenting voices than Ollivier cared for, but when it came to a vote, 245 deputies were in favour, including many members of the opposition; only ten voted against.[26] Though the official declaration came a few days later, after the debate in the Corps législatif everyone knew France was at war.

———

When it was announced that the celebrated opera star Marie Sasse would sing the 'Marseillaise' at the Théâtre Impérial, Parisians invaded the ticket offices. On the day of the performance, like the deputies sitting through the minutes before Ollivier's appearance, the packed audience watched the show before the main event with increasing impatience in the stifling auditorium. When Sasse appeared in a white dress, cloak dotted with imperial bees, carrying the tricolour flag, the audience was awed into silence. As the orchestra attacked the first bars of the hymn, it was as if the music lit a trail of gunpowder from the front of the hall to the back. Someone shouted, 'Stand up!' Everyone did. The excitement turned to patriotic ecstasy when Sasse sang the lines, '*Aux armes, citoyens, formez vos bataillons!'* Then there was wild applause, cheers, delirium, sweat and the sound of nearly two thousand Parisians screaming the chorus, possessed with a nationalist fervour beyond anything that anyone had seen in their lifetime.

Scenes like this were repeated across France, though often with more alcohol and less tuneful singing, as the 'Marseillaise' became an unofficial anthem. The French army was mobilised and its young men were feted as heroes wherever they passed. Ever since war had seemed inevitable, the main Parisian boulevards were so full that people could barely move – all in a state, as one British journalist noted, of 'perfectly frantic excitement' which 'none but a Frenchman can attain'.[27] Not everyone shared the feverish optimism: there were occasional – and brave, given the circumstances – shouts in favour of peace. Other sceptics kept quiet, but feared that the war would not be the triumphal march that most assumed it would be.

One of these was the emperor who was supposed to lead France's armies to victory. Throughout the diplomatic crisis, Louis-Napoléon had prevaricated, swinging between war and peace. The demonstrations in Paris, the urgings of his cabinet, the enthusiasm at court and the righteous self-belief of his wife in her desire for a showdown with Prussia had worn down a man who at the height of his power would patiently listen to his advisers before ignoring them all. Now, sick, tired, old beyond his years, he had become passive.

Plon-Plon, who believed war against Prussia madness, thought he knew whom to blame: Eugénie. Not a man to keep his views to himself, not long after the declaration of war – which had made him especially angry because his summer holiday had been cut short – he stormed into Saint-Cloud and insulted Louis-Napoléon's ministers. Then he turned his ire on the empress: 'I told you that this woman would bring you misfortune.' Brushing aside his cousin's weak protests, Plon-Plon shouted: 'Let us pack our trunks, and pack them well, because we are screwed!'[28]

That was not, of course, the emperor's view, but he was anxious, not least because of his health. As the nephew of Napoléon Bonaparte, he felt honour-bound to command the army. When his cousin and one-time fiancée Mathilde learned this, she hurried to Saint-Cloud. He received her in his study. 'His face was ashen, his eyelids puffy, his eyes dead, his legs wavering, his shoulders bowed,' as she described him.

'Is it true', she asked him, 'that you are taking command of the army?'

'Yes,' he replied.

'But you're not in a fit state to take it! You can't sit astride a horse! You can't even stand the shaking of a carriage! How will you get on when there is fighting?'

Mathilde continued to argue. Eventually, with an air of resignation, he waved her away.[29]

One person who did not care about his sorry physical state was Eugénie. Louis-Napoléon kept the worst of his condition from her, but like many, she erroneously ascribed his ill health to his sexual misadventures, and therefore sympathy for her husband was in short supply. Less time chasing women and more time fighting Prussians was exactly what the doctor ordered. In fact, his doctor ordered bladder surgery, but Louis-Napoléon refused to undergo a dangerous operation, preferring the Prussians to the surgeon's knife.

Everyone expected him to leave for the front immediately after the declaration of war on 19 July. Yet his health meant he delayed in Paris. It was not until 28 July that he was ready to make his way to Metz on France's eastern border, where the army was concentrating. As riding a horse was agony and he did not want the people of Paris to see how weak he was, he went to the front by rail from Saint-Cloud. It was a melancholy departure from his summer palace which had all the joviality of a funeral. In one of the grand rooms, Louis-Napoléon, smoking, said goodbye to his court and ministers.

'In a fortnight your Majesty will be in Berlin,' said one obsequious man.

'No, don't expect that, *even* if we are successful,' replied the emperor, before whispering to Ollivier, lingering as he embraced him, 'I'm counting on you.'

With the slow, deliberate movement of a man for whom each step exacts a considerable price, the emperor made for a waiting carriage. Alongside his fourteen-year-old son, who was accompanying him on campaign and whose eyes were filled with tears, he was driven to a nearby train station. Here, he said more goodbyes, turning to Eugénie and hugging her. Then father and son climbed into the imperial carriage, Louis-Napoléon waving to his wife, Eugénie fixing her eyes on her son and watching the train disappear into the distance, while the men on the platform raised their hats and shouted, '*Vive l'empereur!*'[30]

———

When Louis-Napoléon arrived at his headquarters in Metz on 28 July, everything was in chaos. The mobilisation of hundreds of thousands of soldiers and their provisioning had been shambolic. Men reached the front with ammunition, but without rifles, or with rifles, but without ammunition. 'Can't find my brigade, can't find my commanding officer; what should I do? I don't even know where my regiments are,' telegrammed one officer in despair.[31] 'Things are not as advanced as I thought them,' Louis-Napoléon wrote decorously to Eugénie on 29 July.[32]

To offset the confusion, much was made of past Napoleonic glories and Louis-Napoléon recalled his uncle's campaigns against Prussia, proclaiming: 'Whatever may be the road we take beyond our borders we will find the glorious traces of our fathers.'[33] The subjunctive about the route was not a rhetorical flourish: neither Louis-Napoléon nor his generals had any idea what road they would take. For, with staggering incompetence, the French emperor had declared war with only a sketch of a plan to invade Germany, one that required efficient mobilisation and Austrian support to be viable. But with mobilisation anything but efficient, when Louis-Napoléon presided over a war council at the end of July, he was reduced to asking for suggestions.

'Well, Sire, where are we with Austria?' enquired one of his marshals.

'We are negotiating,' replied the emperor.

'Negotiating!' exclaimed the marshal. 'But in two or three days we have to begin the campaign. If we don't march, we will be attacked.'[34]

This lack of allies was Louis-Napoléon's fault. 'War is declared,' ran a *Times* article reflecting neutral opinion, 'an unjust, but premeditated war. This dire calamity, which overwhelms Europe with dismay, is, it is now too clear, the act of France – of one man in France.'[35] In fact, it was Bismarck's war, but he had played international opinion perfectly. After France's declaration, he leaked secret proposals made by the French emperor years ago that in return for acquiescing in Prussia's rise in 1866, France would be given Belgium or Luxembourg. In the eyes of Europe, Louis-Napoléon was an untrustworthy aggressor.

Without allies, without a plan and, predictably, without maps, the French emperor fell back on a vague idea for a defensive war. France had two weapons that made this a sound strategy. The first was the chassepot rifle, which meant that French infantrymen could fire quicker, further and more accurately than their counterparts. They also had another miracle of technology for killing Germans, the mitrailleuse. An early form of machine gun, this could unleash between one and two hundred rounds a minute – near science-fiction rates of fire for the time. Armed with the chassepot and the mitrailleuse, French army corps would take up strong positions on the border and break the Prussian invasion in defensive battles.

This, however, did not have the Napoleonic panache the army and public opinion expected, and underemployed officers gathered in cafes, criticising the lack of initiative. Soldiers who had been fired with patriotic fervour got bored, then drunk, then started going absent without leave to get the coffee and tobacco they craved, but which, through incompetent organisation, had not been distributed.

At the military camp of Châlons, it was much worse. Here, six battalions from Paris of the *garde mobile* – the name given to what remained of Louis-Napoléon's unpopular attempts to create a reserve to match Prussian numbers – had assembled. As it was made up of young men who had avoided conscription into the regular army, no one expected the *garde mobile* to fight, least of all those in it. Before boarding trains for Châlons, there was nearly a riot as, emboldened by huge quantities of alcohol, they shouted, 'Down with Napoléon!', 'Down with Ollivier!' and 'Long live the Republic!'[36] The party continued on the way; one of the first casualties of war was an inebriated reservist dancing on top of a wagon who failed to duck in time before a tunnel.

When they arrived at Châlons, disgusted officers saw them as unfit for anything other than manual labour. Not that they did much work, preferring to wander through the nearby town in various states of undress, spending their time in bars and brothels and fights. In camp, some of them smashed up a statue of the prince imperial. Aware that all was not well, their commander, a marshal of France, thought a few encouraging words might be in order. While the marshal reviewed the battalions, one soldier insulted him; then complaints, invective and cries of 'Long live the Republic!' erupted from the rest of the men.

'You are insulting a marshal of France,' shouted the commander in disbelief. Other men broke ranks, surrounding him and crying, 'To Paris! To Paris!' Imperiously extending his hand to the east, the marshal replied, 'It is to the border, to the enemy, that you want to go.' It was not. The *garde mobile* knew where the enemy was, which was why they did not want to go there. 'To Paris! To Paris!' they repeated in case there was still some mystification as to their preferred destination. As thousands sang 'To Paris!' to the tune of a revolutionary song, the marshal rode away, his officers following. Eventually, order was restored, but only just – it had nearly been a mutiny.[37]

As dispatches detailing the confusion poured into his headquarters, Louis-Napoléon reasoned something had to be done. For want of a better plan, it was decided to attack the small German town of Saarbrücken. On the morning of 2 August, the French swept towards a place the Prussians regarded as strategically unimportant. After token resistance, therefore, the defenders fell back. French soldiers quaffed beer, bayoneted sausages and set fire to the railway station. It was nothing more than a skirmish – eighty-three Prussian casualties to eighty-six French.

Not far behind the fighting a far more serious struggle was taking place: Louis-Napoléon was trying to mount a horse. Determined to join his soldiers in battle, he struggled into the saddle, but trotting hurt too much. He had to go at walking pace. With his son by his side, they ambled forwards. Once victory was certain, Louis-Napoléon had to turn to one of his officers and ask for help as he painfully tried to struggle out of the saddle. Before 4 p.m., he was back in Metz.

Their son, the emperor excitedly telegrammed his wife, had 'received his baptism of fire' and 'shown admirable sangfroid'. He told Eugénie that the prince imperial had picked up a bullet which had landed close to him on the battlefield. 'There were men who cried on seeing him so calm,' he concluded.[38] This account found its way into the French press and Parisians never tired of lampooning this so-called 'baptism of fire', especially when it became clear that the position before Saarbrücken was too precarious to hold. French troops hurried back across the frontier. They were needed elsewhere; the Prussians were coming.

21

THE DEBACLE

Through the night and into the early hours of 4 August, it had poured with rain in the picturesque French town of Wissembourg, near the German border. Now, General Abel Douay, commanding a small defending force, peered into the thick morning mist. Unable to see much, he was relieved when reconnoitring cavalry returned and reported that although there had been a skirmish with Prussian mounted troops, there was no sign of massed enemy ranks. At 8 a.m., Douay ordered coffee, telling a fellow officer that he did not expect a serious attack.

It came as a surprise, then, when moments later shells exploded in the town and Bavarian soldiers in blue uniforms and plumed helmets emerged from the haze. It was a serious attack – so serious, in fact, that three hours later Douay was dead. The defenders fought ferociously, but they were outnumbered four to one and soon surrendered or fled. Taking Douay's headquarters, the Germans were struck by the general's field kitchen, which was befitting of a French officer: a custom-made wagon with special cages for live poultry and game birds. Douay was a Frenchman's Frenchman: enemy soldiers were also delighted to discover women's underwear, corsets, crinolines and negligees among his personal effects.

The defeat was a shock for the French high command, but what happened two days later was a catastrophe. On 6 August, the French lost two more battles. Prussian artillery proved more lethal than the chassepot or the mitrailleuse. Firing faster, further and more lethally than anything at the time, Prussian heavy guns smashed shells into French lines with awesome power, killing and wounding many, terrifying still more. In one battle, fifty thousand Frenchmen were overrun, nine thousand taken prisoner. On the same day, another army corps was routed, and in what was becoming a familiar scene, terrified civilians fled enemy-occupied villages, carrying

394

what they could, mothers screaming for lost children, old men and women stumbling towards safety. Stating the obvious, a retreating officer told a general leading reinforcements that arrived too late: 'Everything is lost.'[1]

Prussia and its German allies, including southern states such as Bavaria, had invaded France with 426,000 men. Facing them, France had haphazardly cobbled together 304,000 soldiers spread thinly across a wide front. Hitting the French fast and with superior numbers, the Germans smashed and then enveloped isolated French forces, showing the hastily concocted defensive strategy to be woefully inadequate at stopping the German invasion.

From Metz, Louis-Napoléon did his best to rally his troops. Riding was now impossible, but even jolts from his carriage caused the emperor extreme discomfort. On one journey to visit troops, the carriage halted and Louis-Napoléon made his way to a nearby tree, resting his head against the trunk and digging his nails into the bark in a futile attempt to alleviate the pain. On another occasion, his aides-de-camp watched in disbelief as, sitting at a table, Louis-Napoléon began convulsing and writhing uncontrollably, tears rolling down his cheeks. Napoleonic feats of leadership were required. Yet the emperor's physical condition combined with the enormity of the situation – France invaded and three defeats in forty-eight hours – plunged him into a state of paralysis. And that was before he received news of what was happening in Paris.

———

On the same day French forces were in retreat, there was jubilation on the streets of Paris. At the Bourse, a young man waving what he claimed was a dispatch from the front told a crowd that a great French victory had been won. As the rumour spread through the capital there was delirium. People cried, strangers embraced, flags were unfurled. The unfortunate opera star Marie Sasse was recognised travelling in a carriage and was forced to sing the 'Marseillaise' from it as people cheered. But, wondered some, if there had been such a victory, why had it not been posted up in the streets? Then they got their answer. The report was cruel misinformation, an attempt to manipulate the stock market. Now, word spread of defeats and the mood in the streets turned ugly.

It was not until that evening that Ollivier's cabinet received a telegram from Louis-Napoléon confirming the disasters. The emperor urged the capital to prepare for attack. Ollivier immediately telegrammed him, begging for more information. 'If we have no news other than your Majesty's vague dispatch [to give people], there will be an uprising in Paris.'[2] To prevent this, Eugénie, acting as regent, convened an emergency cabinet meeting where martial law was proclaimed and, against Ollivier's advice, the Corps législatif was recalled.

Despite the measures, when the Assembly opened on 9 August, angry protesters congregated outside. The army was there to keep the peace. 'Cowards!', 'To the frontier!' and 'Fight the Prussians!' shouted the mob, alongside cries of 'Down with Ollivier!' and 'Long live the Republic!'[3] Inside the chamber, deputies hurled insults at Ollivier as he explained that despite fighting with 'sublime heroism', the army had suffered defeats. 'By the incompetence of its commander!' shouted the republican Jules Favre, meaning the emperor. Favre proposed a motion that all but deposed Louis-Napoléon and called for the people to be armed. 'It is the beginning of a revolution!' shouted a Bonapartist.[4] Having lost the confidence of the Corps législatif, and never having had that of the empress, Ollivier was forced to resign that evening.

With Ollivier gone, far from rallying behind the regime, the nation's leading politicians played politics. Republicans saw in the military humiliation of France a revival of their hopes – dashed after the plebiscite – to end the Empire. Right-wing Bonapartists spied an opportunity to end the liberal experiment. In the streets, the mood was threatening. 'If France suffers another defeat,' the British ambassador wrote, 'revolution will be inevitable.'[5]

———

Back in Metz, behind a table precariously piled with papers, Louis-Napoléon was usually to be found slumped on a sofa, chain-smoking. Thick clouds of smoke obscured his pale, exhausted face. In the rare moments his hand was free of a cigarette, he obsessively twirled the ends of his moustache. In front of him, his generals argued. Plans changed hourly. First, Louis-Napoléon determined to take the offensive. At 3 a.m.

on 7 August, he and his general staff were sitting in railway carriages ready to move to the front; however, when reports of enemy advances reached him, Louis-Napoléon abandoned the idea.

Panicked, he returned to headquarters, where he hunched over a map, nervously dabbing his mouth with a handkerchief. Several arguments and hours later, a new plan was devised: orders were given for the army to fall back to the camp at Châlons. Though deep inside France, this would have the advantage of extending Prussian supply lines and meeting the enemy armies in force on ground the French chose. While this made military sense, it was pointed out that the political fallout from a retreat that abandoned large parts of eastern France would be disastrous. On 8 August, therefore, and for the second time in twenty-four hours, the emperor countermanded his own orders. 'I don't know what we're doing,' wrote one French soldier involved in the seemingly endless marches and counter-marches in unusually wet August weather, speaking for the whole army, 'but I think we're in retreat.'[6]

'I don't know what they're doing in Paris,' a similarly bewildered Louis-Napoléon said to the minister of war in Metz when he heard that Ollivier's ministry had fallen. 'They've lost their heads.' To Plon-Plon he remarked, 'It is not in the middle of a storm that one changes captain and crew.'[7] Once the master of France, Louis-Napoléon now found his control, military and political, slipping away. After days of agonising over what to do, he reluctantly relinquished his military role and on 12 August appointed Marshal Achille Bazaine to command what was called the Army of the Rhine.

Outrageously brave, Bazaine was not only the army's choice, but also the people's. He had worked his way up from the lowest to the highest rank in the French army. Seriously wounded in action twice, he had always been courageous and led from the front. His service record read as a history of the Second Empire's wars: Algeria, Russia, Italy and Mexico. If this last had been a disaster, most ascribed that to political failings rather than military ones, and besides, it was in Mexico that Bazaine had been elevated to the rank of marshal.

Yet Louis-Napoléon undermined Bazaine's command. Instead of orders, he expressed desires, which, Bazaine grumbled, felt a lot like orders. They disagreed over how to save France. Bazaine wanted to stand his ground at

Metz. The emperor's 'desire' was now the plan he had rejected days before: retreat to Châlons, join up with reserves and regroup. In the end, Bazaine grudgingly agreed. With the urgency of someone doing something they believe to be utterly pointless, he slowly readied his 180,000 men to march west on 14 August.

It was too late. While the French were vacillating, the Prussians were manoeuvring to encircle Bazaine's army. On the same day that Bazaine began the laborious retreat, the advanced German forces crashed into the French rear. After a day's fighting, the French had held their ground and fought off the enemy. Buoyed by finally receiving some good news, that evening Louis-Napoléon shook Bazaine's hand. 'Well, Marshal,' he said, 'you have broken the spell.'[8] But the fighting delayed the retreat and it was not until the next day, 15 August, that the army began slowly to move again.

Louis-Napoléon was not moving much faster. With his son and Plon-Plon in his entourage, the imperial baggage train was immense, carrying all the luxuries considered necessary on campaign. Given the dire provisioning of French soldiers, this was another sign of the emperor's impaired judgement – when he had gone to war in Italy he had made much of travelling as simply as possible on horseback. Now, a convoy of vehicles driven by valets in opulent green and gold imperial livery swept past soldiers and civilians. 'Where's the fresh lobster wagon?' quipped one onlooker.[9]

There was little luxurious about the emperor's retreat, however, when he emerged from a decrepit roadside auberge at 4.30 a.m. on 16 August. Physically struggling, with Herculean exertion he got into his carriage with the help of his aides before sinking into his seat. Then the carriages and escort left. The emperor did not expect to be away from the army for long; Bazaine was to follow him. The Prussian army's commander, Moltke, however, had other ideas. He resolved to stop the marshal's retreat. Unless Bazaine could fight his way out, France's only well-trained, professional army would be cut off from the rest of the country.

———

'You must not worry yourself because it started badly,' said a reservist to the emperor while his convoy changed horses on the road to Châlons. 'Here we are, the rest of us, the reserves, and it is going to go better from now on.' His comrades agreed, 'Yes, yes, long live the emperor!' they cried, waving their hats in the air. At this unexpected outburst of loyalty, Louis-Napoléon's sombre face brightened.[10]

These soldiers and the emperor had reasons to be optimistic. The defeats had led to panic in Louis-Napoléon's headquarters and Paris, but cooler analysis told a different story. The French army had fought well, the chassepot rifle had shown its superiority and well-aimed fire cut down scores of German soldiers long before they saw their opponents. Prussian artillery was terrifying, but the discipline of French troops to maintain their position under awesome firepower was barely believable. Moreover, the German victories had been against isolated and outnumbered army corps. With only a fraction of French forces engaged, if Bazaine met the invaders in force with a coherent plan, there was hope. For once Bazaine marched the Army of the Rhine to Châlons, there would be three hundred thousand at the camp and another hundred thousand defending Paris. Combined, they would be a match for a tired, depleted enemy fighting deep in French territory with precariously extended lines of supply.

Though physically broken, Louis-Napoléon was not, then, as pessimistic as he had been. On the evening of 16 August, he arrived at Châlons. Here, discipline among the *garde mobile* had not improved, nor did Louis-Napoléon's arrival instil lofty sentiments of patriotism. When a detachment passed the imperial headquarters, one man shouted in a comedy high-pitched voice, 'Long live the emperor!' Then a thousand men cried, 'One, two, three, *merde*!'

They were not the only men in the camp who had a low opinion of the emperor: Plon-Plon was there too. 'One might as well go into battle with a plate of soup on one's head and be ordered not to spill anything,' he told one officer with characteristic frankness, the soup being Louis-Napoléon. There was a council of war later that day, and Plon-Plon was briefing anyone who would listen that the soup must return to Paris. In this he was preaching to the converted. 'Sire,' said a general at the meeting, 'the emperor no longer commands the army and he is no longer on the throne. The emperor must be either at the head of his troops or at the head of his government.'

'It is true,' Louis-Napoléon murmured weakly, 'I seem to have abdicated.'

'You have abdicated the government in Paris,' thundered Plon-Plon less diplomatically than the general. 'At Metz, you have just abdicated the command . . . you must take back one or the other. For the command, it is impossible; for the government, it is difficult and dangerous . . . but, what the hell! if we must fall, let us fall like men.'

Plon-Plon's plan was to appoint General Louis-Jules Trochu as governor of Paris and commander-in-chief of its forces. A mild critic of the imperial government, Trochu had received no important command during the war. Both these facts made him admired by the opposition. Plon-Plon reasoned that a popular military man could prepare the capital for the return of the no longer popular or military emperor. Desperate for anything that looked like a solution, Louis-Napoléon welcomed the idea, but he did not trust Trochu. 'I will write to the empress and the ministers,' he said. 'Write to the empress!' shouted Plon-Plon. 'Are you no longer sovereign? Trochu must leave at once.'[11] Bullied into it, Louis-Napoléon sent Trochu to Paris. The emperor would follow. Bazaine's army and the one at Châlons would fall back to defend the capital.

But the Prussians were making plans, too. With little indication that Bazaine was using his much-wanted freedom to get his army moving, on 16 August the officers of a cavalry regiment decided to breakfast in fields about fifteen miles west of Metz. On long tables with spotless tablecloths, bright silver knives and forks were laid out for the meal. Prussian gunners used the glinting cutlery to sight their artillery. The explosions amid trestle tables were the first step in a move to cut off Bazaine's retreat and encircle the Army of the Rhine.

———

The contrast between the French and Prussian leadership was striking. Though he was more than ten years older than Louis-Napoléon, King Wilhelm was a picture of rude Prussian health. Imposingly tall with a rotundness that became his soldierly bearing, he was a military man in nominal command, but he deferred to two supremely talented and devoted subjects, Bismarck and Moltke. In politics, Bismarck dominated. With his rapacious appetite, enormous frame and relentless energy, the juxtaposition with Louis-Napoléon was even more pronounced than with the king Bismarck served. Though Bismarck had little military background, he donned a uniform for the campaign, including a spiked Prussian helmet and oversized riding boots. To Prussian officers, he was ridiculous; to the German public, his look became iconic. Wilhelm and Bismarck were formidable enough, but Prussia also boasted the foremost military thinker and practitioner of the age in Helmuth von Moltke. He had long prepared for war with France, including, unlike his opponents, issuing officers with detailed maps. Now, he was planning the *coup de grâce* against Bazaine.

By the evening of 16 August, the Germans had the numbers in front of Bazaine to make his retreat even more difficult. The marshal telegrammed Louis-Napoléon that he had to first fall back towards Metz and then reorganise, before resuming his march towards Châlons. Bazaine's army was now retreating from the retreat, trudging along the same roads and fields that it had so laboriously traversed in the last two days. 'It is impossible to describe the shock that seized everyone on learning of such an order,' wrote one officer.[12] As they grumbled their way to Metz, the poorly provisioned men stared in disbelief at an enormous bonfire. To stop supplies falling into enemy hands, coffee, camping equipment, linen, even shoes, most of which had never been issued to the soldiers, fuelled a conflagration.

On 18 August, King Wilhelm, Bismarck and Moltke watched on as 190,000 Germans launched what their leaders expected to be a decisive victory. But the French defiantly held their ground against the advancing infantry. Seeing his men falter, Wilhelm rode towards the action to rally them. Instead, his soldiers ran past him as he swore at them for cowardice. But the Prussians brought forward their heavy guns. Despite the French being pounded with artillery more intense than anything seen up to that point in history – trenches collapsed, buildings caught fire, men screamed and died as tens of thousands of shells created an inferno – somehow they weathered it.

At 5 p.m., the elite Prussian Guard launched itself at the beleaguered French right wing. What came next, recalled a young Lieutenant Paul von Hindenburg (later commander of the Imperial German Army in the First World War and the man who, when president of the Weimar Republic, appointed Adolf Hitler as chancellor), was like 'a hurricane'.[13] Apocalyptic rifle fire tore into the Guard. Some eight thousand fell dead or wounded;

others ran. 'I'll shoot down anyone who doesn't stop here!' screamed a Prussian officer helplessly as his men fled.[14]

This defence was nothing short of miraculous. Having somehow withstood bombardment and massed waves of infantry attacks, Bazaine had a chance to counterattack and deal a crushing blow against German forces that were everywhere in disarray. Instead, he did nothing. Two miles from the front, the man who many thought would be the saviour of France was getting ahead of his paperwork. With the satisfaction of someone who knows he is saving himself a job later, he penned a list of senior officers killed that day. Then, rather than command the battle that was raging outside, he thought the moment apposite to write a glowing report of how he had performed in one two days previously. Having ticked that off his to-do list, Bazaine then entered into a telegram exchange with Louis-Napoléon over what best to do with supplies at a nearby town. With all of this to get through, he was understandably annoyed when he was interrupted by runners, sent by generals desperate for orders to seize the moment. Looking up with the irritation of one stopped in the middle of vital work, he repeated what he had said many times that day: they were in good positions. They must defend them.

By evening, that proved impossible. Tired, demoralised and without leadership, French soldiers fell back on Metz. In terms of casualties, it looked like a French victory: twenty thousand Germans to twelve thousand French. But Moltke had got what he wanted: unless Bazaine fought his way out of Metz, France's most effective army was cut off.

———

When the empress discovered her husband was coming back to Paris, she was furious. 'No!' Eugénie shouted. 'I do not want him to return.'[15] As far as she was concerned, the only way Louis-Napoléon returned to the capital was victorious, or dead. Otherwise, she thought, there would be an uprising. 'I cannot return to Paris,' an embarrassed Louis-Napoléon informed Plon-Plon hours after resolving to return to Paris; 'the empress tells me that my position there would be untenable.' After a long pause, his eyes filling with tears, he added: 'The truth is that I am being chased away: they do not want me in the army; they do not want me in Paris.'[16] Preferring to face Prussian artillery than his wife's anger, Louis-Napoléon stayed with what was now called the Army of Châlons. He did keep his resolution to abandon military leadership and gave command to Marshal Patrice de Mac Mahon, hero of the 1859 war in Italy.

That still left the question of what to do with the Army of Châlons. Mac Mahon and Louis-Napoléon knew military logic dictated falling back on Paris to meet the coming German onslaught. Having left behind enough men to keep Bazaine under siege, Moltke still had more than two hundred thousand troops ready to march on the capital. Eugénie and the minister of war, however, were adamant: retreat was politically unacceptable. The Army of Châlons must march to rescue Bazaine.

This might play well for public opinion, but Mac Mahon and Louis-Napoléon knew it was a dangerous move. The Army of Châlons was inferior to the forces that had already failed to defeat the enemy, consisting of a mixture of demoralised regulars who had escaped earlier routs, marines drafted into the army from the navy and untested reservists and volunteers. On top of that, it was not clear what, if anything, Bazaine was doing. On 19 August, the telegraph line from Metz was cut. The last word that got through was that Bazaine would try to rendezvous with Mac Mahon near the Belgian border. So the Army of Châlons, just over a hundred thousand men, moved reluctantly, chaotically and slowly in the general direction of Belgium.

It was a wretched march. Unseasonable rain hammered down, and in the deluge men sank up to their knees in mud as roads became waterlogged. The soldiers were drenched, weighed down by soaked packs, and saw what bread there was, carried in uncovered wagons, turn to a porridge-like substance that oozed through cracks and onto the dirty ground. Discipline broke down. Badly supplied, hungry soldiers left their regiments and seized whatever they could from locals, which meant that they left in their wake a countryside ravaged as though an enemy army had pillaged it.

After a few days of painfully slow progress, Mac Mahon and Louis-Napoléon had had enough. There had been no further word from Bazaine, which surely meant he was not in a position to break out from Metz. What was now certain, though, was that the Germans were in pursuit. The only advantage the Army of Châlons had was that the move away from the capital was so militarily irrational that the Prussians refused to believe it was going towards Belgium, but reports soon confirmed it – 'strange and somewhat foolhardy', noted Moltke with the disappointed tone of a professional watching amateurs.[17]

On 27 August, aware the Germans were close, Mac Mahon, in agreement with the emperor, telegraphed Paris that he would stop the madness. If he continued, he wrote, he would be encircled by superior numbers. 'If you abandon Bazaine,' the minister of war telegrammed the emperor, 'there will be revolution in Paris.'[18] To Mac Mahon, the minister sent a direct order: he must find Bazaine. After reading the telegram, Mac Mahon crumpled the paper in his hands and threw it to the floor. 'They want us to go and get our backs broken,' the marshal said. 'Let's go.'[19] The emperor thought it absurd, but was in no position to exert his authority. He did, however, send to safety the one person he could still command: his son.

On 30 August, Louis-Napoléon was dining in a small village when an officer burst in and said that less than twenty miles away the French had suffered another defeat. 'But that is impossible!' the emperor interrupted. 'Our positions were magnificent.' Then, covered in dust, a general arrived and confirmed the news. 'The marshal', he said, 'asks your majesty to go by train to Sedan.'[20] Louis-Napoléon refused. His place, he argued, was among the soldiers covering the retreat. The general insisted: if the emperor did not leave now, he would be captured.

After a short train ride, Louis-Napoléon reached the nearby town of Sedan. He arrived late; only a few lamps gave a reddish light to the near-deserted station located on the outskirts. At the gate into the town, he pretended to be a general with his staff so as to slip in unrecognised. Wrapped in an overcoat, Louis-Napoléon stumbled painfully down long, straight, dark streets on the arm of an aide towards hastily arranged headquarters in the town centre. It was a hot night and every few minutes he had to rest, asking how much further it was. As they went deeper into the town, lights from the few bars still open lit the way; late-night drinkers stared at the mysterious procession. Finally, after nearly half an hour, they reached their destination.

Exhausted and hungry, the Army of Châlons lurched with a similar lack of grace into the town and its environs. A towering citadel built on the site of a medieval castle loomed over Sedan, but its fortifications dated from the seventeenth century and offered little protection in modern warfare. Mac Mahon did not want to fight, but with enemy forces pursuing him, he had been driven, as if in a hunt, into holding defensive positions shaped like a small triangle around the town. Beyond these, German armies, outnumbering the French almost two to one, were manoeuvring for the kill. 'Now', von Moltke said, rubbing his hands with delight as he surveyed the maps showing his troops encircling Mac Mahon's army, 'we have them in a mousetrap.'[21] Inside the mousetrap, a French general, Auguste-Alexandre Ducrot, was less decorous: 'We are in a chamber pot, about to be shat upon,' he remarked with Gallic charm.[22]

———

Before dawn on 1 September, under cover of darkness and thick fog, Bavarian troops rushed unseen along the main street leading into the small village of Bazeilles, to the south-east of Sedan. Believing they had taken their objective without a struggle, some of the Bavarians cheered. Then came rifle fire from fortified stone buildings. Half of the first Bavarian platoon fell dead or wounded. The Bavarians had blundered into crossfire laid down by experienced, highly trained French marines drafted into the army.

They were not the only defenders. Many inhabitants were armed and, as one Bavarian officer noted with disgust, had the temerity to protect their homes: 'even women took part in the battle and brazenly brandished shotguns'.[23] Shells smashed into the houses and streets, setting much of the village ablaze. Other fires were started deliberately as Bavarians smoked out the enemy in house-to-house fighting. After the attackers stormed one home, a civilian surrendered; a Bavarian raised his weapon and executed him. Fighting their way into another, the Bavarians found the stairs blocked by a woman with a child in her arms. She swore there was no one on the floor above. After hearing a noise, the soldiers barged past and ran into a room littered with rifle cartridges just in time to see men escaping over rooftops. By the time they got downstairs, the woman had gone, which was just as well, as one Bavarian soldier noted, 'because the murder of a woman could probably not have been ruled out'.[24]

When he heard there was fighting at Bazeilles, Mac Mahon mounted his horse and galloped towards the sound of the guns. Amid the rubble, fire and smoke, the marshal saw that the marines were holding the village; then a shell exploded near him, a fragment flying into his leg. As he dismounted his horse, the pain made him lose consciousness. When he regained it, he was in no state to command and designated General Ducrot in his place. Not that Mac Mahon shared with Ducrot what his plan was, possibly because he did not have one. Determined not to be shat upon, Ducrot ordered a breakout towards the west, abandoning Bazeilles. When the marines heard they were pulling out, they could not believe it. Not only had they held the enemy, inflicting devastating casualties, but they were taking back positions lost earlier.

When Louis-Napoléon heard that Mac Mahon had been wounded, he was getting dressed. As the officer explained what had happened, two large tears rolled down the cheeks of the emperor's pale face. What came next was even more painful: he mounted his horse. Knowing the discomfort this would cause, he had towels stuffed into his underwear to ease the distress and soak up the blood from his haemorrhoids. Riding stiffly, he led his entourage towards the fighting to rally his troops.

As he made his way, he passed Mac Mahon as he lay wounded in a wagon coming in the other direction. After a brief exchange, the emperor rode on. Beyond the city walls, sheltering by a brickworks with his entourage, Louis-Napoléon watched the fighting retreat. Bullets hissed past, smashing into a wall behind them; shells exploded all around. Then the emperor turned to his staff, commanding them to shelter in a narrow lane nearby. He wanted to ride to high ground and survey the battlefield. With cool resignation, and chain-smoking, Louis-Napoléon advanced through the storm of iron and lead towards an exposed artillery battery. The weather was now splendid, with a bright sun replacing the morning mist. Below, the emperor could see the enveloping movements of the German armies, bayonets glistening and forests of spiked Prussian helmets on the move, rushing into positions to encircle the French. Whatever his qualities as a general, Louis-Napoléon could see that soon there would be no escape and he was astonished that the order had been given to retreat from the one direction where it looked like a breakout might be possible. He sent an aide to Ducrot, asking the general to explain what he was doing – but not only did it no longer matter what the emperor thought, now it did not matter what Ducrot thought either.

In Paris, the minister of war could not understand Mac Mahon's dithering and defeatist talk. Convinced that enemy forces were only a small advanced guard rather than massive numbers, the regency in Paris sent General Emmanuel Félix de Wimpffen to Sedan. A warrior of the old school, Wimpffen could be relied upon for an impetuous attack whatever the circumstances. Unbeknown to anyone else, he had in his pocket a piece of paper naming him commander in the event of anything happening to Mac Mahon. Just before 9 a.m., Ducrot received word that Wimpffen had taken over – the third commander in as many hours – and was countermanding the orders the army had been following. Instead of moving west, Wimpffen wanted to exploit the Bavarians' weakness at Bazeilles and press an attack eastwards.

Ducrot was furious. He galloped across the battlefield to find Wimpffen. 'In the name of the salvation of the army,' pleaded Ducrot, 'I implore you to allow the retreat to continue. In two hours it will be too late.' An unedifying argument ensued, but Wimpffen held firm. 'What is needed', he said, 'is not a retreat, but a victory!'

'Ah! You need a victory?' retorted Ducrot. 'We will be very lucky if we even have a retreat by this evening.' With that, he rode off.[25]

Once again, Louis-Napoléon was worried. Though he thought breaking out through Bazeilles the better plan, he was somewhat alarmed, to say the least, that after trying to carry out the exact opposite manoeuvre, the order of battle had now been completely changed. 'Don't worry about it, your Majesty,' replied Wimpffen after the emperor had voiced doubts; in two hours, the general insisted, the enemy would be thrown into the river. 'Please God', murmured an officer in the imperial retinue, loud enough to be heard, 'that it is not we who are thrown there!'[26]

———

Fire, rubble, dead bodies: Bazeilles was an inferno. Most of the French soldiers had got out, but some were still holed up, fighting against overwhelming odds. In one fortified mansion, marines held back swarms of Germans with bayonets and rifle fire. But as soon as one enemy soldier fell, another clambered over the dead body and charged at the house. Inside, sabres and bayonets clashed, bullets pounded into masonry and walls collapsed under artillery fire, though this cacophony did little to drown out the screams.

Seeing they could no longer hold on, a few surviving Frenchmen dashed onto the main road. As comrades laid down covering fire, they fell back on the last remaining house in the village held by the French. Here, they beat off wave after wave of attack. After four hours, and having rummaged through the packs of the wounded and dead, the French were out of ammunition. A captain symbolically fired the last round at the enemy before the beleaguered men emerged under a white flag. Only the presence of a Bavarian officer prevented executions.

Others were not so lucky. With the French gone, the Bavarians unleashed their fury. They torched the few remaining buildings not on fire – asphyxiating, among others, a father and his thirteen-year-old daughter, who were hiding in their cellar. Those who came out of their houses were beaten, tied up and marched off to the train station. One Bavarian recounted the fate of a woman caught with a weapon in hand. 'She was seized by a patrol and forcibly led towards the woods. A circle formed around [her]. Within it the soldiers worked.' What the soldiers' 'work' consisted of was left unsaid, but 'after several minutes the circle opened; white clouds of smoke announced an execution'.[27]

While the Bavarians were taking Bazeilles, the rest of the German forces completed the encirclement of the French army. With Mac Mahon's, Ducrot's and Wimpffen's dithering, the day had turned into exactly what all three wanted to avoid: a defensive battle. Ordered to hold the triangle around Sedan, German artillery deployed on the surrounding hills pulverised the French infantry beyond the range of any reply.

Under this barrage, French infantry were supremely brave, lying down to minimise casualties, listening to the whistle of incoming fire and wondering if they were next to die. In one regiment undergoing this torture, the commander was stretchered away immediately when the first shells landed, barely breathing after shrapnel blasted a hole through his neck; another soldier died instantly, most of his skull removed, what remained of his head lying in a pool of blood. Dreadful high-pitched screeches that hurt the ears were heard, before each earth-shattering detonation killed many more. After one such impact, a trembling officer opened his eyes to see his tunic stained with gore, brains and blood from the mutilated men next to him. Turning away from the horror, he saw his lieutenant colonel, who stood throughout the bombardment, grimacing with every explosion.

A captain screamed for help after a blast crushed his knee and tore open his thigh from top to bottom; his orderly was disembowelled by shrapnel. Others had heads, limbs, entire torsos blown away, resembling little more than a mass of flesh held together with their torn uniforms, which dripped with blood. One young lieutenant stood up to order his men to stay lying down. Grapeshot smashed into him; he sank to one knee, then fell gracefully backwards without a word. His face was peaceful, as if dreaming, and his blond moustache glistened in the sun. If it had not been for the blood seeping out of two large wounds on his left side, he might have been asleep. Finally ordered to fall back into a nearby wood after hours of bombardment, the regiment lost hundreds of men without firing a shot. With no further orders, surrounded on all sides, men headed for wherever seemed safest. By early afternoon, with defensive positions everywhere crumbling, the only place that seemed to offer shelter was Sedan.

With infantry melting away, Ducrot ordered a cavalry charge to hold what remained of the line. The officer charged with galloping downhill into massed ranks of Prussian infantry supported by artillery surveyed the hellscape below and saluted without saying a word. While he was reconnoitring the terrain, a bullet hit the cavalry commander in the jaw. Somehow staying on his horse, with two aides supporting him on either side, blood streaming down his face, the general trotted back to his men, weakly raised one arm and pointed at the enemy.

'Avenge him!' came the cry as eighteen hundred magnificent battle horses with riders in resplendent uniforms, sabres raised, breastplates shimmering in the sunshine, started down the slopes towards the Prussians. An avalanche swept across the hill as the charge reached full speed in what looked like an unstoppable mass of men and horses. Facing it, the Prussians held their fire until the charge was two hundred yards away.

Shots rang out, and the front ranks of the cavalry collapsed, horses falling, men screaming, the rows behind tripping over the ones in front. Those who could rode off to the left and the right, leaving the Prussian infantry barely touched. More charges followed, meeting the same fate. Rallying the returning survivors of what had been a massacre, Ducrot asked an officer whether they might try again. 'As often as you like, *mon général*,' came the cheerful response; but the courage of each attempt was matched only by its pointlessness.[28]

One man who had not given up the fight, however, was General Wimpffen. Hastily, he penned a note to the emperor while under fire. Rather than be taken prisoner, the general wrote, he would break out through Bazeilles. 'Let your Majesty come and place himself in the middle of his troops. They will be honoured to open a passage for him.'[29]

———

The streets of Sedan were carnage as panicked soldiers poured into the town. Wagons, horses and men blocked the roads; shells exploded among them, setting buildings on fire. The wounded and the dead lay in the streets, skulls shattered, legs blown off bodies, disembowelled corpses barely held together with the red and blue rags that were once pristine uniforms. Through this, Louis-Napoléon rode back to headquarters. A few paces away, a shell exploded, covering him in a shower of dirt. Another blast knocked several of his aides and their horses to the ground, leaving two dead. An abandoned wagon and its horse blocked the way across a bridge, forcing the emperor to stop. Moments later, a shell landed in front of the wagon where the emperor would have passed, killing the animal. Despite constant danger, Louis-Napoléon had to go on foot several times, so painful was it to remain in the saddle. Finally, he made it to his headquarters.

Inside, Louis-Napoléon remembered that he was emperor. Ill, in mental anguish and broken by the enormity of events, he had doubted his judgement over the last few weeks. Now, though, he had had enough. He made a decision, a brave one, braver than his uncle in similar circumstances. After all, when faced with defeat, Napoléon Bonaparte ran away: from Egypt, from Russia and finally from Waterloo. Not the nephew: he would stay with his army and ensure what remained of his men would survive. Louis-Napoléon was going to surrender.

The emperor's decision, however, went against the code of honour that ran deep in the French army officer corps. For many, it was cowardice. Explosions all around him, picking his way through the debris of a routed army and terrified civilians, as shells crashed into buildings the man charged with taking the white flag to the citadel stumbled on, crying with shame, 'Me! Me! The grandson of a marshal of France!'[30] But when raised, the flag did not stop the murderous Prussian artillery. Inside the emperor's headquarters, the army's generals congregated. 'I don't understand', said a bewildered Louis-Napoléon as shells landed in the garden outside, 'why the enemy continues to fire.'

'Under the laws of war,' explained a kindly officer, 'it is not, in fact, by raising a white flag that one requests an armistice.'

'How', asked the emperor dejectedly, 'is it done, then?'

A formal request for a ceasefire, explained the officer, had to be sent to the enemy by the French commander-in-chief, Wimpffen, and he was nowhere to be seen. This was not, reasoned Louis-Napoléon, the time for labyrinthine military niceties. In desperation, he implored the generals who were there to sign in Wimpffen's place. 'Oh no, Sire, I cannot sign,' came the repeated refrain from commanders who preferred to let their men die rather than affix their name to what they knew would be one of the greatest humiliations in French history.[31] They were adamant: Wimpffen must sign.

Wimpffen, however, was on the front line, trying, almost singlehandedly, to win the battle. After sending his missive to the emperor asking him to join a glorious charge, the French commander-in-chief was going about his business with suicidal vigour, scraping together what men he could and throwing them into costly counterattacks. It came as a surprise, then, when not only did the emperor not come, but one of his aides arrived and explained that he carried a message asking Wimpffen to surrender. 'I will not read the letter, I refuse to negotiate,' said Wimpffen before storming off. Not long afterwards, a general accompanied by a cavalryman carrying a white flag galloped up to him. Seeing the flag, Wimpffen flew into a rage. 'No, no,' he shouted, 'I do not want a capitulation.' Then he disappeared into the fray, beseeching men to join him. Most refused, pointing to the white flag fluttering over the citadel, but he somehow managed to convince two thousand to fling themselves at the Germans. 'Could we not still', Wimpffen said with grim determination to an officer, having led his ragtag band down the road out of Sedan, 'try to make a breakthrough?'

'We certainly can,' replied the officer. He pointed out, though, that it would end in failure and the sacrifice of more men. Still, 'since you've suggested it, let's march'.[32] By now, nearly half the men Wimpffen had brought with him had disappeared. The orders were given and what remained of the Army of Châlons – an army that when it marched out of camp was over a hundred thousand men – and was willing to fight lurched in disorder down the road towards the thick, black smoke which spread like an immense cloud over the rubble that was Bazeilles.

Rifle fire from three sides cut into the ragged column. Men fell, the wounded crawled to the side of the road, others flung themselves into doorways or behind houses. Turning to look behind him, Wimpffen, with the weary resignation of a late-night drinker realising that everyone else has gone home, saw that no one was following him. As the bullets whistled past, at 5.30 p.m. – over three hours after Louis-Napoléon first tried to surrender – Wimpffen finally accepted that he could not defeat two German armies on his own. He would not, though, put his name to the request for a ceasefire. Instead, he resigned. Louis-Napoléon then asked Ducrot to sign his name. He refused. As did all the other generals. Finally, Wimpffen was dragged into headquarters.

'Sire, if I lost the battle, if I was defeated, it is because my orders were not carried out, it is because your generals refused to obey me,' he exclaimed, striding towards the emperor, gesticulating wildly. Ducrot, who had been sitting in the corner, jumped up. 'Alas!' he shouted. 'Your orders have been executed only too well. If we have suffered a dreadful disaster, more dreadful than anything that could have been dreamed, it is to your foolish presumption that we owe it.'

'Well!' said Wimpffen with the flourish of a man who sees a way out. 'Since I am incapable, all the more reason for me not to retain the command.'[33] There then followed a furious argument, which nearly came to blows; other officers held the two men back while they screamed at each other.

In fact, seeing that his generals were, if anything, worse at surrendering than they were at fighting, the emperor had gone direct to the King of Prussia. Noticing the white flag flying above the citadel, Wilhelm had sent an envoy to discover what it meant. 'Having been unable to die amongst my troops,' Louis-Napoléon explained in a letter given to the envoy for Wilhelm, 'it only remains for me to place my sword in your Majesty's hands.'[34]

———

While chaos reigned in Sedan, the German high command watched the drama unfold below from a nearby hill while enjoying a late lunch of bread, chops and peas, accompanied by copious amounts of red wine and fine sherry. Congratulating Bismarck on the impending victory, a US general there to observe the battle remarked that Louis-Napoléon would likely be among the prisoners taken later in the day. 'Oh no,' replied Bismarck, 'the old fox is too cunning to be caught in such a trap; he has doubtless slipped off to Paris.'

It came as a shock, then, when at about 6.30 p.m., an aide brought the old fox's letter to Wilhelm. After reading it, Wilhelm consulted with Bismarck and Moltke. They advised him to reply, accepting the surrender and asking Louis-Napoléon to nominate an officer to negotiate. Try as he might to get out of it, that ended up being Wimpffen. Later that evening, as Bismarck made his way to the house where Wimpffen would meet him and Moltke to arrange terms, he met a nephew serving in the army who offered him a drink. Grabbing the bottle and raising it to his lips, Bismarck said, 'Here's to the unification of Germany!'[35] Then he knocked back the contents in one gulp.

After that, he met with Wimpffen, launched into an anti-French tirade and informed him that unless he surrendered unconditionally, the Germans would bombard what remained of his army and Sedan the next morning. At 1 a.m., Wimpffen reported this to Louis-Napoléon, who was in bed. 'General,' said the emperor, 'at five o'clock in the morning, I will leave for the German headquarters and I will see whether the king is more favourable to us.'[36]

Early the next morning, in great physical pain, the emperor set out in a carriage to meet the King of Prussia. Bismarck, worried that his king might give Louis-Napoléon a more sympathetic audience, intercepted him on the way. The pair retired to a ramshackle weaver's cottage by the side of the road. They spent about fifteen minutes inside this dilapidated hut before deciding that the porch was a more salubrious place for discussions.

Chain-smoking and talking in German, Louis-Napoléon repeatedly begged to be allowed to see the king. Bismarck declined, insisting that the surrender was signed first. Frustrated, Louis-Napoléon refused to consider peace terms to end the war, maintaining that as a prisoner he could not enter into negotiations. In which case, Bismarck pointed out triumphantly, there was no point talking to the king. After about forty-five minutes of haranguing Louis-Napoléon, the Prussian rose, saluted and strode off. The French had no choice but to accept Prussia's terms, though Louis-Napoléon only surrendered on behalf of the Army of Châlons, refusing to discuss an end to the war.

With the capitulation signed, the emperor was granted the audience he had requested, though there was now no point to the interview other than courtesy. Retiring to a nearby chateau, Louis-Napoléon waited to meet King Wilhelm, reading a collection of Montaigne's essays to pass the time. When the king arrived, the emperor carefully marked his place in his book and went to meet him. After the exchange of pleasantries, a short discussion followed. Louis-Napoléon insisted he had never wanted war, but had been forced into it by French public opinion. That claim astonished the king, but it was Louis-Napoléon's turn to be shocked when he learned that Bazaine and the main French army were still besieged at Metz. The emperor had assumed that the entirety of the German forces had honed in on him at Sedan, leaving Bazaine free to break out and make for Paris. When he learned otherwise, he cried. After fifteen minutes, the interview was over.

Leaving the room, Louis-Napoléon met the king's son, the crown prince. With tears still rolling down his cheeks, he shook the Prussian's hand. Awkward small talk followed. Had the emperor managed to get much sleep? No, he had not. Then the crown prince commented that the conflict had been particularly bloody. Yes, frightful, replied Louis-Napoléon, all the more so when 'one has not wanted war'. That left the Prussian prince speechless, greatly surprised, as he recorded in his diary, 'to hear such a statement' from 'the prime originator of the present war'.[37] But his royal manners soon returned and he asked after the prince imperial and Eugénie. Louis-Napoléon said he had not heard from either and asked permission to write to his wife. His only other request was that as far as possible, he be spared the humiliation of having to face his troops and the French people. He asked, therefore, that he be taken prisoner via Prussian lines and then through Belgium into Germany. That was granted.

So it was that the next morning, shivering and barely able to support himself, Louis-Napoléon climbed into the carriage that would take him on the first step of his journey to Wilhelmshöhe, a German castle where he was to be imprisoned. It was raining, and with tender care, two aides helped him into a thick overcoat. But the nearest town in Belgium was over ten miles away – the emperor would have to see the French people one last time. His entourage behind him, the mournful procession rattled towards the border.

With one hand twisting the end of his moustache and the other behind his back in an attempt to lessen the pain from the jolting carriage, Louis-Napoléon surveyed the people lining the streets. Onlookers stared in silence; occasionally, he raised a hand to his face to wipe away a tear. The debris of war was everywhere – abandoned weapons and wagons, freshly covered graves, unburied bloody and mutilated corpses. The jangle of horses' bells, the rhythmic beat of hooves, rain and German soldiers marching: these were the only sounds. Then the cortège passed dishevelled French soldiers walking into captivity; Louis-Napoléon, crying, pushed himself as far back into the carriage as he could, trying to disappear.

'It is impossible for me to tell you what I have suffered and what I am suffering,' wrote Louis-Napoléon to Eugénie that evening when he reached Belgium. 'We have made a march contrary to all principles and common sense. It was bound to lead to a catastrophe. It was complete. I would have preferred death to witnessing such a disastrous capitulation. However . . . it was the only way to avoid the slaughter of sixty thousand people.' Concluding his letter, he wrote, 'I see that my career is broken, that my name has lost its shine. I am in despair.'[38] He also feared there would be revolution in Paris.

22

THE TERRIBLE YEAR

On 3 September, late in the afternoon, screams could be heard in the Tuileries. 'No!' howled Eugénie. 'The emperor has not surrendered! A Napoléon never surrenders! He is dead, and they're trying to hide it from me.' Moving from disbelief to acceptance, she asked, 'Why didn't he have himself buried under the walls of Sedan? Could he not feel that he was disgracing himself? What a name to leave his son!'[1] She said more, 'pale and terrible, her eyes brilliant with anger, her face distorted with emotion', recorded one eyewitness; she poured out a diatribe against her husband that lasted five minutes.[2]

Parisians shared Eugénie's shock and anger. In the absence of government confirmation, reports from Brussels and London fuelled rumours that Mac Mahon had been defeated and the emperor captured. Crowds swarmed onto the streets, and, passing the column of Napoléon Bonaparte in the Place Vendôme, people insulted the first emperor. Outside the Tuileries, they yelled for the overthrow of the regime. Inside, the enormity of events paralysed the empress and ministers. A cabinet meeting broke up that evening without a plan. Deciding there was nothing to be done but sleep, Eugénie went to bed at 9 p.m., to the backdrop of revolutionary cries.

Meanwhile, after midnight, at an emergency session of the Corps législatif, the minister of war – greatly annoyed at being dragged out of bed – confirmed the debacle at Sedan. Keen to get back to sleep, the minister irritably suggested that they discuss the matter tomorrow. Much to the chagrin of the tired minister, Jules Favre was not sleepy. While the government was in a state of stunned inertia, republicans had been plotting for weeks to end a regime they had long detested. Standing to speak, Favre demanded that the deputies declare that the emperor no longer reigned.

After he spoke, nervous republicans expected ministers to leap up in righteous outrage. Instead, they remained sitting on the government bench, impassive. Only one deputy half-heartedly protested that they could not pronounce the end of the Empire. Determining that the best course was to wrap up proceedings, the president announced that the session would resume at midday tomorrow. Finally, there was an objection: 'Not tomorrow, Monsieur le Président, but today, Sunday . . . It's already past midnight.'[3] The fate of the Empire would have to wait a few hours.

The next morning, bright sunshine shone as Parisians congregated in the streets to read posters plastered across the capital. These confirmed that the army had surrendered at Sedan and the emperor was a prisoner. Republicans called on their supporters to march to the Palais Bourbon, where the Corps législatif was to meet at noon. The people outside, reasoned republicans, would add the necessary revolutionary pressure should any Bonapartists in the chamber, emboldened after a sleep, dare to defend the Empire. For republicans were determined to reverse what had happened when Louis-Napoléon launched his *coup d'état* on 2 December 1851. Then, the executive power illegally shut down parliament. This time, parliament would legally end the executive by voting out the emperor.

But as politicians inside the Palais Bourbon read through competing motions, the crowds outside were restless. They had come to see the overthrow of the Empire, and they were not going to stand around while deputies debated exactly what form this took. Patience was lost, shouts of '*Vive la République!*' rang out and a human wave surged through the gates, into the courtyards, corridors and, finally, the chamber.[4] After vain attempts to restore order, the president fled. With great delight, two young men took his seat and passed the time by incessantly ringing his bell.

As citizens and politicians argued over what to do next, the firebrand republican Léon Gambetta shouted that Louis-Napoléon and his dynasty had ceased to reign. The crowds cheered. Then the familiar rhythms and cadences of revolution kicked in. Favre insisted that the republic must be declared at the Hôtel de Ville, as it had been in 1848. There then followed a dash to the city hall as rival republican factions hurried to get there first and proclaim a provisional government and, crucially, themselves as ministers.

Pushing his way through the throng outside the Hôtel de Ville, Henri Rochefort had to smash the glass pane of a locked door to get into the room where the republicans were deliberating on who would lead France. His dramatic entry saw his name added to the list. The preliminary theatrics of the revolution having been accomplished, it remained to be seen what other scenes would be performed. The one that Eugénie feared most was the storming of the Tuileries and the massacre of the royal guard, as in 1792.

———

Drums beating, sunlight glinting off bayonets, National Guardsmen marched on the Tuileries, and thousands of people came to watch the spectacle. Word spread that a republic had been proclaimed. Cheers resounded; the 'Marseillaise' was sung. In the streets, people tore down imperial eagles. On a lamp post on the corner of the Place de la Concorde the distinctive cocked hat of a policeman had been stuck up.

Inside the palace, Eugénie had already refused a request from a group of deputies to abdicate; but when word arrived that the Corps législatif had been invaded, the fear of mob violence decided the issue. Hastily putting on a hat, veil and cloak, and wolfing down some bread, Eugénie, one of her ladies-in-waiting and a few men hurried through the palace's corridors to the adjoining Louvre, from where they hoped to make their escape.

By the time they reached the museum, they heard crowds surging into the Tuileries and shouting, 'Down with the Spanish woman!' Rushing through the galleries of the Louvre, Eugénie paused in front of Théodore Géricault's gargantuan canvas, *The Raft of the Medusa*. They then ran to the main entrance, but the gates were locked. In desperation they shook the side doors until a porter opened one. As people flowed past, Eugénie flung herself into a waiting cab, which drove, at an agonisingly slow place, along the congested rue de Rivoli.

Seeking refuge in a nearby friend's house, Eugénie was dismayed to find that there was no one home. She thought that perhaps the US ambassador might give her sanctuary, but she could not recall his address. It was then that she thought of her American dentist, Dr Thomas Evans. His address was easy to remember – he lived off the avenue de l'Impératrice. After procuring another cab, Eugénie discovered that he was not at home either, but she insisted on waiting for him in his library.

'Perhaps you are surprised to see me here,' said Eugénie when Dr Evans came home.[5] Evans was surprised, but drawing on decades of experience of peering into people's mouths and finding the unexpected, he did his profession proud and replied that the empress could count on his services. Her eyes filling with tears, she thanked him and explained that she must get out of Paris before she fell into the hands of a revolutionary mob.

Though he was resolved to help, this presented a problem for Evans. He had a working dinner that evening: members of the American Sanitation Committee were due any minute, and such august guests could not be cancelled at a moment's notice. In the end, he resolved that an associate would host the dinner, while he and Eugénie planned her escape. So it was that as men discussed Paris's sewers in the next-door dining room, Eugénie and her dentist alighted on the plan to drive the next morning in a carriage to the Normandy seaside resort of Deauville and from there take a boat to England.

After a sleepless night, they set off at 5 a.m. As they made their way through Paris, there was no sign of the tumult of the day before – workers swept the streets, shopkeepers opened their shutters, milk wagons made their rounds. At the city gates, they were only cursorily questioned and the carriage rumbled out of the city, past the fortifications and earthworks that were being hastily reinforced in anticipation of the German army's arrival.

As they passed monuments heavy with historical significance – Malmaison, the former home of Louis-Napoléon's grandmother, the Empress Joséphine, to name but one – Eugénie's mood brightened, though she was still angry at being forced to flee. 'The French people', she complained, 'have great and shining qualities, but they have few convictions, and lack steadfastness.'[6] The Frenchman she was most furious with was General Trochu, the man Plon-Plon had recommended sending back to Paris to act as governor. After learning from a newspaper that he was now head of what was called the Government of National Defence, she exclaimed, 'How was it possible for him to so betray me?' She claimed that he had sworn as a soldier, a Catholic and a Breton to protect her, telling her 'he would never desert me; that whoever might wish to harm me, would have to pass first over his dead body'.[7]

They reached Deauville on 6 September. She and her dentist were paranoid, an anxiety not eased by Eugénie retelling the story of the flight to Varennes, when Louis XVI and Marie Antoinette tried to escape Paris during the first revolution in 1791, only to be recognised along the way, arrested and dragged back to the capital, before being put on trial and guillotined. In the end, though, it was the journey of another fallen sovereign, Louis-Philippe, that was the apposite example. The French king had taken a similar route when fleeing Paris after his overthrow in February 1848.

At Deauville, Evans found an Englishman with a yacht who was persuaded to help the fallen empress.[8] Light rain was falling early the next morning, 7 September, as the yacht ventured into a rough sea en route for the port of Southampton. By early afternoon, a ferocious gale was raging. The yacht plunged up and down in the swell, wind lashed sheets of rain into the ship, lightning shone brilliantly against black clouds and thunder broke like cannon fire. Eugénie thought they would sink, but by midnight the storm had died down. Blown off course and damaged, they limped into harbour at Ryde on the Isle of Wight at 4 a.m. on 8 September. Eugénie refused to rest. There were rumours that her son had made it across the Channel too and was now at Hastings. When this was confirmed, she left at once. Reunited with her son, Eugénie smothered him in a desperate, loving, tearful embrace while he sobbed in her arms.

After a few days in Hastings, Eugénie was keen to procure a more permanent and, crucially, more private residence – locals had taken to staring through the hotel's bay windows in an attempt to catch sight of her. Adding estate agent to empress smuggler in his list of tasks, Evans found Camden Place, in the bucolic Kent village of Chislehurst. Located just over ten miles from London and with a direct train line to Charing Cross, as well as being close to a Catholic church, the mansion was set apart in beautiful, secluded grounds, making it an ideal retreat. Indeed, it was so perfect that it is likely Evans did not 'find' Camden Place at all. It was owned by a man known to Louis-Napoléon who had received money from the French civil list. He had developed Camden House, furnishing it opulently in French style, including magnificent wood panelling bought at great expense from an elegant French chateau a few years earlier. Rather than renting it at market value, he let it to Eugénie for a nominal sum. The life of a nineteenth-century French sovereign usually ended in exile, and if one of Louis-Napoléon's mistresses is to be believed, Camden Place had been prepared as a bolthole for the imperial family.

———

Wilhelmshöhe was an extravagant palace that had once been the residence of Jérôme Bonaparte when he was King of Westphalia. Now, it was where Louis-Napoléon was to spend the rest of the war as a prisoner. Wandering wearily through the cavernous rooms, he looked on with dejected indifference at the walls, paintings, tapestries. Stopping before one portrait, he let out a gasp and took a couple of paces back. It was his mother, Hortense. Staring at the picture for a few moments, Louis-Napoléon then asked his aides to leave him. After spending time alone before the portrait, his confidence was restored. 'My mother was here, waiting for me,' he told a friend, and the painting 'moved me more than I can say'.[9]

He was further cheered when he learned that Eugénie and his son were safe. Having lost a battle and his throne, Louis-Napoléon thought his wife, understandably, might be angry. Instead, she was loving and reassuring in her letters. 'The darker the future becomes, the more the need to lean on each other is felt,' she wrote to him.[10] Plagued by anxiety as he was, this comforted him. 'Tell your mother to write to me,' he wrote to his son. 'Her letters are my sole consolation in prison; at least she has society to distract her – I have only my memories and my regrets.'[11]

An Anglophile, he was delighted mother and son were in Britain. 'I know,' he wrote to Eugénie, 'from the experience of my early years, that, in our position, one is only comfortable in free countries like England.' Once released from captivity, he continued, it was there he would like to 'live with you and [the prince imperial] in a small cottage with bay windows and climbing plants'.[12] They were not extravagantly wealthy. 'I have with me 260,000 francs,' he told Eugénie. 'It is everything I have, but, like you, I am proud of falling from the throne without having placed money abroad.'[13] Money, perhaps not, but property he did have, and he sold some in Italy. For her part, Eugénie had plenty of real estate too, and diamonds.

Few former sovereigns were better suited to captivity than Louis-Napoléon. After all, this was not the first time he had been locked up, and he even had with him his friend Henri Conneau, who had been imprisoned with him in the 1840s. Louis-Napoléon spent most of his time in a small but elegantly furnished study. He worked daily on pamphlets justifying his conduct over the war, trying to counter the powerful republican narrative that his corrupt regime, his incompetence and his wife's stupidity were the root of all France's misfortunes.

He was not deluded as to his role in France's cataclysm, but insisted that responsibility must be shared between himself, his ministers, the Corps législatif and public opinion. He did not have a bad word to say about anyone, except for General Trochu. He lambasted the betrayal when he learned that the man he had personally entrusted with the safety of his regime and wife weeks earlier had not only done nothing to protect Eugénie on 4 September, but had also gone over to the republicans. And he was still haunted by what he had witnessed at Sedan. 'When I think of all the good people I have seen die,' he wrote to his wife, 'and all for no reason, it breaks my heart.'[14]

Apart from his aides, he was imprisoned with French generals taken prisoner at Sedan, which led to awkward five-course dinners washed down with sherries and fine wines. Though he was no gourmand – something the prison governor put down to his ward having lived in England for too long – Louis-Napoléon made his usual quip that he had rarely dined so well. After dinner, everyone retired to his study for coffee and cigars. Chain-smoking, Louis-Napoléon was his usual affable self, making conversation while playing patience and flicking cigarettes into the fireplace.

Free from the day-to-day stresses of state and war, his health improved remarkably. He went for walks in the scenic grounds of the castle. Fluent in German, he got on famously with the prison governor, especially impressing his captor when he asked if the Prussian guards could be issued with warmer clothes because of an unseasonably cold autumn. Soon the initially sceptical prison commander was won over by his nation's enemy, struck by Louis-Napoléon's 'fundamental kindness, his love of humanity and his good nature'.[15]

When not working or walking, Louis-Napoléon received visitors. When one woman asked why he was working so tirelessly to seize power, he replied, 'Madame, it is my vocation.'[16] In part, Louis-Napoléon's good mood and hard work were because, only weeks after reaching a nadir of despair, his belief in his Napoleonic star burned so brightly he thought that he would soon be restored to the throne. He was not the only one. In London, his cousin Plon-Plon had a plan to resurrect the Empire, which, astonishingly, had the blessing of the one person who could bring it about: Otto von Bismarck.

———

On 15 October, at a meeting in Camden Place, Plon-Plon, with Persigny seconding him, blamed Eugénie for the collapse of the Empire. He believed she should have stayed in Paris and crushed the revolution. It was not too late, however, to make amends. 'It is you, Prince,' Eugénie replied, clenching her fist, 'who are in great part the cause of all the bad.' For twenty years, she said, instead of 'shutting up', he had criticised the Empire. Worse, Plon-Plon had sent the disloyal Trochu to Paris. 'You are our most dangerous enemy,' she said. Concluding her rant, she shouted, 'When I return as regent, I will know how to make all heads bow and yours as well – I am Spanish!'[17]

Regardless of how much she hated him, Plon-Plon had a proposal to restore Eugénie and Louis-Napoléon to the French throne, backed by Prussia. For Bismarck's war had been too successful. When he had kicked down the door of what he saw as the decadent Second Empire, he had not expected the whole champagne-drenched chateau to collapse. In its place, there was a republic which refused to surrender and preached a national war to the death in the name of the French people. For Bismarck, this was all very tedious and, frankly, unfair. Having defeated the French at Sedan and taken Louis-Napoléon prisoner, the war should have been over, a humiliating peace signed and a suitably chastised and weakened Empire still in place.

If Eugénie was willing to make peace, therefore, Bismarck, an arch-reactionary who hated republicans, was happy to give her and husband back their Empire. Plon-Plon put the plan to Eugénie: Bazaine's army, still holding out at Metz, would surrender in the name of the Empire and then, after Eugénie signed a peace treaty, these soldiers would march on Paris and

restore the Empire. Eugénie's political judgement had so often proved atrocious. Here, however, she showed a rare moment of perspicacity, for the
plan to return, in connivance with France's sworn enemy, was an absurd
one. After she rejected Plon-Plon's advice, he stormed out, refusing, as he
had countless times before, to have anything more to do with her.

'Misfortune embitters people and divides instead of uniting those who
have the same interests,' wrote Louis-Napoléon wearily in his customary
role as family counsellor to his cousin after learning of the quarrel.[18] As to
the plan, though he was briefly tempted, he thought it 'all quite extraordinary'.[19] With Paris under siege since mid-September, he wrote to Eugénie
that we must 'say nothing and do nothing which would have the air of
favouring dynastic interest over the national interest'.[20] Rather, everything
'done in France must have the character of spontaneity . . . and not of
an intrigue hatched by us'.[21] Besides, on 27 October, Bazaine surrendered.
Louis-Napoléon now reasoned that it was 'a thousand times better to remain
in oblivion and even in misery than to owe one's elevation to an abandon-
ment of one's dignity or the interests of one's country'.[22]

'For the moment there is nothing we can do,' Louis-Napoléon therefore
concluded in a letter to Plon-Plon. 'A reaction in our favour will come of
itself, for the anarchy reigning in France cannot last.'[23] It was not a time for
conspiracies, the arch-conspirator wrote to Eugénie after she had outlined
another madcap scheme, whereby she would present herself in France at
the head of a military revolt. 'We cannot', he added, offering advice that
would have surprised his younger self, take part in adventures that might
lead to the ridicule of being 'arrested by four gendarmes'.[24]

The months went by, and despite all that had befallen him, Louis-
Napoléon ended 1870 on an optimistic note. 'It is difficult for the year
that is coming to be sadder for France than the one that has just passed,'
he wrote to his wife on 29 December 1870, 'so we must hope.'[25] But the
first weeks of January 1871 were appalling. In Paris, thousands were dying
each week from malnutrition, the emperor's model city was being bombarded daily and inexperienced conscript armies continued to suffer awful
casualties.

'Oh, she is quite well,' replied Bismarck casually at dinner after someone enquired about his wife, though she still suffered from a hatred of the

French, 'whom she would wish to see shot and stabbed to death, down to the little babies'.[26] Though it was not quite as bad as this, Bismarck encouraged German soldiers to commit atrocities to force the French into surrender. Towns and villages were burned, civilians caught resisting were executed, near-starved women and children foraging on the outskirts of Paris were fired upon. There was no choice, therefore, but for the Government of National Defence to finally sign an armistice. In response to this, Louis-Napoléon abandoned his newfound scruples about conspiracy. Instead, he plotted to put himself back on the throne.

———

'Virtue and cleverness', wrote Louisa de Mercy-Argenteau, 'have no place in society.' What mattered, she continued, 'are charm and beauty, and these are nothing without the right dress'. That statement showed Mercy-Argenteau was very much a Second Empire woman, proud of the fact that she 'only walked to go from one room to the other or up and down the stairs; or to dance when there were balls'. Or to go to her bathroom, which was the talk of Paris, the bath a giant pink marble seashell sunk into the ground, making the water level with the floor.

She met the emperor at a charity bazaar organised by Eugénie in the late 1860s. Here Mercy-Argenteau was struck by Louis-Napoléon's 'big moustache' and imperial goatee beard, his 'proud nose' and 'wonderful eyes, always half hidden under heavy eyelids, veiled and dreamy, but deep and commanding all the same'. She liked him, thinking him shy, gentle and kind. For his part, 'it was my appearance that had attracted him; what he called my Olympic beauty, my white skin, and my fair hair'. More prosaically, 'he loved blondes', she concluded. The position of emperor's favourite mistress had been around for so long by the time they met that it had become semi-official and was one she now held. At court, she was fawned over. Eugénie, of course, was less impressed. The feeling was mutual. 'As ignorant as a Spanish cow,' was Mercy-Argenteau's verdict on the empress. 'I often wondered how these two could fare together, he so learned and refined and she unable even to spell properly.'[27]

Mercy-Argenteau claimed that their affair was platonic. But she also claimed that they had secret assignations via a tunnel running under the

Élysée Palace to the house that she had bought from Persigny, who, out of spite towards Eugénie, sold it to her at a knockdown price. Whether they slept together or not, the two were extremely close.

After the fall of the emperor, Mercy-Argenteau determined to do what she could to restore his Empire. So when in February 1871 Louis-Napoléon summoned her to Wilhelmshöhe, she dropped everything, leaving a sick daughter behind. Over lunch, Louis-Napoléon explained his plan. Though an armistice had been signed, a peace treaty was yet to be ratified. It was urgent, therefore, that Mercy-Argenteau speak to Bismarck. As part of the treaty, there should be a clause stipulating that the people should be consulted on what form of government they wanted for France – another plebiscite.

Mercy-Argenteau would be negotiating with a new nation state. On 18 January 1871, in a monotonous tone that had all the joy of a delayed train announcement, Bismarck read a declaration to the German people proclaiming the German Empire. Then, in the Hall of Mirrors at Versailles, a location designed to inflict maximum humiliation on the French, there was a shout of 'Long Live His Imperial Majesty the Emperor Wilhelm!', followed by loud hurrahs as German kings, princes and soldiers cheered.[28] Louis-Napoléon's disastrous decision to go to war meant that he had a strong claim, albeit unwittingly, to be one of the founding fathers of Germany.

Arriving at Versailles in mid-February, Mercy-Argenteau discovered it overrun with Prussian soldiers and full of noise – the clinking of spurs, the pounding of military boots and what she called 'rough' German voices. Tables were covered with bottles and glasses, 'a continuous orgy of strong spirits and tobacco'. In her own colourful account, her interview with Bismarck concluded when he tried to seduce her in return for lenient peace terms. 'If I had been sure of winning anything for the emperor or for France, I would have yielded, would have sold myself,' she reminisced; but she did not trust Bismarck. Instead, she fought him off and ran out of the room before slumping on a sofa, hair dishevelled and falling around her shoulders.

Mercy-Argenteau returned to Wilhelmshöhe and related to Louis-Napoléon what had happened. In a drawing room, beside a roaring fire and in the soft glow of a few lamps, he lay down on a sofa, his hopes dashed. Finding an old traditional French instrument, he asked her to play some songs. As the music drifted over him, he closed his eyes. She came to rest her head on his shoulder; he put his arm around her neck with 'infinite gentleness'.[29] And there they stayed until it was time for her to leave.

Bismarck thought Mercy-Argenteau charming, but it was political events that would determine his actions. Elections were held on 8 February 1871 for an assembly charged with discussing peace, and these were a disaster for Bonapartists, with only about twenty returned. Intransigent republicans who wanted to continue the fight also did poorly. The majority was royalist and in favour of the war ending. Soon the Assembly appointed Adolphe Thiers, the great survivor of French politics, as chief executive. For Bismarck, Thiers, with his disdain for the 'vile multitude', was as effective a bulwark against a radical republic as the Empire, but with the added advantage of being in power. Bismarck no longer had a use for Louis-Napoléon.

———

The former emperor thought that such a hastily convened assembly was a 'comedy'; however, he also saw its advantages. Bismarck's peace terms were harsh, he explained in a letter to his wife, and therefore it was preferable that the Assembly agree to them 'rather than us'.[30] That was written on his wedding anniversary, though he failed to mention it. 'Today is our wedding anniversary,' Eugénie wrote the same day. 'I am very deeply attached to you,' she added – in fact, more attached to her wayward husband than she had been for many years. 'In happiness,' she explained, 'these ties loosened. I thought they were broken, but it took a stormy day to show me how strong they are.' Concluding, she soared into biblical rhetoric: 'May my devotion make you forget for a moment the trials your great soul has gone through. Your adorable gentleness makes me think of Our Lord.'[31]

After it was clear Bismarck would do nothing for him, the former emperor had rationalised away any desire to return to power immediately. In a letter to Eugénie, he wrote, 'As long as the country has not had the hard experience of a government without strength, incapable of ensuring order and therefore prosperity, it will not come back to us.'[32] When the preliminary peace terms became public knowledge at the end of February, though, Louis-Napoléon was astonished at the price required to end the war he had started. France would lose territory on its eastern border in Alsace and Lorraine and had to pay five billion francs in reparations within five years. The German army would occupy France until this debt was settled. Such punitive terms, Louis-Napoléon wrote prophetically, could only be a fragile truce, storing up problems for Europe in the decades to come. 'Instead of re-establishing peace,' he wrote, 'it will sow hatred and distrust in the future.'[33] Furthermore, 'If France . . . had a government strong enough to work tirelessly for a resurrection, one could begin to hope, but what do we see? Madmen or egoists.'[34]

Victor Hugo, who could be described as both, agreed with Louis-Napoléon about the peace treaty's danger to Europe. Overjoyed at the end of the Empire, he had arrived in Paris the day after Eugénie fled. He kept busy throughout the siege; the sixty-nine-year old went through forty different sexual partners in five months. Though Paris had been desperately short of food – Hugo noted that rat pâté was on the menu, though he preferred to dine on zoo animals, including bear, stag and antelope – there were free performances of Hugo's vast oeuvre of anti-Bonapartist poetry.

Elected in Paris on a radical ticket in February 1871, Hugo said in the Assembly that the treaty's only redeeming feature was that it was so unfair that one day the French would rise up in revenge to seize the German side of the Rhine. Then, in gratitude for having toppled Louis-Napoléon, the French people would help the Germans overthrow Kaiser Wilhelm and proclaim the United States of Europe. Representatives found this vision of forced European unity no more appealing than they had the previous times Hugo had suggested it; however, a proposal by another politician resulted in wild cheers: Louis-Napoléon was responsible 'for all our misfortunes, the ruin, the invasion and the dismemberment of France'.[35]

'I protest', wrote Louis-Napoléon when he heard the Assembly had judged him solely to blame for the catastrophe, 'against this unjust and illegal declaration.' It was unjust, he maintained in a rather weak defence, because public opinion had pushed him into war. It was illegal, he believed, as the Assembly had gone beyond its powers, which were solely to decide on war or peace. On stronger ground now, he came out fighting. Only by consulting the will of the French people could a legitimate government be founded. 'I am ready to bow before the free expression of the national will, but before it only.'[36] This became the Bonapartist rallying cry: let the people decide who should govern them.

Whatever radical republicans like Hugo might say, there was no choice but to ratify the peace terms, and the same day French politicians debated them, the Germans held a victory parade in Paris. With regular precision, Bavarians, in their distinctive plumed helmets, and then Prussians, in their even more distinctive spiked ones, marched or rode down the Champs-Élysées and under the Arc de Triomphe. Some officers, pausing like children on a school trip before this monument to the military genius of Napoléon Bonaparte, read the names of French victories over their ancestors on German soil under the First Empire. As they did so, crowds of impassive, gaunt Parisians looked on in silence, occasionally punctuated by jeers and hisses. Just as his uncle's had, Louis-Napoléon's reign ended in foreign occupation. With the war over, the former emperor was released from prison. In March 1871, he went to England. Here, many expected him to spend his time exactly as he had twice previously: plotting to seize power.

23

THE END

On 20 March 1871, thousands of people stampeded towards Dover harbour as the steamer carrying Louis-Napoléon approached. When he disembarked, cheers rang out. Dressed in a dark blue overcoat, he smiled and lifted his hat in salute, but the horde was so thick that he struggled to get much further ashore. In the end, policemen had to clear the way. Then he saw his wife. She embraced him tenderly, showering him with kisses before taking one arm; his son clasped his other tightly. As this reunion played out, people lining the streets or leaning out of windows waved handkerchiefs, lifted hats and shouted, 'Long live the emperor! Long live the empress!'[1] It was an imperial welcome to rival the heyday of the Empire, and Louis-Napoléon never stopped smiling on the way to the train station. From there, he went to Camden Place.

A day later, one of his oldest friends, James Harris, 3rd Earl of Malmesbury, who had first met him in Rome in the 1820s, came to see him. 'After a few minutes he came into the room alone,' reminisced Malmesbury, 'and with that remarkable smile which could light up his dark countenance he shook me heartily by the hand.' What Malmesbury found so impressive was Louis-Napoléon's lack of rancour after his decades-long rise to, and then spectacular fall from, supreme power. Guessing what Malmesbury was thinking, Louis-Napoléon shook his hand again and said that such is life. He did not have a bad word to say about anyone, except Trochu. 'Ah,' he said when Malmesbury mentioned him, 'what a rascal.'[2]

A week later, he embraced Queen Victoria, who had invited him to Windsor Castle and was moved by Louis-Napoléon and Eugénie's plight. It was, the queen recorded, an emotional moment, which starkly contrasted with the state visit in 1855. There were tears in Louis-Napoléon's eyes. 'It's been a long time since I saw your Majesty,' he managed to say.

430

'He is grown very stout and grey and his moustaches are no longer curled or waxed,' wrote the queen, 'but otherwise there was the same pleasing, gentle and gracious manner.'[3]

On 3 April, Victoria returned the visit, travelling to Camden Place. There, in a stifling drawing room which the queen found extremely uncomfortable, they made awkward conversation about French politics. Louis-Napoléon said even less than usual. He was, once again, in great pain. At Wilhelmshöhe, his health had made a seemingly miraculous recovery, but the nature of bladder stones made remission followed by flare-ups frequent. For the next few months, he was in agony.

When he was not bedridden, quotidian life at Camden Place recreated the former emperor's habitual routine. Louis-Napoléon rose early, then read the British and French papers, as well as his correspondence. After that, he would retire to his study, which was adorned with a set of hunting guns, a comfortable chair and his writing desk. This was where he spent most of his time, penning letters, overseeing Bonapartist activity in France and, as ever, writing pamphlets, shaping, as far as he could, the narrative over his responsibility for the war, the military debacles and the hated peace.

In the afternoons, he saw visitors. Pacing up and down and chain-smoking, he discussed everything from his new invention – a slow-burning stove to provide cheap heating for the masses – to his plans for an organisation to settle international disputes through mediation rather than war. If there were no audiences, he passed the time reading. Sometimes he subjected Eugénie and his son to passages from his mother's letters. If the weather was fine, he went for walks. When it rained, he worked at a lathe in the billiards room, turning out woodwork. Among other things, he produced finely fluted egg cups. Tea and brioche were then served in the late afternoon.

Dinner was always at 7 p.m. and, as usual, it was a brief affair. His favourite dish, *perdrix aux choux* – rustic French cuisine featuring partridge and cabbage – was rarely served because his chef did not like to cook it and Louis-Napoléon was too kind to insist. After eating, he would retire to smoke more cigarettes and play patience. There was even a miniature court that joined the exile, and a grand piano meant that at least the music was better than at Compiègne, where the awful mechanical one had reigned.

On Sundays, he and Eugénie attended Mass at the local Catholic church. Outside, tourists flocked to catch a glimpse of the celebrities. Sometimes he took the train to London, where he could be found in fashionable clubs. Other than this, sightings of the former emperor were rare because Louis-Napoléon preferred to walk in the grounds of Camden Place, keeping apart from village life. Occasionally, though, he wandered over to the common.

Here, in the summer, cricket intrigued and baffled him. On one occasion, when he saw a fielder pull off a spectacular catch, the player was surprised to receive, in the middle of the game, a note from the fallen emperor congratulating him, and asking if he could repeat the performance. On another, Louis-Napoléon enquired as to whether cricket was played for money. 'No Sire,' came the response, 'for honour.'[4]

Louis-Napoléon had always had a sentimental yearning for a bourgeois family existence. At Camden Place, he finally got it and was closer to his wife – a lack of alluring court women no doubt helped – than at any time since the brief honeymoon period after their wedding in 1853. He had always made time for his son, but now Louis-Napoléon could pay him especial attention, busying himself with his education and helping him with his studies. The prince imperial enrolled for mathematics and physics classes at King's College London, though Louis-Napoléon taught him history and politics, the only way for an imperial heir to get the esoteric interpretation of Napoléon Bonaparte required. After Eugénie sold some diamonds and the couple consolidated their overseas properties, they lived a very comfortable existence.

In September 1871, Eugénie went to Madrid while father and son went on holiday to Torquay. On their arrival at Exeter station, a crowd mobbed Louis-Napoléon, cheering him and the prince imperial. Waiting to change trains, they sought refuge in the station cafe. Pushing the door shut, the relieved station master apologised for the crush. 'Oh! Not at all,' replied Louis-Napoléon. 'I thank them all.'[5] Similar scenes played out in Torquay, though as Louis-Napoléon noted, fortunately the welcome was 'less brutally enthusiastic'.[6]

He stayed at the aptly named Imperial Hotel. An Indian summer of idyllic weeks followed. Louis-Napoléon went for walks in the town, along the coast and to various historic sights. He spent hours on the hotel terrace watching the waves, the fishermen catching mackerel or his son swimming in the bay. As he wrote to his wife, the 'change of air' did him good. If physically he was somewhat restored, the war still tortured his mind. 'I would like to free myself from memories of 1870,' he wrote to Eugénie, 'but I am always brought back to them like a man swimming in the middle of a swamp making futile efforts to get out.'[7]

Louis-Napoléon had been ahead of his time in using the press to promote his cause. Holiday or not, he was still at it, talking to reporters. In fact, he might well lay claim to having held the first ever press conference, at least for a fallen emperor, when he assembled journalists from provincial West Country newspapers. When one remarked that he would like to see the emperor back on the French throne, Louis-Napoléon replied that it was not an enviable position. France, he explained, was so divided that if you met three French people, each one would have different politics. The *Morning Post* was not impressed with this public relations campaign: 'It is a matter for profound regret . . . that certain members of the English press seem disposed to adopt one of the worst features of the American journals – the "interviewing" of distinguished persons.' Undeterred, Louis-Napoléon gave an exclusive to the illustrious *Bath Argus*. The reporter asked whether the former emperor thought the current government in France was stable. 'That I cannot tell,' responded Louis-Napoléon. 'I do not think so. Nothing is settled.'[8] Given the tumultuous events in Paris earlier that year, this was something of an understatement.

———

In Paris on 18 March 1871, French troops under orders from Thiers's government, safely at Versailles, tried to take guns manned by the Paris National Guard, the civilian militia that had helped defend the city during the siege. Convinced that Thiers's move was the first step in restoring the French monarchy, and despising the peace treaty signed with Prussia, people across Paris joined the guardsmen and fought off the French army trying to take their weapons. By evening, the red flag of revolutionary socialism flew from the Hôtel de Ville. The Paris Commune was born.

For its supporters, the Commune was a socialist utopia, and Bonapartes had no part in this dream. So it was that cake and hot chocolate vendors did a brisk trade on 16 May 1871, as a huge crowd gathered in the Place Vendôme to watch the column that celebrated Napoléon Bonaparte's victories and the statue atop it be pulled down. Ropes were hung round the column and a bed of dung had been laid out to soften the impact. It was terrific entertainment; an excited crowd speculated as to whether the column might be heavy enough to crash through the street into the sewers below.

Revolutionary songs were played, then trumpets sounded, the signal for the statue to come down. One of the ropes snapped. 'Ah,' said one bystander, 'I knew it could not succeed.' Why, opined aloud another spectator, could they not just leave it – after all, it had cost so much to put up in the first place. Yes, replied a man, 'millions of human lives on the plains of Germany and in the Russian snows'. Regardless of the difficulty, the Communards were determined that Napoléon must fall. More ropes were fetched, and fifty sailors heaved on them. The statue swayed, a crack echoed around the square and the column, breaking into pieces as it fell, crashed into the filth below, a cloud of dust obscuring it from sight.

At first, the crowd was stunned into silence, like naughty children who have done something they know is wrong, wrote one British observer. Then there were cheers. Women stood over the statue shouting '*Vive la République!*', spitting on Napoléon Bonaparte's head. Men jumped onto the pedestal waving red flags, and various bands, playing with various tempos, struck up the 'Marseillaise'. Speeches vilified the despotism of the two empires and their emperors, though few heard the words above the loud arguments between civilians and National Guardsmen, who searched pockets for souvenirs and confiscated what they found.[9]

For the government headed by Thiers, the Commune was the reification of long-held nightmares about socialism. It had to be crushed. With none other than the man who had marched the Army of Châlons to its doom, Patrice de Mac Mahon, commanding, the French army stormed Paris during what became known as 'Bloody Week'. From 21 to 28 May, men, women and children defended the Commune against an army that gave no quarter.

It was a tragic, one-sided battle. In desperation, Communards set fire to some of Paris's monuments, including the Tuileries – a symbol of French royalty but especially associated with Louis-Napoléon's reign. At night, an immense cloud of black smoke rolled upwards, blocking out the stars; flames lit up the city that the former emperor had transformed, a red glow dancing on the Seine. In part, the fires were a defensive measure, but they were of little use. Nor was surrender, for many of those not killed fighting were shot against street walls. One of the worst massacres took place in the Père Lachaise cemetery. Here, hundreds of Communards were lined up and shot, falling into mass graves. The mitrailleuse – the machine-gun miracle weapon – proved more effective when used on French citizens than it had against Prussian soldiers. Its coffee-grinder howl mixed with rifle fire and the screams of those who fell, unarmed, before French soldiers.

After Louis-Napoléon's *coup d'état* of 1851, republicans had falsely accused him of similar atrocities. Now, it did not escape their notice that Thiers's government had dealt out a vindictive justice far beyond anything committed under the Second Empire. Indeed, when he learned of it, Louis-Napoléon was appalled. Numbers are disputed, but at least six thousand were confirmed dead, though perhaps as many as seventeen thousand were killed in combat or massacred afterwards. Still more, some thirty-five thousand, were arrested, and thousands were deported to overseas French penal colonies. One of these was the déclassé aristocrat Henri Rochefort, who had done so much to protest against the Empire. The irony was not lost on him. In a letter published in the press, he wrote, 'I, after being condemned by the Republic, shall experience the still more terrible doom of pardon by the Empire.' For Rochefort saw 'hopes for the resurrection of a dynasty thought to be dead, and which I was reputed to have buried'.[10]

––––

In the aftermath of Sedan, resurrection seemed impossible. The fall of the Empire led to a deluge of salacious attacks designed to further discredit the regime. Cheap, pornographic, misogynistic pamphlets fabricated Eugénie's sexual debauchery for prurient readers. Caricaturists, too, had a field day, depicting Louis-Napoléon's head atop a vulture and Eugénie's on a crane as part of the wonderfully grotesque – and popular – cartoons titled the *Ménagerie impériale* which lampooned prominent Bonapartists. To further humiliate Louis-Napoléon and Eugénie, their correspondence from the Tuileries was published; Eugénie's personal possessions, even her chemises, and the prince imperial's toys, including his Punch and Judy theatre, were gawped at and then publicly auctioned.

Yet by the autumn of 1871, there were signs that the reaction in his favour that Louis-Napoléon had prophesied, and Rochefort feared, was beginning. Plon-Plon won an election in Corsica; petitions with thousands of signatures and bouquets of flowers arrived at Camden Place for Eugénie's fete day; and the French press was awash with rumours of Bonapartist conspiracy. The news from France, Louis-Napoléon wrote, was always good. In fact, he was worried it was too good. 'I don't want to repair faults that I haven't committed,' he wrote to his wife when contemplating what would be on his to-do list when he returned to Paris.[11] Yet despite fears in France of a 'descent from Torquay' – a sobriquet that sounded more dramatic in French – Louis-Napoléon had merely gone there on holiday; he was happy to wait.

To further his cause, he took his penchant for interviews to *The Times*. He was not conspiring, he told their reporter. He had been head of state for twenty-three years – a figure which showed he had not stopped counting – and he relied on the wisdom of the French people rather than resorting to 'low intrigues'; nothing the Assembly did or said stopped him from 'being the legitimate sovereign of France'. And to those army officers who had asked him to release them from the oath they had sworn to serve the emperor, he said, 'I could not release them until, by a direct vote, the entire nation shall have chosen a definitive government.'[12] In short, everything was still to play for.

Apart from a few Bonapartist papers, the French press was near unanimous in ridiculing what amounted to a manifesto from Chislehurst. As many journalists pointed out, it was hard to believe a denial of conspiracy from someone who had three times conspired – the last time, in 1851, successfully – to seize power. Besides, editorials reminded readers that Louis-Napoléon had played no small part in bringing about the country's ruin. 'France might perish,' ran one article, 'might be reduced to a heap of blood-strewed mud – he would remain unmoved and trusting to the next plebiscite to make him emperor over the last Frenchman.'[13]

Arguments like these had no impact on the former emperor. During lunch with Eugène Rouher – Louis-Napoléon's right-hand man in the late 1860s, who was so powerful he was dubbed the 'vice-emperor' – they discussed a political problem, and Louis-Napoléon said, with startling certainty, 'When I get back to Paris, I will arrange it.'[14] In part, this was because Bonapartist fortunes were reviving, and it had been Rouher who rallied the party. When he returned to France from exile in March 1871, a mob attacked his carriage, beating it with sticks and shouting death threats. In January 1872, he was elected to the National Assembly.

At Rouher's house on the Champs-Élysées, imperial grandees, generals and former ministers met twice weekly. It became the nerve centre of a Bonapartist network that spread across France. They organised campaigns for by-elections, co-ordinated the Bonapartist press and disseminated propaganda – images of heroes from the Napoleonic canon proved as popular as ever, especially those of the prince imperial. Many army officers remained loyal, and societies and clubs were set up to cultivate devotion to the Empire. Thiers's government was terrified. French secret police agents were all over Chislehurst, and the concierge, the valet and the groom at Camden Place were in their pay. In Paris, they disguised spies as street cleaners to watch Rouher's house.

With Rouher at the top, Bonapartism leaned towards the right, and had it not been for Louis-Napoléon, Rouher would have leaned much further. For the former emperor knew that the political success of Bonapartism depended on appealing across the political spectrum, and, as was his habit, in Chislehurst he cultivated relations with oddballs, misfits and outcasts.

That was why Jules Amigues, a dishevelled man with a lustrous beard, hollow face and brilliant shining eyes, turned up, to its resident's horror, at Rouher's mansion and asked for seventy-five thousand francs to start a newspaper. Amigues was a radical who believed that workers had more to gain under the Empire than under a conservative republic. His visionary ideas – among other schemes, Amigues argued for social care for the elderly and a progressive income tax, the latter not introduced in France until the twentieth century – chimed perfectly with Louis-Napoléon's quixotic thinking when discussed at Chislehurst. This was exactly the kind of socialist nonsense the vice-emperor detested, but Louis-Napoléon forced Rouher to work with Amigues, who had an eye for strikingly performative politics. 'Amigues, a rare candidate who does not want to be elected,' was one political slogan he plastered across Paris on twenty-five thousand posters when seeking to win a seat in the parliament.[15] He got his wish: he was defeated. But in his pamphlets and in the cabarets and cafes of Paris he preached his version of the Bonapartist gospel to the poor.

He was making headway. 'The party of the Empire is the party of France,' harrumphed one pamphlet published in 1872. 'The future belongs to it, because the Empire is the only possible government in France.' These words were not, however, those of long-serving Bonapartists, but of recent converts who used to be considered some of the most dangerous men in Europe, written, as they were, by a leading member of the revolutionary and anarchist international movement founded by the extreme left-wing radical Mikhail Bakunin. 'We have fought the enemies of the people with such energy that the social order has been shaken,' pointed out the authors, adding, as though they were themselves surprised, 'and it is we who are imperialist!'[16]

Absent from the ranks of Bonapartist evangelicals was the original misfit firebrand, Persigny. His faith had burned so brightly that he had gone rogue and tried to found his own sect. Adding to the swirl of confusion surrounding the peace negotiations with Prussia, he had gone to Bismarck with his own plan. Believing his friend had tarnished the Napoleonic brand, he was privately hawking the idea that the emperor should abdicate and the restoration should fall on the prince imperial's head. This, and his hatred for Eugénie, saw him fall, permanently this time, from favour. But in January 1872, Persigny was seriously ill. 'I have forgotten what separated us,' Louis-Napoléon wrote as soon as he learned his friend was sick. 'I only remember the proofs of devotion you have given me for so many years.'[17] Sadly, for this letter would have meant a lot to him, Persigny never read it. He died on the day it was written.

Nonetheless, the Bonapartist message was, as ever, simple, populist and effective: under the Empire, the country prospered. Now, there was political unrest, economic decline, social division; the army was humiliated, France humbled. Moreover, argued Bonapartists, the Republic was an illegal regime and, worse, a German creation headed by the butcher of the Commune and enemy of the people, Thiers, nor would it ever be legitimate unless ratified by the French people through a plebiscite.

With Bonapartist support rising, there was no urgency to act, and Louis-Napoléon was willing to manage the party from Chislehurst and watch events unfold in France. After a lunch of eggs, chops and chicken fricassée, washed down with red wine, Louis-Napoléon told a supporter in May 1872 that he was too old to attempt adventures. Moreover, 'What means would I have? What certainty of success? I will only return recalled. The country, better enlightened, will decide.' Anyway, France was impossible to govern. 'We have tried all forms of government and none have succeeded,' Louis-Napoléon said. 'I too have sought . . . to make the country happy and I have failed.' He added, dryly, that 'I am not thanked for my efforts'. Reflecting on French politics, he sighed, 'How I wish France would take [Britain] as an example.'[18] Confident in the knowledge that the Empire would come back, for now there was nothing for Louis-Napoléon to do but wait for French people to become more British.

———

The Reverend Michael Baxter was as convinced as Louis-Napoléon that the Empire would come back. His vision of how this would play out was slightly different, though. For Baxter had studied the scriptures, the book of Revelation and the Old Testament prophecies, and they all pointed towards one thing: Louis-Napoléon was the Antichrist. Baxter had been peddling this theory for some time, but the emperor's fall in 1870 proved it. Unable to resist the temptation to return to power, Louis-Napoléon would reascend the French throne, ably assisted by the devil. With evil firmly ensconced in the Tuileries, popery would see a revival across the world and the emperor's power base would be in Rome. Universal war would follow, in which Louis-Napoléon would crush all his enemies.

That triumph would be short-lived. 'Noisome and grievous sores will fall upon him, and upon his worshippers . . . the rivers and fountains of waters run with blood . . . the sun scorch their parched and stricken bodies as with fire; and black darkness and dimness of anguish cover the whole of the dominions of the Antichrist.' Rome would then be 'subsumed into the subterranean fires of a vast volcano, the smoke of whose burning shall ascend for ever'.[19] With the modern-day Babylon of Rome thankfully erased from the earth, the Battle of Armageddon would be fought, Louis-Napoléon would lose and then the kingdom of heaven would be established on earth. In fairness to Baxter, if anyone was going to attempt such a foreign policy, it was Louis-Napoléon. On the other hand, the devil would have to be a very poor military strategist indeed to entrust his earthly forces to the command of the fallen emperor.

With the instrument of the Antichrist conveniently located in Chislehurst, it made sense to invite him to one of Baxter's millenarian meetings. Louis-Napoléon declined. He was curious, though, and sent a representative to a dirty music hall in Westbourne Grove, Kensington. When he heard an account of the sermon, Louis-Napoléon listened 'half amused'.[20] Ideas about his role in the end of the world showed the fascination in which the ex-emperor was still held. Hoping to cash in on this, an enterprising American, confirming Louis-Napoléon's worst prejudices about the country's love for the dollar, proposed to exhibit him in US cities, promising accommodation at the best hotels and a large fee.

Rather than getting in league with the devil, or going to the United States, Louis-Napoléon went to Bognor in the summer of 1872. It was meant to be a restorative holiday, but with Eugénie and the prince imperial in Scotland, Louis-Napoléon did not enjoy himself. 'It's such a sad hole,' he wrote to his wife, describing the seaside town, 'at the end of the world.'[21] He moved on to Brighton, where his family joined him, and then they all went to the Isle of Wight. 'I can see now the emperor leaning against the mast,' reminisced one teenager who went on a yachting trip with the imperial family, 'looking old, ill, and sad. His thoughts could not have been other than sorrowful, and even in my young eyes he seemed to have nothing to live for.'[22] But the mother of Winston Churchill, Lady Randolph Churchill, for it was she who caught Louis-Napoléon in this moment of melancholy, was wrong. He had plenty to live for. He wanted his throne back.

———

In the last few months of 1872, Camden Place was a hive of activity. A flurry of Bonapartists was seen coming and going. Rouher hurried across the Channel; Plon-Plon too. Seven hundred thousand signatures on letters and cards from across France were said to have reached Chislehurst. 'There must be something urgent,' wrote an anxious French government agent overseeing the surveillance.[23]

There was. Whether conscious that his health meant time was limited or believing Thiers's government was about to fall, or he simply could not countenance another summer at an English resort like Bognor, the emperor was poised to strike back. He was only sixty-four years old – King Wilhelm of Prussia had invaded France at seventy-three. And after all, as a friend of Plon-Plon noted, surely Louis-Napoléon, who had conspired his whole life, would not abandon the game without having thrown the dice one last time.

The plan was simple, and familiar. Fleury, back in his role as fixer, had squared the imperial restoration with Bismarck via back channels in the Russian aristocracy. After travelling clandestinely across the Channel and into Switzerland, the imperial pretender would wait at the border with France. Meanwhile, under the pretext of manoeuvres, the former commander of the Imperial Guard would march thirty thousand soldiers eastwards. Just as his uncle had done in 1815 – and he had failed to do in 1836 and 1840 – Louis-Napoléon would present himself before the soldiers and they would proclaim him emperor. At their head, he would march on Paris, other garrisons would rally to his cause, the people would cheer him on his way, and in the capital he would, once again, reign as emperor. But, asked Plon-Plon, 'Can you get in the saddle and stay there for a while?' – for an emperor must ride in front of his troops. 'I believe so,' said Louis-Napoléon.[24]

To be sure, a couple of days later he set out on horseback to Woolwich to visit his son, who had enrolled as a cadet at the Royal Military Academy. After a mile, the pain was unbearable. Louis-Napoléon had to do the rest of the journey by carriage. That would not do for a triumphal return. There was only one thing for it: he would have to undergo what he had always refused – an operation to remove his bladder stones.

———

On 13 January 1824, Jean Civiale, a medical student specialising in the treatment of bladder stones, invited eminent doctors to his home in Paris. They had come to watch a performance. Civiale had invented a long, narrow metal tube through which a drill could be passed. At one end, there was a claw. As the audience watched on, Civiale greased his instrument with wax and oil. Then he inserted the tube through the penis of the patient and into his bladder. Using the claw to grab the stone, the drill went to work. There was an audible crack. After forty minutes of excruciating agony, it was over. When the patient urinated, he passed the broken-up stone.

This was, to put it mildly, an unpleasant procedure. Though Civiale's patient survived, many others did not. Louis-Napoléon had, therefore, been reticent about undergoing this treatment. But after consultation with celebrity doctors at the top of their profession, including the Prince of Wales's personal physician and a specialist urinary surgeon, Sir Henry Thompson, it was agreed to go ahead. After all, Thompson had refined the procedure, operating successfully in 1863 on Leopold I, King of the Belgians. And crucially, from Louis-Napoléon's point of view, chloroform, an early anaesthetic, would be used. A preliminary exploration of the bladder was scheduled for 26 December 1872.

———

Three days before that, Louis-Napoléon welcomed to Camden Place a journalist who had spent much time with him at Wilhelmshöhe. Receiving him in his study, the former emperor pointed out of the window at the dull murky sky. '*Voilà*, the cause of my sufferings – these fogs suffocate me.' A couple of sunny weeks, he insisted, and he would be restored. Then they discussed French politics.

The Republic was a disease, the Empire the cure. 'It would', he continued, 'take only one word from me for the flag of the Empire to be raised in fifty places at once, from one end of France to the other.' Ever the conspirator, though, he insisted that was not his plan. He was still the Emperor of the French and had to take the interests of France into account. 'It is my pride and my consolation to be able to say to myself that I have had, in all my actions and in all my thoughts, only one motive: the happiness and greatness of France.' Although he was growing tired from talking, his faith shone: 'The Empire will be re-established – that is certain, as certain as above this yellowish fog shines a clear and resplendent sun.' The journalist could see the conversation was draining for Louis-Napoléon and took his leave. Rising painfully from his chair, the former emperor urged, 'Come and see me here often.' Then, pausing, he added, 'Or perhaps in France . . . in a little while.'[25]

———

'What,' exclaimed Dr Thompson as he strode out of the room after examining Louis-Napoléon on 26 December, 'did that man actually endure five hours on horseback on the field of battle at Sedan? He must have suffered agonies!'[26] The size of the stone he had discovered worried the doctor. It was so large that multiple operations might be necessary, involving considerable risk. After warning Louis-Napoléon's entourage, Thompson was told that there were strong reasons for going ahead regardless. He was paid £2,000 to come to Camden Place for a month and perform the surgery.

He arrived on 30 December, and enjoyed smoking cigarettes with his patient and regaling the empress and her dinner guests with descriptions of the proportions of Louis-Napoléon's stone. Eugénie insisted a plate of dates be brought in so that Thompson could identify one of a similar size. This done, the guests examined it with much curiosity and gasps of astonishment. Having likely put people off their dessert, Thompson played billiards with the prince imperial till late in the evening.

On 2 January 1873, the operation took place. It went well: the stone was crushed and there was only a small trace of blood. Coming round from the anaesthetic, Louis-Napoléon was surprised that it was over. Afterwards, he had much discomfort and a slight fever, but nothing out of the ordinary. Over the next two days, however, he complained of more pain, and there was more blood. A fragment had become stuck and a second operation was required. It took place on 6 January.

As well as chloroform, Louis-Napoléon was given opiates for the pain. This, combined with the shock of the operation, made him sleepy and incoherent. Nurses, doctors, Eugénie and his friend of nearly forty years, Henri Conneau, kept constant watch over him. On the night of 8 January, the patient was sleeping soundly and was stronger than he had been since the second operation. As there were signs that yet another fragment had become stuck, a third operation was scheduled for the next day.

At 8 a.m., the patient was considered well enough to undergo the procedure, but when the doctors came to check on him again two hours later his condition had deteriorated. His pulse was weak, his breathing laboured and he was unresponsive. Word was sent to the prince imperial to come immediately from Woolwich, the local Catholic priest was summoned and Eugénie went to her husband. 'But he is dying!' she shouted.

He was. On a small iron bed in an English country house, the one-time Emperor of the French was struggling to breathe, fading away. At 10.45 a.m., there was a feeble breath, deeply drawn. Then silence. Eugénie lifted up her arms, screamed and collapsed, sobbing, her head resting on the bed. Half an hour too late, her son arrived. After saying a prayer kneeling before his dead father, he clung to his body. He had to be dragged away.

Slipping in and out of consciousness in the days before his death, Louis-Napoléon had turned to his friend Henri Conneau and spoken his last words. 'We were not cowards at Sedan,' he said, 'were we?'[27]

EPILOGUE

The death of Louis-Napoléon on 9 January 1873 caused a sensation in Britain. 'An enormous name has passed out of the living world into history,' wrote *The Times*. Louis-Napoléon 'schemed much that was grander, nobler, more daring than any English statesman', was the *Evening Standard*'s judgement. 'The greatest story of modern times', concluded the *Daily Telegraph*, 'is now finished.' Though some radical newspapers differed, the British press was broadly positive. Even the *Manchester Guardian*, not a newspaper naturally sympathetic to Bonapartism, wrote that 'it may unquestionably be said of him that he was for a time one of the most enlightened rulers France ever had'.[1]

That was not the view of the French press. 'A great criminal has just disappeared from the world stage . . . a monster'; 'It is not a misfortune for France; that is what people will say to each other upon learning of the death'; he was a 'nefarious man' who had led the country to 'unspeakable disasters'; 'this maniac, this sleepwalker, who, like all monomaniacs, was known to be capable of the strangest madness'; 'It is in vain that this great criminal, to escape punishment, tries to take refuge in a coffin. The future will know all his crimes.'[2]

If the most vitriolic comments came from the republican press, there was little defence mounted in other papers, except Bonapartist ones. The trauma of the Franco-Prussian War was too much. Louis-Napoléon was a man who had bewitched France, putting it under a spell which ended with him as the man of Sedan who brought ruin to France: 'invaded and defeated, occupied, emptied of five billion, amputated of two provinces'.[3]

But more striking than venom from political opponents was the French public's indifference over the death of a man who less than three years earlier had been emperor. *The Times* dedicated twelve columns to Louis-Napoléon's obituary, which, an incredulous French journalist noted, would stretch to eighty pages in an octavo volume. By contrast, the official French government newspaper found room for only one sentence: 'Napoléon III died yesterday, 9 January, at Chislehurst,' a laconic utterance the ex-emperor might have appreciated.[4] Some republicans roused themselves to shout insults in theatres on the day news of Louis-Napoléon's death circulated in Paris. For the most part, however, the capital continued as usual.

In London, the contrast was notable. People ran to Fleet Street to get the latest reports, newspapers sold thousands of copies in mere hours and shops put their blinds down out of respect. Days later, huge numbers – including the Prince of Wales – made their way to Chislehurst to see Louis-Napoléon's body lying in state. Special trains were put on and crowds jostled outside Camden Place before entering and shuffling respectfully past the corpse.

Cheeks rouged, distinctive moustache waxed to stiletto-point sharpness and dressed in military uniform, with the grand cordon of the *légion d'honneur* among other medals, the emperor, bathed in flickering candlelight, looked better in death than he had for many years in life. With his head resting on a pillow, tilted slightly to the left, he seemed at peace. Beside him was his sword, at his feet the kepi he had worn at Sedan.

Much to the annoyance of republican French journalists, British Bonapartemania went into overdrive before the funeral. In London, Dickensian street urchins hawked cheap images of the late emperor. 'The fervour, the adulation, the baseness of cockneys and the English bourgeoisie have not slowed for five days,' complained a French correspondent. All this sympathy, he wrote, was proof that 'the English can reach phenomenal heights of political immorality'.[5]

Worse was to come for the journalist, for some twenty thousand turned out for the funeral on 15 January. At most, only a thousand were French. Among these were ambassadors, generals and former high-ranking imperial functionaries, but there was one last Bonapartist *coup de théâtre* for the procession. First out the gates of Camden Place was a delegation of Parisian workers, dishevelled – deliberately, so some alleged – and ostentatiously wearing that signifier of French labourers, billowing, dirty blouses. Their leader carried a tricolour flag. Even in death, Louis-Napoléon retained impressive message discipline: Bonapartism represented all classes.

Pulled by eight black horses, the hearse rumbled out of the grounds, decorated with wreaths of bright violets – a Bonapartist symbol – and the imperial coat of arms. After the coffin, the prince imperial, pale and dressed in black, walked alone and sombrely behind the body of his dead father. Contrasting with black mourning clothes, the gaudy decorations of a defeated Empire glittered in the pale Kent sunshine as thousands of inquisitive British onlookers lined the route while the lugubrious cortège lumbered across a bucolic village heath.

The procession ended at a small Catholic church. In the tenebrific interior, decorated with imperial insignia, there was room for fewer than two hundred people, but the guest list was a roll call of the great names of two Napoleonic empires, and Plon-Plon, who sat in silence save for muffled tears during the funeral. At the end, the coffin was lowered into its resting place as the Benedictus prayer was sung. And so, in an obscure, dimly lit Kent village church, the nephew of Napoléon Bonaparte, and the man who against all probability had restored his uncle's Empire to become the last Emperor of the French, was laid to rest.

———

The Zulu warriors tracking their prey had no idea that the man sipping coffee in the uniform of a British officer, with his back to a stone wall, was the prince imperial, known to his supporters as Napoléon IV. He had come to southern Africa to take part in the Anglo-Zulu War of 1879, hoping to win military renown worthy of his name. Now, relaxing after a hard day's riding while reconnoitring routes for the invasion of Zululand, he showed himself to be very much his father's son. Surrounded by abandoned huts in a small Zulu homestead nestled in a wide valley, and with the southern African sun shining down, he was holding forth on the Italian campaign in 1796 of his great-uncle, Napoléon Bonaparte. But it was getting late, and with the urgency of someone reluctantly winding up a picnic, the prince imperial readied his small band of soldiers to leave.

At that moment, rifle shots and war cries announced an ambush. Thirty Zulus armed with assegai spears and guns rushed from the long grass. Though the bullets missed their targets, the noise panicked the horses. Some men managed to scramble onto their mounts; others were not so lucky. One soldier whose horse bolted fled towards a nearby hut; a Zulu plunged a spear into his back.

The prince imperial was in trouble. He had not managed to get on his terrified horse, Percy, but was clinging on to a holster strap attached to the saddle. Sprinting alongside, he desperately tried to bring his horse under control. But Percy would not slow down. The prince imperial felt his grip weaken before the strap slipped from his grasp. Losing his balance, he tumbled to the ground. As he fell, a flailing hoof smashed into his right arm. Rolling in the dust before he sat up, he watched his horse race after his fleeing comrades. Stumbling to his feet, he turned round. He saw ten Zulus were stalking him. The prince imperial reached for his sword, but in his flight it had fallen from its scabbard. The blow to his right hand meant he had to use his weaker left to clumsily draw his revolver. Instead of fighting, he turned and ran down a slope – zigzagging to avoid spears – into a dry ravine, hoping to catch up with his men. They, however, were disappearing into the distance.

At a small knoll, he stopped and turned to face his pursuers. They, too, stopped, not expecting their quarry to halt. The Zulus were even more astonished when the prince imperial started to walk slowly towards them. As a spear was flung, he fired shots wildly, missing each time. Then an assegai lodged in his thigh. Pulling it out and holding it in one hand, revolver in the other, the prince imperial fought the warriors as they closed in. Soon, though, he was on the ground, deflecting blows as best he could. Then a warrior stabbed his spear through the prince imperial's eye and into the brain. Dying, he fell onto his back. Later, his attackers said he 'fought like a lion'.[6]

The next day, a British army search party found the bloodied body of the would-be emperor, pierced with seventeen stab wounds. Lying in the southern African dirt, the prince imperial's body had been stripped naked except for a gold necklace with medallions attached to it, including a miniature portrait of his mother, Eugénie, and a seal of the emperor Napoléon Bonaparte which his father had always kept on his person and left to his son. In the grass nearby, soldiers found one blue sock with 'N' for Napoléon emblazoned on it.

———

In the 1870s, Bonapartism had enjoyed a renaissance, winning electoral success in France; in 1879, the death of the prince imperial put an end to this. The Bonapartist party became embroiled, fittingly, in a tremendously enjoyable if suicidal family dispute. Plon-Plon designated himself the party's heir, but the prince imperial, who hated his uncle and his left-leaning politics, had named Plon-Plon's right-wing son as leader. Predictably, both factions haemorrhaged support as the Third Republic consolidated.

All this petty politicking was in marked contrast to Louis-Napoléon's skill, which had held together a disparate coalition. As he supposedly quipped, 'The Empress is a legitimist, Morny is an Orleanist, [Plon-Plon] is a republican, and I myself am a socialist. There is only one Bonapartist, Persigny – and he is mad!'[7] The witticism illustrates the eclecticism of his political thought, which he developed in his long years far from power.

In this time, he built on the myth that Napoléon Bonaparte was a modern-day Christ, which had put down deep roots in France during and, especially, after the First Empire. In this story, from humble origins Napoléon went on to perform miracles and ruled in the interests of the people, before being betrayed and dying a martyr. Like Christ, however, the original object of worship had little to do with the shape it later took. If Napoléon was Jesus, Louis-Napoléon was Paul.

About the only trait Louis-Napoléon shared with his uncle was that both were brilliant storytellers. Of course, Louis-Napoléon started with a good story, but through his writings, actions and faith in his destiny in the 1830s and 1840s, he almost single-handedly transformed the Napoleonic legend into a political programme with mass appeal. As its prophet, he believed absolutely in his own star and that his uncle watched over him. From this, he drew self-belief that did not border on the delusional but rather leaped across that frontier and became a fantasy so firmly internalised that for Louis-Napoléon it was real.

Then he willed his fantasy into reality, changing France. Like religion, the Bonapartism that Louis-Napoléon fashioned spoke to feelings, a yearning for a better world, a second coming of Napoleonic greatness. Though the practice never reflected the gospel according to Louis-Napoléon, he made his centrist message pitched between revolution and reaction radical, popular and perfectly attuned to mass democratic politics. Eradicate poverty, end revolutions, make France great again – these were the messages at the heart of Bonapartism that were preached before the December 1848 presidential elections.

Bar some noisy dissenters, the congregation received the sermon with rapture. Louis-Napoléon's landslide election as President of the Second Republic in December 1848 was an unprecedented moment. He became the first directly elected head of state in history. Once president, and despite having little knowledge of France, let alone politics, he outmanoeuvred opponents with years of experience who thought they were far more intelligent than a playboy adventurer with a famous name. In 1852, one year after his ruthless *coup d'état*, he realised the dream that he had long been mocked for dreaming: he became emperor.

This was one of the more improbable rises in modern history. Growing up in rural seclusion in Switzerland, he imbibed the intellectual currents of the time and became an incorrigible romantic, dreaming up unrealistic schemes and conspiring in smoke-filled taverns. Three derisory failures – the Italian revolt in 1831, in which his brother died, and his two abject attempts to seize power in 1836 and 1840 – should have disabused him of any notion that these plans might one day succeed. When he was imprisoned for life after being fished out of the harbour at Boulogne, only someone with extraordinary self-confidence – or insane – could boast that his incarceration had brought him closer to power than ever. In 1846, he walked through the front door of the fortress dressed as a workman and fell back into the life of an English dandy, with an outrageously glamorous mistress, the daughter of a Brighton bootmaker.

In 1848, aged forty, he became President of France. For the French elite, this was a travesty. That a man like Louis-Napoléon could be elected head of the French state was shocking; that he became emperor, even worse. It belittled the mental image they had of the grandeur of the nation. Alexis de Tocqueville maintained that Louis-Napoléon's ascent was the result of the outpouring of political illiteracy by the French people combined with social and economic forces that saw 'a dwarf' – Louis-Napoléon – 'reach the top of a cliff that a giant placed on dry ground could not scale'.[8] Victor Hugo seasoned this view with sublime language and deep hatred, first in prose, in *Napoléon le pétit*, and then in verse, *Les Châtiments*. These crystallised Louis-Napoléon's image as a mendacious, idiotic tyrant in the mind of any self-respecting progressive young French person for generations to come.

It was excoriation from the pen of a man whose fame transcends even Hugo's, Karl Marx, that fossilised the emperor's historical reputation. In his essay analysing Louis-Napoléon's ascent to power, Marx characterised him as a 'grotesque mediocrity'. Then he provided the eulogy for the Second Empire at its inception: 'the first time as tragedy, the second time as farce'.[9] The first Napoléon was history on an operatic scale; the nephew was pastiche, vaudeville, farce. The epithet stuck. After all, there was something faintly ridiculous about Louis-Napoléon – the waxed moustache, the gentle billow of imperial silk pyjamas as he philandered his way through an archaic court, and the incompetence with which the emperor met the tragedy of the Franco-Prussian War. Marx seemed to prophesy this in 1852, when the essay was published.

Arguments about Louis-Napoléon's fitness to rule were not new – he had heard them his whole life. Born into imperial power under the First Empire, he grew up as an outsider, mocked by French high society. What he shared with the French electorate in 1848, and even when emperor, was a disdain for the elites that had governed France from 1815 to 1848. They spoke in hifalutin terms about the importance of liberty, representative parliamentary institutions or respect for the rules-based international order set up after the defeat of his uncle at Waterloo in 1815. As his long-time friend Hortense Cornu said, to Louis-Napoléon these appeared as the 'silliest trash'.

Instead, with remarkable foresight – he was one of the first to realise that conservative ideas could be popular to a mass electorate – Louis-Napoléon spoke the plain language of stability, the will of the people and French power. His name gave him a platform, but it was a message voters wanted to hear and proved far more attractive than alternative offers. 'The people and he, therefore, perfectly agree,' remarked Hortense Cornu.[10] One of the great theorists of democracy, Tocqueville, who also predicted its rise, may have had nothing but disdain for Louis-Napoléon, but whatever his intellectual merits, Tocqueville was a terrible politician who twice cowered as mobs invaded the parliament he sat in. Rather than fearing the people,

Louis-Napoléon embraced the future and proved a precociously skilled political practitioner.

He believed that the art of politics lay in anticipating what was to come. Long before many of his contemporaries, who thought themselves infinitely more sophisticated, he realised mass democracy must legitimate power. Not only was this a prescient insight, but also, in its embrace of popular politics, the regime he created after his *coup d'état* in 1851 was a new phenomenon. Democracy did not, as many feared, mean revolution, and Louis-Napoléon ruled France for longer than anyone – including his uncle – since Louis XV, who died in 1774. Whatever his detractors said, this required dextrous skill and an innovative political construct.

Part of that involved institutionalising regular universal male-suffrage elections in France. This, Louis-Napoléon believed, would be one of his greatest achievements. Indeed, ever the dilettante, in 1868 he sketched out the plot for a novel he never wrote. The narrative sees a Frenchman who has lived abroad for decades return to France. He is astounded by the material progress, the railways, telegraphs, the wide, clean streets of Paris, and people going to the Hôtel de Ville to vote rather than overthrow the government. In an ironic real-life plot twist, this latter point remained unrealised – the Republic that replaced the Empire was proclaimed at the Hôtel de Ville after revolt.

Yet the regime he created was, at times, thrillingly confident, with tremendous bombast, pageantry – never again would the French state party as hard and as extravagantly as it did under the Second Empire – and self-confidence. It was capable of audacious acts. Smashing the old Paris to build a new one, or creating the Suez Canal – these were policies of colossal ambition that harnessed technical expertise, manpower and capital on a vast scale, reshaping cities and global trade.

But they were not vanity projects, for another of Louis-Napoléon's insights was that the state should occupy itself not just, as it had in the past, with security, foreign affairs and law, but with what would today be termed 'economic growth'. As ever with the Second Empire, rhetoric far outstripped reality, but much was achieved. As one of the regime's publicists put it, the Empire had on its side 'universal suffrage and a glorious parvenu who represents admirably all those who want to parvenir'.[11]

Paris, of course, was the centrepiece, a monumental legacy. The reconstruction of the capital was the Second Empire's most imperious feat of creative destruction. It was the emperor's personal project and would not have happened without his vision and Haussmann's monomaniacal obsession. Money was procured by whatever means necessary, leveraging the city's accounts to eye-watering levels to produce one of the most magnificent urban environments in the world.

The people of Paris, however, did not thank him for it. As the years went by, the city became a centre of resistance, particularly as the economic boom of the 1850s gave way to regular downturns in the 1860s. Again, Louis-Napoléon showed political talent. He did what recent French rulers had failed to do: reform to preserve. The process that resulted in the liberal Empire saw a revitalisation of imperial politics in 1870. Drawing on men of talent regardless of party, he created a country that – the British ambassador said as much – was more democratic than Britain. It was brimming with ideas, confidence and hope; millions of Frenchmen endorsed in 1870 what they had backed in 1851. After twenty years in power, it was a stunning political éclat.

For all the mistakes, the missteps, the misery of those who suffered from the economic crises or faced arbitrary repression, and the failure to do as much as he had hoped, Louis-Napoléon had created and sustained an extraordinary edifice, crowned with liberty as he promised it would be. Had he died on 9 May 1870, he would have been remembered as one of the most successful rulers of modern France and a politician of enormous ability. But he died in 1873, having led France into a cataclysmic abyss, presiding over one of the most spectacular, staggeringly incompetent and self-inflicted catastrophes in modern history.

––––––

In foreign affairs, the only checks on Louis-Napoléon's power were the limits of his imagination and what was possible. As he was a dreamer who frequently attempted the improbable, these proved weak restraints. Furthermore, he conducted foreign policy as he had his life in the shadows before he came to power. It was conspiracy conducted at the level of international diplomacy. Back channels, informal agents and secret meetings with cigarette smoke hanging heavy in the air were the modus operandi of a man who held the destiny of Europe, and much of the globe, in his hands.

He wanted to make France great again, a diplomatic, economic and cultural superpower. But he also wanted his country to be a progressive force on the right side of history. As in domestic politics, Louis-Napoléon thought that the skill of a statesman lay in anticipating irresistible change. Tearing up the treaties imposed after his uncle's defeats in 1814–15 was not only driven by a desire to overturn France's humiliation, but as the Vienna settlement was intended to put Europe back into a conservative slumber after the tumult of the revolutionary and Napoleonic wars, it was also an attempt to create a new European order based on liberal national-ism and presided over by France.

With the demands of nationalism met – German and Italian unifications were the main questions, but there were others – and greater economic integration, Europe would enter a golden age. In this ideal world, conflict would be settled by international organisations; trade and currency and much besides would be regulated to the mutual benefit of neighbouring nations. Some have seen in this the germ of the European Union or the United Nations.

It was a laudable dream, but a naive one, not least because it clashed with the more cynical demands Louis-Napoléon made. He would help liberate Italy; France must have Nice and Savoy in return. Prussia could lead Germany; France must have Luxembourg or Belgium as compen-sation. Moreover, though Bismarck would later perfect the art, the way Louis-Napoléon engineered war against Austria in 1859 shocked European powers, especially France's then ally Britain. Duplicitous, mendacious and entirely disregarding means in favour of ends, Louis-Napoléon conducted international relations in a way that meant that by 1870 no one trusted him and France had no allies.

Moreover, his opportunism and penchant to gamble – traits that tended to serve him well in domestic politics – resulted in short-term decisions that damaged France's longer-term interests. His first foray into foreign policy in 1849 backfired spectacularly. Expecting to be welcomed as a lib-erator, Louis-Napoléon sent a French army to end the Roman Republic, restore the pope to power and usher in a liberal settlement between radicals and reactionaries. In 1870, twenty-one years later, French troops were still there propping up the pope and denying the newly unified Italy what many saw as its rightful capital. Yet Louis-Napoléon had also gone to war in 1859 to drive Austria out of Italy and help Italian nationalism. Thus the self-proclaimed friend of Italy was, in the minds of many Italians, its number-one enemy. Joined-up realpolitik this was not, particularly as Italy might have been an ally against Prussia.

Then there was Mexico. Louis-Napoléon was one of the few European statesmen to attempt to stop rising US power, which he believed, correctly as it turned out, would one day enable the United States to dictate terms to Europe. Regime change with thirty thousand French troops propping up a Habsburg archduke south of the Rio Grande was, to put it mildly, a quixotic solution to the perceived problem. It ended in disaster, with a humiliating withdrawal and the execution of the man he sent to rule Mexico, Ferdinand Maximilian, who happened to be the brother of the Emperor of Austria, hardly endearing Louis-Napoléon to what should have been another key ally in 1870.

At the time, contemporaries thought such outlandish foreign policy misadventures were hardwired into a Bonapartism they caricatured as militaristic, in thrall to popular opinion and desperate to emulate the feats of his uncle's Empire. The Crimean War, however, was the only conflict that vaguely fits that model. Though there were other reasons, Louis-Napoléon entered into it with the hope of bringing lustre to his regime, which, for once, it did.

But the war was unpopular in France. Despite his British ally urging him to prolong it, Louis-Napoléon ended it as soon as he could. Similarly, in 1859, the invasion of Italy was met with bewilderment in France. When it looked like becoming a protracted, Europe-wide conflagration, Louis-Napoléon brought hostilities to a close barely two and a half months after declaring war. In Mexico, when it became clear even to him that only more French lives and money could prop up Maximilian, he put an end to French intervention.

Napoleonic foreign policy this was not. As he had never seen war at first hand, the horrors of the Italian campaign – the relatively small number of casualties would have barely registered with the first Napoléon – deeply moved the emperor. After 1859, he was anything but bellicose. In 1863, he refused to countenance war to defend Poland against Russian repression, perhaps the only war that might have been popular in France. In 1864, 1866 and 1867, many urged him to fight Prussia. He would not.

Perhaps he should have done. Far from reckless military adventures, Louis-Napoléon's foreign policy was a mix of the bold, the indecisive and the artless. In Italy, he could have fought on, uniting the peninsula in a crusade against Austria and, if necessary, Prussia and perhaps Russia too. After all, that is not only what his uncle might have done, it was what he did. Or he could simply not have invaded – Austria did not pose any threat to France. Instead, he tried, and failed, to accomplish his goals with the minimum of effort. In Mexico, the pattern repeated itself. He could have done more, or nothing. Instead, he did something, but not enough.

Yet despite over twenty years of counterproductive foreign policy, Louis-Napoléon and France came out relatively unscathed. There were even some successes – for example, victories in Crimea and ones he personally commanded in Italy against Austria in 1859. The commercial treaty with Britain was built upon with agreements between other European powers which liberalised the continent's trade. The Suez Canal was constructed under French aegis, and its opening in 1869 appeared to show France at the height of its global prestige.

There was, then, no reason to suspect 1870 would be any different to what had gone before, or more tense than the last tense few years with Prussia. Thus Émile Ollivier could stand up in the Corps législatif and proclaim on 30 June 1870 that at 'no time has the peace of Europe seemed more assured'.[12] Three weeks later, France was at war.

This came from a series of stunning blunders which escalated at speed. There were longer-term factors that meant the cold war between France and Prussia was likely to become hot, but there did not need to be a war in July 1870. Haunted by the decision, for the last three years of his life Louis-Napoléon insisted that public opinion had compelled him to fight. There was febrile chauvinism on the streets of Paris, but the government had done much to encourage it. Moreover, it showed just how impaired illness and old age had made Louis-Napoléon's judgement that he made the mistake he had spent his political career not making: he interpreted the mood in Paris as being that of the nation. Outside the capital, there was little clamour for war.

Where there was a crescendo of bravado was in Louis-Napoléon's court, not least from his rabidly anti-Prussian wife, Eugénie. Weak, tired, ill, Louis-Napoléon, who had weathered tirades from his wife for seventeen years, and had happily ignored opinions from his ministers and courtiers throughout his reign, now caved in to angry men and one woman.

This is all the more shocking given that he was one of the few among the Empire's military and political elite who understood the dangers of fighting Prussia. After Prussia's victory against Austria in 1866, Louis-Napoléon realised that the size of the French army needed to be dramatically increased. The French emperor's plan would have seen the army and its reserve total one million men. This was so unpopular that it was watered down in the Corps législatif to next to nothing. In a revealing contrast, when Prussia's parliament opposed Bismarck's reforms that helped turn the army into an instrument that could achieve his aggressive aims, he bypassed the constitution and did it anyway.

Given the outcome, the decision to go to war against Prussia seems absurd; but French generals and many informed neutral observers were confident of French victory. Even Queen Victoria's daughter, who had married into the Prussian royal family, wrote that the odds were stacked against Germany. If the decision to fight was not so ridiculous, the lack of planning was. The French strategy was little more than a number of unlikely assumptions. One of these was that France would have international support, and it would not have taken great diplomatic skill to have secured allies. Denmark, Austria and Italy were all hostile towards Prussia. A convincing pitch from a trustworthy friend might have won sympathy in Britain. After all, the first half of the twentieth century saw Britain embroiled in two titanic struggles against Germany – 1870 would have been a prescient time to intervene. The indecorous lurch to war, however, meant that in the eyes of European opinion, French braggadocio combined with Napoleonic bellicosity ensured France was seen as the aggressor.

In no small part because he self-mythologised it, the French rush to war is often seen as the culmination of Bismarck's Machiavellian genius, the triumph of masterful, years-long realpolitik with which he sealed France's fate, goading the Gallic bull into a conflict for which it was ill prepared. Louis-Napoléon was unfortunate to come up against a statesman of Bismarck's calibre, who, unlike the French emperor, was ruthless, who had a long-term vision and whose thinking was not clouded with Louis-Napoléon's vague idealism. In this instance, however, Bismarck required all the wit of a chess grandmaster defeating the local pub drunk.

Then, imprisoned by his Napoleonic destiny, Louis-Napoléon felt compelled to command his army. Physically debilitated, in agony and with his mental faculties diminished, he meddled in what passed for French military planning, making a confused situation worse. The calamitous first weeks of the war broke Louis-Napoléon. His indecision, self-doubt and mental and physical agony reduced him to the ignominious role of luxurious baggage, being dragged along in agony with his army to the camp he had so lovingly created at Châlons, where in happier years he could pretend to be a soldier. Here, he was bullied into returning to Paris by Plon-Plon. Then his wife bullied him into staying with the scraped-together Army of Châlons. Finally, Eugénie, along with the minister of war, bullied Louis-Napoléon and the army's commander into a march that went against all military logic. Shattered, resigned, fatalistic, he acquiesced to disaster.

What followed was not farce, but tragedy – for Louis-Napoléon, for the hundred thousand or so men in the Army of Châlons, for France. The French emperor rode through the battlefield almost certainly looking for death. He did not find it. Instead, he found courage. In the midst of his world crumbling, with shells smashing into his headquarters, he realised that he was still emperor. He could stop the nightmare. Unlike Napoléon Bonaparte, he would not abandon his army, nor would he insist on suicidal resistance. Louis-Napoléon showed himself to be a man of tremendous bravery who put the lives of his soldiers before his honour. He surrendered. He was not thanked for it. Rather, he became the most vilified man in France.

———

That one man was responsible for the ruin of France was a convenient fiction few wanted to challenge in the aftermath of 1870. For Hugo and many republicans, Sedan was the inevitable denouement of an illegitimate regime. 'His terrible destiny was to begin with the black flag of massacre,' wrote Hugo – a man who, unlike Louis-Napoléon, had helped massacre Parisians in person – 'and to end with the white flag of dishonour.'[13] Republican historians adopted this caricature, seeing the Second Empire as little more than the history of two unforgivable crimes – the *coup d'état* and Sedan.

After the Second Empire came the Third Republic. It was intended as a prophylactic against Bonapartism. With a weak president elected not by the people but by parliament it was hoped that a man like Louis-Napoléon would never again rule France. This proved to be one of the Third Republic's rare successes. Unimaginatively conservative, the early Republic abandoned the Empire's radical, controversial economic programme and returned to protectionism. The kind of social reform beloved by Louis-Napoléon was anathema to the Republic's early leaders.

Decades of inertia should have cast a more positive light on the dynamism of the Second Empire, but alongside secularisation, the area where the Republic proved most energetic was education. It was under the Third Republic that the republican tradition – Marianne as the embodiment of the nation, the 'Marseillaise' as the national anthem, Bastille Day, for example – became hegemonic. The Second Empire was condemned as an aberration on the ineluctable march towards republicanism. Indeed, it was easy to agree that there was something not quite French about an empire with a Spanish empress and an emperor who had lived most of his life abroad before coming to power. 'They are charming,' quipped a famed literary critic, talking about the imperial couple after spending a week with them at court, 'but they are foreigners.'[14]

So accepted was the view that Empire was as foreign to French history as its rulers were to France that in the decades following its fall it was not seen as a subject of serious historical enquiry. Charles Seignobos, a professor at the Sorbonne who claimed to have turned the art of history into a rigorously researched science, could happily write that only electors indifferent to politics voted for the Empire, 'because it was there'.[15] That after Sedan it so suddenly was not there seemed to prove the narrative. In fact, few states could have weathered such a calamity, especially not the Second Empire, which, as Persigny understood, required a succession of miracles to sustain it; the Franco-Prussian War was the debacle that ended the spell.

Few challenged the black legend that shrouded Louis-Napoléon. Émile Ollivier tried. He spent decades writing a history of the Second Empire which aimed at rehabilitating its reputation, its emperor's and, crucially, his own. Given its aim, perhaps never have so many words – over three million – been so pointlessly written; hardly anyone read his seventeen volumes. Bonapartist fanatics aside, there were not many other defenders. A leading French economist and statistician argued that Louis-Napoléon did more for workers than any other French regime, including the Third Republic, a claim that the British historian A. J. P. Taylor repeated in 1962, thereby including the Fourth Republic and the first four years of the Fifth in his sweeping assertion.

By then, the Third Republic had shown itself to be as calamitous, if not more so, in leading a woefully underprepared France into war with Germany. The First World War was a pyrrhic victory, in which disaster was only narrowly avoided by the fact that, unlike in 1870, France had allies. In 1940, the invasion of France by Nazi Germany made 1870 look like a relatively trivial mistake.

As fascism rose in Europe in the 1930s, some saw its seeds in the Second Empire. There were superficial similarities – the claim to represent the will of the people, the use of plebiscites and unconstitutional means to gain power, to name a few. But far more than the similarities, the Second Empire's contrasts with brutal twentieth-century dictatorships showed the regime in a more realistic light.

The Second Empire was not a militarist state, nor, as the Franco-Prussian War showed, an especially militarised one. Neither was the Second Empire a police state: its internal security forces were not that much different to what came before or after in France. Moreover, the Second Empire was not a one-party state, not least because Louis-Napoléon actively prevented the creation of a Bonapartist party. Enormous pressure was deployed to deliver the government the election results it desired, but people were free to vote against the regime – by 1869 more than three million did exactly that.

Though republican opponents painted him as a tyrant, Louis-Napoléon's temperament made him ill suited to the role. His was a strange authoritarianism whereby, certainly by the late 1860s, the emperor seemed almost as trapped by his own system as his republican opponents who railed against it. Certainly, a leader with a more autocratic streak would have pushed through much-needed army reform, whatever its popularity. Instead, the emperor was kind, compassionate, loyal, generous, sensitive and, with a horror of bloodshed, unlike many an absolute ruler or dictator. Thus the main emotion felt at Louis-Napoléon's court was boredom – a random execution might have proved welcome relief from another game of charades.

Though there were moments of harsh repression, particularly in the aftermath of the *coup d'état* in 1851 or the Orsini assassination attempt in 1858, these were relatively few and tempered by a penchant for impulsive pardons. Indeed, the most arbitrary killing and persecution of French citizens occurred during the June Days under the Second Republic, before Louis-Napoléon became president, and Bloody Week in 1871, when the Paris Commune was crushed after the emperor's fall.

Unlike fascism, the amorphous concept of populism would have been familiar to nineteenth-century observers even if the word was not yet used. Instead, so unlike anything else in the nineteenth century was the Empire's political system that critics turned to events nearly two thousand years old and dubbed it 'Caesarism'. Louis-Napoléon fits many of the tropes associated with populism today. An imperial prince, he positioned himself as an outsider against elites. As president, he painted the French parliament as thwarting the will of the people. He said what many believed was unsayable. His opponents insisted that his popularity was due to the lies he told and the stupidity of the millions who kept voting for him. If he was not venal himself, many close to him were and became scandalously rich through government connections. And, of course, with his *coup d'état*, he shut down democratic institutions, repressed his opponents and arrogated the awesome authority of the French state to himself, making him one of the most powerful men in the world.

The Second Empire was indeed an illiberal democracy, and for much, if not all, of its existence a popular dictatorship. This was another striking innovation: democracy could be co-opted for elite interests. The so-called will of the people had long been invoked, but it had always been a claim.

Now, through the ballot box, it could be demonstrated. Those who disagreed were excluded, censored or repressed.

Just how radically new Louis-Napoléon's system was has been forgotten, because it was copied so much it became commonplace. Up to that time, a regime that embraced technocracy, social reform and economic development through government intervention to manage a mass electorate based on universal male suffrage had never existed. The reactionary Bismarck was one of the first to see the potential. Seeing what Louis-Napoléon had done in France, Bismarck, without any of Louis-Napoléon's genuine belief in popular sovereignty, cynically introduced male universal suffrage into Prussia because he thought he could harness it to his advantage. Later, he launched state socialism, again without any of Louis-Napoléon's vague utopian convictions about helping people, to manipulate the electorate. Louis-Napoléon was, then, not only the accidental father of Germany thanks to the Franco-Prussian War, but also a key influence on how the Second Reich was governed.

When the Second Empire was established in 1852, Europe still resembled the world set up in 1815 – a patchwork of semi-autocratic dynastic states with a few liberal outliers, many of which, notably Britain, had no intention of letting all men vote (alongside limited female suffrage, universal male suffrage was not introduced in Britain until 1918 – sixty-six years after the Second Empire was founded), nor of embarking on anything like the radical programme Louis-Napoléon envisaged for France. By the 1900s, from Germany to the United States, all major powers and many Latin American republics had implemented some or all of the Second Empire's measures, or gone much further, but Louis-Napoléon was the first.

If today voters in many countries can remove the government at elections, and the means parties employ to stay in power are more subtle and more legitimate than those used under the Second Empire, many of the techniques are recognisably the same as those pioneered from 1852 to 1870. As one of the writers persecuted under the Second Empire wrote in a short story published a year before it fell, 'Never forget, when you hear the progress of enlightenment praised, that the devil's finest trick is to persuade you that he does not exist.'[16]

Unlike populist leaders today, however, having accrued near-absolute power, Louis-Napoléon gradually gave his away. Except for his belief that France was best ruled by a Bonaparte – an admittedly quite significant exception – he was a pragmatist who praised Britain's liberal institutions, including parliament and a free press. The history of French politics, and 1848 particularly, meant he thought France was not ready for such liberties, but had the liberal Empire endured, the regime would have continued to evolve towards them. For as many of the Empire's opponents came to realise, Louis-Napoléon was something rare in history: a kind man with genuine beliefs who wielded immense power. 'At heart, a good man,' said the novelist Émile Zola, who had impeccable republican credentials and had dedicated much of his literary career to lambasting the Second Empire, 'haunted by generous dreams, incapable of any wicked action.'[17]

His story, then, is not the usual tale of absolute power corrupting absolutely. Rather, Louis-Napoléon serves as a different kind of warning. To millions of French people, he seemed a simple solution to complex problems. For many years, he repaid the faith voters put in him as an elected monarch; but in foreign policy at least, he proved woefully inadequate to the task of single-handedly directing the French state.

If the Second Empire was, as Hugo insisted, a crime, then the conspiracy went much wider than one man. It was another novelist, George Sand, who proved more perceptive in her analysis. She understood that France was as much to blame as Louis-Napoléon for its fate in 1870. She recognised that as an individual, the emperor had many good qualities, but, she wrote, 'entrusting the destinies of all to a single person is the most culpable and most senseless act that a civilised people can commit'.[18]

———

From the 1930s, Louis-Napoléon and the Empire were partially rehabilitated in French academia, but in public discourse something that the former emperor would have considered far worse than academic disdain happened. He was forgotten. The only time he was recalled was as a faintly ridiculous wolf in a fairy tale or as an insult to political opponents. Thus when Charles de Gaulle launched what amounted to a political *coup d'état* without violence and founded the Fifth Republic in 1958 with a strong, directly elected president and recourse to referendums, some critics accused him of Bonapartism, citing the example of Louis-Napoléon. But such insults were politics, not history; Gaullism was not Bonapartism.

Sometimes branded a republican monarchy, the Fifth Republic – with a strong executive supported by technocrats and focused on government-led economic development – occasionally recalls the Second Empire. Though the legacy of the First and Second Empires influences the modern French state and politics in myriad ways, no one is reading Louis-Napoléon's *Des idées napoléoniennes* for inspiration. There are only echoes of his regime. If the echoes are occasionally heard, it is not because he is shaping the present, but because the present resembles the past. That a description of the Fifth Republic in the twenty-first century can be applied to the Second Empire, which ended in 1870, shows how far ahead of its time Louis-Napoléon's regime was.

Yet Louis-Napoléon is not popular today. At times French presidents are compared to Louis-Napoléon – Nicolas Sarkozy, François Hollande and Emmanuel Macron have all been likened to him – but the allusion is not intended to flatter, though in Hollande's case the likeness was in terms of secret trysts rather than politics. If none of these men have reached the levels of opprobrium heaped on Louis-Napoléon after Sedan, none matched his popularity in 1848, or held it for so long once in power. Aside from being a useful occasional insult – British Conservative politician Michael Gove even accused Tony Blair of resembling the former French emperor – Louis-Napoléon is largely forgotten in France.

The Paris beloved of tourists, films and glossy television series is his most visible legacy, but the man who imagined the wide boulevards, the famous opera house, the beautiful parks, the monumental train stations is absent from his creation. There are no public statues of Louis-Napoléon in the French capital. Though victories such as Sebastopol or Solferino, won under the Second Empire, were too precious to efface, other imperial names were removed after 1870 and there are no grand boulevards or even minor streets named after him. Marshal Mac Mahon, the man who blundered his army into Sedan and commanded forces that killed at least ten thousand Parisians when crushing the Commune, has a grand avenue leading up to the Arc de Triomphe.

In fact, it was only in 1987 that Louis-Napoléon received the modest award of Place Napoléon III outside the Gare du Nord. Such was the enthusiasm that no one got around to publicly unveiling the plaque until three years later. Outside the main entrance to the station, the only people who want to be there are travellers desperate for a cigarette before or after a long journey, a tribute the chain-smoking emperor might have enjoyed. If the *place* is unloved, the facade of the station is a testament to the Second Empire in all its confident, opulent, internationalist glory. Statues embody the great northern cities of Europe – including London, Berlin and Amsterdam – as well as French destinations. Top, front and centre, a figure represents Paris, the city that Louis-Napoléon helped redesign and put back at the heart of European diplomacy, power and culture.

The amnesia in France regarding Louis-Napoléon is all the more conspicuous given the shadow his uncle still casts over the nation. Unlike Louis-Napoléon's waxed moustache and wispy beard, the bicorne hat, the military greatcoat and hand tucked into waistcoat are instantly recognisable. There is a Napoléon industrial complex, from museum gift shops to cinema, adverts to history books. The historical reputation is complex and controversial – it always was – but as President Macron said in a speech commemorating the two-hundredth anniversary of Napoléon Bonaparte's death in 2021, 'he is part of us'.[19]

Macron made his speech before Napoléon's tomb at the Invalides in Paris. More than a million people visit this site every year, and though there is more to see than the mausoleum, it is reasonable to assume that most descend into the crypt where Napoléon's body lies. It seems unlikely that a French president will say before Louis-Napoléon's tomb that 'he is part of us'. Certainly, millions of people do not visit his resting place, for he is not buried in the bombastic memorial to his uncle's grandeur, but in a Benedictine abbey in Hampshire, England, in the decidedly un-imperial satellite town of Farnborough.

After the death of the prince imperial, Eugénie found Camden Place full of painful memories. She moved to Farnborough Hill, a sprawling mansion which is today, aptly, a Catholic girls' school. She founded St Michael's

Abbey, where a crypt was built for her husband and son, and their bodies were moved there in 1888. Very occasionally – not as often as his name is used as an insult – a French politician will call for the former emperor's corpse to be brought to France. No one takes them seriously. And so the body of the first ever directly elected French president and France's last reigning sovereign, a person who for over twenty years was not only the most powerful man in France, but one of the most powerful in the world, lies forgotten in a corner of England.

———

Having so often been wrong as empress, in the fifty years of life she had after the Empire's fall Eugénie seemed determined to be on the right side of history. She befriended suffragettes and became an enthusiast for aviation, as well as newfangled inventions such as the telephone. During the First World War, she turned a wing of Farnborough Hill into a hospital for convalescing British soldiers. It was run by Lady Haig, wife of Douglas Haig, who became the commander of British forces on the Western Front. Eugénie also gave her private yacht to the Royal Navy, a ship upon which she had received Kaiser Wilhelm II in 1907. When meeting the former empress, the grandson of the man who had defeated Louis-Napoléon at Sedan wore garishly inappropriate bright yellow shoes.

Eugénie claimed that she had died in 1870 and often insisted that her curse was to live so long, but she delighted at the French victory in 1918 and was ecstatic to see Alsace and Lorraine returned. She was, however, dismayed by the punitive Treaty of Versailles, seeing it as an incubator of German grievances that would lead to future war. If the story is to be believed, she descended into the crypt, reading, disapprovingly, to Louis-Napoléon's corpse the treaty which, from a French perspective, reversed the humiliation of the one imposed upon France in 1871.

'I am tired; it is time for me to go away,' said Eugénie just before she died, aged ninety-four, while visiting her Spanish homeland on 11 July 1920.[20] The body was transported from the land of her birth to the country where she became empress, where it lay in state briefly at the Gare d'Austerlitz in Paris. There, old men wearing the *légion d'honneur* and sporting side whiskers and oversized moustaches that betrayed the fact that they were out of time tottered past. Then her remains were brought across the Channel to Farnborough for her funeral on 20 July at St Michael's Abbey.

Rather incongruously for a former French empress, when the coffin arrived at Farnborough it was draped in the Union Jack. British cavalry and inquisitive onlookers lined the short route from the train station. As the casket was brought into the abbey, the band of the East Lancashire Regiment played the 'Marseillaise'. No one remembered, or cared, that this was a revolutionary song whose message Eugénie detested and which had been banned for much of the Second Empire, before becoming the national anthem of the French Republic. For just like the Empire, Eugénie was a relic of an ephemeral world, one that Louis-Napoléon had done so much to will into existence, and one that his successors tried so hard to forget.

ACKNOWLEDGEMENTS

I am eternally grateful to all those who made this book possible, especially Patrick Walsh and everyone at PEW Literary, as well as the wonderful people at Faber & Faber – in particular Alex Bowler and Fiona Crosby for believing in the work and providing magnificent notes. Robert Davies went through the manuscript with astonishing attention to detail and I am very thankful for his help. Also, Ian Bahrami's brilliant proofreading was enormously helpful.

I would also like to thank everyone at Camden Place for being so welcoming, especially Angela Hatton for her generosity and enthusiasm for all things Napoléon III. Thanks as well to Ian Sygrave, who was kind enough to show me his remarkable Second Empire collection.

My friends have been supportive and some even kindly feigned interest in nineteenth-century history. I apologise to them for long, rambling monologues on the French Second Empire; Orazio, Ben, Albert and David have had to endure more than most and their patience is much appreciated. Especial thanks to Ben, who has accompanied me on the trail of the emperor, from obscure Italian battlefields to the imperial satellite town of Farnborough. The look of despair on his face as I pointed out another nondescript house in the suburbs of Sedan after a punishing day touring the battlefield gave me unique insight into what it must have felt like for an ordinary French soldier on the seemingly endless marches and counter-marches in August 1870.

I would also like to thank my brother Alex for his love and help over the years. Christabel and Peter, too, have been especially kind, encouraging and caring. I must thank Ian and Catherine for all their support and for being so generous with their time, helping look after my two daughters. My mother died a long time ago, but she always encouraged my passion for history and I like to think she would be proud of this book.

When I wrote the final scene, Louis-Napoléon's death, I cried. Not because I was especially moved by his plight or my prose, but because it reminded me of my own father, who died unexpectedly on 27 August 2022. Like the prince imperial, I was unable to see my father before he died. Unfortunately, I wrote the scene in the British Library. Feeling it was inappropriate to cry in a library, I tried to mask my muffled sobs with laughter (it didn't occur to me that it might be worse to laugh in a library). The end result, a strange mix of tears and forced joviality, must have been disconcerting for others – I apologise. My father was a brilliant storyteller, whether inventing bedtime tales when I was little or in his journalism and writing. Growing up, I assumed that everyone was good at telling stories. I now realise how rare his talent was and how much I owe him. He is greatly missed. My thoughts are with his partner, Margaret, who loved him dearly.

My two beautiful daughters, Ena and Rose, may well lay claim to being the youngest people to know who Napoléon III is. I love them immensely and this book is dedicated to them. As it is to Hannah; without her love and support, it would not have been possible to write it – *tout à toi*.

NOTES

This work draws on archival research as well as newspapers, memoirs, diaries, published correspondence, secondary works, etc. Space precludes a wider bibliography and I have restricted notes to the sources of quotations only.

Prologue

1 Rachel Chrastil, *Bismarck's War: The Franco-Prussian War and the Making of Modern Europe* (London: Penguin, 2023), 145.

2 Alexis de Tocqueville to Gustave de Beaumont, 29 January 1851, in J. P. Mayer (ed.), *Correspondance d'Alexis de Tocqueville et de Gustave de Beaumont*, 3 vols (Paris: Gallimard, 1967), II, 369.

3 Emmanuel-Félix de Wimpffen, *Sedan par le général de Wimpffen* (Paris: A. Lacroix, Verboechhoven et Cie, 1871), 170.

1 The Wondrous Destiny

1 Louis Bonaparte, *Historical Documents and Reflections on the Government of Holland* (London: Lackington, Hughes, Harding, Mavor, and Jones, 1820), 56.

2 Ibid., 125–7.

3 Hortense de Beauharnais, *Memoirs of Queen Hortense*, 2 vols, trans. Arthur Griggs (London: Thomas Butterworth, 1928), I, 77–8.

4 Comte de Saint-Leu to Hortense, 23 November 1809, in André Duboscq, *Louis Bonaparte en Hollande d'après ses lettres, 1806–1810* (Paris: Émile-Paul, 1911), 228–30.

5 Hortense to Eugène de Beauharnais, 2 September 1808, in Jean Hanoteau (ed.), *Les Beauharnais et l'Empereur: lettres de l'impératrice Joséphine et de la reine Hortense au prince Eugène* (Paris: Librairie Plon, 1936), 218–22.

6 William Blanchard Jerrold, *The Life of Napoleon III*, 4 vols (London: Longman, Green, and Co., 1874–82), I, 76–7.

7 Charles Vellay, *Oeuvres complètes de Saint-Just*, 2 vols (Paris: E. Fasquelle, 1908), I, 369.

8 Jean Tulard, *Napoléon, ou, Le mythe du sauveur* (Paris: Fayard, 1986), 84.

9 George Duruy, *Mémoires de Barras*, 4 vols (Paris: Hachette et Cie., 1895–6), II, 56.

10 Louis Bonaparte, *Historical Documents*, 8.

11 Michael Broers, *Napoleon*, 3 vols (London: Faber & Faber, 2014–22), II, 61–2.

12 Louis Bonaparte, *Historical Documents*, 131, 4–5.

13 *Le Moniteur universel*, 22 July 1810.

14 Napoléon Bonaparte to Hortense, 28 May 1809. Fondation Napoléon, napoleonica.org, Correspondence of Napoleon, CG9-21085.md, 1809-05-28. www.napoleonica.org/en/collections/correspondance/CG9-21085.md.

15 Hanoteau (ed.), *Les Beauharnais et l'Empereur*, 259–60.

16 Napoléon-Louis to Hortense, 13 March 1813. 400AP/27, Dossier 1. Fonds Napoléon des Archives nationales 400 AP (Paris).

17 Louis-Napoléon to Hortense, undated. 400AP/39, Dossier 2.

18 Louise Parquin, *Mémoires sur la reine Hortense et la famille impériale par Mlle Cochelet* (Paris: Albin Michel, 1926), 112.

19 Hortense, *Memoirs*, II, 66–7.

20 Broers, *Napoleon*, III, 431.

21 Philip Dwyer, *Citizen Emperor: Napoleon in Power* (London: Bloomsbury, 2013), 483.

22 Hortense, *Memoirs*, II, 72.

23 Ibid., 83–4.

24 Parquin, *Mémoires*, 109–11.

25 Guillaume Peyrusse, *1809–1815, mémorial et archives de M. le baron Peyrusse, trésorier général de la couronne pendant les cent-jours: Vienne–Moscou–Ile d'Elbe* (Carcassonne: P. Labau et Lajoux, 1869), 286.

26 Hortense, *Memoirs*, II, 147–8.

27 Broers, *Napoleon*, III, 560.

2 An Unsentimental Education

1 Hortense, *Memoirs*, II, 212, 214.

2 Ibid., 225.

3 Ibid., 321, 239.

4 Comte de Saint-Leu to Louis-Napoléon, 28 July 1819. 400AP/33, Dossier 2.

5 Napoléon-Louis to Louis-Napoléon, 1818. 400AP/27, Dossier 2.

6 Hortense, *Memoirs*, II, 253.

7 Stéfane-Pol (ed.), *La jeunesse de Napoléon III, correspondance inédite de son précepteur, Philippe Le Bas* (Paris: F. Juven, 1902), 34.

8 Ibid., 68.

9 Ibid., 50, 54

10 Ibid., 79–80.

11 *Morning Advertiser*, 28 August 1867, 5.

12 Louis-Napoléon to Hortense, 21 July 1821. 400AP/39, Dossier 2.

13 Stéfane-Pol (ed.), *La jeunesse*, 112, 131.

14 Jérôme and Catherine, *Mémoires et correspondance du roi Jérôme et de la reine Catherine*, 7 vols (Paris: Dentu, 1861–6), VII, 420.

15 Emmanuel de Las Cases, *Mémorial de Sainte-Hélène*, 2 vols (Paris: Ernest Bourdin, 1842), II, 260.

16 Stéfane-Pol (ed.), *La jeunesse*, 227.

17 Augustin Cabanès, *Moeurs intimes du passé*, 12 vols (Paris: Albin Michel, 1908–36), VIII, 518–19.

18 Stéfane-Pol (ed.), *La jeunesse*, 322–3.

19 Henry Edward Fox, *The Journal of Henry Edward Fox (afterwards fourth and last Lord Holland) 1818–1830* (London: Thornton Butterworth, 1923), 351.

20 Ibid., 277.

21 Margaret Gardiner Blessington, *The Idler in Italy* (Paris: A. and W. Galignani, 1839), 397.

22 Fox, *Journal*, 216.

23 John Vincent (ed.), *The Diaries of Edward Henry Stanley, 15th Earl of Derby between 1878 and 1893* (Oxford: Leopard's Head Press, 2003), 845–6.

24 James Howard Harris Malmesbury, *Memoirs of an Ex-Minister: An Autobiography* (London: Longmans, Green, and Co., 1885), 26.

25 Louis-Napoléon to Comte de Saint-Leu, 19 January 1829. 400AP/40.

26 Comte de Saint-Leu to Louis-Napoléon, 1 September 1829. 400AP/33.

27 Louis-Napoléon to Louis, 3 March 1829, 30 April 1830. 400AP/33.

3 The Column

1 *Le National*, 27 July 1830.

2 David Pinkney, *The French Revolution of 1830* (Princeton, NJ: Princeton University Press, 1972), 109–10.

3 Ibid., 162.

4 Louis-Napoléon to Hortense, August 1830. 400AP/39, Dossier 2.

5 Louis-Napoléon to Hortense, 12 August 1830. 400AP/39, Dossier 2.

6 Louis-Napoléon to Hortense, 15 August 1830. 400AP/39, Dossier 2.

7 Comte de Saint-Leu to Louis-Napoléon, 3 January 1825. 400AP/33, Dossier 2.

8 Valérie Masuyer, *Mémoires, lettres et papiers de Valérie Masuyer . . . Avec une introduction et des notes par Jean Bourguignon, etc.* (Paris: Plon, 1937), 4.

9 Louis-Napoléon to Hortense, 21 January 1831. 400AP/39, Dossier 2.

10 Joseph Orsi, *Recollections of the Last Half Century* (London: Longmans, Green, and Co., 1881), 76, 79.

11 Jerrold, *Life of Napoleon III*, I, 165–6.

12 Louis-Napoléon to Hortense, 22 February 1831. 400AP/39, Dossier 2.

13 Napoléon-Louis to comte de Saint-Leu, 1 March 1831. 400AP/27, Dossier 2.

14 Louis-Napoléon to comte de Saint-Leu, 14 February 1831. 400AP/40.

15 Hortense de Beauharnais, *La reine Hortense en Italie, en France et en Angleterre pendant l'année 1831: fragments extraits de ses mémoires inédits, écrits par elle-même* (Paris: Alphonse Levavasseur, 1834), 106.

16 Louis-Napoléon to Comte de Saint-Leu, 15 March 1831. 400AP/40.

17 H. Roccaserra, *Notice biographique de Son Altesse le Prince Napoléon Louis Bonaparte* (Corfu, 1831), 31–4.

18 Masuyer, *Mémoires*, 146.

19 Ibid., 174.

20 Louis-Napoléon to Louis-Philippe, undated, quoted in Jerrold, *Life of Napoleon III*, I, 183–4.

21 Hortense de Beauharnais, *En Italie*, 192.

22 Ibid., 218.

23 Masuyer, *Mémoires*, 274.

24 Ibid., 243–4.

25 Ibid., 252–3.

26 Ibid., 277, 275, 274.

27 Louis-Napoléon to Charlotte, 28 August 1831. 400AP/13, Dossier 1.

4 Some New Napoléon Might Arise

1 Comte de Saint-Leu to Louis-Napoléon, 22 March 1831. 400AP/33, Dossier 2.

2 Louis-Napoléon to comte de Saint-Leu, 15 December 1831. 400AP/40.

3 Louis-Napoléon to Joseph, 9 September 1831. 400AP/13, Dossier 1.

4 'Rêveries politiques' in Louis-Napoléon, *Oeuvres de Napoléon III*, 5 vols (Paris: Amyot, 1854–69), I, 373–87.

5 Louis-Napoléon to Hortense, 4 July 1834. 400AP/39, Dossier 3.

6 Louis-Napoléon, *Oeuvres*, 374.

7 Ruth Scurr, *Napoleon: A Life in Gardens and Shadows* (London: Penguin, 2022), 280.

8 Louis-Napoléon to Hortense, 14 November 1832. 400AP/39, Dossier 3.

9 Louis-Napoléon to Joseph, 12 July 1837. 400AP/41, Dossier 3.

10 Louis-Napoléon to Hortense, 7 December 1832. 400AP/39, Dossier 3.

11 Louis-Napoléon to Hortense, 20 February, 1833. 400AP/39, Dossier 3.

12 Jerrold, *Life of Napoleon*, I, 266–80.

13 Louis-Napoléon to comte de Saint-Leu, 31 July 1833. 400AP/40.

14 *Allgemeine Schweizer Zeitung*, 21 August 1834.

15 Jerrold, *Life of Napoleon III*, I, 257.

16 Louis-Napoléon, *Manuel d'artillerie à l'usage des officiers d'artillerie de la République helvétique, par le prince Napoléon-Louis Bonaparte, capitaine au régiment d'artillerie du canton de Berne* (Zurich: Orell Füssli, 1836), ii.

17 Louis-Napoléon to comte de Saint-Leu, 15 December 1831. 400AP/40.

18 Louis-Napoléon to comte de Saint-Leu, 31 July 1833. 400AP/40.

19 François-René Chateaubriand, *Mémoires d'outre-tombe. Édition nouvelle . . . Avec une introduction, des variantes, des notes, un appendice et des index, par Maurice Levaillant et Georges Moulinier*, 2 vols (Paris: Gallimard, 1958), II, 604.

20 *Gazette de Lausanne*, 25 December 1835. Louis-Napoléon, 11 December 1835.

21 Louis-Napoléon to Hortense, 5 December 1835. 400AP/39, Dossier 3.

22 Louis-Napoléon to Charlotte, 18 January 1836. 400AP/13, Dossier 1.

23 Masuyer, *Mémoires*, 291–2.

24 Louis-Napoléon to Narcisse Vieillard, 30 January 1835. 400AP/41, Dossier 1.

25 Pascal Clément, *Persigny, l'homme qui a inventé Napoléon III* (Paris: Perrin, 2006), 37.

26 Quoted in Sudhir Hazareesingh, *The Legend of Napoleon* (London: Granta, 2005), 199–200.

27 Eugène Roch, *Insurrection de Strasbourg, le 30 octobre 1836, et procès des prévenus de complicité avec le prince Napoléon-Louis, devant la cour d'assises du Bas-Rhin* (Paris, 1837), 78.

28 Louis-Napoléon to Théophile Voirol, 14 August 1836, in ibid., 146.

29 Jerrold, *Life of Napoleon III*, I, 318–20.

30 Louise Wernert (Louis-Napoléon) to Claude-Nicolas Vaudrey in 'Le Prince Louis-Napoléon a Strasbourg', *La Revue de Paris*, 22 (November–December 1899), 303–4.

31 Armand Laity, *Le prince Napoléon à Strasbourg, ou Relation historique des événements du 30 octobre 1836* (Paris: Thomassin et compagnie, 1838), 77–9.

32 Ibid., 50–2.

33 Roch, *Insurrection*, 127.

34 Albert Fermé, *Les Grands procès politiques. Strasbourg, d'après les documents authentiques, réunis et mis en ordre par Albert Fermé* (Paris: A. Le Chevalier, 1868), 220.

35 Roch, *Insurrection*, 153–4.

36 Ibid., 159–60.

37 Fermé, *Les Grands procès*, 221.

38 Louis-Napoléon to Hortense, 1 November 1836. 400AP/39, Dossier 3.

5 Citizen of Nowhere

1 François Guizot, *Mémoires pour servir à l'histoire de mon temps*, 8 vols (Paris: Michel-Lévy frères, 1858–67), IV, 200.

2 Fermé, *Les Grands procès*, 221.

3 Louis-Napoléon to Vieillard, 19 November 1836. 400AP/41, Dossier 1.

4 Louis-Napoléon to Hortense, 19 November 1836. 400AP/39, Dossier 3.

5 Fermé, *Les Grands procès*, 197.

6 Ibid., 208.

7 Jerrold, *Life of Napoléon III*, I, 412.

8 Augustus Bozzi Granville, *Autobiography of A.B.G. . . .*, 2 vols (London: Henry S. King & Co., 1874), II, 315.

9 Louis-Napoléon to Joseph, 22 April 1837. 400AP/33, Dossier 3.

10 Louis-Napoléon to Hortense, 10 April 1837. 400AP/39, Dossier 3.

11 *New York Herald*, 19 April 1837.

12 Lousi-Napoléon to Hortense, 24 April 1837. 400AP/39, Dossier 3.

13 Louis-Napoléon to Vieillard, 30 April 1837. 400AP/41, Dossier 1.

14 Jerrold, *Life of Napoleon III*, II, 15.

15 Louis-Napoléon to M. le President des États-Unis, 6 June 1837. 400AP/41, Dossier 3.

16 Joseph to Louis-Napoléon, 10 July 1837. 400AP/33, Dossier 1.

17 Louis-Napoléon to Hortense, 16 July 1837. 400AP/39, Dossier 3.

18 Louis-Napoléon to comte de Saint-Leu, 12 July 1837. 400AP/40.

19 Louis-Napoléon to Joseph, 12 July 1837. 400AP/41, Dossier 3.

20 Masuyer, *Mémoires*, 430–4.

21 Hortense to Louis-Napoléon, 3 April 1837, in 'Testament de la Reine Hortense'. 400AP/34.

22 'Testament de la Reine Hortense'. 400AP/34.

23 Comte de Saint-Leu to Louis-Napoléon, 12 October 1837, in 'Valerie Masuyer, Souvenirs et journal: I: De la reine Hortense à Alfred de Musset', *Revue des Deux Mondes*, 71 (1942), 235–7.

24 Louis-Napoléon to Laity, 2 July 1838, quoted in Jerrold, *Life of Napoleon III*, II, 58–60.

25 Comte de Saint-Leu to Louis-Napoléon, 4 August 1838, in Egon Corti, 'La correspondance du roi Louis et de Louis-Napoléon interceptée par la police de Metternich, 1833–1840. Deuxième partie: les complots de Louis-Napoléon et l'état d'âme de son père', *Revue des études napoléoniennes*, 26 (1926), 243–6.

26 Louis-Napoléon to the Grand Council of Thurgau, 20 August 1838, in Jerrold, *Life of Napoleon III*, II, 68.

27 *The Times*, 9 October 1838.

28 *The Times*, 10 October 1838.

29 Benjamin Disraeli, *Endymion* (New York: D. Appleton and Company, 1880), 204.

30 Flora Tristan, *Flora Tristan's London Journal: A Survey of London Life in the 1830s* (London: George Prior, 1980), 29, 37.

31 Jerrold, *Life of Napoleon III*, II, 84–5.

32 William Flavelle Monypenny, *The Life of Benjamin Disraeli, Earl of Beaconsfield*, 6 vols (London: John Murray, 1910–20), 93–4.

33 George Augustus Sala, *The Life and Adventures of George Augustus Sala* (London: Cassell and Company, 1896), 43.

34 William Archer Shee, *My Contemporaries, 1830–1870* (London: Hurst and Blackett, 1893), 74.

35 Edmund Yates, *His Recollections and Experiences*, 4th edn (London: Richard Bentley and Son, 1885), 99–100.

36 Dorothy Nevill, *The Reminiscences of Lady Dorothy Nevill* (London: Edward Arnold, 1906), 50–1.

37 Louis-Napoléon, *Des idées napoléoniennes* (Paris: Imprimerie de Félix Malteste et Cie, 1839), 36.

38 Ibid., 145.

39 Reviews, 3 August 1839, in the *Athenaeum Journal* (January–December), 571–2.

40 *The Times*, 31 October 1839.

41 *Journal des Débats*, 13 August 1839.

42 Louis-Napoléon to *The Times*, 17 May 1839, printed in the *Morning Post*, 18 May 1839.

43 Granville, *Autobiography*, 317–9.

44 Ibid., 327–8.

6 The Eagle Has Landed

1 Orsi, *Recollections*, 133–6.

2 Ibid., 149.

3 'Cour des Pairs', *Le Moniteur universel*, 30 September 1840.

4 Ibid.

5 Ibid.

6 Ibid.

7 'Proclamation of the Municipality of Boulogne', printed in *The Times*, 10 August 1840.

8 François Guizot to Dorothée de Lieven, 7 August 1840. Marie Dupond & Association François Guizot, projet EMAN (Thalim, CNRS-ENS-Sorbonne nouvelle). eman-archives.org/Guizot-Lieven/items/show/424.

9 *Journal des Débats*, 9 August 1840.

10 *Le Constitutionnel*, 7 August 1840.

11 *The Times*, 7 August 1840.

12 Anonymous, *Procès de Louis-Napoléon Bonaparte, jugé par la chambre des pairs, sur l'attentat de Boulogne, du 6 août 1840* (Paris: Maldan, n.d.), 29.

13 *The Times*, 12 August 1840; Anonymous, *Procès de Louis-Napoléon*, 44.

14 Éric Anceau, *Napoléon III: un Saint-Simon à cheval* (Paris: Tallandier, 2008), 86.

15 Louis-Napoléon to comte de Saint-Leu, 6 September 1840. 400AP/40.

16 Anceau, *Napoléon III*, 86.

17 'Cour des Pairs', *Le Moniteur universel*, 29 September 1840.

18 'Cour des Pairs', *Le Moniteur universel*, 30 September 1840.

19 Anonymous, *Procès de Louis-Napoléon*, 176.

20 Jerrold, *Life of Napoleon III*, II, 180.

7 The Prisoner

1 'Aux Manes de l'empereur', 15 December 1840, in Louis-Napoléon, *Oeuvres*, I, 435–7.

2 Louis-Napoléon to Ferdinand Barrot, in Jerrold, *Life of Napoleon III*, II, 191–2.

3 Louis-Napoléon to Hortense Cornu, 5 October 1842, in Marcel Emerit, *Lettres de Napoléon III à Madame Cornu, en grande partie inédites*, 2 vols (Paris: Éditions des Presses Modernes, 1937).

4 Louis-Napoléon to Hortense Cornu, 28 January 1843, in ibid.

5 Louis-Napoléon to Hortense Cornu, 29 August 1842, in ibid.

6 Louis-Napoléon to Hortense Cornu 23 June 1845, in ibid.

7 'Boulogne, Saturday Afternoon', *The Times*, 10 August 1840.

8 Louis-Napoléon to Hortense Cornu, 16 October 1843, in Emerit, *Lettres*.

9 Louis-Napoléon to Hortense Cornu, 2 February 1845, in ibid.

10 Louis-Napoléon to Hortense Cornu, 28 August 1841, in ibid.

11 Louis-Napoléon to Hortense Cornu, 26 August 1843, in ibid.

12 Louis-Napoléon to Hortense Cornu, 19 September 1845, in ibid.

13 Louis-Napoléon to Vieillard, 10 June 1842, in Jerrold, *Life of Napoleon III*, II, 230–4.

14 'Fragments historiques 1688 et 1830', in Louis-Napoléon, *Oeuvres*, I, 342.

15 Louis-Napoléon to Vieillard, 10 June 1842, in Jerrold, *Life of Napoleon III*, II, 233.

16 'Extinction du paupérisme', in Louis-Napoléon, *Oeuvres*, II, 151.

17 Louis-Napoléon to Hortense Cornu, 2 February 1843, in Emerit, *Lettres*.

18 Louis Blanc, *Historical Revelations* (London: Chapman and Hall, 1858), 487–500.

19 George Sand to Louis-Napoléon, in B. Renault, *Histoire du prince Louis-Napoléon, président de la République* (Paris: R. Ruel ainé, 1852), 174.

20 Louis-Napoléon to Peauger, 9 March 1844, in Marc Peauger, 'Lettres du Fort de Ham', *La Nouvelle Revue*, 89 (1894), 448–50.

21 Anceau, *Napoléon III*, 102.

22 Louis-Napoléon to comte de Saint-Leu, 19 September 1845. 400AP/40.

23 Louis-Napoléon to Hortense Cornu, 3 February 1846, in Emerit, *Lettres*.

24 Frédéric Briffault, *The Prisoner of Ham* (London: T. C. Newby, 1846), 284.

25 Jerrold, *Life of Napoleon III*, II, 347.

26 Malmesbury, *Memoirs of an Ex-Minister*, 127.

27 John Forster, *Walter Savage Landor: A Biography*, 2 vols (London: Chapman and Hall, 1869), II, 469.

28 *The Satirist; or, the Censor of the Times*, 25 April 1847.

29 Louis-Napoléon to Prince Napoléon-Jérôme Bonaparte, 28 April 1848, in *Napoléon III et Le Prince Napoléon, correspondance inédite* (Paris: Calmann-Lévy, 1925), 39–40.

30 Louis-Napoléon to Prince Napoléon-Jérôme Bonaparte, 24 August 1845, in *Napoléon III et Le Prince Napoléon*, 33–5.

31 Louis-Napoléon to Vieillard, 10 December 1846, in Jerrold, *Life of Napoleon III*, II, 381.

32 Louis-Napoléon to Hortense Cornu, June 1846, in Emerit, *Lettres*.

33 Louis-Napoléon to Vieillard, 15 August 1846. 400AP/41, Dossier 1.

34 Louis-Napoléon to Vieillard, 15 February 1847, in Jerrold, *Life of Napoleon III*, II, 382.

35 *The Satirist; or, the Censor of the Times*, 14 March 1847.

36 'Haymarket', *The Atlas*, 18 January 1840.

37 Ernest Alfred Vizetelly, *Court Life of the Second French Empire* (London: Chatto & Windus, 1908), 183.

38 *The Times*, 1 October 1847.

8 Napoléon's Ghost

1 *Le Moniteur universel*, 28 January 1848.

2 *Le Moniteur universel*, 27 March 1847.

3 Alexis de Tocqueville, *The Recollections of Alexis de Tocqueville*, trans. Alexander Teixeira de Mattos (New York: Macmillan, 1896), 71.

4 Roger Price, *The French Second Empire: An Anatomy of Political Power* (Cambridge: Cambridge University Press, 2001), 15.

5 Orsi, *Recollections*, 226–7.

6 Louis-Napoléon to the provisional government, 28 February 1848, in Louis-Napoléon, *Oeuvres*, III, 5–6.

7 Ibid., 6–7.

8 'Haute-Cour de Justice', *Le Moniteur universel*, 17 March 1849.

9 Quoted in Sarah Wassermann, *Les clubs de Barbès et de Blanqui en 1848* (Paris: Édouard Cornély, 1913), 179.

10 Christopher Guyver, *The Second French Republic 1848–1852: A Political Reinterpretation* (New York: Palgrave Macmillan, 2016), 68.

11 *Le Moniteur universel*, 14 June 1848.

12 Robert Pimienta, 'La propagande bonapartiste en 1848 (suite)', *Revue d'Histoire du XIXe siècle – 1848*, 38 (1910), 99.

13 'Paroles d'un Revenant ou Lettre de l'Empereur à son neveu Louis-Napoléon', *L'Aigle républicaine*, 17 June 1848.

14 Louis-Napoléon to President of the Constituent Assembly, 15 June 1848, in Louis-Napoléon, *Oeuvres*, III, 14–15.

15 Jonathan Beecher, *Writers and Revolution: Intellectuals and the French Revolution of 1848* (Cambridge: Cambridge University Press, 2021), 180–2.

16 Vallon to Mérimée, 24 June, in Prosper Mérimée, *Correspondance generale* (Paris: Le Divan, 1941–61), V, 332–3n.

17 Charles de Rémusat, *Mémoires de ma vie*, 5 vols (Paris: Plon, 1958–67), IV, 360.

18 Hippolyte Thirria, *Napoléon III avant l'Empire*, 2 vols (Paris: E. Plon, Nourrit et Cie, 1895–6), I, 338.

19 *Journal des Débats*, 22 September 1848. The song was 'Veillons au salut de l'Empire'.

20 *L'Union*, in Thirria, *Napoléon III*, I, 351; *La Presse*, 27 September 1848.

21 *The Sun*, 28 September 1848.

22 *Le Moniteur universel*, 10 October 1848.

23 Émile Ollivier, *L'Empire libéral*, 18 vols (Paris: Garnier frères, 1895–1918), II, 100–1.

24 *Le National*, 10 October 1848.

25 In Pierre-Joseph Proudhon, *Qu'est-ce que la propriété? ou Recherches sur le principe du droit et du gouvernement* (Paris: J.-F. Brocard, 1840).

26 Proudhon to Émile de Giradin, 11 July 1849, printed in *The Times*, 16 July 1849.

27 *Le Constitutionnel*, 24 September 1850.

28 *Le Moniteur universel*, 15 June 1847.

29 *L'Événement*, 25 September 1848.

30 *Le Moniteur universel*, 26 October 1848.

31 *Le Moniteur universel*, 27 October 1848.

32 *The Times*, 30 October 1848.

33 Thirria, *Napoléon III*, I, 442.

34 Ibid., 414–15.

35 'À M. le Directeur de la Liberté de Pensée', *La Liberté de penser: revue philosophique et littéraire*, II (1848), 481–97.

36 *The Times*, 23 September 1848.

37 Thirria, *Napoléon III*, 443–5.

38 Eurydice Dosne, *Mémoires de madame Dosne, l'égérie de M. Thiers*, 2 vols (Paris: Plon, 1928), I, 286–8.

39 'Louis-Napoléon Bonaparte à ses concitoyens', in Louis-Napoléon, *Oeuvres*, III, 24–8.

40 *The Times*, 2 December 1848.

41 *Morning Post*, 12 December 1848.

42 *The Times*, 14 December 1848.

43 André-Jean Tudesq, *L'élection présidentielle de Louis-Napoléon Bonaparte 10 décembre 1848* (Paris: A. Colin, 1965), 203–5.

44 Thirria, *Napoléon III*, I, 472.

45 *The Times*, 11 December 1848.

9 The Chosen One

1 Victor Hugo, *Napoléon le Pétit* (Paris: J. Hetzel et Cie., 1870), 3.

2 *Le Moniteur universel*, 21 December 1848.

3 *The Times*, 1 January 1849.

4 Tocqueville, *Recollections*, 287–8.

5 Guyver, *Second Republic*, 223.

6 Odilon Barrot, *Mémoires posthumes*, 4 vols, 2nd edn (Paris: G. Charpentier, 1875–6), III, 362–3.

7 Thirria, *Life of Napoléon III*, II, 29.

8 William Nassau Senior, *Conversations with M. Thiers, M. Guizot and Other Distinguished Persons during the Second Empire*, 2 vols (London: Hurst and Blackett, 1878), I, 45.

9 *Morning Post*, 16 February 1849.

10 *The Times*, 22 February 1849.

11 Horace de Viel Castel, *Mémoires du Comte Horace de Viel Castel sur le règne de Napoléon III*, 2 vols (Paris: Chez tous les libraires, 1883), I, 45–6.

12 Persigny, *Mémoires*, 28–33.

13 Peter McPhee, *The Politics of Rural France: Political Mobilization in the French Countryside, 1846–1852* (Oxford: Clarendon Press, 1992), 126.

14 Price, *Second Empire*, 27.

15 Tocqueville, *Recollections*, 284–8; 331–2.

16 George Macaulay Trevelyan, *Garibaldi's Defence of the Roman Republic* (London: Longmans, Green, and Company, 1907), 101.

17 'Constitution de 1848, IIe République'. www.conseil-constitutionnel.fr/les-constitutions-dans-l-histoire/constitution-de-1848-iie-republique.

18 Louis-Napoléon to Vieillard, 4 June 1849, in Jerrold, *Life of Napoleon III*, III, 82.

19 Tocqueville, *Recollections*, 151; *Le Moniteur universel*, 12 June 1849.

20 Printed in *Le Peuple*, 13 June 1849.

21 *Morning Post*, 15 June 1849.

22 Tocqueville, *Recollections*, 295.

23 'Proclamation au peuple français, 13 June 1849', in Louis-Napoléon, *Oeuvres*, III, 83–4.

24 Jasper Ridley, *Napoleon III and Eugenie* (London: Constable, 1979), 237.

25 Jerrold, *Life of Napoleon III*, III, 83–4.

26 Karl Marx, *The Class Struggles in France, 1848 to 1850*, in Karl Marx and Frederick Engels, *Selected Works*, 3 vols (Moscow: Progress Publishers, 1969), I, 267.

27 Barrot, *Mémoires*, III, 443.

28 'Message à l'Assemblée legislative, 31 October 1849', in Louis-Napoléon, *Oeuvres*, III, 111–13.

29 *Le Moniteur universel*, 25 May 1850.

30 Senior, *Conversations*, II, 338.

10 Countdown

1 Guyver, *Second Republic*, 176.

2 Germain Bapst, *Le maréchal Canrobert, souvenirs d'un siècle*, 6 vols (Paris: E. Plon-Nourrit et Cie, 1898–1913), I, 498–9.

3 Dosne, *Mémoires de madame Dosne*, II, 252.

4 Victor Hugo, *The History of a Crime: The Testimony of an Eye-Witness*, 4 vols, trans. T. H. Joyce and Arthur Locke (London: Sampson, Low, Marston, Searle & Rivington, 1877), I, 38–9.

5 A. de Morny, 'La genèse du coup d'État. Mémoires', *Revue des Deux Mondes*, 30 (1925), 524.

6 Persigny, *Mémoires*, 153–4.

7 Ibid., 159–65.

8 Émile-Félix Fleury, *Souvenirs du général Cte Fleury Tome Ier*, 2nd edn (Paris: E. Plon, 1897), 123.

9 *Le Moniteur universel*, 11 January 1851.

10 *Le Moniteur universel*, 18 January 1851.

11 Barrot, *Mémoires*, IV, 94.

12 Auguste Romieu, *Le Spectre rouge de 1852* (Paris: Ledoyen, 1851), 14, 12.

13 *The Times*, 14 November 1850, 2–3.

14 Adolphe Thiers, *Discours parlementaires de M. Thiers*, 16 vols (Paris: M. Calmon, 1879–89), IX, 40.

15 Fleury, *Souvenirs*, I, 127.

16 Ibid., 131.

17 Ibid., 136.

18 Saint-Arnaud to Madame de Saint-Arnaud, 12 May 1851, in Armand Jacques Achille Leroy de Saint-Arnaud, *Lettres du maréchal de Saint-Arnaud*, 2 vols (Paris: Michel Levy Frères, 1855), II, 325.

19 *The Times*, 4 June 1851.

20 'Inauguration de la section du chemin de fer de Lyon entre Tonnerre et Dijon', 1 June 1851, in Louis-Napoléon, *Oeuvres*, III, 210–12.

21 *The Times*, 15 July 1851, 5.

22 *Le Moniteur universel*, 18 July 1851.

23 Ibid.

24 Morny, 'La genèse', 526–7.

25 Fleury, *Souvenirs*, I, 147.

26 Morny, 'La genèse', 531.

27 Ollivier, *L'Empire libéral*, II, 436.

28 Charlemagne de Maupas, *The Story of the Coup d'État*, trans. Alfred Vandam (New York: D. Appleton and Company, 1884), 139.

29 *Le Constitutionnel*, 24 November 1851.

30 'Distribution des récompenses aux exposants français par le Président de la République', 25 November 1851, in Louis-Napoléon, *Oeuvres*, III, 267–71.

31 *Le Moniteur universel*, 22 November 1851.

32 *Le Moniteur universel*, 18 November 1851.

33 Louis Véron, *Nouveaux mémoires d'un bourgeois de Paris depuis le 10 décembre 1848 jusqu'aux élections générales de 1863. Le Second-Empire* (Paris: A. Lacroix, Verboeckhoven et Cie, 1866), 345.

34 Granier de Cassagnac, *Souvenirs du Second Empire*, 3 vols (Paris: E. Dentu, 1879), I, 217.

11 History of a Crime

1 Maupas, *The Story*, 264.

2 Maupas, *The Story*, 268–9; Véron, *Noveaux mémoires*, 351–3; Cassagnac, *Souvenirs*, I, 224–5.

3 Hugo, *History of a Crime*, I, 40–2.

4 Ibid., 99–101.

5 Viel Castel, *Mémoires*, 244–6.

6 Louis-Napoléon, *Oeuvres*, III, 271–2.

7 Hugo, *History of a Crime*, III, 108–9.

8 Victor Schœlcher, *History of the Crimes of the Second of December* (London: Library & Agency of the Universal Printing Establishment in Jersey, 1853), 108, 122.

9 Flahault to Madame de Flahault, 3 December 1851, in Henry William Edmund Petty Fitzmaurice (ed.), *The Secret of the Coup d'État: An Unpublished Correspondence of Prince Louis Napoleon, MM. de Morny, de Flahault, and Others, 1848 to 1852* (London: Constable & Co., 1924), 120–2.

10 Rémusat, *Mémoires*, IV, 483.

11 M. C. M. Simpson (ed.), *Correspondence and Conversations of Alexis de Tocqueville with Nassau William Senior from 1834–1859*, 2 vols (London: Henry S. King & Co., 1872), II, 9–10.

12 Barrot, *Mémoires*, IV, 231.

13 Hugo, *History of a Crime*, I, 57–60.

14 Ibid., 252–3.

15 Ibid., II, 30–1, 47, 53–4.

16 Ibid., 110.

17 Schœlcher, *History of the Crimes*, 141–4; Hugo, *History of a Crime*, II, 110.

18 Hugo, *History of a Crime*, II, 114.

19 Fleury, *Souvenirs*, I, 175–7.

20 Claude Vigoureux, *Maupas et le coup d'état de Louis-Napoléon: Le policier du Deux-Décembre* (Paris: SPM, 2002), 189.

21 Hugo, *History of a Crime*, II, 207.

22 Ibid., III, 67, 133–4, 138.

23 Canrobert, *Souvenirs*, I, 537.

24 'The Late Scenes in Paris', *The Times*, 13 December 1851.

25 Hugo, *History of a Crime*, III, 157.

26 Louis-Napoléon, *Oeuvres*, III, 280.

12 *Vox Populi, Vox Dei*

1 Rudolf Apponyi, *Journal du comte Rodolphe Apponyi, attaché de l'ambassade d'Autriche-Hongrie à Paris: vingt-cinq ans à Paris 1826–1850*, 4 vols (Paris: Plon-Nourrit, 1913–26), IV, 368.

2 Maupas, *The Story*, 418.

3 *The Times*, 11 December 1851.

4 *Le Moniteur universel*, 3 December 1851.

5 Maupas, *The Story*, 427.

6 Hugo, *Napoléon le Pétit*, 180.

7 In Matthew Truesdell, *Spectacular Politics: Louis-Napoleon Bonaparte and the Fête Impériale* (Oxford: Oxford University Press, 1997), 34.

8 'Présentation du résultat des votes émis sur le projet de plébiscite', 31 December 1851, in Louis-Napoléon, *Oeuvres*, III, 282.

9 'Ouverture de la session du Sénat et du Corps législatif au palais des Tuileries', 29 March 1852, in Louis-Napoléon, *Oeuvres*, III, 319.

10 Article 2 of the Constitution, 14 January 1852, in Louis-Napoléon, *Oeuvres*, III, 298.

11 'Ouverture de la session du Sénat et du Corps législatif au palais des Tuileries', 320, 322.

12 'Constitution', 14 January 1852, in Louis-Napoléon, *Oeuvres*, III, 293.

13 Ibid., 292.

14 Theodore Martin, *The Life of His Royal Highness the Prince Consort*, 5 vols (New York: D. Appleton and Company, 1875–80), III, 108.

15 Sudhir Hazareesingh, *From Subject to Citizen: The Second Empire and the Emergence of Modern French Democracy* (Princeton, NJ: Princeton University Press, 1998), 64.

16 Marx and Engels, *Selected Works*, I, 442.

17 Anonymous, *Le Tiers Parti et les libertés intérieures* (Paris: E. Dentu, 1866), 13.

18 Viel Castel, *Mémoires*, II, 23–4.

19 Alfred Frédéric, comte de Falloux, *Mémoires d'un Royaliste*, 2 vols (Paris: Perrin, 1888), II, 223.

20 Persigny, *Mémoires*, 173.

21 'Ouverture de la session du Sénat et du Corps législatif au palais des Tuileries', 325.

22 Persigny, *Mémoires*, 179–80.

23 *The Times*, 17 September 1852.

24 Truesdell, *Spectacular Politics*, 51.

25 'Discours de Bordeaux', 9 October 1852, in Louis-Napoléon, *Oeuvres*, III, 341–4.

26 *The Times*, 18 October 1852.

27 *Morning Chronicle*, 18 October 1852.

28 'Proclamation de l'Empire', 1 December 1852, in Louis-Napoléon, *Oeuvres*, III, 352.

13 The Imperial Cloak

1 Fleury, *Souvenirs*, I, 210.

2 Augustin Filon, *Recollections of the Empress Eugenie* (London: Cassell and Company, 1920), 21–2.

3 Ibid., 8.

4 Eugénie to Count of Montijo, 2 January 1837, in F. de Llanos y Torriglia and Pierre Josseran (eds), *Lettres familières de l'impératrice Eugénie*, 2 vols (Paris: Le Divan, 1935), I, 8.

5 Maxime du Camp, *Souvenirs d'un demi-siècle: Au temps de Louis-Philippe et de Napoléon III, 1830–1870*, 2 vols (Paris: Hachette, 1949), I, 148.

6 Joseph Primoli, 'L'Enfance d'une souveraine – Souvenirs intimes I', *Revue des Deux Mondes*, 17 (1923), 783.

7 Jerrold, *Life of Napoleon III*, III, 424.

8 Rémusat, *Mémoires*, IV, 358–9.

9 Fleury, *Souvenirs*, I, 221.

10 Maurice Paléologue, *The Tragic Empress: Intimate Conversations with the Empress*

Eugénie, 1901–1911, trans. Hamish Miles (London: Thornton Butterworth, 1928), 80.

11 Filon, *Recollections*, 23–4.

12 F. A. Wellesley (ed.), *The Paris Embassy During the Second Empire* (London: Thornton Butterworth, 1928), 17.

13 Mérimée to Francisque-Michel, 28 January 1853, in Mérimée, *Correspondance Générale*, VII, 16.

14 George Villiers, *A Vanished Victorian: Being the Life of George Villiers, Fourth Earl of Clarendon, 1800–1870* (London: Eyre & Spottiswoode, 1938), 262.

15 'Communication relative au mariage de l'empereur', 22 January 1853, Louis-Napoléon, *Oeuvres*, III, 357–60.

16 Eugénie to Paca, 22 January 1853, *Lettres familières*, I, 50.

17 Malmesbury, *Memoirs*, 302.

18 Viel Castel, *Mémoires*, II, 55.

19 Thomas Evans, *Memoirs of Dr Thomas W. Evans: Recollections of the Second French Empire*, 2 vols (T. Fisher Unwin, 1905), I, 64.

20 Edmond and Jules de Goncourt, *Journal: mémoires de la vie littéraire*, 3 vols (Paris: R. Laffont, 1989), I, 864.

21 Hugo, *Napoléon le Pétit*, 71–2.

22 Price, *Anatomy of Power*, 406–7.

23 Tocqueville, *Recollections*, 320.

24 Viel Castel, *Mémoires*, II, 148.

25 Anceau, *Napoléon III*, 237.

26 Anonymous, *A History of the Sudden and Terrible Invasion of England by the French, in the Month of May, 1852* (London: T. Bosworth, 1852), 17.

27 Alfred Tennyson, 'The Third of February 1852', in *The Complete Works of Alfred Lord Tennyson* (New York: Frederick A. Stokes Company, 1891), 92.

28 *The Times*, 29 September 1852.

29 Alexander Kinglake, *The Invasion of the Crimea: Its Origin, and an Account of Its Progress Down to the Death of Lord Raglan*, 8 vols, new edn (London: William Blackwood and Sons, 1890), I, 302–3, 323.

30 Jonathan Philip Parry, 'The Impact of Napoleon III on British Politics, 1851–1880', *Transactions of the Royal Historical Society*, 11 (2001), 152.

31 Jasper Ridley, *Lord Palmerston* (New York: E. P. Dutton & Company, 1971), 398.

32 Victoria to King Leopold, 4 December 1851, in Arthur Christopher Benson (ed.), *The Letters of Queen Victoria: A Selection from Her Majesty's Correspondence between the Years 1837 and 1861*, 3 vols (London: John Murray, 1908), II, 334.

33 Tsar Nicholas I to Louis-Napoléon, 17 January 1853. 400AP/47, Dossier 1.

14 War and Peace

1 Isabella Frances Romer, *A Pilgrimage to the Temples and Tombs of Egypt, Nubia, and Palestine, in 1845–6*, 2 vols (London: Richard Bentley, 1846), II, 264–76.

2 Edgar Holt, *Plon-Plon: The Life of Prince Napoleon* (London: Michael Joseph, 1973), 76.

3 Benjamin Disraeli papers, Oxford, Bodleian Libraries. Anecdotes and accounts, numbers 1–49, by Disraeli, *c.*1825–63, Hughenden 26/2 fols 48–50, 133v–140v, 154, Napoleon III.

4 Saint-Arnaud to Madame de Saint-Arnaud, 17 September 1854, in Saint-Arnaud, *Lettres*, II, 489.

5 Adolphus Slade, *Turkey and the Crimean War: A Narrative of Historical Events* (London: Smith, Elder and Co., 1867), 355.

6 Louis Noir, *Souvenirs d'un simple zouave: campagnes de Crimée et d'Italie; mœurs militaires* (Paris: Bureaux du Siècle, 1872), 227.

7 Alain Gouttman, *La guerre de Crimée, 1853–1856* (Paris: SPM, 1995), 218.

8 Saint-Arnaud to Louis-Napoléon, 21 September 1854. 400AP/55, Dossier 4.

9 Louis-Napoléon to Prince Napoléon, 23 November 1854, in *Napoléon III et Le Prince Napoléon*, 75.

10 Louis-Xavier de Ricard, *Autour des Bonaparte: Fragments de mémoires* (Paris: A. Savine, 1891), 238.

11 Orlando Figes, *Crimea: The Last Crusade* (London: Allen Lane, 2010), 311.

12 Queen Victoria's Journals – Princess Beatrice's Copies 1855. 'Monday 16th April 1855'.

13 Martin, *Prince Consort*, III, 202.

14 Theo Aronson, *Queen Victoria and the Bonapartes* (London: Cassell, 1972), 26.

15 Queen Victoria's Journals – Princess Beatrice's Copies 1855. 'Tuesday 17th April 1855'.

16 Villiers, *Vanished Victorian*, 254–5.

17 Aronson, *Victoria and the Bonapartes*, 34.

18 Queen Victoria's Journals – Princess Beatrice's Copies. 'Wednesday 18th April 1855'.

19 Queen Victoria's Journals – Princess Beatrice's Copies. 'Thursday 19th April 1855'.

20 Queen Victoria's Journals – Princess Beatrice's Copies. 'Friday 20th April 1855'.

21 Anna Bicknell, *Life in the Tuileries under the Second Empire* (New York: Century Co., 1895), 94.

22 Queen Victoria's Journals – Princess Beatrice's Copies. 'Saturday 21st April 1855'.

23 Persigny, *Mémoires*, 254–5.

24 Villiers, *Vanished Victorian*, 259.

25 Queen Victoria's Journals – Princess Beatrice's Copies. 'Saturday 25th August 1855.'

26 Queen Victoria's Journals – Princess Beatrice's Copies. 'Friday 24th August 1855'.

27 Jane Ridley, *Bertie: A Life of Edward VII* (London: Chatto & Windus, 2012), 31.

28 Martin, *Prince Consort*, III, 289–90.

15 The Beginning of the Affairs

1 Wellesley, *Paris Embassy*, 275.

2 Louis-Napoléon to Eugénie, 29 August 1854. 400AP/43.

3 Ridley, *Napoleon III and Eugenie*, 410.

4 Louis-Napoléon to Queen Victoria, 17 September 1856, in William Smith, *Eugénie: impératrice et femme, 1826–1920* (Paris: O. Orban, 1989), 88.

5 Antoine Barthez, *The Empress Eugénie and Her Circle*, trans. Bernard Miall (London: T. Fisher Unwin, 1912), 70.

6 Paléologue, *Tragic Empress*, 28.

7 'Réponse de l'empereur aux félicitations du Corps législatif sur la naissance du Prince Impérial', in Louis-Napoléon, *Oeuvres*, V, 11–12.

8 *The Times*, 16 June 1855.

9 Viel Castel, *Mémoires*, IV, 337.

10 Robert de Montesquiou, *La divine comtesse: étude d'après madame la comtesse de Castiglione* (Paris: Manzi, Joyant et Cie, 1913), 35.

11 Viel Castel, *Mémoires*, IV, 23.

12 Montesquiou, *La divine comtesse*, 80.

13 Viel Castel, *Mémoires*, IV, 337.

14 Ibid., 336.

15 Irène de Chauffailles de Gengoux marquise de Taisey-Chatenoy, *À la cour de Napoléon III* (Paris: A. Savine, 1891), 258.

16 Gustave Flaubert to Achille Flaubert, 23 January 1857. flaubert-v1.univ-rouen.fr/correspondance/edition.

17 Gustave Flaubert to Louise Pradier, 17 February 1857. flaubert-v1.univ-rouen.fr/correspondance/edition.

18 *The Times*, 22 June 1857.

19 Louis-Napoléon to Eugénie, 7 July 1857. 400AP/43.

20 Fleury, I, *Souvenirs*, 389–90.

21 Queen Victoria's Journals – Princess Beatrice's Copies. 'Saturday 8th August 1857', 'Sunday 9th August 1857', 'Monday 10th August 1857'.

22 Wellesley, *Paris Embassy*, 111.

23 Louis-Napoléon to Eugénie, September 1857. 400AP/43.

24 Louis-Napoléon to Eugénie, 8 September 1857. 400AP/43.

25 Prosper Mérimée, *Correspondance generale*, VIII, 435; Joseph Alexander von Hübner, *Neuf ans de souvenirs d'un ambassadeur d'Autriche à Paris sous le second Empire, 1851–1859*, 2 vols (Paris: Plon-Nourrit, 1904), II, 91.

26 Anceau, *Napoléon III*, 300.

27 Malmesbury, *Memoirs*, 425.

28 Conspiracy to Murder debated in House of Commons, Monday 8 February 1858, *Hansard*, vol. 148.

29 *The Sun*, 17 April 1858.

30 Malmesbury, *Memoirs*, 422.

31 Wellesley, *Paris Embassy*, 163–4.

32 *Le Moniteur universel*, 27 February 1858.

33 Camillo Benso di Cavour to Victor Emmanuel II, 24 July 1858, www.camillocavour.com/archivio/lettere/cavour-camillo-benso-di-a-savoia-vittorio-emanuele-ii-di-1858-07-24-3684/.

34 Viel-Castel, Mémoires, IV, 336.

35 Villiers, *Vanished Victorian*, 295.

36 Malmesbury, *Memoirs*, 455.

37 *La Presse*, 23 November 1858.

38 Holt, *Plon-Plon*, 126–7.

39 Wellesley, *Paris Embassy*, 141.

40 *The Times*, 27 and 28 April 1859.

16 War and Peace Revisited

1 Bapst, *Le maréchal Canrobert*, III, 367.

2 'Ordre du jour de l'Empereur à l'Armée d'Italie', 12 May 1859, in Louis-Napoléon, *Oeuvres*, V, 81–2.

3 Louis-Napoléon to Eugénie, 14 May 1859. 400AP/43.

4 Fleury, *Souvenirs*, II, 13.

5 Bapst, *Le maréchal Canrobert*, III, 270.

6 Louis-Napoléon to Eugénie, 31 May 1859. 400AP/43.

7 Léon Laforge, *Histoire complète de Mac-Mahon, maréchal de France, duc de Magenta, d'après des documents originaux et des pièces officielles*, 3 vols (Paris: Lamulle et Poisson, 1898), I, 114.

8 Louis-Napoléon to Eugénie, 4 June 1859. 400AP/57, Dossier 1.

9 Louis-Napoléon to Eugénie, 8 June 1859. 400AP/43.

10 'Napoleon III in Italy', in *The Poetical Works of Elizabeth Barrett Browning*, 6 vols (London: Smith, Elder, & Co., 1890), IV, 171–89.

11 Bapst, *Le maréchal Canrobert*, III, 463–4.

12 Fleury, *Souvenirs*, II, 88.

13 Louis-Napoléon to Eugénie, 24 June 1859. 400AP/57, Dossier 1.

14 'Proclamation au people français', 3 May 1859, in Louis-Napoléon, *Oeuvres*, V, 79.

15 Anceau, *Napoléon III*, 306.

16 Fleury, *Souvenirs*, II, 71.

17 Augustin Filon, *Memoirs of the Prince Imperial* (London: William Heinemann, 1913), 11.

18 Fleury, *Souvenirs*, II, 121.

19 Holt, *Plon-Plon*, 150.

20 Elizabeth Browning to Sophia Eckley, 17 July 1859. www.browningscorrespondence. com/correspondence/4841/?rsId=400849&returnPage=1#D-00T0004.

21 Bapst, *Le maréchal Canrobert*, II, 519.

22 Ridley, *Napoleon III and Eugénie*, 457.

23 Robb, *Victor Hugo*, 373.

24 François Charles du Barail, *Mes Souvenirs, etc.*, 3 vols (Paris: E. Plon, Nourrit et Cie, 1895–6), II, 252.

25 Louis-Édouard Pie, *Oeuvres de monseigneur l'évêque de Poitiers*, 8 vols (Paris: H. Oudin & Cie, 1883–4), IV, 42–3 ('Lettre circulaire aux curés de la ville épiscopale, ordonnant des prières pour l'armée pontificale, 29 septembre 1860').

26 Queen Victoria's Journals – Princess Beatrice's Copies. 'Sunday 18th March 1860'.

27 Wellesley, *Paris Embassy*, 206.

28 Martin, *Prince Consort*, V, 37.

29 Viel Castel, *Mémoires*, VI, 75–6.

30 Marie de Saint-Germain, *Relation du voyage de LL. MM. l'Empereur & l'Impératrice à Nice 12 et 13 septembre 1860* (Nice: Impr. Canis frères, 1860), 87–8.

31 Fleury, *Souvenirs*, II, 163.

32 'Discours de l'émpereur prononcé au banquet offert à sa majesté par la ville d'Algiers', 19 September 1860, in Louis-Napoléon, *Oeuvres*, V, 126–7.

33 'Lettre de l'empereur au gouveneur de l'Algérie', 6 February 1863, in Louis-Napoléon, *Oeuvres*, V, 189–94.

34 Louis-Napoléon to Eugénie, 2 December 1860. 400AP/43.

35 Louis-Napoléon to Eugénie, 4 December 1860. 440AP/43.

36 Bicknell, *Life in the Tuileries*, 146.

37 Armand Lucy, *Lettres intimes sur la campagne de Chine en 1860: souvenirs de voyage* (Marseille: J. Barile, 1861), 96.

38 Maurice d'Hérisson (ed.), *L'Expédition de Chine: d'après la correspondance confidentielle du Gal Cousin de Montauban* (Paris: E. Plon, 1883), 223.

39 Henry Knollys (ed.), *Incidents in the China War of 1860: Compiled from the Private Journals of General Sir Hope Grant* (Edinburgh: W. Blackwood & Sons, 1875), 332.

40 Robert Swinhoe, *Narrative of the North China Campaign of 1860: Containing Personal Experiences of Chinese Character, and of the Moral and Social Condition of the Country; Together with a Description of the Interior of Pekin* (London: Smith, Elder, 1861), 330.

41 'Discours de l'empereur à l'ouverture de la session législatif', 4 February 1861, in Louis-Napoléon, *Oeuvres*, V, 136.

42 Queen Victoria to Louis-Napoléon, 3 January 1861. 400AP/45, Dossier 5.

43 'Discours de l'empereur à l'ouverture de la session législatif', 5 November 1863, in Louis-Napoléon, *Oeuvres*, V, 207–8.

44 'Allocution de l'empereur aux troupes partant pour la Syrie', 7 August 1860, in Louis-Napoléon, *Oeuvres*, V, 122.

17 Blood and Iron

1 'Ouverture de la session législative de 1853', 14 February 1853, in Louis-Napoléon, *Oeuvres*, III, 361–4.

2 Louis-Napoléon to Eugénie, 26 November 1860. 400AP/43.

3 Pierre de la Gorce, *Histoire du second Empire*, 7 vols, 11th edn (Paris: Plon Nourrit, 1907–10), III, 447.

4 Pamela Pilbeam, *Saint-Simonians in Nineteenth-Century France: From Free Love to Algeria* (Basingstoke: Palgrave Macmillan, 2014), 49–50.

5 Louis-Napoléon, *Oeuvres*, I, 21.

6 'Discours prononcé par l'empereur à l'inauguration du boulevard Malasherbes', 13 August 1861, in Louis-Napoléon, *Oeuvres*, V, 144.

7 Émile Zola, *Le Ventre de Paris* (Paris: G. Charpentier, 1882), 218.

8 Anceau, *Napoléon III*, 362.

9 Bicknell, *Life in the Tuileries*, 46.

10 Stéphanie Tascher de la Pagerie, *Mon séjour aux Tuileries . . . Deuxième série, 1859–1865* (Paris: P. Ollendorff, 1894), 183.

11 Gustave Flaubert to Caroline Commanville, 17 November 1864, flaubert.univ-rouen.fr/correspondance/correspondance/17-novembre-1864-de-gustave-flaubert-%C3%A0-caroline-commanville/?year=1864&page=12.

12 Maxime du Camp, *Souvenirs littéraires*, 2 vols (Paris: Hachette, 1882), II, 269.

13 Bicknell, *Life in the Tuileries*, 48.

14 Émile Ollivier, *Journal, 1846–1869*, 2 vols (Paris: R. Juilliard, 1961), II, 186–7.

15 Senior, *Conversations*, II, 198–203.

16 Ollivier, *L'Empire libéral*, VII, 311–12.

17 *Evening Standard*, 17 March 1865.

18 Wellesley, *Paris Embassy*, 273.

19 Anonymous, *Les petits papiers secrets des Tuileries et de Saint-Cloud étiquetés par un collectionneur. Partie 1*, 2 vols (Paris: E. Dentu, 1871), 5–6.

20 Holt, *Plon-Plon*, 183.

21 Edward Shawcross, *The Last Emperor of Mexico: A Disaster in the New World* (London: Faber & Faber, 2022), 19.

22 Charles Dupin to Louis-Napoléon, 9 November 1863, 'Du Mexique dans ses rapport avec Napoléon III par le baron Charles Dupin, sénateur', Archives des Affaires Etrangères, Paris, Mémoires et documents, Mexique, 10.

23 Éric Taladoire, *Les contre-guérillas françaises dans les terres chaudes du Mexique (1862–1867): Des forces spéciales au XIXe siècle* (Paris: L'Harmattan, 2016), 70–2.

24 Louis-Napoléon to Prince Napoléon, 29 March 1863, in *Napoléon III et Le Prince Napoléon*, 241–5.

25 Prince Napoléon to Louis-Napoléon, 31 March 1863, in ibid., 245–7.

26 Anceau, *Napoléon III*, 433.

27 Holt, *Plon-Plon*, 117.

28 *The Times*, 22 May 1865.

29 *The Times*, 27 May 1865,

30 Ollivier, *L'Empire libéral*, VII, 391–2.

31 Louis-Napoléon to Prince Napoléon, 19 June 1865, in *Napoléon III et Le Prince Napoléon*, 267–9.

32 'Note V – Note sur un conversation entre l'empereur Napoléon et moi, le 19 June 1865, aux Tuileries', in *Napoléon III et Le Prince Napoléon*, 373–82.

33 Jonathan Steinberg, *Bismarck: A Life* (Oxford: Oxford University Press, 2011), 174, 180–1.

34 Mérimée to Fanny Lagden, 9 October 1865, in *Correspondance Générale*, XII, 553–4.

35 Steinberg, *Bismarck*, 180–1.

36 Ollivier, *L'Empire libéral*, VII, 475.

37 Persigny, *Mémoires*, 328–9.

18 The Empire in the Pillory

1 *La France*, quoted in *The Times*, 5 July 1866.

2 Paléologue, *Tragic Empress*, 112.

3 Jacques Louis Randon, *Mémoires du maréchal Randon*, 2 vols (Paris: Lahure, 1875–7), II, 145.

4 Friedrich Ferdinand, Count von Beust, *Memoirs of Friedrich Ferdinand Count von Beust*, 2 vols (London: Remington, 1887), I, 320.

5 Roger Williams, *The Mortal Napoleon III* (Princeton, NJ: Princeton University Press, 1971), 115–17.

6 Maximilian to Degollado, 8 March 1866, in Egon Ceasar Corti, *Maximilian and Charlotte of Mexico*, trans. Catherine Alison, 2 vols (New York and London: Alfred A. Knopf, 1928), II, 605.

7 Louis-Napoléon to Maximilian, 15 January 1866, in Corti, *Maximilian*, II, 930–1.

8 'Discours de l'empereur à l'ouverture de la session législative', 22 January 1866, in Louis-Napoléon, *Oeuvres*, V, 251–9.

9 Émile de Kératry, *L'élévation et la chute de l'empire Maximilien: intervention française au Mexique, 1861–1867* (Paris: A. Lacroix, Verboeckhoven et Cie, 1867), 41, 179.

10 Louis-Napoléon to Maximilian, 18 March 1864, in Corti, *Maximilian*, I, 398.

11 Maximilian to Carlota, 7 August 1866, in Konrad Ratz (ed.), *Correspondencia inédita entre Maximiliano y Carlota*, trans. Elsa Cecilia Frost (Mexico: Fondo de Cultura Económica, 2004), 312–14.

12 Mérimée to Panizzi, 12 August 1866, in Mérimée, *Correspondance Générale*, XIII, 172–3.

13 Maurice Fleury, *Memoirs of the Empress Eugenie*, 2 vols (New York: D. Appleton and Company), 1920, II, 119.

14 Shawcross, *Last Emperor*, 197.

15 José Luis Blasio, *Maximilian, Emperor of Mexico*, trans. Robert Hammond Murray (New Haven, CT: Yale University Press, 1941), 107.

16 Paléologue, *Tragic Empress*, 87.

17 Roger Lawrence Williams, *Gaslight and Shadow: The World of Napoleon III, 1851–1870* (New York: Macmillan, 1957), 266–7.

18 Ollivier, *L'Empire liberal*, IX, 192–201.

19 Ibid., 203.

20 'Lettre de l'Empereur au Ministre du État', 19 January 1867, in Louis-Napoléon, *Oeuvres*, V, 275–7.

21 Ollivier, *Journal*, II, 314.

22 *Le Moniteur universel*, 15 July 1867.

23 Victor Duruy, *Notes et souvenirs*, 2 vols (Paris: Hachette, 1901), I, 183.

24 Félix Dupanloup, *M. Duruy et l'éducation des filles, lettre de Mgr l'évêque d'Orléans* (Paris: C. Douniol, 1868).

25 'Discours d'ouverture de la session de 1867', in Louis-Napoléon, *Oeuvres*, V, 278–86 at 283.

26 Mark Twain, *The Innocents Abroad* (Hartford, CT: American Publishing Company, 1869), 127.

27 *Paris-Guide par les principaux écrivains et artistes de la France; introduction par Victor Hugo* (Paris: Librairie internationale, 1867), xli.

28 *The Times*, 3 April 1867.

29 *Illustrated Times*, 11 May 1867.

30 Ridley, *Napoleon III*, 531.

31 Albert Laprade, *Charles Garnier et l'Opéra* (Paris: Bibliothèque nationale, 1961), 11.

32 *Morning Post*, 3 July 1867; *Express*, 3 July 1867.

33 'Discours de l'Empereur à la distribution des récompenses de l'éxposition', in Louis-Napoléon, *Oeuvres*, V, 286–9.

34 Castelnau to Louis-Napoléon, 28 October and 9 November 1866. 400AP/61, Dossier 3.

35 Konrad Ratz, *El ocaso del imperio de Maximiliano visto por un diplomático prusiano* (Mexico City: Siglo XXI, 2012).

36 Shawcross, *Last Emperor*, 277.

37 *El Boletín republicano*, 21 June 1867.

38 Eugène Forcade, 'Chronique de la Quinzaine', *Revue des Deux Mondes*, 2e période, 70 (1867), 517.

39 *The Times*, 26 August 1867; *Morning Herald*, 23 August 1867.

40 Lynn Marshall Case and Warren Spencer, *The United States and France: Civil War Diplomacy* (Philadelphia: University of Pennsylvania Press, 1970), 369.

41 *Le Moniteur universel*, 10 November 1867.

42 *Le Moniteur universel*, 6 December 1867.

43 Ernest Pinard, *Mon journal*, 2 vols (Paris: E. Dentu, 1892), I, 236.

44 Anceau, *Napoléon III*, 458.

45 Henri Rochefort, *The Adventures of My Life*, trans. Ernest Smith, 2 vols (London: Edward Arnold, 1896), I, 141.

46 *La Lanterne*, 30 May 1868, 21.

19 The Liberal Empire

1 Quoted in Émile Ollivier, 'L'Affaire Baudin', *Revue des Deux Mondes*, 5e période, 33 (1906), 299–300.

2 Paléologue, *Tragic Empress*, 81–2.

3 Louis-Napoléon to Eugénie, 23 July 1868. 400AP/43.

4 'Discours d'ouverture de la session législative de 1869', 18 January 1869, in Louis-Napoléon, *Oeuvres*, V, 313–18.

5 Ridley, *Napoleon III*, 544–5.

6 Anceau, *Napoléon III*, 469.

7 Mountstuart E. Grant Duff, *Notes from a Diary, 1886–1888*, 2 vols (London: John Murray, 1900), I, 81.

8 Arnold Wilson, *Suez Canal: Its Past, Present, and Future*, 2nd edn (London: Oxford University Press, 1997), 21.

9 Quoted in K. Bell, 'British Policy Towards the Construction of the Suez Canal, 1859–65', *Transactions of the Royal Historical Society*, 15 (1965), 137.

10 Queen Victoria's Journals – Princess Beatrice's Copies. 'Thursday 6th July 1876'.

11 Eugénie to Louis-Napoléon, 27 October 1869, in Smith, *Eugénie*, 144.

12 Louis-Napoléon to Eugénie, 15 October 1869. 400AP/43.

13 *Journal officiel de l'Empire français*, 30 November 1869.

14 *The Times*, 13 December 1869.

15 Ollivier, *L'Empire libéral*, XII, 198.

16 Ibid., 137.

17 *Journal officiel de l'Empire français*, 8 January 1870.

18 *Irish Times*, 28 February 1870.

19 *The Times*, 6 January 1870.

20 Anceau, *Napoléon III*, III, 482.

21 Roger Lawrence Williams, *Manners and Murders in the World of Louis-Napoleon* (Seattle: University of Washington Press, 1975), 133–4.

22 Rochefort, *Adventures*, I, 228–9.

23 Williams, *Manners*, 137.

24 Ollivier, *L'Empire libéral*, XII, 415.

25 *Journal officiel de l'Empire français*, 12 January 1870.

26 *Morning Post*, 13 January 1870.

27 Éric Anceau, 'Le plébiscite du 8 mai 1870: un monument oublié de notre histoire politique', *Napoleonica. La Revue*, 43 (2022), 8.

28 *Journal officiel de l'Empire français*, 24 April 1870.

29 Philippe de Massa, *Souvenirs et impressions 1840–1871*, 2nd edn (Paris: C. Lévy, 1897), 264.

30 Anceau, 'Le plébiscite', 86.

31 Ollivier, *L'Empire libéral*, XIII, 401–2.

32 Lord Lyons to Lord Clarendon, 24 May 1870, in Thomas Wodehouse Legh, Lord Newton (ed.), *Lord Lyons: A Record of British Diplomacy*, 2 vols (London: Edward Arnold, 1913), I, 290.

33 *Journal officiel de l'Empire français*, 1 July 1870.

20 War or Peace

1 Alfred Grafen von Waldersee, *Denkwürdigkeiten des General-Feldmarschall*, 3 vols (Berlin: Deutsche Verlags-Anstalt, 1922), I, 54–5.

2 Ollivier, *L'Empire liberal*, XIV, 23.

3 *Journal officiel de l'Empire français*, 7 July 1870.

4 Ollivier, *L'Empire libéral*, XIV, 108.

5 Wetzel, *Duel of Giants*, 112.

6 Ollivier, *L'Empire libéral*, XIV, 43.

7 *Le Rappel*, 13 July 1870.

8 Ollivier, *L'Empire liberal*, XIV, 118.

9 *Evening Standard*, 11 July 1870.

10 *The Times*, 9 July 1870.

11 Williams, *Mortal Napoleon III*, 137.

12 Ollivier, *L'Empire libéral*, XIV, 239–41.

13 Pierre Muret, 'Émile Ollivier et le duc de Gramont les 12 et 13 juillet 1870', *Revue d'Histoire Moderne & Contemporaine*, 13.3 (1909), 306.

14 Otto von Bismarck, *Bismarck, the Man and the Statesman: Being the Reflections and Reminiscences of Otto Prince von Bismarck*, trans. A. J. Butler, 2 vols (London, Smith, Elder & Co., 1898), 94–6.

15 Paléologue, *Tragic Empress*, 138.

16 *Les origines diplomatiques de la guerre de 1870–1871: recueil de documents publié par le Ministère des Affaires étrangères*, 29 vols (Paris: G. Ficker, 1910–32), XXVIII, 479–80.

17 Bismarck, *The Man and the Statesman*, 97–102.

18 Ollivier, *L'Empire libéral*, XIV, 285–6.

19 Ibid., 292.

20 *Le Pays*, 14 July 1870.

21 Ollivier, *L'Empire libéral*, XIV, 355–6.

22 Ibid., 358.

23 Gorce, *Second Empire*, VI, 289.

24 Ibid., 292.

25 Ollivier, *L'Empire libéral*, XIV, 370–3.

26 *Journal officiel de l'Empire français*, 16 July 1870.

27 *The Times*, 20 July 1870.

28 Pierre de Lano, *L'Empereur Napoléon III* (Paris: Victor Harvard, 1893), 113.

29 Paléologue, *Tragic Empress*, 145.

30 Evans, *Memoirs*, I, 231–2; Ollivier, *L'Empire libéral*, XV, 306.

31 Geoffrey Wawro, *The Franco-Prussian War: The German Conquest of France in 1870–1871* (Cambridge: Cambridge University Press, 2003), 47–8.

32 Louis-Napoléon to Eugénie. 400AP/43.

33 *Journal officiel de l'Empire français*, 29 July 1870.

34 Ollivier, *L'Empire libéral*, XV, 309.

35 *The Times*, 16 July 1870.

36 *Liverpool Daily Post*, 2 August 1870.

37 Bapst, *Le maréchal Canrobert*, VI, 154.

38 Louis-Napoléon to Eugénie, 2 August 1870. 400AP/68, Dossier 1.

21 The Debacle

1 Gorce, *Second Empire*, VI, 432.

2 Ollivier, *L'Empire libéral*, XVI, 317–18.

3 *Morning Post*, 11 August 1870.

4 *Journal officiel de l'Empire français*, 10 August 1870.

5 Wawro, *Franco-Prussian War*, 140.

6 Chrastil, *Bismarck's War*, 82.

7 Anceau, *Napoléon III*, 516.

8 Charles Fay, *Journal d'un officier de l'armée du Rhin*, 4th edn (Paris: J. Dumaine, 1871), 71.

9 Bapst, *Le maréchal Canrobert*, VI, 373.

10 Massa, *Souvenirs*, 290.

11 Gorce, *Second Empire*, VII, 167–71.

12 Gaston d'Andlau, *Metz, campagne et négociations par un officier supérieur de l'armée du Rhin* (Paris: J. Dumaine, 1871), 78.

13 Paul von Hindenburg, *Out of My Life*, trans. F. A. Holt (New York: Harper & Brothers, 1921), 43.

14 Wawro, *Franco-Prussian War*, 176.

15 Ollivier, *L'Empire libéral*, XVII, 276.

16 Ibid., 269.

17 Helmuth von Moltke, *The Franco-German War of 1870–71*, trans. Clara Bell and Henry Fischer (New York: Harper & Brothers, 1892), 71.

18 Comte de Palikao to Louis-Napoléon, 27 August 1870. 400AP/68, Dossier 1.

19 Émile Ollivier, 'La Guerre de 1870 – Les Tourmens de Mac Mahon', *Revue des Deux Mondes*, 6e période, 16 (1913), 751.

20 Gorce, *Second Empire*, VII, 291.

21 Wawro, *Franco-Prussian War*, 211.

22 Chrastil, *Bismarck's War*, 144–5.

23 Mark Stoneman, 'The Bavarian Army and French Civilians in the War of 1870–1871: A Cultural Interpretation', *War in History*, 8.3 (2001), 276.

24 Ibid., 278.

25 Auguste-Alexandre Ducrot, *La journée de Sedan* (Paris: E. Dentu, 1871), 31–2.

26 Massa, *Souvenirs*, 320.

27 Stoneman, 'Bavarian Army', 279.

28 Paul and Victor Margueritte, *Les Braves gens*, 4 vols (Paris: E. Plon, Nourrit et Cie, 1897–1904), 121.

29 Wimpffen, *Sedan*, 170.

30 Massa, *Souvenirs*, 324.

31 Ducrot, *Sedan*, 51; B.-L.-J. Lebrun, *Guerre de 1870: Bazeilles–Sedan* (Paris: E. Dentu, 1884), 130–3.

32 Lebrun, *Guerre de 1870*, 135–9.

33 Ducrot, *Sedan*, 52.

34 Wawro, *Franco-Prussian War*, 226.

35 Philip Sheridan, *Personal Memoirs of P. H. Sheridan, General, United States Army*, 2 vols (New York: Charles L. Webster & Company, 1888), 403, 405.

36 Wimpffen, *Sedan*, 245.

37 Frederick III, *The War Diary of the Emperor Frederick III, 1870–1*, trans. A. R. Allinson (New York: Howard Fertig, 1988), 99.

38 Louis-Napoléon to Eugénie, 2 September 1870. 400AP/43.

22 The Terrible Year

1 Paléologue, *Tragic Empress*, 194.

2 Filon, *Recollections*, 134–5.

3 *Journal officiel de l'Empire français*, 4 September 1870.

4 Ernest Dréolle, *La journée du 4 septembre au Corps législatif avec notes sur les journées du 3 et du 5 septembre: souvenirs politiques* (Paris: F. Amyot, 1871), 73–4.

5 Evans, *Memoirs*, II, 295.

6 Ibid., 318.

7 Ibid., 329–30.

8 Ibid., 365–7.

9 Louise, comtesse de Mercy-Argenteau, *The Last Love of an Emperor: Reminiscences of the Comtesse Louise de Mercy-Argenteau* (London: William Heinemann, 1926), 214.

10 Eugénie to Louis-Napoléon, 14 October 1870. 400AP/43.

11 Louis-Napoléon to prince imperial, 9 September 1870. 400AP/75, Dossier 2.

12 Louis-Napoléon to Eugénie, 29 September 1870. 400AP/43.

13 Louis-Napoléon to Eugénie, 17 September 1870. 400AP/43.

14 Louis-Napoléon to Eugénie, 29 September 1870. 400AP/43.

15 General Monts, *La Captivité de Napoléon III en Allemagne: souvenirs traduits de l'allemand par Paul Bruck-Gilbert et Paul Lévy* (Paris: P. Lafitte, 1911), 35.

16 Ibid., 65.

17 'Récit de ce qui s'est passé entre l'impératrice et le Prince Napoléon à Londres le 15 October 1870'. 400AP/53, Dossier 2.

18 Louis-Napoléon to Prince Napoléon, 25 November 1870, in *Correspondance*, 317.

19 Louis-Napoléon to Eugénie, 5 October 1870. 400AP/43.

20 Louis-Napoléon to Eugénie, 6 October 1870. 400AP/43.

21 Louis-Napoléon to Eugénie, 20 October 1870. 400AP/43.

22 Louis-Napoléon to Eugénie, 29 October 1870. 400AP/43.

23 Louis-Napoléon to Prince Napoléon, 8 and 25 November 1870, in *Correspondance*, 316–17.

24 Louis-Napoléon to Eugénie, 22 December 1870. 400AP/43.

25 Louis-Napoléon to Eugénie, 29 December 1870. 400AP/43.

26 Moritz Busch, *Bismarck: Some Secret Pages of His History, Being a Diary Kept by Dr Moritz Busch during Twenty-Five Years' Official and Private Intercourse with the Great Chancellor*, 3 vols (London: Macmillan and Company, 1898), 273.

27 Mercy-Argenteau, *Last Love*, 273, 132, 119, 45, 119, 150.

28 Frederick III, *War Diary*, 272.

29 Mercy-Argenteau, *Last Love*, 246–8, 258.

30 Louis-Napoléon to Eugénie, 30 January 1871. 400AP/43.

31 Eugénie to Louis-Napoléon, 30 January 1871. 400AP/43.

32 Louis-Napoléon to Eugénie, 17 February 1871. 400AP/43.

33 Louis-Napoléon to Mercy-Argentau, 2 March 1871, in Mercy-Argentau, *Last Love*, 268–70.

34 Louis-Napoléon to Eugénie, 28 February 1871. 400AP/43.

35 *The Times*, 6 March 1871.

36 Louis-Napoléon to Monsieur le President de l'Assemblée nationale, 6 March 1871. 400AP/43.

23 The End

1 *The Times*, 21 March 1871.

2 Malmesbury, *Memoirs*, 666–7.

3 Queen Victoria's Journals – Princess Beatrice's Copies. 'Monday 27th March 1871'.

4 Ivor Guest, *Napoleon III in England* (London: British Technical and General Press, 1952), 183.

5 *Exeter and Plymouth Gazette*, 15 September 1871.

6 Louis-Napoléon to Eugénie, 12 September 1871. 400AP/43.

7 Louis-Napoléon to Eugénie, 27 September 1870. 400AP/43.

8 *Morning Post*, 23 October 1871.

9 *The Times*, 19 May 1871.

10 *Daily News*, 27 October 1871.

11 Louis-Napoléon to Eugénie, 29 October 1871. 400AP/43.

12 *The Times*, 23 October 1871.

13 *Journal des débats* quoted in *Evening Standard*, 26 October 1871.

14 Du Camp, *Souvenirs*, II, 279.

15 John Rothney, *Bonapartism after Sedan* (Ithaca, NY: Cornell University Press, 1969), 96.

16 Albert Richard and Gaspard Blanc, *L'empire et la France nouvelle: appel du peuple et de la jeunesse à la conscience française* (Brussels: V. Devaux et Cie, 1872), 70, 8.

17 Joachim Kühn (ed.), *Napoleon III: Ein Selbstbildnis in ungedruckten und zerstreuten Briefen und Aufzeichnungen* (Arenenberg: Napoleon-Museum, 1993), 858–9.

18 Alfred Magne, 'Deux visites à Chislehurst en 1872', *Revue hebdomadaire*, 17 August 1912, 306–7.

19 Michael Baxter, *Coming Wonders Expected between 1867 and 1875* (Toronto: M. Sherwin, 1867), 409. He was still predicting the emperor's return in 1872: see *Twelve Future Acts of Napoleon III* (London: J. Snow & Co., 1872).

20 Filon, *Recollections*, 245.

21 Louis-Napoléon to Eugénie, 7 August 1872. 400AP/43.

22 *The Reminiscences of Lady Randolph Churchill* (London: Edward Arnold, 1908), 31.

23 Rothney, *Bonapartism*, 40.

24 Du Camp, *Souvenirs*, II, 291.

25 Alfred Mels, *Wilhelmshoehe: Souvenirs de la captivité de Napoléon III* (Paris: Paul Dupont, 1880), 214–16.

26 Filon, *Recollections*, 260.

27 Augstin Filon, *Souvenirs sur l'impératrice Eugénie* (Paris: Calman-Lévy, 1920), 275.

Epilogue

1 *The Times*, 11 January 1873; *Evening Standard*, 13 January 1873; *Daily Telegraph*, 10 January 1873; *Manchester Guardian*, 10 January 1873.

2 *Le Siècle*, 11 January 1873; *Journal des débats*, 10 January 1873; *Le Temps*, 11 January 1873; *Le Figaro*, 12 January 1873; *Le Rappel*, 12 January 1873.

3 *Le Rappel*, 17 January 1873.

4 *Le Moniteur universel*, 11 January 1873.

5 *Le Rappel*, 17 January 1873.

6 John Laband, '"He Fought Like a Lion": An Assessment of Zulu Accounts of the Death of the Prince Imperial of France during the Anglo-Zulu War of 1879', *Journal of the Society for Army Historical Research*, 76 (1998), 199.

7 Jerrold, *Life of Napoleon III*, IV, 378.

8 Alexis de Tocqueville to Gustave de Beaumont, 29 January 1851, in *Correspondance d'Alexis de Tocqueville*, II, 369.

9 Marx and Engels, *Selected Works*, I, 395, 398.

10 Senior, *Conversation*, I, 211.

11 Theodore Zeldin, *The Political System of Napoleon III* (London: Macmillan, 1958), 49–50.

12 *Journal officiel de l'Empire français*, 1 July 1870.

13 Victor Hugo, *Histoire d'un Crime*, in *Complete Works*, XVI, 151.

14 Du Camp, II, *Souvenirs*, 294.

15 Charles Seignobos, *Le Déclin de l'Empire et l'établissement de la troisième République, 1859–1875* (Paris: Hachette, 1921), 248. See also 'La Révolution de 1848. Le Second Empire, 1848–1859', in Ernest Lavisse (ed.), *Histoire de France contemporaine, depuis la Révolution jusqu'à la paix de 1919* (Paris: Hachette, 1921–2).

16 Charles Baudelaire, 'Le Joueur généreux', *Figaro: journal non politique*, 7 February 1864.

17 *Le Gaulois*, 20 August 1895.

18 George Sand, 'Dans les bois', in *Dernières pages* (Paris: Calman Lévy, 1877), 3–20.

19 'Déclaration de M. Emmanuel Macron, président de la République, à l'occasion du bicentenaire de la mort de Napoléon Ier, à Paris le 5 mai 2021'. www.vie-publique.fr/discours/279807-emmanuel-macron-05052021-napoleon-ier.

20 Seward, *Eugénie*, 277.

PICTURE CREDITS

L'Empereur Napoléon Ier sur la terrasse de Saint-Cloud by Louis Ducis: Chateaux de Versailles et de Trianon, Versailles, France – RMN-Grand Palais / Christophe Fouin / Dist. Foto SCALA, Florence

L'impératrice reçoit le Tsar Alexandre Ier à Malmaison by Victor Viger du Vigneau: Chateaux de Malmaison et Bois-Préau, Rueil-Malmaison, France – RMN-Grand Palais / Franck Raux / Dist. Foto SCALA, Florence

Louis-Napoléon Bonaparte à Boulogne (Débarquement en Août 1840): The Picture Art Collection via Alamy

Manifeste de Louis-Napoléon / Bonaparte / Aux électeurs: CC0 Paris Musées / Musée Carnavalet – Histoire de Paris

Portrait d'Elisabeth-Ann, dite Miss Harriet Howard, épouse Trelawny, comtesse de Beauregard, 1850 by Henriette Jacott Cappelaere: Musée du Chateau, Compiègne, France – RMN-Grand Palais / Dist. Foto SCALA, Florence

Portrait de Louis Napoléon Bonaparte en Prince-Président, futur empereur Napoléon III by Gustave le Gray: CC0 Paris Musées / Musée Carnavalet – Histoire de Paris

Louis-Napoléon, président de la République, élu pour 10 années par plus de 7 000 000 de voix: CC0 Paris Musées / Musée Carnavalet – Histoire de Paris

Frontispiece de l'Histoire d'un crime by Fortuné Louis Méaulle: CC0 Paris Musées / Musée Carnavalet – Histoire de Paris

Napoléon III empereur by Henri Walter: CC0 Paris Musées / Musée Carnavalet – Histoire de Paris

L'impératrice Eugénie en prière by Gustave le Gray: The Met Collection – Public Domain Open Access

Portrait de Napoléon-Joseph-Charles-Paul Bonaparte, Prince Napoléon: CC0 Paris Musées / Musée Carnavalet – Histoire de Paris

Napoleon III on the Battlefield at Sedan, 1877 by Wilhelm Camphausen: Gainew Gallery via Alamy

Les Génies de la Mort (Napoleon III) by Edmond Guillaume: CC0 Yale University Art Gallery

Scène d'intérieur de la famille impériale: CC0 Paris Musées / Musée Carnavalet – Histoire de Paris

Mort de Charles Louis Napoléon Bonaparte (1808–1873), dit Napoléon III, Empereur des Français: CC0 Paris Musées / Musée Carnavalet – Histoire de Paris

INDEX

Abbreviations: LNB refers to Louis-Napoléon Bonaparte, and Napoléon refers to Napoléon Bonaparte.

agricultural colonies (LNB's views on), 119–20, 173
Aix-les-Bains, 23
Aladenize, Jean-Baptiste-Charles, 100, 103, 104
Albert, Prince, 241, 248, 254, 260–3, 273, 329
Alexander I, Tsar, 10, 15–16
Alexander II, Tsar, 264, 274–5, 345–6
Algeria: counterproductivity of LNB's measures, 326; deporting French activists to, 215–16; French military 'pacification' campaign, 185–7; LNB's visits and visions as 'Arab kingdom', 299–301, 325–6; Zouaves (French army elite), 251, 263–4
Allsop, Thomas, 275–6
Amigues, Jules, 437–8
Ancona, 47–8
Anglo-Zulu War (1879), 447–8
Antichrist, LNB as, 439–40
Antoinette, Marie, 6, 269
Arc de Triomphe, Paris, 15, 69, 113, 429, 465
Arenenberg (Hortense de Beauharnais's chateau), 24, 27–8, 33, 41, 55, 56, 61–2, 63, 66, 67, 85, 90
Army of Châlons, 403–5, 412
Army of the Rhine, 397–8, 399, 400, 401–2, 403
assassination attempts: on LNB (and trial), 275–80; on Tsar Alexander II, 346
Assembly of Second Republic: arrest of deputies during *coup d'état*, 198–9, 201–3; bill and vote for dissolution, 163–4, 165; by-election boycotts, 194; creation of, 139; debates female suffrage, 196; deputies' stipend, 203; elections to, 139, 141–2, 145, 146–7, 167, 168; invasion of (1848), 139–41; LNB dissolves in *coup d'état*, 200; LNB prepares ruin of, 176–7; LNB's absences from, 150; LNB's appearances at, 147–9, 150–1; LNB's attempt to revise constitution, 183, 184, 185, 188–9, 190–1; 'the Mountain' in, 163–4, 165, 167–8, 172, 193, 194, 203–13; no-confidence motion vote in the ministry, 181–2; 'Party of Order' in, 154, 155, 161, 166, 167–8, 170, 176–7,

178–9, 203; passes law limiting power of president, 159; relationship with military, 180, 186, 195; resistance against *coup d'état*, 203–13; support for Changarnier in, 178; votes to keep law limiting suffrage, 194
Assembly of Third Republic, 427, 428, 437–8
Augsburg, 29, 30, 350–1
Austria: and Austro-Prussian War (1866), 331, 332, 333, 334; Duke of Reichstadt's virtual imprisonment in Vienna, 40, 60; and Italian Campaign (1859), 280–1, 283, 284–6, 287–8, 289–91, 292, 294; and Italian Revolts (1831), 45, 46, 47, 49; LNB visits Franz Joseph, 350–1; and Napoleonic Wars, 6, 13, 15, 20, 285; reasserting control of Italy, 169; recognises Second Empire, 242; and Second Schleswig War (1864), 328–9; signs Treaty of Paris (1815), 241; *see also* Joseph, Franz
Austro-Prussian War (1866), 329, 330–4

Baden, 69–72
Bakunin, Mikhail, 438
banking reforms, 221, 258
Barbès, Armand, 140
Barrot, Odilon, 161, 174–5, 182–3, 203
Baudelaire, Charles, 271–2
Baudin, Alphonse, 207–8
Baudin, Jean-Baptiste, 355
Bavaria: Augsburg, 29, 30, 350–1; and Franco-Prussian War, 394, 395, 405, 408, 429
Baxter, Michael, 439–40
Bazaine, Achille, 397–8, 399, 401–2, 403, 423
Bazeilles, 405–6, 407–8, 412
Beauharnais, Eugène de, 9, 13, 24, 32
Beauharnais, Hortense de:
    CHARACTER: calmness and strength in crisis, 14, 43, 47; expertise in misinformation, 28, 48; liveliness, 3; opportunism, 86
    LIFE: in Aix-les-Bains, 23; assists political fugitive, 43; births of children, 4; childhood, 9; composes 'Partant pour la Syrie', 247; death, 85, 86–7; death of first child, 4; death of second son, 47; escapes Italy with LNB, 47–9; flees France, 22–3; flees Paris, 14–15; in France and London with LNB, 50–3, 54; gives Joséphine's wedding ring to

LNB, 72; illegitimate child (with comte de Flahaut), 179; illness, 83, 86; loses custody of Napoléon-Louis, 17, 23; marries comte de Saint-Leu, 3–4, 9; plans to 'rescue' sons in Italy, 45–6; returns to Switzerland, 55; salons and entourage, 27–8, 33, 34, 35, 40–1; sends children into hiding, 17–18, 21, 22; settles in Switzerland, 24; travels to Rome with LNB, 41–2
  RELATIONSHIPS: comte de Flahaut (lover), 179; comte de Saint-Leu (husband), 3, 17, 25; Edward Henry Fox, 34; LNB (son), 4, 5, 11–13, 23–4, 26, 30, 34, 35, 72, 79, 83, 86–7, 421; Napoléon, 9, 11, 18–19, 21, 24; Napoléon-Louis (son), 11–13; Tsar Alexander I, 16
Beauharnais, Joséphine de (Empress Joséphine), 4–5, 8–9, 11, 15–16, 72; children see Beauharnais, Eugène de; Beauharnais, Hortense de
Beauregard, comtesse de see Howard, Harriet
bee, as Napoleonic emblem, 219, 224, 253, 388
Bellanger, Marguerite, 317–19
Beneditti, Count Vincent, 377–8, 382–4
Benso, Camillo see Cavour, Count of
Berryer, Pierre-Antoine, 108, 110–11
Bertie, Prince of Wales, 262, 346
Biarritz, 268, 321, 329–30
Bismarck, Otto von: and Austro-Prussian War, 329–31, 333; 'blood and iron' vision for German unification, 328–9, 375; and Franco-Prussian War/peace terms, 381–2, 383–4, 391, 400–1, 413–14, 423–4, 425, 427; mimics LNB's policies, 462; and plots for imperial restoration, 438, 441; proclaims the German Empire, 426
bladder stones, 313–14, 359–60, 380, 431, 441–2, 443
Blanc, Louis, 120, 136
Blanquist Insurrection (1839), 96
Blessington, Earl of, 35
Blessington, Lady, 34–5, 93
'Bloody Week' (1871), 434–5
Bognor, 440
Bologna, 44, 46
Bonaparte, Carlo, 5, 8
Bonaparte, Caroline, 8
Bonaparte, Charlotte, 41
Bonaparte, Elisa, 8
Bonaparte, Jérôme: attends Napoléon's funeral, 130; breaks off daughter's engagement to LNB, 82; celebrates LNB's reconciliation with Joseph, 97; character, 237, 261; children, 31, 65, 68 see also Bonaparte, Napoléon-Jérôme ('Plon-Plon'); death, 298–9; defends

Plon-Plon's return from Crimean War, 252; as governor of the Invalides, 162, 166; jostles with siblings, 8; as president of the Senate, 237; rides out in Paris during LNB's coup d'état, 200–1; in Rome, 31; wife see Bonaparte, Mathilde
Bonaparte, Joseph: anger with LNB over political activity, 81, 84–5, 96–7; approves LNB's marriage to Mathilde, 67; children, 10, 41; death, 127; exile in United States, 31, 69; ill health, 97; jostles with siblings, 8; as King of Spain, 10, 229; LNB pins hopes on (but is disappointed), 56, 60–1; reconciliation with LNB, 97–8
Bonaparte, Joséphine see Beauharnais, Joséphine de (Empress Josephine)
Bonaparte, Letizia (Madame Mère), 31
Bonaparte, Louis see Saint-Leu, comte de
Bonaparte, Louis-Napoléon:
  AFTER DEATH: as forgotten, 463, 464; French and British reaction to death, 445–6; funeral, 446–7; historical reputation, 451, 460, 464; lack of public monuments to, 464–5; memorabilia, 446; resting place in Farnborough, 465, 466
  APPEARANCE: ageing, 343, 374; attire, 90–1, 92, 93, 108, 127–8, 153, 165, 201, 213; in caricatures, 152–3; disguises, 48–9, 122–4, 137; eyes, 343, 374, 425; facial hair, 55, 82, 123, 137, 146, 147, 155, 232, 271, 343, 425, 431; hands, 42; mixed opinions of attractiveness, 36, 42, 54, 82, 94, 146, 232; nose, 425; stature and figure, ix–x, 36, 42, 71–2, 123, 146, 147, 188, 232, 255, 431; unfavourable with a cold, 70
  CHARACTERISTICS: accent, 104, 147, 148, 152, 188, 257; amiability, 32, 263, 422; calmness, 54, 92, 108–9, 147, 173, 263, 289, 346; charm, 5, 64, 232, 255; courage, 458; empathy, 5, 25; as father, 301–2, 432; impassivity, 147, 239, 289–90; kindness, 5, 12, 25, 232, 422, 425, 431, 461, 463; laughing at own jokes, 268; loyalty, 162, 236–7, 238, 248, 461; 'madness', 168; melancholic tendencies, 42, 61, 79, 116, 263, 440; pragmatism, 463; public-speaking confidence, 188; public-speaking nerves, 104, 109, 138, 148; romanticism, 29, 33–4, 64, 66, 450; sangfroid, 164; self-belief, 67, 78, 81, 82, 85, 92, 94, 113–14, 117–18, 126, 131, 168–9, 437, 442–3, 449, 450; shyness, 23, 24, 425; smoking, 163, 262, 285, 313, 314, 396, 406, 422, 431; storytelling abilities, 449; sweet nature, 24, 425; taciturnity, 23, 24, 92, 93, 149, 268,

291, 431; voice, 255; weakness for women, 54, 63–4, 82, 93, 128, 130, 152, 163, 269, 271, 315, 425

CHILDREN: illegitimate (with Éléonore Vergeot), 117, 127; Napoléon Eugène *see* Bonaparte, Napoléon Eugène

HEALTH: bladder stones, 431, 441, 442, 443–4; improved health during imprisonment, 422; measles, 48; physical decline, 313–14, 317, 334, 356, 357, 359–60, 374, 380, 389, 395, 406; weariness, 357, 364, 389

IDEOLOGIES AND VISIONS: Bonapartism, 40, 52–4, 56–7, 58–61, 62–3, 66, 67, 84–5, 86, 94–6, 107, 109, 119, 121, 131, 364, 449–50; expressed in *Rêveries politiques*, 57–8, 59; Italian nationalism, 41, 42, 43; patriotism, 39; revisionism, 330; socialism, 119–21, 146, 155, 173, 312; views on agricultural colonies, 119–20, 173; views on second Empire, 59; views on suffrage, 57, 58, 95, 96, 120, 154, 176, 218, 452; vision for reforms and programmes, 221, 240, 258, 259–60, 265, 274, 310, 311–12, 339–43, 359, 367, 452–3

INTERESTS: ancient history, 32; artillery, 63, 69, 115, 132, 291; fencing, 91; gambling, 93, 126; horse racing, 93, 126; horse riding, 24, 36, 97, 163, 188, 200–1; hunting, 127–8, 315, 369; ice skating, 66; swimming, 24, 34; technology and steam engines, 61, 115, 274, 431; woodwork, 431

LIFE: EARLY YEARS: birth, 4; education, 5, 25–7, 28–9, 30–1, 32–3, 350–1; infancy and childhood, 4–5, 10, 11–13, 14–16, 17–18, 19, 22–4; obsession with Napoléon, 24, 28; older childhood and youth, 24–8, 29–31, 32–4, 35–6

LIFE: BEFORE GAINING POWER: Assembly appearances/absences, 147–9, 150–1; Assembly elections, 141–4, 146–7; banishment from France, 40, 59, 142; Boulogne Conspiracy and trial, 99–110, 111; challenged to duel, 97; death of brother, 47, 49, 55, 56; death of Duke of Reichstadt, 60; death of father and inheritance, 126–7; death of mother, 83, 84, 85–7; evades Austrian troops in Italy, 46–9; exile in Britain, 90–4, 97–8, 152, 153; exile in United States, 78–9, 81–3; expulsion from Rome, 43; expulsion from Switzerland, 89–90; in France and London with Hortense, 49–54; growing support for, 142, 143, 144, 149–50, 153–4, 156–8; involvement with Bonapartist conspiracist in London, 53–4; involvement with Carbonari

and Revolts of 1831 (Italy), 41, 42–3, 44–5, 56; in London after prison escape, 125–7, 128–9, 131–2, 138–9, 143, 144, 146, 153; London residences, 92, 96, 128–9, 131; in Paris after February Revolution, 137–8; presidential candidacy and campaign, 149–57; presidential election victory, 157–60, 450; prison sentence and escape, 111, 113–25; returns to Switzerland with Hortense, 55; Strasbourg insurrection, 67–77; in Swiss militia, 36, 39; tours industrial English cities, 61

LIFE: IN POWER (*see also under coup d'état* of LNB (1851); Second Empire (1852–70); Second Republic (1848–52); *under specific conflicts*): attempts to buy Grand Duchy of Luxembourg, 337–8; becomes emperor, 227; birth and baptism of Napoléon Eugène, 266–8; confiscates property of Louis-Philippe, 220; considers marriage options, 228–9; continued association with the 'footman class', 162; death of half-brother, 328; decision for neutrality in Second Schleswig War and Austro-Prussian War, 329–32, 333–5; decision not to intervene in Poland, 323–4, 325; distances himself from own government, 173–5; drives trade treaties with Europe, 305; engagement and marriage to Eugénie, 233–5; hosts Victoria and Albert's state visit, 260–3; Isle of Wight holiday, 273; lessens personal powers, 309–10, 365–7; lifestyle, 162–3, 196, 231–2, 238–9, 268, 374–5; pardons political crimes, 296, 364, 461; popular support, 160–1, 164, 165–6, 188, 189, 221–2, 224–5, 226–7, 358, 372–3; as populist leader, 461, 463; powers as emperor, 239–40; receives Order of the Garter, 255–6; recreates portrait of Napoléon on horseback, 220; relationship with Party of Order, 161–2, 166, 168, 175, 176–7; restores universal male suffrage, 200; role in Suez Canal construction, 360–1; speeches, 184, 234, 342, 347–8, 357, 364; state visit to London, 253–7; tours Nice and Savoy, 299; visits Algeria, 299–301, 325–6; visits Austria, 350–1

LIFE: AFTER LOSING POWER: Camden Place life, 430, 431–2, 439; death, 444; exile to Britain and reunion with Eugénie and Napoléon Eugène, 429–30; growing support and plots for return to power, 436–9, 440–1; hopes to reinstate Empire, 425, 426–9; imprisonment at Wilhelmshöhe Palace, 421–3, 424, 426–8; press conferences and interviews, 433, 436, 442–3; seaside holidays, 432–3, 440

RELATIONSHIPS: Charles de Morny (half-brother), 179, 328; comte de Saint-Leu (father), 25, 32, 36, 44–5, 56, 64, 66, 67, 87, 88–9, 108, 122, 125, 126; Countess of Castiglione, 269–71; Éléonore Vergeot (mistress and mother of his children), 117, 128, 302; Eugénie (wife) *see under* Eugénie, Empress; Harriet Howard (mistress), 130, 132, 146, 162–3, 228, 235–6, 269; Hortense Cornu (friend), 33, 115–16, 117, 120, 316–17; Hortense (mother), 4, 5, 11–13, 23–4, 26, 30, 34, 35, 72, 79, 83, 86–7, 421; James Harris, 3rd Earl of Malmesbury (friend), 35–6, 430; Joseph (uncle), 60–1, 81, 84–5, 96–8; Joséphine (grandmother), 4–5; Louisa de Mercy-Argenteau (mistress), 425–7; Marguerite Bellanger (mistress), 317–19; Mathilde (cousin and fiancée), 65–7, 69, 79, 82, 389–90; Miss Godfrey of Tunbridge Wells (romantic attachment), 55; Napoléon-Louis (brother), 23, 25, 42, 47, 55; Napoléon (uncle), 10, 11, 19, 99; Nicolas Changarnier (political opponent), 178–9, 180; Philippe Le Bas (tutor), 28–9, 30; Plon-Plon (cousin), 127–8, 130, 166, 167, 237, 252, 323–4, 327–8; Queen of Portugal (rumoured attachment), 65; Queen Victoria, 255–6, 257–8, 260, 261–3, 273, 430–1; Rachel Félix (mistress), 128, 130; Tsar Alexander I, 16; Tsar Alexander II, 274–5; Tsar Nicholas I, 242, 246; Victor vicomte de Persigny (friend), 68, 92, 97, 232–3, 273, 356–7, 438; other liaisons, 64, 130, 269, 271, 281, 315, 334

WIFE *see* Eugénie, Empress

WRITINGS: collected writings in single volume, 120, 121; *Considérations politiques et militaires sur la Suisse*, 63; *Des idées Napoléoniennes*, 94–6; edits pamphlet on Strasbourg insurrection, 87; *The Extinction of Pauperism*, 119–20, 154, 157; *Historical Fragments*, 119; history of artillery, 115, 132; history of Charlemagne (abandoned), 115; manual on artillery, 63, 69; newspaper articles, 118–19; pamphlet on sugar import tariffs, 119; pamphlets justifying conduct over Franco-Prussian War, 422, 431; plot to unwritten novel, 452; presidential manifesto, 155–6; published letter about political reforms, 340; published letter about prison escape, 126; published letter to Eugène Rouher, 341; published letter to

European sovereigns, 325; published letter to Pope Pius IX, 174; published letter to president of United States, 83–4; *Rêveries politiques*, 57–8, 59, 95; two volumes on the life of Julius Caesar, 315–16, 317, 341

Bonaparte, Lucien, 8, 31

Bonaparte, Mathilde, 65–7, 69, 79, 82, 162, 165, 271, 389–90

Bonaparte, Napoléon: *The Memorial of Saint Helena*, 30, 32, 66

AFTER DEATH: anniversary of death, 51, 52; birthday as public holiday, 220, 296, 360; body is returned to France, 99, 107, 112–13; Column of the Grande Armée, 102, 105, 106; diorama of tomb, 51; enduring interest in, 465; journals by 'ghost' of Napoléon, 143; London theatre shows about, 53; memorabilia, 52, 69, 92, 108, 126, 128, 131, 465; Queen Victoria visits tomb, 262; statues, 50, 69, 143, 213, 327, 416, 434; two-hundredth anniversary of death, 465; voters dress up as, 157

CHARACTER: charisma, 7; leadership, 6–7; personal mythology, 7–8, 17, 21, 23, 30, 220, 230, 449; running away from defeat, 8, 13, 20

CHILDREN: illegitimate sons, 97, 271; son *see* Reichstadt, Duke of

LIFE: admits defeat and renounces throne, 15; birth, 5; commander of Army of Italy, 7; death, 29–30, 99, 110; defeat at Waterloo, 20; as emperor, 9–10, 11; exile on Elba, 15; exile on Saint Helena, 21, 99; as First Consul, 8; military offensives, 4, 6–8, 10–11, 13, 15, 20; name change, 7; officer-training school, 5–6; returns to France, 17; returns to power, 17–18, 19–20, 68

RELATIONSHIPS: comte de Saint-Leu (brother), 3, 4, 8, 9–10, 14; Eugène (stepson), 9; Hortense (stepdaughter), 9, 11, 18–19, 21, 24; Napoléon-Louis and LNB (nephews), 10, 11, 19, 99; other siblings, 8

WIVES *see* Beauharnais, Joséphine de (Empress Joséphine); Marie Louise, Empress

Bonaparte, Napoléon Eugène: in Anglo-Zulu War, 447–8; baptism, 267–8; birth, 266–7; at Camden Place, 431, 432; childhood, 316, 436; death, 448; death and funeral of LNB, 444, 447; early childhood, 293, 295, 296, 299, 301–2; education, 432; and Franco-Prussian War, 390, 393, 398, 404; reunions with Eugénie and LNB in England, 420, 430; at Royal Military Academy, 441; Torquay holiday with LNB, 432

Bonaparte, Napoléon II *see* Reichstadt, Duke of

Bonaparte, Napoléon-Jérôme ('Plon-Plon'): absents himself from politics, 324; after LNB's death, 449; as ambassador to Spain, 166; appearance, 319; as 'Craint-Plomb', 252; and Crimean War, 248, 252; criticises/undermines LNB, 166, 232, 237; death of father, 298–9; defends LNB in Assembly, 150; and Franco-Prussian War, 397, 398, 399, 400, 402; is unsatisfied by Ollivier's dinner parties, 366; liberal Bonapartism, 327–8; LNB continues to support, 237; at LNB's funeral, 447; marries Princess Maria Clotilde of Savoy, 281, 282–3; meets President Lincoln, 319–20; mutual hatred with Eugénie, 326–7, 389, 423, 424; orgies, 282; others' poor opinions of, 166, 248, 260, 261; plots for imperial restoration, 440–1; relationship with LNB, 127–8, 130, 166, 167, 237, 252, 323–4, 327–8; relationship with Rachel Félix, 130, 175, 281; unfaithfulness to wife, 283; urges LNB to intervene in Poland, 323–4; wins election in Corsica, 436; wishes to resurrect Empire, 423–4

Bonaparte, Napoléon-Louis: birth, 4; character, 41; childhood, 10, 11–13, 14–15, 16, 17–18, 19, 22–3; contracts measles, 46–7; death, 47, 55; evades Austrian troops in Italy, 46–7; father obtains custody of, 17, 23; interment of body in France, 130; involvement with Carbonari and Uprisings of 1831 (Italy), 41, 43, 44–5; marries Charlotte, 41; political views, 41, 42 RELATIONSHIPS: Charlotte (wife), 41; comte de Saint-Leu (father), 44–5; Hortense (mother), 11–13; LNB (brother), 23, 25, 42, 47, 55; Napoléon (uncle), 10, 11, 19, 99

Bonaparte, Pauline, 8, 31

Bonaparte, Pierre, 82–3, 150, 368–9

Bonaparte, Plon-Plon see Bonaparte, Napoléon-Jérôme ('Plon-Plon')

Bonapartism: after LNB's death, 449; Bonapartist and Democratic Banquet, Paris, 160–1; Boulogne Conspiracy (1840), 99–111; and build-up to Franco-Prussian War, 379–80, 382; at comte de Saint-Leu's funeral, 130–1; demonstrations on anniversary of death of Napoléon, 51, 52; and Denis-Charles Parquin, 101; and European Union, 95; growing popular support, 142, 147, 153, 154, 157–8; and Hortense, 22, 24, 62, 86; journals and Napoléon's 'ghost', 143; and LNB, 40, 52–4, 56–7, 58–61, 62–3, 66, 67, 84–5, 86, 94–6, 107, 109, 119, 121, 131, 364, 449–50; LNB on factions of, 449; in London after death of LNB, 446; in London during LNB's state visit, 253–4; memorabilia of LNB, 143, 446; memorabilia of Napoléon, 52, 69, 92, 108,

126, 128, 131, 465; and the military, 22, 23, 28, 41, 70–1, 186, 189, 195, 210–11; and mythology/propaganda around Napoléon, 9, 21, 22, 23, 69; and Plon-Plon, 327–8; republicans swayed towards, 121; Société du Dix-Décembre, 175–6; Strasbourg insurrection (1836) see Strasbourg insurrection; during Third Republic, 437–9, 440–1; and Victor Hugo, 149–50, 190–1, 195; and Victor vicomte de Persigny, 67–8, 83, 110, 143, 156–7, 167, 438

Bordeaux, 225, 358

Boulogne: Column of the Grande Armée, 102, 105, 106; LNB and Hortense travel through, 55

Boulogne Conspiracy (1840), 99–111

Bourbon family: and Legitimists, 58; see also Charles X, King of France; Louis XVI, King of France; Louis XVIII, King of France

Britain: Anglo-Zulu War (1879), 447–8; commercial treaty with France, 305, 311; Conspiracy to Murder Bill (defeated), 278; and Crimean War, 245–8, 249–50, 251, 253, 263–4; Eglinton Castle, Scotland, 90–1; Eugénie flees to, 418–21; Eugénie's solo tour to, 301, 302; and First World War, 466; LNB is exiled to, 90; LNB visits industrial heartland, 61; LNB visits Isle of Wight, 273; LNB's state visit, 253–8; and Napoleonic Wars, 6, 7, 13, 20; recognises Second Empire, 242; and Second Opium War, 303, 304–5; signs Treaty of Paris (1815), 241; suffrage, 57, 138, 462; see also Albert, Prince; Bognor; Camden Place, Kent; Farnborough; Isle of Wight; London; Victoria, Queen

Browning, Elizabeth, 288, 294

Byron, Lord, 35

Cabet, Étienne, 96

Café Anglais, Paris, 318, 345–6

Camden Place, Kent, 420–1, 430, 431, 436, 437, 439, 440–1, 443–4

canal construction, Second Empire, 225, 311, 387; see also Suez Canal

Carbonari (terrorist organisation), 41, 43

Carl, Crown Prince of Württemberg, 275

Castiglione, Countess of, 269–71

Catholic Church: dispute with Greek Orthodox Church in Palestine, 243–4; and educational reform, 341–2; in Italy, 297, 298, 351; in Mexico, 320; and obscenity trials, 271–2; in Poland, 323; Pope Pius IX, 169–70, 174, 267, 298, 336, 341; and Second Empire, 219–20, 244, 246, 271–2

Cavaignac, Louis-Eugène, 151–2, 153, 157

Cavour, Count of, 270, 280–1, 294

Châlons-sur-Marne, military camp, 274, 392–3, 398, 399

Champs-Élysées, Paris, 15, 113, 164, 201, 370, 371, 429, 437

Changarnier, Nicolas: in Algeria, 186; arrested during *coup d'état*, 198; as 'general Bergamot', 178; as head of armed forces and deputy in Assembly, 164, 178; LNB sacks, 181–2; LNB wishes to sack, 179, 180; low opinion of LNB, 164, 178, 179, 182; at the Opéra-Comique, 196; opposes revision of constitution, 191; republicans' views of, 195

Charge of the Light Brigade, 253

Charles X, King of France, 37–8, 58

Charlotte, Empress of Mexico, 335, 336–7

Chartist demonstration, London (1848), 138–9

chassepot rifle, 351–2, 392, 399

Chevalier, Michel, 310–11

China: Second Opium War (1856–60), 302–5

Christianity *see* Catholic Church; Greek Orthodox Church

Churchill, Lady Randolph, 440

Civiale, Jean, 441–2

Clarendon, 4th Earl of, 233–4, 261, 282, 297

Closeburn y Grivegnée, María Manuela de, 229, 230, 231, 233–4

Cobden–Chevalier Treaty (1860), 311

Col-Puygellier, Pierre, 103–5

Colonna-Welewski, Alexandre, 271

Column of the Grande Armée, nr Boulogne, 102, 105, 106

commercial treaties, French–European, 305, 311

Compiègne, chateau of, 232, 270, 271, 282, 314–15, 365

Conciergerie (prison), Paris, 107, 261

Congress of Vienna (1815), 246, 265, 330, 331

Conneau, Henri, 100, 114, 123, 124–5, 314, 444

conscription to French military, 342–3

Conspiracy to Murder Bill (defeated), England, 278

Constance, 24, 64, 66; *see also* Arenenberg (Hortense de Beauharnais' chateau)

Cornu, Hortense, 33, 115–16, 117, 120, 177, 316–17, 451

Corps législatif of Second Empire: creation, size and initial powers, 218; debates going to war with Prussia, 386–8; elections to, 221, 272, 324–5, 338, 356, 357–9, 363–4; electoral corruption and fraud, 324, 325; emergency session announcing liberal reforms, 359; emergency session announcing martial law, 396; increased powers, 309–10; opposition voices in, 292, 323, 326, 338–9, 350, 352, 359, 382, 396

Corsica, 299, 327, 368, 436

Council of State of Second Empire (creation and powers), 218

coup d'état of LNB (1851): arrest of Assembly deputies, 198–9, 201–3; casualties, 207–8, 209, 212, 213, 215; LNB appeals to people, 200; LNB courts foreign opinion immediately after, 213; LNB courts society and public opinion before, 165–6, 174, 187–90, 195–6; LNB initially rejects idea of, 160, 164; LNB prepares ground for, 175–7; LNB's decisions and movements during, 199–201, 208–9; LNB's presidential tour following, 223–6; military occupation of Paris, 198–9, 200; planning, 187, 192–3, 196–7; plebiscite supporting, 213–14, 216–17; popular endorsement by plebiscite, 213–14, 216–17; rumours of, 175, 176; success of, 213; suppression of republican resistance, 203–13, 215–16

Cowley, Lord, 213

Crédit Foncier de France (mortgage bank), 221

Crédit Mobilier (bank), 258

cricket, 432

Crimean War (1853–6), 244–53, 263–4; LNB's decisions and actions during, 246, 247, 248, 250, 253, 257, 261, 264

crinoline dresses, 267, 268–9

Crow, James (captain of *Edinburgh Castle*), 100, 102, 107

Daguerre, Louis, 51

David, Jacques-Louis: *Napoléon Crossing the Alps* (painting), 220

Delacroix, Eugène: *Liberty Leading the People* (painting), 39

démoc-socs (left-leaning alliance), 168, 193–4

Denmark: and Second Schleswig War (1864), 329

Dijon, 187–8, 190

Directory (government), 7, 8

Disraeli, Benjamin, 92, 93, 328–9, 360

dogs, of LNB: Fido, 43; Ham, 115, 124, 146; Nero, 353

Douay, Abel, 394

Ducrot, Auguste-Alexandre, 405, 406, 407, 409, 410, 412

duels: LNB, 97; Pierre Bonaparte, 368–9

Dumas, Alexandre *fils*, 231

Dumas, Alexandre *père*, 62

Dunant, Henry, 291

Duruy, Victor, 341–2

eagles: distributed by LNB to troops, 220; in Dover (upside-down wings), 254; live bird purchased by Boulogne conspirators, 101,

106; on LNB's clasp, 92; in London, 253; in Notre-Dame, 235; in Paris during Victoria and Albert's state visit, 260; on standard and flags, 20, 68, 73, 74, 75, 130, 290; on streets during LNB's tour of France, 224; torn down during fall of Second Empire, 418; *see also* Flight of the Eagle
economic programmes, Second Empire, 221, 240, 258, 311, 312–13, 452
Edinburgh Castle (steamer used by Boulogne conspirators), 100–1, 102, 105–6
educational reform, Second Empire, 341
Égalité, Philippe, 38
Eglinton Castle, Scotland, 90–1
Egypt, 7–8, 132
electoral corruption and fraud, Second Empire, 324, 325
Élysée Palace, Paris, 162, 165, 196
Espinasse, Charles-Marie-Esprit, 198, 199
Eugénie, Empress (born Eugenia de Palafox y Kirkpatrick):
  CHARACTERISTICS: appearance, 231, 236, 254, 255, 299; attire, 268–9, 362, 374; boldness, 231, 268; Catholicism, 321, 351; enjoys parlour games, 268, 314; practical joker, 268, 330; reactionary tendencies, 326, 380
  LIFE: after LNB's death, 465–6; assassination attempt on LNB, 277, 279; attends Exposition universelle, 345; attends opening of Suez Canal, 361–3; birth and baptism of Napoléon Eugène, 266, 267; Camden Place life, 431, 432, 436, 443; childhood, 229–31; court lifestyle, 238; creates museum at Fontainebleau, 303–4; death and funeral, 466; death of LNB, 444; death of sister, 300–1; early meetings with LNB, 229, 231–2; engagement and marriage to LNB, 233–5; as fashion icon, 268–9, 299; flees to England after fall of Second Empire, 418–21; LNB falls in love with, 232–3; LNB returns from Italian Campaign, 295–6; LNB's unfaithfulness, 269, 270–1; marital relations with LNB, 266, 269, 301, 318, 325, 334, 361, 390, 416, 421, 425, 430, 432; misogyny towards, 269, 435; political involvement and influence, 331, 334, 356–7, 367, 382, 389, 396, 400, 402, 403; public auction of personal possessions from Tuileries, 435–6; publication of personal correspondence, 435; as regent during LNB's absences, 286, 292, 293, 326–7, 396; reunion with LNB in England, 430; solo tour of Scotland and England, 301, 302; state visit to London, 254–5, 256; tour of Nice and Savoy, 299; visits Algeria, 299–301; wealth, 421, 432
European Union, (LNB's views on), 95
Evans, Thomas, 418–20
Executive Commission of Second Republic, 139, 142, 143–4; June Days uprising against, 144–5, 153
Expedition of the Thousand, 298
Exposition universelle, Paris: of 1855, 258, 259–60, 265; of 1867, 343–5, 347–8

Farnborough, 465–6
fascism (1930s), 460
Favre, Jules, 142, 279, 323, 326, 350, 358, 363, 372, 396, 416
February Revolution (1848), 135–6
Félix, Rachel, 128, 130, 175, 281
Ferry, Jules, 355–6
Fialin, Jean Gilbert Victor *see* Persigny, Victor vicomte de
Fido (LNB's dog), 43
Fifth Republic (1958–), 464
financial scandal, and Second Empire, 312–13, 356
First World War, 460, 466
Flahaut, comte de, 179, 200–1
Flaubert, Gustave, 232, 271, 315
Fleury, Émile Félix: accompanies LNB to Isle of Wight, 273; advises LNB to marry, 232; as ambassador to Russia, 377; conversion to Bonapartism, 186; doesn't want LNB to go to Crimea, 256; on Harriet Howard, 228; involvement in *coup d'état*, 192, 208; is wary of republicans' support of Italian Campaign, 292–3; and Italian Campaign, 286, 290, 294; as LNB's military fixer, 181, 186, 187; plots for imperial restoration, 441; as *premier écuyer*, 238
Flight of the Eagle, 17, 68
Florence, 42, 43–4
Fontainebleau: palace of, 231, 303–4, 314; Treaty of, 15
food, Parisian, 345–6; *see also* Café Anglais, Paris
Forlì, 46–7
Fortress of Ham (LNB's imprisonment and escape), 114–15, 116, 122–5
Fox, Edward Henry, 34
France: Boulogne Conspiracy (1840), 99–111; Directory (government), 7, 8; February Revolution (1848), 135–6; Fifth Republic (1958–), 464; French Revolution (1789–99), 6–7, 8, 11, 26, 38; Hundred Days (1815), 17–21, 22; July Monarchy (1830–48) *see* July Monarchy; July Revolution (1830), 37–9, 43, 57, 119; June Days uprising (1848), 144–5,

153; main political movements (overview), 58; Napoleonic Wars, 4, 6–7, 10–11, 13–15, 20, 26; nearly goes to war with Switzerland over LNB's expulsion, 89–90; plebiscites (nationwide votes) *see* plebiscites; Second Empire (1852–70) *see* Second Empire; Second Republic (1848–52) *see* Second Republic; Strasbourg insurrection (1836) *see* Strasbourg insurrection; suffrage, 57, 58, 95, 120, 135, 137, 154, 158, 176, 194, 196, 200, 218, 452; Third Republic (1870–1940) *see* Third Republic; *see also* Bazeilles; Biarritz; Bordeaux; Boulogne; Châlons-sur-Marne; Dijon; Franco-Prussian War; Ham; Lyon; Metz; Paris; Sedan

Franco-Prussian War (1870–1): armistice and peace terms, 425, 426, 427, 428, 429; Bazaine surrenders at Metz, 423, 424; build-up, 375–86, 456–8; events before LNB surrenders, ix, x–xi, 390–410, 458; LNB attempts to avoid conflict, 376, 379–80, 386; LNB surrenders at Sedan, 410–15, 458; LNB's decisions and actions during, 390–2, 393, 395, 396–7, 398–400, 402–4, 406, 407, 410–11, 412–15, 456–8

Frederick William III, King of Prussia, 15

French Revolution (1789–99), 6–7, 8, 11, 26, 38; *see also* February Revolution (1848); July Revolution (Second French Revolution) (1830)

Gambetta, Léon, 355, 372, 417

gambling dens, London, 92

Garibaldi, Giuseppe, 169, 171, 293, 298, 349, 351

gas lighting, Second Empire, 258, 259

Gaulle, Charles de, 463–4

German Confederation, 329

Germany: Austro-Prussian War (1866), 329, 330–4; counter-revolution, 169; fascism, 460; Franco-Prussian War (1870–1) *see* Franco-Prussian War; French occupation, 428; Schleswig-Holstein territory, 329; Second Schleswig War (1864), 328–9; unification (German Empire), 426, 462; *see also* Baden; Bavaria; Prussia; Westphalia; Wilhelmshöhe Palace; Württemberg

Godfrey, Miss, of Tunbridge Wells, 55

Gordon, Eleonore, 71–2, 77, 79–80, 81, 100, 229

Government of National Defence of Third Republic, 419, 425

Gramont, Agénor de, 375–7, 379, 381, 382, 385

Gravier, Marie-Thérèse, 367

Great Exhibition, London, 257, 259–60

Greater Poland Uprising (1848), 139–40, 325

Greek Orthodox Church: dispute with Catholic Church in Palestine, 243–4

Guiccioli, Teresa, 35

Guizot, François, 135, 380–1

Guzman Palafox y Portocarrero, Don Cipriano de, 229–30, 231

Les Halles, Paris, 312

Ham (LNB's dog), 115, 124, 146

Ham, Fortress of (LNB's imprisonment and escape), 114–15, 116, 122–5

Hamilton, Duke of, 213

Haussmann, Georges-Eugène, 259, 311–12, 313, 335, 347, 355–6, 365–6

Heine, Heinrich, 69

Hindenburg, Paul von, 401–2

hippopotamus, in the Seine, 380

Holland: comte de Saint-Leu as King of, 4; Napoléon annexes, 10

Hôtel de Ville, Paris, 26, 38, 136, 140, 142, 147, 417–18

Howard, Harriet, 129–30, 132, 146, 162–3, 228, 235–6, 269

Hugo, Charles, 378–9

Hugo, Victor: appeals for Maxmilian's pardon, 349; and Bonapartism, 149–50, 190–1, 195; on Charles de Morny, 179; elected to Assembly of Second Republic, 145; on elections to Corps législatif, 221; Flaubert defends at Compiègne, 315; on Franco-Prussian War and peace treaty, 428, 458–9; on June Days uprising, 144–5; on LNB's court lifestyle, 238–9; on LNB's presidential election victory, 160; on LNB's stature and character, x, 450–1; *Les Misérables*, 63; *Notre-Dame de Paris*, 52; pamphlet criticising LNB's state visit to England, 256; on plebiscite endorsing *coup d'état*, 217; promiscuity, 428; refuses pardon, 296; rejects LNB's liberal reforms, 372; in resistance movement against *coup d'état*, 203–6, 208, 209–10, 212–13; speech against constitutional revision, 190–1; supports *La Lanterne* magazine, 354; writes introduction to official guide to Paris, 344

Hundred Days (1815), 17–21, 22

industrial action, 354, 358, 367

industrialisation and infrastructure programmes, Second Empire: canal construction, 225, 311, 387; and France's importance as world power, 305; gas lighting, 258, 259; iron and steel production, 311; manufacturing expansion, 265; rail expansion, 221, 225, 240, 258, 259, 265, 274, 311, 465; road building, 311; sewage improvements, 259, 311, 419; telegraphy, 221, 267, 291, 311

Invalides, Paris, 112, 113, 166, 262, 465

iron and steel production, Second Empire, 311
Isle of Wight, 273, 420, 440
Italian Campaign (1859): build-up, 275, 280–3;
 end and peace terms, 294–5, 297; events,
 284–92, 293–4; French people's opinions of,
 292–6; immediate aftermath and outcomes,
 296–8; LNB's decisions and actions during
 (and immediate aftermath), 283, 284–6,
 287–92, 293–4, 295, 297–8, 454–5
Italy: Battle of Mentana (1867), 351–2; French
 Roman Expedition (1849) see Roman
 Expedition; partial annexation by France
 (1860), 297–8, 302; partial annexation by
 Piedmont (1860), 297; Revolts of 1831, 44–5,
 56; Second War of Independence (1859) see
 Italian Campaign; unification, 298, 319; see
 also Ancona; Bologna; Florence; Forlì; Milan;
 Nice; Piedmont; Rome

Jacquerie (1385), 183; later allusions to, 183,
 190, 215
Joseph, Franz, 283, 288, 294, 333, 350, 351, 363
Joséphine, Empress, 4–5, 8–9, 11, 15–16,
 72; children see Beauharnais, Eugène de;
 Beauharnais, Hortense de
Juárez, Benito, 320, 349
July Monarchy (1830–48): Blanquist Insurrection
 (1839), 96; Boulogne Conspiracy against
 (1840), 99–111; end of, 136; LNB's views on,
 57–8, 59, 60; Paris Uprising against (1832),
 62–3; Strasburg insurrection (1836) see
 Strasbourg insurrection; widespread discontent
 with, 51, 58, 62–3, 68, 69; see also Louis-
 Philippe, King of France
July Revolution (Second French Revolution)
 (1830), 37–9, 43, 57, 119
June Days uprising (1848), 144–5, 153

Karl Philipp, Prince of Schwarzenberg, 15

Lafayette, marquis de, 38
Laity, Armand, 87–8, 162
Lamartine, Alphonse de, 136, 139–40
La Lantern (satirical magazine), 353–4
Le Bas, Philippe, 26–7, 28–9, 30–1, 32–3, 54
Le Boeuf, Edmond, 384–5
Leboeuf, Justine Marie see Bellanger, Marguerite
Ledru-Rollin, Alexandre Auguste, 172–3
legitimists (France), 58, 108
Leopold, Prince of Prussia, 375–8, 380–1,
 382–3, 414–15
'Liberté, Égalité, Fraternité' (revolutionary
 legend), 219
Lincoln, Abraham, 319–20
London: Chartist demonstration, 138–9; Great

Exhibition, 257, 259–60; LNB and Hortense's
 brief sojourn in, 52–4; LNB lives in after
 prison escape, 125–7, 128–9, 131–2; LNB
 remains in during February Revolution and
 aftermath, 138–9, 143, 144, 146, 153; LNB
 spends exile in, 91–4, 97–8, 152; LNB stays
 in to secure passage back to Switzerland, 84–5;
 LNB's state visit, 253–8
Louis-Philippe, King of France: abdicates, 136;
 appearance, 39; banishes Bonapartes from
 France, 40, 54, 59; becomes king, 38, 39;
 character, 39; exiles LNB after Strasburg coup,
 78; invites LNB to ask for pardon in exchange
 for freedom, 122; LNB confiscates property
 of, 220; overlooks death penalty for LNB
 and Hortense, 50–1; refuses to concede to
 demands for universal suffrage, 135; supporters
 (Orléanists), 58; see also July Monarchy
Louis XVI, King of France, 6, 38
Louis XVIII, King of France, 15, 17, 22
Louvre, Paris, 261
lumpenproletariat (Karl Marx theory), 222
Luxembourg, 337
Lyon, 225

Mac Mahon, Patrice de, 287, 288, 403–6, 464–5;
 see also Army of Châlons
Macron, Emmanuel, 465
Magenta, Battle of, 287
Malmaison (chateau of Empress Joséphine), 4–5,
 21
Malmesbury, 3rd Earl of (James Harris), 35–6,
 91, 125, 236, 279, 282, 430
Manet, Édouard: The Execution of Maximilian
 (painting), 350
manufacturing expansion, Second Empire, 265
maps, and the French army, 171, 250, 285, 322,
 392
Maria Clotilde, Princess of Savoy, 281, 282–3
Marie Louise, Empress, 11, 14
La Marseillaise (newspaper), 368–9, 372–3
'Marseillaise' (revolutionary anthem): as anthem
 of Franco-Prussian War, 379, 389, 395; LNB's
 opinion of, 161; as national anthem, 459;
 played at Bonapartist and Democratic banquet,
 161; played at Eugénie's funeral, 467; sung
 at the Théâtre Impérial, 388–9; sung during
 fall of Second Empire, 418; sung during Paris
 Commune, 434; sung during Paris riots, 358;
 sung during protest march in Paris, 371; sung
 in resistance to LNB's coup d'état, 209; see
 also 'Partant pour la Syrie' (anthem of Second
 Empire)
Martyn, Francis Mountjoy, 129–30
Marx, Karl, 174, 222, 354, 451

Masuyer, Valérie, 41–2, 47, 49, 52–4, 55
Maupas, Charlemagne de, 194–5, 196–7, 208, 209
Maussion, Ernest-Louis-Marie de, 103
Maximilian, Archduke Ferdinand, 322, 335–7, 348–50
mechanical piano, 314–15
medieval revivalism, 90–1, 153
Mentana, Battle of (1867), 351–2
Mercy-Argenteau, Louisa de, 425–7
Mère, Madame (Letizia Bonaparte), 31
Metz, 391, 395, 396–8, 401, 402, 403, 423
Mexico see Second Franco-Mexican War (1861–7)
Milan, 288
mitrailleuse (machine gun), 392, 435
Moltke, Helmuth von, the Elder, 291, 381, 398, 401, 404, 405
Montholon, marquis de (Charles Tristan), 99–100, 101–2, 110, 114, 116–17
Montijo, Eugénie de see Eugénie, Empress (born Eugenia de Palafox y Kirkpatrick)
Montmartre cemetery, Paris, 355
Morny, Charles de, 179–80, 191–2, 193, 194, 196–7, 208–9, 215, 221, 238, 313, 321–2, 328
Mountain (radical Assembly representatives), 163–4, 165, 167–8, 172, 193, 194; resistance against coup d'état, 203–13
moustache fashions, 82
Murat, Lucien, 200–1, 238

Napoleonic Wars, 4, 6–7, 10–11, 13–15, 20, 26; see also Congress of Vienna (1815)
Nero (LNB's dog), 353
New York, 82–3
Ney, Edgar, 200–1, 238
Nice: annexation by France, 297–8, 302; LNB visits, 299
Nicholas I, Tsar, 242, 244–5, 246, 264
Noir, Victor, 369–71
Notre-Dame, Paris, 217, 235, 261, 267–8

obscenity trials, France, 271–2
Oldoini, Virginia see Castiglione, Countess of
Ollivier, Émile: appearance, 338; and build-up to Franco-Prussian War, 376, 379, 380, 384, 385, 386–7, 388; character, 338, 375; leadership as first minister, 365–7, 371, 373; LNB appoints as first minister, 365; as republican deputy of Corps législatif, 310, 338–9, 340–1; resignation, 396; writings on Second Empire, 460
Opéra-Comique, Paris, 196
opera house, Paris, 346

Orleanists (France), 58
Orléans, duc d' see Louis-Philippe, King of France
Orsay, Alfred d', 35, 93–4, 125, 126
Orsi, Joseph, 43, 100–2, 137
Orsini, Felice, 275–7, 278–80, 295
Ottoman Empire: Crimean War (1853–6), 244–53, 263–4; French intervention in Syria (1860), 306; Russo-Turkish wars, 36; and Suez Canal, 361
Oudinot, Charles, 170–1

Palafox y Kirkpatrick, Eugenia de see Eugénie, Empress
Palafox y Kirkpatrick, Francisca (Paca), 230–1, 234, 300–1
Palais Bourbon, Paris, 139, 160, 179–80, 198–9, 417; see also Assembly of Second Republic; Corps législatif of Second Empire
Palais du Champ-de-Mars, Paris, 344, 345, 347–8
Palestine: dispute between Catholic and Orthodox Christians, 243–4
Palmerston, Lord, 242, 246, 264, 273, 278, 282, 297, 329, 360
pan-Latinism, 321
Panthéon, Paris, 219–20
Paris: Allied soldiers march on, 15; Arc de Triomphe, 15, 69, 113, 429, 465; Blanquist Insurrection (1839), 96; Bonapartist and Democratic Banquet, 160–1; Café Anglais, 318, 345–6; Champs-Élysées, 15, 113, 164, 201, 370, 371, 429, 437; Conciergerie (prison), 107, 261; coup d'état of LNB (1851) see coup d'état of LNB; Élysée Palace, 162, 165, 196; expansion, 312; Exposition universelle, 258, 259–60, 265, 343–5, 347–8; false reports of success in Franco-Prussian War, 395; February Revolution, 135–6; German victory parade, 429; Les Halles, 312; Hôtel de Ville, 26, 38, 136, 140, 142, 147, 417–18; international food in, 345–6; Invalides, 112, 113, 166, 262, 465; July Revolution (1830), 37–9, 43, 57, 119; June Days uprising (1848), 144–5, 153; LNB and Hortense's brief sojourn in, 50–2; LNB returns to after Assembly election success, 147; LNB rides through in proto-imperial procession, 226; LNB's brief visit following February Revolution, 137–8; Lord Raglan attends military review, 247; Louvre, 261; Malmaison (chateau of Empress Joséphine), 4–5, 21; under martial law, 173, 396, 400; military parade after Italian Campaign, 296; modernisation and remodelling, 240, 258–9, 265, 311–12, 335, 347, 419, 452, 453; Montmartre cemetery, 355; Napoléon's state funeral, 112–13;

Notre-Dame, 217, 235, 261, 267–8; Opéra-Comique, 196; opera house, 346; Palais Bourbon, 139, 160, 179–80, 198–9, 417; Panthéon, 219–20; Père Lachaise cemetery, 435; Place Napoléon III, 465; Place Vendôme, 50, 51, 69, 143, 213, 296, 416, 434; poverty, 347, 358; protest march following shooting of Victor Noir, 369–71; protests during Franco-Prussian War, 395, 396; Quay d'Orsay barracks, 202–3; riots (1869), 358; Salle Roysin, 206; sex workers, 346–7; siege, 428, 433; tourism, 346–7; Treaty of Paris (1815), 241; Tuileries (palace) *see* Tuileries; unrest after LNB's surrender, 416–19; uprising protesting Roman Expedition (1849), 172–3; Victoria and Albert's state visit to, 260–3; war fever takes hold (1870), 378–9, 388–9

Paris Commune (1871), 433–5

Paris Exposition *see* Exposition universelle, Paris

Paris Uprising (1832), 62–3

parlour games, 268, 314, 315

Parquin, Denis-Charles, 28, 35, 70–1, 72, 74, 76, 77, 79, 80–1; and Boulogne Conspiracy, 100, 101, 102, 103, 107

'Partant pour la Syrie' (anthem of Second Empire), 247, 254, 257

Party of Order, 154, 155, 161, 166, 167–8, 170, 176–7, 178–9, 203

peasant's revolt (Jacquerie) (1385), 183; later allusions to, 183, 190, 215

Père Lachaise cemetery, Paris, 435

Persigny, Victor vicomte de: as absurd figure, 166–7; approves Haussmann's appointment, 259; argues for war with Russia, 242; as 'bad melodrama actor', 222; believes LNB should abdicate, 438; blames Eugénie for collapse of Empire, 423; and Boulogne Conspiracy, 100, 104, 105, 110; as 'con artist', 97; conversion to Bonapartism, 68; criticises Eugénie and is exiled from power, 356–7; death, 438; disapproves of LNB writing about Caesar, 316; early life, 67; encourages LNB to take action against Russia, 245; as French ambassador in London, 273, 278, 293–4, 297; friendship with LNB, 68, 92, 97, 232–3, 273, 356–7, 438; given *légion d'honneur*, 162; imprisonments, 114, 132, 143; interest in Egyptology, 132; involvement in *coup d'état*, 192, 196–7; and LNB's ascendancy, 137, 143, 156–7; military discharge, 67, 68; as minister of the interior, 222, 324, 325; musical choices for LNB's wedding, 235; name change, 67; and Napoleonic Wars, 438; opinion on 1869 election results, 358; opposes French neutrality during Austro-Prussian War, 331–2; opposes LNB's marriage, 232–3; predicts imminent restoration of Napoléon's Empire, 132; promotes Bonapartism to elites, 166–7; pushes case for LNB as Napoléon III, 222–4; reorganises Bonapartists in London, 83; and Strasbourg insurrection, 68–9, 72, 73, 75, 77; suggests second *coup d'état* in face of republican opposition to reforms, 352; supports Italian Campaign, 293–4; and threat of Changarnier and military attack on LNB, 180–1; urges LNB to perform *coup d'état*, 160, 176; writes propaganda piece about LNB and Napoléon, 99

Piedmont, 270, 280, 281, 282–3, 297; *see also* Cavour, Count of; Italian Campaign (1859); Victor Emmanuel II

Place Napoléon III, Paris, 465

Place Vendôme, Paris, 50, 51, 69, 143, 213, 296, 416, 434

plebiscites (nationwide votes): supporting annexation of Nice and Savoy, 297–8; supporting LNB's *coup d'état*, 213–14, 216–17; supporting LNB's liberal reforms, 371–3; supporting Napoléon and hereditary empire, 11; supporting Second Empire with LNB as hereditary monarch, 227

Poland: Greater Poland Uprising (1848), 139–40, 325; January Uprising (1863), 323; refugees from, 63; Russian occupation, 45, 57, 63, 323, 325

Pope Pius IX, 169–70, 174, 267, 298, 336, 341

Portugal, Queen of, 65

presidential election of Second Republic, 149–59, 450

press conferences, 433, 436

press, freedom of, 37–8, 39, 136, 173, 176, 194, 216, 219, 272, 277, 309, 340, 350, 352–3, 355

Proudhon, Pierre-Joseph, 149, 164, 205

provisional government of Second Republic, 136–7

provisional government of Third Republic, 417–18, 419

Prussia: and Austro-Prussian War (1866), 329, 330–4; and counter-revolution in Germany, 169; as dominant power, 334, 342, 343; Franco-Prussian War (1870–1) *see* Franco-Prussian War; military attaché attends ball at Tuileries palace, 374–5; and Napoleonic Wars, 6, 15, 20; recognises Second Empire, 242; and Second Schleswig War (1864), 328–9; signs Treaty of Paris (1815), 241; suffrage, 462; thwarts LNB's attempt to buy Grand Duchy of Luxembourg, 337; *see also* Bismarck, Otto von; Leopold, Prince of Prussia; Wilhelm I, King of Prussia

Quay d'Orsay barracks, Paris, 202–3

Raglan, Lord, 246–7, 250, 253
rail expansion: Second Empire, 221, 225, 240, 258, 259, 265, 274, 311, 465; Second Republic, 187–8, 189
Red Cross, founding, 291
Reding, Mademoiselle de, 63–4
Reichstadt, Duke of: birth, 11, 234; conspiracists supporting, 53–4; death, 60; infancy and early childhood, 14; LNB and Hortense's imagined cabinet for, 52–3; LNB supports cause of, 40, 59–60; as Napoléon II in name, 223–4; Napoléon steps aside for, 20; virtual imprisonment in Vienna, 40, 60
Revolts of 1831 (Italy), 44–5, 56
Rio de Janeiro, 79
road building, Second Empire, 311
Robespierre, Maximilien, 6, 7, 26
Rochefort, Henri, 353–4, 358, 363–4, 367, 368–9, 370, 371, 418, 435; see also La Marseillaise (newspaper)
Roman Expedition (1849), 169–72, 173, 174–5; uprising in protest to, 172–3
Romanticism (LNB's interest in), 29, 33–4, 64, 66, 450
Rome: Bonaparte family in, 31–2; French Roman Expedition (1849) see Roman Expedition; LNB and Hortense travel to, 42–3; LNB spends winters with family in, 31–3, 34–6
Romer, Isabella Frances, 243, 244
Romieu, Auguste, 183
Rossini, Giochino, 347
Rouher, Eugène, 339–40, 352, 353, 359, 436–7, 440
Russell, Lord John, 360–1
Russia: Crimean War (1853–6), 244–53, 263–4; and Napoleonic Wars, 13, 15; occupation of Poland, 45, 57, 63, 323, 325; recognises Second Empire, 242; Russo-Turkish wars, 36; signs Treaty of Paris (1815), 241; Treaty of Tilsit, 10; see also Alexander I, Tsar; Alexander II, Tsar; Nicholas I, Tsar
Russo-Turkish wars, 36; see also Crimean War (1853–6)

Saint-Arnaud, Armand-Jacques Leroy de: and Algerian 'pacification' campaign, 185–6, 187; colourful past, 186; and coup d'état, 192–3, 196–7, 208–9, 213; and Crimean War, 246, 248–9, 250–3; gambling, 238, 246; illness and death, 250, 252; as minister of war, 194
Saint-Cloud, palace of, 228, 231, 236, 260, 295, 301, 314, 335, 336–7

Saint Helena, 21, 24, 51; The Memorial of Saint Helena (Napoléon Bonaparte), 30, 32, 66
Saint-Leu, comte de (Louis Bonaparte):
    CHARACTER: coldness, 3, 42; controlling misanthropy, 32, 41; erratic behaviour, 25, 32; perversity, 41
    LIFE: in Army of Italy, 36; births of children, 4; death of first child, 4; death of Hortense, 87; flees to Bohemia, 10; flees to Italy, 23; funeral, 130–1; illness and death, 122, 125, 126–7; King of Holland, 4, 10; marries Hortense, 3–4, 9; opposes sons' political and revolutionary activities, 42, 44–5, 46, 56, 87, 88–9; refuses then agrees to LNB's marriage to Mathilde, 66, 67; returns to and flees from France, 14; wins custody of Napoléon-Louis, 17, 23; writes public letter of protest against ill treatment of LNB, 108
    RELATIONSHIPS: Hortense (wife), 3, 17, 25; LNB (son), 25, 32, 36, 44–5, 56, 64, 66, 67, 87, 88–9, 108, 122, 125, 126; Napoléon (brother), 3, 4, 8, 9–10, 14; Napoléon-Louis (son), 44–5
St Michael's Abbey, Farnborough, 465–6
Saint-Simon, Henri de, 310
Saint-Simonians, 310–11
Salle Roysin, Paris, 206
Sand, George, 121, 217, 317, 463
Sardinia, 270
Sasse, Marie, 388–9, 395
seances, 273
Second Empire (1852–70): as ahead of its time, 461–2, 464; annexes Nice and Savoy (1860), 297–8, 302; anthem of ('Partant pour la Syrie'), 247, 254, 257; Battle of Mentana (1867), 351–2; Britain and Europe's concerns, then acceptance of Empire, 240–2; and Catholic Church, 219–20, 244, 246, 271–2; characteristics (overview), x, 452–3, 460–3; commercial treaties with Europe, 305, 311; Corps législatif (lower chamber of parliament) see Corps législatif of Second Empire; Council of State (creation and powers), 218; court life, 237–9, 314–15, 374–5; creation of, 227; economic programmes, 221, 240, 258, 311, 312–13, 452; educational reform, 341; electoral corruption and fraud, 324, 325; fall of, 416–18; financial scandals, 324, 356; foreign policy (overview), 306, 323, 330–1, 453–6; growing republican opposition, 352–4, 355–6; historical reputation and scholarship on, 459, 460; importance of British alliance, 305; importance of military, 219, 220, 274, 342; industrialisation and infrastructure programmes see industrialisation

and infrastructure programmes, Second Empire; liberal reforms, 296, 309–10, 338, 340–1, 352–3, 354, 359, 365–7; limitations of ministerial power, 239–40; LNB relinquishes personal power, 365–7; LNB's updated constitution, 218–19; ministerial appointments, resignations and sackings, 222, 238, 239, 278, 279, 313, 324, 325, 340, 341, 353, 359, 365, 384; Paris remodelling, 240, 258–9, 265, 311–12, 335, 347, 419, 452, 453; plebiscites in, 219, 227, 297–8, 371–3; popular support of Ollivier ministry, 366–7; Second Opium War (1856–60), 302–5; Senate (upper chamber), 218, 227, 237, 309–10; social reforms, 312, 367; state suppression, 272, 277–8, 354, 355, 356; Syrian intervention (1860), 306; Vietnam conquest (1858), 305 see also Crimean War (1853–6); Franco-Prussian War (1870–1); Italian Campaign (1859); Second Franco-Mexican War (1861–7)

second Empire (fictional/imagined): Alexandre Dumas dismisses idea of, 62; LNB believes in necessity of, 59; LNB imagines cabinet for, 52–3

Second Franco-Mexican War (1861–7), 320–3, 335–7, 348–50, 455; LNB's decisions and actions during, 321–2, 335–7, 348, 350, 455

Second French Revolution see July Revolution (Second French Revolution) (1830)

Second Opium War (1856–60), 302–5

Second Republic (1848–52): Assembly see Assembly of Second Republic; banning political clubs, 175; cabinets (appointments, resignations and sackings), 161–2, 168, 174–5, 179, 180, 181–3, 187, 194–5; Executive Commission see Executive Commission of Second Republic; LNB's coup d'état see coup d'état of LNB (1851); presidential election, 149–59, 450; provisional government, 136–7; Roman Expedition (1849) see Roman Expedition (1849); suffrage, 176, 194

Second Schleswig War (1864), 328–9

Sedan (and surrounding area), 404–5, 407, 408–13; Bazeilles, 405–6, 407–8, 412

Seignobos, Charles, 459

Senate of Second Empire, 218, 227, 237, 309–10

Sevastopol: plans to attack, 247, 249, 250; siege, 252, 263–4

sewage improvements, Second Empire, 259, 311, 419

sex workers, Paris, 346–7

social reforms, Second Empire, 312, 367

socialism: beginnings of movement, 119–20; fear of, 141, 146, 155, 168, 183–4; LNB's leanings towards, 119–21, 146, 155, 173, 312; Paris Commune (1871), 433–5; see also démoc-socs (left-leaning alliance)

Société du Dix-Décembre, 175–6

Solferino, Battle of, 289–91

Somerset, FitzRoy (Lord Raglan) see Raglan, Lord

Spain: Joseph Bonaparte as king of, 10, 229; and Napoleonic Wars, 4, 13, 229; Plon-Plon as ambassador to, 166; Prince Leopold's candidacy for throne, 375–8, 380–1, 382–3

steam engines, 61

Stendhal (writer), 230–1

Strasbourg insurrection (1836): conspirators and planning, 67–72; failed execution, 72–7; LNB's exile after, 78–9; pamphlet with LNB's alternative narrative of, 87–8; trial and acquittal of co-conspirators, 79–81

strikes, 354, 358, 367

Stuttgart, 274–5

Suez Canal, 360–3

suffrage: Britain, 57, 138, 462; France, 57, 58, 95, 120, 135, 137, 154, 158, 176, 194, 196, 200, 218, 452; LNB's views on, 57, 58, 95, 96, 120, 154, 176, 218, 452; Prussia, 462; United States, 57

Summer Palace, China, 302–4

Switzerland: government refuses to expel LNB at France's order, 89–90; Hortense de Beauharnais settles in, 24; LNB trains with Swiss artillery, 36; LNB's analysis of politics and history of, 63; Napoléon's imposed political settlement, 63; see also Arenenberg (Hortense de Beauharnais' chateau); Constance

Syria: French intervention (1860), 306

Taylor, A. J. P., 460

telegraphy, Second Empire, 221, 267, 291, 311

Temple, Henry John see Palmerston, Lord

Thelin, Charles, 82, 92, 114–15, 122, 123, 124

Thiers, Adolphe: arrested during coup d'état, 198; Assembly speeches, 182, 184–5; as chief executive of Assembly of Third Republic, 427, 433, 434, 435; elected to Corps législatif, 325; fear of republicans, 176; hatred for the people, 184–5; initially supports LNB, 154–5, 164; as leader of Party of Order, 154–5, 161, 178–9; low opinion of LNB, 154–5, 162, 350; opposes going to war with Prussia, 387–8; opposes revision of constitution, 191; republicans' views of, 195; wishes to restore monarchy, 178–9, 184–5

Third Republic (1870–1940): Assembly elections, 427, 428, 437–8; creation of, 416–18; and First World War, 460; Government of National Defence, 419, 425; Paris Commune

(1871), 433–5; plots for imperial restoration, 438, 440–1; protectionism, 459; provisional government, 417–18, 419
Thompson, Sir Henry, 442, 443
Tocqueville, Alexis de, ix–x, 135, 136, 162, 168–9, 172, 189, 201–3, 239, 450, 451
Torquay, 432–3
tourism, Paris, 346–7
Treaty of Fontainebleau (1814), 15
Treaty of Paris (1815), 241
Treaty of Tilsit (1807), 10
Treaty of Versailles (1919), 466
Tristan, Charles *see* Montholon, marquis de (Charles Tristan)
Trochu, Louis-Jules, 400, 419–20, 422, 430
Tuileries (palace, Paris): Changarnier's official residence at, 178; Communards set on fire, 434–5; Eugénie flees after fall of Second Empire, 418; inscription to LNB over entrance to, 226; LNB invites Ollivier to, 339; LNB returns to after endorsement by plebiscite, 217–18; LNB shows Victoria and Albert around, 261; LNB's court life at, 236, 314, 374–5; Louis XVI and Marie Antoinette imprisoned in, 6; Napoléon and family at, 11, 18, 20; publication of LNB and Eugénie's personal correspondence and public auction of possessions, 435–6; seances at, 273
turtle, of Empress Eugénie, 361, 363
Twain, Mark, 343

United States: civil war, 319–20, 335; Joseph Bonaparte is exiled in, 31, 69; LNB is exiled in, 78–9, 81, 82–3; Plon-Plon meets President Lincoln, 319–20; suffrage, 57; supports Mexican Republic, 335

Vaudrey, Claude-Nicolas, 71–5, 76, 78, 80, 81, 92, 162

Vergeot, Éléonore, 117, 128, 302
Véron, Louis-Désiré, 149
Versailles Palace, 261–2, 426, 433
Versailles, Treaty of (1919), 466
Victor Emmanuel II, King of Piedmont-Sardinia/ Italy, 270, 281, 288, 294–5, 298
Victoria, Queen: attire, 254, 256, 261; on China, 305; on Eugénie, 255; hosts Eugénie on solo visit, 302; hosts LNB at Windsor Castle, 430–1; hosts LNB's state visit, 253, 254–6, 257–8; joins LNB at Isle of Wight, 273; on LNB, 242, 255, 257–8, 261, 263, 297, 346, 431; on Plon-Plon, 260; state visit to Paris, 260–3; visits LNB at Camden Place, 431
Vietnam: French conquest (1858), 305
Villiers, George, 4th Earl of Clarendon, 233–4, 261, 282, 297
Voirol, Théophile, 70, 74–5
voting rights *see* suffrage
Vuitton, Louis, 268, 361

Walewska, Marie-Anne, 271, 318
Waterloo, Battle of, 20, 71, 99, 118, 246; LNB visits battlefield, 60
Wellesley, Henry (Lord Cowley), 213
Wellington, Duke of, 91, 138, 152, 246
Westphalia: Jérôme Bonaparte as king of, 68, 421; *see also* Wilhelmshöhe Palace
Wilhelm I, King of Prussia, 376, 380, 382–4, 400, 401, 412–13, 414, 426
Wilhelmshöhe Palace, 415, 421–3, 426–7
William, King of Württemberg, 275
Wimpffen, Félix de, 407, 410, 411–12
Worth, Charles Frederick, 268
Württemberg, 274–5

Zola, Émile, 346, 463
Zouaves (French army elite), 251, 263–4
Zululand: Anglo-Zulu War (1879), 447–8